STO

SO-BXC-620

# The McGraw-Hill Dictionary of national Finance

# The McGraw-Hill Dictionary of International Trade and Finance

Carolyn R. Gipson, J.D., Ph.D.

McGraw-Hill, Inc.

New York   San Francisco   Washington, D.C.   Auckland   Bogotá
Caracas   Lisbon   London   Madrid   Mexico City   Milan
Montreal   New Delhi   San Juan   Singapore
Sydney   Tokyo   Toronto

**Library of Congress Cataloging-in-Publication Data**

Gipson, Carolyn Renee, date.
    The McGraw-Hill dictionary of international trade and finance  /
Carolyn R. Gipson
        p.     cm.
    ISBN 0-07-023600-3 (alk. paper)      —ISBN 0-07-023601-1
    (pbk. : alk. paper)
    1. International trade—Dictionaries.   2. International finance
—Dictionaries.   I. Title.
    HF1373.G57   1993
    332′.042′03—dc20                    92-21390
                                    CIP

1 2 3 4 5 6 7 8 9 0  DOH/DOH  9 9 8 7 6 5 4 3


ISBN 0-07-023600-3 [HC]
ISBN 0-07-023601-1 [PBK]


*The sponsoring editor for this book was Betsy N. Brown, the editing supervisor
was Mitsy Kovacs, and the production supervisor was Donald Schmidt. It was
set in Palatino by McGraw-Hill's Professional Book Group composition unit.*

*Printed and bound by R. R. Donnelley & Sons Company.*

# Acknowledgments

I owe debts of deep gratitude to many people. I am especially indebted to my mother, Hazel Austin Gipson, who has always supported me with great intelligence. She set a splendid example of rectitude, style, and taste. I am also grateful to my late father, McAlester Gipson, who taught me the virtue of work, the value of persistence, and the joy of love.

Two mentors, Professors Russell Fraser and Marvin Feldheim of the University of Michigan, influenced my life more profoundly than they could have known at the time. The late poet Robert Hayden has been a continuing source of inspiration. To them and to Harold Cruse, who enabled me to publish early in my career, I will always be grateful.

In addition, there are few words that can adequately convey my appreciation to McGraw-Hill. I am indebted to Betsy Brown, my editor, whose tenacity and belief in the project made this book possible. David Fogarty and Mitsy Kovacs skillfully shepherded a lengthy and complex manuscript through the final editing and proof stages. My gifted copy editor, Judy Duguid, exhibited a rare facility for language and a keen eye for detail that merit the highest praise. William Hickel brought his superb foreign language skills to bear on the manuscript and greatly improved its quality.

Much of the information in the dictionary was difficult to unearth, and I am grateful to the employees of banks, embassies, government agencies, and financial and commodity markets who took the time to answer many questions. Special appreciation is due the staff of the High Point, North Carolina City Library, particularly June Evans, Sheila O'Neil, Lucy Tyndal, and Josephine Williamson, without whose help this book could not have been completed. Further thanks are owed to Sybil Cunard and Sam Scott of High Point, both of whom gave me highly valued help and encouragement.

The published sources for the dictionary were many and wide-ranging. In particular, The *Journal of Commerce* was a daily companion with its timely coverage of international economic issues. *Export Today* and *The Exporter* were extremely useful in helping me remain close to practical problems and solutions in international trade. *A Concise Dictionary of Business* (eds., Alan Isaacs et al., Oxford University Press, 1990), *Dictionary of Banking Terms* (Thomas Fitch, Barron's Educational Series, 1990), *Directory of World Stock Exchanges* (Economist Publications, Johns Hopkins University Press, 1988),

*Encyclopedia of International Commerce* (William J. Miller, Cornell Maritime Press, 1985), *International Business Dictionary and Reference* (Lewis A. Presner, John Wiley & Sons, 1991), and the *Official Export Guide* (North American Publishing Co., 1992) were invaluable resources.

Finally, setting out to complete a project of this magnitude is never without its perils. The very nature of the book dictated choices that could only leave the most ardent researcher uneasy. Some selections are probably idiosyncratic, reflecting no doubt my own fascination with history and discovering the origins of things. But now that the choices have been made and the information compiled and put on paper, I hope my enthusiasm for the material is contagious, even among the most casual of readers.

*Carolyn R. Gipson*

# Using the Dictionary

**Selections.**   This dictionary is constructed as a broad reference to terms encountered in international trade and finance. It defines banking, customs, economics, financial, insurance, legal, regulatory, and shipping terms. National currencies are identified. Major international trade agreements, regional trading associations, financial institutions, and stock and commodity exchanges are included. Most federal agencies of the United States and trade and investment-related programs available through them also have entries.

**Finding a Term.**   Entries are alphabetized by letter. Abbreviations and acronyms have individual entries.

**Main Entries.**   The dictionary is designed to facilitate the search for information related to a given term. Multiword terms are entered separately, but most can also be found under headings for generic terms. For example, *public corporation* has its own entry, but refers you to *corporation*, where it and other types of corporations are listed and defined.

**Subentries.**   When continuity best serves the interest of defining a heading and placing it in context, related terms are listed under subheadings to a main entry. For example, the various rounds of multilateral trade negotiations and agreements reached by the General Agreement on Tariffs and Trade (GATT) are defined under the main entry for the GATT.

**Multiple Definitions.**   The dictionary treats broad areas of subject matter and defines terms in the variety of ways they are used. When multiple explanations of a single term are appropriate, numbered definitions appear under the main entry.

**Cross-References.**   To enable a reader to scan subjects quickly, synonyms and terms related to a main entry are usually contained within the body of the definition. When similar or contrasting terms are placed at the end of an entry, "See also" and "Compare" precede them.

**Examples**.    Abstract terms are most often defined by example, or where broad generalizations are necessary, examples are included to refine definitions and take into account exceptions to a rule.

**Foreign Language Terms**.    Apart from English, the most common languages used in the dictionary are French, German, and Spanish, although there are occasional entries in other languages. The names of international agreements and organizations are entered in alphabetical order in the language in which they are customarily identified. For example, the Latin American Integration Association is usually referred to as ALADI, the abbreviation for *Asociación Latinoamericana de Integración. Therefore, the main entry defining the term is alphabetized according to its Spanish name. Non-English terms within entries are italicized.*

# Recent Developments

Shortly after the dictionary went to press, the pace of events made it important to mention here changes occurring in three areas. In the United States, the Congress enacted the Omnibus Budget Reconciliation Act of 1993. The act significantly alters U.S. tax and fiscal policies. Canada, Mexico, and the United States concluded a series of supplemental agreements to the North American Free Trade Agreement (NAFTA). The overall accord has been approved by the Canadian Parliament. The Mexican legislature and the U.S. Congress are poised to act on it before the end of 1993. In Geneva, meetings of the General Agreement on Tariffs and Trade (GATT) negotiating committee took on new urgency. The negotiating authority of the United States to conclude a multilateral trade agreement expires December 15, 1993.

The Budget Reconciliation Act raises income taxes, increases the federal gasoline tax, offers tax relief to low-income taxpayers, and provides modest investment incentives. The legislation repealed the luxury tax on all products except automobiles, and it restricts the content of imported tobacco products to 25 percent. Specifically, the act:

- Increases some tax rates from 31 percent to 36 percent retroactive to January 1, 1993. The new rates apply to individuals with taxable incomes above $115,000 per year (or gross incomes of $140,000) and to married couples with taxable incomes exceeding $140,000 per year (or gross incomes exceeding $180,000). The tax rate on incomes above $250,000 is 39.6 percent.

- Increases the federal gasoline tax by 4.3 cents, raising the total to 18.4 cents per gallon beginning October 1, 1993.

- Reduces the tax deduction for business meals from 80 percent to 50 percent.

- Institutes a research and expenditure (R&E) tax credit. The R&E credit extends to research expenditures invested over a 36-month period retroactive to June 30, 1992.

- Reduces by 50 percent the capital gains tax on profits from the sale of stocks owned in small businesses and held for 5 years.

- Modifies the alternative minimum tax (AMT) depreciation schedule for capital-intensive companies. The act also simplifies the AMT formula for computing depreciation.

With regard to NAFTA, negotiators completed work on several supplemental agreements. The supplemental agreements specify remedies and the dispute-resolution process when a NAFTA country violates the accord. Their basic provisions are:

- Systematic import surges trigger a complete withdrawal of NAFTA benefits.

- Systematic violations of trade-connected labor (i.e., child labor, minimum wage, and health and safety) and environmental laws trigger consultations and review by trilateral dispute-settlement panels. When two members of a panel find a pattern of violations, the offending country pays monetary enforcement assessments (i.e., damages) and enforces its own labor and environmental laws.

- The sanctions for systematic violations are damages and, if the offending country is Mexico or the United States, an immediate withdrawal of NAFTA benefits. Damages are fixed at 20 million U.S. dollars in the first year of any violation and a percentage of trade flows thereafter. Canada is exempt from withdrawal sanction because its national courts are competent to enforce international orders without further review. Mexico and the United States are subject to the withdrawal sanction because their national courts lack enforcement powers similar to those available to Canadian courts. The NAFTA general secretariat will be located in Mexico, the environmental secretariat in Canada, and the labor secretariat in the United States.

The fate of the Uruguay Round remains uncertain. Unless an agreement in principle is reached by the end of 1993, United States participation in the negotiations automatically terminates. Drafting a multilateral agreement invariably poses difficult technical problems; however, delays in concluding an agreement caused by mere drafting problems would presumably not kill the round. On the other hand, the failure to agree on substantive issues by the deadline may very well sound the round's death knell. The U.S. Congress can, but need not, extend the President's authority to agree to new multilateral trading rules.

## About the Author

Carolyn R. Gipson is the founder of Foreign Trading Services Company. An international trade attorney who specializes in foreign market access, she offers advice to everyone from exporters experiencing foreign regulatory problems to companies entering international markets. She lives and works in Washington, D.C.

# A

**A.** An abbreviation for account and ampere.

**A.** The marking for United States Generalized System of Preferences Eligible Product. See *Harmonized Tariff Schedule of the United States, Annotated.*

**A\*.** The marking for United States Generalized System of Preferences Eligible Product Subject to Exclusion. See *Harmonized Tariff Schedule of the United States, Annotated.*

**A1.** 1. A symbol for excellent quality or good condition. 2. A seaworthiness rating given by *Lloyd's Register of British and Foreign Shipping* to the highest-quality ships.

**AA/AAA.** The abbreviations for Airforwarders Association and American Arbitration Association.

**AAA/AA/A.** In the United States, bond ratings and credit ratings of banks, companies, and individuals issued by a credit-rating service. AAA-grade bonds are the highest-rated issues. Bonds rated Baa or higher by Moody's Investors Service and BBB or above by Standard & Poor's are considered investment-grade bonds.

**AAEI.** The abbreviation for American Association of Exporters and Importers.

**AAPA.** The abbreviation for American Association of Port Authorities.

**AAR.** The abbreviation for Association of American Railroads.

**AB.** The abbreviation for *aktiebolaget.*

**A/B.** The abbreviation for airbill.

**abandoned goods.** In customs, merchandise or commodities refused by an importer on delivery. Abandoned goods are stored for a short time by the customs agency in the importing country and later sold, destroyed, or otherwise disposed of.

**abandonment.** The voluntary surrender of title to property. In marine insurance, abandonment occurs when a policyholder files notice of relinquishment after an accident or other disaster. The notice constitutes a total-loss claim and entitles an insurer to reclaim the salvage value of an abandoned ship.

**abattement forfaitaire.** Also known as *montant forfaitaire,* the abatement of duties and taxes on goods traded within the European Community (EC). The abatement reduces the price of regional imports while increasing the relative prices of non-EC imports. Compare *common external tariff.*

**ABCC.** The abbreviation for Association of British Chambers of Commerce. See *chamber of commerce.*

**ABI.** The abbreviation for Automated Broker Interface Program and Association of British Insurers.

**ability-to-pay tax system.** A progressive tax system under which rates rise as income increases. Taxes are paid at higher rates on incremental income gains above a fixed nominal rate. See also *progressive tax.* Compare *flat tax.*

**ab Kai.** German: from pier, i.e., goods free at the pier.

**above par.** The premium paid for a stock or bond over its face value. Bond premiums (i.e., interest) are included in quoted prices. For example, a $5000 bond quoted at 105 yields $5250, or 105 percent, at maturity. Premiums are not usually paid on stocks, although some stocks do pay a nominal price above par value.

**above-the-line item.** 1. In business accounting, entries displayed on a company's profit and loss statement above the line dividing profits and losses from distributed profits and the sources of funds subject to losses. 2. In government accounting, above-the-line items, also called autonomous transactions, reflecting private for-profit transactions included in a country's current account deficit or current account surplus. Above-the-line items are excluded from balance-of-payment calculations. 3. In advertising, the cost of public media advertising, including expenditures for television and print media, plus the commission owed to the advertising agency for placing advertisements. Compare *below-the-line item.*

**ABP.** The abbreviation for Associated British Ports.

**ab Quai.** Synonymous with ab Kai.

**ABR.**   The abbreviation for the African Business Roundtable. See *African Development Bank Group.*

**Abrechnung.**   German: settlement, i.e., the settlement of an account.

**abrogation.**   The termination of an international agreement, often by agreement among its signatories.

**ABS.**   The abbreviation for the American Bureau of Shipping. See *classification society.*

**Abschluß.**   German: a closing, i.e., the conclusion of a contract or negotiations.

**absolute advantage.**   Superior efficiency in producing a given product or service. A concept central to Adam Smith's (1723–1790) theory of free trade, absolute advantage reflects one country's natural superiority in some facet of economic competition when compared with its trading partners. Absolute advantage may arise from geography and/or an abundance of natural resources, wealth, human skill, or any combination thereof. Compare *comparative advantage.*

**absorption.**   1. In accounting, the process of factoring the cost of intermediate products and services into the total cost of a product. Absorption is also known as full costing. 2. In shipping, a gratis service provided by a carrier that is not covered by a published freight tariff or included in freight charges. Premium services include free wharfage, switching, and so on. Depending on the law of the jurisdiction in which they are offered, premium services may constitute illegal inducements. Compare *accessorial services.*

**A/C.**   The acronym for account.

**ACAS.**   The abbreviation for Advisory Conciliation and Arbitration Service.

**ACC.**   The abbreviation for Arab Cooperation Council.

**accelerated cost recovery system/schedule.**   See *accelerated depreciation.*

**accelerated depreciation.**   A form of tax accounting for assets with a limited useful life. In theory, an asset has peak value when new and decreases in value with age. Accelerated depreciation reduces a company's tax liability in an amount roughly equal to the reduced value of used buildings and equipment. In the United States, depreci-

ation relief is available under the accelerated cost recovery system, a complicated method of allocating costs over several accounting periods. Accelerated depreciation was authorized by the Economic Recovery Tax Act in 1981 and modified by the Tax Reform Act of 1986, which lengthened the period for depreciating machinery and equipment. Internationally, the availability of tax relief varies from country to country. See also *wasting asset.*

**accelerated tariff elimination.**   An agreement between nations to expedite the removal of import duties. Procedures for eliminating duties vary depending on the terms of a treaty. Normally, however, private businesses or trade associations may petition a government to eliminate duties on specific products. In other instances, customs tariffs provide for eliminating duties on certain products within a prescribed time period.

**acceptability.**   The condition of a draft or bill of exchange deemed eligible for discount or rediscount by a lender of last resort, such as the Bank of England, the Bundesbank, or a U.S. Federal Reserve Bank. Acceptability is determined by the creditworthiness of an instrument's endorser, maker, or payee. In commercial bank financing, a creditworthy endorser or maker often eliminates the need for financial statements. Treasury bills and corporate trade bills are examples of acceptable instruments. See also *eligible paper.*

**acceptable determination.**   In the United States, an official import valuation by the U.S. Customs Service. A determination is acceptable when the value assigned to an import is consistent with the arm's-length value of identical or similar merchandise. See also *binding tariff classification ruling.*

**acceptance (acpt.).**   1. In diplomacy, the procedure by which a country becomes a party to an international accord. See also *accession.* 2. In finance, the promise by a third party, usually a bank, to pay the face amount of a time draft at maturity. An acceptance is a negotiable instrument, which can be sold to another party before it matures. The acceptance occurs when the acceptor inscribes or stamps "accepted" on the face of the instrument. The date of acceptance and the acceptor's signature are also affixed to the instrument. The acceptor looks to the drawer to repay the face amount of the debt at maturity. The selling price of an acceptance can be discounted at the prevailing or a preferred rate of interest. The value of the discount depends on the creditworthiness of the acceptor. See also *acceptability, anticipated acceptance, banker's acceptance, clean acceptance, documentary acceptance, third-country acceptance,* and *trade acceptance.* Compare *accommodation endorsement.*

**acceptance commission.** A bank fee collected for accepting a draft or bill of exchange. The fee is charged for guaranteeing the face amount of the draft until payment. The commission is billed to the customer's account along with interest and other bank charges.

**acceptance financing.** A prearranged line of credit extended to finance imports or exports. The lending bank may require the borrower to pledge, or hypothecate, a warehouse receipt, bill of lading, or other evidence of title to merchandise.

**acceptance house.** 1. Also known as an accepting house, a private institution specializing in guaranteeing bills of exchange. The commission charged for the guarantee is determined by the rate at which the bill is discounted in commercial money markets. 2. In the United Kingdom, a member of the London Accepting House Committee. The members of the committee include the most prestigious merchant banks in London.

**acceptance supra protest.** Also known as acceptance for honor, a third-party payment of a dishonored bill of exchange or draft. The payment is made to preserve the honor of the drawer or endorser. The debt is repaid by the maker or drawer when the instrument matures.

**acceptor.** A person or entity who accepts a bill of exchange or draft, thereby guaranteeing that the instrument will not be dishonored. An acceptor becomes liable to subsequent holders of the bill. See also *acceptance* and *acceptance supra protest.*

**accession.** A nation's agreement to the terms and conditions of an international agreement or treaty. In some instances, a country joins a multilateral agreement through an accession clause contained in the treaty, which obviates the need

for each country to negotiate separately. Countries accede to treaties by having designated officials sign and deposit the treaty instrument with an official agent. If there are few signatories, instruments are exchanged at appropriate ministries. However, instruments for multilateral treaties with numerous signatories are placed with a depository agency, usually the headquarters of a multilateral institution sponsoring the treaty. See also *enter into force.*

**accessorial services.** A premium service offered by a carrier, including preloading and postloading storage of cargo, extending credit to a shipper, and so on. Carriers charge fees for accessorial services. Compare *absorption.*

**accommodation bill.** A document issued by a carrier before the receipt or loading of goods for shipment. The accommodation bill is provided when a shipper must prove that cargo is in the carrier's possession. An accommodation bill may be accepted by a bank for payment under a letter of credit.

**accommodation endorsement.** A third-party's guarantee of a promissory note. The accommodator becomes liable on the instrument if the maker or endorser fails to pay at maturity. As a practical matter, the accommodator is usually a bank or a substantial commercial firm. By endorsing the instrument, the accommodator enhances the creditworthiness of the instrument for discount and sale in secondary markets. See also *bank aval.* Compare *acceptance.*

**accommodation paper.** A bill of exchange to which an accommodation endorsement has been affixed.

**accommodating transaction.** See *below-the-line item.*

**Accord of the Commonwealth of Independent States.** See *Commonwealth of Independent States.*

**account (A/C).** 1. The record of a series of transactions. 2. A debt owed by one party to another. 3. A financial relationship whereby one party holds and accepts and/or disperses funds on behalf of another, e.g., a bank deposit or checking account, a charge or credit account, a trust account. 4. In the United Kingdom, a period of 2 to 3 weeks designated by a stock exchange for trading stocks without immediate cash settlements. There are 25 accounts in a year. Cash settlements are made on account day, or the Monday falling 10 days following an account. In New York, account day is called the settlement date. See also *contango market*. Compare *trade date*.

**account day.**   See *account.*

**accountee/account party.**   The beneficiary of a letter of credit, usually a seller or supplier.

**account executive.**   1. A commission agent who plots investment strategies. In commodity futures and options markets, account executives buy and sell on behalf of customers. 2. In advertising, an employee who manages an advertising firm's business with a given client.

**accounting exposure.**   See *exposure.*

**accounting standards.**   See *Financial Accounting Standards Board* and *statements of standard accounting practice.*

**accreditation.**   1. The process by which an official agency grants approval to a commercial enterprise, nonprofit institution, or individual to engage in specified activities. 2. In international relations, the procedure by which ambassadors present credentials and become official representatives of their governments in foreign countries or at multilateral institutions.

**accretion.**   The augmentation of an investment by interest or additional capital. Accretion is the opposite of amortization.

**accrual basis accounting.**   A method of business accounting whereby expenses and income are realized during prescribed accounting periods, irrespective of when payments are actually made or received. In the United States, accrual basis accounting is authorized by generally accepted accounting principles and required by the Tax Reform Act of 1986 for most business tax reporting. Compare *cash basis accounting.*

**accrued interest.**   Unpaid interest accumulated on an investment in a financial instrument. Accrued interest is factored into the selling price when the instrument is sold.

**accumulation.**   Increasing invested principal by accruing interest and profits. In bond financing, accumulation is the difference between a dis-

counted bond's face value and its purchase price. Compare *amortization.*

**ACE.**   The abbreviation for Active Corps of Executives and the *Association Canadienne d'Exportation.* See *Canadian Export Association.*

**ACH.**   The abbreviation for Automated Clearing House.

**ACI.**   The abbreviation for *Association Cambiste Internationale.*

**ack./ackgt.**   The abbreviation for acknowledgment.

**ACM.**   The abbreviation for Arab Common Market.

**ACP.**   The abbreviation for African, Caribbean, and Pacific countries.

**acpt.**   The abbreviation for acceptance.

**acquisition.**   See *merger.*

**across-the-board (ATB) tariff reduction.**   Also known as linear tariff reduction, a device used in multilateral trade negotiations to avoid negotiating item-by-item reductions. Under ATB reductions, nations consent to binding percentage decreases in tariff rates for specific classes of goods. Compare *item-by-item tariff reductions.*

**ACRS.**   The abbreviation for accelerated cost recovery system/schedule. See *accelerated depreciation.*

**ACS.**   The abbreviation for Automated Commercial System.

**ACT.**   The abbreviation for the advance corporation tax.

**action.**   French: share.

**Active Corps of Executives (ACE).**   In the United States, a private-sector arm of the Small Business Administration that advises small companies on export trade, finances, management, and so on. ACE members are experienced volunteers who help entrepreneurs identify business problems and opportunities. ACE chapters are found in most cities in the United States.

**act-of-state doctrine.**   An international law tenet holding that nations are ultimate legal authorities and submit voluntarily to the jurisdiction of alien courts. The act of state doctrine embodies the principle of sovereign immunity. But its effect is often limited by treaty, as, for example, when a country joining the United Nations consents to the jurisdiction of the International Court of Justice. Similarly, rules governing the treatment of foreign nationals and their property are usually specified in international agreements. In the United States, the jurisdiction of U.S. federal courts extends to cases involving U.S. nationals, including the expropriation of their property, illegal detention, and interference with personal or property rights specifically protected by international law. As a practical matter, a court has recourse only against the assets of another country located within its jurisdiction.

**ACTPN.** See *Advisory Committee on Trade Policy Negotiations.*

**actual gross weight.** The total weight of a shipment, including packaging and containers.

**actuals.** Commodities convertible into cash and sold at the spot rate. Also known as spot goods, actuals are the items underlying option contracts and futures contracts.

**actual value rate.** A freight rate based on a shipper's valuation when the true value of cargo is not readily discernible. Customarily, actual value rates are applied only to certain classes of commodities identified in a carrier's tariff.

**ACTWU.** The abbreviation for the Amalgamated Clothing and Textile Workers Union.

**ACU.** See *artificial currency unit.*

**AD.** The abbreviation for after date and antidumping

**ADA.** The abbreviation for the Anti-Dumping Act of 1921.

**ADB.** The abbreviation for the Asian Development Bank.

**ADBF.** The abbreviation for the African Development Bank and Fund. See *African Development Bank Group.*

**adcom.** The abbreviation for address commission.

**ADD.** An abbreviation for antidumping duty. See *duty: antidumping duty.*

**additional product aid.** A component of the European Community's Common Agricultural Policy which guarantees price-support payments to domestic producers of import-sensitive agricultural commodities. Additional product aid is limited to farm products not covered by tariffs bound under the General Agreement on Tariffs and Trade.

**address.** The process of consigning a ship to an agent who arranges a ship charter. See also *address commission.*

**address commission (adcom).** The percentage fee paid to, or on behalf of, an agent who charters a vessel. The payment of address commissions originated in the maritime practice of compensating any party who put a vessel into active service. The address commission is paid in addition to brokerage fees.

**ADF.** The abbreviation for African Development Fund. See *African Development Bank Group.*

**adjudication.** 1. In law, the process of settling a legal claim by judicial decision. Compare *arbitration.* 2. In some countries, a determination by a taxing authority of the tax payable for affixing an official stamp to a document. An adjudication can usually be appealed to a court for reversal of the determination. 3. In France, the decision awarding a procurement contract to the lowest bidder in open bidding.

**adjusted CIF price.** In the European Community (EC), a cost, insurance, and freight (CIF) price that includes a variable duty on grain exports. Under the Common Agricultural Policy, the duty is used to adjust the price of grain imports in relation to fluctuations in local grain prices. The adjustment reflects a premium or discount, depending on the differences in quality between imported grain and EC grain.

**adjusted gross income (AGI).** In the United States, as distinguished from gross income, a taxpayer's taxable income from all sources. Adjusted gross income is reported to the Internal Revenue Service on Form 1040 and reflects income after allowable deductions for certain personal and business expenses.

**adjustment assistance.** A government program providing economic and retraining assistance to workers dislocated by external trade. Most developed countries provide some form of displaced worker assistance to compensate for liberalized trade. Typically, adjustment programs combine cash payments with fixed hourly stipends for time spent in retraining or outplacement. In the United States, adjustment assistance was first authorized by the Trade Act of 1974. U.S. free trade agreements often also authorize adjustment assistance programs.

**adjustment program.**    A program adopted by a government to modify domestic economic policies, frequently in response to economic contractions. Elements of adjustment programs may include budget reductions (fiscal policy), currency devaluation, increasing bank reserve requirements, or any of a number of devices available to a country's central monetary authority to restrain or expand the monetary supply (monetary policy). Programs imposed by the International Monetary Fund to correct balance-of-payments deficits or by the World Bank as a condition of future lending are known as structural adjustment programs.

**adjustments to price.**    Changes in the declared price of an import to determine its transaction value for levying duties. The invoice price is adjusted to include previously undeclared expenses incurred in producing the import. The cost of assists, some commissions, packing expenses, royalties and licensing fees, and insurance and transportation expenses to the departure port are added to the invoice price. Import duties, taxes, further assembly and construction expenses, and insurance and transportation costs to a point other than the departure port are subtracted from the invoice price. See also *customs entry* and *valuation*.

**ad libitum (ad lib.).**    Latin: as indicated.

**ad locum (ad loc.).**    Latin: (delivery) to the place.

**adm.**    The abbreviation for admitted, e.g., goods admitted.

**administered pricing.**    The process of setting a price without regard to market conditions, usually as an aspect of government policy or price fixing by a cartel. Administered pricing is price regulation by an oligopoly or monopoly used to maintain profit levels or eliminate potential competitors from a market. In the United States, private agreements to regulate prices generally violate antitrust laws unless approved by statute or by the U.S. Department of Justice in a business review letter. In the European Community, the legality of pricing agreements is governed by competition rules established by the European Commission.

**administering power.**    See *non-self-governing territory*.

**administração do porto.**    Portuguese: port authority.

**administración de aduanas.**    Spanish: customs authority.

**administración de puertos.**    Spanish: port authority.

**administration des douanes.**    French: customs authority.

**administration des douanes et accises.**    French: customs and excise tax authority.

**Administration Générale pour la Coopération au Développement.**    See *official development assistance*.

**administrative board.**    In the European Community (EC), a board of directors of a European company. Under the EC single-tier corporate structure, an administrative board combines functions of oversight and management. Compare *supervisory board*.

**administrative law judge (ALJ).**    In the United States, a federal judge who decides regulatory cases. Unlike the authority of judges of the federal district courts, appeals courts, and Supreme Court, the authority of ALJs is statutory rather than constitutional. ALJ decisions are initially reviewable in federal district courts. Appeals lie with the regional courts of appeal and the U.S. Supreme Court. See also *U.S. Courts of Appeals and U.S. District Courts*.

**Administrative Procedure Act of 1946 (APA).** In the United States, a statute establishing uniform procedures for regulatory rule making and the conduct of administrative hearings. The APA requires that a proposed rule, as well as notices of the time and place of hearings held for public comment on it, be published in the *Federal Register*. The act also provides for judicial review of federal agency decisions and mandates that federal rules be reasonable. Federal courts are authorized to set aside arbitrary, capricious, or unauthorized administrative actions.

**administrative protective order (APO).** In the United States, a summary directive issued by a federal agency. For example, the International Trade Commission (ITC) issues protective orders to avoid unauthorized disclosures of business proprietary information released to parties during antidumping or subsidy proceedings. Among others, penalties for intentional or inadvertent APO violations include the exclusion of exculpatory evidence from a proceeding, debarment of an attorney from further practice before the ITC, or criminal prosecution by the U.S. Department of Justice.

**administrator (admr.).** 1. In a bankruptcy proceeding, a person officially appointed by a court to distribute property and dispose of the debts of another. In the United States, an administrator is known as a bankruptcy trustee and authorized to represent the interests of general and secured creditors, determine priorities for payments to creditors, and initiate claims for debts owed to the bankrupt. In some jurisdictions, officials known as U.S. trustees manage all bankruptcy cases within an assigned territory. 2. A person named by a court to settle the estate of one who dies in intestacy. Letters of administration issued by the court authorize the administrator to take charge of the deceased's assets, pay debts, and distribute the remainder to heirs as required by laws governing intestacy. The feminine form of administrator is administratrix. Compare *executor*. 3. Any person designated to manage the affairs of an agency, department, firm, or office.

**admission of seaworthiness.** In marine insurance, a provision whereby the underwriter declines in advance to allege poor ship construction or maintenance as a basis for denying insurance claims. An admission of seaworthiness excuses a shipper from certifying the condition of a ship before each shipment.

**admission temporaire/temporary admission.** See *carnet*.

**admr.** The abbreviation for administrator.

**ADR.** The abbreviation for American depositary receipt.

**ADS.** The abbreviation for American depositary share. See *American depositary receipt*.

**A/DS.** The abbreviation for Agent/Distributor Service.

**aduanas.** Spanish: customs and duty.

**ad val.** See *ad valorem*.

**ad valorem (A/V; ad val).** Latin: according to value. Duties and excise taxes are often computed on an ad valorem basis, i.e., determined by the price rather than the quantity of goods. See also *duty*.

**advance against collection.** Short-term financing advanced to an exporter when the buyer or a third party agrees to pay a draft. The advance may amount to all or a portion of the face value of the draft, less bank fees and interest. The bank collects the amount of the loan when the draft is paid.

**advance against documents.** Short-term financing advanced to a seller, often based on a contract of sale or shipping documents. The advance can be made by a bank or a buyer. The bank is repaid from sales proceeds. A buyer who makes an advance normally deducts the amount from payments owed to the seller.

**advance corporation tax (ACT).** In an imputation tax system, income tax paid by a corporation following a distribution of dividends and before its annual tax liability is settled. For example, corporations in the United Kingdom pay the ACT at the basic rate both on distributed dividends and on amounts owed on corporate taxes. The ACT is later credited against taxes payable by shareholders and the corporation. Any unused portion of an ACT credit is applied against taxes owed for past or future years. In the case of multifirm corporations, unused credits may be transferred between companies. Compare *mainstream corporation tax*.

**advance deposit.** In international trade, a deposit paid to a central bank to obtain an import license from the issuing agency, which may also be the central bank. The amount of the deposit varies. In some instances, it is equal to 100 percent of an import's value. In other instances, the deposit is computed as a percentage of the import's cost, insurance, and freight value. Normally returned to the importer within 60 to 90 days, an advance deposit constitutes a short-term, no-interest loan to the importing country's central bank.

**advertising.**   The distribution of commercial information, often through the public media, intended to create a market for a product or service. Advertising encompasses billboards, flyers, and commercial notices carried by print and electronic media and designed to appeal to prospective buyers in order to stimulate sales. Consumer advertising is directed toward the public at large, while trade advertising reaches buyers within a specific industry, such as manufacturers, distributors, or retailers. See also *advertising agency.*

**advertising agency.**   Popularly known as ad agencies, any one of several types of commercial firms that create and distribute advertising for the benefit of clients. Full-service agencies offer a variety of services, including advertising design and production, marketing advice, and sales promotion consulting. Boutique agencies provide more limited services, specializing, for example, in a facet of advertising or in a particular product, service, or industry. Advertising agencies generally charge commissions based on the size of a client's account. See also *above-the-line item* and *below-the-line item.*

**advice.**   A term synonymous with advice of fate, preadvice, credit advice, and advise fate. See also *advisement.*

**advice of nonconformity.**   See *Société Générale de Surveillance, S.A.*

**advised letter of credit (L/C).**   A letter of credit of which an exporter has been notified. The advisement specifies the conditions for payment.

**advisement.**   Also known as advice, a bank's notice that a letter of credit has been opened in favor of a beneficiary. The advice is forwarded from the issuing bank in the importer's country to the exporter's local bank. Also known as an advising bank, the local bank informs the exporter of the terms and conditions of pay-

ment. Advisement may be by cable, letter, or telex. See also *advising bank* and *operative instrument.*

**advising bank.**   A bank that informs a beneficiary of a letter of credit and the terms of payment. A letter of credit is often advised through two banks. For example, the foreign bank may advise a bank in a financial center, which informs the exporter's local bank. The exporter pays for advice from both the financial center bank and the local bank. See also *negotiating bank.* Compare *confirming bank.*

**advisory capacity.**   A principal's limitation on the scope of an agent's authority. An agent limited to an advisory role may not approve or alter a course of action without prior consent of the principal. See also *agency.*

**Advisory Committee on Trade Policy Negotiations (ACTPN).**   In the United States, a committee of private-industry representatives selected to advise the U.S. Trade Representative (USTR) on international trade policy. Among other things, the ACTPN may advise the USTR to seek tariff concessions or reservations from trade agreements when domestic industries might otherwise be injured. During the 1980s, the role of private business in influencing U.S. trade negotiating strategies grew. For example, a coalition representing U.S. service industries successfully lobbied for the inclusion of services in the Uruguay Round of trade negotiations conducted by the General Agreement on Tariffs and Trade. In their present form, the ACTPN and its sectoral committees, known as Industry Sector Advisory Committees, are authorized by the Omnibus Trade Act of 1988.

**Advisory Conciliation and Arbitration Service (ACAS).**   In the United Kingdom, an official panel established by the government in 1975 to mediate labor disputes. Some members of the panel are appointed by the Confederation of British Industry and the Trade Union Congress. Labor disputes not resolved by mediation are referred by the ACAS for arbitration.

**advisory opinion.**   A view advanced by an administrative agency or a court on facts not before it. Some courts and agencies issue opinions on the legality of statutes or regulations before an actual case has been brought. The U.S. Supreme Court does not render advisory opinions.

**AERP.**   The abbreviation for the Automated Export Reporting Program. See *Automated Export System.*

**AES.**   The abbreviation for the Automated Export System.

**AFA.**   The abbreviation for the Air Freight Association.

**AFDB.**   The abbreviation for the African Development Bank. See *African Development Bank Group.*

**affidavit (afft.).**   A written declaration of fact voluntarily made under oath and sworn before an authorized official.

**affirmative dumping determination.**   In the United States, an administrative finding by the International Trade Administration that an import is priced below the cost of production. The International Trade Commission determines whether the below-market pricing injured a domestic industry. An affirmative dumping determination precedes the imposition of an order to pay antidumping duties in an antidumping action.

**affreightment.**   See *contract of affreightment.*

**afft.**   The abbreviation for affidavit.

**afghani.**   The currency of Afghanistan.

**afloat.**   A description of goods priced in transit when the spot price of a commodity changes before a shipment reaches the destination port. For example, when cargo traveling from London to New York is labeled "afloat New York," the price is the difference between the current spot price and the price fixed for immediate shipments of similar commodities in London.

**AFL-CIO.**   The abbreviation for the American Federation of Labor and Congress of Industrial Organizations.

**à forfait.**   See *forfaiting.*

**aforos.**   An ad valorem duty levied primarily in Latin America. The duty is applied to certain classes of imports based on the value assigned by the local customs agency. The customs value is a theoretical value, distinct from actual market value.

**Africa Growth Fund (AGF).**   In the United States, a private venture-capital fund that provides start-up and expansion capital for private companies located in sub-Saharan Africa. When the United States has a significant interest in a sub-Saharan company's success, the agency invests equity capital for its own account. A significant interest exists when U.S. investors hold substantial equity in a company, or if U.S. exports or management contracts will increase as a consequence of AGF's participation. The Overseas Private Investment Corporation (OPIC) guarantees AGF's investment through its political risk insurance programs. AGF is headquartered in Washington, D.C. Compare *African Public Sector Grant Financing.*

**African Business Roundtable.**   See *African Development Bank Group.*

**African, Caribbean, and Pacific (ACP) countries.**   Beneficiary countries entitled to tariff concessions and official development assistance under the Lomé Conventions, the foreign aid and trade preference program of the European Community (EC). As of 1992, roughly 65 developing countries received EC foreign aid in the form of capital investment, debt relief, duty reductions, subsidies, and technical assistance. The most recent Lomé Convention between the EC and ACP countries was concluded in 1989. It expires in 1999. See also *Stabex* and *Sysmin.*

**African Development Bank Group.**   A multilateral financing agency that includes the African Development Bank (AFDB), the African Development Fund, and the Nigerian Trust Fund. Also known as the *Banque Africaine de Développement,* the African Development Bank was created by the United Nations Economic Commission for Africa to finance regional infrastructure and development projects. The bank's activities are funded by 50 African countries and 25 nonregional members. AFDB shares have a par value of 10,000 units of account each, the equivalent of one special drawing right. The agency's soft-loan window is the African Development Fund (ADF), created to attract capital from non-African states. The AFDB maintains 50 percent of the ADF's voting shares. Non-African states have voting rights in proportion to their subscribed shares. Subscriptions to the fund are measured in fund units of account, each of which equals roughly 0.921052 special drawing right. The African Development Bank and the African Development Fund are headquartered in Abidjan (Côte d'Ivoire) and maintain regional offices in Africa, Europe, and the Middle East. The Nigerian Trust Fund, an additional soft-loan window, is based in Lagos (Nigeria). The African Business Roundtable is the African Development Bank Group's private-sector arm.

**African Development Fund.**    See *African Development Bank Group.*

**African Public Sector Grant Financing.**    In the United States, a program created by the U.S. Trade and Development Program (TDP) to finance U.S. consultancies and feasibility studies in Africa. The program supports projects sponsored by the African Development Bank (AFDB) Group. Applications for public-sector grant financing are approved by the TDP in consultation with the AFDB. Compare *Africa Growth Fund.*

**after date (a.d.).**    A notice affixed to a draft or bill of exchange, indicating that the instrument will be paid after the time noted on it (e.g., 30 days after date). An after-date instrument is a time draft that can mature before acceptance. Compare *after sight* and *at sight.*

**after-hours deal.**    A transaction on a stock exchange concluded after the official close of trading. Normally, the trade is recorded on the following business day.

**after market.**    A secondary market in bonds and other fixed-interest financial instruments. For example, the after market in Eurobonds arises following issue but before the underwriting group dissolves.

**after sight.**    A notice that a draft or bill of exchange will be paid after it has been presented for payment. The seller retains title to a shipment until shipping documents have been presented and accepted by the paying bank. Compare *after date* and *at sight.*

**AFTKA.**    See *Association of Foreign Trading Agents of Korea.*

**A.G.**    The abbreviation for *Aktiengesellschaft.*

**AGCD.**    The abbreviation for the *Administration Générale pour la Coopération au Développement.* See *official development assistance.*

**agcy.**    The abbreviation for agency.

**agency (agcy).**    A relationship created by oral or written agreement, authorizing one party (the agent) to represent another (the principal) in a transaction involving a third party. A general agency entitles an agent to act without restriction on all matters covered by the agency contract. A limited agency restricts an agent's authority to advice or similar activities. An exclusive or sole agency restricts a principal's right to conduct business through other agents. In international agencies, the law applied is often that of the agent's residence. Thus, a principal may be liable under local laws for all damages arising from an agent's breach of contract, torts, or other legal violations, including copyright, patent, or trademark infringement. 1. In common-law countries, the rights of parties in agency are based on the contract between agent and principal. A principal is normally bound by the terms of an agreement negotiated between an agent and third parties only to the extent of the agent's authority as defined in the agency contract. Under the common law, most agencies are construed as "at-will" relationships, allowing either party to terminate an agreement. An agent's compensation at termination is determined by the agency contract. See also *apparent authority.* 2. In civil-law countries, legal codes and decrees define rights acquired in agency and may override the terms of a written contract. Civil-law codes typically place significant restrictions on agency relationships, particularly in the case of termination. The codes often specify damages payable to an agent and provide venues for contesting terminations in protracted legal or arbitration proceedings. Civil codes may also treat certain classes of agents as employees, irrespective of contract terms. In France, for example, an agent falling under the definition of *voyageur, représentant et placier,* is covered by French labor laws and entitled to compensation at termination despite contrary contract terms.

**agency bank.**    A subsidiary created by a parent banking corporation to enter a foreign financial market. In the United States, agency banks do not offer retail banking services, but they are permitted to handle foreign exchange and letters of credit. However, agency banks are exempt from federal interstate banking laws and are permitted to operate branch banks where authorized by state law. See also *Edge corporation.*

**agency bill.**   In the United Kingdom, a bill of exchange drawn on the London branch of a foreign bank.

**agency fee.**   A commission paid according to the terms of an agency agreement. Depending on the nature of the transaction, the fee may be payable as a percentage of the gross value of the transaction or as a negotiated retainer. See also *agency.*

**Agenda 21.**   A global plan for restoring the world's environment by the twenty-first century. Agenda 21 was prepared by the United Nations as a program for sustainable development. The plan contains provisions for universal cooperation in combating global warming and protecting plant and animal species. It was adopted by a majority of the world's nations at the United Nations Conference on the Environment and Development (UNCED), known popularly as the Earth Summit, held in Rio de Janeiro in 1992. The program encourages signatory countries to consider the ecological impact of economic and industrial development policies. It also commits developed countries to finance environmental improvement in developing countries. See also *sustainable development.*

**agent (agt.).**   A person or firm authorized to represent a principal in a transaction. An agent's authority may be limited or general. In common-law countries, agency relationships are governed largely by judicial decision. In civil-law countries, agency relationships are defined by legislation. A subagent is a party authorized to act on behalf of an agent and bound by the agent's contractual obligation to the principal. In commercial transactions, subagents are often regional purchasing agents. See also *agency.*

**agent bank.**   A bank that collects funds for a foreign bank against bills of exchange and letters of credit. An agent bank may also represent the interests of a lending syndicate formed to finance large loans or the interests of an underwriting syndicate created to underwrite a securities offering. See also *lead bank* and *managing underwriter.*

**agent de change.**   French: stockbroker. See also *Bourse.*

**Agent/Distributor Service (A/DS).**   In the United States, a matchmaking service for domestic exporters sponsored by the U.S. & Foreign Commercial Service (US&FCS). US&FCS officers identify international projects, buyers, and representatives for foreign manufacturers and service providers. The information is channeled from overseas embassies through the U.S. Department of Commerce to manufacturers and joint-venture seekers in the United States.

**agente de bolsa.**   Spanish: stockbroker. See also *bolsa.*

**agents of influence.**   In the United States, a phrase popularized in a book of the same title by Pat Choate, an observer of the politics of international trade in Washington, D.C. The term is a pejorative description applied to lawyers, lobbyists, and public relations agents who represent foreign clients on national legislative and regulatory matters. When agency relationships are disclosed in the manner prescribed by official registration procedures, advocating the views of foreign clients to government administrators and legislators is not illegal. Attorneys who represent foreign clients in legal proceedings are not called agents of influence. See also *foreign agent.*

**AGF.**   The abbreviation for the Africa Growth Fund.

**aggregated shipment.**   A consolidated cargo of several small shipments destined for a single importer. The shipment is assembled by a carrier or a consolidator. See also *assembled shipment* and *non-vessel-operating common carrier.*

**aggregate of the intermediaries rule.**   In the United States, a provision in the Interstate Commerce Act of 1887 that permits a shipper to pay a combined freight rate for deliveries along a route with several intermediate stops. The combined rate is lower than the through rate. The rule applies to coastal water carriers and interstate motor carriers and railroads. Freight forwarders and ocean liners are not subject to the act and are exempted from the rule.

**AGI.**    The abbreviation for adjusted gross income.

**agio.**    A premium paid, usually to a bank, in the course of a foreign currency exchange transaction. The cost of the premium reflects the difference between currency exchange values, the relative scarcity of one currency at the exchange site, or both. The term *agio* is rarely used in the United States.

**AGM.**    The abbreviation for annual general meeting.

**AGO.**    The abbreviation for apparent good order.

**AGR.**    The abbreviation for agriculture and American Goods Returned.

**agreement among underwriters.**    See *syndicate agreement.*

**Agreement Establishing a Common Fund for Commodities.**    An international agreement initiated by the United Nations Conference on Trade and Development (UNCTAD) and adopted in 1980 by the United Nations Negotiating Conference on a Common Fund. The agreement proposes a new multilateral institution to oversee and implement international commodity agreements, particularly those affecting the economies of developing countries. The agreement has been ratified by the required 90 countries. The Common Fund's capital subscription is $470 million. See also *Integrated Programme for Commodities.*

**Agribusiness Promotion Council (APC).**    In the United States, a private-sector council that advises the U.S. Department of Agriculture on international trade and investment strategies, including tariff and other barriers to U.S. agricultural exports. The APC also helps domestic farmers and food processors locate export financing and target foreign markets, particularly in the Americas.

**AGRICOLA.**    The acronym for the Agricultural On-Line Access System. See *Agricultural Information and Marketing Services.*

**Agricultural Act of 1956.**    In the United States, an act of Congress approving quantitative limits on textile imports. Section 204 of the act authorizes the President to negotiate bilateral treaties, known as Section 204 agreements. Bilateral agreements limiting textile and apparel imports are negotiated under the MultiFiber Arrangement Regarding International Trade in Textiles. Presidential authority to restrict textile and apparel imports is exercised by the Committee for the Implementation of Textile Agreements.

**Agricultural Adjustments Acts of 1933 and 1938.**    In the United States, statutes limiting imports that interfere with the administration of domestic farm-support programs. The 1933 act was held unconstitutional on other grounds by the U.S. Supreme Court, but its constitutional provisions, including import restrictions, were reenacted in the 1938 act. The acts authorize the President to impose tariffs or quantitative limits on agricultural imports when import surges require the U.S. Department of Agriculture to alter commodity price supports. The authority delegated under the Agricultural Adjustments Acts set precedents for import quotas in the United States, which were subsequently imposed on a number of products, including automobiles, sugar, and textiles and apparels.

**Agricultural Information and Marketing Services (AIMS).**    An information service for domestic agricultural producers sponsored by the U.S. Department of Agriculture (USDA). AIMS supplies data on foreign purchasers and export markets through the following media:

*Agricultural On-Line Access System (AGRICOLA).*    A database of holdings in the USDA library. AGRICOLA is available on CD-ROM.

*Agricultural Products Report (APR).*    A publication that identifies foreign markets for U.S. commodities and provides general international trade information.

*Buyer Alert Program.*    A coordinated advertising program that notifies foreign purchasers of available U.S. commodities. The notices are forwarded to foreign embassies through the Foreign Agricultural Service by way of an information network, known as Telenet.

*Foreign Buyer Lists.* Notices published in the United States containing contact information on prospective foreign buyers of U.S. commodities. Lists are formatted to provide worldwide or country-specific information.

*International Marketing Profiles (IMPs).* A series of automated reports detailing statistical information useful in agricultural trade. Data provided in IMPs include general external market information, analyses of foreign competitors' market positions, and buyer contact lists.

*Trade Leads.* A multiformat service provided by the USDA. Offers to buy U.S. commodities are published in electronic format and in *Export Briefs*, a weekly publication of the Foreign Agricultural Service. The USDA also publishes trade leads in the *Journal of Commerce*, a U.S. international trade and business daily.

**Agricultural On-Line Access System.** See *Agricultural Information and Marketing Services.*

**agricultural paper.** Banker's acceptances, bills of exchange, or promissory notes arising from the sale of agricultural commodities. Agricultural paper is used by farmers to cover the cost of exporting, equipment and feed purchases, and farm operating expenses. In the United States, the largest agricultural lenders are commercial banks and the Farm Credit System. Also known as commodity paper, agricultural paper is often eligible for discount under Federal Reserve Regulation A. See also *land bank.*

**Agricultural Products Report.** See *Agricultural Information and Marketing Services.*

**Agricultural Trade Development and Assistance Act of 1954.** See *PL 480 programs.*

**Agricultural Trade Office (ATO).** In the United States, an overseas office operated by the Foreign Agricultural Service of the U.S. Department of Agriculture. ATOs facilitate exports of domestic agricultural commodities and advise foreign farm producers of U.S. agricultural import requirements.

**agt.** The abbreviation for agent.

**AIA.** The abbreviation for American Insurance Association.

**AIB.** The abbreviation for American Institute of Banking and Arab International Bank.

**AIBD.** The abbreviation for Association of International Bond Dealers.

**AICPA.** The abbreviation for American Institute of Certified Public Accountants.

**AII.** The abbreviation for Automated Invoice Interface.

**AIMS.** The abbreviation for Agricultural Information and Marketing Service.

**AIMU.** The abbreviation for the American Institute of Marine Underwriters.

**AIOEC.** The abbreviation for the Association of Iron Ore Exporting Countries.

**airbill (A/B).** An air carrier's receipt for goods received for shipment. The air waybill (AWB), included in an airbill, consigns goods for transport to a stated destination. Also known as an air consignment note, an AWB names the consignee, consignor, points of departure, and destination. It also describes the content and value of a shipment. A house air waybill is issued by a freight forwarder after small loads from several shippers have been consolidated for delivery to a named destination. A master air waybill is issued for a consolidated shipment of several cargoes from one shipper to a single destination. In the United States, the universal air waybill, a uniform airbill, became mandatory as of January 1984.

**Airbus Subsidies Agreement.** A 1992 agreement between the United States and the European Community (EC) limiting subsidies for the European airbus, a civil aircraft financed by several EC countries. The agreement restricts direct subsidies to the airbus holding company to roughly one-third of the cost of developing new aircraft and requires repayment of subsidized loans over a limited period of time. Various indirect subsidies from military contracts are limited to less than 5 percent of an airbus operating company's annual sales.

**air consignment note.** See *airbill.*

**AJDF.** See *ASEAN-Japan Development Fund.*

**Akkreditiv.** German: letter of credit. Preferred: *Kreditbrief.*

**aktiebolaget (AB.).** In Sweden, a form of business incorporation, which requires an initial minimum capitalization of 5000 kronas. Two-thirds of the company's directors must be Swedish nationals. The abbreviation AB. follows the company 's name.

**Aktien.**   German: shares or stock.

**Aktiengesellschaft (A.G.).**   German: joint-stock company, i.e., a form of business incorporation requiring a minimum of 100,000 Deutsche marks and two incorporators. *Aktiengesellschaften* are large, publicly held companies. The abbreviation *A.G.* follows the name of the company.

**aktieve Veredelung.**   German: inward processing.

**AKV.**   The abbreviation for *Auslandskassenverein.* See *Kassenverein.*

**ALADI.**   The acronym for *Asociación Latinoamericana de Integración.*

**ALAT.**   The abbreviation for the *Asociación Latinoamericana de Traficantes. See Asociación Latinoamericana de Integración.*

**Alexander Committee.**   In the United States, a congressional committee authorized in 1912 to investigate the structure and regulation of the domestic maritime industry. The committee effectively legalized self-regulating shipping conferences, subject to federal oversight. The committee's findings were codified in the Shipping Act of 1916.

**alien corporation.**   See *corporation.*

**ALJ.**   The abbreviation for administrative law judge.

**Alliance for Progress.**   The defunct Latin American economic development program that was the centerpiece of the Kennedy Administration's policy for the Americas in the 1960s. The Alliance for Progress combined official development assistance with programs for local economic and land reform. Approved by the Organization of American States (OAS) at the Punta del Este Conference in 1961, the program became the model for north-south economic cooperation through the 1970s. All OAS members participated in the program except Cuba. Compare *Caribbean Basin Initiative I.*

**allied companies.**   Otherwise unaffiliated manufacturing firms that share foreign and domestic distribution channels.

**all in.**   A pricing term indicating that a quoted rate includes all freight charges to a named destination.

**allocated quota.**   See *quota.*

**allonge.**   A document attached to a negotiable instrument for additional endorsements when the available space has been filled. An allonge is permanently attached to the principal instrument.

**all or none (AON).**   1. A notice from a customer to a broker to execute an entire stock order or cancel it. Compare *fill or kill.* 2. A notice from an issuer that an undersubscribed offering of new securities will be withdrawn.

**allotment.**   A means of distributing newly issued corporate shares in exchange for capital investment. Prospective shareholders obtain allotments by application to the issuer or managing underwriter. The letter of allotment informs subscribers of the number of shares assigned to each applicant. When an issue is oversubscribed, a portion of the total shares is assigned to each applicant. Subscription capital not applied to an issue is refunded to applicants.

**all risks.**   In insurance, a provision protecting a policyholder from financial losses, except when coverage is expressly excluded by the policy. Negligence and intentional misconduct are bases for exclusion.

**all told.**   See *deadweight tonnage.*

**alphanumeric.**   A code composed of letters, numbers, and spaces, often used in an electronic data interchange system. Compare *numeric.*

**alpha stocks.**   See *Stock Exchange Automated Quotations System.*

**alternative minimum tax (AMT).**   In the United States, a federal tax assessed against corporations, estates, individuals, limited partnerships, and trusts. The tax is levied at a flat rate and payable on capital gains to offset revenue losses from low basic income tax rates. The AMT was enacted in the Tax Reform Act of 1986. See also *tax preference items.*

**amb.**   The abbreviation for ambassador.

**ambassador (amb.).**   A diplomat holding the highest rank, often titled ambassador extraordinary and minister plenipotentiary. Ambassadors are accredited to a foreign government once they have presented credentials, known as letters of credence, to the appropriate foreign authority, usually the head of state. See also *diplomat*.

**AmCham.** The acronym for American Chambers of Commerce Abroad. See *chamber of commerce*.

**amdt.** The abbreviation for amendment.

**amendment (amdt.).** 1. A change in the terms of a contract. 2. A change in the terms of a letter of credit, usually to correct a discrepancy.

**American Bureau of Shipping.** See *classification society*.

**American components assembled abroad.** In the United States, domestic exports, also known as American goods returned (AGR), assembled abroad and imported free of duty into the United States. The import preference was implemented to reduce the cost of establishing overseas assembly operations. Under HTS item 9802 of the Harmonized Tariff Schedules of the United States, AGR reenter the United States duty-free to the extent of the value of their American components. The duty-free amount is computed by subtracting the value of U.S. components from the total value of finished imports. Normally, U.S. components must not have been transformed or enhanced in value during the foreign assembly process. An exception in Caribbean Basin Initiative II (CBI II) exempts from duties U.S. imports processed or made from components (or ingredients) produced wholly in the United States and finished in the Caribbean. Most textiles and apparels and petroleum products are not covered by the exemption in CBI II .

**American depositary receipt (ADR).** A certificate issued by a bank in the United States for foreign securities placed in its custody. ADRs are registered with the Securities and Exchange Commission in the name of the shareholder. Similar certificates issued by securities firms are known as American depositary shares. Depositary certificates are denominated in dollars and can be traded in the same manner as stocks issued in the United States. See also *International depositary receipt*.

**American depositary share.** See *American depositary receipt*.

**American Foreign Trade Definitions.** See *Revised American Foreign Trade Definitions—1941*.

**American goods returned.** See *American components assembled abroad*.

**American manufacturing clause.** In the United States, a provision of domestic copyright law enacted to preserve employment in the domestic printing industry. Part of the 1891 Copyright Act, the provision restricted imports of printed material manufactured outside the United States. It did not apply to works created in the first instance by non- U.S. citizens or residents or first published in a country belonging to the Universal Copyright Convention (UCC). The statute established a limited exemption for 2000 copies of nonconforming works when the author obtained an import statement from the U.S. Copyright Office. The manufacturing clause expired July 1, 1986.

**American National Accreditation Program for Registrars of Quality Systems.** See *American National Standards Institute*.

**American National Standards Institute (ANSI).** In the United States, a private nonprofit organization that writes quality standards for U.S. products. Electronic data interchange message formats are developed by American Standards Committees (ASCs), also known an ANSI subcommittees. ASC X9 develops standards for the domestic financial industry, ASC X11 for the securities industry, and ASC X12 for international trade. ANSI also operates the accreditation program for registrars who audit and certify product quality systems in the United States to meet international quality standards. Called the American National Accreditation Program for Registrars of Quality Systems, the program is managed jointly by ANSI and the Registrar Accreditation Board, based in Milwaukee, Wisconsin. ANSI standards are administered by the Data Interchange Standards Association (DISA), established in 1987 and based in Alexandria, Virginia. ANSI is headquartered in Washington, D.C. See also *National Institute of Standards and Technology* and *ISO 9000*. Compare *EDIFACT*.

**American option.**  See *option*.

**American selling price (ASP).**  In the United States, a customs valuation method authorized by the Tariff Act of 1930 for a limited number of imports. Imports covered by the ASP were appraised according to the price of equivalent U.S. goods without regard to actual market price. Applied to imports of clams in containers, benzoid chemicals, certain footwear, and some low-cost knit wool gloves and mittens, the ASP was abolished by the Trade Agreements Act of 1979. See also *customs valuation*.

**American Stock Exchange (AMEX).**  In the United States, a stock exchange established in New York in 1910 to trade unlisted securities. Originally, AMEX did not list stocks carried on the New York Stock Exchange (NYSE), but the exchanges concluded a dual-listing agreement in 1976, which ended AMEX's practice of dropping NYSE-listed securities. AMEX trades American depositary receipts, American depositary shares, currency warrants, index warrants based on foreign indexes, options, stocks, and U.S. government securities. It also lists the largest number of foreign shares of any U.S. stock exchange. AMEX is based in New York.

**American Tanker Rate Schedule.**  In the United States, a defunct publication that listed generic ocean shipping rates. The schedule was supplanted by Worldscale in 1969.

**AMEX.**  The acronym for American Stock Exchange.

**AMF.**  The abbreviation for Arab Monetary Fund.

**am M.**  The abbreviation for *am Main*, German for on (the river) Main.

**AMO.**  The abbreviation for Associated Marine Officers.

**amortization.**  The process of liquidating a debt in installments. 1. In accounting, the prorated writedown of debt over a given accounting period. 2. In bond financing, making periodic payments into a sinking fund to liquidate a debt. 3. For premium bonds, the process of assessing the value of the investment. Value is determined by prorating a bond's yield between its purchase and maturity dates. Compare *accumulation*.

**amp.**  An abbreviation for ampere.

**ampere (A, amp).**  In the metric system of weights and measures, a unit for gauging the intensity of an electric current. See also *Systeme Internationale*.

**AMS.**  The abbreviation for Automated Manifest System.

**AMSO.**  The abbreviation for Association of Market Survey Organizations.

**amt.**  The abbreviation for amount.

**AMT.**  The abbreviation for alternative minimum tax.

**AMU.**  The abbreviation for Arab Mahgreb Union.

**ancillary restraints doctrine.**  In the United States, a legal defense used by companies engaged in international trade to avoid prosecution under domestic antitrust laws. The doctrine exempts from prosecution for restraining trade those firms combining to avert unjust losses of profits from a foreign venture.

**ANCOM.**  The acronym for the Andean Common Market.

**Andean Common Market.**  See *El Pacto Andino*.

**Andean Free Trade Zone.**  See *El Pacto Andino*.

**Andean Trade Preference Act (ATPA) of 1991.**  In the United States, a law permitting duty-free imports of most products originating in *El Pacto Andino*, also called the Andean Common Market. The trade preferences are in addition to those available under the U.S. Generalized System of Preferences. Like Caribbean Basin Initiative I (CBI I) and Caribbean Basin Initiative II (CBI II), the ATPA excludes most textile and leather products. Unlike CBI II, however, the ATPA is not a perpetual program and expires in 2001.

**ANERA.**  The abbreviation for the Asia–North American Eastbound Rate Agreement. See *conference*.

**Angell Plan.**  The proposal advanced by James Angell, an American economist, to reorganize the International Monetary Fund (IMF) into a global central bank. The plan also proposed restricting the activities of national central banks to domestic banking operations. Although the Angell proposal was never adopted, its concept of a universal unit of account was realized when special drawing rights were created by the IMF in 1969.

**Anglophone.**    A description of the English-speaking countries of West Africa, including Gambia, Ghana, and Nigeria. Anglophone countries adhere largely to the language and legal traditions inherited from nineteenth-century British colonialism. Most remain loosely associated with the British Commonwealth. Compare *Francophone.*

**Ankft.**    The abbreviation for *Ankünft.*

**Ankunft (Ankft.).**    German: arrival.

**Anleihe.**    German: bond or loan. *Öffentliche Anleihen* are government bonds. *Industrieanleihen* are privately issued bonds.

**Annecy Round.**    See *General Agreement on Tariffs and Trade.*

**annex.**    A separately negotiated supplementary text to an international treaty, often adopted by accession.

**annual general meeting (AGM).**    Also known as a shareholders' meeting, a yearly meeting held for the benefit of a corporation's shareholders. AGMs typically follow a preset agenda that includes a review of the company's performance in the preceding year, plans for future years, the appointment of directors and officers, and discussions of corporate community service projects. In most countries, rules governing the notice and timing of AGMs for publicly owned corporations are prescribed by national statute, particularly regarding proxy requirements. In the United States, the conduct of AGMs is determined by the law of the state of incorporation and federal securities laws. In the European Community, broad requirements for AGMs are contained in the statute authorizing a European company. See also *annual report* and *proxy statement.*

**annual percentage rate (APR).**    In the United States, the yearly rate of return earned on a consumer loan. Under the Truth in Lending Act of 1968, the true cost of credit must be disclosed to a consumer at the time a loan is made. The APR reflects real credit costs because it discloses finance charges, including fees and interest. APRs are also the advertised rates of return on certificates of deposit in the United States. Compare *effective annual yield.*

**annual report.**    A yearly summary of a corporation's business activities provided by its directors and executive officers to shareholders. The annual report includes an audited statement of corporate income, losses, and capital investments. In the United States, the Securities and Exchange Commission (SEC) establishes guidelines for publicly held corporations' annual reports, which must include a summary of Form 10K filed annually with the SEC. Most U.S. corporations also publish quarterly financial reports, including brief earnings statements. The British term for annual report is directors' report, a document prepared by a corporation's directors and filed with the Registrar of Companies. See also *auditor's report.*

**annuity.**    A personal investment contract extending over a fixed period of time. The investor, or annuitant, pays into the fund at regular intervals and receives installment payments of principal and interest at retirement. A deceased annuitant's remaining benefits are paid to survivors, either in a lump sum or in installments determined by the annuity contract. In the United States, annuities are purchased through life insurance companies.

**ANRPC.**    The abbreviation for the Association of Natural Rubber Producing Countries.

**ANSI.**    The abbreviation for the American National Standards Institute.

**ANSI/ASQC 90b series.**    In the United States, documents issued by the American National Standards Institute/ American Society for Quality Control that contain ISO 9000 product quality assurance standards.

**ANSI X9.**    In the United States, the format for electronic transfers of financial data between financial institutions, federal agencies, corporations, and trade suppliers. See also *American National Standards Institute* and *electronic data interchange.*

**ANSI X11.**    In the United States, the format for electronic transfers of securities data. See also *American National Standards Institute* and *electronic data interchange.*

**ANSI X12.**   In the United States, the format for electronic transfers of international trade data. See also *American National Standards Institute* and *electronic data interchange.*

**antedated instrument.**   A draft, bill of exchange, or other financial instrument that carries a date earlier than the date of its making. An antedated instrument is negotiated at the time of its presentment.

**antiboycott regulations.**   In the United States, federal rules prohibiting domestic firms from joining foreign commercial boycotts. U.S. antiboycott regulations were originally adopted to thwart the boycott against Israel initiated by the Arab League in 1948 and implemented by its Central Boycott Office. In 1965, the U.S. Department of Commerce requested that domestic companies not participate in the boycott of Israel, and stricter regulations banning compliance with the boycott were implemented in 1975. Additional antiboycott regulations were implemented following the enactment of the Export Administration Act of 1979, which subjects U.S. firms participating in economic boycotts of friendly countries to civil and criminal penalties. Regulations authorized by the act are implemented by the Office of the Near East in the International Trade Administration. See also *international boycott factor, Tax Reform Act of 1976*, and *Unified Law on the Boycott of Israel.*

**anticipated acceptance.**   An acceptance honored or redeemed before it matures, usually by a commercial bank.

**anticipated bunker price.**   The fuel-cost freight factor stipulated in a charter party. The anticipated bunker price provision allocates fuel costs reflecting price changes over the life of a charter party.

**antidiversion clause.**   See *destination control statement.*

**antidumping action.**   A government proceeding undertaken to resolve an unfair trade complaint. In the United States, antidumping actions are initiated when a domestic manufacturer, industry association, or trade union files a petition for relief jointly with the International Trade

Administration (ITA) and the International Trade Commission (ITC). The ITA determines whether the import was sold at less than fair value, i.e., below the cost of production or the price of comparable products in the exporter's home market. The ITC determines the extent of injury to a domestic industry. Following affirmative findings, the ITA issues antidumping orders to the U.S. Customs Service.   A duty is imposed on the dumping margin, i.e., the difference between the exporter's home market price and the foreign import price adjusted for export expenses. A complainant or defendant may appeal an adverse ITA decision to the U.S. Court of International Trade.

Antidumping actions are often criticized as a form of trade protection, since imports may be priced below market prices because of exchange rate fluctuations, the exporter's home market power, and so on. Some trade theorists see flexible tariffs as more transparent remedies for actual injuries resulting from harmful import surges. In their view, antidumping measures should be restricted to clear cases of predatory pricing. Intentional dumping causes economic harm to victimized industries, but cheap imports generally benefit consumers. See also *Antidumping Act of 1921; General Agreement on Tariffs and Trade: Tokyo Round, Antidumping Code; dumping*; and *Tariff Act of 1930.* Compare *countervailing duty action.*

**Antidumping Act of 1921.**   In the United States, an act of Congress authorizing antidumping proceedings. The act required the imposition of a duty equal to the difference between the invoice price of dumped goods and their home market price. When home market price was uncertain, the cost of producing like goods under the same conditions was used instead. The 1921 Antidumping Act was supplanted by the Trade Agreements Act of 1979.

**Antidumping Code.**   See *General Agreement on Tariffs and Trade: Tokyo Round.*

**antimarket disruption laws.**   The term for antidumping laws in some countries.

**Anti-Monopoly Law of 1947.**   In Japan, a law enacted to encourage business competition that authorizes the Japan Fair Trade Commission

(JFTC) to regulate anticompetitive practices. The JFTC has used provisions of the act to issue guidelines instructing *keiretsu* to reduce trade-restraining practices and to achieve similar administrative purposes, but the effect of its stronger provisions is a subject of debate. Criminal indictments in Japan for price conspiracy are rare, and the extent to which a criminal verdict is enforceable remains unclear. See also *Structural Impediments Initiative.*

**antitrust laws.**    In the United States, laws prohibiting predatory pricing, price fixing, and other anticompetitive practices. The Antitrust Division of the U.S. Department of Justice and the Federal Trade Commission share enforcement jurisdiction. Antitrust regulation is authorized by the Sherman Antitrust Act of 1890, the Clayton Act of 1914, the Federal Trade Commission Act of 1914, the Robinson-Patman Act of 1936, the Miller-Tydings Act of 1937, and the Antimerger Act of 1950. Limited antitrust exemptions are available under the Export Trading Company Act and the National Cooperative Research Act. The penalties for antitrust violations are injunctive relief and treble damages, which amount to three times the value of financial injury suffered by competitors.

Broadly, two types of activities are prohibited under U.S. antitrust law:

*per se violations.*    Conspiracies to fix prices, divide markets, and drive competitors from markets. Certain forms of business boycotts and tying arrangements are also illegal per se.

*rule-of-reason violations.*    Anticompetitive practices involving otherwise legal conduct, e.g., business cost-sharing arrangements or combinations to negotiate lower supplier rates. Among others, business justification may succeed as a defense to rule-of-reason violations.

**any quantity (AQ) rate.**    A carrier price term offering a uniform freight rate without regard to the quantity of a shipment. Freight tariffs specify AQ rates for certain categories of goods, often for bulk commodities.

**AP.**    The abbreviation for account payable.

**APA.**    The abbreviation for Administrative Procedure Act.

**APACS.**    The abbreviation for Association for Payment Clearing Services.

**APC.**    The abbreviation for the Agribusiness Promotion Council and the Asian and Pacific Council.

**APEC.**    The abbreviation for the Asia-Pacific Economic Cooperation Group.

**APEMF.**    The abbreviation for the *Association des Pays Exportateurs de Minerai de Fer.* See *Association of Iron Ore Exporting Countries.*

**apertura.**    A policy adopted in some Latin American countries relaxing prior import licensing restrictions. *Apertura* involves a gradual shift from issuing licenses to assessing duties as the primary means of import regulation.

**APO.**    The abbreviation for administrative protective order and Asian Productivity Organization.

**apostille sheet.**    A cover sheet used in international trade to authenticate commercial documents when an importing country requires legalization of export papers. Legalization is the process used by consular officials to validate documents. Countries belonging to The Hague Convention Abolishing the Requirement of Legalisation for Foreign Public Documents accept the apostille sheet in lieu of legalization. An apostille sheet is attached to certificates notarized in the exporting country, usually by a local chamber of commerce. Shipping documents are not covered by The Hague Convention and often require separate consular approval.

**apparel twin-plant operations.**    See *maquiladora.*

**apparent authority.**    In common law, an agency doctrine whereby principals become accountable for the actions of their agents. When a third party relies in good faith on an agent's representations, the principal may not usually claim the agent lacked authority in defending against a legal action.

**apparent good order (AGO).**    A notation on shipping documents by a carrier's agent when merchandise is delivered for shipment or arrives at the destination port. An AGO notice indicates that the exterior packaging is undamaged and the cargo appears sound. When noted on a consignee's arrival notice, apparent good order usually satisfies one condition for letter-of-credit payment to an exporter.

**appel d'offres.**   French: tender call, i.e., an invitation to bid.

**appellation of origin.**   A brand name identifying the place where a product originated. For example, Bordeaux wines (France) and Florida oranges (the United States) are appellations of origin. An exclusive right to use a product name is claimed by a country when an appellation of origin becomes a universal symbol of product quality. The extent of international protection afforded origin appellations was a subject of negotiations in the Uruguay Round of The General Agreement on Tariffs and Trade multilateral trade negotiations.

**appended declaration.**   A sworn and notarized statement attached to export documents. Some countries require the declaration in addition to other export certifications. Appended declarations are attached to bills of lading or insurance documents. The forms are usually available through an importing country's local consulate in the exporting country.

**application for a validated export license (Form BXA-622P).**   In the United States, a form used to obtain an export license for regulated exports. A successful application contains a detailed description of the shipment, including the exporter's explanation of how the product will be used abroad. Dual uses or possible adaptations of the product for purposes other than originally intended are also explained in the application, which is accompanied by technical manuals and specification sheets. Preapplication information is available from the Office of Export Control in the U.S. Department of Commerce.

**application identifier.**   A two-letter code for opening a computer application file in an electronic data interchange system. The identifier indicates the task to be performed.

**apportionment.**   The method of allocating economic value among the component parts of a given product. Apportionment is a part of the customs valuation process.

**appraisal.**   The procedure used to determine the economic value of a good.

**appraised value.**   1. The market value ascribed to an asset by a qualified appraiser. An item's appraised value may be more or less than the price paid for it, depending on current market prices for comparable property. An appraisal can be based on an item's replacement cost or appreciated (or depreciated) resale value. 2. The dutiable value of an import determined by customs valuation. Compare *market value.*

**appreciation.**   An increase in the value of an investment. An asset appreciates when market prices for comparable goods decrease. Compare *depreciation.*

**approved deferred share trust (ADST).**   In the United Kingdom, a trust created for the benefit of employees by a company and funded through purchases of its own shares. Taxes on ADST dividends, which are deferred until the shares are sold, are paid at a reduced rate. ADSTs are approved by Inland Revenue.

**APR.**   The abbreviation for Agricultural Products Report. See *Agricultural Information and Marketing Services.*

**APTA.**   The abbreviation for the Automotive Products Trade Act.

**AQ.**   The abbreviation for any quantity (rate).

**A/R.**   The abbreviation for account receivable.

**Arab Bank for Economic Development in Africa (ABEDA).**   An economic development bank created by the Arab League in 1973 to recycle petrodollars to African countries. The bank finances development projects in non–Arab League African countries. ABEDA, also known as *Banque Arabe pour le Développement Économique en Afrique* (BADEA), is headquartered in Khartoum, Sudan.

**Arab Common Market (ACM).**   An economic association created in 1965 by the Council of Arab Economic Unity.   The ACM encompasses Egypt, Iraq, Sudan, Syria, the United Arab Emirates, and Yemen. Since the 1980s, the goal of creating an integrated ACM market has been stymied by war in Sudan and the global economic sanctions imposed on Iraq following its invasion of Kuwait in 1990.

**Arab Cooperation Council (ACC).**   An economic association formed by Egypt, Iraq, Jordan, and

Yemen in 1989. Shortly after the ACC was created, the United Nations Security Council imposed worldwide economic sanctions on Iraq. During the Gulf War in 1991, substantial economic damage was inflicted on Iraq and Jordan. As of 1993, universal sanctions against Iraq remain in force, and the ACC is largely inactive.

**Arab dinar.**    See *Arab Monetary Fund.*

**Arab Fund for Economic and Social Development.**    A financing facility established in 1968 to fund projects of common interest in Arab countries. All Arab League countries are members, except Djibouti and Mauritania. The Arab Fund is based in Kuwait City.

**Arab International Bank (AIB).**    A multilateral bank owned principally, but not exclusively, by the governments of Egypt, Libya, Oman, Qatar, and the United Arab Emirates. The bank finances trade and development projects in Arab countries. Created in 1971, the AIB is based in Cairo.

**Arab League.**    An association of Arab nations created by agreement in 1945. Known formally as the League of Arab States, many of the organization's early efforts revolved around the continuing Arab-Israeli conflict. Arab League members are Algeria, Bahrain, Djibouti, Egypt, Iraq, Jordan, Kuwait, Lebanon, Libya, Mauritania, Morocco, Oman, Palestine, Qatar, Saudi Arabia, Somalia, Sudan, Syria, Tunisia, United Arab Emirates, and Yemen. The Arab Monetary Fund and the Arab Bank for Economic Development in Africa are Arab League organizations. The Arab League is headquartered in Cairo. See also *Council of Arab Economic Unity.*

**Arab Mahgreb Union.**    See *Mahgreb Common Market.*

**Arab Monetary Fund (AMF).**    A multilateral financial institution created by the Arab League at Rabat, Morocco, in 1977. The AMF, founded primarily to assist member countries facing balance-of-payments deficits, also encourages other forms of cooperation among its members. The organization is composed exclusively of Arab states and the Palestine Liberation Organization. The AMF's accounting unit is the Arab dinar, which is equivalent to one special drawing right. The AMF is based in Abu Dhabi.

**arbitrage.**    The process of leveraging assets for profit. In arbitrage transactions, a commodity is purchased at a low price in one market and sold at a higher price in another. Arbitrage can involve buying money-market instruments in one banking center and selling the instruments in a different banking center, trading financial instruments denominated in different currencies, or exchanging short-term futures for longer-term contracts. In futures arbitrage, the investor gains from a higher-risk premium set for the longer-term contract. See also *hedge* and *swap.*

**arbitrageur.**    A specialist in arbitrage.

**arbitration.**    Dispute resolution without resort to litigation. Unlike litigation, arbitration does not set a legal precedent for future cases or require a finding of misconduct. In international transactions and treaties, parties often agree in advance to be bound by arbitration, primarily because the process enables them to avoid unfamiliar courts and resolve disputes within accepted international rules. Arbitration is especially useful in countries where lawsuits are uncommon, as in Asia, or where local custom cedes legal jurisdiction over commercial disputes to religious rather than civil courts, as in some Middle Eastern countries. Some countries distinguish between de jure arbitration (i.e., ordinary legal principles are applied to dispute settlement) and de facto arbitration (i.e., disputes are resolved according to principles of equity and fairness). In Chile, for example, de jure arbitrators must be lawyers and nationals, and nonnationals may only serve as de facto arbitrators. Arbitration may be the subject of a contract clause or an entire agreement, which specifies the issues to be arbitrated, the mediating agency, and procedures governing the dispute-settlement process. In the United States, commercial arbitration is governed by the Arbitration Act of 1947 and often conducted by an authorized agency, such as the American Arbitration Association. The International Centre for the Settlement of Investment Disputes, a World Bank affiliate, provides arbitration facilities for international dispute settlement. Rules for international commercial arbitration have been established by the United Nations Convention on Arbitration and the United Nations Convention on the Recognition and Enforcement of Foreign Arbitral Awards .

**Arbitration Act of 1947.**   In the United States, a law authorizing dispute-settlement procedures when parties to foreign commercial contracts agree to be bound by arbitration. A 1970 amendment to the act authorizes federal courts to remove from state courts those cases subject to international arbitration. The federal courts are also allowed to appoint arbitrators and enforce arbitral awards. The 1970 and 1990 amendments conform the act to international rules created by the United Nations Convention on the Recognition and Enforcement of Foreign Arbitral Awards.

**Arcru.**   A rarely used artificial currency unit based on a basket of Arab national currencies. The Arcru was introduced in 1974 and tied to the value of the U.S. dollar.

**A record.**   See *transaction control header.*

**Argentina-Brazil Agreement.**   See *Mercosur.*

**Arms Export Control Act of 1976.**   In the United States, an act of Congress authorizing the President to regulate arms exports, including exports of technical data. The act also covers ammunition and other implements of war. See also *International Traffic in Arms Regulations.*

**arr.**   The abbreviation for arrival.

**Arrangement Regarding Bovine Meat.**   See *General Agreement on Tariffs and Trade: Tokyo Round.*

**Arrangement Regarding Trade in Textiles.**   See *MultiFiber Arrangement Regarding International Trade in Textiles.*

**arrest.**   In maritime law, the seizure of an ocean vessel pending final determination of an admiralty suit.

**arrival draft.**   A financial instrument accepted on or near the date of a shipment's arrival at a port of destination. An arrival draft is customarily payable without additional documentation.

**arrival notice.**   A notice issued by a common carrier informing a consignee of a shipment's arrival time. The condition of the merchandise and fees payable are also described in the notice.

**arrived ship.**   A charter party term specifying when lay time for a chartered carrier begins. An arrival has occurred when a vessel is docked *and* ready for loading and unloading. The exporter or consignee must also have been notified, usually in writing, of the ship's readiness to load and unload.

**articles of association.**   The articles of incorporation or articles of partnership required to form a company.

**articles of incorporation/partnership.**   A document creating a firm, setting forth the purpose of the organization, the initial investment, the rights of owners, and rules for operating the business. In the United States, articles of incorporation are filed with the secretary of state in the incorporating state. The document names incorporators and specifies the number and the par value of authorized shares. Articles of partnership, also known as partnership agreements, identify the partners of a firm and clarify the rights, duties, and share of firm profits and losses attributable to each partner. In Britain, these documents are known as articles or memoranda of association. See also *authorized shares* and *certificate of incorporation.*

**artificial currency unit (ACU).**   A financial accounting unit established by international agreement. The value of an artificial currency unit is based on a basket of currencies, an international reserve currency, or a commodity, usually gold. Broadly, most ACUs are monetary units, held and traded exclusively for the accounts of official bodies or major international banks. Except when specially designated for commercial transactions, ACUs are not used to settle private accounts. See also *European currency unit, North American currency unit*, and *special drawing right.*

**Aruba vrijgestelde vennootschap (AVV).**   In Aruba, a foreign corporation exempt from the local profits tax and created to attract offshore investment. AVVs are operated as licensed local trusts.

**ASAM.**   The abbreviation for Automated Search and Match. See *Intermarket Surveillance Information System.*

**ASC X9.**   See *American National Standards Institute.*

**ASC X11.**   See *American National Standards Institute.*

**ASC X12.**   See *American National Standards Institute.*

**AsDB.**   The acronym for the Asian Development Bank.

**ASEAN.**   The abbreviation for the Association of Southeast Asian Nations.

**ASEAN Free Trade Area.**   See *Association of Southeast Asian Nations.*

**ASEAN-Japan Development Fund (AJDF).**   In the Pacific, an official development assistance fund established in Tokyo for the benefit of the Association of Southeast Asian Nations (ASEAN) and Pacific Rim countries. The agency finances joint ventures and investments in member countries through the Japan-ASEAN Invest-ment Corporation. The AJDF funds the New Asian Industrial Development Plan, which finances infrastructure and industrial estates development, and supports activities of the Asian Productivity Organization. See also *Asian Development Bank.*

**as freighted.**   A carrier pricing term indicating that surcharges will be determined on the same basis as the base freight for a shipment.

**A-shares.**   See *B-shares.*

**Asian and Pacific Council (APC).**   An informal discussion group created in Tokyo in 1966. APC was formed to forge closer regional cultural and economic ties. Australia, Japan, New Zealand, the Philippines, South Korea, Taiwan, and Thailand are APC members. Compare *Asia-Pacific Economic Cooperation Group.*

**Asian Clearing Union.**   A settlement association formed to clear international payments for member countries. The Asian Clearing Union's unit of account is the Asian monetary unit, which is equal to one special drawing right. Its members are Bangladesh, Myanmar, India, Iran, Nepal, Pakistan, and Sri Lanka.

**Asian currency unit (ACU).**   The unit of account created in Singapore in 1968 for Asian dollar deposits. ACUs are held in separate accounts in Asian banks for nonresident depositors. See also *Singapore interbank offered rate.*

**Asian Development Bank (AsDB, ADB).**   A multilateral bank established to finance economic and industrial development in Asia and the Pacific region. Created in 1966 by the United Nations Economic and Social Commission for Asia and the Pacific, the bank has 31 regional and 14 nonregional members. Concessional loans are made through the Asian Development Fund, AsDB's soft-loan window. AsDB's activities are financed by contributions from its members of which Japan and the United States are the largest contributors. The bank's per-share par value is 10,000 special drawing rights. AsDB is located in Manila.

**Asian Development Fund.**   See *Asian Development Bank.*

**Asian dollar.**   A U.S. dollar or other foreign currency deposited in an Asian bank.

**Asian dollar market.**   A financial market located primarily in the international banking centers of Singapore and Hong Kong. The market encompasses Asian dollar deposits and Eurobonds.

**Asian monetary unit.**   See *Asian Clearing Union.*

**Asian Productivity Organization (APO).**   A regional economic development organization founded in 1971. Fourteen Asian states are APO members. The APO promotes sharing of management and technical assistance among member states. The organization is based in Tokyo. See also *ASEAN-Japan Development Fund* and *New Asian Industrial Development Plan.*

**Asia-Pacific Economic Cooperation Group (APEC).**   Also known as the Pacific Economic Cooperation Conference Group, APEC is a loosely organized group of Pacific nations formed to promote regional economic cooperation. Australia, Canada, Hong Kong, Japan, New Zealand, People's Republic of China (PRC), South Korea, Taiwan, the United States, and the countries of the Association of Southeast Asian Nations (ASEAN) are APEC members. Founded at Canberra, Australia, in 1989, APEC is seen by some experts as a future Pacific rival to the European Community. The contrary view holds that the disparate and conflicting interests of APEC members preclude the formation of an integrated Pacific trading bloc. Compare *Asian and Pacific Council.*

**Asociación Latinoamericana de Integración (ALADI).**   Also known as the Latin American Integration Association (LAIA), ALADI is the successor to ALALC, the Latin American Free Trade Association (LAFTA), founded in 1960. Reorganized as ALADI by the Treaty of Montevideo of 1980, the association consists of Argentina, Bolivia, Brazil, Chile, Colombia, Ecuador, Mexico, Paraguay, Peru, Uruguay, and Venezuela. *El Pacto Andino* and *Mercosur* are ALADI subgroups. The Montevideo Treaty contemplates bilateral agreements negotiated among member countries as the first step toward integrated trade in the region. In 1988, ALADI established the *Asociación Latinoamericano de Traficantes* (ALAT), also known as the Latin American Association of International Trading Companies, at Rio de Janeiro. ALAT is ALADI's private-sector arm formed in association with the Inter-American Development Bank. ALADI has headquarters in Montevideo, Uruguay.

**ASP.**   The abbreviation for American selling price.

**assembled shipment.**   Cargo consolidated by a commercial carrier or freight forwarder for shipment to one consignee. Normally, an assembled shipment is covered by one invoice and a single through bill of lading. Compare *installment shipments.*

**assembly operation.**   See *American components assembled abroad* and *maquiladora.*

**assembly service.**   See *assembled shipment.*

**assented stock.**   Equity subject to an approved takeover bid. Compare *nonassented stock.*

**asset-based lending.**   Short-term secured financing obtained from a bank or finance company and collateralized by business assets, usually a mixture of inventories and accounts receivables. Asset-based loans are used for a variety of purposes, such as business expansion or interim financing for international trade transactions.

**assignment.**   The transfer of title and rights in property owned by one party to another. A portion or the entire proceeds of a sale or other transaction may be assigned. 1. In sales, the transfer of a seller's right to payment to a supplier or other third party. 2. In finance, the transfer of a beneficiary's rights to proceeds under a letter of credit. An assignment must usually be confirmed by the advising bank. 3. In securities transactions, the transfer of stocks or bonds to another party. 4. In commodities trading, the naming of an option writer to buy or sell contracts.

**assistant regional commissioner (ARC).**   In the United States, an official of the U.S. Customs Service assigned to a customs region. ARCs supervise regional port operations, inspect imports, and enforce domestic customs laws and regulations. See also *district area office.*

**assists.**   Domestic exports inserted (or otherwise integrated) into finished products abroad for import to the exporting country. In the United States, duties are levied on manufacturing assists on the first U.S. reentry; subsequent reimportations enter duty-free. Research and design assists enter duty-free on the first U.S. reentry.

**Associated British Ports (ABP).**   The port authority in the United Kingdom. The port authority is managed by Associated British Ports Holding plc.

**associated financing.**   A term used by the Organization for Economic Cooperation and Development to denote government-to-government financing. Associated financing includes official development assistance and export financing credits, whether granted on concessional or market terms.

**associated foreign corporation.**   In the United States, a subsidiary of a domestic international sales corporation (DISC) authorized by the Tax Revenue Act of 1971. Associated companies received tax deferments on export earnings when no more than 10 percent of their voting shares were owned by a DISC or by the corporate parent of a DISC. The DISC was modified by the Tax Reform Act of 1984.

**Association Cambiste Internationale (ACI).**   A worldwide association of foreign exchange dealers. The Forex Club facilitates social contacts among ACI members. ACI is based in Paris. See also *cambist.*

**Association Européenne de Libre Echange.** French: European Free Trade Association.

**Association for Payment Clearing Services (APACS).**   In the United Kingdom, a banking association that clears payments and international funds transfers. Different APACS companies provide clearing services, depending on the nature and value of the financial instrument. APACS services available to UK commercial banks are identical to those performed by the Federal Reserve System for member banks in the United States.

**Association of British Insurers (ABI).**   In the United Kingdom, a trade association representing the nation's largest insurers. ABI's members control roughly 90 percent of the domestic insurance market. ABI is headquartered in London.

**Association of Foreign Trading Agents of Korea (AFTAK).**   A semiprivate trade association, which registers import agents on behalf of the Korean government. Only registered traders may import goods into Korea unless the importer is also the end user of the goods. AFTAK is based in Seoul.

**Association of Iron Ore Exporting Countries (AWAKE).**   An international commodity group established in 1975 to promote cooperation in the marketing and pricing of iron-ore products and share exploration information. AWAKE members are Algeria, Australia, India, Liberia, Mauritania, Peru, Sierra Leone, Sweden, and Venezuela. Also known as the *Association des Pays Exportateurs de Minerai de Fer (APEMF)*, AWAKE is headquartered in Geneva.

**Association of Natural Rubber Producing Countries (ANRPC).**   An international commodity group established in 1970 to stabilize and maintain prices for natural rubber products. ANRPC's founding agreement, the International Rubber Agreement, was among the first to establish buffer stocks. ANRPC members are India, Indonesia, Malaysia, Papua New Guinea, Singapore, Sri Lanka, and Thailand. The organization is headquartered in Kaula Lumpur, Malaysia.

**Association of Southeast Asian Nations (ASEAN).**   A regional economic development and trade promotion association founded in 1967 and revived in 1976. ASEAN members are Indonesia, Malaysia, the Philippines, Singapore, Thailand, and Brunei. In 1992, ASEAN members established the ASEAN Free Trade Area, agreeing to implement regional economic integration by the year 2008, beginning with internal tariff reductions in 1993. ASEAN's secretariat is located in Jakarta, Indonesia. See also *ASEAN-Japan Development Fund.*

**assurance.**   The British term for personal insurance, especially life insurance.

**ASYCUDA.**   The acronym for the Automated System for Customs Data.

**ATA.**   The abbreviation for the American Truckers Associations.

**ATA carnet.**   The abbreviated term for *admission temporaire*/temporary admission. See *carnet.*

**ATB.**   The abbreviation for across-the-board tariff reduction.

**at best.**   An investor's instruction to a broker to buy or sell equity or commodities for the best price. The notice requires a broker to execute a transaction immediately. Compare *at limit.*

**ATC.**   The abbreviation for air traffic control.

**at call.**   See *call money.*

**ATFI.**   The abbreviation for the Automated Tariff Filing Information system.

**Athens Convention Relating to the Carriage of Passengers and Their Luggage by Sea.**   An international agreement adopted in 1974 defining ocean carrier liability for passenger injuries and personal property losses. Except where a carrier acted recklessly or with knowledge of impending injury or loss, a negligent carrier's liability is limited under the convention. Certain of its protocols denominate liability in Poincaré francs (1976) and increase limits from 55,000 to 225,000 U.S. dollars for death or injury and from 2322 to 12,900 U.S. dollars for personal property losses (1990). The Athens Convention is administered by the International Maritime Organization.

**at limit.**   An investor's instruction to a broker to buy or sell equity or commodities at a specified price. In an at-limit transaction, the investor also sets a time limit for the broker to execute a sale (e.g., within 2 days). Compare *at best.*

**ATM.** The abbreviation for automated teller machine or automated transaction machine. See *electronic funds transfer.*

**ATMI.** The abbreviation for the American Textile Manufacturers Institute.

**ATO.** The abbreviation for Agricultural Trade Office.

**at sight.** A payment term indicating that a draft or bill of exchange will be paid when presented to the drawee.

**attaché.** See *consul.*

**at the market.** In commodities trading, an order to buy or sell a futures contract or options contract at the best available price.

**at the money.** In options trading, a market price for futures equal to the strike price. Compare *in the money* and *out of the money.*

**attn.** The abbreviation for attention.

**auction.** 1. The sale of a commodity based on bids. 2. In financial markets, the sale of Treasury bills or bonds, often to the highest bidder. Treasury auctions are held in Australia, Belgium, Canada, France, Germany, Italy, the Netherlands, Spain, Switzerland, the United Kingdom, and the United States. In some countries, auctions are known as tenders.

**aucune valeur commerciale.** French: without commercial value. Samples imported for display or professional purposes and bearing an *aucune valeur commerciale* marking are usually admitted duty-free in French-speaking countries that are not members of a carnet convention.

**audit.** An external auditor's or certified public accountant's survey of a company's accounts. The auditor's opinion, also known as the auditor's report, is included in a company's annual report. The auditor's opinion may be qualified or unqualified. Most companies also conduct internal audits to determine whether financial accounts are in order. Compare *customs audit.*

**auditor's report.** An annual certified accountant's report used to verify a company's accounts. In the United States, the Securities and Exchange Commission requires audited financial statements from companies whose securities are publicly traded. In the United Kingdom, audits of limited companies are filed with the Registrar of Companies. See also *directors' report.*

**au jour le jour.** In France, the daily lending rate in money markets. Rates available for Treasury bills are more favorable than those for private bills. The Banque de France influences rates through its dealings with discount houses. See also *maison de réescompte.*

**Ausfuhr.** German: export. The plural forms are *Ausfuhrwaren* and *Ausfuhrartikel* (export goods). *Ausfuhrschein* is an export permit.

**Ausfuhrkredit GmbH (AKA).** In Germany, an export credit company formed by commercial banks to provide medium- and long-term foreign trade financing. AKA lends pooled funds to exporters against discounted promissory notes. It also extends market-rate credit to foreign buyers and preferential credit to developing countries and Eastern European countries.

**Auslandskassenverein.** See *Kassenverein.*

**Auslandsobligation.** German: foreign (issue) security.

**austral.** The currency of Argentina.

**Australian Dollar Area.** A group of eight island countries in the South Pacific with national currencies linked, or "pegged," to the Australian dollar. The countries are Fiji, Kiribati, Papua New Guinea, Solomon Islands, Tonga, Tuvalu, Vanuatu, and Western Samoa.

**Australian Stock Exchange (ASX) Limited.** A national exchange created in 1987 by a merger of local exchanges. ASX is a self-regulating organization that trades listed securities, financial futures, and options. Membership is open to foreign corporations. Prices are quoted in Australian dollars and published daily in the national and international financial press. Investments are insured by the National Guarantee Fund owned by the ASX. Corporate takeovers are governed by the Companies (Acquisition of Shares) Act of 1980 and regulated by the exchange. ASX member exchanges are located in Adelaide, Brisbane, Hobart, Melbourne, Perth, and Sydney. See also *International Options Clearing Corporation.*

**autarchy.**    Also known as autarky, a national policy of economic self-sufficiency. Autarchy discourages foreign trade and investment, while promoting internal industrial development. Several regimes around the world implemented autarchic policies in the twentieth century. By most economic measures, those policies failed. Compare *economic nationalism.*

**authority to purchase.**    A type of financing encountered in Asia. A seller's bank authorizes its correspondent bank to draw a draft against an importer's account. The authority to purchase may be drawn with recourse or without recourse. When the importer's credit is backed by a bank, the instrument resembles a letter of credit.

**authorized dealer.**    An agent approved by an owner to distribute or allocate merchandise or commodities, often within a limited geographical area. See also *agency.*

**authorized shares.**    Common stock or preferred stock approved for issue by a company's articles of incorporation. The number of authorized shares in each class of stock is changed by amending the articles of incorporation, which is accomplished by a majority vote of holders of voting stock.

**Automated Broker Interface.**    See *Automated Commercial System.*

**Automated Clearing House (ACH).**    In the United States, the electronic clearing facility for financial institutions. The ACH system consists of a network of regional clearing associations, most of which subscribe to Federal Reserve System data processing services. ACH facilities are used to transmit deposits for personal accounts and transfer payments between commercial institutions.

**Automated Commercial System (ACS).**    In the United States, the electronic data interchange (EDI) message system used by the U.S. Customs Service to track and process trade data. ACS enables the Customs Service to enter and clear goods without paper documents and determine the tariff status of imports from information transmitted through the EDI systems of brokers or manufacturers. ACS is composed of several dedicated electronic modules, or integrated systems, including the Census Interface System, the Drawback System, and the Quota System. The ACS Automated Manifest System (AMS) enables airlines, freight forwarders, and container shippers to send manifest data to the Customs Service. Carriers using AMS are given cargo clearance preference over carriers filing paper documents. The Automated Broker Interface (ABI) is the portion of the ACS used by importers and brokers to send customs entry and clearance data. ABI uses the automated broker interface/nonstatement to notify the Customs Service when a broker pays duties and fees for a single customs entry. The automated broker interface/statement notifies the Customs Service when a broker pays duties and fees for a bulk customs entry. The Automated Export System (AES) is used by exporters to file electronic manifests and declarations. AES also bills exporters for customs fees. The ACS, partially operational since 1988, is to be fully implemented by 1996.

**Automated Export System.**    See *Automated Commercial System.*

**Automated Manifest System.**    See *Automated Commercial System.*

**Automated Search and Match.**    See *Intermarket Surveillance Information System.*

**Automated System for Customs Data (ASYCUDA).**    The electronic data interchange system for customs processing in Africa developed by the United Nations Conference on Trade and Development. Implemented in 1985, the system became operational in 1991. Countries on several continents are actual or prospective participants in ASYCUDA.

**Automated Tariff Filing Information (ATFI).**    The electronic data interchange system developed by the Federal Maritime Commission to process ocean freight rate data. The ATFI automates carrier filings, including rules and formulas applied by carriers when transporting cargo and computing tariffs. The system contains a customized version of the Harmonized Commodity Description and Coding System, an optional service for ocean carriers and freight forwarders. The automated system was implementated on January 1, 1993.

**automated teller machine.**   See *electronic funds transfer.*

**automated transaction machine.**   See *electronic funds transfer.*

**Automotive Products Trade Act of 1965.**   See *Automotive Products Trade Agreement.*

**Automotive Products Trade Agreement.**   A bilateral trade agreement eliminating tariffs on new automobiles and automobile parts traded between Canada and the United States. Also known as the Auto Pact, the agreement was reached in 1965.   Replacement parts are not covered by the agreement. The Auto Pact was implemented in the United States by the Automotive Products Trade Act of 1965.

**autonomous duty.**   See *duty.*

**autonomous transaction.**   See *above-the-line item.*

**autoridad portuaria.**   Spanish: port authority.

**autorité portuaire.**   French: port authority.

**aval.**   See *bank aval.*

**average (avg.).**   In insurance, a partial loss incurred as a consequence of a marine accident. Also called general average, the concept of average survives an ancient principle of maritime law, which required that salvage costs arising from a maritime accident be justly and fairly apportioned among participants in the voyage. The shipper's contribution, known as general average security, is usually covered by marine insurance. Average claims are paid from a common salvage fund financed by contributions from parties to the transaction. The contributions are normally secured by average bonds posted by the contributors' insurers before claims are paid. Maritime liens automatically attach to defensible average claims. A claim is deemed defensible when (1) the loss is partial; i.e., the voyage, or some portion of it, is completed ; (2) the disaster imperils the ship and its cargo; and (3) costs are incurred to mitigate the disaster. See also *average adjuster* and *York-Antwerp Rules.* Compare *aversio* to *average,* and to *total loss.*

There are three possible insurance policy provisions for average:

*free of all average (FAA).*   The policy covers total-loss-only claims and excludes average or partial-loss claims.

*free of particular average (FPA).*   The policy covers partial losses if the salvage operation benefits all parties to the voyage. FPA clauses may contain American or English conditions, which describe the origin of the condition rather than the place where a policy is written. FPA-American conditions (FPAAC) exclude partial-loss claims, except when caused by collision, sinking, burning, or stranding. Losses incurred when cargo is transported by light vessels, such as sailing craft or barges, are excluded. FPA-English conditions (FPAEC) cover claims for any partial loss from collision, sinking, burning, or stranding.

**particular average (P/A).**   A marine policy provision that excludes partial-loss claims when the salvage operation was meant to benefit only one party to a shipping transaction.

**average adjuster.**   A marine insurance adjuster who calculates the pro rata liability of parties to a shipping transaction when average (partial-loss) or hull damage claims are filed. The adjuster is often hired by the shipowner.

**average bond.**   See *general average security.*

**aversio.**   1. In commerce, the sale of a bulk (or gross) unit rather than a component part. 2. In insurance, *aversio periculi* means total-loss coverage, including the costs of avoiding a shipping disaster. Compare *average.*

**avg.**   The abbreviation for average.

**avoir fiscal.**   In France, a tax credit applied to 50 percent of some dividend income. The credit is granted to compensate shareholders for taxes previously paid by a corporation. The *avoir fiscal* is primarily available to residents of France. Nonresident individuals are eligible only when they reside in specified countries. To qualify for the credit, a nonresident corporation must have substantial capital investments in France. See also *imputation tax system.*

**AVV.**   See *Aruba vrijgestelde vennoostchap.*

**AWB.**   The abbreviation for air waybill.

# B

**B-13.** The Canadian export declaration form.

**BAA.** The abbreviation for British Airports Authority plc.

**back.** The short form of backwardation.

**back contract.** Also called a distant contract, a futures contract that expires at a distant time in the future. Compare *front contract.*

**back date.** A draft or contract carrying a date other than the date of its making. The instrument must be negotiated within 6 months of the date noted on it.

**back door/front door.** In the United Kingdom, the means used by the central bank, the Bank of England, to increase the domestic money supply. When securities are purchased, the term *back door* is used. Back-door purchases are known as open-market operations in the United States. Conversely, when the Bank of England expands the money supply by lending to discount houses, the term *front door* is used. A similar process in the United States is known as raising or lowering the discount rate. In the UK, the interest rates on central bank transactions with discount houses are known as Bank of England dealing rates. See also *interest rate policy.*

**back-end load.** A mutual fund on which a sales commission, or load, is paid when an investor cashes out. Compare *front-end load.*

**back freight.** The charge for returning cargo to the destination port after it has been miscarried to a distant port. The carrier or shipper may bear the cost, depending on the reasons for overcarriage.

**Background Notes.** In the United States, an information series published by the U.S. Department of State. The publication provides miscellaneous data collected abroad by the Foreign Service. *Background Notes* cover foreign countries' demographics, political and foreign policy positions, as well as trade and economic data.

**backhander.** See *baksheesh.*

**back letter.** 1. A letter clarifying the details of a charter party. 2. A letter of indemnity.

**backspread.** In finance, an arbitrage term. A backspread is a price lower than the anticipated difference between the purchase price of a commodity and its selling price.

**back-to-back credit.** Also known as a countervailing credit, and not to be confused with a back-to-back letter of credit, a back-to-back credit conceals the identity of a seller from a buyer. The financier of the transaction makes a purchase for its own account and issues documents in its own name. The details of the transaction are not disclosed to the buyer.

**back-to-back letter of credit (L/C).** A letter of credit with two instructions, one to pay an exporter and the other to pay a supplier. The supplier's L/C is based on an irrevocable letter of credit issued to the exporter. Back-to-back L/Cs are a common form of supplier financing.

**back-to-back loan.** 1. A two-party loan made to a multinational parent company in one country and a subsidiary in another. Usually, the parent pledges collateral for the loan. If the subsidiary defaults, a lender has recourse against the parent. 2. A loan made in one currency against a loan denominated in another currency. Compare *parallel financing.*

**back-to-back transaction.** A transaction completed in two parts. 1. In international trade, buybacks and various other forms of countertrade. 2. In finance, various forms of multiparty loans, e.g., a purchaser in country A from a seller in country B sells goods to a third party in country C. The buyer in country A may use the receivable from country C as security for credit to pay the seller from country B.

**back translation.** A second translation of the same subject matter into the original language. For example, a document is "back translated" when it is translated from English to French to English.

**backup.** In finance, an increase in interest rates that causes bond prices to fall. When prices drop, yields rise and bonds are more difficult to sell. Investors who anticipate the change swap long-term bonds for shorter-term issues, thereby "backing up" their portfolios.

**backup line.** A bank line of credit, usually secured by a confirmed letter of credit or a revolving credit facility. Backup lines are issued in support of commercial paper that may not be sold at maturity. The borrower pays a fee or maintains a compensating balance sufficient to pay the cost of the bank line of credit.

**backup withholding.**    In the United States, a type of withholding tax, or an amount retained for taxes by one party from another's earnings. For example, the Internal Revenue Service requires banks to withhold a percentage of dividends and interest payable to some taxpayers. Reported on Form 1099, the withholding affects taxpayers who have not previously paid taxes on income or disclosed Social Security numbers to the bank.

**backwardation.**    1. The difference between a commodity spot price and the forward (or futures) price. When used to denote price differentials, backwardation describes a market condition in which the spot price for a commodity is lower than the futures (or forward) price quoted for delivery in subsequent months. 2. In stock trading, a penalty paid by a seller to delay delivery of securities. See also *contango market*. 3. In the Eurobond market, the difference between one market maker's bid and another's lower offer.

**BACS.**    The acronym for Bankers' Automated Clearing House.

**BAD.**    The French abbreviation for *Banque Africaine de Développement* and *Banque Arabe de Développement*. See also African Development Bank Group.

**bad check/cheque.**    A draft returned unpaid. Checks are returned for insufficient funds, lack of endorsement, and so on. In the United States, banks are required to charge a returned-check fee.

**bad debt.**    A sum payable that a debtor seems unlikely to repay. Bad debts are written off as losses, usually against a reserve fund maintained for that purpose.

**BADEA.**    The abbreviation for *Banque Arabe pour le Développement Économique en Afrique*. See *Arab Bank for Economic Development in Africa*.

**bad order.**    A railway term for a decrepit or unrepaired railcar.

**bagged cargo.**    See *bale cargo*.

**bag operation.**    An industrial espionage operation, usually involving foreign government theft of proprietary business secrets. The term is also used when one government attempts to uncover the international trade negotiating strategies of another.

**baht.**    The currency of Thailand.

**bailee.**    A party in temporary possession of property belonging to another. The bailee does not acquire title and surrenders the property to the owner when the bailment terminates. Common carriers and warehouses are bailees, and liens for transport and storage fees arise on goods in their possession. The party entrusting property to a bailee's custody is known as a bailor.

**bailee receipt.**    A document of title transferred to a lender by an importer of bailed goods. In return for the receipt, the importer obtains the bill of lading needed to sell the goods, repaying the lender from sales revenues. Bailed goods are sold on open accounts or as cash-with-order sales. Cash or installment payments are deposited with the lender, and the balance remaining after the lender has been repaid is remitted to the importer. Compare *trust receipt*.

**bailment.**    See *bailee* and *bailee receipt*.

**baksheesh.**    Sometimes called *bakshish*, a gratuity paid to facilitate a business deal in the Middle East. Also known as a backhander, the payment is a customary and expected business practice in some Middle Eastern countries and is not generally understood to constitute a bribe. In the United States, payments to foreign officials to obtain government contracts or financial favors are illegal under the Foreign Corrupt Practices Act of 1977.

**bal.**    The abbreviation for balance.

**balance commerciale.**    French: (merchandise) balance of trade. See also *balance of payments*.

**balance des paiements courants.**    French: current accounts balance. See also *balance of payments*.

**balance of concessions.**    A term roughly synonymous with reciprocity in international trade negotiations during which countries agree to exchange economic benefits. When concessions are reciprocal, countries trade objectively equal economic benefits. When concessions are made "on balance," the benefits exchanged are of equal economic value only in relative (i.e., subjective) terms.

**balance of payments (BOP).**   The difference in real value between a country's income and liabilities as reflected by its current accounts over a fixed time period, usually 1 year. A balance of payments may be positive or negative, may be in surplus or in deficit, and is based on the following factors:

*balance of trade.*   The difference between merchandise export inflows and merchandise import outflows.

*services balance.*   Income from sales of services in foreign markets minus purchases of services provided by foreigners.

*balance of goods and services.*   The sum of the balance of trade added to the services balance.

*transfer payments account.*   Income from foreign sources other than sales and investment transactions.

*balance on current account.*   The sum of the balance of goods and services added to the transfer payments balance.

*capital account.*   Investment inflows minus investment outflows.

*basic balance.*   The sum of the balance on current account added to the capital account balance.

*reserve transaction account.*   The difference between sales and purchases of reserve assets (e.g., hard currencies, gold, or special drawing rights).

*official settlements balance.*   The basic balance added to the reserve transaction account balance.

**balance sheet.**   A company's statement of assets, liabilities, and retained capital at the end of an accounting period. The assets listed on a balance sheet equal a company's liabilities and capital.

**balboa.**   The currency of Panama.

**bale cargo.**   Commodities packed in canvas or cloth sacks.

**bale space.**   A carrier's interior shipping capacity.

**ballast.**   Superfluous stock used to stabilize an ocean carrier operating below its stowage capacity.

**ballast bonus.**   A fee charged by an ocean carrier for an intermediate port stop. The freight includes a surcharge for loading cargoes too small to fill a ship's cargo capacity.

**balloon cargo.**   A shipment that fills the interior cargo space of a carrier without fulfilling the carrier's weight capacity.

**balloon payment.**   A payment made on a loan at longer than usual intervals. Balloon payments are usually annual or semiannual.

**Baltic Exchange.**   In London, a private exchange that specializes in commodity trading and freight charters. Brokers trading on the Baltic Exchange arrange ocean charters and air charters under the auspices of the Baltic International Freight Futures Exchange, the premier international exchange for arranging freight and passenger charters. The Federation of Oils, Seeds and Fats Associations and the London Grain Futures Market (barley and wheat) are also located at the Baltic. The Baltic's Grain and Free Trade Association supervises trading in dry-cargo freight futures. Brokers transact business at the Baltic during daily face-to-face meetings on the trading floor.

**Baltic Freight Index.**   A charter price index published in London and used primarily by owners and charterers of bulk-shipping vessels. The index is based on freight charges along 15 international shipping routes. It is published each business day by the Baltic International Freight Futures Exchange. See also *Baltic Exchange.*

**Baltic International Freight Futures Exchange (BIFFEX).**   See *Baltic Exchange.*

**Baltic Market.**   A common market proposed in 1991 to be composed of Estonia, Latvia, and Lithuania. The Baltic Republics of the former Union of Soviet Socialist Republics (U.S.S.R.) plan a new economic union to coordinate economic, environmental, financial, and social policies.

**banco central.**   Spanish: central bank.

**Banco Centroamericano de Integración Económica (BCIE).**   Also known as the Central American

Bank for Economic Integration, BCIE is the central bank of *Mercado Común Centroamericano* established at Managua, Nicaragua, in 1960. Costa Rica, El Salvador, Guatemala, Honduras, and Nicaragua are BCIE members. BCIE is headquartered at Tegucigalpa, Honduras.

**banco del estado.**    Spanish: state bank. Depending on the country, the term may denote a central bank or an economic development bank. See also *central bank* and *development bank*.

**banco de reserva.**    Spanish: reserve bank. See also *central bank*.

**bancogiro.**    See *giro*.

**band.**    1. In foreign exchange management, the range of movement permitted a currency. 2. In the United Kingdom, the duration of the Bank of England's periodic interventions in the money market measured by its purchases of bills of exchange. A band is the length of a bill's maturity. For example, Band I matures in 1 to 14 days, Band 2 in 15 to 33 days, Band 3 in 34 to 63 days, and Band 4 in 64 to 91 days.

**bank.**    A financial institution that receives deposits, lends funds, and settles accounts. Banks also act as agents when buying and selling securities or managing trust accounts. As government-regulated institutions, banks are limited to activities approved by the laws of the jurisdiction in which they are chartered. Compare *nonbank*.

**bankable.**    A financially sound deal or borrower. A bankable borrower is creditworthy enough to receive credit without collateral or a third-party guarantor. A bankable deal promises a safe return, except under unusual and unexpected circumstances.

**bank advance.**    A bank loan.

**bank annuity.**    See *consolidated annuity*.

**bank aval.**    A bank's endorsement inscribed on a bill of exchange to guarantee payment to a subsequent holder. The practice is common in Europe but rare in the United States. See also *accommodation endorsement*. Compare *acceptance*.

**bank discount rate.**    1. A bank's fee for accepting a draft. The fee, called a discount, is the difference between the amount the bank pays to the borrower and the face value of the instrument. 2. The rate of interest deducted from a loan at the time it is made. The borrower receives the balance of the note less interest.

**bank draft.**    A check drawn by a bank on its own funds or against deposits in a correspondent bank. A sight draft drawn on a foreign bank is paid in the correspondent's local currency. When drafts are paid at the spot exchange rate, the foreign exchange risk is reduced.

**banker's acceptance.**    An acceptance guaranteed by a bank. Banker's acceptances are high-quality financial instruments, often eligible for discount, and frequently used in international trade transactions. A banker's acceptance becomes a third-country acceptance when a bank in country A guarantees payments from an importer in country B to a seller in country C. See also *bank discount rate*.

**Bankers' Automated Clearing House (BACS).** In the United Kingdom, an interbank electronic funds transfer system created in 1968. Routine payments are cleared through BACS.

**banker's bill.**    A bill of exchange issued by a bank. When also accepted or guaranteed by the bank, a banker's bill is stronger than a commercial bill and discounted at a better rate. Compare *trade bill*.

**banker's credit.**    A letter of credit.

**Bank Export Services Act of 1982.**    See *Export Trading Company Act*.

**Bank for International Settlements (BIS).**    An international bank that services central banks of major industrialized countries. The BIS was created at The Hague in 1930 by Belgium, France, Germany, Italy, and the United Kingdom. Canada, Japan, and the United States later became affiliated with the BIS. The bank accepts deposits, makes short-term investments, lends to member banks, and settles accounts among central banks. It is also the funds transfer agent for the International Monetary Fund and the clearinghouse for European currency unit interbank transfers. BIS voting shares are proportional to members' subscriptions. Its unit of account is the gold franc. The BIS is located in Basel, Switzerland.

**bank guarantee.**   A bank's unconditional promise to pay a third party's debt when presented with a demand for payment.

**bank holding company.**   A holding company that controls one or more commercial banks. In the United States, the Bank Holding Company Act of 1956 requires a bank owning another bank or acquiring between 5 and 25 percent of a bank's shares to register with the Federal Reserve Board. The Douglas Amendment to the act prohibits bank holding companies from acquiring banks across state lines unless the law of the host state approves such acquisitions. The term *Bancorp* or *Bancshares* identifies U.S. banks owned by holding companies. U.S. branches of foreign banks are designated as regulated bank holding companies. See also *McFadden Act of 1927.*

**bank holiday.**   1. In the United States, public holidays. Interbank payments are made on the next business day after a holiday. 2. In the United Kingdom, certain days specifically designated as bank holidays, which vary in Britain, Ireland, and Scotland. Drafts payable on bank holidays are paid on the following day. In Britain, Christmas and Good Friday are public holidays but not bank holidays. See also *Saints' days.*

**Banking Edge.**   See *Edge corporation.*

**Bank Negara.**   The central bank of Malaysia.

**bank note.**   Paper currency or legal tender in most countries, but a term not generally used in the United States. Originally backed by gold, most bank notes are no longer fully convertible into a commodity. Contemporary bank notes are supported by the issuing government's credit.

**Bank of.**   When followed by a country name, usually a central bank.

**Bank of Central African States (BCAS).**   See *Banque des États de l'Afrique Centrale.*

**Bank of China (BOC).**   The foreign exchange bank of the People's Republic of China. Compare *Central Bank of China.*

**Bank of England dealing rate.**   The rate at which the Bank of England lends to London discount houses. See also *back door/front door.* Compare *London interbank offered rate.*

**bank paper.**   A negotiable instrument to which a bank's acceptance or endorsement has been affixed.

**bank rate.**   Broadly, the rate of interest at which a central bank lends within its national banking system. See also *minimum lending rate.*

**bank release.**   A receipt issued by a bank after a bill of exchange or draft has been paid or accepted. The document removes the bank's claim on shipped goods, which are released to the buyer.

**bankruptcy.**   The procedure by which a debtor or the debtor's creditors petition a court for relief. A proceeding initiated by a debtor's petition is known as voluntary bankruptcy. When creditors file a petition, the proceeding is called involuntary bankruptcy. In either case, the debtor's assets are held for distribution by a court-appointed trustee or, if the bankrupt is a business, by the debtor in possession. Debts are repaid at a discount from the amount originally owed. See also *administrator, liquidator,* and *receiver.* 1. In the United Kingdom, bankruptcy proceedings may be initiated by creditors, a debtor, or the director of public prosecutions. Repayments are supervised by a court-appointed liquidator. The Insolvency Act of 1986 determines the order in which creditors are paid. 2. In the United States, insolvency proceedings are governed by the Bankruptcy Reform Act of 1978, subsequently amended by the Bankruptcy Reform Act of 1984. The main provisions of the Reform Act are:

*Chapter 7.*   A liquidation in which a court-appointed trustee distributes a debtor's assets among creditors. If the debtor has no assets, debts are discharged.

*Chapter 11.*   A business reorganization supervised by a creditors' committee representing the interests of secured creditors. Bankruptcies involving large companies often require several creditors' committees.

*Chapter 12.*   A farm liquidation involving debts of more than $1 million. Repayment is apportioned based on the fair market value of assets rather than book value.

*Chapter 13.* A wage earner plan permitting partial repayments from wages. Repayments are spread over 3 to 5 years.

**bankruptcy trustee.** See *administrator.*

**Bankschuldverschreibung.** German: bank debenture.

**Bank Wire.** In the United States, a defunct electronic system used to confirm credits and debits. Used largely by large corporations, Bank Wire provided notice of electronic funds transfers. Compare *Federal Reserve Wire Network.*

**banque centrale.** French: central bank.

**Banque Centrale des États de l'Afrique de l'Ouest (BCEAO).** Also known as the Central Bank of West African States, BCEAO was created at Dakar, Senegal, in 1955. It is the central bank for Benin, Burkina Faso, Côte d'Ivoire, Niger, Senegal, and Togo. The bank's official currency is the CFA franc. BCEAO is headquartered at Dakar.

**banque d'affaires.** French: bank of affairs. See *investment bank.*

**Banque de.** French: Bank of; a phrase that, when followed by a country name, denotes a central bank.

**Banque de Développement des États de l'Afrique Centrale.** See *Communauté Économique des États de l'Afrique Centrale.*

**Banque des États de l'Afrique Centrale.** See *Communauté Économique des États de l'Afrique Centrale.*

**Banque Française du Commerce Extérieure (BFCE).** In France, a quasi-government bank formed to provide export credit. Medium-term credits extended by commercial banks are guaranteed by BFCE and rediscounted by the Banque de France. Long-term credits are financed by BFCE.

**Banxquote Money Markets Index.** A price index compiled by Banxquote On-Line Inc. The index records rates paid on negotiable certificates of deposits and high-yield savings accounts under $10,000. The index is published weekly in New York.

**bareboat arrangement.** A charter agreement used to finance the purchase of ships. The charterer pays a fixed fee to the owner and operational costs during the life of the charter. At the end of the charter, the charterer acquires title to the ship. Bareboat arrangements are often used by developing countries to purchase ships.

**bareboat charter.** See *charter party.*

**bareboat component.** A ship subject to a bareboat charter. See also *charter party.*

**bargain.** 1. An agreement between parties to exchange goods and/or services. A good or bad bargain is determined by its value to one or both parties to a transaction. 2. In the United Kingdom, a transaction on the London Stock Exchange (LSE). Trades are published in the *Daily Official List,* the organ of the LSE.

**barge.** An oceangoing vessel, whether motorized or not, that is smaller than a carrier or tanker.

**barge-aboard-catamaran.** A Scandinavian system for hauling cargo. A barge is loaded with cargo and hauled aboard a catamaran, or a twin-hulled vessel. The barge is transported to and from ocean carriers. See also *lash.*

**barge-on-board.** A system of hauling cargo similar to the barge-aboard-catamaran. A barge is preloaded at a small waterfront facility, placed aboard a large ocean carrier for shipment to an intermediate port, and later towed to another destination point for unloading. See also *flash* and *seabee.*

**barque.** A small sailing vessel.

**barratry.** Intentional misconduct on the part of a ship's crew, causing injury to a shipper or shipowner. Diverting cargo and carrying contraband are examples of intentional crew misconduct. Losses from barratry are covered by marine insurance.

**barrel.** A unit used to measure the volume of liquid cargo. In the United States, 1 barrel is equal to 42 gallons. See also *United States Customary System.*

**barrels per day.** In the petroleum industry, a measure of an oil field's or a refinery's daily rate of production.

**Barriers Report.** See *Omnibus Trade Act of 1988.*

**barter.** A sale settled by exchanging goods or services. Barter is frequently used when hard currency is unavailable to settle a sale. The exchange may, but need not, be simultaneous. The terms of the sale in a barter are fixed by a barter agreement. See also *countertrade*. Compare *counterpurchase*.

**base freight.**   The charge for transporting cargo. Freight is priced according to weight (e.g., tonnage) or measurement (e.g., cubic meter or foot).

**Basel Agreement.**   1. Any of several informal agreements among central bankers associated with the Bank for International Settlements to cooperate in managing exchange rates. The first agreement was reached in 1961. 2. The 1972 agreement among European Economic Community (EEC) central bankers to create the European currency snake, a system of exchange rate management used by the EEC until 1979. Compare *Basel Concordat*.

**Basel Concordat.**   An agreement among members of the Basel Club, i.e., the central bankers of the Group of Ten (G-10) and Luxembourg, to supervise international banking practices. The central banks are affiliated through the Bank for International Settlements in Basel, Switzerland. The Basel Club's oversight committee, the Basel Committee on Banking Supervision, has established uniform capital-to-risk ratios for commercial banks and considered measures to supervise interest rates and securities trading in international markets. The first Concordat was adopted in 1975. See also *Cooke Committee*.

**Basel Convention on the Control of  Transboundary Movement of Hazardous Wastes and Their Disposal.**   An international agreement to control the cross-border movement of hazardous waste, including sewage sludge, solvents, and oil pollutants. The agreement binds nations to collect data on hazardous waste disposal. The Basel Conven-tion became effective in 1992. See also *dangerous goods*.

**Basel credits.**   Lending facilities created by the Bank for International Settlements. Basel credits are available to central banks and some multilateral financial institutions. The credits are created on an ad hoc basis.

**base metals.**   Copper, lead, tin, and zinc. Compare *precious metals*.

**base price.**   Also known as the intervention price, the price that triggers government interven-

tion in a commodity market. Under the European Community's Common Agricultural Policy, governments purchase commodities or increase duties when prices fall below the base price. The intervention tightens supplies of the commodity and raises the market price above the base price.

**base produce.**   Unprocessed bulk agricultural commodities.

**base rate.**   1. In finance, the interest rate used to price a loan. The base rate may be a banker's acceptance rate, a certificate of deposit rate, the London interbank offered rate, the U.S. prime rate, or another index rate. The difference between the bank's borrowing rate and lending rate is added to, or subtracted from, the base rate. The differential is known as the margin or the lending spread. 2. In shipping, the rate assigned to a specific commodity or class of commodities in a carrier's freight tariff. Fuel price adjustments or exchange rate changes are reflected in surcharges added to the base rate.

**basic balance.**   See *balance of payments.*

**basing point.**   A generic shipping site. When a basing point is used, shipping charges are calculated according to the cost of transporting cargo from a nominal point without regard to the actual place of first shipment.

**basis.**   1. In the United States, the historical cost of an asset plus capital additions less depreciation. Capital gains or losses are determined by the basis value of an asset. 2. In commodity markets, the difference between the spot price and the forward price of a commodity. 3. In foreign exchange markets, the rate of discount used to equalize currency values. When bases are adjusted, a currency reflecting a higher interest rate trades on par with a lower-interest-rate currency.

**basis grade.**   Also known as par grade, the minimum standard of quality for a commodity underlying a futures contract. Deviations from basis grade often result in discounts or premiums over the original contract price.

**basis point.**   A method of quoting changes in bond yields at maturity. A basis point is one-hundredth of 1 percent, or 0.01 percent. For example, when a bond yield goes from 7.50 percent to 8.50 percent, it has moved 100 basis points.

**basket of currencies.** A currency basket, or the mechanism for assigning value to an artificial currency unit. The value of one artificial currency unit is based on the average market values of a group of currencies. For example, the European currency unit and special drawing rights are based on weighted-average values of several national currencies.

**BATF.** The abbreviation for the Bureau of Alcohol, Tobacco, and Firearms.

**Bay Street.** In Canada, the Toronto Stock Exchange or, more generally, financial institutions operating in Toronto.

**B/B.** The abbreviation for bank balance and break bulk.

**bbl.** The abbreviation for barrel.

**BC, B/C.** See *bill of credit.*

**BCAS.** The abbreviation for the Bank of Central African States. See *Communauté Économique des États de l' Afrique Centrale.*

**BCEAO.** The abbreviation for *Banque des États de l'Afrique Centrale.* See *Communauté Économique des États de l' Afrique Centrale.*

**BCIE.** The abbreviation for *Banco Centroamericano de Integración Económica.*

**BC-NET.** See *Business Cooperation Network.*

**bd.** The abbreviation for board, bond, and bound.

**BD.** The abbreviation for bill discounted. See *bill of exchange.*

**B/D.** The abbreviation for barrels per day.

**bd. ft.** The abbreviation for board foot.

**BDI.** The abbreviation for both dates inclusive.

**bdl, bdls.** The abbreviation for bundle(s).

**BDR.** The abbreviation for bearer depositary receipt.

**BE, B/E.** The abbreviation for bill of exchange.

**bearer.** The holder of a negotiable instrument marked "payable to bearer," i.e., anyone in possession of it. Title to a bearer instrument is transferred without endorsement and by delivery of the instrument to a subsequent holder.

**bearer bond.** A bond not registered in the name of a particular owner. The holder of the bond certificate transfers the instrument by delivery without endorsement. Interest is received by submitting detachable coupons to a paying agent. See also *Eurobond.* Compare *registered bond.*

**bearer depositary receipt (BDR).** A receipt for stock made to the bearer. BDRs are issued for shares in foreign companies. See also *international depositary receipt.*

**bearer deposit note.** A bearer certificate issued for bank deposits. While certificates of deposit are interest-bearing deposits, bearer deposit notes are discount instruments.

**bear market.** A financial or commodity market with declining values. Dealers reacting to low economic expectations are known as bears, who are more likely to sell than buy in anticipation of decreasing prices. Compare *bull market* and *stag market.*

**bear note.** See *bull note.*

**bear position.** See *short selling.*

**bear raid.** A type of dealing in a bear market. A bear raid occurs when dealers attempt to push prices down by prolonged selling. A dealer selling short in a bear market needs to buy securities or commodities to deliver on contracts. By forcing prices down, the dealer earns the difference between the item's purchase price and the contract selling price.

**bear spread.** In options trading, a transaction designed to protect a customer against losses from price declines. The transaction combines long and short call options or put options, permitting one to be sold at a lower strike price while another is bought at a higher strike price. Conversely, a bull spread is a transaction of the same type, except one contract is bought at a lower strike price and another sold at a higher strike price. See also *short selling.*

**bear squeeze.** Central banks intervening in foreign exchange markets to stop speculation. The central banks drive prices higher by bidding for more than the available supply of a national currency, thereby forcing short sellers to cover their positions quickly. Speculators forced to buy at higher prices can suffer large losses.

**bed and breakfast.**    Securities sold late in the day on a stock exchange and repurchased the following morning. The trader intends to create a loss to offset taxable capital gains. If the next day's purchase price falls substantially below the selling price, the trader has no loss to offset.

**beggar thy neighbor.**    The goal of protectionist trade policies, designed to stimulate domestic production at the expense of other countries. High tariffs and other walls against imports arise from beggar-thy-neighbor policies. In the United States, the term recalls the high tariff policy codified in the Smoot-Hawley Tariff Act.

**Beige Book.**    In the United States, a report issued by the Federal Reserve Board on domestic regional economic activity. *Beige Books* are primary references for the Federal Open Market Committee, which sets U.S. monetary policy.

**Belgisch-Luxembourgs Institut voor de Wissel.** See *Belgium-Luxembourg Economic Union.*

**Belgium-Luxembourg Economic Union (BLEU).**    A single market formed in 1921 between Belgium and Luxembourg. BLEU maintains uniform import and foreign exchange policies. Import controls are administered by the Joint Belgium-Luxembourg Administrative Commission. The *Belgisch-Luxembourgs Institut voor de Wissel* in Luxembourg and the *Institut Belgo-Luxembourgeois du Change* in Belgium enforce a dual foreign exchange policy. Foreign currencies are traded in the free market; export earnings and remittances for imports are controlled in the official market. When the values of foreign trade items exceed a prescribed limit, documents are approved by exchange authorities before funds are released.

**Belgium-Netherlands-Luxembourg Economic Union (Benelux).**    A common market created in 1947 encompassing Belgium, the Netherlands, and Luxembourg. Benelux grew out of the Belgium-Luxembourg Economic Union, or BLEU, originally established in 1921 as a customs union, which became the pioneering example of mutual economic cooperation in Europe. When the Netherlands joined, Benelux was formed and accomplished the free movement of persons, capital, goods, and services between the three coun-

tries. The Benelux countries joined the European Economic Community in 1958.

**below par.**    See *par value.*

**below-the-line item.**    1. In business accounting, entries displayed on a company's profit and loss statement below the line dividing profits and losses from distributed profits and the sources of funds subject to losses. 2. In government accounting, an item, also known as an accommodating transaction, in a nation's reserve transaction account. The item reflects the transfer of a domestic or foreign reserve asset. The transfer is computed as a part of the national balance of payments. 3. In advertising, an item for which an advertising agency does not charge a commission for placing advertisements in the public media. Below-the-line expenditures include the costs of displaying commercial samples and direct-mail services. Compare *above-the-line item.*

**belt line.**    An intermediate rail line that transports cargo between long-distance carriers. In international trade, a belt-line railway moves goods between railways and shipping ports, usually under a through bill of lading.

**beneficial interest.**    See *beneficiary.*

**beneficiary.**    1. A party owning a beneficial interest in an asset (such as an insurance policy, investment trust, etc.) and designated to receive income or proceeds deriving from it. 2. In foreign trade, the party authorized to draw against the proceeds of a draft, bill of exchange, or letter of credit. The beneficiary is usually an exporter or supplier.

**benefit-of-insurance clause.**    A provision in some ocean bills of lading exempting a carrier from liability when cargo is covered by insurance. The provision eliminates an insurer's right to sue a carrier and recapture sums paid against a policyholder's claim. In the United States, a benefit-of-insurance clause is not valid for shipping transactions governed by the Carriage of Goods by Sea Act. See also *loan receipt.*

**Benelux.**    The acronym for Belgium-Netherlands-Luxembourg Economic Union.

**BERD.**    The abbreviation for *Banque Européenne pour la Reconstruction et la Développement.* See *European Bank for Reconstruction and Development.*

**Berne Convention for the Protection of Literary and Artistic Works.**    An 1886 international agreement protecting holders of copyrights. The oldest international copyright agreement, the Berne Convention adopted the principle of assimilation, known now as national treatment, with regard to the enforceability of copyrights in signatory nations. The convention extends protection to all written works, films, music, and visual arts. An author's property rights are protected for life plus 50 years. The United States is not a member of the Berne Convention, which is administered by the Berne Union and the World Intellectual Property Organization. Compare *Universal Copyright Convention.*

**Berne Treaty.**    The agreement that created the Universal Postal Union. The treaty authorizes universal cooperation regarding the handling of mail. It was signed at Berne in 1874 and became effective in 1875.

**Berne Union.**    1. Also known as the International Union of Credit and Investment Insurers and *Union d'Assureurs des Credits Internationaux,* an association of public and private providers of export credit insurance. Created at Berne, Switzerland, in 1934, the Union was established to develop uniform procedures for issuing export credit insurance. Members of the Union review and adjust credit insurance premiums annually. The Berne Union is headquartered in London. 2. The organization that administers the Berne Convention for the Protection of Literary and Artistic Works in association with the World Intellectual Property Organization.

**berth clause.**    A charter party term stipulating when lay time begins. Normally, lay time commences when a ship is positioned in a berth, without regard to its actual time of arrival. The berth clause is also called a term clause two or in regular turn.

**berth–no-berth.**    A charter party provision giving a carrier the option of beginning lay time upon notice to the charterer. A berth need not be available when the ship arrives at port. The phrase *whether in berth or not* has the same meaning.

**Bestätigung.**    German: confirmation, e.g., the confirmation of a letter of credit.

**best effort.**    A qualified commitment made by the underwriter of a new securities issue, usually involving shares of a new or unestablished company. In a best-effort offering, the underwriter acts as the issuer's agent without promising to purchase shares that remain unsold after an initial public offering. This form of underwriting normally occurs in over-the-counter markets. Compare *firm commitment.*

**beta stocks.**    See *Stock Exchange Automated Quotations System.*

**Bevollmächtigung.**    German: authorization, e.g., as in authorizing the actions of an agent.

**BEXA.**    The acronym for the British Exporters Association.

**beziehungsweise (bzw.).**    German: means both or and respectively; appears frequently in German documents.

**BFCE.**    The abbreviation for Banque Française du Commerce Extérieure.

**B/G.**    The abbreviation for bonded goods.

**B/H.**    The abbreviation for bill of health.

**b.i.d.**    The abbreviation for *bis in die,* or twice a day.

**bid.**    An offer to buy or sell a product or service at a given price. The buyer or seller may make a counteroffer for a higher or lower price. A firm offer is the final offer made by a party to the bidding. See also *bid price.*

**bid and ask.**    In a market, the highest offer from a buyer and the owner's proposed selling price. Brokers' quotations are usually a combination of the bid and asked prices.

**bid bond.**    A surety of performance provided by a party bidding for an international project contract. The surety is posted as evidence of the bidder's ability to perform the terms of the contract. Standby letters of credit are the usual method of posting bid bonds.

**bidder's mailing list.**    A procurement list of eligible contractors and suppliers. Most government procurement agencies compile long and short lists of suppliers whose goods and services meet their quality standards. Often eligible suppliers are registered with the procurement agency and notified of tender offers by mail. Usually, a prospective supplier must apply to be placed on a procurement mailing list. Articles of incorporation and business financial data are included in the application.

**bid price.** The price a buyer is willing to pay for securities. The bid price is normally lower than the asked price, or the price at which a seller proposes to sell.

**BIFFEX.** The abbreviation for Baltic International Freight Futures Exchange. See *Baltic Exchange.*

**Big Bang.** In the United Kingdom, the date on which major changes were implemented on the London Stock Exchange (LSE). On October 27, 1986, the LSE was reorganized into the International Stock Exchange of the United Kingdom and Republic of Ireland Ltd. Under the reforms, nonnegotiable brokerage commissions were eliminated; program trading was introduced; banks, foreign brokerage houses, and insurance companies were accepted as members; and member firms were permitted to trade for the general public or to act as market makers.

**Big Eight.** 1. The British pound sterling, Canadian dollar, French franc, German mark, Italian lira, Japanese yen, Swiss franc, and U.S. dollar. These are hard (key) currencies, which are freely convertible into other currencies and constitute a portion of central banks' reserve assets. 2. The premier international accounting firms: Arthur Andersen, Arthur Young, Coopers and Lybrand, Deloitte Haskins and Sells, Ernst and Whinney, Peat Marwick Mitchell, Price Waterhouse, and Touche Ross.

**Big Four.** In the United Kingdom, the major commercial banks: Barclays, Lloyds, Midland, and National Westminster.

**bilateral.** A description of any official contact between two governments. Agreements, negotiations, trade, and so forth represent bilateral exchanges. See also *bilateral restraint agreement* and *bilateral investment treaty.*

**bilateral central rate.** The stability factor in the European monetary system (EMS). The EMS has an exchange rate mechanism (ERM) that ties the European Community (EC) national currencies to the European currency unit (ECU). The central

rate is the rate of exchange between a given national currency and the ECU. The values of national currencies are maintained within a fixed range of the ECU's value, known as the parity grid. When an EC currency moves outside the parity grid, EC governments intervene in the currency markets to restore equilibrium to the system. For example, if the central rate is 2 percent, a deviation in the value of the French franc by more than 2 percent above or below parity requires intervention to keep the franc within the ERM. Alternatively, a government may choose to withdraw from the ERM rather than expend vast sums of its reserve assets to stay within the system. The central rate is also known as the bilateral exchange rate, the bilateral parity rate, and the bilateral ratio.

**bilateral exchange rate.** See *bilateral central rate.*

**bilateral investment treaty (BIT).** In the United States, an agreement between the federal government and a foreign government to protect the assets and investment owned by nationals of the other. BITs provide for national treatment of investment, fair compensation for expropriated property, and investors' rights to remove and repatriate capital. The treaties also establish a legal framework for dispute settlement, including recourse to local courts or arbitration through the facilities of the International Centre for the Settlement of Investment Disputes. Compare *friendship, commerce, and navigation treaty.*

**bilateral parity.** See *bilateral central rate.*

**bilateral restraint agreement.** Also known as a quantitative export restraint, an agreement between two governments to manage trade in specific products. Bilateral restraints may also be negotiated between governments and foreign private trade associations or trade unions. Restraint agreements are implemented when one country fears a loss of market share to the other. The competing country agrees to bilateral negotiations to avoid unilateral quotas or steep tariff increases. The precedent for widespread bilateral trade management was set with the adoption of the MultiFiber Arrangement Regarding International Trade in Textiles (MFA). Bilateral restraint agreements, also known as selective safeguards, may be called orderly marketing agreements, voluntary export restraints, or voluntary restraint agreements.

**bill broker.** In Britain, a broker that trades bills of exchange or specialized securities. Bill brokers are discount houses, which arose to trade bills of exchange between banks when one bank faced a cash shortage and another had a surplus. Although still known as brokers, bill brokers now also deal for their own accounts.

**bill of credit (BC, B/C).** A guarantee by a third party recommending that credit be extended to another.

**bill of entry.** A document prepared by a shipper describing the content and value of cargo. In some countries, these documents are required for customs entry.

**bill of exchange (BE, B/E).** An instruction from a drawer advising a drawee to pay a sum certain to another party in the future. The bill of exchange is drawn by the creditor (the drawer) and accompanied by an instruction letter forwarded by the creditor's bank. It need not be negotiable and may require accompanying documents of title for negotiation. When bills of exchange are issued in sets, a notation is placed on each bill in a set (e.g., first of exchange denotes the original bill). A bill issued alone bears a notation "sola," "solus," or "sole of exchange." International rules governing bills of exchange are contained in the Uniform Law on Bills of Exchange, adopted by the Convention on Bills of Exchange signed at Geneva in 1932. The Uniform Law has been wholly or partly enacted into national law in some countries. In 1987, the United Nations Convention on International Bills of Exchange and International Promissory Notes was submitted by the United Nations Commission on International Trade Law and opened for signature by UN member states. The primary instrument of international trade, bills of exchange are usually called drafts in the United States. See also *banker's bill of exchange, clean bill of exchange, continental bill of exchange, documentary bill of exchange, dollar bill of exchange, long bill of exchange, sterling bill of exchange, trade bill of exchange,* and *Treasury bill.*

**bill of lading (BL, B/L).** A shipping document that expresses the contract terms between a ship-

per and a carrier, including the freight rate and the shipping route. When goods are shipped by common carrier, the bill of lading is a contract of carriage, document of title, and receipt for cargo. When goods are carried under charter, the contract terms are contained in the charter party and the bill of lading serves as a receipt and document of title. In the United States, rights acquired by the holder of a bill of lading are governed by the Federal Bill of Lading Act of 1915 (the Pomerene Act). Uniform bills of lading conform to the specifications of the Pomerene Act. See also *accommodation bill of lading, clean bill of lading, foul bill of lading, multimodal bill of lading, negotiable bill of lading, straight bill of lading,* and *through bill of lading.*

**bill of quantities.** In Britain, a description of building materials required to construct a building, which includes the costs of materials and labor. The bill is provided by a quantity surveyor and is sent with tender offers to prospective bidders.

**bill of sale (B/S).** A receipt for goods purchased with cash or on account. The bill of sale is also a document of title and transfers ownership in the underlying goods. The transfer of title may be conditional ( when goods are purchased on credit) or absolute (when goods are purchased with cash).

**bill of sight.** A document submitted by an importer to customs authorities in some countries. A bill of sight authorizes a customs inspection of cargo when the importer cannot accurately describe a shipment prior to entry.

**bill rate.** See *discount rate.*

**binational dispute-settlement mechanism.** See *Canada-U.S. Free Trade Agreement.*

**Binational Secretariat.** See *Canada-U.S. Free Trade Agreement.*

**bind/bound.** 1. In finance, a firm commitment. 2. In international trade, a country's commitment to maintain a specified tariff level. See also *bound tariff.*

**binding arbitration.** See *arbitration.*

**binding tariff classification ruling.** A written confirmation of an import's dutiable status and the rate of duty payable. In most countries, an official ruling is binding for identical products imported under like conditions. Upon written request, the U.S. Customs Service provides binding rulings, which can be obtained based on product samples forwarded to the agency. Classification rulings are binding on all U.S. ports of entry unless subsequently revoked by the Office of Regulations and Rulings in the Customs Service. Prior customs tariff classification rulings can be obtained under the Freedom of Information Act. See also *preclassification.*

**BIPM.** The abbreviation for *Bureau International des Poids et Mesures.*

**birdyback.** A colloquial term for shipping a multimodal container by air freight.

**birr.** The currency of Ethiopia.

**BIS.** The abbreviation for Bank for International Settlements.

**BIT.** The abbreviation for bilateral investment treaty.

**B/L.** The abbreviation for bill of lading.

**black knight.** A prospective investor engaged in a hostile takeover or an unwelcome bid to purchase controlling shares in a company. Compare *gray knight* and *white knight.*

**black market.** A market for trading in contraband or illegal services. Black markets emerge when consumer markets develop for banned or scarce products. Black markets thrive in highly regulated economies and during national emergencies. Compare *gray market.*

**Black Monday.** In the United States, one of two Mondays on which the stock market crashed. The first occurred Monday, October 28, 1929, when the Dow Jones Industrial Average lost 13 percent of its value. On Monday, October 19, 1987, the Dow fell by 23 percent. In both instances, global markets fell sharply in response to the Wall Street collapse.

**blanc.** French: clean.

**blank endorsement.** Also known as an endorsement in blank, a signature on a negotiable instrument made "payable to bearer." Bearer instruments are negotiated by delivery to the appropriate party.

**blanket policy.** An insurance policy insuring several items. A blanket policy is written for a total sum up to a ceiling, without regard to the value of individual items covered by the policy. Compare *open policy.*

**blank transfer.** A transfer of equity without naming the transferee. A subsequent holder becomes the registered owner of the shares by adding a name and a date. Blank transfers are held by banks as security for loans or by trustees acting on behalf of equity owners.

**BLEU.** The abbreviation for the Belgium-Luxembourg Economic Union.

**bloc.** A group of nations trading or otherwise acting in concert. Normally, a trading bloc lowers tariffs and other barriers to trade among its members, thereby encouraging internal trade. Conversely, a bloc maintains or increases trade barriers against outsiders and discourages external trade. Compare *common market.*

**block.** Securities bought and sold as a single unit in one transaction. Blocks are usually composed of up to 10,000 shares.

**block control header record.** Also known as the B record, the file used to select, group, and sort data according to specific categories for the Automated Commercial System. Compare *transaction control header record.*

**block control trailer record.** Also known as the Y record, the file used to interface with the header record and conclude the transmission of a group of data in the Automated Commercial System. Compare *transaction control trailer record.*

**blocked account.** 1. A frozen account from which money cannot be withdrawn. A domestic account may be blocked during bankruptcy or other judicial proceedings. 2. In foreign trade, a blocked funds account frozen under foreign exchange controls. Sales revenues or investment proceeds are held on deposit with a local foreign exchange dealer, but they cannot be repatriated. Foreign exchange dealers are usually commercial banks authorized as depositories by the blocking country's central bank. 3. In the United States, an account frozen for national security reasons. These accounts are blocked or released by the U.S.

Department of Treasury under authority delegated by presidential executive orders.

**blocked currency.** See *blocked funds.*

**blocked funds.** In foreign trade, profits held in a blocked account that cannot be moved except by government order. Countries with foreign exchange controls have different regimes, but most prohibit free reinvestment or repatriation of profits payable in foreign currencies. A fixed percentage of distributed partnership shares, declared dividends, or foreign subsidiary earnings are normally subject to blocking.

**Blue Book.** In the United Kingdom, the *UK National Accounts,* which provide data on the national economy. Blue Books record income, expenditures, and gross national product. They are published monthly by the Central Statistical Office. See also *Pink Book.*

**blue chip.** A security issued by an established company, known for its stable growth, valuable assets, and sound management. Blue chips make up the largest share of institutional investments.

**Blue List.** Formally known as *The Blue List of Current Municipal Offerings,* a trade listing of municipal bond and note coupon rates, par values, and yields to maturity. The *Blue List* is published daily in New York by Standard & Poor's.

**blue sky laws.** In the United States, the popular name for state securities laws, patterned largely after federal securities laws. The laws vary, but uniformly prohibit fraudulent securities issues and require that most securities be registered with local and/or federal authorities.

**BMZ.** The abbreviation for *Bundesministerium für Wirtschaftliche Zusammenarbeit.* See *official development assistance.*

**b.o.** The abbreviation for branch office and buyer's option.

**Board.** 1. The short title for board of directors. 2. The popular name for the New York Stock Exchange, also called the Big Board.

**board of customs and excise.** The customs authority in most English-speaking countries. Apart from collecting duties, customs and excise agencies collect value-added taxes and excise taxes. In the United Kingdom, the Board of Customs and Excise enforces revenue laws and trade regulations and collects international trade data.

**board of directors.** The trustees of an incorporated entity authorized to act on behalf of its shareholders or contributors. The duties of directors' boards vary in different jurisdictions, but board members are generally presumed to owe a fiduciary duty of care to the shareholders of a company or, if the entity is a nonprofit institution, to its contributors. Directors can be discharged for insider trading, fraudulent conduct, negligence, breach of trust, and so on. Directors of public corporations are registered with the Securities and Exchange Commission in the United States and with the Registrar of Companies in the United Kingdom. Under European company law, the board of directors may be a supervisory board or an administrative board.

**board of foreign trade (BOFT).** A government agency that authorizes foreign sales and purchases. Usually, the board coordinates trade regulations and issues import-export licenses. In the case of imports, a BOFT's authority may be limited to recommending that an import license be issued by the central bank or another regulatory agency. In the case of exports, the board may be the only agency authorized to issue export licenses, particularly for commodities subject to cartel agreements.

**Board of Inland Revenue.** In the United Kingdom, the revenue agency that collects direct taxes. UK direct taxes are the income tax, capital-gains tax, corporate tax, inheritance tax, and gasoline tax. The stamp duty on the transfer of securities is scheduled for repeal. The members of the Board are known as commissioners of Inland Revenue.

**board of investment (BOI).** A government agency that authorizes foreign investment. In most developing countries, an investment agency approves joint-venture and other foreign investment applications. Some BOIs require better than 50 percent local participation in joint ventures. The board may also require that a foreign applicant demonstrate conformity between its foreign investment goals and the government's social and economic objectives. Investment agencies are usually authorized to rule on these matters.

**BOC.** The abbreviation for the Bank of China, the foreign exchange bank of the People's Republic of China.

**BOFT.** The abbreviation for board of foreign trade.

**BOI.** The abbreviation for board of investment.

**boilerplate.** Language, mostly legal, regularly inserted in business documents. Boilerplate is common in commercial contracts and insurance policies.

**BOJ.** The abbreviation for the Bank of Japan.

**bolsa.** Spanish: stock exchange.

**Bolsa de Comercio de Santiago.** In Chile, a stock exchange organized in 1893. Bonds, certificates of deposit, and equities are traded on the exchange. Prices are quoted in pesos and published in the *Daily Stock Exchange Report* and in the exchange's monthly, quarterly, and annual publications. Corporate takeovers are unregulated. Information detailing special restrictions on foreign investment is available through the Central Bank of Chile. The operations of the exchange are overseen by the Insurance and Value Superintendency. Brokerage companies are known as *corredores de la bolsa*.

**Bolsa de Valores do Rio de Janeiro.** In Brazil, the principal securities exchange founded in 1845. Bonds, debentures, and shares are traded on the Bolsa, which also operates an options market and a futures market. Prices are quoted in cruzados and published in the daily *Bolsa Hoje* and the weekly *Revista Bolsa*. No nationality restrictions apply to membership in the Bolsa, but foreign investment is regulated by the *Comissão de Valores Mobiliarios* and *Banco Central do Brazil*.

**Bolsa Mexicana de Valores SA de CV.** In Mexico, the stock exchange based in Mexico City and organized in 1894. The Bolsa trades banker's acceptances, bonds, commercial paper, petrobonds, stocks, and Treasury bills. Prices are quoted in pesos and published daily in the *Boletín Bursatil, Desglose Mercado de Capitales,* and *Desglose Mercado de Dinero.* Foreign participation is generally limited to certain approved investments. The exchange's price index, the Bolsa Index, is based on weighted-average share prices of 40 leading companies. Exchange brokers are known as *agentes de bolsa.* The Bolsa is regulated by the *Comisión Nacional de Valores.*

**bona vacantia.** Any goods whose ownership reverts to the state because no valid legal claim has been laid to them, e.g., the personal property of a person who dies in intestacy. Compare *escheat.*

**bond (bd.).** A fixed-interest debt obligation. Also known as fixed-income securities, bonds are interest-bearing instruments that pay predetermined rates of interest. A bond may be issued by a government, local agency, or corporation. A bond debt is created by an indenture, which obligates the issuer to repay a specified sum over the life of the instrument. In the United States, bonds (debt) are distinguished from stocks (equities). See also *senior security.*

**bond anticipation note (BAN).** In the United States, a short-term instrument offered by a local government prior to a bond issue. Principal and interest are repaid when the bonds are issued. BANs are exempt from federal taxes. Compare *revenue anticipation note.*

**Bond Buyer Index.** A daily index of municipal bond yields published in the United States. The index covers the average yield of 40 long-term bonds quoted by bond brokers and the composite yields of 20 general obligation bonds and 11 select bonds.

**bonded goods (B/G).** Also known as goods under bond, imports held in a bonded warehouse. Bonded goods are released when they are to be reexported or when duties and excise taxes have been paid.

**bonded warehouse.** A warehouse where imports are stored before they are reexported or until duties and taxes are paid. In the United States, bonded warehouses are licensed by the U.S. Customs Service. Stored goods may be repackaged or reassembled in the custody of the warehouse. Duties are suspended until the merchandise is shipped from the warehouse zone. See also *field warehouse.*

**bond note.** In the United Kingdom, a warehouse receipt issued by Customs and Excise. The note effects the release of warehoused goods, usually for reexport.

**bond rating.** An estimate of the probability that a bond issuer will default on an obligation. The rating companies in the United States are Standard & Poor's, Moody's Investor Service, Fitch Investor's Service, and Suff & Phelps. Bonds are rated from AAA (highest quality) to D (questionable value). Standard & Poor's BBB and Moody's Baa or better ratings are given to investment-grade bonds.

**bond stripping.** See *stripped bond.*

**bon du Trésor.** French: Treasury bill. A *bon du Trésor en compte courant* is a marketable security of 3 to 18 months maturity. A *bon du Trésor sur formule* is a nonmarketable security with a 5-year maturity.

**bond washing.** See *stripped bond.*

**bonus.** 1. Money or an extra benefit received outside the normal course of business, usually as a reward, incentive, or compensation for facing a special hazard. 2. A performance reward received by an employee for superior work. 3. A payment earned by an employee as a share of company profits.

**bonus issue.** See *stock split.*

**bonus payment.** In insurance, a share of the insurer's profits paid to a policyholder in addition to proceeds from a policy. Bonus payments are made to holders of life insurance policies containing investment provisions. The policyholder receives a share of the net profits earned from investments managed by the insurer. Compare *terminal bonus.*

**bonus scheme.** A government incentive offered to local producers, generally to those who increase exports every year. Export bonus schemes must be carefully constructed to comply with international trade rules, which penalize most government export subsidies, although limited exemptions are granted for developing countries that do not harm trading partners' domestic industries. A payment scheme is considered prima facie legal if the bonus offsets the cost of foreign inputs imported to produce finished goods for sale in local markets. See also *General Agreement on Tariffs and Trade: Tokyo Round, Subsidies (and Countervailing Measures) Code.* Compare *bounty or grant.*

**book.** In securities underwriting, the sum of indications of interest in an offering. In the United States, underwriters are limited to soliciting expressions of interest from prospective investors before an issue is registered with the Securities and Exchange Commission. The number of indications received are known as the book, a primary factor in the pricing of a securities issue.

**booking number.** The shipper's identification number affixed to a bill of lading.

**book runner.** In the Eurocurrency market, the most visible member of a loan or bond underwriting syndicate. Book runners disseminate information and generally maintain communications between borrowers and lenders.

**book transfer.** Any means used to convey title to a buyer without the actual physical transfer of a commodity or a document of title. In contemporary trading, most book transfers are accomplished by electronic means.

**book value (bv.).** The accounting value of an asset carried on a company's books. When an asset is new, its book value is roughly equal to its market value. For used assets, the book value is the difference between the purchase price and market price reduced by depreciation. If a used asset is revalued, its book value is its appraised value reduced by any subsequent depreciation. Compare *market value.*

**boot.** In the United States, a dissimilar asset received in exchange for securities or stock, e.g., an option received for stock. The gain earned on the option probably becomes taxable if it is exercised to purchase underlying stock.

**bootstrap.** In finance, the first offer by a prospective purchaser to acquire the number of shares needed to control a corporation. A second offer is made for the remaining shares at a price lower than the bootstrap price.

**BOP.** The abbreviation for balance of payments.

**bordereaux.** Documents used to report individual shipments covered by an open insurance policy. An insurer will frequently issue a blanket policy for several shipments by a single policyholder. Open policies are written for large-volume exporters who make regular shipments. Bordereaux record the details of a given shipment. See also *errors and omissions clause.*

**border tax adjustment.** A rebate of indirect taxes paid on exports. Indirect taxes include sales and value-added taxes paid by the end user and included in the selling price of a product. Refunds of indirect taxes on exports are legal, but rebates of direct taxes violate international trading rules. See also *General Agreement on Tariffs and Trade: Tokyo Round, Subsidies (and Countervailing Measures) Code.*

**borsa.** Italian: stock exchange, e.g., *Borsa Valori di Milano.*

**Börse.** German: stock exchange. See *Frankfürter Wertpapierbörse Aktiengesellschaft.*

**BOT.** The abbreviation for balance of trade.

**bottomry.** See *hypothecation.*

**bought deal.** 1. A form of placement used by corporations to raise capital. Bought deals involve invitations issued to banks and market makers to bid for new shares. The shares are sold to the highest bidder. Compare *rights offering* and *vendor placing.* 2. A bond issue purchased entirely by one or a small number of managers, who assume the risk of a lower market price before the issue is sold. Bought deals are purchased at a firm price.

**bound duty.** See *bound tariff.*

**bound tariff.** A rate of duty agreed to in international trade negotiations that a signatory is obliged to maintain. Binding a tariff avoids unilateral increases in the rates of duty. Tariff reductions negotiated under the General Agreement on Tariffs and Trade are bound when the agreement is adopted and are often phased in over a number of years. See also *compensation.*

**bounty or grant.** An illegal export subsidy paid by a government to stimulate exports among domestic producers. Subsidies commonly involve below-market-rate loans, guarantees, direct payments, rebates of direct taxes, or tax forgiveness. Outside the United States, export subsidies are often seen as means of advancing domestic economic policy. Strong antisubsidy policies were written into the General Agreement on Tariffs and Trade largely at the insistence of the United

States. See also *countervailing duty* and *General Agreement on Tariffs and Trade: Tokyo Round, Subsidies (and Countervailing Measures) Code.* Compare *bonus scheme.*

**Bourse.** 1. In France, the Paris Stock Exchange founded in 1141 and known officially as the *Société des Bourses Françaises.* Bonds, convertibles, options, stocks, and warrants are traded on the Bourse. Its main market is divided between the *marché au comptant* (the spot market) and the *marché à règlement mensuel* (the forward market). The Bourse's over-the-counter market is known as the *marché hors cote.* The Bourse's index, *Cotation Assistée en Continue,* or CAC 40, lists weighted averages for 40 leading stocks. Securities prices, quoted in French francs and European currency units, are published in the *Bulletin de la Cote Officielle,* the official daily list. Bourse brokers are called *agents de change.* Some limitations are imposed on foreign investors. The Bourse is regulated by the *Commission des Opérations de Bourse.* See also *contango market.* 2. Other European stock exchanges, e.g., *Bourse de Bruxelles,* the Brussels Stock Exchange. Prices of shares listed in Brussels are published daily in the *Cote de la Bourse de Fonds Publics et de Change de Bruxelles.*

**box (bx.).** A shipping container.

**box spread.** In options arbitrage, combining a bear spread and a bull spread to eliminate the risk of loss.

**boycott.** See *antiboycott regulation.*

**boycottage.** The European term for a commercial boycott formed to damage the competitive interest of an outside company. Commercial boycotts are per-se violations of U.S. antitrust law. Compare *antiboycott regulation.*

**BPT.** The abbreviation for business profit tax.

**bracket.** In financial markets, groupings of underwriters of bond issues and syndicated loans. The groupings are determined by the amount committed to underwrite the borrowing. The order of ranking is lead manager, special underwriters, underwriters, and selling-group managers. See also *tombstone.*

**branch-plant economy.** A national economy dependent on foreign investment.

**brand name.**    A trade name identified with a specific product. Manufacturers invest large sums in advertising brand names to gain market share. Brand names familiar in a given market are usually protected trade names or registered trademarks. See also *brands and labels protection* and *private brand.* Compare *generic.*

**brands and labels protection.**    An insurance clause covering a trade name identifying a manufacturer's product in consumer markets. When products bearing brands and labels are damaged, the goods are sold for salvage value, usually with labels removed. Losses suffered by the manufacturer are insured through brands and labels insurance. Compare *control of damaged goods.*

**breach date.**    The day on which one party to a contract fails to perform an obligation. In international breach-of-contract suits, damages and court costs are paid in the currency of the jurisdiction in which a case is heard. Foreign exchange values for settling legal claims are fixed on the breach date. The rate of exchange for damages and court costs is the rate in effect on the date the contract was breached.

**breach of contract.**    The failure of a party to a contract to fulfill a term or condition of the agreement. When the party indicates that an obligation will not be performed, the contract is repudiated. When the party indicates that an obligation will not be performed at some future time, an anticipatory breach occurs. In common-law courts, the remedies for breach of contract are determined by the nature of the breach. Depending on the circumstances, an injured party may affirm or rescind the contract. Remedies for breach of contract are monetary damages, injunction, or specific performance.

**breach of warranty.**    See *warranty.*

**break.**    In futures trading, a rapid price decline. By contrast, a bulge denotes a sudden increase in prices.

**break-bulk shipment.**    Cargo broken into lots (i.e., deconsolidated) and transported in the hold of a ship. Break-bulk cargo is packaged in cartons, drums, or other packing equipment. A break-bulk shipment is smaller than an intermodal container shipment. Compare *bulk cargo.*

**break clause.**    In Eurocurrency lending agreements, a clause modifying a lender's obligations and increasing the borrower's risks when changes in Euromarket conditions occur. Compare *jeopardy clause.*

**break-forward.**    A forward exchange contract with a currency option. The option is exercised at the exchange rate fixed by the contract.

**breakpoint.**    A volume discount or the point at which a broker's commission, known as brokerage, is lowered for large transactions.

**break-up value.**    The current per-share value of a company if its assets are sold separately. When companies are dissolved, their assets are usually discounted and sold at distress prices for less than current market value. See also *unbundling.*

**B record.**    See *block control header record.*

**Bretton Woods Conference.**    The United Nations Monetary and Financial Conference held at Bretton Woods, New Hampshire, July 1–4, 1944. The conference's Final Act contained the Articles of Agreement that created the International Bank for Reconstruction and Development, popularly known as the World Bank, and the International Monetary Fund. The General Agreement on Tariffs and Trade also evolved from Bretton Woods. The conference established the post-World War II international monetary system by agreement among 44 nations. The system was based on a par-value exchange rate system linked to the value of the U.S. dollar fixed at 1/35 ounce of gold. In 1971, the par-value system ended with the Smithsonian Agreement signed in Washington, D.C. A new floating-exchange-rate system replaced the Bretton Woods system in 1973. See also *Basel Agreement* and *Jamaica Accords.* Compare *International Clearing Union.*

**bribery.**    Illicit private gain from public office. Gifts and receipts of money or favors involving public officials are illegal in all countries, though legal and enforcement standards vary. The size of the cash payment, or the value of a favor, is often the determining factor. In highly bureaucratic countries, a small payment (a tip) to expedite a process may not be illegal. In a Western country, payment for a lunch is not unlawful. However, substantial cash payments ( kickbacks) to receive government contracts or favorable administrative rulings are universally illegal. In the United States, an attempt to bribe U.S. or foreign government officials violates the Foreign Corrupt Practices Act of 1977. Elsewhere, anti-corruption laws generally prohibit bribery of local officials but do not actively bar corruption of foreign officials. Compare *baksheesh*.

**bridge loan.**   Also called gap financing, a short-term loan made in anticipation of longer-term financing. For example, in corporate restructurings, bridge loans cover interim expenditures before new stocks or debt bonds are issued. In international public finance, short-term credits are extended by multilateral banks to countries negotiating debt restructurings or new loans with commercial banks.

**Britannia coins.**   In the United Kingdom, gold coins issued in 100-, 50-, 25-, and 10-pound denominations. The coins are held as investments and compete in international markets with the South African Krugerrand.

**British Commonwealth.**   Also known as the Commonwealth, the surviving association of the former British Empire created in 1931 by the Statute of Westminster. In the Ottawa Agreement of 1932, the Commonwealth adopted a program of mutual trade preferences, which was substantially modified when Britain entered the European Economic Community in 1973. Commonwealth members are the United Kingdom, Australia, Bahamas, Bangladesh, Barbados, Botswana, Canada, Cyprus, Fiji, Gambia, Ghana, Guyana, India, Jamaica, Kenya, Lesotho, Malawi, Malaysia, Malta, Mauritius, New Zealand, Nigeria, Sierra Leone, Singapore, Sri Lanka, Swaziland, Tanzania, Tonga, Trinidad and Tobago, Uganda, Zambia, and Zimbabwe. Within the Commonwealth, the British sovereign remains the head of state of some countries. Other heads of state are elected by popular vote or selected by other means. See also *commonwealth preference*.

**British dependent territories.**   Countries afforded special recognition upon Britain's entry into the European Economic Community. All British foreign possessions are dependent territo-

ries, including the British Virgin Islands, except Hong Kong and Gibraltar. See also *overseas countries and territories*.

**British Imperial System.**   The system of Imperial units of weights and measures. The British Imperial System was employed in the United Kingdom before 1985 when the British government fully adopted the metric system, or the *Systeme Internationale*.

**British Standards Institute (BSI).**   An organization chartered by the British government to formulate, among other things, industrial product standards in Britain. The Kite mark logo is the BSI symbol of quality. See also *International Standards Organization*.

**British Technology Group (BTG).**   An organization formed by the British government in 1981 to finance advanced-technology research and development. BTG supports research at local universities, private research institutes, and government research facilities. BTG is based in London.

**broad money.**   The sum total of currency available in a national economy. Broad money consists of currency for immediate use (narrow money) and deferred use (quasi-money). Narrow money is currency in circulation plus private demand deposits. Quasi-money is money on time and savings deposit plus foreign currency deposits. See also *money supply*.

**broker.**   An agent who arranges sales for a commission or fee. When acting on behalf of principals, brokers do not buy for their own accounts. When acting as principals in a trading exchange, brokers are known as dealers, market makers, or specialists.

**brokerage.**   A commission paid to a broker, usually based on a percentage of a transaction's value and sometimes discounted at a breakpoint.

**broker's call loan.**   A short-term loan to a broker collateralized by pledged securities. Advances made to customers on margin accounts are often financed by call loans. Call loans may be repayable on 24-hour notice. Compare *day loan*.

**brown goods.**   Consumer durables in North America. Elsewhere, brown goods are televisions, stereos, and similar consumer electronic equipment, so called because of the wood cabinets in which they were originally encased.

**Brussels Convention on the Valuation of Goods for Customs Purposes.**    See *Brussels definition of value.*

**Brussels definition of value.**    The import valuation method on which the Brussels Tariff Nomenclature is based, which was used throughout most of the world from the 1950s to the 1980s. The Brussels definition derives import value from a nominal price, known as the *normal price,* i.e., the market price for like products produced and exported under similar conditions. It originated with a study group commissioned to recommend proposals for creating a European customs union. The study group submitted three international conventions to Belgium, Britain, France, Luxembourg, and the Netherlands. In 1950, the conventions establishing the valuation of goods for customs purposes, a nomenclature for the classification of goods in customs tariffs, and the Customs Cooperation Council were accepted at Brussels. The conventions became effective in 1953. The Brussels definition was substantially replaced by the Customs Valuation Code approved by the Tokyo Round of the General Agreement on Tariffs and Trade in the 1970s. It is now employed by most countries only when transaction value required by the Customs Valuation Code is inconsistent with declared or other evidence of value. The Brussels definition of value was never adopted by the United States.

**Brussels International Trade Mart.**    In the European Community, the largest market for wholesale buyers of consumer products. The mart is open year-round and offers permanent display facilities.

**Brussels Pact of 1948.**    An agreement among Belgium, France, Luxembourg, the Netherlands, and the United Kingdom to cooperate on military and political matters. The agreement was the product of the Congress of Europe held at the Hague in 1948 following the creation of the Warsaw Pact. Also known as the Brussels Treaty Organization, the Brussels Pact represented the first postwar effort to establish multigovernment political organization in Western Europe. The military component of the Brussels Pact was subse-

quently supplanted by the North American Treaty Organization. However, the agreement reached at Brussels became the basis for international cooperation on several fronts and evolved into the European Coal and Steel Community, the precursor of the European Community.

**Brussels Tariff Nomenclature (BTN).**    Also known as the Customs Cooperation Council Nomenclature, the international standard for classifying goods for customs valuation from 1953 until 1988. The BTN was originally approved by the Convention on Nomenclature for the Classification of Goods in Customs Tariffs signed in 1950, which grew out of the Brussels Pact of 1948. The BTN remains in use in some countries and is administered by the Customs Cooperation Council. Although the United States never adopted the system, the U.S. Customs Service publishes notes explaining BTN classification codes. Since 1988, a growing number of countries have adopted the alternative Harmonized Commodity Description and Coding System. See also *Brussels definition of value.*

**Brussels Treaty Organization.**    See *Brussels Pact of 1948.*

**b/s.**    The abbreviation of bags and bales.

**B/S.**    The abbreviation for bill of sale.

**BSC.**    The abbreviation for Business Service Center.

**B-shares.**    In the People's Republic of China (PRC), equities reserved solely for foreign investors, as compared to A-shares sold only to domestic investors. B-shares are listed mainly on the Shanghai Securities Exchange, the newer exchange in Shenzhen, and the Stock Exchange of Hong Kong, although some are also traded in New York and by mutual funds known as China funds. As investments, B-shares are considered risky because of uncertain accounting standards and financial regulation in the PRC.

**BSI.**    The abbreviation for British Standards Institute.

**BT.**    The abbreviation for berth terms.

**BTG.**    The abbreviation for British Technology Group.

**BTN.**    The abbreviation for Brussels Tariff Nomenclature.

**bu.**    The abbreviation for bushel.

**bucket shop.**    In the United Kingdom, a colloquial term denoting an insubstantial brokerage or agency firm. Bucket shops are unaffiliated with established trade associations.

**Budapest Treaty on the International Recognition of the Deposit of Microorganisms for the Purposes of Patent Procedure.**    See *World Intellectual Property Organization.*

**budget.**    1. A schedule of estimated income and expenditures for a specified period of time. 2. In government, a combined financial plan and policy document issued for a given fiscal year. 3.In the United States, the federal budget drafted by the Office of Management and Budget (OMB) and formally proposed to the Congress by the President in an annual State of the Union address each January. OMB budget proposals are amended by budget authority approved by budget committees in the Senate and House of Representatives. Conflicting budget proposals are reconciled by joint Senate and House committees. Expenditures based on budget authority are set by House and Senate Appropriations Committees.

**budget deficit.**    Expenditures in excess of revenues.

**budget surplus.**    Revenues in excess of expenditures.

**Buenos Aires Convention.**    See *Pan-American Copyright Convention.*

**buffer stock.**    A reserve supply created by a withholding plan and authorized under an international commodity agreement. Buffer stocks are held to avoid selling at low prices during periods of declining demand. When prices decrease, commodities are purchased for the stockpile. As prices increase, commodities from the stockpile are released for sale on world markets. See also *United Nations Trade and Development Programme* and *Common Fund for Commodities.*

**building society.**    A British savings and loan association.

**bulk cargo.**    A shipment of commodities transported without packaging. Mechanical shovels and conveyor belts are used to load and unload bulk shipments. Coal, grains, and ores are transported in bulk. Compare *break-bulk shipment, container,* and *pallet.*

**bulk carrier.**    A ship constructed to transport bulk cargoes.

**bulk freight container.**    A shipping container for bulk cargoes. The container is designed to accommodate unloading through discharge hatches.

**bulk stowage.**    See *bulk cargo.*

**bulk tank container.**    A shipping box constructed to transport hazardous liquids. Tank containers are gradually replacing metal drums, which are more prone to leakage.

**bull.**    A dealer who buys in anticipation of rising prices. The bull hopes to profit by selling at a higher market price. See also *bull market.* Compare *bear.*

**bulldog bond.**    In the United Kingdom, a bond issued by a foreign borrower. Bulldog bonds are denominated in pound sterling, offered at fixed rates of return, and normally pay interest semiannually.

**bullet.**    1. In finance, the repayment of a loan balance in one installment. 2. In securities markets, a bond or note offered at a predetermined interest rate with a fixed maturity date.

**bullion.**    Precious metals, such as gold or silver, poured into bars or other bulk form and often used by central banks to settle international debts. London and Zurich are major gold bullion trading centers. New York is the center of gold bullion futures trading.

**bull market.**    A securities market or commodity market in which dealers buy, anticipating rising prices. The growth in buying activity contributes to price increases. Bulls who sell at the height of a bull market before prices decline reap substantial profits. Compare *bear market* and *stag market.*

**bull note.**    In the United Kingdom, a bond with a hedge option. The value of the bond is based on a financial index or a commodity price at redemption. The redemption value of a bull note exceeds the principal if the reference price increases, but is less than the principal if the reference price decreases.

**bull spread.**    See *bear spread.*

**Bundesbank.**  The central bank of Germany. See also *Landeszentralbank, Privatdiskont AG,* and *interest rate policy.*

**Bundesministerium der/für Finanzen.**  German: ministry of/for finance. Finance ministries are the customs authorities in Bonn and Vienna.

**Bundesministerium für Wirtschaft.**  German: ministry of commerce.

**Bundesschatzschein.**  German: federal Treasury bill, i.e., of 1 to 3 years maturity.

**Bundesobligation.**  German: federal Treasury debenture, i.e., of more than 5 years maturity.

**bundled pricing.**  A selling price that includes the cost of the product plus the value of peripheral goods or services.

**bundling.**  A method of financing small trade transactions. In a bundling transaction, a government agency packages several export receivables for transfer to a commercial bank. The bank converts the package to commercial paper for sale in the money market, usually at a discount.

**B-unit.**  An artificial currency unit weighted in terms of British pound sterling, Deutsche marks, French and Swiss francs, and U.S. dollars. B-units were created in London by Barclays Bank in 1974.

**bunker.**  The maritime term for heavy fuel used to power ship engines.

**bunker clause.**  A charter party term that determines who pays the costs of fuel price increases over the life of the contract. Normally, a charter agreement estimates fuel consumption from origin port to destination port. Fuel charges are based on the price in effect at both ports. The charterer usually pays for the fuel aboard the ship when the voyage begins. The shipowner refunds an amount equal to the value of fuel remaining on the ship when the voyage ends. Compare *bunker surcharge.*

**bunker price clause.**  See *bunker clause.*

**bunker surcharge.**  A surcharge imposed by an ocean carrier for fuel price increases not anticipated in the carrier's published tariff. The surcharge is based on a fixed percentage of the basic tariff rate. Compare *bunker clause.*

**bur.**  The abbreviation for bureau.

**Bureau Benelux des Marques.**  One of two trademark (*marque de produit* or *marque de fabrique*) registration offices in the Benelux countries. Bureau Benelux des Marques is located in the Hague. The other registration office, the International Bureau, is located in Geneva. Trademark registrations in Benelux are controlled by the Benelux Uniform Law, which applies the first-to-register test. A judicial decision establishing an exclusive right of trademark use in one Benelux country is honored in other Benelux countries.

**bureau de change.**  A place where foreign currency is exchanged and checks are cashed. Eurocheques are cashed worldwide at *bureaux de change* that display a European Community sign.

**bureau des marques.**  French: office of trademarks.

**Bureau International des Poids et Mesures (BIPM).**  Also known as the International Bureau of Weights and Measures, an organization founded to standardize units of measurement. Founded in Paris in 1875, BIPM administers the international metric system. The organization is based in Sèvres, France. See also *Systeme International.*

**Bureau of Alcohol, Tobacco, and Firearms (BATF).**  In the United States, an agency of the U.S. Department of Treasury that regulates commerce in alcohol, tobacco, and firearms. BATF also administers U.S. international traffic in arms regulations by issuing occupational licenses to U.S. arms manufacturers and importers and setting registration requirements and procedures for weapons exports. A police agency, BATF also seizes and destroys contraband.

**Bureau of Export Administration (BXA/BEA).**  In the United States, an agency of the U.S. Department of Commerce that issues Export Administration Regulations and validated export licenses. The agency implements antiboycott regulations and U.S. export policy based on foreign policy, national security, and short-supply directives issued by other federal agencies. BXA operates the U.S. Export/Import Regulations database, popularly known as USER; the Export License Application and Information Network (ELAIN); and the System for Tracking Export

License Applications (STELA). The agency also maintains a list of firms whose export privileges have been withdrawn for violations of U.S. export regulations.

**Bureau Veritas.**    See *classification society.*

*Business America.*    In the United States, a biweekly international trade magazine published by the International Trade Administra-tion, an agency of the U.S. Department of Com-merce. The magazine features articles on global trade trends, external trade, and investment data. Announce-ments of U.S. government-sponsored trade shows are also carried in *Business America.*

**Business Cooperation Network (BC-NET).**    The European Community's electronic information service for small- to medium-sized businesses. BC-NET was implemented by the EC in 1988. The network is accessible to businesses in countries outside the EC. Euro Info Centres are the nerve centers of BC-NET.

**business cycle.**    Periods of economic recession and recovery endemic to market economies. Also known as the trade cycle, the business cycle is measured by expansions or contractions in a nation's gross national product. Employment, credit, investment, manufacturing output, and worker productivity are affected by the business cycle. In some instances, a government will attempt to manage the extremes of the cycle through fiscal (spending) or monetary (interest rate) policies. In other instances, a government will refrain from interfering in the market. See also *countercyclical policy* and *tight money.*

**Business Development Corporation Lending Program.**    In the United States, a state loan guar-antee program sponsored by the Export-Import Bank. The program provides federal guarantees for loans made by state development corporations to U.S. exporters of capital goods. The program became effective in the state of New York in 1992.

**Business Entry Service.**    See *Business Service Center.*

**business-interruption policy.**    An insurance pol-icy that covers policyholders' claims for business losses resulting from fire, storm damage, or other insurable risks.

**Business Monitor.**    In the United Kingdom, a magazine of domestic business and trade data. *Business Monitor* is published by the Business Statistics Office, an agency of the Central Statistical Office.

**business name.**    The trade name under which a business operates. In the United Kingdom, a busi-ness operated under a name other than that of a sole proprietor must be registered with the Registrar of Companies. Under the Business Names Act of 1985, business names (other than those of sole proprietors) are posted at the place of business. Business stationery also carries a company's business name and the names of the owners.

**business profit tax (BPT).**    A tax on foreign imports and the net profits of a foreign-owned company. Methods of computing the tax vary. For imports, determining the amount of the tax usually involves multiplying a nominal tax rate by the nor-mal selling price of the import. The normal selling price is an estimated price based on prices of like products imported under similar circumstances. For foreign subsidiary profits, the tax is normally based on the subsidiary's net profits above a base corporate tax rate. See also *tax.*

**business proprietary information (BPI).**    Trade secrets, or data, generated by a business for profit or internal use. Unauthorized disclosure of a busi-ness secret injures the property interest of the business owner. In the United States, intentional or inadvertent disclosures of proprietary informa-tion in the course of a government proceeding are punishable by civil and criminal statutes. A party injured by unauthorized disclosures also has com-mon-law judicial remedies. See also *industrial espi-onage.*

**business review procedure.**    In the United States, the process used by the Antitrust Division of the U.S. Department of Justice (DOJ) to deter-mine the legality of a proposed acquisition, merger, or price-setting combination. The review is based on information provided by a company seeking a statement of DOJ's position in the event an agreement is concluded. DOJ issues an advi-sory opinion, known as a business review letter, stating its view of the proposed agreement.

Business review letters are confined to the facts of a given case and do not set precedents for subsequent cases. Compare *FCPA review procedure* and *no-action letter*.

**Business Service Center (BSC).**   In the United States, a satellite office of the U.S. Customs Service staffed by import entry processing teams, called entry specialist teams. BSC offices are fully automated and designed to streamline entry processing by placing all import filings within one unit.

**butterfly.**   See *straddle*.

**Buy America Act of 1933.**   In the United States, the buy-national law that requires domestic content in goods and services procured by the federal government and by some federal contractors. To comply with the terms of the Procurement Code adopted by the Tokyo Round of the General Agreement on Tariffs and Trade, the Trade Agreements Act of 1979 waived nationality requirements for most federal procurements on a reciprocal basis. The reciprocity requirements of the 1979 act were eliminated for Caribbean Basin Initiative I countries by presidential directive in 1986.

**buyback.**   1. In corporate finance, a repurchase of shares from an investor who financed the start-up, expansion, or takeover of a company. 2. In foreign trade, a counterpurchase whereby exports are purchased for resale in another market. In a buyback, the exporter is paid in hard currency earned from the resale of exports. Buyback deals are attempted when the exporter cannot pay for capital goods needed to manufacture products for export. Compare *barter*. 3. In international debt restructuring, an agreement by an indebted country to repurchase its unretired loans, usually at less than fair market value. The International Monetary Fund often provides or arranges financing for buybacks to cure an indebted country's balance-of-payments problems. See also *debt conversion program*.

**Buyer Alert Program.**   See *Agricultural Information and Marketing Services*.

**buyer's market.**   A market in which supply exceeds demand. During these intervals, buyers drive prices down. When prices fall too low, sellers create scarcity by leaving the market and so prices increase.

**buyer's option (b.o.).**   An option in a forward contract allowing a buyer to choose between commodities originating in different places or between different delivery dates. The option prescribes the period for settlement.

**buyer's premium.**   A premium paid by the European Community (EC) to domestic tobacco processors under the Common Agricultural Policy. The premium reduces the cost of EC tobacco to local tobacco processors. The subsidy makes higher-priced EC tobacco competitive with tobacco imports from Turkey and the United States.

**buying on margin.**   A method of investor financing. The investor makes an advance (the margin) against the purchase price of securities and borrows the balance from a bank or broker. In the United States, the amount of the margin is determined by Federal Reserve Regulation G, Federal Reserve Regulation T, and Federal Reserve Regulation U.

**buyout.**   See *leveraged buyout*.

**bv.**   The abbreviation for book value.

**BVI.**   The abbreviation for the British Virgin Islands.

**BWI.**   The abbreviation for the British West Indies.

**bx.**   The abbreviation for box.

**BXA.**   The acronym for the Bureau of Export Administration.

**bzw.**   The abbreviation for *beziehungsweise*.

# C

©. The copyright symbol of the Universal Copyright Convention.

c. An abbreviation for consul.

C. The symbol for the Canadian dollar.

CA. The mark of origin of imports from Canada. See also *Harmonized Tariff Schedule of the United States , Annotated*.

c/a. The abbreviation for capital account.

CAA. The abbreviation for the U.S. Civil Aviation Administration, the civil aviation authority in the United States.

CAAA. The abbreviation for Comprehensive Anti-Apartheid Act.

CABEI. The abbreviation for Central American Bank for Economic Integration. See *Banco Centroamericano de Integración Económica*.

cable. An international telegram or wire funds transfer. Cable is also a colloquial term for British pound sterling, dating to the period when all international funds transfers were denominated in sterling.

cabotage. Transporting cargo between two destinations within one country. Cabotage licenses are issued for road, maritime, and air carriage. By tradition, cabotage laws are national in scope, often granting local carriers monopolies for domestic transport. Recent trade negotiations have attempted to reduce the impact of cabotage laws on international commerce. For example, liberalized laws in the European Community (EC) removed restrictions on ground cross-border pickups and deliveries. Single-carrier registries and EC-wide cabotage rules are expected to reduce limitations on interregional EC air and water carrier transport in 1993. Compare *cartage*.

CAC 40. See *Bourse*.

CACM. The abbreviation for Central American Common Market. See *Mercado Común Centroamericano*.

CAD. The abbreviation for cash against documents and computer-aided design.

CADEX. The abbreviation for Canadian Data Exchange. See *electronic data interchange*.

C.A.F. The abbreviation for *coût, assurance, frêt*. See *cost, insurance, and freight*.

CAIC. The abbreviation for the Caribbean Association of Industry and Commerce.

Cairns Group. A coalition of agricultural exporting countries formed in the 1980s to influence negotiations during the Uruguay Round of the General Agreement on Tariffs and Trade. It was created at Cairns, Australia, in 1986 and composed of 14 Latin American and Asian nations. During the Uruguay Round, the Cairns Group attempted unsuccessfully to mediate disputes between the European Community (EC) and the United States involving the EC's Common Agricultural Policy.

Caisse Centrale de Coopération Économique. See *official development assistance*.

calendar. A published notice of scheduled securities issues.

calendar spread. Also known as a horizontal spread, in options trading the buying and selling of equivalent options contracts with different expiration dates but carrying the same strike prices.

call. 1. In bond financing, the right of an issuer to retire a debt and demand surrender of its bonds at a prearranged call price. Bond indentures specify a period of call protection for bond purchasers. Call protection is a form of bondholder insurance against income losses from lower-yield investments made to replace a called bond. 2. In equity finance, a demand for callable capital. 3. In commodities markets, the period for fixing prices of certain futures contracts. 4. In international trade, a country's request for consultations to alter a textile or apparel import quota under the MultiFiber Arrangement Regarding International Trade in Textiles.

callable capital. See *paid-up capital*.

call date. 1. The day when additional payments are demanded from owners of partly paid shares. 2. The earliest time a bond issuer may redeem a bond at the price stated in the indenture. Call dates protect bondholders' earnings for a specified period of years by penalizing early redemptions. In bond quotations, prices are frequently quoted as yield to the first call date rather than the yield to maturity date. Issuers pay the highest premium to redeem bonds at the first call date to compensate investors for capital lost when a security is trading above par. Lower premiums are paid thereafter for subsequent redemptions before maturity. See also *maturity date* and *noncallable.*

**call loan.**  See *broker's call loan.*

**call money.**  Demand deposits, primarily deposits placed in money-market funds. Also known as money at call, call money is repayable at demand. In Germany, France, Japan, and the United Kingdom, call money is a reserve asset when placed by the central bank with discount houses or similar financial institutions.

**call option.**  A contract allowing the buyer of an option to purchase securities, commodities, or futures at a fixed price during a specified interval. Call options are purchased in anticipation of rising commodity or securities prices. See also *option.*

**callover.**  A meeting of traders on the floor of an exchange. Callovers are common in futures dealing where brokers make buy and sell offers.

**call price.**  1. In bond markets, the price at which an issue can be redeemed by the issuer after a specified period of time. 2. In options trading, the price of a call option.

**call protection.**  See *call.*

**Calvo doctrine.**  A legal doctrine advanced by Carlos Calvo, an Argentine jurist, and adhered to in Latin America. Under the doctrine, a foreign firm is subject to the jurisdiction of the country in which it operates. National laws are deemed fairly applied to foreign nationals, so long as legal treatment is nondiscriminatory. Thus, the local law of a country where an agreement is made may supersede and disallow rights granted under international law.

**CAM.**  The abbreviation for computer-aided manufacturing.

**camara de comercio.**  Spanish: chamber of commerce.

**camara do comercio.**  Portuguese: chamber of commerce.

**cambist.**  1. A foreign exchange dealer who specializes in trading foreign currencies and bills of exchange. See also *Association Cambiste Internationale.* 2. A book of tables used to convert one foreign currency to another.

**cambiste.**  French: cambist.

**CAMEL rating.**  In the United States, the abbreviation for capital, assets, management, earnings, and liquidity. A CAMEL rating is an estimate of a commercial bank's soundness. Banks are rated from 1 to 5. A 4 or 5 is a poor rating. CAMEL ratings are not disclosed to the general public.

**camera di commercio.**  Italian: chamber of commerce.

**can.**  The abbreviation for canceled.

**Canada Account.**  A concessional lending and insurance program offered to developing countries by the Canadian Export Development Corporation. Also known as the Government Account, the lending facility was authorized by the Canadian Export Development Act. Canada Account borrowing is available to countries not otherwise qualified for the Canadian loan guarantees or export credit insurance.

**Canada Customs Invoice.**  The customs form required for import shipments to Canada valued in excess of $1200 Canadian dollars.

**Canada Data Exchange.**  See *electronic data interchange.*

**Canada-U.S. Free Trade Agreement (CFTA, FTA).**  A bilateral trade accord that began eliminating Canadian-U.S. import tariffs on January 1, 1989. The agreement contemplates unimpeded cross-border movement of most goods, investment, and labor, excluding Canada's cultural derogation for its entertainment, publishing, and telecommunications industries. For covered products, progressive annual phaseouts of import duties are scheduled for completion on January 1, 1999. Staging Category A ended duties on animal fur apparel, data processing equipment, telephones, and whiskey in 1989. Staging Category B began the elimination of tariffs on, among others, chemicals, furniture, machinery, paper goods, and petroleum products on January 1, 1993. Staging Category C completes the phaseout by ending tariffs on the most import-sensitive goods, including agricultural products, remaining alcoholic beverages, rubber, steel, textiles, and some wood products. The FTA eliminates cross-border quotas, except those negotiated by agreement or specifically authorized by the General Agreement on Tariffs and Trade. It contains detailed country-of-origin rules to avoid diversions and transshipments of third-country exports. To qualify for eliminated duties, a third-country export must undergo substantial transformation in Canada or the United States, giving the product a regional content of 50 to 70 percent of its finished value. The FTA extends national treatment to investment, procurement, and services. It also contains dispute-settlement provisions, which authorize the FTA Binational Secretariat, a permanent review panel with offices in Ottawa and Washington. See also *dispute settlement* and *North American Free Trade Accord*.

**Canadian Export Association (CEA).** Also known as *Association Canadienne d'Exportation (ACE)*, a private trade association formed in 1943 to promote Canadian exports. CEA licenses members of the Council of Canadian Trading Houses (CCTH), an association of trading houses specializing in arranging foreign trade transactions. The organization is based in Ottawa.

**Canadian Import Tribunal (CIT).** See *Canadian International Trade Tribunal*.

**Canadian International Trade Tribunal (CITT).** In Canada, the agency that succeeded the Canadian Import Tribunal and investigates dumping and subsidy complaints. The Special Import Measures Act of 1984 authorizes CITT to rule on unfair import practices and report to the Canadian government on the trade impact of its findings.

**canalization fee.** In some countries, a surcharge imposed on imports by local trade organizations authorized to license certain imports. For example, the National Film Development Corporation (NFDC) of India approves domestic film imports. Foreign film export associations pay NFDC a canalization fee on behalf of their members. The fee is paid for U.S. film exporters by the Motion Picture Export Association of America.

**Canal Zone.** See *Panama Canal Zone*.

**cancellation date.** 1. In international trade, the date when a charterer may terminate a charter party if a ship is not available for loading. 2. In

stock purchases, the date on which an order is filled or canceled.

**C&D.** The abbreviation for collected and delivered.

**C & F.** The abbreviation for cost and freight.

**C & I.** The abbreviation for cost and insurance.

**cap.** A limitation on a term in a loan agreement. For example, a limitation on the maximum interest rate payable to a lender and ceilings on a borrower's revolving line of credit are caps.

**CAP.** The abbreviation for Common Agricultural Policy.

**capacity stabilization agreement.** Also known as rationalization, an agreement between ocean carriers to maintain rates and reduce expenses by sharing assets. Carriers use capacity stabilization agreements to reduce competition by retiring ships from a given trade route, to eliminate excess container and vessel space, and to share technology.

**capital.** Assets invested in a firm. Business capital covers physical assets (e.g., plants and equipment) and human assets (e.g., employee skill and creativity). Financial capital includes assets acquired by way of retained earnings, loans, and securities issues.

**capital account.** See *balance of payments*.

**capital allowance.** See *depreciation*.

**capital consumption allowance.** An accounting item used to compute national income. The entry reflects the aggregate value of capital depreciation and losses claimed by a nation's business sector over a specified period of time. See also *balance of payments*.

**capital flight.** The wholesale removal of capital investments from a country. Capital flight occurs when a country is politically or economically unstable, or both.

**capital formation.** A description of the aggregate financial value of a nation's privately held assets. Capital formation is measured by the value of private capital assets, including inventory, reduced by deductions for depreciation and consumption.

**capital-gains tax (CGT).** An income tax levied on the difference between the purchase price and selling price of an asset. The capital-gains rate for short-term assets (i.e., those held for less than a year) is higher than that for longer-term assets. The CGT applies to net gains, attributable to holding the asset, less losses and exemptions. Allowable capital losses and exemptions vary in different tax jurisdictions. Capital-gains taxes are levied only against assets sold by a person not normally engaged in trading assets of the type taxed. See also *capital loss.*

**capital gearing.**   See *leverage.*

**capital good.**   See *good.*

**capital intensive.**   See *labor intensive.*

**capitalism.**   An economic system characterized by relatively free markets in which individuals and companies accumulate capital in the form of private wealth. In capitalistic economies, goods and services are produced and distributed by private individuals or firms with limited government intervention. Compare *socialism.*

**capitalize.**   1. In accounting, to treat expenditures as assets rather than expenses. 2. In finance, to sell shares and use the profits to convert debt into stock.

**capital loss.**   A loss attributable to holding a capital asset. The loss results when an asset is destroyed or when liabilities are associated with owning the asset. Capital losses offset capital gains.

**capital market.**   A market where funds are raised by governments and corporations. Stocks, bonds, and notes are issued in capital markets through investment banks, merchant banks, and other financial institutions. The issues are purchased by private investors, banks, pension funds, and insurance companies. Capital markets in the United States and other industrialized countries are divided into stock markets for equities, bond markets, and money markets for short-term debt issues. Compare *central market.*

**Capital Movements Code.**   Officially known as the Code of Liberalization of Capital Movements, an international agreement initiated by the Organisation for Economic Cooperation and Development. The code encourages the uninhibited flow of capital resources and investment between signatory countries, but derogations from its provisions are permitted when influxes of foreign capital threaten domestic industries. The Capital Movements Code was opened for signature in 1961. See also *OECD Codes.*

**capital-redemption reserve.**   In the United Kingdom, a fund maintained by a company to redeem shares from retained earnings. Maintenance of reserve funds is required by the British Companies Act of 1985. The act does not apply to redemptions financed through new securities issues.

**CAPRI Project.**   See *World Intellectual Property Organization.*

**captive market.**   Purchasers of goods or services without alternative sources of supply.   Prices paid by consumers in captive markets are generally higher than those in competitive markets, particularly where alternative suppliers are abundant.

**CAR.**   The abbreviation for compound annual return.

**CARDIS.**   The abbreviation for Cargo Data Interchange System.

**car float.**   A barge used to transport railway freight cars to piers. The freight cars are hauled from barges onto ocean vessels.

**cargo.**   Goods consolidated into one shipment and transported to a destination point. General cargoes contain several lots of goods destined for different consignees. A special cargo contains a single lot of goods, sometimes stowed in bulk in the hold of a ship. Compare *freight.*

**cargo broker.**   Also called a freight broker, an agent who locates ships for hire. Brokers are compensated based on a percentage of a cargo's value and may receive an address commission.

**Cargo Capacity Measurement System (CCMS).** An electronic system developed to calculate the cargo capacity of ships entering the Panama Canal Zone. The system is scheduled for activation in 1994.

**cargo-carrying capacity.**   The total deadweight tonnage of a ship when loaded with cargo, passengers, and supplies. Compare *cargo deadweight tonnage.*

**cargo container sealer.**   A device designed to reveal and prevent product tampering. Types of sealing devices include electrical circuits, dye vials, photographic fiber-optic wire, and so forth. When manipulated or broken, the devices reveal container tampering.

**cargo control document (CCD).**    A notice from a carrier or freight forwarder to a consignee that a shipment has arrived for customs clearance. The notice may be in the form of a shipping manifest, airway bill, or other document.

**Cargo Data Interchange System (CARDIS).**    An electronic data interchange system that transmits trade documents, including bills of lading. The system was developed by NCITD–The International Trade Facilitation Council in conjunction with the U.S. Department of Transportation. Implementation of CARDIS was delayed by legal questions surrounding the negotiability of electronic bills of lading. Normally, a bill of lading cannot be negotiated without a signature to authenticate the transfer. To facilitate authentication, NCITD recommended the use of an electronic identifier code known only to the shipper. The CARDIS system was originally demonstrated in 1979.

**cargo deadweight tonnage.**    The total shipping capacity of a carrier when loaded with cargo minus the *weight* of equipment, supplies, and water. Compare *cargo-carrying capacity.*

**Cargo Preference Act of 1954.**    In the United States, an amendment to the Merchant Marine Act of 1936, requiring that at least 50 percent of all U.S. government cargoes be transported aboard U.S.-flagged ships. The rule covers national defense supplies, agricultural surplus commodities, official development assistance shipments, and exports financed by the Export-Import Bank of the United States. See also *Jones Act of 1920.*

**Caribbean Association of Industry and Commerce (CAIC).**    A private trade association representing commercial and manufacturing interests in the Caribbean. CAIC was founded in 1917 and reorganized in 1981. CAIC is based in Barbados.

**Caribbean Basin Development Program.**    See *Caribbean Basin Projects Financing Authority.*

**Caribbean Basin Division.**    In the United States, an office of the International Trade Administration in the U.S. Department of Commerce. The division is staffed by specialists on the Caribbean region and advises the secretary of commerce on Caribbean-U.S. economic policies. The Caribbean Basin Division also responds to inquiries from companies concerning trade and investment in the region.

**Caribbean Basin Economic Recovery Act (CBI I).**    See *Caribbean Basin Initiative I.*

**Caribbean Basin Economic Recovery Expansion Act (CBI II).**    See *Caribbean Basin Initiative II.*

**Caribbean Basin Initiative.**    See *Caribbean Basin Initiative I* and *Caribbean Basin Initiative II.*

**Caribbean Basin Initiative I (CBI I).**    In the United States, a trade and aid program authorized by the Caribbean Basin Economic Recovery Act of 1983, also known as CBI I. The CBI I program was enacted to provide markets for Caribbean exports and to encourage investment in the region. It was supplanted by Caribbean Basin Initiative II in 1990. CBI I combined tax benefits, tariff exemptions, and technical assistance. The program also waived duties on most Caribbean imports meeting regional content requirements for a period of 11 years. To qualify for the import preference, an article must have been grown, produced, manufactured, or substantially transformed into a "new and different" product in the Caribbean region. A 35 percent local content requirement also applied to CBI imports. The program, which became effective January 1, 1984, was scheduled to expire September 30, 1995. See also *substantial transformation* and *35 percent value added.*

**Caribbean Basin Initiative II (CBI II).**    In the United States, the revision of Caribbean Basin Initiative I (CBI I) enacted by the Caribbean Basin Economic Recovery Expansion Act of 1990. CBI II improved on CBI I by granting perpetual U.S. trade preferences to eligible Caribbean countries and eliminating duties on most Caribbean exports assembled from U.S. components. For CBI exports manufactured or otherwise produced entirely from U.S. components or ingredients, the 35 percent value-added and substantial transformation requirements were also eliminated. As of 1993, the following countries are CBI beneficiaries: Antigua, Aruba, Bahamas, Barbados, Belize, British Virgin Islands, Costa Rica, Dominica, Dominican Republic, El Salvador, Grenada, Guatemala,

Guyana, Haiti, Honduras, Jamaica, Montserrat, Netherlands Antilles, St. Kitts and Nevis, St. Lucia, St. Vincent and the Grenadines, and Trinidad and Tobago. See also *Caribbean Basin Projects Financing Authority.*

**Caribbean Basin Initiative Agribusiness Information Center.**    In the United States, a matchmaking and information service sponsored by the U.S. Department of Agriculture. The center provides U.S. farmers and food processors with information on investment and trade opportunities in the Caribbean Basin.

**Caribbean Basin Projects Financing Authority (CARIFA).**    In Puerto Rico, the agency of Economic Development Administration of Puerto Rico (FORMENTO) authorized to administer funds dedicated to Caribbean Basin economic development under Section 936 of the U.S. Internal Revenue Code. Section 936 covers qualified possession source investment income funds maintained by U.S. businesses in Puerto Rico. CARIFA approves Section 936 applications under FORMENTO Regulation 3582, primarily to promote twin-plant operations in the Caribbean. CARIFA is headquartered in San Juan. See also *Caribbean Basin Initiative I* and *Caribbean Basin Initiative II.*

**Caribbean-Canada Economic Trade Development Assistance Program (CARIBCAN).**    The trade development, official development assistance, and technical aid program sponsored in the Caribbean region by the Canadian government. Roughly 90 percent of Caribbean exports from British Commonwealth countries enter Canada free of duty. CARIBCAN exempts textiles and apparels, most leather goods, and some oil-based products from trade preferences.

**Caribbean/Central American Action Committee.**  See *Caribbean Latin American Action Committee.*

**Caribbean Development Bank (CDB).**    A multilateral development bank established in 1969 under the auspices of the United Nations Economic Commission for Latin America and the Caribbean. The bank provides financing and technical assistance for projects in member countries, primarily for agricultural, infrastructure, and economic development programs. CDB members are Antigua, Bahamas, Barbados, Belize, British Virgin Islands, Canada, Cayman Islands,

Colombia, Dominica, Grenada, Guyana, Jamaica, Montserrat, St. Kitts and Nevis, Trinidad and Tobago, Turks and Caicos Islands, the United Kingdom, and Venezuela. The bank is based in St. Michael, Barbados.

**Caribbean Economic Community (CARICOM).**  Also known as the Caribbean Common Market, an association of English-speaking Caribbean, Central American, and South American countries. CARICOM was established in 1973 to coordinate the economic, foreign, and social policies of member states. The successor to the defunct Caribbean Free Trade Association, CARICOM imposes a common external tariff on imports that range from 5 to 45 percent. The highest import rate is levied on agricultural products; the lowest on agricultural inputs. The community plans monetary union, including a single currency, by the year 2000. CARICOM members are Antigua, Bahamas, Barbuda, Barbados, Belize, Dominica, Grenada, Guyana, Jamaica, Montserrat, St. Kitts and Nevis, St. Lucia, St. Vincent and the Grenadines, and Trinidad and Tobago. CARICOM's secretariat is located in Georgetown, Guyana.

**Caribbean Free Trade Association.**    See *Caribbean Economic Community.*

**Caribbean/Latin American Action Committee (C/LAA).**    In the United States, a nongovernmental organization established in 1980 to promote economic development and foreign private-sector investment in the Caribbean Basin and Latin America. C/LAA publishes *Caribbean/Latin America in Action,* a quarterly report on Caribbean Basin economic trends and policy issues. The organization has also sponsored the Miami Conference on the Caribbean each year since 1977. The Miami Conferences provide wide-ranging information about the Caribbean Basin, as well as trade show and matchmaking opportunities. C/LAA is based in Washington, D.C.

**CARIBCAN.**    The acronym for Caribbean-Canada Economic Trade Development Assistance Program.

**CARICOM.**    The acronym for Caribbean Common Market.

**CARIFA.**    The acronym for Caribbean Basin Projects Financing Authority.

**CARIFTA.**    The acronym for Caribbean Free

Trade Association. See *Caribbean Economic Community.*

**Carmack Amendment.**   In the United States, a 1906 amendment to the Interstate Commerce Act of 1887 defining liability and legal rates for U.S. ground carriers. The amendment imposes liability on a carrier to the extent of total cargo losses when goods are transported under a through bill of lading. It also alters the Interstate Commerce Act to permit lower shipping rates in exchange for reduced carrier liability. The Interstate Commerce Act and the Carmack Amendment do not apply to air or ocean carriers.

**carnet.**   A book of vouchers used to suspend duties and taxes for temporary imports entered into a customs territory for reexport. The carnet system covers samples and equipment imported for business or professional purposes or en route to another destination. Carnets are issued and guaranteed by international business or trade associations, certified in the exporting country, and accepted in countries belonging to carnet conventions. Quotas on textiles, apparels, and other products may apply to carnet entries. Carnets are usually valid for 1 year. Types of carnets include the following:

*Admission Temporaire/Temporary Admission (ATA) carnet.*   ATA carnets cover most types of temporary imports, except goods entered for processing or repair. Nearly all countries accept ATA carnets, under either other carnet conventions or national laws and regulations. ATA carnets are obtained from local chambers of commerce or through the International Bureau of the International Chamber of Commerce in Paris.

*Echantillon Carnet Sample (ECS).*   ECS carnets suspend duty, import license, and import entry requirements for commercial or trade samples, but not for imports entered for reexport. Because of its limitations, the ECS carnet has been largely supplanted by the ATA carnet.

*Transport International Routier/International Road Transport (TIR) carnet.*   TIR carnets are issued for shipments en route from one country to an interior destination in another. The carnets are authorized by the Customs Convention on the International Transport of Goods under Cover of TIR Carnets, which provides for shipments across national borders without intermediate reloading. The TIR carnet is used as security for import duties and taxes payable at the destination point. Goods traveling under TIR carnets are not subject to customs inspection at intermediate stops. In the United States, the Equipment Interchange Association is the guarantor of TIR carnets. See also *Convention relative au contrât de transport international de marchandises par route.*

**carriage and insurance paid to (CIP).**   An international commercial term (INCOTERM). The seller pays the cost of delivery and insurance to a named destination. The buyer bears all subsequent costs.

**carriage cost.**   The cost of transporting goods within a country's interior. A price quoted as carriage forward means the buyer pays delivery costs. A carriage paid/free quotation means the seller pays delivery costs.

**carriage forward.**   See *carriage cost.*

**carriage free.**   See *carriage cost.*

**Carriage of Goods by Sea Act of 1936 (COGSA).** In the United States, a federal law restricting ocean carrier liability for damage or loss to cargo. The act limits a carrier's liability to $500 per package (or per customary freight unit), although a shipper may usually recover the higher declared value of goods. When cargo losses are attributable to certain causes, including fire or sinking, the insurer is not entitled to subrogation in a legal action against the carrier. COSGA requires that U.S. bills of lading covering ocean shipments incorporate its provisions by reference. See also *Hague-Visby Rules* and *Hamburg Rules.*

**carriage paid to (CPT).**   An international commercial term (INCOTERM). The seller pays transportation costs to a named destination. The buyer pays all other costs. See also *carriage cost.*

**carrier.**   A firm transporting passengers or cargoes for a fee. Most jurisdictions have different licensing requirements, depending on whether the carrier is a common carrier licensed to operate for the general public on a regulated tariff basis, a contract-limited carrier licensed to operate under negotiated rates stipulated by contract, or a private carrier licensed to operate for a parent or affiliated company.

**carrier's certificate.**   A document provided by a common carrier to customs officials to verify the identity of the consignee named in a bill of lading. The certificate is required to take delivery of goods following customs clearance. In the United States, the carrier's certificate, known as the carrier's certificate and release order, is mandated by the Tariff Act of 1930.

**carta de credito.**    Spanish: letter of credit.

**cartage.**    The process of moving goods between short-haul sites over ground routes within the same country. Cartage also means the freight charged for local transport. Compare *cabotage*.

**cartel.**    An agreement between two or more entities to regulate internal competition. Cartels are formed to control supplies and increase profits or stabilize prices. In the United States, except where specifically permitted by statute, private business combinations are illegal under antitrust laws. Cartels are not prohibited, however, by international law, and international commodity groups and similar cartels are common among producers of raw commodities.

**cash.**    For accounting and tax purposes, coins and currency plus any financial instrument immediately convertible to coins and currency with the bearer's signature. The instruments are cashier's checks, bank drafts, money orders, and traveler's checks.

**cash against documents (CAD).**    A term of sale requiring a buyer to pay cash for purchases in exchange for documents of title. In CAD sales, documents and payments are usually exchanged through third-party intermediaries, such as banks or commission houses. See also *documentary collection*.

**cash basis accounting.**    A form of business accounting whereby expenses and income are realized when payments are made and received. Cash basis permits a business to manipulate income for tax-reporting purposes by accelerating or delaying payments or receipts. Under the Tax Reform Act of 1986, a corporation, corporate partnership, or trust may not use cash basis accounting when annual gross receipts exceed $5 million. Compare *accrual basis accounting*.

**cash before delivery.**    See *cash in advance*.

**cash commodity.**    See *commodity*.

**cash deal.**    See *cash settlement*.

**cashflow.**    The amount of cash held in current accounts for expenses and payments to creditors. Cashflow determines the amount of money available for immediate use and is a clearer indicator of liquidity than profit and loss projections. A company has a positive or negative cashflow, depending on whether it has sufficient assets readily convertible to cash to pay current debts. Compare *discounted cashflow*.

**cashier's check.**    See *check*.

**cash in advance (CIA).**    Also known as cash before delivery (CBD), a term of sale conditioning shipment on receipt of the cash purchase price before goods are shipped. CIA is normally required when a buyer's creditworthiness is uncertain or when goods are manufactured to special specifications. Compare *cash with order*.

**cash management.**    In corporate finance, maintaining adequate cash balances by accelerating collections and controlling disbursements. Corporations frequently deposit funds collected from receivables in concentration accounts. Controlled disbursements enable a corporation to invest excess funds in certificates of deposit or money-market funds. Earnings from investments increase cash assets.

**cash management bill.**    In the United States, a short-term security introduced in 1975 by the U.S. Department of Treasury to avoid temporary cash shortages. Cash management bills are sold to institutional investors for minimum investments of $1 million. The bills carry maturities from 2 to 167 days and have average maturities of 50 days. Cash management bills have largely replaced tax anticipation bills and are issued shortly before a tax receipt deadline. Compare *Treasury bill* and *Treasury note*.

**cash market.**    See *spot market*.

**cash price.**    A term of sale requiring a buyer to pay cash for a purchase. Cash payments often entitle buyers to discounts because the seller collects money immediately without the carrying expenses of a credit sale. See also *spot price*.

**cash settlement.**    1. In securities markets, an option to receive stock on the day a trade is concluded rather than on the payment date. 2. A cash deal in which payment is made on the day following the purchase of securities. 3. In options trading, a payment to the holder of an option of the difference between the settlement price and the exercise price specified in the option contract. 4. In futures trading, payment of the market price for a futures contract. The market price for futures is the settlement price at the time of a transaction determined by the policy of the futures exchange on which the contract is traded.

**cash with order (CWO).**    A term of sale requiring a buyer to pay cash at the time goods are ordered. Cash-with-order terms are required when a buyer's creditworthiness is uncertain, when goods are manufactured to special specifications, or when the seller is unable to bear the cost of producing goods without certainty of payment. Compare *cash in advance.*

**Cassis de Dijon.**    In the European Community (EC), a landmark case decided by the European Court of Justice in 1987 concerning the right of one EC country to ban imports from another. Germany had invoked its own national legislation to prohibit imports of liqueur made in France, although the liqueur conformed to French food standards. Deciding in favor of France, the Court affirmed an EC country's right to export goods for sale in another EC country absent defensible health and safety objections. See also *consumer protection.*

**CAT.**    The abbreviation for computer-aided trading.

**CATS.**    The abbreviation for certificate of accrual on Treasury securities.

**cautionnement forfaitaire.**    French: cautionary payment, e.g., a lump-sum guarantee, usually in the form of a bond, required to enter goods for inward processing.

**caveat.**    Latin: Let one beware. In law, a caveat is a notice to an administrative officer or a judge in a legal proceeding to await further action until an underlying issue has been resolved. For example, a caveat may halt the issuance of a patent until essential facts related to a patent application have been determined.

**caveat emptor.**    Latin: Let the buyer beware. *Caveat emptor* is a legal rule under which a buyer bears the risks of a purchase. In most common-law countries, consumer protection laws and contractual warranties have reduced the impact of the doctrine.

**Caymanian Protection Board.**    In the Cayman Islands, the agency identified by the national government to issue operating licenses to foreign firms. The board is authorized by the Local Companies Law.

**CB.**    The abbreviation for *Customs Bulletin.*

**CBD.**    The abbreviation for cash before delivery. See *cash in advance.*

**CBERA.**    The abbreviation for Caribbean Basin Economic Recovery Act. See *Caribbean Basin Initiative I.*

**CBEREA.**    The abbreviation for Caribbean Basin Economic Recovery Expansion Act. See *Caribbean Basin Initiative II.*

**CBI.**    The abbreviation for Caribbean Basin Initiative and Confederation of British Industry.

**CBI I.**    The abbreviation for Caribbean Basin Initiative I.

**CBI II.**    The abbreviation for Caribbean Basin Initiative II.

**CBOE.**    The abbreviation for Chicago Board of Exchange.

**CBOT, CBT.**    The abbreviations for Chicago Board of Trade.

**c.c.**    The abbreviation for civil commotions and current cost.

**CC.**    The abbreviation for carrier's certificate.

**CCC.**    The abbreviation for Commodity Credit Corporation and Customs Cooperation Council.

**CCCE.**    The abbreviation for *Caisse Centrale de Coopération Économique.* See *official development assistance.*

**CCCN.**    The abbreviation for Customs Cooperation Council Nomenclature.

**CCD.**    The abbreviation for cargo control documents.

**CCE.**    The abbreviation for *Communauté Economique Européenne.* See *European Economic Community.*

**CCFF.**    The abbreviation for Compensatory and Contingency Financing Facility.

**CCIE.**    The abbreviation for chief comptroller of imports and exports.

**CCPA.**   The abbreviation for U.S. Court of Customs and Patent Appeals.

**CCT.**   The abbreviation for common customs tariff. See *common external tariff.*

**CD.**   The abbreviation for certificate of deposit.

**CDB.**   The abbreviation for Caribbean Development Bank.

**CD-ROM.**   The abbreviation for compact disk–read-only memory.

**CDS.**   The abbreviation for construction differential subsidy.

**CE.**   The abbreviation for caveat emptor, Communauté Européenne, Conseil de l'Europe, country of exportation, and consumption entry. See *Council of Europe* and *customs entry.*

**CEAO.**   The abbreviation for *Communauté Économique de l'Afrique de l'Ouest.*

**CEDEL.**   The acronym for *Centrale de Livraison de Valeurs Mobilières.*

**cedi.**   The currency of Ghana.

**cedule.**   A European term for a negotiable warehouse receipt.

**CEEC.**   The abbreviation for Central and Eastern European countries.

**cellularized vessel.**   Sometimes called a slot ship, a ship furnished with slots or other internal ribbing for transporting stacked containers.

**CEM.**   The abbreviation for combination export manager.

**CEN.**   The abbreviation for Committee for European Normalization, commonly known in long form as the Committee for European Standardization. See *Communauté Européenne.*

**Cenelec.**   The acronym for Committee for Electrotechnical Standardization. See *Communauté Européenne.*

**Census Automated Reporting Program.**   See *Automated Export System.*

**CENTO.**   The acronym for Central Treaty Organization.

**Central American Bank for Economic Integration.**   See *Banco Centromericano de Integración Económica.*

**Central American Common Market.**   See *Mercado Común Centroamericano.*

**Central and Eastern European countries (CEEC).**   In international parlance, the post-Cold War designation loosely applied to countries of the former western and eastern European blocs. CEEC is generally used to mean Austria, Germany, the Czech Republic, Hungary, Poland, Romania, Slovakia, and the countries contiguous to them. Depending on the context, the term covers all or only the western republics of the former Soviet Union.

**central bank.**   Also known as a reserve bank, one of a nation's central monetary institutions. Central banks are lenders of last resort, which also regulate the national money supply, principally by setting interest rate policy and lending to local banks, issue currency, manage transfers of foreign exchange when controls are in place, hold reserve assets, manage public debt, and finance government expenditures through the sale of government securities. In broad terms, central banks attempt to achieve price stability and maintain reasonable levels of employment. Compare *currency board.*

**Central Bank of China.**   The central bank of Taiwan.

**Central Bank of North America.**   The central bank of the proposed North American Free Trade Accord (NAFTA). The proposal for monetary integration in North America, advanced largely by academics, has not been adopted as policy by the national governments of North America. NAFTA covers Canada, Mexico, and the United States. See also *North American currency unit.*

**Central Bank of West African States.**   See *Banque Centrale des États de l'Afrique de l'Ouest.*

**Centrale de Livraison de Valeurs Mobilières (CEDEL).**   An electronic clearing system created in 1970 by international financial institutions for the delivery and settlement of securities. Bank members of the Society of Worldwide Financial Interbank Telecommunications transmit advice and settlement instructions through CEDEL. CEDEL is based in Luxembourg.

**centrally planned economy.**   Also called a non-market or command economy, a national economy in which financial and capital resources are allocated by government directive. Frequently associated with communist countries, limited central planning also occurs in various forms in socialist and in some nonsocialist countries. Compare *market economy.*

**central market.**    A national or regional commodities market where trading functions are performed by brokers or dealers. Central markets are often also distribution centers for spot commodities. Compare *terminal market.*

**central monetary institutions.**    Government units responsible for managing a nation's fiscal affairs. Central monetary institutions are composed of central banks and finance (or treasury) ministries. These institutions manage balance of payments, credit, foreign exchange, reserve assets, and monetary policies. In the United States, central monetary functions are performed by the Federal Reserve System, the U.S. Department of the Treasury, and the comptroller of the currency.

**central rate.**    In a multilateral monetary system, the index rate for fixing the value of national currencies. In the European Monetary System (EMS), the central rate is ostensibly fixed by the European currency unit (ECU). In reality, however, the Deutsche mark, the strongest national currency in the European Community (EC) currency basket, determines the central rate. A currency deviation from the central rate in excess of a certain range triggers intervention by one or more EC central banks to restore balance to the EMS.

**Central Statistical Office.**    The British equivalent of the U.S. Bureau of the Census. The Central Statistical Office publishes *Economic Trends,* a monthly economic forecast for the United Kingdom; the *Monthly Digest of Statistics*; and two surveys of national economic statistics, *The Blue Book* and *The Pink Book.*

**CER.**    The abbreviation for Closer Economic Relationship.

**CERN.**    The abbreviation for *Organisation européenne pour la recherche nucléaire,* the Geneva-based European Organization for Nuclear Research.

**cert.**    An abbreviation for certificate and certify.

**certificate (cert., ctf.).**    1. A document issued by a bank, insurance underwriter, customs authority,

or other government or private agency to authenticate a fact needed to facilitate a transaction. Compare *declaration.* 2. An instrument representing money on deposit with a financial institution. See also *certificate of deposit.*

**certificate of accrual on Treasury securities (CATS).**    In the United States, an instrument that serves the purposes of a zero-coupon Treasury bond. Treasury securities purchased by an investment bank are deposited with a trustee. Receipts are issued against scheduled principal repayments and coupon payments. The receipts are sold for present discounted value. Known collectively as felines, CATS were first issued by Solomon Brothers in 1982. Merrill Lynch felines are known as TIGRS (Treasury investment growth securities).

**certificate of admeasurement.**    A document verifying the cargo-carrying capacity and tonnage of a newly constructed or refurbished ship. Certificates of admeasurement are furnished by independent inspection firms and used to support shipbuilders' claims that a vessel's construction complies with insurance and regulatory standards. Taxes and fees are normally assessed on the tonnage specified in certificates of admeasurement.

**certificate of analysis.**    A document issued by an exporter or inspection firm to an importer. Certificates of analysis verify the testing, inspection, quality, and quantity of goods entering an importing country.

**certificate of consumer protection.**    A certificate of health, sometimes required in addition to a certificate of free sale. In some countries, the consumer protection certificate must be legalized by the importing country's local consulate.

**certificate of damage.**    A certificate signed by a dock agent when damaged cargo is received. The document verifies the nature of the damage, usually for insurance purposes.

**certificate of deposit (CD).**    1. A receipt issued for a time deposit with a fixed maturity date. Time CDs can be negotiable or nonnegotiable, normally maturing in 7 days or more and paying fixed market rates of interest. See also *consumer certificate of deposit, Euro certificate of deposit, negotiable certificate of deposit, roly poly certificate of deposit, savings certificate, variable-rate certificate of deposit,* and

*Yankee certificate of deposit.* 2. A nonnegotiable, non-interest-bearing receipt payable to a holder on demand. Demand CDs are issued against funds deposited for the benefit of another, usually as a surety.

**certificate of free sale.**    A document provided by a health agency in an exporter's home market. The certificate verifies that goods meet minimum local standards for sale and consumption. In the United States, a letter of comment is issued in lieu of the certificate of free sale.

**certificate of health.**    A document required in some form by all countries for imports entered for human consumption, including food, pharmaceuticals, and blood products. Health certificates verify the purity of the imported product, particularly its freedom from pest and disease, and are usually required in addition to certificates of free sale. In some instances, import health requirements may be determined by bilateral agreement. Minimal standards for consumable products traded in international commerce have been established by the World Health Organization and the Food and Agricultural Organization. Health certificates must often be legalized by the importing country's local consulate in the exporting country. See also *Codex Alimentarius* and *food manufacturer's/food ingredient certificate.*

**certificate of incorporation.**    A certificate issued to the founding shareholders of a new company chartered to operate in a given jurisdiction. The certificate is issued after articles of incorporation, also called articles of association, and other documents have been filed with the incorporating agency.

**certificate of indebtedness.**    A short-term unsecured note issued by a corporation or government agency. In the United States, certificates of indebtedness were issued by the U.S. Department of Treasury until 1981 when they were replaced by U.S. Treasury bills.

**certificate of inspection.**    A document furnished to an importer by a private agency, usually an independent inspection firm. Certificates of inspection verify the condition and other characteristics of goods under shipment. Depending on the country of importation, plants, animals, cosmetics, and products for human consumption may

require special inspection certificates. See also *clean report of findings* and *phytosanitary inspection certificate.*

**certificate of insurance.**    A document supplied by a seller to a buyer certifying cargo insurance coverage. The coverage may have been obtained under the seller's own policy or under an open policy maintained by a freight forwarder. When a transaction is financed by a letter of credit, the insurance certificate is presented to the paying bank along with other shipping documents. Certificates of insurance are negotiable instruments endorsed by the bank financing a sale.

**certificate of label approval.**    In the United States, a document required for imports of distilled spirits. The certificates are issued to importers by the Bureau of Alcohol, Tobacco, and Firearms. Certificates of label approval are filed with the U.S. Customs Service to obtain release of distilled spirits for sale in the domestic consumer market.

**certificate of manufacture.**    Also called a manufacturer's certificate, a document provided by a manufacturer to a bank or other issuer of a letter of credit. Certificates of manufacture are required when a letter of credit stipulates the finished manufacture of goods before a seller is paid. A letter of credit may require that the manufacturer's certificate be notarized.

**certificate of origin.**    A document provided to customs authorities in an importing country confirming the country of origin identified in shipping documents. Certificates of origin are usually issued by a local chamber of commerce in the exporting country. The certificates may cover a single shipment or multiple shipments of identical goods. Origin certificates determine whether and at what rate imports are dutiable. In the United States, origin certificates are of two types: (1) Customs Form 3229 (or approved alternative documentation) is used for imports not entering free of duty, and (2) UNCTAD Certificate of Origin Form A is used for duty-free imports entering under the Caribbean Basin Initiative and the U.S. Generalized System of Preferences.

**certificate of weight and inspection.**    See *certificate of inspection.*

**certification.**    The act of authenticating a fact or attesting to an expert evaluation of quality. A certification is contained in a written document and signed by a party who is privy to the fact, who is authorized to verify the quality of a product or service, or who is competent to attest to a person's qualifications or reputation.

**certified check.**   See *check.*

**certified stock.**   See *commodity exchange.*

**Certified Trade Fair Program.**   In the United States, a program sponsored by the U.S. Department of Commerce to certify international trade fairs for domestic industries. To obtain certification, a foreign trade fair must be a leading industry event capable of attracting at least 20 U.S. exhibitors. Trade fair promoters must also provide adequate local trade show services and exhibition space.

**CET.**   An abbreviation for common external tariff.

**C et F.**   The abbreviation for *coût et fret.* See *cost and freight.*

**ceteris paribus (cet. par.).**   Latin: other things being equal.

**cet. par.**   The abbreviation for *ceteris paribus.*

**cf.**   The abbreviation for cubic foot and customs form.

**CFA.**   The abbreviation for *Communauté financière africaine* and *Coopération Financière en Afrique Centrale.* See *Franc Zone.*

**CFP.**   The abbreviation for *Comptoirs Français du Pacifique.* See *Franc Zone.*

**CFR.**   The abbreviation for cost and freight.

**CFS.**   The abbreviation for container freight station.

**CFTC.**   The abbreviation for Commodity Futures Trading Commission.

**chaebol.**   In Korea, a vertically integrated business combination that includes manufacturers, suppliers, and distributors. The *chaebol* fixes delivery terms and controls distribution channels. In the United States, interlocking business combinations are presumed to restrain competition and impede trade. See also *keiretsu.*

**chamber of commerce.**   A business and trade association that represents the commercial and political interests of its members. Chambers are organized in most countries around the world. In the United States, local and state chambers are linked through the U.S. Chamber of Commerce. National chambers are affiliated through the International Chamber of Commerce located in Paris.

**chamber of commerce certificate.**   A document issued by a local chamber of commerce in an exporting country. Normally, chamber certificates verify country of origin, home country prices, or the identity and reputation of an exporter. Some countries accept similar certifications from other organizations.

**chambre de commerce.**   French: chamber of commerce.

**CH&H.**   The abbreviation for the (European) continent between Le Havre and Hamburg.

**change à terme.**   French: forward exchange.

**channel/channel length.**   The length of a product distribution chain from the manufacturer to end users. Intermediaries along the chain include agents, brokers, dealers, and distributors. The manufacturer is usually the most powerful member in the chain and is sometimes called the channel captain. Disputes between members of a distribution chain are called channel conflicts. A dispute is horizontal when members at the same level of the channel (e.g., distributors) are involved. The conflict is vertical when members at different levels of the chain (e.g., brokers and distributors) are involved.

**Channel Tunnel.**   See *Eurotunnel.*

**CHAPS.**   The abbreviation for Clearing House Automatic Payments System.

**charter.**   1. The legal document authorizing the formation of a corporation. 2. In the United States, a license granted to a bank. A chartered bank must meet state and federal capital-adequacy requirements and obtain federal deposit insurance. 3. See *charter hire.*

**chartered company.**   See *company.*

**charterer's liability.**   An insurable risk borne by the charterer of an ocean vessel. The liability arises from loss, damage, or injury caused by a ship during the course of a charter. Marine policies cover charterer's liability, except in cases expressly excluded from coverage.

**charter hire.**   1. The renting of a ship or aircraft. 2. The freight, or tariff, charged by the owner of a chartered vessel.

**charter party/charterparty.**   A written agreement to rent or hire an entire ship or aircraft. Under a bareboat charter, also called a demise charter, the charterer pays all crew, fuel, and stores expenses. In a time charter, a ship is hired for a specified period of time, the shipowner operates the ship, and the hirer provides fuel and other expenses. Under a voyage charter, a ship is hired for a specific voyage and the shipowner pays all expenses. When a charter is open, the charterer pays all expenses, controls the ship, and is free to transport cargo to any destination. See also *disponent owner*.

**chassis.**   The frame of a truck on which containers and trailers are transported.

**chattel paper.**   Documents confirming a creditor's security interest arising from the purchase of goods. Chattel paper vests title to the property in the creditor. A security interest is eliminated when the debt is paid.

**check.**   Also known as a cheque, a negotiable demand draft drawn on a bank promising to pay a named party a specified sum at a stated time. A check must be signed by the drawer or maker, but it can be made payable to the maker or a third party. A check is negotiated by endorsement and voided by a stop-payment order. A check canceled by endorsement cannot be renegotiated. A bank certifying a check, known as a certified check, verifies the maker's signature and promises to pay the draft. By contrast, a cashier's check is drawn by a bank on its own funds and signed by a bank officer.

**checker.**   The employee designated by an ocean carrier to inspect shipments and issue receipts for cargo delivered to a departure port.

**check with order (CWO).**   A term of sale requiring payment by draft at the time a purchase order is issued. Compare *cash with order*.

**cheque.**   See *check*.

**chg., chgd.**   The abbreviations for charge and charged, respectively.

**Chicago Board of Trade (CBOT, CBT).**   In the United States, a commodity exchange and futures market established in 1848 to facilitate cash grain sales. The first futures contract was sold on the exchange in 1851. The world's largest grain exchange, CBOT lists deferred Treasury bond options, ferrous scrap metal futures, freight index futures, zero-coupon Treasury bonds, and note futures.The exchange also introduced insurance futures contracts to hedge against large indemnity claims. In 1986, CBOT created the MidAmerica Commodity Exchange (MidAm), a wholly owned affiliate. In 1992, the CBOT implemented Project A, an electronic system for trading unlisted contracts in barge freight-rate index futures, scrap steel futures, some Treasury bond options, and zero-coupon bonds and notes. CBOT's electronic Standard Portfolio Analysis of Risk system is used to match margins to portfolio risks before contracts are cleared through the Board of Trade Clearing Corporation. Trades are surveilled through the exchange's Computerized Trade Reconstruction system, which records trading activity. The CBOT is located in Chicago. See also *Globex*.

**Chicago Board Options Exchange (CBOE).**   An exchange created in 1973 for trading listed stock options contracts. CBOE trades options on stock, stock index options, and other share-price indexes.

**Chicago Convention on International Civil Aviation.**   Also known as the Chicago Convention, a global agreement that governs international civil aviation. The convention and the International Civil Aviation Organization (ICAO) emerged from deliberations of the Chicago International Civil Aviation Conference held in 1944. The conference largely approved bilateral negotiations as the principal vehicles for establishing global civil aviation rules. In 1992, the ICAO began considering revisions of the Chicago Convention to create a multilateral regulatory system. The ICAO is based in Montreal.

**Chicago Mercantile Exchange (CME)–International Money Market (IMM).**   A combined commodity exchange and financial futures market. The CME was created in 1919 and the IMM in 1972. The CME-IMM specializes in trading foreign exchange, Eurodollar, livestock, metals, U.S. Treasury bill futures, and options contracts. The

IMM's foreign exchange contracts are standard contracts for specific quantities of currencies (e.g., a contract for 35,000 Deutsche marks) with fixed delivery dates, which fall on the third Wednesday of a given month. The exchanges are located in Chicago. See also *Globex.*

**China Trade Act Corporation.** In the United States, a corporation entitled to special tax benefits under the China Trade Act of 1962. The benefits were limited to companies trading with the People's Republic of China. The China Trade Act was repealed in 1978.

**CHIPS.** The abbreviation for New York Clearing House Interbank Payments System.

**Chunnel.** See *Eurotunnel.*

**churning.** Excessive trading in securities for a single account. Brokers churn accounts to increase brokerage fees. The practice is illegal in the United States.

**CI.** The abbreviation for cost and insurance.

**CI, C/I.** The abbreviation for certificate of insurance and consular invoice. See *consular documents.*

**CIA.** The abbreviation for cash in advance.

**CIDA.** The abbreviation for Canadian International Development Agency. See *official development assistance.*

**Cie.** The abbreviation for *compagnie.*

**CIF.** The abbreviation for cost, insurance, and freight.

**CIF&C.** The abbreviation for cost, insurance, freight, and commission.

**CIF&E.** The abbreviation for cost, insurance, freight, and exchange.

**CIFCI.** The abbreviation for cost, insurance, freight, commission, and interest.

**CINS.** The abbreviation for Committee on Uniform Securities Identification Procedures International Numbering System. See *CUSIP number.*

**CIP.** The abbreviation for carriage and insurance paid and Commodity Import Program.

**circuity of action.** The process of returning a bill of exchange to the original signer before it matures. Although a returned bill of exchange remains negotiable, the original signer loses rights of action against subsequent endorsers.

**circular letter of credit (L/C).** A letter of credit addressed to a local bank's foreign correspondents, authorizing drafts drawn by a payee up to a specified credit limit. Also known as traveler's credits, circular credits are negotiable letters of credit used for multiple payments, often to a single business traveler. See also *letter of indication.*

**circulating medium.** A term usually used in reference to currency or gold. However, a circulating medium is any commodity with convertible value suitable to settling an account.

**CIS.** The abbreviation for Commonwealth of Independent States.

**CISG.** The abbreviation for United Nations Convention on Contracts for the International Sale of Goods.

**CITA.** The abbreviation for Committee for the Implementation of Textile Agreements.

**CITES.** The abbreviation for Convention on International Trade in Endangered Species.

**City.** The popular name for the City of London, or the merchant district of London. The premier financial center in the world, the City of London dates to medieval times when its merchant banks controlled international finance. The London Stock Exchange, major international banks, insurance companies, and commodity, foreign currency, and metal exchanges are located in the City of London.

**City Code on Takeovers and Mergers.** In the United Kingdom, a professional code of conduct for firms engaged in mergers and acquisitions (M&As), which has been adopted by major corporations and banks operating in London. Among other things, the code imposes a fiduciary duty on corporate directors to act in the interest of shareholders and requires full disclosure of terms and conditions proposed in the course of M&A negotiations.

**City/State Program.** In the United States, an export counseling program for state and municipal agencies sponsored by the Export-Import Bank of the United States (Eximbank). To enter the program, local agencies must dedicate funds to the project, prepare marketing plans, and sponsor agency employee participation in Eximbank export seminars. Participating agencies are authorized to prescreen local applicants for Eximbank loan and guarantee programs.

**civil and commercial codes.**   See *civil law.*

**civil embargo.**   See *embargo.*

**civil law.**   1. The principal body of law in most European and Latin American countries, as well as some African countries. Civil law looks to statutes, rather than judicial decisions, as the basis for determining legal rights. Among other things, the interpretation of commercial contracts and agency agreements is governed primarily by statute. Civil and commercial codes originated in the Roman statutes published during the reign of Justinian I in A.D. 529. Modern codes derive largely from the *Code Napoléon* promulgated in France in 1804. In contemporary French law, the principal codes are *Code de Commerce* (regulating commerce), *Code de Procédure Civile* (regulating civil procedure), *Code d'Instruction Criminelle* (regulating criminal procedure), and *Code Pénal* (the criminal code). 2. In common-law countries, statutes and judicial decisions governing noncriminal matters. Compare *code law.*

**ck.**   The abbreviations for cask and check.

**ckd.**   The abbreviation for completely knocked down.

**CL.**   The abbreviation for carload.

**cl.**   The abbreviation for clause.

**C/LAA.**   See *Caribbean/Latin American Action Committee.*

**class code.**   In the United States, an identification code used in the Automated Commercial System. The code identifies specific accounts for deposits of duties and customs fees. Multiple codes are used to allocate deposits to the proper accounts.

**classical economics.**   A school of economics originating principally with Adam Smith, the eighteenth-century Scottish philosopher. Smith advocated neutral markets and free trade, based on supply and demand, as the best devices for creating and spreading wealth. The concepts of comparative advantage, perfect competition, the invisible hand

of free markets, and the labor theory of value were pioneered by the classical school. The labor theory of value holds that the market value of an item derives from the quantity of labor required to produce it. See also *neoclassical economics.*

**classification.**   In international trade, the identification of an import for data-gathering or customs purposes. Classifications identify products under import bans or on quota lists and determine duty rates. Product classifications are normally entered by the shipper on customs documents, subject to a customs agency's approval. Most countries apply the Standard International Trade Classification developed by the United Nations. In the United States, however, the Standard Industrial Code is used. The U.S. Customs Service uses two methods to classify imports:

*eo nomine method.*   An import is classified by finding its name in the exporting country's tariff schedule. If the name is not found, the import is classified in terms of its presumed use *or* the classification normally applied to its component materials.

*general description method.*   An import is classified according to a class of like products *or* the class ascribed to its component materials. Alternatively, an import is classified according to the actual or probable use of similar products.

**classification society.**   In the shipping industry, a private association that defines classes of ocean liners and establishes seaworthiness guidelines for vessel construction. Classification societies issue safety certificates, which are required by banks, insurers, and regulatory agencies, attesting to the design and structural soundness of newly constructed or refurbished ships. Of the 50 existing classification societies, 11 are members of the London-based International Association of Classification Societies. In recent years, the marine insurance industry has shown relatively less confidence in the validity of inspection certifications issued by classification societies. Duplicate inspections undertaken by insurers, charterers, and port authorities have become the rule rather than the exception. The U.S. classification society, the American Bureau of Shipping (ABS), was founded in 1862. ABS is headquartered in New York. Other national classification societies are *Bureau Veritas* (Paris), *Det Norske Veritas* (Hovik, Norway), Germanischer Lloyd (Hamburg), Lloyd's Register of Shipping (London), *Nippon Kaiji Kyokai* (Tokyo), *Polski Registr* (Gdansk), and *Registro Italiano Navale* (Genoa).

**claused bill.**   See *clausing*.

**clause paramount.**   A uniform contract provision that automatically incorporates certain national laws and international agreements into ocean bills of lading. See also *Carriage of Goods by Sea Act of 1936*.

**clausing.**   The process of identifying the transaction underlying a bill of exchange or the rate of exchange for payment. For example, a claused bill would indicate "export of cotton to France per *SS. Rotterdam*." See also *bill of lading*.

**Clayton Act.**   See *antitrust laws*.

**CLC.**   The abbreviation for Convention on Civil Liability for Oil Pollution Damages. See *International Maritime Organization*.

**clean.**   1. In finance, the description of a draft or bill of exchange that is negotiable without additional documents, or a letter of credit payable without shipping documents. See also *clean remittance*. 2. A fixed-interest security, the price of which excludes accrued interest. 3. In international trade, a bill of lading without a cautionary qualification. 4. In commercial law, a contract without onerous provisions. 5. In accounting, an auditor's unqualified opinion that an audit revealed no financial irregularities. See also *clean float*.

**clean acceptance.**   An acceptance of a draft or bill of exchange by a bank without additional documentation, e.g., shipping documents.

**Clean Air Act of 1990.**   In the United States, a law that prohibits the import of products not conforming with Environmental Protection Agency (EPA) emission- and pollution-control standards. For example, the law covers imports of new and used vehicles and vehicle components. Conforming imports carry a Vehicle Emission Control Information label, which includes the manufacturer's name and trademark. Automobiles or motorcycles imported solely for racing or testing are exempt from the act, so long as they are not

sold in the United States and EPA approval is obtained before importation. See also *DOT-registered importer, EPA Form 3520-1*, and *independent commercial importer*.

**clean bill of exchange.**   A bill of exchange that does not require additional documentation, e.g., shipping documents, for acceptance or payment. Compare *documentary bill of exchange*.

**clean bill of lading.**   A bill of lading issued by a carrier when cargo is in apparent good order. Compare *foul bill of lading*.

**clean collection.**   See *clean remittance*.

**clean float.**   The process by which a national currency finds its market value without government intervention. In modern economies, clean float is a relative term, since all central banks regularly monitor the performance of their currencies in international financial markets and intervene to some degree to influence currency exchange values.

**clean product carrier.**   An ocean carrier used exclusively to transport refined, as opposed to crude, petroleum products.

**clean remittance.**   A term that replaced *clean collection* in the Uniform Rules for Collections issued by the International Chamber of Commerce. A clean remittance denotes an accepted or unaccepted bill of exchange, check, promissory note, receipt, or similar instrument used to obtain payment and not attached to a document of title, invoice, or shipping documents.

**clean report of findings (CRF).**   A certificate of inspection issued by an authorized agency, usually an independent inspection firm, before exports are shipped to a destination point. The report verifies the conformity of goods to conditions identified in a letter of credit. In some instances, importing countries require clean reports of findings for both procured and consumer imports. Conversely, an advice of nonconformity is issued for cargoes not meeting an importer's specifications. See also *declaration of importation* and *Société Générale de Surveillance, S.A.*

**clean ship.**   An ocean carrier transporting refined petroleum products. Compare *dirty ship*.

**clearance.**   1. In banking, the settlement procedures used when one bank offsets claims against another for drafts drawn against its accounts. 2. In commodities dealing, the process of settling accounts during a specific accounting period. 3. In international trade, the process of clearing customs.

**clearance papers.**    Documents issued by customs, health, and other regulatory authorities verifying that a ship has complied with port regulations and is free to depart the harbor.

**clearance permit.**    See *import permit.*

**clear day.**    A day when trading exchanges are open for business.

**clearing arrangement.**    A form of countertrade in which firms operating from different countries establish trading partnerships. A clearing arrangement involves an agreement to swap or counterpurchase goods or services over a predetermined period of time. See also *countertrade.*

**clearing customs.**    Meeting customs entry requirements to obtain the discharge of imports. Shipping documents and required certifications are submitted to customs officials at the port of entry. Once customs completes inspections and receives payment for duties, imports are cleared.

**clearinghouse.**    1. In banking, an office where banks clear checks, draw drafts, and settle interbank accounts. In most countries, clearinghouse functions are performed by electronic systems. See also *Clearing House Automatic Payments System* and *Clearing House Interbank Payments System.* 2. In commodity trading, an agency of the exchange that intermediates between sellers and buyers. The clearinghouse buys from the seller and sells to the buyer, thereby eliminating transaction risks. Settlements occur through the delivery of a commodity or through purchases of alternative futures or option contracts. See also *International Commodities Clearing House.*

**Clearing House Automated Payments System (CHAPS).**    In the United Kingdom, the interbank payment system for same-day clearing of payments denominated in pound sterling. CHAPS is an operating company of the Association for Payment Clearing Services and is located in London.

**Clearing House Interbank Payments System (CHIPS).**    In the United States, the interbank payment system for same-day clearing of payments denominated in U.S. dollars. Accounts are settled

through adjustments to special balances deposited with the Federal Reserve Bank of New York. Interbank transfers are made through the Federal Wire (Fed Wire), the electronic funds and securities network owned by the Federal Reserve System. CHIPS is located in New York and operated by the New York Clearing House Association.

**clear title.**    See *marketable title.*

**CLI.**    The abbreviation for cost-of-living index. See *price index.*

**client.**    A person who purchases professional services from an advertising firm, lawyer, investment adviser, and so on. Compare *customer.*

**close.**    1. The price paid for a security on a public exchange. 2. The exchange of money for securities when stock or bond issues have been placed. 3. In securities markets, the end of trading activity on a business day. In the United States, trades at the close occur within 30 minutes of the closing bell.

**closed conference.**    See *conference.*

**closed-end fund.**    See *mutual fund.*

**closed indent.**    A purchase order sent to a foreign indenting agent that does not name the manufacturer.

**Closer Economic Relationship (CER).**    An agreement between Australia and New Zealand that supersedes the New Zealand–Australia Free Trade Agreement of 1966. The CER establishes a schedule for phasing out duties on goods traded between the two countries. New Zealand has relatively small consumer markets and benefits most from the CER. See also *South Pacific Bureau for Economic Cooperation.*

**closing call.**    On a commodity exchange, the time allotted at the end of a trading day for traders to cover positions.

**closing date.**    1. In shipping, the deadline for a shipper to deliver cargo to a pickup site for shipment. 2. In finance, the date on which securities are delivered to a buyer and payments delivered to the seller.

**closing price.**    The purchase or selling price recorded on a commodity or stock exchange at the end of a trading day. Compare *after-hours deal.*

**cluster filing.**    To protect inventions, a technique used by companies awaiting approval of foreign patent applications. Cluster filers attempt to build a wall around a main invention by filing serial applications for related inventions. Multiple filings can be especially useful in countries where details of inventions are released before patents are approved. In Japan, for example, patent approval may take 6 to 7 years, although inventions are customarily disclosed within 18 months of filing.

**CME.** The acronym for Chicago Mercantile Exchange.

**CMEA.** The abbreviation for Council for Mutual Economic Assistance.

**CMR.** The abbreviation for *Convention relative au contrat de transport international de marchandises par route.*

**CNAR.** The abbreviation for compound net annual rate.

**Co.** The abbreviation for company.

**COAP.** The abbreviation for Cottonseed Oil Assistance Program.

**coaster.** In the United Kingdom, a short-run cargo ship that travels between local ports.

**COB.** The abbreviation for *Commission des Opérations de Bourse.* See *Bourse.*

**Cocoa Producers' Alliance (COPAL).** An international association of African and Latin American cocoa-producing nations. COPAL was established in 1962 to maintain global cocoa prices at acceptable levels and to facilitate the exchange of production and marketing information among its members. COPAL is headquartered in Lagos, Nigeria.

**COCOM.** The abbreviation for Coordinating Committee on Multilateral Export Controls.

**COCOM Lists.** The lists of products controlled under the International Import Certificate/Delivery Verification System. The lists are used to prevent diversions of armaments or similar products to unauthorized importers. The import verification system is supervised by the Coordinating Committee on Multilateral Export Controls (COCOM), which oversees international traffic in weapons, military equipment, and dual-use materials and technologies. The COCOM Lists include the International Atomic Energy List (regulating trade in nuclear weapons, components, and fuel), the International Munitions List, and the International Industrial List (covering dual-use components and materials). In 1991, COCOM reduced the number of controlled products noted on its core lists. In the United States, individual validated licenses and special import licenses are required to trade items covered by COCOM Lists. See also *Commerce Control List.*

**C.O.D.** The abbreviation for cash on delivery.

**code law.** A legal system based on a codex, or a revealed body of law. In code-law countries, legal decisions derive from scrutiny of a sacred text. A codex is ordinarily divided into civil, commercial, and criminal codes. See also *Shari'a* and *Talmud.* Compare *civil law* and *common law.*

**Code Napoléon.** See *civil law.*

**code of conduct.** A set of principles adopted by a professional association or self-regulating organization. Conduct codes incorporate minimum standards of behavior widely accepted in a profession or trade. These codes are not usually legally binding on the parties adopting them, but they establish an authoritative standard by which a member's conduct can be judged in administrative or legal proceedings. In most instances, conduct codes are adopted after an industry's reputation has been damaged by the misconduct of its members.

**Code of Conduct for Liner Conferences.** See *Convention on a Code of Conduct for Liner Conferences.*

**Code of Liberalization of Capital Movements.** See *Capital Movements Code.*

**codetermination.** In labor relations, the practice of requiring employee representation on corporate boards of directors. Also known as *Mitbestimmung,* the concept was pioneered in the former West Germany. The principle of codetermination was incorporated into the European Economic Community's labor and social policies and adopted in the Community Charter of the Fundamental Rights of Workers. In the European Community, company law provides for employee "participation in the supervision and strategic development" of a European company, though not in its "day-to-day" management. See also *Vredling Directive.*

**Codex Alimentarius.**   The formal name for *Codex Standards,* a list of minimum health standards for food products sold in international trade. The list is published by the Codex Alimentarius Commission, a United Nations-affiliated body organized in 1963 by the Food and Agriculture Organization and the World Health Organization. The commission is based in Rome. See also *certificate of health.*

**coemption.**   The process of cornering a market, or buying all or most of the available supply of a commodity. Speculators attempt to corner markets to create scarcity and position themselves to set prices.

**COFA.**   The abbreviation for contract of freight affreightment.

**COFACE.**   The acronym for *Compagnie Française d'Assurances pour le Commerce Extérieure.*

**COFC.**   The abbreviation for container-on-flatcar.

**cofinancing.**   A method of financing whereby commercial lenders participate jointly with official lenders in financing international trade and development projects. Cofinancing is preferred by development banks and export-import banks, primarily as means of imposing commercial lending standards on sovereign borrowers and spreading financial risk.

**COGSA.**   The abbreviation for Carriage of Goods by Sea Act.

**coinsurance.**   A form of risk sharing used by insurance underwriters. Coinsurance policies are issued by lead insurers, who collect premiums and distribute shares among several coinsurers. The policy schedule identifies coinsurers and their risk shares. A coinsurer's premium share depends on the degree of risk assumed. Compare *reinsurance.*

**collars.**   Interest rate options that protect investors when interest rates fluctuate. The cap (or top) limits the percentage by which interest payable can rise. The floor (or bottom) limits the percentage by which interest owed can fall.

**collateral.**   An asset pledged to secure payment of a debt or the performance of a contract obligation. When a debtor or contractor defaults on an obligation, collateral is seized and sold to satisfy the debt. In the United States, acceptable collateral is defined by the Uniform Commercial Code as cash, negotiable paper and documents of title, trade goods, and intangibles (i.e., accounts receivable, copyright and patents royalties, etc.).

**collections.**   Procedures for receiving payment on financial instruments and outstanding debts. See also *documentary collection.*

**collection letter of credit.**   A letter of credit against which a buyer's bank agrees to pay upon receipt and acceptance of shipping documents.

**collection papers.**   Documents forwarded by a seller or agent, usually the seller's bank, to a buyer in order to collect payment for a shipment. Collection papers include shipping documents and various certificates and declarations required by a contract of sale.

**collective bargaining.**   Negotiations between employers and an organized entity, i.e., labor union, over wages, benefits, working conditions, etc. In the United States, several federal statutes regulate collective bargaining, including the National Labor Relations Act of 1935.

**collective farm.**   The basic farming unit in a centrally planned economy. In a collective-farm system, the state owns the land and capital assets. Resources are allocated and managed by a government agency according to a fixed economic plan, and products are distributed within quota systems. In some collective-farm systems, farmers tilling communal land are given plots to cultivate for family use or private gain.

**collective reserve unit (CRU).**   A gold-based artificial currency unit proposed by Valéry Giscard d'Estaing of France in 1965. The Giscard plan, contemplating a gold-based reserve asset funded by the Group of Ten, was never implemented. The plan did, however, contribute to the consensus for creating an international settlement currency. The special drawing right, known popularly as paper gold, was created in 1969.

**colliery turn.**   A phrase found in charter parties when the chartered vessel is powered by coal. The contract specifies a particular mine as the source of coal used to fuel the ship.

**Colombo Plan for Cooperative Economic and Social Development in Asia and the Pacific.** Commonly known as the Colombo Plan, an economic development association created in 1950 by members of the British Commonwealth. The

Colombo Plan provides financing and technical assistance for development projects in 26 member countries. The organization is headquartered in Colombo, Sri Lanka.

**colón.**    The currency of Costa Rica and El Salvador.

**COLREGS.**    The acronym for Convention on the International Regulations for Preventing Collisions at Sea.

**column rate.**    In the United States, rates of duty in the Harmonized Tariff Schedules. Some column rates are based on negotiated agreements and are granted in exchange for reciprocal trade concessions. Other column rates prescribe the statutory rate of duty. A statutory rate is a unilateral rate determined by law and remains unaffected by rates negotiated under international agreements.

**com., comm.**    The abbreviations for commission, committee, and commonwealth.

**comandancia de marina.**    Spanish: port authority.

**combination export manager (CEM).**    A private firm that locates and manages foreign sales for a manufacturer.  Although combination export managers usually specialize in a given industry, their clients are not competitors. CEMs often sell for their own accounts, but are sometimes compensated on a commission basis.

**combination rate.**    The total freight charge, or through rate for a shipment. The charge combines intermediate rates for cargo transported over land.

**combined transport bill of lading.**    See *multimodal bill of lading.*

**combined transport operator (CTO).**    A common carrier offering multimodal carriage, i.e., it transports goods by different transportation modes. For example, the combined transport operator might contract to move goods by air, rail, road, or water. Some services may be provided under subcontracts. See also *multimodal bill of lading.*

**COMECON.**    An acronym for Council for Mutual Economic Assistance.

**COMEX.**    The acronym for the Commodity Exchange of New York.

**comfort letter.**    1. A letter from a parent financial or commercial institution guaranteeing a debt owed by a subsidiary. 2. An auditor's letter

explaining the methods used to prepare the prospectus and registration statement for a new securities offering.

**comisión...de aduanas.**    Spanish: customs authority.

**comisión consultiva de aranceles de aduanas.**    Spanish: consultative commission on customs classification, i.e., an agency that hears appeals from customs classification and valuation determinations.

**comissão de...aduaneira.**    Portuguese: customs authority.

**comité nacional de regalías.**    Spanish: national royalties committee, i.e., an agency that approves copyright, patent, and trademark applications and licensing agreements.

**command economy.**    See *centrally planned economy.*

**Commerce Business Daily.**    In the United States, a publication of the U.S. Department of Commerce. Notices of international tender offers and contract awards are published daily (except Sundays) in *Commerce Business Daily.*

**Commerce Control List (CCL).**    In the United States, a list issued by the U.S. Department of Commerce and also known as the Commodity Control List. The list identifies products and countries subject to export bans or controls by Schedule B number. A periodic requirements license, a form of individual validated (export) license, is required for CCL-controlled exports. CCL items include products regulated by the Coordinating Committee for Multilateral Export Controls (COCOM) or controlled under unilateral U.S. regulatory measures. On August 29, 1991, following the dissolution of the Warsaw Pact, a revised list was published in the *Federal Register*. A further revision in 1992 removed most high-technology products destined for other COCOM countries. Rules governing validated export licenses are published at 15 *Code of Federal Regulations*, Section 799.1 (Supplement No.1). See also *COCOM Lists, Coordinating Committee on Multilateral Export Controls, country groups, Export Administration Act of 1979,* and *Schedule B number.*

**commercial bank.**    A private financial institution chartered by a government to accept deposits from the general public and make personal and business loans. In the United States, commercial banks are called full-service banks when they provide trust and international banking services. See also *Glass-Steagall Act of 1933* and *McFadden Act of 1927*. Compare *nonbank bank*.

**commercial bill.**    See *bill of exchange*.

**commercial controls.**    Government-imposed restrictions on domestic or international commerce. Controls arise from government policies that may be expressed (official) or unexpressed (unofficial). Economic sanctions and trade quotas are forms of commercial controls.

**commercial documents.**    A term used by the International Chamber of Commerce to distinguish documents of title and shipping documents from financial instruments.

**commercial free zone.**    A free trade zone dedicated to mixing, repackaging, sampling, screening, and sorting products for export. Compare *industrial free zone*.

**Commercial Information Management System (CIMS).**    In the United States, an export service available to domestic exporters through the U.S. Department of Commerce (DOC). The service provides detailed analyses of foreign industrial and service sectors through DOC district offices located in major cities in the United States.

**commercial interest reference rates (CIRRs).**    Also known as OECD rates, the interest rate guidelines established for official lending by the Organisation for Economic Cooperation and Development (OECD). The CIRR is set at a fixed margin above a member country's base rate to keep government-to-government lending rates near the market interest rate in OECD countries. Base rates are determined by government bond yields with various maturities. Normally, the fixed margin is 100 basis points over the base rate. The CIRR is expressed as an OECD currency CIRR, as, for example, the yen CIRR or the ECU CIRR.

**commercial invoice.**    A business form containing pricing and other sales information. In international trade, the commercial invoice is one of the documents used to identify consignees and value imports for duties. In the United States, the information provided in a commercial invoice is prescribed by the Tariff Act of 1930 and by U.S. Customs Regulations Sections 141.86 and 141.89.

The invoice must specify (1) the buyer and seller of goods, (2) the nature and quantity of a shipment, (3) the purchase price of the shipment in the currency of sale, (4) rebates or drawbacks attributable to the import, (5) costs incurred in producing the import omitted from the invoice price, (6) the country of origin, and (7) the destination port. Compare *pro forma invoice*.

**Commercial News USA.**    In the United States, a newsletter published 10 times a year and distributed abroad by the U.S. Department of Commerce to promote exports of domestic goods and services. Information contained in *Commercial News USA* is compiled by the International Trade Administration.

**commercial paper.**    An instrument that requires a drawer's endorsement, specifies the amount to be paid, and is payable on demand. In international commerce, commercial paper is a draft or other instrument presented for payment.

**commercial risk.**    1. In finance, the circumstances that raise uncertainty about a seller's ability to collect the full value of a debt. Lenders use different measures to determine commercial risk. The quality of a debtor's creditworthiness, which can be based on past credit history, insolvency, unreliability, or other predisposition to default, is one factor in calculating commercial risk. 2. In international transactions, commercial risk factors are (1) creditworthiness; (2) market risk, i.e., potential losses from fluctuating exchange rates; and (3) interest rate risk, i.e., potential losses from mismatched interest rates or maturities on different instruments. See also *country risk* and *hedge*.

**commingled merchandise.**    Goods packaged so that particular items cannot be easily distinguished during a customs inspection. Unless the importer documents the quantity and value of individual parts of a shipment, the duty assessed on the total cargo is based on the discernible item having the greatest dutiable value. Methods of identifying commingled goods vary from country to country. In the United States, the Customs Service verifies the contents of commingled shipments by inspecting packing lists, samples, or other evidence.

**commission.**    A fee paid to an agent or broker, usually computed as a percentage of a transaction's value.

**commission agent.** A manufacturer's representative who specializes in arranging sales of certain types of products. Commission agents do not usually maintain inventories, but take orders for shipment. Depending on the jurisdiction, commission agents may be registered with a government authority or local trade association. Registered agents are known as indenting agents and may be required to meet minimum local paid-in capital requirements.

**commissionaire.** A local distributor who sells manufactures on a commission basis.

**commission house.** A firm that specializes in trading commodities or futures and options contracts on behalf of customers for a commission.

**commissioner of customs and excise.** The primary customs officer in some English-speaking countries. In the United States, the commissioner of customs implements customs directives issued by the secretary of the treasury. The commissioner also administers import regulations but is not authorized to change or modify import quotas. In the United Kingdom, commissioners of customs and excise are members of the Board of Customs and Excise. The board collects revenues, administers British international trade regulations, and compiles trade data from customs documents.

**Committee for Electrotechnical Standardization.** See *Communauté Européenne.*

**Committee for European Standardization.** See *Communauté Européenne.*

**Committee for the Implementation of Textile Agreements (CITA).** In the United States, the committee that administers the U.S. Textile and Apparel Import Program, known popularly as the Textile Program. The committee was created by executive order in 1970 to oversee the implementation of U.S. textile agreements. CITA is headed by the secretary of commerce and composed of representatives from the Department of Labor, Department of State, Department of Treasury, and Office of the U.S. Trade Representative. The committee issues import quota directives to the U.S. Customs Service and initiates requests for bilateral discussions, known as calls, with trading partners to review textile and apparel import levels. See also *fiber constraints* and *MultiFiber Arrangement Regarding International Trade in Textiles.*

**Committee of Marketing Organizations (COMO).** In the United Kingdom, an association of domestic marketing organizations formed to promote the expansion of marketing activities in the UK. COMO members include the Incorporated Society of British Advertisers, the Institute of Marketing, and the Market Research Society. The organization is based in London.

**Committee on Banking Regulations and Supervisory Practices.** See *Cooke Committee.*

**Committee on Uniform Securities Identification Procedures.** See *CUSIP Number.*

**Commodities Futures Trading Commission (CFTC).** In the United States, an independent federal agency established in 1974 to regulate the commodity futures market. The CFTC succeeded the Commodity Exchange Authority originally created in 1947. The commission sets margin requirements and regulates trade in commodity option contracts. Commodities traders, known as futures commission merchants, are registered with the CFTC.

**commodity.** A tradable item of commercial value. 1. Staples, or low-value products sold in natural form, including agricultural produce. 2. Simple manufactures, or wares standardized through basic technology and indistinguishable from like products. 3. A good with physical attributes as distinguished from a service.

**commodity agreement.** See *international commodity agreement.*

**commodity broker.** A broker who buys and sells commodities in a commodity market. Brokers trading commodities other than metals are sometimes called produce brokers. A broker who transacts business on behalf of a principal acts as an agent. When the rules of given exchange permit brokers to trade for their own accounts, they are known as dealers or market makers. When acting as agents, brokers often need not reveal the identities of their principals, although they usually must reveal that they are acting on behalf of another. See also *commodity exchange.*

**Commodity Control List.** See *Commerce Control List* and *COCOM Lists.*

**Commodity Credit Corporation (CCC).** In the United States, an agency of the U.S. Department of Agriculture created in 1933 to fund domestic farm price-support programs. CCC-financed programs are intended to stabilize farm income, maintain the orderly distribution of farm commodities, and promote foreign sales of U.S. agricultural products. CCC pays cash bonuses to farmers and food processors and guarantees commercial bank loans to farmers. Funding for current CCC programs is authorized by the Food, Agriculture, Conservation, and Trade Act of 1990. See also *Dairy Export Incentive Program, Export Enhancement Program, and Market Promotion Program.*

**Commodity Credit Corporation Credit Guarantee Programs.** See *GSM-102* and *GSM-103.*

**commodity exchange.** A site where bulk commodities are sold. Commodities underlying contracts traded on major exchanges must meet industry certification or international quality standards. In addition to trading, established exchanges also offer clearinghouse facilities for traders and hedge options for commodities speculators. The Chicago Board of Trade, the Chicago Mercantile Exchange, the Commodity Exchange of New York, and the London Futures and Options Exchange are major international commodities exchanges.

**Commodity Exchange of New York (COMEX).** A commodity exchange and futures market established in 1933 for trading in metals, including gold, silver, copper, etc. COMEX has the largest volume of trading in gold and gold futures in the United States. COMEX also trades palladium and platinum futures, as well as gold futures options.

**commodity paper.** A bill of exchange or draft representing the sale of commodities. When commodity paper is negotiable or accompanied by a document of title, a holder may sell the underlying goods to collect an unpaid debt. See also *agricultural paper.*

**commodity price index (CPI).** A weighted reference for commodity spot prices or futures prices. Commodity price indexes are compiled by government agencies and private exchanges to monitor changes in market prices. A price index uses a base year to measure price fluctuations over a fixed time period, often daily, monthly, and annually. In the United States, the wholesale price index, the official index of agricultural and industrial prices, is published by the U.S. Department of Commerce. The CRB Futures Index, a weighted price index of 21 agriculturals, industrials, and precious metals, is published by the Commodity Research Bureau, a subsidiary of Knight-Ridder, Inc. See also *Journal of Commerce Industrial Price Index.*

**commodity terms of trade.** See *terms of trade.*

**Common Agricultural Policy (CAP).** In the European Community (EC), the agricultural price-support system implemented in 1961. The CAP originally covered only raw commodities, known as Annex II products, enumerated in the Treaty of Rome. In 1969, non-Annex II products (processed foods) were also brought under the CAP. The elements of the CAP are common pricing, common financing, and community preference. Sometimes referred to as the single-market concept, common pricing removes barriers to internal EC commodity trade. A threshold price determines the floor price, or minimum price, for a commodity. Declines below the threshold price trigger the intervention price, or the price at which EC governments buy commodities to increase prices. The intervention achieves a target price, or the optimum local wholesale price for a given commodity. When a commodity shortage occurs in one EC country, its target price is reduced to account for the cost of transporting replenishments from other EC countries. The community preference is implemented through the sluice-gate price, or internal guide price, for CAP commodities. An ad valorem duty is levied on all foreign imports. A variable levy is imposed on some imports to achieve a maximum tariff, which raises the import price to the sluice-gate price; it is recomputed each quarter. Common financing is the cost-sharing aspect of CAP. EC member states share CAP costs through the European Agricultural Guidance and Guarantee Fund. Revenues generated by a common external tariff are paid into a common budget. Currency values used to determine contributions to the common budget and import prices are based on a green rate, which fixes the rate of exchange between the European currency unit (ECU) and EC national currencies; monetary compensation amounts (MCAs) make up for exchange rate differences. The MCA is variable and adjustable over a specified period of time. MCA adjustments are known as franchises, or neutral margins. See also *common external tariff.*

**Common Budget.** See *Common Agricultural Policy.*

**common currency area.**  See *monetary union.*

**Common Customs Tariff (CCT).**  1. The customs tariff schedule of the European Economic Community, which has been supplanted by the Harmonized Commodity Description and Coding System. The CCT was based on the Brussels Tariff Nomenclature. See also *NIMEXE.* 2. A common external tariff.

**common external tariff (CET, CXT).**  Also known as a common customs tariff, a duty imposed on imports from nonmember countries by a customs union, free trade area, or common market. A CET reflects a trading association's priorities in allocating internal economic resources. High duties are usually placed on imports that compete with protected domestic industries or primary local products of significant foreign exchange value. Lower CETs are imposed on imports of components or ingredients used in priority domestic industries.

**Common Fisheries Policy.**  In the European Community (EC), an agreement between member states imposing catch limits for certain fish species. The policy was instituted in 1983 for a 20-year period and establishes both exclusive economic zones and equal-access fishing zones for EC countries. See also *territorial waters.*

**Common Fund for Commodities (CFC).**  A multilateral financing facility established by the United Nations Negotiating Conference on a Common Fund in 1980. The CFC was created by the Agreement Establishing the Common Fund for Commodities. A common facility for financing commodity buffer stocks maintained by international commodity organizations was first proposed by the United Nations Conference on Trade and Development (UNCTAD) at Nairobi in 1976. The CFC came into being in 1989 at Geneva as a component of UNCTAD's Integrated Programme for Commodities. CFC buffer stock financing is currently available to members of the International Cocoa Agreement and the International Rubber Agreement. Stocking loans are guaranteed by warrants against existing commodities stocks. CFC also finances commodity organization research, quality control, and marketing activities in countries belonging to international commodity agreements.

**common law.**  1. The case law containing judicial precedents on which the legal systems of English-speaking countries are based. As a rule, in common-law jurisdictions, matters of law are decided by judges and issues of fact by juries. In Australia, Canada, the United Kingdom, and the United States (except Louisiana), interpretations of contract and agency are determined by common law as opposed to legislation. See also *equity.* 2. In the United Kingdom, the law of a nation, as opposed to local or foreign law. Compare *civil law* and *code law.*

**common margins arrangement.**  See *European currency snake.*

**common market.**  1. An agreement among nations to cooperate on economic matters. Members of common markets typically eliminate duties on internal trade, impose a common external tariff, adopt uniform fiscal and monetary policies, harmonize health and product standards, and limit restrictions on the internal movements of capital and labor. 2. The European Common Market.

**common pricing.**  See *Common Agricultural Policy.*

**common stock.**  Equity in a corporation. Owners of common stock are entitled to collect dividends, elect directors, and vote on company policy. In corporate bankruptcies, the rights of common-stock holders are subordinate to those of bondholders, preferred shareholders, and general creditors. Outside the United States, common stocks are known as ordinary shares.

**Commonwealth Development Corporation.**  In the United Kingdom, a public corporation created in 1948 to provide official development assistance (ODA) to members of the British Commonwealth. The Commonwealth Development Corporation provides equity and debt financing, loan guarantees, and funding for feasibility studies in Commonwealth countries. The most common form of ODA is offered through long-term, low-interest loans.

**Commonwealth of Independent States (CIS).**  In the former Union of Soviet Socialist Republics (U.S.S.R.), a federation of nations created by the Accord of the Commonwealth of Independent States in December, 1991. As of 1993, CIS members are Armenia, Belarus, Kazakhstan, Russia, Tajikistan, Turkmenistan, Uzbekistan, and Ukraine. Azerbaijan, Georgia, Moldova, and the former Baltic Republics of Estonia, Latvia, and Lithuania are not CIS members.

**commonwealth preference.** In the United Kingdom, nonreciprocal tariff concessions extended by Britain to other members of the British Commonwealth. The preference was formalized during the Ottawa Imperial Conference of 1932. Following Britain's entry into the European Common Market in 1973, the commonwealth preference was largely supplanted by the Generalized System of Preferences (GSP) authorized by the General Agreement on Tariffs and Trade and the Lomé Conventions adopted by the European Community.

**Communauté Économique de l'Afrique de l'Ouest (CEAO).** Also known as the West African Economic Community, a regional trading association formed at Abidjan, Côte d'Ivoire, in 1973 and composed of the Francophone West African countries of Benin, Burkina Faso Côte d'Ivoire, Mali, Mauritania, Niger, and Senegal. CEAO established a common external tariff, harmonized import regulations and tax laws, and removed barriers to border traffic. Member countries also created a regional economic development fund, known as *Fonds de Solidarité et D'Intervention Pour le Développement de la CEAO.* According to a 1989 agreement, CEAO plans a future merger with the Economic Community of West African States (ECOWAS). CEAO is based in Ouagadougou, Burkina Faso. Compare *Conseil de l'Entente.*

**Communauté Économique des États de l'Afrique Centrale (CEEAC).** Also known as the Economic Community of the States of Central Africa and the Central African Economic Community, a regional association composed of Burundi, Cameroon, Central African Republic, Chad, Congo, Equatorial Guinea, Gabon, Rwanda, São Tomé and Principe, and Zaire. Formed at Yaounde, Cameroon, in 1983, CEEAC has a common central bank, the *Banque des États de l'Afrique Centrale (BEAC),* also known as the Bank of Central African States. Established in 1955, BEAC is headquartered in Yaounde A soft-loan window is available through the *Banque de Développement des États de l'Afrique Centrale,* located at Brazzaville, Congo. The CFA franc is CEEAC's official currency. CEEAC has headquarters in Libreville, Gabon. See also *Union Douanière des États de l'Afrique Centrale.*

**Communauté Économique des Pays des Grands Lacs (CEPGL).** Known unofficially as the Economic Community of the Great Lakes Countries (ECGC), a regional economic association of three central African states. Created at Gisenyi in 1976, CEPGL's members are Burundi, Rwanda, and Zaire. CEPGL is headquartered in Gisenyi, Rwanda.

**Communauté Européenne (CE).** 1. French: the European Community (EC). 2. CE is the product quality marking for goods distributed in the EC and European Free Trade Association. European standards are written by private testing organizations and overseen by the European Organization for Testing and Certification. The testing bodies are (1) the European Committee for Standardization, (2) the European Committee for Electrotechnical Standardization, (3) the European Quality System, and (4) the European Telecommunication Standards Institute. European standards typically mirror those approved by the International Standards Organization (ISO) and the International Electrotechnical Commission. The EC adopted ISO 9000, known in Europe as EN 29000, which consists of quality-assurance guidelines issued by the ISO. Testing and certification procedures depend on the nature of the product. For some products, plant facilities are inspected; for others, documented design and manufacturing information or testing by EC-approved laboratories is required. Special requirements apply to, among others, gas appliances, industrial safety equipment, medical devices, and some telecommunications equipment. Manufacturers of these products are required to operate in-house quality assurance systems that meet ISO 9000 standards. Declarations of product conformity are available through local EC distributors. The European Committee for Standardization is based in Brussels. See also *consumer protection.*

**Communauté financière africaine.** See *Franc Zone.*

**Community Charter of the Fundamental Rights of Workers.** In the European Community, a document proposed by Jacques Delors of France and adopted by the European Council in 1989. The charter derives from the earlier worker protection arrangements accepted by the Council of Europe and various international labor conventions. It guarantees to European workers freedom of movement between countries and occupations, freedom of association and collective bargaining, fair remuneration, safe living and working conditions, annual paid leave and weekly rest periods, codetermination, nondiscrimination based on gender, and social security protection for workers, children, the aged, and the disabled. The charter was substantially adopted by the Treaty of Maastricht creating a single European market in 1992. The United Kingdom derogated from the labor provisions of the Maastricht Treaty.

**Community Patent Convention.**    See *European Patent System.*

**community preference.**    See *Common Agricultural Policy.*

**compact disk–read-only memory (CD-ROM).**    A computer-based technology for storing large quantities of data. CD-ROM reproduces animated images, sound, and texts. Future applications of CD-ROM technology to ground and other transport modes are promising, primarily because of its capacity to combine road maps, routing, billing, and tariff data in a single system. In the United States, CD-ROM systems are developed by firms known as service bureaus.

**Compact of Freely Associated States (FAS).**    In the United States, an agreement between the Trust Territories of the Pacific Islands and the United States. Since 1947, the territories have been administered by the United States under the supervision of the United Nations Trusteeship Council. The beneficiaries of the accord are the Federated States of Micronesia, including the Caroline, Marshall, and Mariana Islands (except Guam). Duty-free rates are extended to most FAS exports identified by the special programs indicator in the U.S. Automated Commercial System, including some products not protected under the U.S. Generalized System of Preferences or bilateral agreements. U.S. rules of origin apply to all FAS exports. The current trade and aid program became effective October 18, 1989, and is perpetual unless specifically terminated by the United States or beneficiary territories.

**compagnie (Cie.).**    French: company.

**Compagnie Française d'Assurances pour le Commerce Extérieure (COFACE).**    In France, an export credit insurance agency founded in 1946. COFACE insures some country risks and commercial risks that preclude commercial bank financing. The agency is financed by, among others, Banque Française du Commerce Extérieure.

**Companies Act of 1985.**    In the United Kingdom, an act of parliament that governs the conduct of companies organized under UK laws. The act is administered by the Registrar of Companies, an agency that maintains records of registered companies. Registered names and offices, registries of company members, charges against company assets, etc., are listed with the Registrar of Companies. The Companies Act also mandates annual general meetings of shareholders, known as statutory meetings. The law further requires that the annual report and company accounts be compiled in a statutory report and reported to members of a company. See also *Companies House.*

**Companies House.**    In the United Kingdom, the Registrar of Companies, also known as the Companies Registration Office. Private and public companies operating in the UK are registered with Companies House. A business provides the following information for registration: the company name, the business address, and the names of the corporate directors and shareholders. Company balance sheets must also be filed and maintained for inspection. Companies House is located in Cardiff. See also *Companies Act of 1985* and *European company.*

**company (Co.).**    An incorporated or unincorporated business firm. 1. A chartered company is authorized by royal charter or government decree. Early for-profit companies were formed under monarchs, but modern chartered companies are usually nonprofit organizations. 2. An incorporated company, also known as a corporation, is organized under the laws of the jurisdiction in which it was established and is subject to local regulation. 3. A joint-stock company is an enterprise in which capital and equity are jointly held by its owners. 4. A limited company is known as a corporation in the United States. Elsewhere, it is a company in which the liability of the owners is limited to the extent of their share in the firm's assets and equity. A limited company is indicated by "Ltd" after its name. 5. A listed company, also known as a quoted company, is one whose share prices are quoted on an organized stock exchange. To qualify for listing, a company enters into a listing agreement with an exchange and meets its listing requirements, including minimum earnings and assets, a minimum number of shareholders, and regular financial disclosures. Listed companies that fail to meet listing requirements over a predetermined period of time are delisted. See also *listed security*. 6. Also called a proprietary company, a private limited company is a limited liability company that does not offer its equity to the general public. Private limited companies may be required to register with a government agency, but are usually exempt from paid-in capital and public disclosure requirements. They are identified by "Ltd" or "Pty" after the company's name. 7. A proprietary company is a private limited company. 8. A public limited company (plc) sells shares of its securities to the general public and is required to have a minimum amount of paid-in capital, which can be less than the minimum number of authorized shares. Public limited companies must meet accounting and reporting requirements mandated by law. In most instances, public limited companies are said to "go private" when they repurchase shares from outside investors and re-register as private companies. A public limited company is identified by "plc" after its name. In the United States, public limited companies are known as publicly held corporations. 9. A registered company is an enterprise that has filed the necessary registration documents in countries requiring official registration of privately owned and publicly held companies. 10. A statutory company is a firm authorized by legislation. Statutory companies are formed to carry out public purposes and may, but need not, be financed wholly or partly with public funds. In the United Kingdom, statutory companies are privately owned public utilities governed by special acts of Parliament. 11. An unincorporated company, also known as an unlimited company, is a firm whose owners face unlimited liability for the debts of the business. In the United States, an unincorporated company can operate without registration or incorporation, but its owners are personally liable for the firm's debts. 12. In the European Community (EC), a European company is defined by EC statute.

**company law.**    1. In the United States, corporate law, which includes the local law of the state where a company is incorporated (or operates) *and* federal laws governing publicly held corporations administered by the Securities and Exchange Commission. 2. In most countries, national laws and procedures regulating the formation and operation of companies. In the United Kingdom, company law is composed of the Companies Act of 1985, the Company Directors' Disqualification Act of 1986, the Financial Services Act of 1986, and the Insolvency Act of 1986. In the European Community, company law is contained in the European Company statute.

**company seal.**    In the United Kingdom, a seal on which a company's name is engraved. A company's articles of association indicate how and when the seal will be used. British law requires that the seal be affixed to certain contracts. Where laws stipulate, a contract without a seal is not enforceable.

**comparable uncontrolled price.**    A synonym for arm's-length price.

**comparative advantage.**    Superiority of one country over another in a facet of economic competition. Comparative advantage results from abundant or accessible natural resources, the skill of a work force, or planned specialization. In free trade theory, advanced in Britain by David Ricardo (1772–1823), a country specializes in economic activities where it has a price, resource, or other advantage. Artificial barriers to trade distort natural affinities and rob the global economy of the benefits of specialized production. See also *classical economics* and *law of one price*. Compare *competitive advantage*.

**compensating product.**    A locally manufactured product used by a manufacturer to replace an imported component.

**compensation.**    1. In international commerce, countertrade. 2. In multilateral trade, a concession made when a treaty obligation has been breached. Compensation usually takes the form of reduced duties. Compare *reciprocity*.

**compensation fund.**    A fund created by a trading exchange to compensate investors when a member firm fails to meet its obligations. A compensation fund was established by the London Stock

Exchange (LSE) following the Big Bang in 1986, which initiated reforms in many of the LSE's operations. Compensation funds are usually financed by members of a trading exchange.

**compensation trade.**    A form of countertrade whereby the parties agree to reciprocal purchases of equivalent value. When one party purchases and sells less (or more) than another, the transaction is called a counterpurchase. Compare *barter, buyback,* and *countertrade.*

**Compensatory and Contingency Financing Facility (CCFF).**    An International Monetary Fund (IMF) lending facility created in 1963. CCFF provides short-term lending to developing countries, which depend on income from sales of primary commodities. When commodity prices decline, the CCFF extends temporary financing to compensate for the impact on payments imbalances. Like other IMF programs, CCFF financing is contingent on the implementation of structural adjustment programs (SAPs) to reduce inefficiencies and improve economic growth. See also *balance of payments* and *conditionality.*

**compensatory duty.**    See *duty.*

**compensatory suspension.**    See *suspension.*

**competition.**    A contest to supply goods and services to consumers. In market economies, governments attempt to increase economic competition through antitrust laws or deregulation. Imperfect competition is sometimes accepted when pure competition would damage the public interest, as in the case of public utilities. See also *competition policy.*

**competition and credit control.**    In the United Kingdom, reforms adopted by the government in 1971 to increase commercial bank competition and regulate credit through interest rate policy. The reforms changed the role of the Bank of England in the gilt-edged securities market. Among others, a major reform in 1981 eliminated the minimum lending rate (MLR), or the minimum rate at which the Bank of England lends to discount houses. The MLR is subject to revival by the British government. See also *interest rate policy.*

**competition policy.**    In Europe, the synonym for antitrust regulation. Cartels, price fixing, certain exclusive market-sharing agreements,etc., are pro-

hibited in the European Community, except where consumers benefit or predominant market power does not develop. Competition rules are enforced by the European Commission, which, in 1990, also acquired regulatory power over mergers and acquisitions involving more than 5 billion European currency units and monopoly market power. In the United Kingdom, the Department of Trade and Industry and the Monopolies and Mergers Commission share jurisdiction on competition matters.

**competitive advantage.**    A firm's superiority in some facet of selling in the marketplace. A company achieves a competitive advantage by virtue of offering better products, lower prices, creative advertising, employee talent, or other attributes that make its products or services more attractive to purchasers than those provided by its competitors. Compare *comparative advantage.*

**competitive bid.**    An offer to make a purchase or supply a good at a stated price. The highest price is usually accepted by a seller and the lowest price by a purchaser. But other factors, such as quality, may be as important as price in determining winners and losers in competitive bidding. Compare *noncompetitive bid.*

**complementary export agreement.**    See *allied companies.*

**composite.**    In the United Kingdom, an insurance company that provides various types of insurance, e.g., fire insurance and life assurance.

**composite rate tax.**    In the United Kingdom, a tax deducted by banks and building societies from interest paid to resident depositors. The composite rate tax was abolished in 1991.

**compound annual return (CAR).**    Invested principal increased by interest earned. Interest payments raise the value of the annual return on an investment. When taxes are deducted, the balance remaining on earnings is called the compound net annual return.

**compound duty.**    See *duty.*

**Comprehensive Anti-Apartheid Act of 1986 (CAAA).**    In the United States, the law that authorized federal economic sanctions against the Republic of South Africa. In 1977, the United Nations Security Council imposed a mandatory arms embargo against South Africa. Selective economic sanctions were adopted by most governments during the mid-1980s. In the United States, federal sanctions imposed under the CAAA were lifted by executive order in 1991. As of 1993, economic sanctions against South Africa remained in some U.S. states and municipalities, which are unaffected by the federal executive order.

**Comprehensive Export Schedules.**    See *general license.*

**Comptroller of Customs.**    In the United States, an agency of the U.S. Customs Service. The Comptroller's office manages funds and allocates resources dedicated to the Customs Service. The Comptroller also supervises customs administrative support services, including data processing facilities.

**comptroller of the currency.**    In the United States, the head of the national bank regulatory system. A U.S. national bank files periodic condition reports with the Office of the Comptroller of the Currency. Compliance with federal regulations is monitored through an electronic system, called the National Bank Surveillance System. Banks are also examined by national bank examiners, who are agents of the Comptroller's Office. The comptroller, appointed by the President and confirmed by the Senate for a 5-year term, is also a director of the Federal Insurance Deposit Corporation.

**compulsory licensing.**    A grant by a government to a third party of the right to exploit copyrighted or patented property without seeking permission from the copyright or patent holder. Normally, conditions under which licensing is compelled are specified by statutes, which also mandate the payment of royalties and an accounting of profits to the property owner. For example, in the United States, the Copyright Revision Act of 1976 permits cable television systems and noncommercial broadcasters of musical works, among others, to use protected works under compulsory licensing.

**computed value.**    In customs valuation, the total cost of materials, undeclared assists, fabrications, and processing used to produce imported merchandise. Packing costs, ordinary profit, and general expenses are also included in computed value. See also *merchandise of the same class or kind.* Compare *deductive value.*

**computer-aided design (CAD).**    Designs created with the aid of computers. Drawing devices enable designers to sketch pictures and images on computer screens. Designs can also be analyzed and altered by computer. CAD helps manufacturers adjust to changing market demands by substantially reducing the time lag between product design and production.

**computer-aided manufacturing (CAM).**    The use of computers to carry out manufacturing processes, often from computer-aided designs. Computer-operated machines can be programmed to perform tasks in automobile manufacturing, chemical processing, and so on.

**computer-assisted trading (CAT).**    The use of computers to display prices, record transactions, and settle trades on a stock or currency exchange. Computerized trading has not replaced face-to-face dealing in most commodity exchanges.

**con.**    The abbreviation for consul and consolidated annuity.

**concealed damage protection clause.**    Insurance covering latent cargo damage. The clause indemnifies an owner against losses not detectable until cargo has been unpacked and inspected. When cargo damage is intentionally concealed at the manufacturing or packing site, the losses are not covered by the clause.

**consensus rate.**    See *OECD Consensus rates.*

**concession.**    A description of terms of sale, lending conditions, and import regulations negotiated by agreement or granted by unilateral action. In international trade, concessions reduce or eliminate tariffs or extend low rates of interest and longer-than-average repayment terms on loans to another country. In concessional sales, the seller grants preferential terms, often in relation to tied aid. To encourage purchases, a government offering concessional sales may agree to accept payment in the buyer's soft currency, reduce interest rates, or provide similar inducements. See also *Generalized System of Preferences, most favored nation,* and *reciprocity.* Compare *compensation.*

**concessional duty.**    See *duty.*

**concessional sale.**    See *concession.*

**conditional exemption.**    The contingent elimination of duties on certain imports. In the United

States, conditional exemptions cover American goods returned, some personal items, and materials imported by schools, government agencies, and research institutes. Conditionally exempted imports become dutiable when used for nonexempt purposes. See also *conditionally free goods.*

**conditionality.** The general approach to lending adopted by the International Monetary Fund (IMF). Countries receiving IMF balance-of-payment financing are required to adopt specific measures to improve efficiency and economic performance, usually as components of a structural adjustment program. IMF conditions typically require price-policy reform, exchange rate realignment, deficit reduction, less regulation, and so on. Paris Club debt restructurings and commercial bank loan renegotiations are often tied to IMF conditionality.

**conditionally free goods.** Goods allowed to enter a customs territory free of duties for specific purposes. A duty is imposed on conditionally free goods in the absence of proof that the import meets a required condition. See also *conditional exemption.*

**conduit.** An organization that assembles several loans into a package and sells the packaged securities in the secondary market. The securities are issued in the name of the conduit.

**conex containers.** In the United States, ocean containers used to transport official cargoes, which consist of government supplies or goods purchased under U.S. trade preference programs.

**Confederation of British Industry (CBI).** In the United Kingdom, a voluntary trade association representing the interests of British industry. CBI was created in 1965 by a merger between the National Association of British Manufacturers and other British trade associations. The organization is governed by a council of member associations.

**conference.** Also known as a rate agreement, a shipping association composed of several ocean carriers plying the same trade routes. Ocean carriers that belong to conferences are called conference carriers or conference line ships. Nonmember lines are called independent carriers or nonconference line ships. Conferences are loosely regulated cartels, which set uniform freight and service standards for their members. To obtain beneficial shipping rates from conferences, shippers agree to ship all or a specific portion of their cargoes on ships controlled by the cartel. In the United States, conferences are required to file tariffs with the Federal Maritime Commission (FMC). The Shipping Act of 1984 also requires conferences to give notice of independent actions. 1. A closed conference sets collective rates and service standards. Carriers that do not agree to collective rate making are barred from membership. Closed conferences are illegal in the United States but are legal in Europe. However, European Community competition rules may eventually reduce the number of closed conferences traveling European trade routes. 2. An open conference can be joined by any carrier applying for membership and does not preclude independent pricing. 3. A dual-rate conference offers two-tier tariffs, depending on the nature of the agreement with a given shipper. Normally, a shipper who executes a loyalty agreement pays a higher rate than a shipper who signs an exclusive patronage contract. However, the Shipping Act of 1916 that authorized conferences in the United States does not distinguish between exclusive patronage contracts and loyal agreements. Dual-rate conferences are required by the FMC to notify shippers before freight rates are increased. 4. A single-rate conference applies a uniform tariff to all shippers. In the United States, single-rate conferences are permitted to modify rates by giving notice as prescribed by the FMC. See also *Convention on a Code for Liner Conferences.*

**Conference on Security and Cooperation in Europe (CSCE).** A multilateral organization that originated with the Helsinki Final Act of 1975. The CSCE began with discussions between members of the North Atlantic Treaty Organization and the Warsaw Pact. CSCE provides a framework for a global security alliance, possibly to be created before the year 2000. The organization's secretariate is located in Prague. See also *Paris Charter.*

**conference signatory.** See *loyalty agreement.*

**confirmation note.** A broker's summary of terms proposed for a charter party. When principals approve the terms, the confirmation note becomes the basis for a charter contract.

**confirmation patent.** In some countries, a form of patent protection extended where national patent systems have not been developed. Used primarily in former European colonies, confirmation protection is based on patents awarded in another country. The duration of a confirmation patent is coterminous with the underlying patent. Regarding former colonies of the United Kingdom, a confirmation patent must usually be registered within 3 years of the original patent grant in the United Kingdom.

**confirmed letter of credit (L/C).** A letter of credit that guarantees payment to the beneficiary, even if the buyer defaults or the buyer's bank fails to pay. To ensure payment, a confirmation by the issuing bank must be backed by funds on deposit with a correspondent in the exporter's country. When a letter of credit is unconfirmed, the foreign bank remits funds after goods are shipped. See also *irrevocable letter of credit.*

**confirming bank.** See *confirmed letter of credit.*

**confirming house.** A business organization that specializes in without-recourse financing. When a confirming house remits purchase orders for a principal, it becomes the guarantor of the transaction. A confirming house may also be the consignee authorized to transfer goods on behalf of a principal.

**confiscation.** The seizure of private property by a government. Typically, confiscated property is taken without adequate or reasonable compensation, often on the theory that the owner has forfeited it by virtue of some deed or circumstance. See also *country risk.* Compare *expropriation.*

**Conformity Assessment Systems Evaluation Program.** See *National Institute of Standards and Technology.*

**congestion surcharge.** See *port congestion surcharge.*

**conglomerate.** A business entity composed of several companies, which may specialize in different products or services. Typically, conglomerates are highly diversified, e.g, an oil company that also owns a film company and an automobile-rental company. Companies often conglomerate when the long-term prospects of a principal industry, such as oil or tobacco, begin to fade.

**coning.** A means of securing containers on an ocean vessel. Cones are devices used to lock containers in stacks. The containers are lashed to the deck of a ship.

**connecting conveyance.** An intermediate mode of carriage by which goods are transported from an origin point to a departure point for shipment to a final destination.

**conocimiento de embarque.** Spanish: bill of lading.

**cons.** The abbreviation for consolidated and consul.

**Conseil de l'Entente.** Also known as the Entente Council, a regional economic cooperation group composed of Benin, Burkina Faso, Côte d'Ivoire, Niger, and Togo. Members of the Entente Council contribute to common financial aid funds used to finance regional development projects. The *Conseil de l'Entente* was founded at Abidjan, Côte d'Ivoire, in 1959.

**Conseil Intergouvernemental des Pays Exportateurs de Cuivre (CIPEC).** Also known as the Inter-Governmental Council of Copper Exporting Countries, an international commodity group established in 1967 to improve marketing and increase world prices for copper products. CIPEC members are Australia, Chile, Indonesia, Mauritania, Papua New Guinea, Peru, Zaire, and Zambia. The former country of Yugoslavia was an associate member. CIPEC is based in Neuilly-sur-Seine, France.

**consensus rate.** See *OECD consensus rates.*

**consent decree.** A contract between parties to a legal dispute setting forth terms for settlement. The terms are adopted as an order of the court. In the United States, a party signing a consent decree need not admit prior fault.

**consignee.** See *consignment.*

**consignee mark.** A symbol affixed to cargo indicating the port of entry and other identifying information.

**consignment.** The assignment of goods to an agent. Goods on consignment are sold by the agent (consignee) for the benefit of the owner (consignor). The owner, usually the shipper named in a bill of lading, retains title to the goods. The consignee receives a consignment note, or a detailed receipt, on delivery of the shipment. Consignment notes, which are not negotiable documents, are sometimes called waybills. When the goods are sold, the consignee is compensated on a commission basis. The details of the transaction are settled through a consignment account in which expenses associated with the sale, the consignee's commission, and proceeds owed to the owner are recorded.

**consignor.**   See *consignment.*

**consol.**   An abbreviation for consolidated annuity.

**consolidated annuity (con.).**   In the United Kingdom, bonds issued by the British government. Also known as consols or consolidated stocks, consolidated annuities do not have a redemption date but do pay interest. The return on a consol is equal to the annual yield on long-term gilt-edged securities in Britain.

**consolidator.**   See *non-vessel-operating common carrier.*

**consolidation.**   The process of grouping smaller shipments into a larger shipment. Consolidations are provided by carriers and freight forwarders. Consolidated shipments qualify for volume-discounted freight rates, which are lower than average tariff rates. See also *assembled shipment.*

**consolidation and deconsolidation coverage.**   In insurance, protection for a policyholder whose cargo is handled at an intermediate terminal. The coverage extends to packing and unpacking cargo at a temporary facility other than the policyholder's place of business.

**consortium.**   See *syndicate.*

**constructed price.**   See *constructed value.*

**constructed value.**   A method used by customs officials to value an import in nominal terms. Constructed price is the sum of the cost of materials, manufacturing and packaging expenses, and profit margins associated with the production of like goods in the country of origin. Customs officials use constructed value when the invoice price is inconsistent with the value evidenced in shipping documents or elsewhere. Appraising imports in terms of transaction value is the preferred method of valuation.

**construction differential subsidy (CDS).**   In the United States, a government subsidy authorized by Title V of the Merchant Marine Act of 1936 to finance the purchase of ships from domestic shipbuilders. The subsidy enables a carrier to recapture

up to 50 percent of the cost of labor and materials. Its purpose is to equalize the costs of U.S.-built ships with those made in foreign shipbuilding yards where labor and materials may be more expensive. As a matter of policy, no CDS projects were financed between 1982 and 1992. The CDS is administered by the Maritime Administration. Compare *operating differential subsidy.*

**consul (c., con., cons.).**   An embassy official. Known variously as economic attachés, commercial counselors, or consular officials, consuls often manage an embassy's trade and investment portfolio, provide business and trade information to firms in the exporting country, validate documents, and serve as resident ambassadors' emissaries at local business functions. See also *diplomat.*

**consular documents.**   Official statements issued by an embassy or consulate in an exporting country, documenting the contents of cargo for a foreign customs agency. 1. A consular declaration certifies the nature of exported goods. 2. A consular invoice verifies the quantity and price of exported goods, or other conditions specified by the importing country, and determines import duties. Consular invoices are presented to the embassy or consulate in an importing country's official language for legalization, or stamping.

**consular fee.**   Also called consulage, a charge for preparing and certifying consular documents. Consular fees generate revenues for local consulates and are usually paid to a bank designated by the importing country. The fees are later deducted at the port of entry from duties payable on imports. See also *legalization.*

**consumer.**   See *end user.*

**consumer certificate of deposit (CD).**   In the United States, a nonnegotiable time-deposit instrument issued by a financial institution. Consumer CDs are protected by the Federal Deposit Insurance Corporation for amounts up to $100,000 in principal and interest. Some U.S. banks and savings and loan associations also issue zero-coupon CDs with all interest paid at maturity.

**consumer good.**   See *good.*

**consumer price index.**   See *price index.*

**consumer protection.**   Laws and regulations creating a legal right of action for injury caused by unfair business practices, which range from consumer credit fraud to sales of falsely labeled products. In common-law countries, both statutory and breach-of-contract (warranty) damages and tort remedies are available to consumers injured by unethical business practices. 1. In the United States, consumer protection laws are administered by the Consumer Protection Agency and the Federal Trade Commission. 2. In Europe, consumer protection regulation is more complex. Various consumer groups are highly organized at the national level, e.g., *Arbeitsgemeinschaft der Verbraucherverbände* (Germany), *Cooperazione Italiana* (Italy), *Union Française des Consommateurs* (France). In the European Community (EC), Article 100 (a) (3) of the Single European Act mandates that the European Commission establish a "high level of [consumer] protection." Directives setting uniform "essential" health and safety standards for products are approved by the European Commission. However, the consumer protection provisions of the Single Act have been construed to mean that EC national standards need not be identical so long as they comply with a directive's essential standards. On the other hand, products approved by European standards organizations are generally acceptable in all EC national markets, although the legal enforceability of regional standards in the face of a strong challenge by a member state remains uncertain. See also *Cassis de Dijon* and *Communauté Européenne*.

**consumption entry.**   See customs entry.

**consumption tax.**   A sales tax or value-added tax paid by consumers for the privilege of consuming goods or services.

**cont.**   An abbreviation for contract.

**container.**   A large rectangular shipping box that can be loaded and unloaded from different types of transport vehicles without unpacking. Containers are standardized to conform roughly to the International Standards Organization Standard 688 for containers. Most containers used in international trade are slightly higher (8 feet 6 inches) and are capable of transporting somewhat more weight (24 tons maximum gross weight) than Standard 688 specifies. The space allotted for transporting containers is expressed as TEUs (20-foot equivalent units) or FEUs (40-foot equivalent

units), which measure the number of shipping containers a lot can accommodate. Compare *high cube*.

**container equivalent unit.**   See *container*.

**containerization.**   See *container*.

**container load.**   A cargo of sufficient bulk to fill a shipping container.

**container-on-flatcar (COFC).**   A means of transporting cargo that has been preloaded into a shipping container at a factory or other packing site. The cargo is transported to and from a port by railroad.

**container pool.**   An agreement between common carriers to share shipping containers. These agreements guarantee an adequate supply and efficient use of container inventories.

**container-sealing device.**   See *cargo container sealer*.

**container ship.**   A ship designed to accommodate shipping containers.

**contango market.**   1. A special forward market that operates monthly on the day after settlement day. For example, transactions on the Paris Bourse are normally concluded on the settlement date. On the contango market, also known as the *marché des reports,* however, stocks are sold (or bought) at a fixed price on the day after the settlement and repurchased (or sold) at the same price the following month. Contango rates are the prices paid by buyers or the backwardation paid by sellers. 2. A market where prices are higher in distant delivery months than at earlier delivery dates.

**content requirement.**   See *domestic content requirement*.

**continental bill.**   A bill of exchange drawn on a European bank. Compare *dollar bill of exchange* and *sterling bill of exchange*.

**contingency planning.**   The process of developing a plan to manage difficulties arising from unforeseen circumstances; e.g., a company plans in advance to reduce costs and expenditures, including wages and salaries, in the event of a recession or decline in its business.

**contingent liability.**   On a balance sheet, a debt that becomes payable if a future event occurs. Self-insured companies have contingent liability when claims are filed, as do companies facing damage claims in lawsuits. Normally, the nature and sum of potential liabilities are noted on a company's balance sheet.

**continuation statement.**    See *security interest.*

**contr.**    An abbreviation for contract.

**contraband.**    Smuggled goods that cannot be legally sold. Possession of contraband is a criminal offense, and contraband is subject to seizure by customs agents or other police authorities. Articles smuggled during wartime are known as contraband of war and may be seized by belligerents. Contraband of war includes weapons and munitions (known as absolute contraband), dual-use items, and staples and supplies that can be used to fortify troops. Under international law, a belligerent may seize a neutral ship transporting contraband on the high seas. However, neutral nations are not obligated to seize contraband on behalf of wartime belligerents. See also *interdiction.*

**contract (cont.).**    An agreement entered into between parties to a transaction. A contract may be oral, written, or implied from the conduct of transacting parties. It can be made by a principal or an agent authorized to contract on a principal's behalf. An agent's authority may be express or implied. Formation of a contract requires an offer, acceptance, and consideration paid to create it. Both parties must intend and have the legal capacity to form a contract (i.e., the parties must be of legal age, sober, and sane). The contract must be legal (i.e., murder for hire is an illegal contract) and not void for vagueness or public policy reasons. Sales contracts are usually in writing. In the United States, the Uniform Commercial Code (UCC) requires a written contract for the sale of goods exceeding $500. The UCC does not apply to contracts for the sale of services, although a services contract is usually enforceable on equitable grounds when one party benefits at the expense of another. Certain other contracts (e.g., promissory notes) are not enforceable unless in writing. The written form of a contract is usually inconsequential unless prescribed by law, although courts do not enforce agreements omitting any reference to the terms and conditions under which obligations are to be performed and payments collected. See also *breach of contract.*

**contract demurrage.**    The rate paid by a shipper for delays in delivering merchandise to a carrier for loading. Demurrage terms are specified in a carriage contract.

**contract grade.**    In a commodity futures market, the quality ascribed to goods deemed suitable by a trading exchange for delivery under a futures contract.

**contracting parties.**    The official name of signatories to the General Agreement on Tariffs and Trade.

**contract of affreightment.**    A written agreement, usually supported by a bill of lading, evidencing a contract between an exporter and a carrier. The contract specifies the details of the transaction, including a description of the goods, the destination of the shipment, and the transport company's liability for damage or loss. A long-form bill of lading defines the terms and conditions of a carriage contract. A short-form bill of lading summarizes information contained in the contract.

**contract of carriage.**    A transport agreement between a shipper and a carrier. See also *contract of affreightment.*

**contractor.**    A general contractor, also known as a principal contractor, prime contractor, or prime. Construction or supply contracts are let to prime contractors, who respond to tenders and assume primary liability for the contract. Work not performed by the general contractor is let to a subcontractor, who is usually liable for failure to perform an obligation specified in the subcontract. In most instances, the general contractor and subcontractor share joint and several liability, giving a principal legal recourse against both.

**contract note.**    A notice from a broker to a principal confirming the details of a completed securities trade or commodities transaction. The note is called a bought or sold note, depending on whether the principal is a buyer or seller.

**contract rate.**    The preferential freight rate applied to merchandise covered by an exclusive patronage contract between a shipper and a shipping conference.

**contract shipper.**    An exporter who executes an exclusive contract with a shipping conference.

**contra proferentem.** Latin: against the proclaimer. A legal doctrine holding a party who drafts a document (or attempts to base a claim against another on it) responsible for any ambiguity in its terms. For example, in a breach-of-contract action ambiguities are resolved against the plaintiff.

**controlled carrier.** In the United States, an ocean carrier owned by a foreign government or controlled by directors or executive officers appointed by a foreign government. The Federal Maritime Commission (FMC) regulates controlled carriers to prevent predatory pricing. The FMC is authorized by the Controlled Carrier Act of 1980 to suspend predatory freight rates.

**controlled currency rate.** A currency value fixed by exchange controls, which are imposed as a part of a government's economic stabilization policy. In dual-exchange-rate systems, there is normally a controlled rate and a floating exchange rate. The controlled rate yielding a higher per-unit foreign exchange value is reserved for official uses and international trade transactions. The floating rate applies to less favored activities, such as tourism and consumer imports. For example, the controlled peso rate established by the Bank of Mexico is used for specific types of transactions, including foreign trade. See also *exchange control* and *secondary exchange market.*

**controlled foreign corporation.** In the United States, an overseas company in which U.S. nationals own or control 51 percent or more of the corporation's voting shares at any time in a tax year. See also *Subpart F.*

**controlling interest.** In a corporation, the interest of a shareholder who owns or controls more than 50 percent of the voting common stock. Depending on the number of authorized voting shares, shareholders may control more voting shares than they own, since a controlling interest in common stock can be owned in combination with others.

**control of damaged goods.** In insurance, protection for a manufacturer who suffers economic loss to prevent the sale of damaged or salvaged goods. See also *brands and labels protection.*

**conventional duty.** See *duty.*

**Convention for the Unification of Certain Rules Relating to International Transportation by Air.** See *Warsaw Convention.*

**Convention on a Code of Conduct for Liner Conferences.** An international agreement reached in 1974 under the auspices of the United Nations Conference on Trade and Development (UNCTAD). The convention became effective in 1983. The UNCTAD Code establishes international shipping rules for shipping conferences and ocean carriage of government cargoes. It permits closed conferences but requires that membership be open to carriers along members' trade routes. The code clarified international rules for conference rate making and adopted the 40-40-20 rule, regulating the division of cargoes between carriers of different countries. The rule authorizes governments to reserve 40 percent of official cargoes for ships flying an exporting country's flag, 40 percent for ships flying the importing country's flag, and 20 percent for ships registered in other countries.

**Convention on Conditions for Registration of Ships.** See *United Nations Conference on Trade and Development.*

**Convention on International Trade in Endangered Species of Wild Fauna and Flora (CITES).** An international agreement regulating trade in endangered species of plants and animals signed at Washington, D.C., in 1973. The agreement accords different levels of protection to covered species, although trade in the most endangered species is banned entirely. Globally threatened species are licensed by the exporting nation, and locally threatened species are placed on a protected list for supervised importation. A signatory nation may exempt itself from regulations involving any category of species. CITES became effective in the United States in 1977 with the enactment of the Endangered Species Act, administered by the Fish and Wildlife Service and the National Marine Fisheries Service. Permits for U.S. imports of endangered species are issued by the Fish and Wildlife Service.

**Convention on Limitation of Liability for Maritime Claims.** A 1976 agreement covering ocean carrier liability for personal injury, loss of life, and property damage. The convention supplants the Brussels Convention Relating to the Limitation of the Liability of Owners of Seagoing Ships, signed in 1957. Under the new convention, liability limitations are determined by the size of a ship and valued in special drawing rights, or, in the case of countries not members of the International Monetary Fund, the gold franc. The convention is administered by the International Maritime Organization.

**Convention on the Contract for the International Carriage of Goods by Road.** See *Convention relative au contrât de transport international de marchandises par route.*

**Convention on the Facilitation of International Maritime Traffic.** See *International Maritime Organization.*

**Convention on the International Maritime Satellite Organization.** See *International Maritime Satellite Organization.*

**Convention on the International Regulations for Preventing Collisions at Sea.** See *International Convention for the Safety of Life at Sea.*

**Convention on the Prevention of Marine Pollution by Dumping of Wastes and Other Matter.** An international agreement adopted at London in 1972 to prevent the spread of marine pollution. Also known as the London Dumping Convention, the agreement bans dumping of hazardous materials from aircraft, vessels, and so on unless a prior permit has been issued. The convention does not apply when human life or a transport craft is at risk or when wastes are created by mineral exploration. Annexes identify wastes requiring special dumping permits and rules governing the issuance of permits. The convention is administered by the International Maritime Organization.

**Convention Relating to Civil Liability in the Field of Maritime Carriage on Nuclear Materials.** A 1971 agreement clarifying the liability of ocean carriers transporting nuclear materials. The convention exonerates a carrier for injury caused by a nuclear incident when the operator of the nuclear facility is liable. The agreement is administered by the International Maritime Organization and the International Atomic Energy Agency.

**Convention Relating to a Uniform Law on the Formation of Contracts for the International Sale of Goods.** See *United Nations Convention on Contracts for the International Sale of Goods.*

**Convention Relating to a Uniform Law on the International Sale of Goods.** See *United Nations Convention on Contracts for the International Sale of Goods.*

**Convention relative au contrât de transport international de marchandises par route (CMR).** Also known as the Convention on the Contract for the International Carriage of Goods by Road, the CMR governs contracts covering goods shipped by road in international trade. The convention was adopted at Geneva in 1956.

**conversion.** In arbitrage, the use of a futures contract, a long put option, and a short call option to eliminate the risk of a transaction. For a conversion to succeed, the put option and the call option must have the same expiration date and the same strike price.

**convertible.** 1. A currency freely exchangeable for gold or another currency. 2. Also known as a conversion issue, a bond or debenture that can be exchanged for preferred or common stock, or preferred shares that can be exchanged for common stock. The price and period for conversion are fixed at the time of issue.

**convertible bond.** A debt obligation that can be exchanged for stock. The terms of convertibility are determined by the bond indenture. A convertible debenture in usually unsecured and can be exchanged for common stock.

**convertible debenture.** See *convertible bond.*

**Cooke Committee.** Formally known as the Committee on Banking Regulations and Supervisory Practices, an organ of the Bank for International Settlements (BIS). Established in 1974, the committee is composed of the central bankers of the Group of Ten nations and Luxembourg. The committee meets regularly at the BIS and considers uniform measures for supervising international banking activities. See also *Basel Concordat.*

**Cooley Loan Program.** See *PL 480 programs.*

**cooperage.**    External packaging used in shipping, such as crates.

**cooperation agreement.**    A joint venture between governments involving buybacks. In a cooperation agreement, one government agrees to transfer technology to another and to purchase a portion of the venture's output. Some ventures of this type have been successfully undertaken by Western and Eastern European countries, particularly for large industrial or development projects. Supplies and construction are provided by commercial firms under subcontracts from their governments. Cooperation agreements are long-term arrangements, usually lasting for periods of 10 years or more.

**Coordinating Committee on Multilateral Export Controls** (COCOM).    A group of nations made up of the North American Treaty Organization (except Iceland), Australia, and Japan, which monitors exports of strategic weapons, materials, and dual-use high technology. COCOM was preceded by the Consultative Group, established after the United States adopted the Export Control Act of 1946. Originally designed to isolate the former Warsaw Pact, COCOM now attempts to control the proliferation of dangerous weapons around the world. COCOM Lists itemize export-controlled products. The committee also groups countries into certain categories (e.g., Country Group Y), indicating their eligibility to receive certain imports. COCOM member states may impose unilateral restraints stricter than the committee's controls. COCOM is headquartered in Paris.

**copyright.**    A limited, exclusive right of ownership in a work created by an author. Copyrights apply to written works, musical compositions, visual works, designs, films, broadcasts, performance works, and computer software. In most legal jurisdictions, infringing a copyrighted work is a civil and criminal offense. The usual test for copyright infringement is whether the unauthorized copy is substantially similar to the original work. The copyright holder's remedies are an accounting of profits, damages, and injunction. Limited exemptions exist for copying solely for educational and research purposes. The principal international copyright agreements are the Berne Convention for the Protection of Literary and Artistic Works and the Universal Copyright Convention. 1. In the United States, copyrights for works created after January 1, 1978, are governed by the Copyright Revision Act of 1976. Works created, or fixed in tangible form for the first time, are automatically protected from the moment of creation. U.S. copyright protection lasts for the author's life plus 50 years. Anonymous or pseudonymous works and works for hire are protected for 75 years from the date of publication or 100 years from creation, whichever is longer. If the author's identity is revealed, protection reverts to the author's life plus 50 years rule. The Copyright Act is administered by the U.S. Copyright Office of the Library of Congress. 2. In the United Kingdom, copyrights are protected by the Copyright Act of 1988. The British Copyright Act of 1911 still has effect in some former British colonies. For example, the 1911 law (as amended in 1971) is still in force in Israel. The 1988 British law follows the author's-life-plus-50-years rule.

**Copyright Revision Act of 1976.**    In the United States, the law that governs copyright protection and covers, among other things, international trade in copyrighted articles. Section 602 defines unauthorized imports of works copyrighted elsewhere as copyright infringement. Infringing works are forfeited, seized, and destroyed. When the violation was unintentional, the infringing items are returned to the exporting country. The act is administered by the U.S. Copyright Office.

**cordoba.**    The currency of Nicaragua.

**Core List.**    See *COCOM List.*

**Corp.**    An abbreviation for corporation.

**corporate average fuel efficiency (CAFE).**    In the United States, fuel-efficiency standards required for automobiles by the Clean Air Act of 1990. Under CAFE standards, foreign and domestic automobiles must obtain 27 miles per gallon of gasoline. Proposed increases in CAFE standards would require automobiles to reach 36 to 45 miles per gallon. As of 1993, proposed changes in CAFE standards have not been enacted.

**corporate tax.**    See tax.

**Corporate Trade Exchange (CTX) Network.**    In the United States, the electronic data interchange system used by corporations and government agencies for foreign funds transfers. CTX is owned by the Automated Clearing House system. The CTX format combines payment data with an addendum record, also called a variable-length record. The addendum record contains invoice information and facilitates payments to multiple creditors from a single funds transfer. The format conforms to ANSI X12, the American National Standards Institute format for electronic international trade data transfers.

**Corporate Trade Payment (CTP) Network.**    In the United States, the electronic data interchange system used by corporations and government agencies to pay creditors. Created primarily for payments to corporate suppliers, CTP is owned by the Automated Clearing House system. CTP records contain standard remittance information. CTP is an older, less flexible system than the corporate trade exchange network.

**corporation (Corp.).**    A registered business with a legal existence apart from its owners. A corporation has limited liability; i.e., creditors have claims against its owners up to the extent of the corporation's assets. It can make contracts and own property in its own name. Corporations can also transfer equity to shareholders other than founding or existing shareholders. Corporations are named differently, depending on their ownership and purpose. 1. A corporation sole is a private corporation owned by one party. 2. A corporation aggregate is owned by several or many shareholders. 3. An alien corporation is a company incorporated in a foreign country. 4. In the United States, a domestic corporation is a company doing business within the state of incorporation. Elsewhere, a domestic corporation is a company incorporated, or registered, in the home country. 5. In the United States, a foreign corporation in one state is technically a company incorporated in another state (i.e., a New York corporation is a foreign corporation in California). Under U.S. federal tax law and elsewhere, a foreign corporation is a company incorporated in another country. 6. A multinational corporation is a parent company that owns one or more foreign subsidiaries. 7. A quasi-public corporation is a privately owned company created to fulfill a public purpose. Quasi-public compa-

nies are often partially backed by a government, but they also issue publicly traded stock and borrow on private capital markets. 8. A public corporation is a nonprofit government company organized to carry out a public purpose. Public corporations usually provide a service (e.g., the British Broadcasting Company or the Corporation for Public Broadcasting in the United States). A public corporation may also be created to manage a nationalized industry. The chief executive officer and board members are often appointed by a ministerial agency. In the United States, these officers are appointed by the President and confirmed by the U.S. Senate. 9. A publicly held corporation is a private, for-profit company whose shares are traded on an organized stock exchange. Outside the United States, a publicly held corporation is called a public limited company. In the United States, a corporation is indicated by "Inc." after its name. See also *associated foreign corporation, company, controlled foreign corporation, discount corporation, domestic international sales corporation, export trade corporation, export trading company, foreign international sales corporation, foreign sales corporation*, and *subchapter S*.

**corporation tax.**    See *tax*.

**correction.**    1. An amendment to a letter of credit to eliminate a discrepancy. Banks charge additional fees for corrections. 2. A fall in stock prices when investors take profits and withdraw from a market. Corrections are often caused by unfavorable external events, creating pessimism about future earnings. A technical correction occurs when a market has more sellers than buyers, irrespective of market sentiment. Compare *rally*.

**correspondent bank.**    A bank that serves as an agent for local or foreign banks. Funds on deposit in a correspondent bank are often used to reconcile the accounts of another bank. In the United States, correspondent banks buy participations in loans for smaller respondents when a loan exceeds legal lending limits. Correspondent services enable smaller institutions to enter costly international financial markets. Compare *respondent*.

**cost accounting.**    An accounting method that allocates the direct and indirect costs of producing goods (or delivering services) to various units of a business organization. Expenditures are divided into overhead (building and maintenance expenses, administrative expenses, and executive salaries), selling costs (advertising, promotion, and sales commissions and salaries), and borrowing costs. See also *cost center* and *costing software*.

**cost and freight (CFR, C&F).** An international commercial term (INCOTERM). The seller pays the cost of shipping goods to a named destination port and insures cargo until it is loaded on a ship or aircraft. The risk of loss and associated costs then pass to the buyer.

**cost and insurance (C&I).** A term of sale. The seller pays insurance to a named destination. The buyer pays freight.

**cost, assurance, and freight (CAF).** See *cost, insurance, and freight*.

**cost center.** In cost accounting, a unit in an organization that generates expenditures without producing earnings. In business organizations, a cost center normally services profit centers.

**costing software.** A business software system that enables a carrier to determine the actual costs of moving a shipment. The software aggregates capital expenditures and depreciation, as well as the cost of fuel, labor, maintenance, overhead, taxes, and insurance.

**cost, insurance, and freight (CIF).** 1. An international commercial term (INCOTERM). The seller pays insurance and freight to a named destination. A buyer is obligated on a CIF contract to pay for exported goods once documents of title have been presented. If the seller has forwarded the bill of lading, commercial invoice, insurance certificate, and other shipping documents, the risk of loss passes to the buyer, even though the cargo is lost or damaged in transit. Since sellers purchase minimum insurance coverage, buyers often also insure shipments to make up the difference. 2. In customs, the CIF price is the basis for import valuation in most countries. F.O.B. (free on board) price is used in the United States. See also *adjusted CIF price* and *valuation*. Compare *free on board*.

**cost, insurance, freight, and commission (CIF&C).** A term of sale. The seller pays insurance, freight, and the importer's commission. See also *cost, insurance, and freight*.

**cost, insurance, freight, and exchange (CIF&E).** A term of sale. The seller pays insurance, freight, and the difference in foreign exchange rates. See also *cost, insurance, and freight*.

**cost, insurance, freight, commission, and interest (CIFCI).** A term of sale. The seller pays insurance, freight, an importer's commission, and the interest owed to a bank for negotiating a letter of credit. See also *cost, insurance, and freight*.

**cost-plus contract.** An open-ended contract whereby the contractor is paid the cost of goods and services plus the contract's value. Cost-plus contracts are used when the cost of work and materials cannot be determined in advance. Buyers are disadvantaged under these contracts because the contractor is not bound by specific cost terms. Construction contracts are often let on a cost-plus basis.

**Cote Officielle.** French: Official List.

**COTP.** The abbreviation for captain of the port.

**Cotton Marketing Certification Program.** In the United States, a cotton price-support program created in 1990 and administered by the U.S. Department of Agriculture. U.S. cotton exporters are given rebate certificates. The rebate is available if the cheapest U.S. cotton price exceeds a competing country's cotton price by a fixed amount for a specified period. The value of a certificate is equal to the difference between the U.S. price and the competing country's price.

**Cottonseed Oil Assistance Program (COAP).** In the United States, a program offered by the U.S. Department of Agriculture for domestic cottonseed oil exporters. The Sunflowerseed Oil Assistance Program assists domestic vegetable oil producers on similar terms. The programs enable these producers to sell below the U.S. price in targeted export markets. Exporters are required to post performance bonds in exchange for cash bonuses. The value of the bonus is the difference between the U.S. price and the prevailing world market price.

**Council for Mutual Economic Assistance (CMEA).** Also known as COMECON, the defunct economic cooperation organization of the Warsaw Pact. CMEA was created in 1949 by the former Union of Soviet Socialist Republics to foster economic integration among its satellites. COMECON members were Cuba, the Eastern bloc of European states (excluding Albania), Mongolia, the U.S.S.R., and Vietnam. Finland and the former country of Yugoslavia were associate members. Although CMEA was originally conceived as a multilateral trading union, member states cooperated largely on a bilateral basis. CMEA dissolved in 1991 and was reconstituted into an economic advisory committee, known as the Organization for International Economic Cooperation (OIEC). The successor organization deals largely with quota and tariff issues. OIEC is also an intermediary in relations between its members and the European Community. See also *International Investments Bank.*

**Council of Arab Economic Unity (CAEU).** A regional economic cooperation association created by the Arab League in 1957. CAEU is composed of 10 Moslem countries in Africa and the Middle East, including Iraq, Jordan, and Syria. The Palestine Liberation Organization represents Palestinians in CAEU. Egypt and Saudi Arabia are not CAEU members.

**Council of Canadian Trading Houses.** See *Canadian Export Association.*

**Council of Entente.** See *Conseil de l'Entente.*

**Council of Europe (CE).** Also known as the Conseil de l'Europe, a regional body composed of 21 European States created by the Statute of the Council signed at London in 1949. The Council of Europe was established to facilitate economic and political cooperation in Western Europe. Belgium, Denmark, France, Ireland, Italy, Luxembourg, the Netherlands, Norway, Sweden, and the United Kingdom were original members, but all Western European countries are now represented on the Council. The Council's executive body is the Committee of Ministers, composed of foreign ministers. Its legislative arm is known as the Consultative Assembly. The European Commission on Human Rights and the European Court of Human Rights are affiliates of the Council. Largely due to exceptions by Britain and the Scandinavian countries, the Council of Europe was never granted significant decision-making power. Unanimous (rather than majority) approval of its initiatives hampers the authority of

the Council. Its secretariat is located in Strasbourg, France. Compare *European Council of Ministers.*

**Council of Lloyd's.** The governing body of Lloyd's.

**Council of Ministers.** See *European Community.*

**Council of Representatives.** See *General Agreement on Tariffs and Trade.*

**Council of the European Communities.** See *European Council of Ministers.*

**count certificate.** A document issued by an independent inspection firm verifying the volume of merchandise contained in a shipment.

**countercyclical policy.** A policy designed to assist unemployed workers and increase employment during economic downturns. Countercyclical policies combine fiscal (increased government spending) and monetary (loosening of money and credit) measures. Deficit government spending joined with increased consumer spending is intended to stimulate economic activity. Countercyclical expenditures tend to produce periods of higher growth, often followed by periods of inflation. See also *business cycle.*

**counterfeit article.** A copy or imitation of an original or trademarked item produced to defraud prospective purchasers. International traffic in counterfeit goods is prohibited by the Counterfeit Code of the General Agreement on Tariffs and Trade and under international copyright, patent, and trademark conventions. Sales of counterfeit goods in domestic markets are prohibited by national civil and criminal statutes.

**Counterfeit Code.** See *General Agreement on Tariffs and Trade: Tokyo Round.*

**counterpurchase.** A form of countertrade in which an exporter contracts to buy all or part of the importer's inventory. Unlike a buyback arrangement, counterpurchased goods are unrelated to the original transaction, but sales proceeds are used to pay the exporter.

**countertrade.** A transaction settled through the exchange of goods and services. Countertrades are used in international transactions when an importer lacks sufficient foreign exchange to close a sale. Many countertrade transactions are offset trades; i.e., the exporter accepts goods or services from the importer as a product input in lieu of cash. In a direct offset, the exporter uses the input to finish a product. In an indirect offset, the exporter accepts peripheral goods or services. Other forms of countertrade include barter, buy-back, clearing, compensation deals, counterpurchase, swapping, and switching.

**countervailing credit.**    See *letter of credit.*

**countervailing duty (CVD).**    An import duty imposed to counter the effects of a government subsidy. Countervailing duties are paid in addition to ordinary duties. In the United States, CVDs are levied against imports produced with "excessive" subsidies. An excessive subsidy is a bounty or grant paid solely to stimulate exports. The process of determining countervailing duties is known as a countervailing duty (or subsidy) action.

**countervailing duty (CVD) action.**    An administrative remedy for economic injury caused by subsidized imports. In the United States, countervailing duty actions are authorized by the Tariff Act of 1930. An action is initiated when an interested party, usually a U.S. manufacturer or trade association, files a petition with the International Trade Administration. The petitioner complains of injury from subsidized imports. Injury is determined by the International Trade Commission. Countervailing duty actions are infrequent outside the United States. See also *General Agreement on Tariffs and Trade: Tokyo Round, Subsidies (and Countervailing Measures) Code,* and *U.S. Court of International Trade.* Compare *antidumping action.*

**Country Agricultural Report.**    In the United States, a publication of the U.S. Department of Agriculture. *Country Agricultural Reports* carry trade tables showing the volume of U.S. farm exports and identify principal foreign competitors.

**Country Backgrounder Report.**    In the United States, a publication of the U.S. Department of Agriculture. *Country Backgrounder Reports* cover international markets for high-value agricultural products. The reports include market descriptions, trends, and statistics on international markets.

**country-controlled buying agent.**    A government agency or a firm that serves as the primary purchaser of foreign imports. Controlled purchasing agents are usually found in countries with for-

eign exchange controls, although government agencies in other countries may be the sole authorized purchasers for highly regulated products, such as arms or chemicals, or heavily taxed products, such alcohol and tobacco.

**Country Exposure Lending Survey.**    In the United States, a quarterly report issued by bank regulators. The report summarizes foreign lending by domestic banks and identifies foreign borrowers by country and type of loan (e.g., public or private). The survey is published by the Interagency Country Exposure Review Committee, composed of federal bank regulators who determine the country risk exposure of U.S. banks. The Comptroller of the Currency, Federal Deposit Insurance Corporation, and Federal Reserve System are represented on the nine-member committee. Delinquent foreign loans are classified as substandard, value impaired, or losses. Banks are required to write down or increase reserves against nonperforming loans.

**country groups.**    A system of classifying countries to implement export control measures. In the United States, all countries (except Canada) are classified by groups represented by a letter of the alphabet (e.g., Country Group Z covers Cuba, Cambodia, North Korea, and Vietnam). U.S. exports to Canada are not, as a rule, subject to export controls. See also *Coordinating Committee on Multilateral Export Controls.*

**country information kits.**    In the United States, background reports prepared by the Overseas Private Investment Corporation (OPIC). Compiled by OIPC's Investor Information Service, the backgrounders provide business, economic, and political data on developing countries eligible for OPIC's investment and insurance services. OPIC also publishes regional information kits.

**country limit.**    The maximum amount a given national bank will lend to a foreign country. The limit covers all lending, including loans to public and private borrowers.

**Country Limitation Schedule.**    In the United States, a publication of the Export-Import Bank of the United States (Eximbank) that outlines restrictions on its lending programs and guarantees. A country is ineligible for the Eximbank programs when it violates a policy of the United States. Among others, human rights policies, labor standards, and the failure to protect intellectual property rights may bar Eximbank lending under various statutes.

**country of origin.**    The country in which an import was created, grown, manufactured, processed, or produced. Rules of origin are factors in assessing import duties, enforcing trade bans, and granting trade preferences. A shipper's declaration of origin is prima facie evidence of an import's source. The symbol indicating an import's national origin is called a country-of-origin marking.

**country-of-origin marking.**    See *country of origin*.

**country risk.**    One of several factors in a foreign investment decision. Country risks include political instability, currency devaluation, or any of a variety of risks arising from a sovereign's exercise of power. 1. A cross-border risk is any risk taken in an international transaction. 2. A currency risk, also known as currency availability risk, arises when a currency may be devalued or remittances blocked. 3. A domicile risk occurs when a debtor's assets may be seized or destroyed or when a sovereign debtor is predisposed to repudiate a debt. 4. A nationality risk results if debtors are natural persons or corporations whose nationality may cause seizure of their assets. A corporate branch or subsidiary can be a national of its parent's incorporating country *or* a national of a country where it has business operations or assets. 5. Political risks include war, insurrection, civil instability, or any event resulting from a government's inability or unwillingness to protect foreign investments. 6. Sovereign risks arise from the nature of a government. A prior default on debt or a threat of insurrection creates sovereign risk. See also *Country Exposure Lending Survey*. Compare *commercial risk*.

**coupon.**    A certificate attached to a note or bond. Bearer bond coupons are negotiable and guarantee interest to a holder when the coupon is clipped and sent to the issuer's paying agent. The coupon specifies the amount of interest payable. Coupon interest, also called the coupon rate, is computed on an annual basis but may be payable semiannually.

**coupon rate.**    See *coupon*.

**coupon swap.**    See *swap*.

**cours acheteur.**    French: bid price.

**cours du change.**    See *échanger*.

**cours vendeur.**    French: offer price.

**courtage.**    French: (brokerage) commission.

**courtier.**    French: broker.

**Court of Arbitration.**    An agency of the International Chamber of Commerce that oversees international commercial arbitrations. Matters in dispute are voluntarily submitted by the parties, who agree in advance to be bound by the court's decision. The Court of Arbitration sits in Paris. Compare *Permanent Court of Arbitration*.

**covenant.**    An enforceable promise made in a contract. For example, in a bond contract, a bond issuer pledges to prevent impairment of a bondholder's investments. The pledge is a covenant.

**cover.**    Measures adopted to protect the value of an investment. In finance, collateral is a form of cover. In investments, hedges are covers for short selling in commodities and currency futures trading.

**covered transaction.**    A transaction in which principals are indemnified against future losses from exchange rate fluctuations. See also *forward exchange contract*.

**C/P.**    The abbreviation for charter party, chemically pure, clearance permit, contracting party, and customs of the port.

**CPA.**    The abbreviation for certified public accountant.

**CPD.**    The abbreviation for charterer pays dues.

**CPI.**    The abbreviation for consumer price index and commodity price index.

**C.P.Q.**    The abbreviation for customary quick dispatch.

**CPSC.**    The abbreviation for Consumer Product Safety Commission.

**CPT.**    The abbreviation for carriage paid to.

**cr.**    The abbreviation for credit.

**CR.**    The abbreviation for carrier's risk, current rate, and customs regulations.

**C.R.A.**    The abbreviation for customs regulations amendment.

**craft and lighter.**    In insurance, a policyholder's indemnity for cargoes traveling by light craft. The provision covers damage or loss when light vessels travel between a port and an ocean carrier. Light craft include rafts, barges, and similar vessels.

**crawling peg.**    See *pegged exchange rate.*

**credit (cr.).**    1. In accounting, a positive asset entered on the right side of an accounts ledger. 2. In finance, an agreement to provide money, goods, or services in exchange for a borrower's promise to pay at a future date.

**crédit de mobilisation de créance commerciale.**  French: a short-term trade bill of exchange.

**credit d'impôt.**    In Belgium, a tax credit applied to dividend income. See also *advance corporation tax* and *avoir fiscal.*

**credit enhancement.**    The upgrading of a loan to improve a borrower's creditworthiness. Enhancement is normally achieved by adding a third-party guarantee or pledging collateral exceeding the value of the loan. Among others, third-party enhancements are standby letters of credit from banks or surety bonds issued by insurance companies. Credit enhancements are used to obtain investment-grade bond ratings or to improve the marketability of money-market securities.

**credit line.**    Also known as a line of credit, the amount of credit made available to a customer by a lender.

**crédit mixte.**    Credit terms granted to developing countries by members of the Organisation for Economic Cooperation and Development (OECD). Under the OECD Consensus, some credits are repayable at commercial lending rates and others at concessional rates. Concessional rates are granted for official development assistance.

**creditors' committee.**    See *bankruptcy.*

**credit rating.**    A lender's evaluation of personal or business creditworthiness. The rating is based on the credit report provided by a credit-rating service. Consumer-credit ratings are obtained from national consumer-credit-reporting agencies. Business-credit services provide reports on commercial firms, including capitalization, debt oblig-

ations, and ownership. Creditworthiness may also be determined by an application, financial statement, and tax return. See also *rating.*

**credit risk.**    The likelihood that a borrower will default on a loan obligation. See also *commercial risk* and *country risk.*

**credits.**    At the World Bank, loans provided by the International Development Agency (IDA). The World Bank Group distinguishes IDA credits from International Bank for Reconstruction and Development loans. IDA credits are concessional loans, typically extended for a period of 50 years or more. Repayment of principal begins after a 10-year grace period.

**credit tranche.**    See *International Monetary Fund.*

**CREW.**    The abbreviation for combined rewarehouse entry and withdrawal.

**CRF.**    The abbreviation for clean report of findings and cost and freight.

**cross-currency exposure.**    See *currency exposure.*

**cross-border.**    A transaction or activity that transcends the territorial boundaries of one country and reaches into those of another.

**crossed check.**    In some banking jurisdictions, a check with a restriction on its negotiability. When a general crossing is used, the check must be deposited in a bank account and cannot otherwise be cashed. A special crossing imposes an additional restriction, as when the check must be deposited with a specified bank. Compare *open check.*

**cross hedge.**    The purchase of a financial future in a different asset. Cross-hedges are devices used to avoid losses on interest-rate fluctuations. When a hedge is successful, the interest rate risk is reduced by dealing in a different market.

**cross rate.**    The rate of exchange between two currencies priced against a third currency. Cross rates for major currencies are published in cross-rate tables.

**cross retaliation.**    A form of retaliation for unfair trade practices. Normally, when a domestic economic sector is injured, a country raises tariffs or imposes quotas against the same sector in the offending country. Cross retaliation occurs when a country retaliates against an economic sector other than that charged with the original trade violation.

This form of trade sanction is used (or threatened) when the strongest export industries in the offending country cannot be affected by simple retaliation. In the United States, the U.S. Trade Representative publishes a list of prospective targets in the *Federal Register* and invites comments from domestic industries before selecting an industry for cross retaliation. As a general matter, cross retaliation is a departure from the settled international trade principle that unfair conduct in one economic sector invites retaliation against the same sector.

**cross subsidy.**    The use of earnings from one market to support operations in another. Cross subsidies allow firms to launch products in new markets, often engaging in predatory pricing to capture larger market share. When cross subsidies are used, the impact of short-term losses in one market is minimized by higher returns in the other.

**cross trader.**    A shipping line engaged in business outside its home territory.

**crown corporation.**    In Canada, a limited-liability company formed to engage in international trade and partly or wholly owned by the Canadian government. The Canadian Commercial Corporation and the Export Development Corporation are crown corporations. A provincial crown corporation is one owned by a provincial government.

**CRU.**    The abbreviation for collective reserve unit.

**cruzado.**    The currency of Brazil, which replaced the cruzeiro in 1985. See also *revalorization*.

**CSA.**    The abbreviation for Canadian Shipowners Association and Customs Simplification Act.

**CSCE.**    The abbreviation for Conference on Security and Cooperation in Europe.

**ct.**    The abbreviation for carat and cent.

**ctf.**    An abbreviation for certificate.

**ctge.**    The abbreviation for cartage.

**ctn.**    The abbreviation for carton.

**CTO.**    The abbreviation for combined transport operator.

**CTR.**    The abbreviation for currency transaction report. See *laundered money*.

**Cuban Assets Control Regulations.**    In the United States, the mechanism for enforcing trade and investment sanctions against Cuba. Authorized by the Trading with the Enemy Act of 1917, as amended, the regulations ban all U.S. trade with Cuba, except humanitarian exports licensed at the discretion of the U.S. Department of Treasury. Violations of the Cuban embargo are punishable by civil and criminal penalties.

**cultural derogation.**    An exemption of cultural industries from liberalized trade provisions of an international agreement, usually on the grounds that a country has a special interest in regulating the artifacts embodying its cultural traditions. The Canada-U.S. Free Trade Agreement excepts art, book publishing, films, music, television, and similar genre from liberalized trade and subjects foreign investments in cultural industries to review by Investment Canada.

**cum.**    Latin: with, i.e, indicating a right conferred on a buyer. For example, a bond sold "cum coupon" denotes the buyer's right to collect the next interest payment due. Compare *ex*.

**cur.**    The abbreviation for current and currency.

**currency (cur.).**    Any mixture of coins, paper money, or bank notes. In broad terms, currency is a medium used to settle financial transactions.

**currency adjustment factor.**    In international finance, a foreign exchange surcharge added to the cost of a loan to compensate a lender for exchange rate fluctuations.

**currency area.**    A group of countries where local currencies are pegged to the strongest foreign currency, e.g., the Australian Dollar Area and the French Franc Zone.

**currency band.**    The range of prices in which currencies move in relation to reference currencies. In the international floating-exchange-rate system, the Deutsche mark, Japanese yen, and U.S. dollar are the base exchange rate units for currency markets. Central banks intervene in international currency markets to maintain relative alignments of these currencies.

**currency basket.**    A basket of currencies, or the basis for fixing the value of an artificial currency unit. A basket consists of constituent currencies that maintain relatively stable market values. The value of a basket changes as the prices of its constituent currencies fluctuate against one another. See also *numeraire system.*

**currency board.**    An institution that issues domestic bank notes backed by reserve assets. The bank notes are exchanged at fixed rates of interest. A currency board does not accept deposits or issue bonds, notes, or other debt instruments. Unlike central banks, currency boards do not use debt monetization to manage reserve assets.

**currency exposure.**    The difference between debts owed in one currency and liquid assets held in another when a transaction is settled in more than one currency. Debtors are exposed if their assets are priced in a currency of undetermined value at closing. If a debtor sells assets to pay a debt, proceeds may be lower than the face amount of the debt. See also *exposure* and *hedge.*

**currency option.**    See *option.*

**currency risk.**    See *country risk.*

**currency spread.**    The range within which several currencies fluctuate before a government intervenes. When currency swings occur, usually as a result of speculation, governments intervene in currency markets to stabilize exchange rates and restore equilibrium to the international financial system.

**currency swap.**    The exchange of one currency for another. Currency swaps often enable companies to dispose of excess holdings in one currency or obtain lower interest rates on loans. When the swap involves exchanging a fixed-rate debt in one currency for a floating debt in another, the exchange is called a cross-currency swap.

**currency transaction report.**    See *laundered money.*

**currency warrant.**    An option coupon attached to some securities permitting a holder to purchase additional securities in a different currency. The coupon is detachable and priced according to terms set by the issue.

**current account.**    1. An account maintained by an individual or organization with a bank or savings and loan association. Withdrawals by check or electronic debit are made from funds deposited in the account. Depending on the bank and the juris-diction in which it operates, interest may be paid on current accounts. Customers are sometimes charged a fee for each transaction, or the fee may be waived when a specified balance is maintained. 2. The internal accounts of an organization reflecting receipts and expenditures. See also *cashflow.* 3. The accounts showing a country's current account deficit or current account surplus.

**current account deficit.**    A negative balance in a country's annual income from all foreign sources and obligations payable on foreign accounts. See also *balance of payments.*

**current account purchases.**    A factor in computing a nation's gross national product (GNP). The factor measures the value of manufacturing inputs in relation to domestic production. Current account purchases, also known as intermediate products, are included in GNP to avoid undervaluing national net worth. Current account purchases do not include inventory, which is the sum of goods stocked for sale or consumption.

**current account surplus.**    A positive balance in a country's annual income from all foreign sources and foreign obligations payable on foreign accounts. See also *balance of payments.*

**current yield (cy).**    The annual interest earned on a bond. The interest rate is the difference between the coupon rate and the bond's original purchase price. Current yield reflects annual changes in a bond's financial value. Compare *yield: yield to maturity.*

**CUSDEC.**    The acronym for customs declaration message.

**cushion.**    1. In finance, a reserve account maintained by a bank or corporation to cover bad debts or unanticipated expenses. 2. In investments, the period between the date a security is issued and the earliest call date, providing an investor with call protection.

**cushion bond.**    A bond with a call option minimizing the difference between the higher coupon price and the market price. The issuer can redeem a cushion bond at a call price lower than the coupon price.

**CUSIP number.**    In the United States, a number provided by the American Bankers Association's

Committee on Uniform Securities Identification Procedures (CUSIP), which identifies U.S. securities issued in book-entry or certificate form. CUSIP numbers for stocks and bonds are alphanumeric; i.e., they are composed of seven digits and two letters. Since 1989, foreign securities have been identified in the United States by a nine-digit number known as CINS, or the CUSIP International Numbering System.

**CUSRES.**    The acronym for customs response message.

**customary freight unit.**    See *Carriage of Goods by Sea Act of 1936*.

**customer.**    A person or firm that purchases goods or services from a company in the regular course of trade. Compare *client*.

**customhouse.**    A government building designated as the site for collecting duties and clearing ships for port entry or departure.

**customhouse broker.**    A private agent licensed by a government to clear imports through customs. In the United States, customhouse brokers are licensed by the U.S. Customs Service and must have power of attorney to clear imports on a principal's behalf.

**customs.**    See *customs authority*.

**Customs and Economic Union of Central Africa.**    See *Communauté Économique des États de l'Afrique Centrale*.

**Customs & Excise.**    A common term for the customs authority in English-speaking countries.

**Customs and Trade Act of 1990.**    In the United States, a statute authorizing the U.S. Customs Service to collect fees from users of the Automated Commercial System. The act also increased federal regulation of logging on public lands when the wood is for export.

**customs audit.**    1. The initial step in customs clearance to determine an import's eligibility for immediate release. In some instances, further examination or inspection is required before clearance. 2. In the United States, an import or export transaction review by the Office of Regulatory Audit, an agency of the U.S. Customs Service. The audits are designed to protect federal revenues and ensure compliance with U.S. customs laws. 3.

In international trade, a firm's internal controls to prevent violations of customs laws. In the United States, periodic updates are presented to customs audit teams during compliance audits.

**customs authority.**    A government agency authorized to clear imports and exports and collect duties, taxes, and trade data. Customs agents inspect and classify imports and exports, enforce local port laws, and exercise police powers to prevent illegal trade.

**customs bond.**    A contract assuring payment of duties, taxes, and fees. The contract must be in writing and inscribed with the witnessed signatures of the parties. The usual parties to a bond are the principal, the beneficiary, and the surety.

**customs broker.**    See *customhouse broker*.

**customs broker fee.**    A commission paid to a customhouse broker for preparing documents, certifying a bill of lading, and clearing goods through customs. The fee is based on a minimum bulk weight with an additional charge for tonnage in excess of the minimum weight.

**customs classification.**    See *classification*.

**customs clearing agent.**    See *customhouse broker*.

**Customs Cooperation Council (CCC).**    An international agency established in 1950 to administer the Brussels Tariff Nomenclature, also known as the Customs Cooperation Council Nomenclature. A newer classification system, the Harmonized Commodity Description and Coding System, was developed by CCC and implemented in some countries in 1988. A research and advisory body, CCC provides technical assistance to the General Agreement on Tariffs and Trade, regional customs unions, and countries harmonizing national tariff classification systems under the Kyoto Convention on the Simplification and Harmonization of Customs Procedures.

**Customs Cooperation Council Nomenclature.**    See *Brussels Tariff Nomenclature*.

**Customs Court.**    See *U.S. Court of International Trade*.

**customs declaration.**    A traveler's verification of imported items. In the United States, declarations are required for articles imported for personal use. U.S. declarations are made on Form 6059B, available in Chinese, Dutch, English, French, German, Italian, Japanese, Korean, Polish, Portuguese, Russian, and Spanish. See also *informal entry*.

**Customs Declaration Message (CUSDEC).** With the Customs Response Message, the portion of Electronic Data Interchange for Administration, Commerce, and Transportation dedicated to the U.S. Customs Service.

**customs document processing station.** Special customs offices where inland ground in-bond shipments are processed.

**customs duty.** See *duty*.

**customs enforcement area.** The zone within which a national customs service exercises its legal authority. Customs enforcement zones extend offshore beyond customs waters. In the United States, the customs enforcement area is limited to 50 miles beyond customs waters. U.S. laws are enforced in the zone when the President finds that ships operating in the area are in violation of U.S. law.

**customs entry.** The process of meeting regulatory requirements for importation. Imports are deemed entered when (1) cargo has arrived at the port of entry, (2) documents are processed, (3) imports are valued, and (4) duties and taxes are paid. Customs entry is preceded by a customs audit. In the United States, evidence of the right to make entry must be established. Only attorneys or licensed brokers are authorized to enter imports. Otherwise an importer must grant power of attorney to a customhouse broker. The entry process begins when a carrier's certificate is submitted at the port of entry. If the carrier's certificate is unavailable, an airway bill, bill of lading, other evidence of title, or simple possession of goods may be used to establish the right to make entry. Customs documents are submitted, including a commercial invoice, certificate of origin, entry manifest, special permits, and license applications. Imports must be claimed within a specific period of time, normally within 5 to 10 days of arrival. Unless an extension is granted, unclaimed goods are warehoused, usually under a general order for up to 1 year. In the United States, an entry summary is filed for commercial imports. Items exceeding a statutory limit in value and not imported for personal use are known as formal entries, which require customs classification, valuation, and often inspection. Items imported for personal use (or commercial imports not valued in excess of the statutory limit) are known as informal entries and are cleared under simplified procedures. Informal entries usually involve simple examinations of declaration forms or commercial invoices. The most common formal entries are:

*consumption entry.* An article of commercial value entered for sale. Finished products, manufacturing components, and natural ingredients subject to further processing are entered for consumption. Consumption entries are dutiable according to the product's tariff classification.

*transportation/exportation (T/E) entry.* Imports admitted for reexport. T/E imports are nondutiable. See also *carnet*.

*warehouse entry.* Imports admitted for storage. In most jurisdictions, goods may be warehoused for up to 5 years and repackaged in a warehouse. A warehouse receipt or warrant is produced before goods are released. Warehoused entries are not dutiable when reexported.

**customs invoice.** An invoice required in addition to a commercial invoice. The customs invoice covers information that is requested by an importing country but that is not contained in the commercial invoice.

**Customs Modernization Act of 1991.** In the United States, a law to conform customs procedures to the requirements of electronic data interchange. The act eliminates mandatory paper filings for customs entries.

**customs of the port.** The cargo- and document-handling procedures characteristic of a given port. Customs of the port normally affect local court decisions. For example, a legal action against a carrier or customs broker may be decided based on local port practices.

**customs of the trade.** Practices common to an industry that form the accepted standard of conduct in a given trade. Where statutory or regulatory guidelines are not available, courts often consider customs of the trade when deciding legal disputes.

**customs rate.** See *customs valuation*.

**Customs Reform and Simplification Act of 1978.** In the United States, a law which, among other things, authorizes the U.S. Customs Service to seize and dispose of imports bearing counterfeit trademarks. Imports stripped of false marks are donated to charities or sold at public auctions. When false marks cannot be removed, imports are destroyed.

**Customs Response Message.** See *Customs Declaration Message.*

**Customs Service.** See *U.S. Customs Service.*

**customs tariff.** A document issued by a country listing dutiable items, the rate of duty applied, and products subject to quotas or eligible for duty preferences. 1. A general-column tariff, also known as a unilinear tariff, applies the same rate to all imports within a given product classification, irrespective of the country of origin. 2. A multiple-column tariff contains preferential tariffs and applies different rates of duty to imports depending on the country of origin. Multiple rates are used by countries belonging to customs unions, free trade areas, or common markets or by industrialized countries granting trade preferences to developing countries. 3. A single-column tariff applies a single rate of duty for all imports, irrespective of product classification or country of origin.

**customs territory.** An area claimed by a country in order to control the flow of goods within its borders. A customs territory includes a nation's geographical area, possessions, and customs waters. Customs territory is not synonymous, however, with sovereignty. For example, foreign trade zones are outside the customs (but not the sovereign) territory of the country where they are located. Similarly, the U.S. Virgin Islands are outside the customs territory of the United States and the British Virgin Islands are outside that of the United Kingdom.

**customs union.** A form of economic association that arises when two or more countries eliminate internal duties, share uniform customs tariffs, and impose common duties on nonmember countries.

**customs valuation.** The process of allocation and appraisal whereby an import's economic value is determined, so that import duties and taxes can be paid. In countries adhering to the Customs Valuation Code adopted by the Tokyo Round of the General Agreement on Tariffs and Trade, an import's value is the transaction price recorded on the commercial invoice or customs declaration form plus adjustments. In the United States, when transaction value is inappropriate for customs valuation, deductive value or computed value is used. See also *Trade Agreements Act of 1979.*

**Customs Valuation Code.** See *General Agreement on Tariffs and Trade: Tokyo Round.*

**customs waters.** An area of the high seas over which a nation asserts sovereignty. National police agencies are authorized to board, inspect, or seize vessels or contraband in customs waters. In the United States, customs waters extend to 12 miles beyond the U.S. shoreline. See also *customs territory* and *territorial waters.*

**CVD.** The abbreviation for countervailing duty.

**CWO.** The abbreviation for cash with order and check with order.

**CXL.** The abbreviation for canceled order.

**CXT.** The abbreviation for common external tariff.

**CY.** The abbreviation for current yield.

**CZ.** The abbreviation for Canal Zone. See *Panama Canal Zone.*

# D

**D/A.** The abbreviation for documents against acceptance.

**DAF.** The abbreviation for delivered at frontier.

**dahir.** A royal decree in Morocco.

**DAI.** The abbreviation for *derechos arancelarios de importación*.

**daily hire.** A fee charged by a vessel owner for each day a ship is under charter.

**Dairy Export Incentive Program (DEIP).** In the United States, a farm price-support program sponsored by the U.S Department of Agriculture. DEIP bonuses approved by the Commercial Credit Corporation (CCC) are paid to enable domestic dairy farmers to sell milk, cheese, and butter in foreign markets. The value of the bonus is computed by multiplying the CCC-approved amount by net exports.

**dalasi.** The currency of Gambia.

**damaged goods.** Defective, impaired, spoiled, or otherwise nonconforming goods delivered to a buyer. Normally, the buyer may return defective goods to the seller and seek a refund of the purchase price, require repairs or substitute goods, or pursue legal remedies for breach of contract or breach of warranty. Under the United Nations Convention on Contracts for the International Sale of Goods, a buyer is obligated to give notice of nonconforming goods and permit the seller to remedy the situation. If the seller refuses, the buyer is permitted to reduce the purchase price in an amount equal to the reduced value of the nonconforming goods.

**damage-free car.** A railroad car modified to protect fragile or easily damaged cargoes and equipped with adjustable bulkheads, flexible frames, and cushions. Damage-free cars are used when sensitive equipment or products are shipped.

**damages.** Restitution awarded by a court for injury or loss. The amount of the award is decided by a jury or a judge within guidelines prescribed by precedent or statute. 1. Compensatory damages are based on actual losses suffered and are intended to restore injured parties to the position they were in before a wrongful act occurred. 2. Exemplary damages are punitive damages designed to punish a wrongdoer for malicious or fraudulent acts. Punitive damages are often awarded in tort and product-liability cases. 3. General damages need not be specifically claimed, but are awarded because a wrongful act caused injury. 4. Liquidated damages are fixed in advance by agreement between parties to a contract. 5. Nominal damages are awarded when a victim suffers real but inconsequential injury. 6. Special damages, also known as specific damages, arise from the particular circumstances of a case and must be claimed and proved by an injured party. 7. Statutory damages are prescribed by law and are awarded in the amount set forth by statute.

**D&O.** The abbreviation for directors and officers.

**dandy note.** In the United Kingdom, a release order authorizing the discharge of goods from a bonded warehouse. The goods are released for export at the order of the owner. Release orders must be verified by Customs and Excise.

**dangerous article tariff.** See *dangerous goods.*

**dangerous goods.** The term used by the International Maritime Organization in the Dangerous Goods Code to identify cargo requiring special handling. Combustible (or implosive) materials and inherently dangerous instruments fall in this category. Common carriers charge a higher rate, called a dangerous article tariff, to transport dangerous goods. See also *hazardous cargo.*

**dango.** In Japan, the practice of awarding contracts to affiliated or otherwise favored firms.

**Danube Commission.** A consultative organization founded in Belgrade in 1948 to regulate and oversee navigation between the Danube and the Black Sea. The Danube Commission guarantees open navigation of the waterways and sets standards for customs, harbor and navigation fees, and pollution control. Danube commission members are Austria, Bulgaria, Hungary, Romania, and representatives of the former Czechoslovakia, U.S.S.R., and Yugoslavia. Since 1957, the former Federal Republic of Germany (West Germany) has been an observer at the Danube Commission's proceedings. The commission has headquarters in Budapest.

**DAT.** The abbreviation for dangerous articles tariff. See *dangerous goods*.

**data element.** Information units entered into a computer. The data element comprises a record or file in an electronic data interchange system.

**data freight receipt.** A document that contains the details of a straight consignment and names the consignee. This receipt is sometimes issued by telex in lieu of a bill of lading. Data freight receipts are not negotiable and cannot be used to transfer title to goods.

**data plate.** A notice affixed to an intermodal container, identifying the shipper and the container's manufacturer. The notice is required for ocean shipping containers by the International Convention for Safe Containers. See also *manufacturer's particulars.*

**data protection.** Measures adopted by a government to protect confidential information stored in computer systems. Data protection laws prevent unauthorized disclosures of personal information. Some forms of confidential business information are also protected.

**date draft.** A demand draft payable at a specified time, irrespective of its acceptance date.

**dated security.** A stock with a fixed redemption date.

**date for value determination.** The date used by customs authorities to fix the value of imports for duty determinations. Duties are based on the value of goods at the time goods are shipped. Deteriorations in value from shrinkage or other causes are not factors in customs valuation.

**date of record.** See *record date.*

**DAX.** See *Frankfürter Wertpapierbörse Aktiengesellschaft.*

**day loan.** A bank loan by brokers for morning securities purchases. Securities purchased with day loans can be pledged in the afternoon for brokers' call loans.

**day order.** An order to a broker to buy or sell a specific quantity of stock or commodities at a fixed price. If not filled, the order is automatically canceled at the close of the trading day.

**days of grace.** See *grace period.*

**day trade.** Buying and selling a futures contract or an options contract on the same day.

**DB.** The abbreviation for development bank.

**dba.** The abbreviation for doing business as.

**DC.** The abbreviation for developing country, deviation clause, and dutiable charge.

**DCAA.** The abbreviation for Defense Contract Audit Agency.

**DCF.** The abbreviation for discounted cashflow.

**DCL.** The abbreviation for designated consultation level and discretionary credit limit. See *Foreign Credit Insurance Association.*

**D/D.** The abbreviation for days after delivery, days after draft, delivered, delayed delivery, demand draft, and district director.

**DDP.** The abbreviation for delivered duty paid.

**DDU.** The abbreviation for delivered duty unpaid.

**D/E.** The abbreviation for date of exportation.

**dead freight.** The minimum rate charged by a carrier for transporting a shipment too small to fill a vessel's total cargo capacity. The fee is based on the tariff that would have been earned had the carrier been filled to capacity.

**deadweight cargo.** A shipping charge based on weight rather than volume.

**deadweight tonnage.** A craft's maximum capacity for hauling cargo and transporting passengers, a crew, supplies, and water.

**dealers.** Traders who buy and sell for their personal accounts. Unlike brokers, who are commission agents, a dealer buys as a principal and attempts to profit from the spread between the selling price and the purchase price in a given transaction. See also *market maker.*

**dealing rates.** See *Bank of England dealing rate.*

**dear money.** The British equivalent of tight money. Dear money denotes a period of restrictive monetary policy, i.e., a central bank using reserve requirements or other regulatory measures to discourage commercial lending. The effect spreads through a national economy, making consumers reluctant to spend and businesses slow to invest.

**deb., deben.**   The abbreviation for debenture.

**debasement.**   Real depreciation in a currency's market value. A national currency is depreciated in real terms when it is untied from a reference commodity, such as gold, or when its precious metal content is reduced. A currency is also debased when the quantity of money in circulation exceeds the value of goods and services sold. Compare *devaluation*.

**debenture (deb., deben.).**   Debt paper issued by a company to obtain a loan. Most debentures are redeemable on a fixed date at a specified interest rate. In the United States, debentures are usually unsecured, backed only by the credit of the issuer, and issued under a deed of trust or an indenture. In the United Kingdom, most debentures are secured by the issuer's assets. Unsecured debentures are known as naked debentures. Debentures may be redeemed at a premium, although convertible debentures can be exchanged for common stock at a fixed price. Interest on debentures is paid before dividends are distributed to shareholders.

**debenture stock.**   Also called loan stock, the British term for convertible debentures.

**debt conversion program (DCP).**   In an indebted country, an external debt management program. Beginning in the 1970s, a number of countries in Africa and Latin America accumulated excessive debts and later sought debt relief from official and commercial creditors. Some Western countries (notably France) unilaterally forgave significant sums of bilateral debt. Official debt restructurings are supervised by the Paris Club; commercial renegotiations are conducted by the London Club. The World Bank and International Monetary Fund participate in restructurings by providing financing and technical assistance on conditional terms. The United Nations Conference on Trade and Development (UNCTAD) has developed an electronic system to help indebted countries formulate adequate debt reduction programs. UNCTAD's electronic system is called the Debt Management and Financial Analysis System.

Typically, commercial debt conversion programs involve one or more of the following debt reduction techniques:

*buyback.*   An indebted country purchases its debt from a bank creditor or on the secondary market. The country buys back the loan documents in its own currency at fair market value, which may be substantially below the discounted price received by the bank in a secondary-market sale.

*debt-for-bond swap.*   An indebted country's central bank issues long-term bonds, called stabilization bonds, in exchange for its discounted debt. The bonds may be backed by a creditor country's bonds. Repayment of principal and interest are guaranteed by a creditor country or by the IMF.

*debt-for-equity swap.*   An indebted country trades equity in state-owned assets, usually a public utility or commodity stock, for discounted debt paper. The debt is purchased in the country's local currency. Purchasers of equity for debt usually require guarantees against future nationalization of their investments and clear guidelines for capital repatriation. See also *debt for equity* (q.v.).

*debt-for-nature swap.*   See *debt swap*.

*debt swap.*   Discounted debt paper is sold by a bank to a third party and converted into the debtor's local currency. The converted debt is invested in nonprofit or commercial ventures. In debt-for-nature swaps, funds are invested in local environmental programs. See also *rescheduling*.

**debt for equity.**   The purchase of long-term debt, usually at a discount, in exchange for equity. Debt-for-equity swaps can be used as a part of a heavily indebted country's debt conversion program, by private firms seeking to reduce indebtedness, or as a part of a privatization program converting nationalized industries.

**Debt Management and Financial Analysis System.**   See *debt conversion program*.

**debt monetization.**   The use of public debt offerings to increase a country's money supply. Debt is monetized when a central bank purchases its own bills or bonds. The proceeds become reserve funds for depository banks, which are able to expand the supply of money and consumer credit.

**debtor nation.**   1. A country whose external debt exceeds its foreign receivables. Debtor nations have net foreign trade outflows and internal investment deficits. 2. A country with principal and interest arrearages to commercial banks and official lenders. Heavily indebted nations adopt debt conversion programs and request debt reschedulings by commercial and official creditors. See also *debt service ratio*.

**debt overhang.**   The consequence of too much borrowing, which leaves the debtor with a high debt service ratio in relation to income.

**debt rescheduling.**   See *rescheduling*.

**debt service ratio (DSR).**   1. In finance, the proportion of income to debts that determines a borrower's ability to repay a loan after other obligations have been met. 2. In international trade, a country's export income relative to its annual external debt payments, including principal and interest. See also *debtor nation*.

**debt swap.**   See *debt conversion program*.

**debt-to-equity ratio.**   The proportion of convertible assets to debt. In corporate finance, the ratio of shares (when liquidated) to debt obligations.

**DEC.**   The abbreviation for District Export Council.

**declaracões de despacho.**   Portuguese: customs declaration.

**declaration.**   A formal unsworn statement by a principal. In court cases, declarations are admissible evidence under most circumstances. In import regulation, customs declarations are often accepted in lieu of certificates when third-party certification is impractical.

**declaration day.**   In the United Kingdom, the last day the holder of a stock option is permitted to exercise the claim. Declaration day is 2 days before the account day on which the transaction must be completed.

**Declaration on the Establishment of a New International Economic Order.**   See *new international economic order*.

**declaration of importation.**   A declaration submitted by an importer to a bank, often along with a pro forma invoice and other documents. Import declarations are usually required in countries with foreign exchange controls. A commercial bank forwards the declaration to the central bank, which decides if cargo inspection is required to obtain foreign exchange.

**declaration of origin.**   A variation of the import certificate of origin. For example, South Africa requires that an origin declaration be attached to the commercial invoice in lieu of a certificate of origin. The special declaration form is available from commercial printers.

**declaration of ownership.**   A declaration establishing title to goods or intellectual property. For example, Myanmar (formerly Burma) does not enforce patent and trademark statutes, but a declaration of ownership filed with the Office of the Registrar of Deeds establishes an intellectual property claim protectable by local courts.

**Declaration of Particulars Relating to Customs Value.**   See *Single Administrative Document*.

**declaratory judgment.**   A decision by a common-law court defining the rights of parties in a legal action. The decision is binding, but compliance is not enforced. A declaratory judgment is sought to determine the rights of parties to a dispute.

**deconsolidation.**   The process of dividing a large shipment of goods into smaller lots for transport or sale. Frequently, a shipment is deconsolidated and combined with lots from different shipments. Carriers and freight forwarders normally charge extra fees for deconsolidation services. Compare *consolidation*.

**decree.**   1. A court order that determines the rights of parties in a suit. See also *consent decree*. 2. A sovereign or legislative act having the force of law.

**dedicated service.**   An exclusive carriage contract. The exporter agrees to hire a single carrier for export shipments for a fixed period of time.

**dedicated to a single-use test.**   A method of customs valuation for imported components. The dutiable value of a single-use input is its pro rata value in relation to the finished product.

**deduction at the source.**   A tax collection method whereby one party, usually a corporation, deducts the tax on income paid to another and pays a taxing authority. Both the corporation and the income recipient receive tax credits for deductions at the source. This system is common in Europe where corporations pay an advance tax on distributed dividends and interest. See also *imputation tax system*.

**deductive value.**   A method of customs valuation sometimes used in lieu of transaction value. Deductive value is computed by adjusting an import's selling price. Packing costs are added to the selling price. Administrative expenses, commissions, duties and taxes, further processing costs, profits, and transportation and insurance costs are deducted from the selling price. See also *unit pricing.* Compare *computed value.*

**deed.**    A document of title conveying a seller's interest in property to a buyer. To accomplish a transfer of title, a deed must be signed by the seller, affixed with a seal, and delivered to the buyer or a trustee. See also *quitclaim deed, title, trust deed, and warranty.*

**deed of arrangement.**    In some countries, a transfer of property rights as an alternative to bankruptcy. In the United Kingdom, a debtor may agree to a partial discharge of debt through a process known as a scheme of arrangement. The deed of arrangement verifies the debtor's agreement to a proportional distribution of income and assets to creditors. The deed is filed with the Department of Trade and Industry.

**deed of assignment.**    A document of title transferring property to another. A party may transfer rights to proceeds from a contract, patent, lease, or trust.

**deed of covenant.**    In some countries, a legal document used to receive tax deductions for transfers of income. In the United Kingdom, the taxpayer must pay out income in regular payments. The payments are usually made to a charity. The taxpayer deducts the payments from taxable income at the basic rate.

**deed of trust.**    See *trust deed.*

**deep discount.**    1. In bond trading, a bond discounted at 20 percent or more. Bonds with lengthy maturities carry higher discounts than those with shorter maturities. 2. In finance, the discount on a loan traded in a secondary market at less than its book or acquisition value.

**deep tank.**    A ship designed to transport bulk liquid cargoes.

**def.**    The abbreviation for deferred.

**de facto.**    Latin: in fact, i.e., a legal term denoting a situation arising from the fact of its existence rather than a right conferred by law. For example, a manufacturer selling a high-quality product at a reasonable price may achieve de facto dominance in a market arising from the fact of its conduct in the marketplace. Compare *de jure.*

**defalcation.**    The misappropriation of funds by a fiduciary. A defalcation is a wrongful diversion by a corporate officer or public official in breach of trust.

**default.**    A failure to meet a contractual obligation. In an unsecured transaction, a noteholder or bondholder has legal recourse to accelerate payment on a debt. When the debt is secured, the creditor can foreclose or repossess the borrower's assets.

**defeasance.**    1. In banking, a redemption clause in a loan agreement. The clause allows a debtor to redeem pledged property when the loan is repaid. 2. In bond financing, a means of refinancing debt without redemption on the call date. The issuer pays interest until maturity from assets held in an irrevocable trust. Although interest is paid, the bond liability no longer appears on the issuer's balance sheets. 3. In law, any legal instrument that nullifies another, e.g., a deed or will. In real property law, a defeasance is sometimes called a collateral deed.

**défection.**    French: default.

**defective title.**    1. In commercial law, a title to a negotiable instrument obtained by fraud or other illegal conduct. 2. In real property law, title to property claimed by one whose ownership is subject to the claims of others. Compare *marketable title.*

**Defense Contract Audit Agency (DCAA).**    In the United States, the auditing arm of the U.S. Department of Defense. DCAA also audits contracts for other federal agencies.

**deferred asset.**    A description of an asset from which profit will be realized at a future time. Deferred assets include credits, dividends, income, interest, rents, and royalties scheduled for future receipt. Deferring income by postponing payments and collections delays tax liability. Deferred liabilities include taxes and payments definitely due on a future date. See also *deferred ordinary share.*

**deferred income.**    See *deferred asset.*

**deferred liability.**    See *deferred asset.*

**deferred ordinary share.**    In the United Kingdom, common stock on which dividends are remitted after all other dividends are paid or after a fixed number of years. Deferred ordinary shares may entitle a shareholder to substantial profit or to the same dividend distributed to other shareholders.

**deferred payment credit.**   See *credit.*

**deferred tax accounting.**   An accounting method in which funds are allocated and deposited in separate accounts for tax payments covering prior or future tax periods. Deferred tax accounting is used when current accounts reflect a difference between capital allocations and claimed depreciation expenses. The discrepancy arises when tax-reporting rules and accounting conventions differ.

**deficiency judgment.**   A court order instructing a creditor to collect part of a debt by foreclosing on assets or repossessing property. Creditors seek deficiency judgments when a debtor's assets are valued below the book value of a debt.

**deficiency payment.**   A subsidy authorized under an agricultural price-support program. The amount of the subsidy is determined by the difference between the market price of a commodity and its official floor price. The differential is paid by the government to commodity producers. See also *subsidy.*

**definitive securities.**   In the United States, a security evidenced by a certificate. Many securities are issued as electronic book entries without paper documents.

**deflation.**   A trough in the business cycle, i.e., a decrease in the average price levels of goods and services. See also *recession* and *tight money.*

**deg.**   The abbreviation for degree.

**DEG.**   The acronym for *Deutsche Gesellschaft für Wirtschaftliche Zusammenarbeit.* See *official development assistance.*

**deindustrialization.**   A decline in a nation's manufacturing productivity and output. The decline can result from poor labor relations, inadequate capital investment, or a short-term management bias. Government polices can also contribute to misallocated resources and poor national investment strategies.

**de inspecteur der invoerrechten en accijnzen.** Dutch: inspector of customs and excise.

**DEIP.**   The abbreviation for Dairy Export Incentive Program.

**de jure.**   Latin: in law. A legal term denoting the existence of a legal right. Compare *de facto.*

**del.**   The abbreviation for deliver and delivery.

**del credere agent.**   A sales agent who assumes the credit risk of a principal. These agents finance a manufacturer's sales or guarantee payment if a buyer fails to pay.

**delincuencia organizada.**   Spanish: a criminal organization. A *delincuencia organizada* is one engaged in illegal narcotic or contraband traffic.

**delivered duty paid (DDP).**   An international commercial term (INCOTERM). The seller makes all arrangements and pays all costs, including duties, to a named foreign destination. The buyer pays all subsequent costs. See also *duty paid.*

**delivered duty unpaid (DDU).**   An international commercial term (INCOTERM). The seller makes all arrangements and pays all costs to a named foreign destination. The buyer pays duties and all subsequent costs.

**delivered price.**   A term of sale. The seller pays all costs to a destination point.

**delivered weight.**   A price adjustment term. The seller discounts the invoice price to compensate for shrinkage or deterioration in the volume of goods.

**delivery (D/y).**   1. The process of presenting a negotiable instrument for payment. 2. The transfer of commodities or securities to the purchaser.

**delivery month (D/M).**   In futures trading, the period designated in a contract for physical delivery of a commodity.

**delivery notice (D/N).**   An official notice issued by the clearinghouse of a trading exchange that a commodity will be delivered according to the terms of a contract.

**delivery order (D/O).**   A manufacturer's order specifying the type, quantity, and quality of goods ordered and the delivery site.

**delivery point (D/P).**   In commodities trading, a site designated by an exchange for delivery and tender of goods.

**Delors Report.**   Officially known as the *Report on Economic and Monetary Union in the European Community,* a 1989 report recommending the creation of a single currency and a unified central bank in the European Community. The report was issued by a committee chaired by Jacques Delors of France, the president of the European Commission. The report's recommendations were substantially adopted in the Treaty of Maastricht in 1992.

**delta.**  In options trading, the value of a change in the premium paid for a contract in relation to equivalent changes in the price of an underlying contract. The change in the contract price reflects fluctuations in gamma, i.e., a change in the price of the reference commodity. The delta is positive or negative, depending on whether the trader holds a bullish or bearish position. A delta is roughly equivalent to 0.5 in an at-the-money option, 1 in an in-the-money option, and zero in an out-of-the-money option.

**delta stocks.**  See *Stock Exchange Automated Quotations System.*

**demain-après.**  French: tomorrow-next, i.e., a two-day transaction.

**demand draft.**  A check or bill of exchange payable at sight.

**demise.**  See *bareboat charter.*

**demurrage.**  1. A penalty paid by a charterer for exceeding lay time, or the time allotted for loading and unloading goods from a ship. 2. Extra storage charges when goods are not removed from a warehouse at the time specified in a warehouse contract. Compare *dispatch.*

**Department of External Affairs (DEA).**  In Canada, the foreign trade bureau, also known as External Affairs and International Trade Canada. DEA negotiates international trade treaties and implements national trade policy. The department was created in 1982 as a successor to the Department of Industry, Trade and Commerce. Its counterpart in the United States is the Office of the U.S. Trade Representative. The Department of Trade and Industry performs similar functions in the United Kingdom. Compare *Industry, Science and Technology Canada.*

**Department of National Savings.**  In the United Kingdom, a government agency that administers savings programs, including the National Savings Stock Register. Unlike Bank of England Register share earnings, taxes on National Savings Register securities are paid after income is received on investments. Taxes on earnings from Bank of England Register shares are treated as deductions at the source.

**Department of Trade and Industry (DTI).**  In the United Kingdom, an executive department that enforces competition and consumer protection laws, manages international trade policy, and regulates the domestic insurance industry. DTI also oversees the British Patent Office and implements laws concerning the formation and operation of companies.

**dependent territories.**  See *non-self-governing territory* and *overseas countries and territories.*

**déport.**  French: discount.

**deposit.**  1. Funds placed in the custody of a bank or savings and loan. The depositor can normally withdraw funds up to the amount of the deposit, less bank service charges. Interest is earned on deposits placed in interest-bearing deposit accounts. 2. Funds paid by a buyer as security to preserve a purchase option or as the first payment on an installment contract. In securities transactions, deposits are paid by clients to brokers to cover potential trading losses.

**deposit account.**  1. A bank account from which funds cannot be withdrawn without prior notice to the bank. In the United States, deposit accounts are known as interest-bearing deposit accounts. Interest is paid at the deposit interest rate or an unregulated market rate. Ceilings on deposit interest rates were eliminated in 1986. 2. Money-market deposit accounts authorized in the United States by the Garn–St. Germain Depository Institutions Act of 1982. These deposit accounts have no interest rate ceiling. Compare *negotiable order of withdrawal account.*

**depositary.**  A bank or commercial firm authorized to hold funds or securities as a third-party fiduciary. Compare *depository.*

**depositary receipt.**  A document issued by a financial institution holding securities for the benefit of a third party. See also *American depositary receipt* and *International depositary receipt.*

**deposit bond.**  In the United Kingdom, a national savings bond. Deposit bonds offer premium interest on investments in specified denominations. Taxes on interest earned from deposit bonds are reported by the taxpayer. Compare *deduction at the source.*

**deposition.**   A written record of a witness's oral responses to questions posed by a lawyer in a legal action. Depositions can be limited to discovering information in a meeting or can be entered as evidence at a trial.

**deposit note.**   In the United States, a federally insured security issued by a bank and exempt from federal registration. Deposit notes are usually purchased by institutional investors, although some are issued in small denominations and sold to individual investors. The notes mature in 2 to 5 years and pay a fixed interest rate on a 360-day basis.

**depository.**   A bank authorized to accept deposits of private and public funds and hold securities by agreement with the owner. See also *licensed deposit taker.* Compare *depositary.*

**Depository Trust Company (DTC).**   In the United States, a New York corporation that holds securities certificates for Wall Street brokerage firms. DTC maintains computerized records of transfers and registrations, thereby reducing physical transfers of securities certificates. The firm settles brokerage firm accounts daily for members of the National Securities Clearing Corporation.

**depósitos francos.**   Portuguese: bonded (free) trade zones.

**dépôt.**   French: deposit.

**depreciation.**   A diminution in the economic value of an asset. 1. In currency markets, a decline in the market price of a currency, which adversely affects a holder's purchasing power. 2. In accounting, a decline in the value of business assets due to wear and tear. An equivalent amount is charged off as a loss in a company's profit and loss statement. When diminishing-value depreciation is used, a base percentage is applied to the reduced value of an asset in the first year. In subsequent years, progressively lower percentages are deducted, each reduced by accumulated depreciations. When straight-line depreciation is used, an equal percentage of the cost of an asset is allocated over each year of its service. The diminishing-value method better approximates the actual loss in an asset's value over its useful life. See also *accelerated depreciation.* Compare *amortization.*

**depression.**   A deep and prolonged recession. More severe than ordinary business-cycle troughs, depressions are characterized by high levels of unemployment, deflation, and panicky runs on bank deposits. They seem to recur periodically, usually after a financial collapse, such as the Wall Street crash in 1929. Following the Great Depression of the 1930s, Western governments generally pursued Keynesian economic policies and instituted programs to avert depressions, e.g., bank deposit insurance, social security, etc. In the United States, the Glass-Steagall Act of 1933 was enacted to prevent commercial banks from putting depositors' funds at risk by engaging in investment banking activities. See also *Kondratieff cycle.*

**DEQ.**   The abbreviation for delivered ex quay (duty paid).

**derechos arancelarios de importación.**   See *Nomenclatura Arancelaria Uniforme Centroamericana II.*

**deregulation.**   The process of minimizing government control over an economic sector. In theory, deregulated markets are the most efficient allocators of capital and other resources. However, some government intervention is accepted in most national economies, particularly where monopolies are licensed by government agencies in the public interest.

**derivative product.**   In banking and finance, any one of several contracts used to hedge against changes in the price of an underlying asset. Derivative products include foreign exchange and interest-rate futures and swaps, as well as commodity and equity contracts.

**derogation.**   An official notice from a nation that it will not adhere to a specific annex, protocol, or provision of an international agreement.

**DES.**   The abbreviation for delivered ex ship.

**designated consultation level (DCL).**   A negotiated quota on a class of textile imports reached by agreement between nations. The quota can be altered following a call for consultations by either party. See also *bilateral restraint agreement, guaranteed access level,* and *MultiFiber Arrangement Regarding International Trade in Textiles.*

**despatch.** See *dispatch.*

**destination clause.** A contract provision that specifies a destination for a shipment. Destination clauses often appear in contracts for the sale of cartel-controlled commodities. The clause prevents diversions of commodities, thereby reducing the availability of supplies and protecting the price set by the cartel.

**destination control statement.** In the United States, a document issued to prevent diversions of U.S. exports to unauthorized destinations. When a destination control statement is issued, air waybills, bills of lading, and commercial invoices display notices that export licenses are valid for specified consignees.

**Deutsches Institut für Normen.** See *DIN.*

**Deutsche mark (DM).** The currency of Germany.

**devaluation.** 1. In a fixed-exchange-rate system, an adjustment in the value of a currency to restructure a country's balance of trade. 2. In the contemporary floating-exchange-rate system, the realignment of a currency's exchange rate in relation to other currencies. A de facto devaluation occurs when a central bank fails to buy enough of its currency or raise interest rates high enough to reduce the effects of a sell-off by speculators. When a currency is devalued, the country's exports become more competitive, but its holders become poorer relative to other purchasers. Compare *debasement.*

**developed country.** See *industrialized country.*

**developing country (DC).** One of a group of low- to middle-income countries, located primarily in the Southern Hemisphere. Some developing countries have abundant natural resources, but all are characterized by modest levels of skilled labor and limited financial and infrastructure resources. Most developing countries are dependent on primary products for export income, usually commodities or simple manufactures. When prices fall for primary commodities relative to import prices for other products, developing countries tend to accumulate large balance-of-payments deficits. Developing countries, collectively called the Third World, include most of Africa, Asia, and Latin America. See also *newly industrialized country.*

**development bank (DB).** A government-owned bank that provides financial and technical assistance to official agencies for economic growth and development. A development bank can be global (World Bank Group), regional (African Development Bank Group), or national (Japan Development Bank). The activities of development banks are financed by government subscriptions and/or from capital raised in international money markets. Development banks normally have a soft-loan window for lending to the poorest countries on concessional terms.

**Development Bank Trust Funds.** In the United States, a program administered by the U.S. Trade and Development Program that finances consulting studies. The program funds grants for projects sponsored by the African Development Bank, the International Finance Corporation, and the World Bank, primarily for feasibility studies undertaken by U.S. consultants in Africa. The trust fund financing is available for projects that increase U.S. exports.

**Development Committee.** A committee of the International Monetary Fund (IMF) established in 1974 as the Joint Ministerial Committee of the Boards of Governors of the Bank and the Fund on the Transfer of Real Resources to Developing Countries. The committee consists of 22 members, usually finance ministers, and advises the IMF on the resources and needs of developing countries. See also *Group of Twenty-Four.* Compare *Interim Committee.*

**development finance company (DFC).** A nonprofit developing country corporation created under the auspices of the World Bank. The corporations finance investments in private-sector development from funds provided largely by multilateral lenders. Loans to DFCs are based on currency baskets tied to the Deutsche mark, Japanese yen, Swiss franc, and U.S. dollar.

**deviation.** A limitation on a carrier's defenses when cargo is damaged or lost. A carrier is ordinarily liable for direct losses or damage when a ship departs from an agreed trade route or course of conduct during a voyage. See also *Carriage of Goods by Sea Act of 1936.*

**devisen.** 1. A short-term negotiable instrument. 2. German: foreign exchange.

**Devisenkassamarkt.** German: spot foreign exchange market.

**Devisenmarkt.** German: foreign exchange market.

**Devisenterminmarkt.** German: forward foreign exchange market.

**devises.** French: foreign exchange.

**DFC.** The abbreviation for development finance corporation.

**DFP.** The abbreviation for duty-free port. See *foreign trade zone.*

**dft.** The abbreviation for draft.

**DFZ.** The abbreviation for duty-free zone. See *foreign trade zone.*

**DG.** The abbreviation for *directeur général.* See *managing director.*

**D.I.A.N.E.** The acronym for Direct Information Access Network.

**dies non.** Latin: nonbusiness day.

**differential duty.** See *duty.*

**differential exchange rate system.** A system of foreign exchange management used by a country with persistent balance-of-payments deficits. Foreign exchange is allocated under a two-tier system, which ascribes a higher value to activities that yield additional foreign exchange. A lower value is assigned to nonessential expenditures, such as consumer imports. See also *dual-exchange market.*

**differential rate.** A carrier's charge when the through rate to a destination has not been established. The differential rate is based on the cost of transporting goods by way of several intermediate points.

**differentiated marketing.** See *differentiated product line.*

**differentiated product line.** A line of like, but variegated, products offered by a single manufacturer. A manufacturer differentiates the content or form of a product in anticipation of sales to different types of consumers. Alternative advertising and marketing strategies are also used for differentiated product lines. See also *product differentiation.*

**différentiel.** French: commission (paid for securities).

**Dillon Round.** See *General Agreement on Tariffs and Trade.*

**diminishing-value depreciation.** See *depreciation.*

**DIN.** The abbreviation for *Deutsches Institut für Normen,* or German Institute for Standards.

**dinar.** The national currency of Algeria, Bahrain, Iraq, Jordan, Libya, Tunisia, the former Yugoslavia Republics (Bosnia, Croatia, Macedonia, Montenegro, Serbia, Slovenia), and Kuwait.

**dingo.** The acronym for discounted investment in negotiable government obligations.

**dipl.** The abbreviation for diplomat.

**diplomat (dipl).** In international relations, a person appointed by a government to represent its interests in a foreign country or before a multilateral institution. Under the principle of diplomatic immunity adopted in 1961 by the Vienna Convention on Diplomatic Relations, persons holding diplomatic rank are immune from civil process and criminal prosecution in the jurisdictions to which they are accredited. An ambassador holds the highest diplomatic rank. See also *consul.*

**Dir./ dir.** The abbreviations for director and direction.

**dirección...de aduanas.** Spanish: customs authority.

**dirección de aprovisionamiento del estado.** Spanish: bureau of government, i.e., a procurement agency.

**dirección de comercio exterior.** Spanish: bureau of foreign trade.

**dirección...de sanidad pública.** Spanish: bureau of public health.

**dirección de tributación aduanera.** Spanish: customs tribunal, i.e., a council that issues import classification rulings.

**direção...das alfândegas.** Portuguese: customs authority.

**direct controls.** Measures adopted by a government to regulate economic activity. Quotas and tariffs are direct controls, while regulatory barriers and surcharges are indirect controls.

**direct costs of processing.** 1. Costs associated with producing a product, but excluding general business and administrative expenses. Direct costs include the cost of materials and wages paid for finishing a product. 2. In international trade, local processing costs used to meet value-added requirements for preferential trade programs. See also *substantial transformation and 35 percent value added.*

**direct endorsement.** See *endorsement.*

**directeur des douanes.** French: director of customs.

**direct export.** A sale to a foreign importer without intermediaries. Exporters are liable for direct exports to countries under sanctions or embargo. An exporter avoids liability by indirect exporting, i.e., transshipping goods through a third-country intermediary.

**direct foreign investment.** See *foreign direct investment.*

**directie douane-aangelegenheden.** Dutch: director of customs.

**direct importation.** A requirement for reduced or duty-free customs entry under trade preference programs. In the United States, imports must be shipped directly from a beneficiary country port to a U.S. border or entry port.

**Direct Information Access Network for Europe.** See *Euronet.*

**directional rate.** In marine shipping, freight based on the direction of a ship, often a factor in determining cargo weight.

**direction des douanes et des droits indirects.** French: bureau of customs and excise (taxes).

**direction...des travaux.** French: bureau of ( public) works.

**direction du commerce.** French: bureau of commerce.

**direction du commerce exterieur.** French: bureau of foreign trade.

**direction...du port.** French: port authority.

**directive.** 1. An official statement of policy. 2. The primary law making tool of the European Community (EC). Directives are proposed by the European Commission, reviewed by the European Parliament, and approved by the European Council. A directive is not a statute in the ordinary sense, but a mandate for harmonizing national laws to conform to a broad policy. EC countries are permitted to choose different approaches to legislation, as long as national laws substantially reflect policies adopted by directive. See also *subsidiarity.*

**direct marketing.** Soliciting sales directly from a customer. Direct marketing eliminates retailers and sales agents from the distribution chain. Mail-order selling and telemarketing are forms of direct marketing.

**direct offset.** 1. The cost of an import reduced by the value added in the importing country. Imported components are usually eligible for a duty drawback. 2. The cost of a local component used to manufacture an end product. The purchase price of local components is a tax-deductible cost.

**director (Dir.).** A person elected by an organization's owners to act as a fiduciary, implement policies, oversee expenditures, select executive officers, and, in the case of corporations, approve dividend distributions and executive compensation. Collectively, directors constitute the board of directors. Outside directors are recruited for their standing in the community. Inside directors are company employees and are usually active in its executive management. Directors may be compensated on a salary or fee basis. In the United States, directors are registered with the incorporating agency in the state of incorporation and, in the case of publicly held companies, with the Securities and Exchange Commission. They are liable for fraud, defalcation, negligence, misfeasance, and, in the case of publicly held companies, insider trading. Bank directors guilty of abuse of office are removed by bank regulators; directors of nonbank corporations can only be removed by company shareholders. Outside the United States, companies normally have a managing director who exercises authority roughly equivalent to that of a chief executive officer in the United States. In the United Kingdom, directors are registered with the Registrar of Companies. See also *European company, proxy* and *proxy statement.*

**directors and officers (D&O) insurance.**  Liability insurance for corporate directors and executive officers that indemnifies them from legal damages sought by creditors, government agencies, plaintiffs in product-liability cases, shareholders, and so on. Some corporations are self-insured through in-house accounts or pooling arrangements sponsored by trade associations.

**directors' report.**  See *annual report*.

**direct placement.**  See *private placement*.

**direct subsidy.**  See *subsidy*.

**direct taxation.**  A tax on a taxpayer's assets. Corporate, estate, income, and property taxes are direct taxes. By contrast, value-added taxes and excise taxes are indirect taxes.

**dirham.**  The currency of Morocco and the United Arab Emirates.

**dirigisme.**  French: design, denoting a pattern of government regulation.

**dirty float.**  See *managed float*.

**dirty ship.**  A ship that transports unrefined petroleum products, usually crude oil or residual fuel, which leave behind traces of residue. Compare *clean ship*.

**dis., disc.**  The abbreviation for discount.

**disaster clause.**  See *jeopardy clause*.

**disbursement.**  An expenditure that settles a debt or otherwise reduces liabilities.

**DISC.**  The abbreviation for Domestic International Sales Corporation.

**discharge.**  The result of a court order in a personal bankruptcy proceeding. The order relieves debtors of personal obligations not voluntarily repaid. In the United States, debts are not discharged when corporations reorganize in bankruptcy.

**disclosure.**  1. In the United States, information provided to consumers by creditors. State and federal laws require creditors to disclose the annual percentage rate of interest, the method of computing interest, minimum monthly payments, and disputed billing resolution procedures. 2. In law, the obligation to inform a party of the relevant facts in a legal proceeding. 3. In securities markets, information provided to purchasers of securities.

In the United States, the Securities Act of 1933 and Securities and Exchange Commission regulations require brokers and dealers to inform buyers of facts relevant to a transaction. The information must be sufficiently detailed to enable buyers to make informed decisions regarding the soundness of a securities purchase.

**discount (dis., disc.).**  1. In sales, a deduction from the selling price of goods for bulk, cash, or trade buyers. 2. In securities markets, the difference between the lower market price and the par value of a security. 3. In banking, the difference between the face value of a bill of exchange and its value at maturity. A bank accepting a bill of exchange pays the discount price. It profits if the risk of nonpayment at maturity is not fulfilled. See also *acceptance* and *federal funds rate*.

**discount brokerage.**  A firm that executes securities transactions but does not offer investment advice. Sometimes called cut-rate brokers, discount brokers usually settle accounts through a trading exchange. See also *bill broker*.

**discount corporation.**  A bank or other commercial institution that trades and discounts acceptances and bills of exchange.

**discounted cashflow (DCF).**  A technique for evaluating future capital investments. The anticipated income and costs of the project are discounted to present value in relation to current income and costs. Interest that would accumulate until the investment becomes profitable is factored into the decision. If anticipated interest exceeds profits projected for a project, the investment is not financially sound. Compare *cashflow*.

**discounted investment in negotiable government obligations (dingo).**  In Australia, a zero-coupon bond resembling the certificate of accrual on Treasury securities.

**discount house.**  A firm or bank that discounts banker's acceptances, bills of exchange, commercial paper, and trade acceptances. In the United Kingdom, discount houses are the only institutions to which the Bank of England traditionally lends, permitting some London bill brokers to deal exclusively in trading Treasury bills to discount houses. The houses balance their books by 3 p.m. daily, often through a lending facility, known as privilege money, extended by a few commercial banks. 2. In France, a *maison de réescompte,* i.e., one of a very small number of financial institutions authorized for dealings with Banque de France. The operations of discount houses in France resemble those of similar institutions in the United Kingdom.

**discount market.** A money market where securities are discounted. Banks, brokers, and discount houses make up the discount market. Brokers normally borrow short-term funds from banks or discount houses and profit by discounting bills of exchange.

**discount rate.** See *bill rate, discount window,* and *interest rate policy.*

**discount window.** A facility through which local financial institutions borrow directly from a central bank. The discount window enables central banks to manage short-term reserve assets, but its operation varies in different countries. In the United States, the Federal Reserve rediscounts acceptances and notes previously discounted by commercial banks. The Fed also advances funds secured by a commercial bank's Treasury holdings. Banks use the advances to cover reserve account deficiencies. The interest rate obtained at the discount window, known as the discount rate, is lower in the United States than short-term lending rates obtained from Federal Reserve advances. By contrast, the Bundesbank discount rate is higher than short-term rates, and the discount window is used by commercial banks as a last resort. In the United Kingdom, there is no official discount window. See also *Federal Open Market Committee, Federal Reserve discount rate,* and *interest rate policy.* Compare *federal funds rate.*

**discrepancy.** A disparity between the terms specified in a letter of credit and information contained in shipping documents. The most common discrepancies are late shipments, late presentation of documents, and nonconforming descriptions of goods. When banks uncover discrepancies, a letter of credit is amended or the exporter is not paid. Extra bank fees are charged for amendments. See also *telex for authority to pay.*

**discretionary cargo.** Government cargo that can be transported by any available carrier. Discretionary cargo is exempt from laws giving an exclusive right of carriage to domestic carriers. Military shipments are never discretionary cargoes, and commodities sold on concessional terms are rarely transported by foreign carriers. See also *Convention on a Code for Liner Conferences* and *Jones Act of 1920.*

**discretionary credit limit.** See *Foreign Credit Insurance Association.*

**discriminating duty.** See *duty.*

**discrimination.** In international trade, unequal duties applied by one country to another's exports when compared to duties levied on competing imports of equal status. Tariff preferences based on treaties do not constitute discrimination against other trading partners. For example, most-favored-nation (MFN) rates do not discriminate against non-MFN countries, but substantially different rates applied to imports from two non-MFN countries constitute trade discrimination if all other factors are equal.

**dishoarding.** A government's reduction in surplus supplies of commodities. The process may involve auctioning, exporting, or releasing goods for consumption. Goods are dishoarded to obtain foreign exchange, to reduce the cost or risk of maintaining a surplus, or to benefit from favorable world market prices.

**dishonor.** A financial institution's refusal to accept or pay a draft, bill of exchange, or letter of credit. Instruments are dishonored because the drawer's or maker's account has insufficient funds. To collect payment on a dishonored instrument, a holder notifies the endorser, who is usually the drawer of a bill of exchange, the maker of a check, or a guarantor. The notification is known as a protest. In the United States, a dishonored draft must be returned by the bank within a day of presentment, or the holder loses the right to collect payment from the endorser.

**disinflation.** Lowering the inflation rate by reducing credit available to businesses and consumers. Governments restrict the money supply when price increases encourage speculation by rising at a faster rate than overall economic growth. Tight money policies are designed to deflate prices.

**disintermediation.** An investor's withdrawal from investments that require intermediaries when the costs of intermediation exceed the value of the services provided. Disintermediation is a frequent market response to regulatory lending ceilings, leading investors to seek other means of financing transactions. Governments tend to deregulate markets when investments are removed in search of higher yields. The opposite of disintermediation is reintermediation, i.e., the reinvestment of funds for purposes that require transfer by an intermediary, as when a depositor places funds with a bank for lending to borrowers.

**disinvestment.**    A foreign investor's removal of assets from a country in the grip of political or economic instability. Foreign companies usually disinvest because of a country's economic conditions. In rare instances, objections to a foreign country's social or political policies are raised in a company's home country causing it to disinvest when it might otherwise remain. Compare *divestment.*

**dispatch.**    Also known as despatch, a bonus received by the charterer of a ship when cargo is loaded or unloaded before lay time expires. Charter parties typically contain provisions giving charterers a fixed amount of time for loading and unloading cargo. Compare *demurrage.*

**disponent owner.**    The party who has operational control of a ship under the terms of an ocean charter. In maritime trade, legal responsibility is fixed by contract without regard to the actual ownership of the ship. See also *charter party.*

**dispute settlement.**    The method of conflict resolution consented to by parties to an agreement. International commercial contracts frequently contain arbitration provisions, which enable the parties to avoid local courts and resolve disputes before an impartial tribunal. International trade accords typically contain dispute-settlement mechanisms. The General Agreement on Tariffs and Trade has a dispute-settlement process, available to member countries when bilateral treaties do not contain a mechanism for settlement. Bilateral conflict-resolution procedures are known as binational dispute-settlement mechanisms. The Canada-U.S. Free Trade Agreement (FTA) has elaborate dispute-settlement procedures. For example, Article 1807 of the FTA authorizes a binational panel composed of two members from each country. The panel chooses a fifth person

who chairs the body. It arbitrates dumping and subsidy disputes, effectively by-passing the jurisdiction of national courts and binding parties by agreement. Appeals from the panel's decisions lie with a binational committee authorized to overturn arbitration rulings. The committee may also propose the creation of a new panel when rulings are deemed unfair or unfounded.

**distance freight.**    An ocean carrier's surcharge imposed when weather conditions force a ship's captain to divert a ship. Distance freight is charged when the ship must dock at a port other than the original destination port. The amount of the surcharge depends on the carriage rate specified in the charter.

**distance selling.**    An offer to sell directly to consumers by mail, telephone, television, or facsimile. Consumer protection laws may impose a mandatory cooling-off period and require written notice of a consumer's right to cancel a sales contract before its payment terms become binding. Typically, the laws also require delivery of consumer products within a fixed time from the date of a sales contract.

**distortion.**    In conventional international trade theory, the result of excessive trade regulation and unfair trade practices. A government raises trade barriers to minimize the natural effects of absolute advantage or comparative advantage. Theoretically, free trade enables consumers to buy cheaper or higher-quality products than producers in the country regulating trade can produce. In practice, most countries accept some distortion and higher consumer prices to preserve jobs in vital economic sectors.

**distress dumping.**    See *dumping.*

**distress freight.**    Cargo shipped at a discounted rate to attract business. Discount rates are offered when a vessel would operate below capacity without additional cargo.

**distribution.**    A corporation's dividend payments to shareholders. Dividends must be paid from profits or assets that can be legally distributed, such as cash on hand, property, or stock. When there are no profits, dividends represent a return on capital. In some jurisdictions, publicly held corporations may not legally distribute cash dividends that reduce capital reserves or share capital.

**distribution center.**    A warehouse used by a manufacturer to store bulk goods for shipment to retailers or wholesalers.

**distribution channel.**    The delivery chain from manufacturer to consumer. Normally, a product passes from the manufacturer through wholesalers to retailers for sale to consumers. Depending on the product, the chain may also include suppliers, agents, or other intermediaries.

**distribution resource planning (DRP).**    A software system used by manufacturers to control inventory. DRP enables manufacturers and distributors to avoid delays and waste by coordinating inventories and shipping schedules. See also *just-in-time* and *zero inventory*.

**distributor.**    A manufacturer's sales agent. In international sales, the distributor is often a foreign firm that also markets and services products. A distributorship is exclusive when the distributor acquires the sole right to sell and service a manufacturer's product in a given territory.

**district/area (customs) office.**    In the United States, a local office of the U.S. Customs Service. There are forty-five area offices subordinate to seven regional offices. A district office has a district director and two assistant district directors. Assistant district directors are responsible for import classification, valuation, inspection, and control. District offices review petitions to reclassify imports, reduce fines, or forestall seizures. They also conduct administrative proceedings involving suspensions or revocations of customhouse broker licenses.

**District Export Council (DEC).**    In the United States, a committee of local business representatives who work with the U.S. Department of Commerce to promote U.S. exports. DECs cooperate with district Commerce Department offices to sponsor workshops and trade shows for local firms. The councils also provide advisory services and technical assistance to new-to-export companies.

**district/port entry code.**    In the United States, a four-digit computer code in the Automated Commercial System that identifies U.S. Customs districts and ports of entry.

**diversity of citizenship.**    In the United States, a condition required to have most civil suits heard in a federal court rather than a state court. Diversity of citizenship exists, subject to a specific dollar limitation, when the parties to a lawsuit are citizens of different U.S. states or when one is a foreign national. If the Constitution of the United States, a federal statute, or an international treaty is not a factor in a case, the federal court applies the law of the state in which the case is heard.

**divestment.**    A policy adopted by a government to sell state-owned enterprises to private business interests. Enterprises are usually sold off in stages. The sales are typically arranged through a nonprofit corporation created for that purpose. Compare *disinvestment*.

**dividend.**    The share of a corporation's cash income or stock distributed to its owners. In the United States, dividends are declared by a company's board of directors, usually quarterly. Both the corporation and shareholders pay taxes on distributed dividends. In the United Kingdom, dividends are normally paid biannually. A company mails a dividend mandate notifying shareholders of pending dividend distributions. The dividend check is called a dividend warrant. The first is a modest interim dividend that accompanies a company's midyear report to investors. The larger dividend, known as the final dividend, is paid after the annual general meeting of shareholders. When a company cannot afford to pay dividends, it notifies shareholders by way of a dividend waiver. See also *advance corporation tax*.

**dividend restraint.**    See *wage and price controls*.

**dividend stripping.**    See *stripped bond*.

**dividend warrant.**    A dividend check with the amount of the dividend and taxes deducted shown on its face. In some countries, the dividend warrant is filed with the taxing authority to claim refunds when no taxes are owed.

**division.**    The apportionment of earnings among different carriers transporting a single cargo shipment. A portion of the total rate is allocated to each carrier on a pro rata mileage basis. Mileage is computed using the distance from the origin point (along intermediate points) to the destination point. See also *multimodal bill of lading*.

**division des risques.**   French: limitation of risks, e.g., a bank's limit on lending to a given customer.

**Division of Energy and Product Information.** In the United States, an office of the Federal Trade Commission. The office administers consumer-appliance labeling standards, including import labeling. False product safety markings and performance labeling are within the agency's jurisdiction.

**DJIA.**   The abbreviation for Dow Jones Industrial Average.

**dlo.**   The abbreviation for dispatch loading only.

**D/M.**   The abbreviation for delivery month.

**DMFAS.**   The abbreviation for Debt Management and Financial Analysis System. See *debt conversion program.*

**D/N.**   The abbreviation for delivery notice.

**D/O.**   The abbreviation for delivery order.

**DOA.**   The abbreviation for documents on acceptance. See *documents against acceptance.*

**dobra.**   The currency of São Tomé and Principe.

**doc.**   The abbreviation for document.

**DOC.**   The abbreviation for U.S. Department of Commerce.

**dock.**   A port or harbor designated for loading and unloading a ship. See also *dockage.*

**dockage.**   1. Positioning a ship at a dock. 2. In sales, an offset against the invoice price of defective goods.

**dock receipt (D/R).**   1. A document issued by an ocean carrier at a pier. The dock receipt is not negotiable, but entitles the recipient to obtain a bill of lading. When cargo is damaged or miscounted, a notation is made on the dock receipt. It determines whether a foul bill of lading is issued. 2. A warehouse receipt when issued for goods destined for storage by a shipping company. See also *warrant.*

**dock warrant.**   See *warrant.*

**documentary acceptance.**   An acceptance not honored without additional documentation, usually shipping documents.

**documentary bill of exchange.**   A bill of exchange attached to shipping documents. A documentary bill is usually presented to a bank with a letter of instructions. Documentary bills of exchange are also known as documentary drafts.

**documentary collection.**   Also known as cash against documents, an alternative to letter-of-credit financing. A financial institution, usually a seller's bank, sends shipping documents with collection instructions to the importer's bank. When the documents are received, the importer's bank pays the seller's bank. Shipping documents (including an endorsed bill of lading) are used by the importer to obtain the goods from the carrier or warehouse. In countries with a stamp tax or other enhanced transaction costs, payment against documents at sight or deferred payment against documents is common. Documentary collections are less expensive than letter-of-credit financing, but they lack the payment guarantees of irrevocable letters of credit.

**documentary credit.**   A letter of credit instructing a bank to pay a seller on receipt of shipping documents.

**documentary draft.**   An instrument, usually a sight or time draft, paid only when attached to shipping documents.

**documents against acceptance (D/A).**   Also known as documents on acceptance, a notice from an exporter to a bank setting forth conditions for releasing documents of title to an importer. The documents are released when a bank accepts the buyer's draft or bill of exchange. Under a documents against payment/presentation notice, the buyer is entitled to goods when the draft has been paid or presented for payment.

**documents against payment/presentation (D/P).** See *documents against acceptance.*

**DOJ.**   The abbreviation for U.S. Department of Justice.

**dol.**   The abbreviation for dollar.

**DOL.**   The abbreviation for the U.S. Department of Labor.

**dollar (dol.).**   The currency of Australia, Bahamas, Barbados, Bermuda, Canada, Dominica, Fiji, Guyana, Hong Kong, Jamaica, Liberia, New Zealand, Singapore, Taiwan, Trinidad and Tobago, the United States, and Zimbabwe.

**dollar bill of exchange.** A bill of exchange payable in U.S. dollars, irrespective of where the payment is made.

**dollar bond.** A bond denominated in U.S. dollars but issued outside the United States.

**dollar standard.** An exchange rate system based on the U.S. dollar. The dollar standard was first adopted by the Bretton Woods Conference of 1944 and replaced by the floating-exchange-rate system in 1973. See also *Smithsonian Agreement.*

**dollar stocks.** In the United Kingdom, securities denominated in Canadian or U.S. dollars.

**dollar zone.** A term loosely applied to exports originating in the Americas.

**dom.** The abbreviation for domestic.

**domaines et territoires d'outre-mer.** French: overseas countries and territories. The overseas dependent territories of France include French Polynesia, New Caledonia, and Wallis and Fortuna Islands. Metropolitan France includes the overseas departments of the French West Indies, Mayotte, Reunion, and St. Pierre and Miquelon.

**domestication.** The forceable transfer of assets owned by foreign nationals to local residents or entities. When foreign property is domesticated, adequate compensation is paid to the owners. See also *expropriation* and *nationalization.*

**domestic content requirement (DCR).** Also called a local content requirement, a mandate that a prescribed portion of an import have value added in the importing country. Most countries and regional trading unions require that an import have some local content to qualify for a trade preference. In the United States and elsewhere, DCRs are imposed by statute to maintain employment in local industries. DCRs are a nontariff barrier to international trade.

**domestic corporation.** See *corporation.*

**domestic international sales corporation (DISC).** In the United States, a company that qualified for special tax deferments before 1984. A DISC is a domestic corporation earning 95 percent of its income from foreign export sales. Taxes were deferred on all earnings from equity held by the corporation. The DISC was modified by the Tax Reform Act of 1984, after U.S. trading partners

complained to the General Agreement on Tariffs and Trade that DISC deferments constituted an illegal subsidy. Although the DISC was disallowed in its original form, the 1984 tax law permanently forgave DISC deferments claimed before its effective date and authorized the interest-charge DISC. See also *associated foreign corporation* and *foreign international sales corporation.* Compare *foreign sales corporation.*

**domestic offshore trade.** In the United States, trade involving the state of Hawaii, Guam, Puerto Rico, and the U.S. Virgin Islands. Domestic offshore trade falls under the jurisdiction of the Federal Maritime Commission. The term defines the physical area covered by U.S. shipping laws, particularly the Jones Act of 1920, the primary U.S. ocean cabotage law.

**domicile.** Sometimes called domicil, a person's or a firm's permanent home. The domicile is the place where a party intends (or expresses an intention) to remain. More than nationality or the place where one is a resident, domicile determines civil status, including tax liability and other legal rights. A corporation is domiciled in the place of incorporation.

**doomsday tax.** In the United States, tax liability incurred by a U.S. firm when it liquidates a subsidiary tax haven. The Internal Revenue Code treats overseas liquidation proceeds as dividends earned by the parent corporation. The dividends are taxed as corporate income.

**DOP.** The abbreviation for documents on payment. See *documents against payment/presentation.*

**Doppelsteuerabkommen.** German: double-taxation treaty.

**dossier.** In France, a loan secured by the book transfer of an accounting asset. The security for a *dossier* is known as *effets privés,* or private paper.

**DOT.** The abbreviation for the U.S. Department of Transportation.

**DOT bond.** In the United States, security required for nonconforming or uncertified imports of motor vehicles. Imported motor vehicles must meet U.S. emissions standards, or the importer is required to obtain a temporary import certificate. Dealers registered with the U.S. Department of Transportation, called DOT-registered importers, are authorized to alter nonconforming vehicles and certify modifications. Motor vehicles imported for permanent use must conform to U.S. standards within 120 days of entry. A DOT bond equals 150 percent of the dutiable value of the vehicle.

**DOT-registered importer.**    See *DOT bond.*

**douane.**    French: customs office or duty.

**douanier/douanière.**    French: custom agent, masculine and feminine.

**double-stack train (DST).**    A train with double the freight capacity of conventional freight trains.

**double substantial transformation.**    The process of increasing the local content of an import through additional manufacturing processes to qualify for preferential duties. Most countries require a fixed percentage of value-added content for imports entering under trade preference programs. Imports entering the United States under the Caribbean Basin Initiative and the U.S. Generalized System of Preferences must have 35 percent of their value added in a beneficiary country. The simple processing of natural products does not usually add sufficient value to products, especially when finished items contain components made outside the beneficiary country. For example, a furniture product made of wood from a beneficiary country may contain insufficient local content. Conversely, if wood components finished locally are used in the product, the 35 percent requirement is probably met. See also *substantial transformation.*

**double taxation.**    Taxation of the same income in different jurisdictions. For example, multinational corporations are subject both to the tax laws of the domicile country and to those of countries where they have operations. Since double taxation discourages trade, most governments grant unilateral tax relief or enter into bilateral tax treaties to apportion tax liability. Different methods are used to reduce the effects of double taxation:

*exemption with progression.*    One hundred percent of income from foreign sources is exempt from taxes in the foreign country. But the foreign income is reported as a part of annual gross income in the home country, thereby increasing the company's effective corporate tax rate.

*full exemption.*    One hundred percent of income from foreign sources is exempt in the foreign country. Foreign income is not calculated as a part of annual gross income and has no effect on the company's corporate tax rate in the home country.

*full tax credit.*    One hundred percent of the taxes paid on foreign income is credited against taxes owed in the home country, thereby reducing corporate taxes payable by the company.

*ordinary tax credit.*    Taxes paid on income from foreign sources are credited against taxes owed in the home country if a company's domestic tax liability would have been comparable. Ordinarily, a country using this method does not allow credits for taxes it does not itself levy. The ordinary tax credit method is used in the United States.

**double-taxation treaty.**    See *double taxation.*

**Dow Jones Industrial Average (DJIA).**    Known popularly as the Dow, a price-weighted industrial index of 30 stocks traded on the New York Stock Exchange. The averages reflect the daily opening, high, and low prices of each component stock quoted in the index rather than the combined average prices of the group. The Dow, which is compiled by Dow Jones & Company, was created in 1884. Dow Jones also issues three other indexes covering composite prices of several industry stocks, 20 transportation stocks, and 15 utility stocks.

**down payment.**    See *deposit.*

**downsizing.**    Any restructuring method employed by a company to streamline production and reduce costs. Downsizing is intended to enhance a company's competitive advantage in the market by increasing employee productivity and overall efficiency. Most contemporary downsizings include closing unprofitable branches and plants, selling off subsidiaries where the market is weak or the management is not expert, laying off workers, hiring temporary employees, or outsourcing work on a need basis to independent firms.

**downstream.**    1. In sales, the movement of a product from the original producer to consumers along the distribution chain. The price paid for a finished product depends on the value added to the base product from factory to end sale. 2. In finance, funds borrowed by a parent for use by a subsidiary. These are known as downstream loans, usually obtained at more favorable rates than upstream loans.

**downtime.**   A period when a machine is idle, often for repairs. Accounting costs are attributed to work time lost during downtimes.

**doz.**   The abbreviation for dozen.

**DP.**   The abbreviation for data processing, direct payment, and direct port.

**D/P.**   The abbreviation for delivery point and documents against payment/presentation.

**d.p.p.**   The abbreviation for dirty petroleum products.

**dr.**   The abbreviation for debtor and dram.

**D/R.**   The abbreviation for dock receipt.

**drachma.**   The currency of Greece.

**draft (dft.).**   An unconditional written demand by one party (a drawer) that a second party (the drawee) pay a fixed sum to a named party on a certain date. In the United States, draft is a synonym for bill of exchange. See also *arrival draft, bank draft, demand draft, documentary draft, sight draft,* and *time draft.*

**drawback.**   See *duty drawback.*

**drawee.**   The party who pays or accepts a bill of exchange or draft.

**drawer.**   The party who receives payment on a bill of exchange or draft.

**drawing unit reserve asset (DURA).**   One of several proposed universal artificial currency units. The special drawing right was the product of prior proposals to create a global settlement unit.

**drayage charge.**   A fee charged by a trucking company for hauling shipping containers and trailers.

**droits.**   French: taxes.

**drop shipper.**   A wholesale dealer who places orders with manufacturers, who ship directly to retailers. Manufacturers are paid by the wholesaler.

**DRP.**   The abbreviation for distribution resource planning.

**Drug Enforcement Administration (DEA).**   In the United States, a police agency of the U.S. Department of Justice that enforces domestic laws restricting sales of controlled substances.

**dry bulk.**   Grain or other solid cargo transported in the hold of a ship without external crating or packaging.

**dry-docking clause.**   A clause in a charter party exempting the charterer from charges when a ship is docked for cleaning and painting. Some charter agreements provide for refurbishing the bottom of a ship at the discretion of the charterer or the ship's master.

**D/S.**   The abbreviation for days after sight.

**DST.**   The abbreviation for double-stack train.

**DTI.**   The abbreviation for the Department of Trade and Industry.

**dual-exchange market.**   See *controlled currency rate* and *exchange control.*

**dual pricing.**   Different prices applied to a single product sold in different markets. A producer differentiates prices when the cost of selling in one market exceeds that of selling in another. Scarcity in one market and abundance in the other can account for price differentiation.

**dual-rate contract.**   A shipping contract with two freight rates. Dual-rate contracts offer discounted rates to shippers who enter into exclusive agreements with a shipping conference. The higher rate is charged to nonexclusive shippers.

**dual-use items.**   Items that can be used for military and nonmilitary purposes. Dual-use items include computers, chemicals, fiber optics, precision machine tools, and some mass-market computer software programs with encryption capabilities. These articles are often covered by export controls. See also *Commerce Control List.*

**due bill.**   In shipping, an invoice issued to a shipper.

**due date.**   The date when a financial instrument matures or is presented for payment.

**dumping.**   The act of selling exports in a foreign market at an unfair price. Distress dumping is sporadic underpricing that occurs when a producer sells a temporary surplus in a foreign market. Predatory dumping is intentional underpricing to monopolize a foreign market by driving out local producers. Persistent dumping reflects a pattern of unfair pricing in a foreign market, sometimes occurring when the exporter's home market is too small for predictable profits. See also *antidumping action*.

**dumping margin.**    See *antidumping action*.

**dumping price.**    An export price below the cost of producing and selling the same product in the home market. Sometimes confused with predatory pricing, a low export price may not reflect anticompetitive conduct under all conditions. For example, a producer may sell at a lower price in a foreign market because of a product's strength in the home market or because exchange rate fluctuations reduce the value of the importing country's currency. See also *dumping*.

**Dun & Bradstreet (D&B).**    In the United States, a corporate credit-reporting agency, which rates companies on capital adequacy, financial performance, and trade payment history. D&B also operates the Data Universal Numbering System composed of codes identifying companies by address, the number of employees, contact names, etc. D&B's directory, *The Reference Book*, lists credit-rating information on U.S. and Canadian companies. Moody's Investors Service, which rates bank certificates of deposits, bonds, and commercial paper, is a Dun & Bradstreet subsidiary.

**dunnage.**    Superfluous packing materials used to balance cargo during shipping.

**dup.**    The abbreviation for duplicate.

**durable good.**    An article manufactured to have a minimum usable life of 3 years. Nondurables or soft goods are the opposite of durables.

**duration clause.**    A marine insurance provision indicating the period covered by a policy.

**Dutch auction.**    A bond auction technique where a given lot of securities is initially offered at a high price that is lowered until an acceptable bid is made. Winning bids are always lower than the starting price, and the lowest price paid is known as the stop-out price. U.S. Treasury securities are infrequently sold at Dutch auctions.

**dutiable list.**    A country's official listing of items subject to duty and the rate of duty per item. The dutiable list is included in a country's customs tariff.

**dutiable status.**    See *status*.

**duty.**    Also called a tariff or a customs tariff, a customs tax collected on foreign products to generate revenues or discourage imports. Normally, a country's tariff schedules specify the amount of duty chargeable to a given class of imports. Duties are discriminatory if applied unequally to products from different countries, protective if designed to limit competition faced by domestic producers, and retaliatory if implemented to punish a trading partner's unfair trade practices. When bound by negotiated agreements, tariffs are called conventional duties. If prescribed by law, tariffs are called statutory duties, which may be ordinary or concessional. Ordinary duties are higher than concessional duties, which are granted unilaterally or by treaty. Duties fall into several other categories:

*ad valorem duty.*    An ordinary duty based on the economic value of an import. Ad valorem duties are computed as a percentage of the invoice price, as in 5 percent of $100.

*antidumping duty.*    A special duty imposed on dumped imports. The duty is equal to the exporter's gain from dumping.

*autonomous duties.*    Sometimes called special duties, tariffs used to safeguard a domestic industry. The safeguard prevents injury from a surge of cheap imports or penalizes exporters attempting to avoid quota or country-of-origin limitations.

*bound duty.*    A concessional duty agreed to by treaty and alterable only by agreement between signatory nations.

*compensatory duty.*    A concessional duty conceded to a trading partner to counter the adverse impact of an increased duty on another class of imports. See also *compensation*.

*compound duty.*    A duty based on both economic value and per-unit weight or measurement. For example, a compound duty would be expressed as 5 percent ad valorem plus $0.10 per pound.

*concessional duty.*   An especially low rate of duty granted on a reciprocal basis by trading partners. Concessional duties are also made available to developing countries by industrialized countries on a unilateral basis under trade preference programs. See also *Caribbean Basin Initiative II, Generalized System of Preferences, Lomé Conventions,* and *most favored nation.*

*countervailing duty (CVD).*   A special duty imposed on subsidized imports equal to the value of the subsidy. See also *bounty or grant.*

*differential duty.*   A duty that can be ordinary or concessional. Differential duties are based on the relationship between an importing and exporting country. Most-favored-nation status or similar concessions reduce duties on an exporting country's products.

*exclusionary duty.*   See *prohibitive duty.*

*flexible duty.*   A duty alterable by executive decision. Most countries' tariff laws authorize an executive officer or committee to set unilateral duties in response to actions by trading partners. A flexible tariff is later revoked or authorized by law. See also *Reciprocal Trade Agreements Act of 1934.*

*marking duty.*   An ad valorem duty imposed on imports with erroneous country-of-origin markings. The marking duty is levied in addition to ordinary ad valorem duties. In the United States, a marking duty amounts to 10 percent of the customs value of an import. Marking duties can be recovered through duty drawback.

*preferential duty.*   A concessional duty.

*prohibitive duty.*   A duty imposed at a rate high enough to deter imports of certain items. A prohibitive duty can be flexible enough to guarantee a continuous supply of the product, while interrupting the flow of imports when permissible levels are exceeded. Prohibitive duties are designed to protect infant or ailing industries from competing imports, or, in some instances, to retaliate against increased duties by trading partners.

*protective duty.*   A duty imposed to protect domestic producers from foreign imports or to discourage imports that drain foreign exchange reserves. Protective duties may be slightly lower than the higher end of a prohibitive duty, but they have the same effect.

*specific duty.*   An ordinary duty based on a import's per-unit weight, measurement, or number, as in 5 percent per pound or 2 percent per 100.

**duty drawback.**   Also known as a manufacturing drawback and inward processing relief, a feature of customs law that permits an exporter to recover duties on imported components used to manufacture exports. In the United States, duty drawbacks were first authorized by the Tariff Act of 1789. There are three categories of drawback: (1) manufacturing drawbacks for imports remade into new products, (2) rejected-merchandise drawbacks for imports unsuited to the purposes for which they were purchased, and (3) same-condition drawbacks for imports exported in the same condition in which they were imported. Duty drawbacks may apply to antidumping, countervailing, marking, and ordinary duties in addition to other revenue taxes. Drawbacks also cover taxes on domestic inputs substituted for foreign components. Products imported, but destroyed or reexported without additional processing, are eligible for a same-condition drawback if destroyed or reexported within the prescribed time period. The value of a drawback is known as the drawback rate, usually 99 to 100 percent of the import's value. See also *manufactured or processed.* Compare *duty remission.*

**duty-free.**   An import entering a country without the levying of a customs tariff. Bonded goods and some imports admitted under trade preference programs enter foreign jurisdictions duty free, but the exemption from duties is lost if the goods are used for purposes other than those for which they are admitted.

**duty-free port.**   See *foreign trade zone.*

**duty-free zone.**   See *foreign trade zone.*

**duty liability.**   A debt for duty owed on an import. The debt creates a lien on imports subject to duty. Imported goods are dutiable upon arrival in a customs territory. The goods need not be discharged to an importer for the duty to be owed. Duty liabilities pass to the importer's assigns, heirs, and successors.

**duty paid.**    A description applied to dutiable imports when duties and taxes have been paid. Fully paid duties entitle the owner or consignee to withdraw the imports from a bonded warehouse or customs facility for sale or other use in the importing country.

**duty remission.**    A conditional refund of duties on imported components used to manufacture exports. Contingent refunds are intended to stimulate export activity in high-value foreign markets. Duty remissions probably violate international trading rules, since they are expressly intended to stimulate exports. See also *General Agreement on Tariffs and Trade: Tokyo Round, Subsidies (and Countervailing Measures) Code.*

**D.V.1.**    See *Single Administrative Document.*

**d.w.**    The abbreviation for deadweight.

**D/W.**    The abbreviation for dock warrant.

**d.w.c.**    The abbreviation for deadweight capacity.

**d.w.t.**    The abbreviation for deadweight ton.

**D/y.**    The abbreviation for delivery.

# E

**E.** The marking for Caribbean Basin Initiative Eligible Product. See *Harmonized Tariff Schedule of the United States, Annotated.*

**E\*.** The marking for Caribbean Basin Initiative Eligible Product, Subject to Exclusion. See *Harmonized Tariff Schedule of the United States, Annotated.*

**EAA.** The abbreviation for Export Administration Act.

**EADB.** The abbreviation for East African Development Bank.

**EAEC.** The abbreviation for East Asia Economic Caucus.

**EAI.** The abbreviation for Enterprise for the Americas Initiative.

**E.& O.E.** The abbreviation for errors and omissions excepted.

**EAON.** The abbreviation for except as otherwise noted.

**EAR.** The abbreviation for Export Administration Regulations. See *Export Administration Act of 1979* and *Bureau of Export Administration.*

**earnings per share (EPS).** The rate of return on common stock, i.e., a company's net profits divided by the number of outstanding common stock after adjustments for taxes and dividends paid on preferred stock. Normally, net profits are expressed as fully diluted earnings per share, reflecting a share's actual value if convertible bonds and preferred stocks were traded for common stock.

**earnings yield.** See *yield.*

**earning the points.** Profit earned from selling foreign currency at a higher spot price and buying at a cheaper forward rate. The profit is the difference between the spot price and the forward price. Selling at a lower spot price and buying at a higher forward price is called losing the points.

**Earthwatch.** An environmental network established by the United Nations Environment Programme. The network is composed of the Global Environmental Monitoring System to track environmental and climatic changes; INFOTERRA, a computerized environmental information and referral service; and the International Register of Potentially Toxic Chemicals, containing scientific and regulatory data on hazardous substances. See also *Agenda 21.*

**East African Economic Community (EAEC).** Also known as the East African Community, the defunct customs union of Kenya, Tanzania, and Uganda. EAEC was established in 1967 and dissolved in 1978. The former EAEC countries are members of the Preferential Trade Area for Eastern and Southern African States.

**East Asia Economic Caucus (EAEC).** A regional trade association proposed by Malaysia in 1990. The association would encompass all Pacific countries, except Australia, Canada, New Zealand, and the United States. As of 1993, EAEC, also known as the East Asian Economic Grouping, had not been formed.

**Eastern and Southern African Trade and Development Bank.** See *Preferential Trade Area for Eastern and Southern African States.*

**Eastern Europe Business Information Center (EEBIC).** In the United States, an office of the U.S. Department of Commerce that provides investment and trade information on Eastern European countries, including import standards, investment regulations, markets, and notices of prospective joint ventures. The center publishes the *Eastern Europe Business Bulletin*, a bimonthly newsletter of business data and opportunities in Eastern Europe.

**East-West trade.** Commerce between the industrialized Western countries and the former Warsaw Pact countries. The Western countries are members of the Organisation for Economic Cooperation and Development. The Soviet bloc countries were members of the defunct Council for Mutual Economic Cooperation. East-West trade was a popular concept in the early 1970s after the United States and China reestablished diplomatic relations, temporarily altering the global balance of power. Compare *North/South.*

**E.B.** The abbreviation for eastbound.

**E bond.** In the United States, a savings bond that was replaced by the Series EE bond in 1980.

**EBRD.** The abbreviation for European Bank for Reconstruction and Development.

**EC.** The abbreviation for European Community.

**E.C.** The abbreviation for east coast.

**ECA.** The abbreviation for Economic Commission for Africa. See *United Nations Economic Commissions.*

**ECB.** The abbreviation for European Central Bank.

**ECCN.** The abbreviation for export control commodity number.

**ECE.** The abbreviation for Economic Commission for Europe. See *United Nations Economic Commissions.*

**ECGD.** The abbreviation for Export Credit Guarantee Department.

**échanger.** French: exchange. The exchange rate is *cours du change.*

**échantillon carnet sample.** See *carnet.*

**échéance.** French maturity (of a bill of exchange).

**ECLAC.** The abbreviation for Economic Commission for Latin America and the Caribbean. See *United Nations Economic Commissions.*

**ECLS.** The abbreviation for Export Contact List Service.

**ECME.** The abbreviation for Economic Commission for the Middle East. See *United Nations Economic Commissions.*

**Economic and Social Commission for Asia and the Pacific.** See *United Nations Economic Commissions.*

**Economic and Social Commission for Western Asia.** See *United Nations Economic Commissions.*

**Economic and Social Council.** A council created by the United Nations Charter to coordinate international economic and social policy. The council oversees UN specialized agencies and regional economic commissions. The council's 54 members are elected by the UN General Assembly for 3-year terms.

**Economic Bulletin Board.** In the United States, a subscription service offered by the U.S. Department of Commerce announcing international trade leads and opportunities. The data are published in electronic format from information collected by U.S. federal agencies.

**Economic Commission for Africa.** See *United Nations Economic Commissions.*

**Economic Commission for Europe.** See *United Nations Economic Commissions.*

**Economic Commission for Latin America and the Caribbean.** See *United Nations Economic Commissions.*

**Economic Commission for the Middle East.** See *United Nations Economic Commissions.*

**Economic Community of the Great Lakes Countries.** See *Communauté Économique des Pays des Grands Lacs.*

**Economic Community of the States of Central Africa.** See *Communauté Économique des États de l'Afrique Centrale.*

**Economic Community of West African States (ECOWAS).** Also known as the Economic Community of West Africa, a regional cooperation area composed of 16 sub-Saharan African states. Created by treaty at Lagos, Nigeria, in 1975, ECOWAS was established to promote uniform economic policies and eliminate regional trade barriers. Internal tariffs on most raw materials and handicrafts were removed in 1990. Gradual reductions in tariffs on industrial materials also began in 1990. A common external tariff, harmonized import standards, and monetary union are contemplated by the year 2000. ECOWAS is the largest regional economic association in sub-Saharan Africa. Its members are Benin, Burkina Faso, Cape Verde, Côte d'Ivoire, Gambia, Ghana, Guinea, Guinea-Bissau, Liberia, Mali, Mauritania, Niger, Nigeria, Senegal, Sierra Leone, and Togo. The ECOWAS Fund for Cooperation, Compensation, and Development is based in Lomé, Togo. ECOWAS is headquartered in Lagos.

**economic development board (EDB).** A government agency responsible for promoting development, usually in the form of foreign direct investment. EDBs propose and administer foreign investment rules and incentives. For example, the Economic Development Board of Singapore is a statutory agency operating under the Ministry of

Trade and Industry. The EDB offers low-cost leases, tax concessions, and other incentives to attract multinational corporations to Singapore.

**economic growth.** In national accounting, an increase in output or gross domestic product.

**economic integration.** The process by which two or more nations adopt uniform fiscal, monetary, and trade policies. Economic integration is accomplished by treaty and gradually eliminates impediments to cross-border flows of capital, goods, labor, and services. See also *economic union.* Compare *common market* and *free trade area.*

**economic nationalism.** A policy of organizing economic priorities primarily in terms of national interests to compete in global markets. Economic nationalism is not synonymous with autarchy, which mostly precludes reciprocal economic cooperation with other countries.

**economic needs test.** A standard applied in some countries as a condition for licensing foreign firms to enter regulated industries. The licenses are granted on an ad hoc basis when the market will absorb additional competitors. For example, Australia applies an economic needs tests in evaluating foreign applicants for banking licenses.

**Economic Recovery Tax Act (ERTA) of 1981.** In the United States, a statute that reformed the federal tax system. The act reduced individual and corporate tax rates, indexed taxes to compensate for inflation, and authorized accelerated depreciation for businesses. Tax-deferred personal savings accounts, known as individual retirement accounts, were also authorized by the act. The ERTA was modified by the Tax Reform Act of 1986.

**economic sanctions.** Also called trade and investment sanctions, restrictions imposed by one country on commerce with another. Sanctions are intended to force policy and political changes in the target country, usually after diplomacy fails. Comprehensive sanctions initiated by the United Nations are universal, restricting all forms of commerce and investment except in instances involving humanitarian aid. Sanctions imposed by one country are known as unilateral sanctions and are often disregarded by other countries. See also *Comprehensive Anti-Apartheid Act of 1986* and *embargo.*

**Economic Trends.** In the United Kingdom, a publication of the Central Statistical Office. *Economic Trends* is published monthly and provides current trade and other economic data on the UK.

**economic union.** The integration of foreign economies. With economic union, member countries form a single market without internal barriers to trade and investment. The elements of economic union are uniform trade and investment standards, as well as harmonized fiscal and monetary policies. The goals of economic union are a single central bank and a common currency. Political union may follow economic union. See also *economic integration.*

**economies of scale.** Also known as the scale effect, a financial advantage gained in large enterprises where per-unit costs presumably decrease as output rises. Returns to scale are gains attributable to the size of an enterprise. If costs and increased output rise in tandem, the effect is known as diseconomies of scale.

**ecosystem.** A social system designed to conform the needs of the human community to preservation of the physical environment. See also *environmental regulation.*

**ECOWAS.** The abbreviation for Economic Community of West African States.

**ECS.** The abbreviation for *Echantillons Commerciaux/Commercial Samples.* See *carnet.*

**ECSC.** The abbreviation for European Coal and Steel Community.

**ectype.** An imitation or copy of an original item.

**ECU.** The abbreviation for European currency unit.

**écu.** Any one of several gold or silver coins minted in France from time to time, especially the silver 5-franc coin.

**EDF.** The abbreviation for European Development Fund.

**EDGAR.** The abbreviation for Electronic Data Gathering Analysis Retrieval.

**Edge Act of 1919.** See *Edge corporation.*

**Edge corporation.** In the United States, a bank subsidiary authorized by the Edge Act of 1919. The act permits domestic banks to establish international branches, known as foreign banking corporations. Originally severely restricted in their functions, banking Edges now act as foreign subsidiaries of domestic bank holding companies. Nonbanking Edges invest in foreign commercial and financial institutions. Banks chartered outside the United States are authorized to buy Edge corporations by the International Banking Act of 1978. See also *agency bank* and *Federal Reserve Regulation K*.

**EDI.**   The abbreviation for electronic data interchange.

**EDIFACT.**   The abbreviation for Electronic Data Interchange for Administration, Commerce, and Transport.

**EDP.**   The abbreviation for electronic data processing.

**EDR.**   The abbreviation for European depositary receipt. See *international depositary receipt*.

**ee/E.E.**   The abbreviation for errors excepted. See *errors and omissions excepted*.

**EEA.**   The abbreviation for European Economic Area.

**EEBIC.**   The abbreviation for Eastern Europe Business Information Center.

**EEC.**   The abbreviation for European Economic Community.

**EEP.**   The abbreviation for Export Enhancement Program.

**EEZ.**   The abbreviation for exclusive economic zone.

**effective annual yield.**   The return on a time deposit maintained in an account for a full year, including accumulated or compounded interest. An effective annual yield quoted for deposits with maturities of less than a year does not reflect true earnings unless the investment is rolled over at the original rate. Compare *annual percentage rate*.

**effective exchange rate.**   The true cost of exchanging one currency for another. Currency conversion costs are determined by premiums and taxes paid for the exchange. Gains or losses attributable to different currency values are also factors in the cost of exchange. See also *agio*.

**effective interest rate.**   Sometimes called the real interest rate, interest costs adjusted for inflation.

The effective interest rate differs from a nominal rate, which omits the inflationary factor.

**effective lending rate.**   The cost of repaying a loan. Real borrowing costs include bank fees added to principal and interest.

**effective rate.**   1. The effective interest rate, or the annual percentage rate paid on a loan (or the interest earned on a deposit account), as opposed to the nominal or quoted rate. 2. The yield on a security after accounting for discounts or premiums, price, and the difference between the purchase date and the maturity date.

**effective rate of protection.**   See *effective tariff rate*.

**effective tariff rate.**   The dutiable cost of an import. The actual duty is the difference between the tariff on a finished import and duties levied on components or raw materials used to manufacture an identical product locally. Tariffs on inputs imported for local use are normally significantly lower than duties on finished imports. The effective rate of protection reflects the higher cost, to consumers, of finished imports.

**effective tax rate.**   The real rate of tax paid under certain circumstances. Unless taxes are paid on a flat-rate basis, the effective tax rate usually differs from the scheduled rate. See also *progressive tax*.

**effective United States control (EUSC).**   In the United States, a description of the authority of the federal government to requisition certain transport vessels in times of national emergency. The term covers U.S.-registered ships and foreign-flagged ships owned by citizens of the United States, usually those registered in Panama, Liberia, or Honduras (known as PANLIBHON countries). The Federation of American Controlled Shipping represents U.S. owners of foreign-flagged ships in negotiations with the federal government.

**Effektengiro.**   In Germany, a system for recording book entries for electronically transferred securities. Physical deliveries are cleared through the *Kassenverein*.

**effets à moyen terme.**   French: medium-term debt paper.

**effets de...catégorie.**   In France, commercial paper traded in a money market. *Effets de première catégorie* (first-class paper) are guaranteed by institutions approved by the Banque de France. *Effets de deuxième catégorie* (second-class paper) are essentially trade paper supported by less substantial guarantors.

**effets privés.**   French: private paper. See *dossier.*

**EFP.**   The abbreviation for exchange of futures for physicals.

**EFT.**   The abbreviation for electronic funds transfer.

**EFTA.**   The abbreviation for European Free Trade Association.

**EFTPOS.**   The abbreviation for electronic funds transfer at point of sale.

**EFTS.**   The abbreviation for electronic funds transfer system.

**EI.**   The abbreviation for entry input.

**EIA.**   The abbreviation for Equipment Interchange Association.

**EIB.**   The abbreviation for European Investment Bank.

**EIN.**   The abbreviation for employer identification number. See *withholding tax.*

**Einfuhrerlaubnis.**   German: import license.

**Einfuhrzoll.**   German: import duty.

**EIS.**   The abbreviation for environmental impact statement. See *environmental regulation.*

**ELAIN.**   The abbreviation for Export License Application and Information Network.   See *Bureau of Export Administration.*

**elasticity.**   In economics, a capacity for expansion, e.g., the ability of a market to absorb increased demand and grow.

**Electronic Data Gathering Analysis Retrieval (EDGAR).**   In the United States, the electronic data interchange system used by publicly held corporations to file registration statements and public disclosure information with the Securities and Exchange Commission. Originally initiated as a pilot program in 1984, the EDGAR system became operational in 1992. See also *Form 8K, Form 10K, Form 10Q, proxy statement,* and *registration statement.*

**electronic data interchange (EDI).**   The electronic transfer of business data between computer systems. EDI uses standardized formats to elimi-

nate routine transaction documents, e.g., invoices, purchase orders, and payments. Most industries have developed special EDI industry standards, such as the Warehouse Information Network Standard (WINS), developed by the American Warehousemen's Association, and the grocery industry standard, developed by the Uniform Standards Committee. In international trade, EDI systems also utilize standardized formats to process customs filings, duty payments, document verification, licenses, and fees. Similarly, electronic entry processing permits brokers and large-volume importers to file customs entries for goods entering a port from any interior location within a country. In the United States, American National Standards Institute formats are used in EDI systems. The international EDI standard is the Electronic Data Interchange for Administration, Commerce, and Transport.

**Electronic Data Interchange for Administration, Commerce, and Transport (EDIFACT).**   The international standard for electronic data interchange message formats. EDIFACT originated with the cargo documentation system developed by the British Simplification of International Trade Procedures Board in the 1970s. Known as Transportation Data Interchange, or TDI, the British standard was adopted initially by the United Nations but never used in the United States. In 1987, the UN created a new protocol, EDIFACT, approved by the International Standards Organization. EDIFACT message formats are reviewed by local EDIFACT boards and approved by the United Nations Working Party on Trade Facilitation. Trade Data Interchange (also known as TDI), the general business document format used in Europe, is based on EDIFACT formats. EDIFACT is incompatible with the ANSI standard used in the United States. See also *Customs Declaration Message.* Compare *ANSI X12.*

**electronic funds transfer (EFT).**   The settlement of financial accounts using electronic data interchange. EFTs are completed without checks or other forms of paper payment and settled through interbank accounts transferred between private clearinghouses and central bank electronic systems. Consumer direct payments to retailers are known as electronic funds transfer at point of sale, or simply point of sale. In the United States, EFTs are governed by the Electronic Funds Transfer Act of 1978, which limits the liability of consumers using automated teller machines and wire transfers when a bank is notified of unauthorized funds transfers. Bank guidelines for handling consumer transfers are contained in Federal Reserve Regulation B. Outside the United States, ATMs are generally known as automated transaction machines. See also *Association for Payment Clearing Services, Clearing House Interbank Payments System, Fed Wire,* and *Uniform Commercial Code.*

**electronic funds transfer at point of sale (EFT-POS).** See *electronic funds transfer.*

**electronic mail (E-mail).** Paper documents transmitted by computer. Mailboxes for E-mail users are retained in the memory of a central computer post office. Messages saved by the computer can be checked by users aided by telephone lines and a modem.

**electronic placing support system.** In the United Kingdom, a computerized system used by insurance companies to transmit underwriting information. Electronic placing usually involves large commercial policies for marine, aviation, and energy transactions. As a rule, the details are transmitted after the terms of a policy have been negotiated and agreed to. See also *London Insurance Market Network.*

**electronic product declaration (Form FD 2877).** In the United States, the manufacturer's certificate required for imports of nonconforming electronic equipment. The certificate verifies that the import (1) was manufactured before product standards regulations were implemented and is imported for research or training purposes, (2) complies with existing regulations, or (3) will be brought into compliance after importation.

**electronic random number indicating equipment (ERNIE).** In the United Kingdom, an electronic system for drawing winners of tax-free prices who purchase premium bonds issued by the Department for National Savings. The maximum holding is 10,000 pounds. The bonds do not have a maturity date and are redeemed at face value.

**eligible banker's acceptance.** See *eligible paper.*

**eligible for discount.** See *eligible paper.*

**eligible paper.** Banker's acceptances, bills of exchange, drafts, notes and trade acceptances,

which qualify for discounting by a central bank. Commercial paper carries lower financing costs when discounted, but it must meet the central bank's requirements for collateral. In the United States, eligible paper arises from a commercial transaction, is endorsed by a bank, and has a maturity of not more than 90 days. Commercial paper previously discounted by a commercial bank is accepted at the Federal Reserve discount window for rediscount. Although access to the discount window was granted to all U.S. financial institutions engaged in business finance by the Monetary Control Act of 1980, the Federal Reserve rarely rediscounts commercial paper. Most Federal Reserve loans to commercial banks are in the form of advances. See also *discount window* and *Federal Reserve Regulation A.*

**El Pacto Andino.** Also known as *El Grupo Andino* and the Andean Subgroup, a regional economic union established by agreement at Cartagena, Colombia, in 1969. *El Grupo Andino* is a subgroup of the *Asociación Latinoamericana de Integración.* Members of the pact created the Andean Free Trade Zone in 1985 as an intermediate regime leading to an Andean Common Market. A common external tariff and harmonized rules of origin are scheduled for full implementation by 1995. *El Pacto Andino* has approved common policies, called Andean Pact decisions or protocols, which cover intellectual property protection, foreign investment, and tariff regulation. The protocols set minimum standards for member states, leaving them the option of establishing more liberal national policies. An investment protocol adopted in February 1987, effective in 1989, liberalized regional foreign direct investment policies. *El Pacto Andino* members are Bolivia, Colombia, Ecuador, Peru, and Venezuela. Chile withdrew from the agreement in the 1970s. See also *Group of Three.*

**Elsecom.** The acronym for European Electrotechnical Sectoral Committee. See *Communauté Européenne.*

**ELVIS.** The abbreviation for Export Licensing Voice Information System.

**EMA.** The abbreviation for European Monetary Agreement. See *European Monetary System.*

**E-mail.** The abbreviation for electronic mail.

**embargo.**   1. A wartime ban on commerce with a hostile country. The term originated in the law of the sea, when belligerents closed local ports to enemy ships. 2. Civil embargoes are a form of economic sanctions, imposing a total or partial ban on commerce with an unfriendly country. Embargoes typically cover trade and air and seaport rights. See also *Foreign Assets Control Regulations* and *Trading with the Enemy Act of 1917.*

**EMC.**   The abbreviation for export management company.

**EMCOF.**   The acronym for European Monetary Cooperation Fund.

**emergency economic law (EEL).**   Any one of several laws enacted in developing countries in the 1980s to attract foreign direct investment, particularly in Latin America. For example, an EEL and regulatory decrees were adopted by Argentina in 1989, modifying the existing foreign investment law. Emergency economic laws usually open procurement bidding to foreign companies and repeal major impediments to foreign trade. An EEL may revoke regulations requiring prior government approval of certain investments, allow majority or total foreign ownership of businesses, and waive payments of duties and taxes on certain imports.

**emergency tariff system.**   A temporary tariff schedule used in some countries to protect vital domestic industries from short-term competition. Usually, the schedule is invoked against specific imports for a predetermined period of time. In South Korea, for example, emergency rates are sometimes in effect for up to 6 months. Compare *flexible tariff.*

**emerging market.**   An economic sector with growth potential. 1. In international trade, a country deregulating markets and liberalizing trade and investment regimes. 2. In sales, a maturing consumer market with adequate disposable income and a predisposition to purchase a given product.

**EMI.**   The abbreviation for European Monetary Institute.

**eminent domain.**   At common law, a sovereign's lawful seizure of private property for public purposes. In the United States, constitutional due process requires that an owner whose property is taken be given just compensation and an opportunity to contest the taking, usually before a jury. A court determines the amount of compensation.

**employment protection.**   Legal and regulatory safeguards against arbitrary employment practices. In civil-law countries, employee rights are protected by labor codes and administrative decrees. In common-law countries, regulations, statutes, and judicial decisions govern labor practices. In the United Kingdom, the Employment Protection Act of 1978 provides statutory remedies for unfair labor practices. In the United States, unfair labor practices are defined primarily by the National Labor Relations Act of 1935, the Fair Labor Standards Act of 1938, the Civil Rights Act of 1964, and court cases arising under the Constitution.

**empresa...de puertos/portuaria.**   Spanish: port authority.

**empresa...dos portos.**   Portuguese: port authority.

**EMS.**   The abbreviation for European monetary system.

**EMU.**   The abbreviation for European Monetary Union. See *European monetary system.*

**EN 29000.**   See *ISO 9000.*

**Endangered Species Act.**   See *Convention on International Trade in Endangered Species of Flora and Fauna.*

**endiguer.**   French: to hedge.

**endorsement.**   Affixing a signature, stamp, or sign to the back of a negotiable instrument to transfer ownership. 1. A financial instrument made to the order of a named payee is negotiated by endorsement and delivery. By virtue of adding an endorsement, the endorser becomes liable to other parties, known as holders, for the face amount of the instrument. 2. A blank endorsement, also called an absolute or general endorsement, creates a bearer instrument, entitling the person in possession of it to payment. 3. A conditional endorsement creates a contingent right to payment, requiring stated conditions to be fulfilled before ownership passes to a holder. For example, bills of exchange usually condition payment on the transfer of title in goods (e.g., "Pay

ABC Company upon delivery of goods"). 4. An endorsement without recourse disclaims a prior holder's liability if the instrument is later dishonored by the maker or a drawee ( e.g., "Pay XYZ, Inc., without recourse"). 5. A direct (or special) endorsement, also called an endorsement in full, creates an order instrument, requiring a named payee's signature before it is paid ( e.g., "Pay to the order of RST Company"). 6. A restrictive endorsement obligates a fiduciary to hold an instrument for the benefit of a third party ( e.g., "for deposit to the account of EFG Company only.") or otherwise limits its negotiability. In the United States, endorsements are governed by the Uniform Commercial Code. See also *enhancement*.

**end-to-end.**    In foreign exchange dealing, the means of fixing maturity dates for forward contracts and currency swaps. End-to-end encompasses the period from the last business day of one month to the last business day of the next month. Normally, a future maturity date, or the spot date for delivery, is the last business day of the month. When the maturity date is a nonworking day, the spot date falls on the next business day.

**end user.**    The ultimate consumer of a good. The end user may be other than the ultimate purchaser, who is the last party to pay the purchase price of a product or service. In international trade, the status of an import's end user often determines whether the import is dutiable or subject to licensing. End-use certificates regulate imports by identifying authorized end users.

**Engineering Multiplier Program.**    In the United States, a loan program administered by the Engineering Division of the Export-Import Bank (Eximbank) to finance feasibility studies. The program is open to domestic architectural and engineering firms that perform preconstruction consulting services. An applicant must demonstrate that a loan is likely to generate exports of $10 million or more, or double the value of the contract awarded to the borrower, whichever is greater.

**English water ton.**    The British measure of the volume of petroleum products. A water ton is equal to 224 imperial gallons of petroleum.

**enhanced structural adjustment facility.**    See *International Monetary Fund*.

**enhancement.**    1. The addition of a creditworthy party's endorsement to a financial instrument. The endorsement enhances the instrument's eligibility for acceptance and may create eligible paper. 2. In official financing, collateral deposited with a lender by a borrowing country to obtain a loan. The collateral is sometimes obtained from a multilateral institution, such as the World Bank or a regional development bank.

**enlargement.**    1. An increase in the membership of a common market or free trade association accomplished by treaty. 2. In Europe, the First Enlargement, or the 1973 entry of Denmark, Ireland, and the United Kingdom into the European Economic Community. The Second Enlargement denotes the entry of Greece in 1979 and Portugal and Spain in 1986.

**entente.**    In continental Europe, a business cartel. More broadly, an agreement between nations.

**Entente Council.**    See *Conseil de l'Entente*.

**enter into force.**    To become effective or acquire the force of law, particularly regarding a treaty, international agreement, amendment, annex, or protocol. Treaties typically contain self-executing provisions that specify the terms and conditions under which they become effective. Ordinarily, an international agreement is opened for signature at a stipulated time and place and requires a predetermined number of nations to sign by a fixed date. To enter into force, a treaty must be accepted, acceded to, approved, or ratified, depending on the nature of the agreement and the status of the signatory country in relation to it. In some instances, to adopt a treaty, governments enact or change national laws to conform to their own constitutional or legal requirements or to fulfill obligations imposed by it. In others, national agencies are created to administer changed laws. An international agreement enters into force in a signatory country when a government takes the measures necessary to execute treaty obligations. See also *accession* and *tacit acceptance*.

**Enterprise for the Americas Initiative (EAI).**    In the United States, a trade and aid program announced on June 27, 1990. The North American Free Trade Agreement, concluded in 1992, is the first step toward the EAI goal of creating a hemispheric free trade zone. The EAI contemplates a series of bilateral framework agreements and free trade agreements (FTAs) negotiated between the United States, Caribbean, and Latin American countries. The proposed framework agreements are preconditions to negotiating FTAs that set forth rules for trade, bilateral consultations, and compliance with the General Agreement on Tariffs and Trade. Beyond trade, the EAI proposes to increase foreign investment through an Enterprise for the Americas Fund administered by the Inter-American Development Bank and financed by the United States, the European Community, and Japan. The EAI also proposes to reduce external debt in the Americas through an Enterprise for the Americas Facility. An additional lending facility, the Environmental Fund, is contemplated to fund environmental programs through debt-for-nature swaps. See also *debt conversion program*. Compare *Caribbean Basin Initiative I* and *Caribbean Basin Initiative II*.

**enterprise zone (EZ).**   An underinvested area suffering from high unemployment. In the United States, several legislative proposals have been advanced, mostly recently in 1993, to target enterprise zones for special investment incentives, including tax benefits and relaxed regulations. For example, under some proposals, a business locating in an enterprise zone would receive a 100 percent allowance for capital expenditures and exemptions from corporate and business taxes for a 10-year period.

**entreposto.**   Portuguese: bonded warehouse.

**entrepôt.**   A warehouse or distribution center for in-transit goods. Known as the entrepôt trade, goods are warehoused for auctioning, sampling, testing, repackaging, etc. Duties are not levied until entrepôt goods are withdrawn for reexport. 1. An *entrepôt fictif* is a private warehouse, usually owned by an importer and not under direct customs control. Basic manufactures, coal, grain, and petroleum products are warehoused, often for up to 2 years. 2. An *entrepôt réel* is a public bonded warehouse controlled by a customs agency and usually located at major ports, such as Hong Kong, Rotterdam, or Singapore. Goods may remain in an *entrepôt réel* for up to 5 years. 3. An *entrepôt spécial* is a privately owned warehouse,

often bonded and equipped with cold storage for perishable products stored for under 3 months.

**entrepôt de douane.**   French: customs warehouse.

**entrepreneur.**   A person who invests capital and time for profit. The entrepreneur assumes the risks of offering goods or services for sale.

**entry.**   See *customs entry*.

**entry documents.**   Documents required to enter goods into a customs territory. In most countries, the documents include a commercial invoice or pro forma invoice, a customs manifest, a packing list, proof of entitlement to merchandise, special permits, and a surety bond. Normally, a summary document can be filed and estimated duties paid for the immediate release of goods for warehousing or sale. Detailed customs document filings are usually required within 30 days of entry. In the United States, the procedure is known as National Entry Processing.

**entry input (EI).**   In the United States, the electronic code for opening the computer application to create an entry summary record in the Automated Commercial System.

**entry manifest.**   In the United States, Customs Form 7533. See also *manifest*.

**Entry Rulings Branch.**   See *U.S. Customs Service*.

**entry specialist team (EST).**   In the United States, U.S. Customs Service employees assigned to a single multitask unit. The units were created to eliminate duplications in customs entry processing. ESTs operate under expedited customs procedures, including accepting entry summary filings to facilitate the entry process. See also *Business Service Center*. Compare *customs document processing station*.

**entry summary.**   In the United States, Customs Form 7501, the standard import form for commercial customs entries. The entry summary is filed with estimated duties within 10 working days of the release of goods to an importer. See also *entry documents*.

**environmental.**   In economics, calculating the costs and benefits of maintaining viable ecosystems. See also *environmental regulation*.

**environmental impact statement.**   See *environmental regulation*.

**Environmental Protection Agency (EPA).** In the United States, a federal agency established in 1970 to set domestic environmental standards. The EPA enforces clean air and water standards, recommends pollution abatement, and mandates waste disposal and toxic substances controls. Environ-mental standards proposed at the state level are approved by the EPA. See also *Clean Air Act of 1990*.

**environmental regulation.** In law, any one of a number of statutes, decrees, and rules issued by a national, regional, or municipal authority to control various forms of pollution, waste disposal, and natural resource exploitation. Most jurisdictions have adopted some form of environmental regulation with varying degrees of penalties for noncompliance. Environmental impact statements or similar measures are used by governments to evaluate the ecological effects of proposed projects, laws, or rule changes in advance of approval. See also *Agenda 21* and *green technology*.

**EO.** The abbreviation for executive order.

**EOHP.** The abbreviation for except as otherwise herein provided.

**EOM.** The abbreviation for end of the month.

**eo nomine.** See *classification*.

**EOTC.** The abbreviation for European Organization for Testing and Certification.

**EP.** The abbreviation for European Parliament.

**EPA.** The abbreviation for Environmental Protection Agency and European Productivity Agency.

**EPA Form 3520-1 (Rev. 7-88).** In the United States, a declaration filed at entry for vehicles not conforming to Environmental Protection Agency clean air regulations. See also *independent commercial importer*.

**EPC.** The abbreviation for European Patent Convention.

**EPO.** The abbreviation for European Patent Office.

**EPR.** The abbreviation for Export Product Review.

**EPU.** The abbreviation for European Payments Union.

**EPZ.** The abbreviation for export processing zone.

**EQS.** The abbreviation for European Quality System. See *Communauté Européenne*.

**equilibrium.** An analytical tool used by economists to predict economic behavior. Equilibrium presupposes a balance between conflicting interests that limits variability in human conduct. When the balance is exact, an economic variable becomes fixed and incapable of changing. For example, theories of the equilibrium between supply and demand provide a tool for reducing the infinite possibilities of pricing and support the concept of a market price. See also *Pareto optimum*.

**equipment interchange receipt and safety inspection report.** See *interchange agreement*.

**equitable treatment.** See *national treatment*.

**equity.** 1. An ownership interest in an asset. 2. The value of a shareholder's stock in a company. Equity is the net value of shareholders' claims on a company's assets once priority creditors and holders of senior security claims have been paid. 3. In common-law tradition, an outcome determined by fairness rather than legal principles.

**equity swap.** See *debt conversion program*.

**equivalent treatment.** See *reciprocity*.

**ERLC.** The abbreviation for the Export Revolving Line of Credit Program.

**ERM.** The abbreviation for exchange rate mechanism. See *European monetary system*.

**ERNIE.** The abbreviation for electronic random number indicating equipment.

**errors and omissions excepted (E&OE).** 1. In insurance, a provision protecting a policyholder from losses due to inadvertent errors or simple negligence. 2. In commercial documents, such as invoices, a phrase that protects a sender from inadvertent errors favoring another party.

**ERTA.** The abbreviation for Economic Recovery Tax Act.

**ESAF.**    The abbreviation for enhanced structural adjustment facility. See *International Monetary Fund.*

**ESC.**    The abbreviation for European Shippers' Council.

**escalation clause.**    A contract clause, usually in a construction contract, that permits a contractor to increase prices under specified conditions. Escalation clauses usually cover the inflation factor when a contract is completed over several years. Price escalators can apply to materials, labor, and services. See also *cost-plus contract.*

**ESCAP.**    The abbreviation for Economic and Social Commission for Asia and the Pacific. See *United Nations Economic Commissions.*

**escape clause.**    1. In contracts, a clause discharging a party from an obligation under certain conditions. 2. In trade treaties, import relief to prevent domestic market disruption. Article XIX contains the escape clause in the General Agreement on Tariffs and Trade (GATT). A GATT member may resort to remedies, including temporary quotas, when a critical domestic industry is threatened. In the United States Section 201 of the Trade Act of 1974 determines when the GATT escape clause may be invoked by the federal government. See also *International Trade Commission.*

**escheat.**    The process by which real property reverts to the state when a valid claim to it has not been established. The reversion is automatic when there are no rightful heirs to realty or when the owner has breached a legal condition of ownership. Compare *bona vacantia.*

**escompte commercial.**    In France, trade finance using a subsequently discounted bill of exchange.

**escrow.**    A contract or deed authorizing funds to be held in trust for a stipulated purpose. Escrow accounts are maintained with banks or trust companies. The account remains in effect until its purpose has been fulfilled.

**escudo.**    The currency of Portugal.

**ESCWA.**    The abbreviation for Economic and Social Commission for Western Asia. See *United Nations Economic Commissions.*

**ESOP.**    The abbreviation for employee share-ownership plan.

**est.**    The abbreviation for estimate, estimated, and estimated weight.

**EST.**    The abbreviation for entry specialist team.

**establishment.**    In external trade, setting up a business in a foreign country. Under free trade theory, the right of establishment complements liberalized trade and encompasses equitable access to leasing, licensing, and financial facilities. Developing rules applying national treatment to establishment, particularly regarding service industries, was an original objective of the Uruguay Round of the General Agreement on Tariffs and Trade. But the process of devising equitable rules of establishment in service industries is especially complex. In most countries, services, such as banking and insurance, have historically been heavily regulated monopolies. As of 1992, the GATT framework for establishment originally proposed in the Uruguay Round had not been adopted.

**estate.**    1. The sum total of a person's interest in real and personal property. 2. In the common law of real property, an ownership interest in land. The interest may be unconditional (a vested estate), limited by the life of a named person (a life estate), due to arise in the future (a future estate), dependent on the occurrence of a specified event (a contingent estate), or implied by a court (an equitable estate). See also *freehold.*

**estate agent.**    Also called a land agent, a realtor in most English-speaking countries outside the United States.

**estoppel.**    A common-law principle that, once having asserted a fact, a person may not later deny its truth. For example, a party proclaiming a material fact during contract negotiations cannot later disclaim it.

**et al.**    The abbreviation for *et alibi* (and elsewhere) and *et alii* (and others).

**ETC.**    The abbreviation for export trading company.

**ETF.**    The abbreviation for electronic transfer of funds.

**ETSI.** The abbreviation for European Telecommunications Standards Institute. See *Communauté Européenne.*

**EUR 1 form.** The European Community import form for products originating in African, Caribbean, and Pacific countries.

**EURAT0M.** The abbreviation for European Atomic Energy Community.

**Eurco.** The acronym for European composite unit.

**Eurobill of exchange.** A negotiable bill of exchange denominated in a foreign currency and payable in a third country.

**Eurobond.** A bond issued in a Eurocurrency, frequently on behalf of a multinational corporation. Eurobonds, often placed simultaneously in several countries, can be denominated in a single currency, multiple currencies, or artificial currency units (ACUs). Types of Eurobonds are floating-rate bonds (at variable rates), perpetual bonds, and straight bonds (fixed-rate loans for up to 8 years). Eurobonds are issued in bearer form through foreign banking syndicates, usually investment banks located in Japan or the United States. The bonds are unregistered, and taxes are not withheld. Interest is paid annually, often at relatively low interest rates pegged to the London interbank offered rate or a similar index rate. Eurobonds are cleared through Cedel, an international clearing system, and Euroclear, operated in Brussels by Morgan Guaranty Trust Company of New York. Compare *Yankee bond* and *yen bond.*

**EUROCAM.** The abbreviation for European chambers of commerce. See *Chamber of Commerce.*

**Euro certificate of deposit (CD).** A dollar-denominated, time-deposit instrument issued outside the United States, mainly in London. The rates of Euro CDs are pegged to the London interbank offered rate.

**Eurocheque.** A check drawn on a European bank and guaranteed by a Eurocheque card. A Eurocheque is usually paid in the local currency where it is made. When the check is written on a foreign bank, a small commission and the foreign exchange conversion value are added to the amount of the check.

**Euroclear.** See *Eurobond.*

**Eurocommercial paper.** A short-term promissory note issued in Europe for payment in the United States. The notes are sold through dealers and paid in U.S. dollars. See also *Euronote.*

**Eurocorde Agreement.** An early 1990s shipping conference agreement, made by independent carriers traveling the North Atlantic trade route, to consult on freight rates. Although the European Commission found the agreement in violation of the European Community's competition rules, continuation of the agreement was permitted until 1995.

**Eurocrat.** An employee of a European Community agency. See also *European Commission.*

**Eurocredit.** See *revolving underwriting facility.*

**Eurocurrency.** A foreign currency on deposit abroad, often, but not always, in Europe. The Eurocurrency money market developed in the 1950s to finance international trade through short-term loans. Short-term loans have largely been supplanted in the Eurocurrency market by longer-term syndicated loans and Eurobond issues for corporate and government finance. Central banks, commercial banks, and multinational corporations borrow and lend in Eurocurrencies at relatively low rates of interest, while also escaping tax and regulatory limits in domestic lending markets. London, the world's largest Euromarket, specializes in Eurobonds. Other Euromarkets are located in the Bahamas, Brussels, Paris, and Zurich.

**Eurodollar.** A U.S. dollar deposited outside the United States, usually in foreign banks or the foreign branches of U.S. banks. International banking facilities also hold Eurodollar accounts, although most Eurodollars are deposited in London. Eurodollar certificates of deposit are issued by foreign branches of U.S. banks, mostly in London, and are pegged to the London interbank offered rate.

**Eurodollar certificate of deposit (EUROCD).** See *Eurodollar.*

**Euroequity.** A stock denominated in a currency other than the local currency of the country in which it is issued.

**EuroFed.** The proposed European Central Bank.

**Eurofeds.** Overnight Eurodollar loans transferred between U.S. banks. Eurofeds are borrowed by banks short of reserves and transmitted by Federal Wire.

**Euro Info Centres.** See *BC-NET.*

**Euro-lending center.** See *Eurocurrency.*

**Euromarket.** See *Eurocurrency.*

**Euromart.** A financial or equity market where foreign-denominated debt or equity is traded.

**Euronet.** The electronic information network of the European Community (EC). Euronet was originally approved by the Council of the European Communities in 1971 to link 192 European databases through the Direct Information Access Network and disseminate commercial, engineering, scientific, and legal information throughout the EC. Although Euronet was implemented in 1980, it has largely been supplanted by the national computer networks of EC member states.

**Euronote.** A short-term unsecured promissory note carrying a maturity of up to a year and sold at a discount. Euronotes are high-quality bearer instruments issued by financial institutions, governments, and large corporations, usually for 30 to 180 days. The notes are denominated in European currency units or U.S. dollars and are offered for sale by tender panels. See also *Eurocommercial paper.*

**Euro-patent.** See *European Patent System.*

**European Agricultural Guidance and Guarantee Fund.** See *Common Agricultural Policy.*

**European Atomic Energy Community (EURATOM).** An organization created in 1957 by the Treaty of Rome. EURATOM was established by the six original members of the European Coal and Steel Community to develop an industrial base for producing nuclear energy. The agreement was subsequently joined by Denmark, Ireland, and the United Kingdom in 1973. Greece became a member in 1979. Portugal and Spain joined in 1986.

**European Bank for Reconstruction and Development (EBRD).** Also known as the European Bank and *Banque Européenne de Reconstruction et Développement,* a development bank created at Paris in 1990. EBRD was established by the European Community (EC) and other countries to finance the economic development of the former Soviet Union and Eastern

Europe following the collapse of the Warsaw Pact. EBRD lends for continental private-sector development, usually at commercial lending rates. A soft-loan window, or a special capital fund, to convert Eastern European military industries to commercial uses has also been proposed, and the bank is a clearinghouse for legal and technical assistance in Eastern Europe. Fifty-one percent of the bank's voting shares are held by EC members. The remaining shares are held by other European and non-European nations, including Pacific Rim and Middle Eastern countries. The United States holds 10 percent of the bank's shares. As the legal successor to the Union of Soviet Socialist Republics, a charter EBRD member, the Russian Republic holds 8 percent of its shares. EBRD is headquartered in London.

**European Central Bank (ECB).** Also called EuroFed, the proposed central bank of the European Community (EC) to be established before the year 2000. A European System of Central Banks was formally proposed to the European Commission by the Delors Report in 1989, a proposal substantially adopted by the EC in the 1992 Treaty of Maastricht. The agreement at Maastricht created the European Monetary Institute, the predecessor of the ECB. As of 1993, important issues surrounding the proposed central bank were not resolved. For example, whether the composition of the bank's capital will be determined by the gross domestic product or the population size of the EC countries was not decided at Maastricht. Responsibility for the EC's foreign exchange policy was also not fixed. Currently, monetary policy in the European monetary system (EMS) is controlled largely by the Bundesbank, which determines domestic interest rate policy, but strongly influences the values of other EC currencies because of the strength of the Deutsche mark. With the advent of the ECB, presumably a reserve board on which all participants in the EMS are represented will moderate the Bundesbank's influence. Ultimately, EC foreign exchange policy may be decided by the Council of Finance Ministers, possibly through a twin-key mechanism of shared responsibility between the council and the ECB 's governing board.

**European Coal and Steel Community (ECSC).** A common market in coal, steel, and iron ore products formed by the six original members of the European Community (EC). The original signatories to the 1951 Treaty of Paris were Belgium, the Federal Republic of Germany (the former West Germany), France, Italy, Luxembourg, and the Netherlands, often simply called the Six. The ECSC was originally conceived to enable France and West Germany to cooperate in rebuilding heavy industries following World War II. The Six agreed to integrate the common market under a single High Authority, the first international governing body in Europe. The ECSC was one of three European Communities created by the six countries in the 1950s. In 1967, the ECSC and the European Atomic Energy Community merged with the European Economic Community to form the European Common Market, or the European Communities, the predecessor of the contemporary European Community.

**European Code of Social Security.**  See *Treaty of Maastricht.*

**European Commission.**  Also known as the Commission of the European Communities, the European Commission is the executive body and international trade negotiator for the European Community (EC). The European Commission was created in 1967 by a merger of the executive bodies of the European Coal and Steel Community, the European Atomic Energy Community, and the European Economic Community. The European Commission collects and disburses revenues, negotiates agreements on behalf of the EC, and drafts directives, the EC's primary policymaking instruments. Among others, anticompetition, dumping, subsidy, and consumer protection complaints are filed with the European Commission, which is authorized to levy duties and fines and to halt injurious business practices. Appeals from unfavorable decisions are heard by the European Court of Justice. The European Commission has 17 commissioners appointed by EC countries. Two commissioners each represent France, Germany, Italy, Spain, and the United Kingdom, the largest countries in the EC. Belgium, Denmark, Greece, Ireland, Luxembourg, the Netherlands, and Portugal are each represented by one commissioner. The European Commission's decisions are independent of EC governments and taken by a majority vote. The European Commission is supported by the European civil service, known pop-

ularly as Eurocrats, which consists of 23 Directorates-General. The body is headed by a president appointed for a 2-year term, renewable by the European Council. The European Commission sits in Brussels.

**European Common Market.**  See *European Economic Community.*

**European Community (EC).**  Also known as *Communauté Européenne* and the European Communities, the merged European Atomic Energy Community, European Coal and Steel Community, and European Economic Community. The communities were integrated in 1967 when the Commission of the European Communities and the Council of the European Communities were formed. The members of the EC in 1967 were Belgium; France, Italy, Luxembourg, the Netherlands, and West Germany, known as the Six. In 1973, Denmark, Ireland, and the United Kingdom joined the EC, then known as the Nine. When Greece, Portugal, and Spain joined the EC between 1979 and 1986, the common market became known as the Twelve. In 1992, the EC adopted the Treaty of Maastricht, designed to create a European single market in 1993. Monetary union is contemplated before the year 2000. The governing organs of the EC are the European Commission, the European Council of Ministers, the European Parliament, the European Court of Justice, and the Economic and Social Committee.

**European Community of Research and Technology (ECRT).**  A series of programs authorized by the Single European Act to finance and coordinate research and development in the European Community. The EC has created regional research facilities, known as Joint Research Centres, in Belgium, Germany, Italy, and the Netherlands. Joint financing is also available to other research centers, universities, and private companies. ECRT funds are allocated in European currency units.

**European company.**  A company organized under European Community (EC) company law. Also known by the Latin name *Societas Europaea*, a European company is formed by creating a holding company, establishing a joint subsidiary, or converting an existing public limited company. There are legal limitations on mergers. The minimum capital requirement is 100,000 European currency units, although the EC country in which a company is registered may require higher capitalization. Bankruptcy and liquidation are also governed largely by the registering country. Boards of directors may be organized under a two-tier system comprising a management board and a supervisory board or under a single-tier system composed of an administrative board. Public disclosure of financial statements and general meetings of shareholders are required. Various proposals mandating some form of employee participation or co-determination are under consideration by the European Community.

**European composite unit (Eurco).** The unit of exchange of the European Investment Bank introduced in 1973. The Eurco is an unofficial artificial currency unit created to settle private accounts. Based on a basket of European Community national currencies, the Eurco's value is established daily. Eurcos are the commercial equivalent of European currency units which are available only for government holders. Compare *Euro-SDR*.

**European Council of Ministers.** The principal decision-making body of the European Community. The council determines EC policies, both domestic and foreign. Its lawmaking instrument is the directive. Directives are adopted by a weighted majority, but a single EC country may veto regional mandates on health and safety issues. The council is composed of 12 members appointed by EC member governments. Although usually made up of foreign ministers, the council may be made up of others holding various government portfolios, depending on the issue before it. The council sits in Brussels. Compare *Council of Europe*.

**European Court of Justice.** A 13-member judicial body appointed by common consent of European Community (EC) countries. The Court is the forum of last resort in the EC and interprets laws and directives. The Court also rules on the validity of EC rules and on internal conflicts between EC countries, institutions, and individuals. The European Court sits in Luxembourg.

**European currency snake.** The exchange rate management system adopted by the European Economic Community (EEC) following the end of the Bretton Woods Conference arrangement in 1971. The common margins arrangement, also known as the snake in the tunnel, was devised at an EEC meeting in Basel in 1972. Each European Community currency was permitted to float within a range, or band, of 2.25 percent of the U.S. dollar. Belgium (franc), Denmark (krone), France (franc), Ireland (punt), Netherlands (guilder), Italy (lira), and West Germany (Deutsche mark) were participants in the snake. Britain did not join the arrangement. The snake was supplanted by the European monetary system in 1978.

**European currency unit (ECU).** The artificial currency unit of the European Community (EC). ECUs are based on a basket of weighted EC national currencies. The ratio of a national currency is determined, among other things, by each national bank's gold reserves, hard currency holdings, and balance of payments. See also *European monetary system*. Compare *Eurco*.

**European depositary receipt.** See *international depositary receipt*.

**European Economic Area (EEA).** Also known as the European Trade Area, an extended free trade zone uniting the European Community (EC) and the European Free Trade Association, which encompasses 19 countries. EEA negotiations began in 1988 and were concluded in 1992. Member countries agreed to adopt uniform trade legislation, authorizing the free flow of goods, investment, and services between EEA states. The EEA treaty ends internal tariff discrimination, brings EFTA imports under EC rules of origin, harmonizes product standards, and simplifies border controls. As of mid-1993, all but two (Iceland and Liechtenstein) of the seven EFTA countries have taken the initial steps needed to join the EC. However, Swiss voters rejected a referendum endorsing the EEA in 1992.

**European Economic Community (EEC).** The European Common Market formed from the European Coal and Steel Community in 1957. The 1957 Treaty of Rome, which created the EEC, also established the European Atomic Energy Community. The EEC eliminated internal tariffs, established a common external tariff, harmonized regulatory standards, and developed the Common Agricultural Policy. The EEC also adopted a common policy on trade with developing countries, which has been approved by four

Lomé Conventions. The Treaty of Maastricht signed in 1992 created a single European market.

**European Economic Space.**    See *European Economic Area.*

**European Electrotechnical Sectoral Committee.** See *Communauté Européenne.*

**European Free Trade Association (EFTA).**    Also known as the *Association Européenne de Libre Echange,* a free trade area created at the Stockholm Convention in 1960. Original EFTA members were Austria, Denmark, Norway, Portugal, Sweden, Switzerland, and the United Kingdom. Iceland and Liechtenstein later joined the EFTA. Between 1973 and 1986, Denmark, Portugal, and the United Kingdom left the EFTA to join the European Community (EC). Finland is an EFTA associate member. The EFTA is governed by the European Free Trade Council, a body of ministers who meet semiannually. Relations between the EFTA and Finland are administered by the Joint Council of the European Free Trade Association and Finland. In 1992, the EFTA and the EC agreed to form the European Economic Area. The EFTA's secretariat is based in Geneva.

**European Free Trade Association Council.**    See *European Free Trade Association.*

**European Investment Bank (EIB).**    A regional development bank founded in 1957. The EIB was created by the Treaty of Rome to finance European Economic Community (EEC) economic development and to fund projects in poor EEC regions. The EIB funds development projects in Europe and provides loan guarantees to banks, agencies, and private businesses. Projects are financed primarily through funds raised in international capital markets. The European currency unit is the EIB's official accounting currency. The EIB issues the Eurco for commercial settlements. The bank is headquartered in Luxembourg. See also *New Community Instrument.*

**European Monetary Cooperation Fund (EMCOF)** Also known by its French acronym, FECOM, the unit within the European monetary system (EMS) that stabilizes exchange rates and settles official European Community (EC) accounts. EC countries deposit a percentage of their gold and reserve assets with the fund, which finances balance-of-payments lending facilities. European Monetary Cooperation Fund loans are made in European currency units (ECUs). The fund is based in Brussels.

**European Monetary Institute (EMI).**    A transitional organization created by the 1992 Treaty of Maastricht to precede monetary union in the European Community (EC). The EMI, to be fully established in 1994, is the predecessor of the proposed European Central Bank. The capital assets of the EMI will be minimal. The EMI is authorized to manage national reserves voluntarily deposited by EC countries.

**European monetary system (EMS).**    The exchange rate system established by the European Community (EC) in 1978 to replace the European currency snake. The EMS is composed of the exchange rate mechanism (ERM) and the European Monetary Cooperation Fund. The ERM requires EC countries to maintain national currency values within a narrow range of the European currency unit (ECU). EC central banks alter interest rate policies or, in extreme cases, purchase currencies in international money markets to maintain values within the band, or grid. In reality, the ECU is primarily valued in relation to the Deutsche mark, the strongest currency in the EMS. In 1992, the parity grid was 2.25 percent. Under the EMS agreement, exchange-rate ratios are reviewed every 5 years or when requested by a member state. The European Monetary Cooperation Fund provides short- to medium-term credit facilities to enable EC countries to stabilize rates and compensate for balance-of-payments deficits. The 12 EC countries are EMS members, although all do not participate in the ERM. In 1992, the British pound and the Italian lira were temporarily withdrawn from the ERM to avert further losses against the Deutsche mark. Turmoil in the international currency market in 1993, reflected in the sharp devaluation of the Irish punt, appeared likely to cause a future restructuring of the EMS.

**European monetary union (EMU).**    The complete economic integration of the European Community (EC) contemplated by the 1992 Treaty of Maastricht and scheduled to take effect between 1997 and 1999. Monetary union envisions a European Central Bank and a single EC currency.

**European option.**    See *option.*

**European Options Exchange.**    See *International Options Clearing Corporation.*

**European Organization for Testing and Certification (EOTC).**    An organization created at Brussels in 1990 to oversee product testing and certification in the European Community and the European Free Trade Association, known jointly as the European Economic Area. EOTC's purpose is to eliminate technical barriers to internal European trade. The standards approved by EOTC are not mandatory, but nonconforming imports must usually be certified by each European country. See also *Communauté Européenne.*

**European Parliament (EP).**    The popularly elected body of the European Community (EC). The EP is the final authority on EC budgetary matters, except those involving agriculture. Apart from its budget authority, the EP is limited to advising and ratifying decisions of the European Commission and the European Council. The Parliament has 518 members, which represent roughly 11 political parties. The EP meets in Brussels. Its secretariat is headquartered in Luxembourg.

**European Patent Convention.**    See *European Patent System.*

**European Patent Office.**    See *European Patent System.*

**European Patent System.**    The system designed to administer the series of multilateral agreements harmonizing European patent laws. The European Patent Convention, also known as the Munich Patent Convention and the Convention on Granting of European Patents, was adopted at Munich in 1973. The convention became effective in 1977 and created the European Patent Office (EPO) at Munich. Applications are filed with the EPO under a unified system. Non-renewable patents are granted for a period of 15 years. Although the EPO has a uniform filing system, EC countries have national patent processing systems, and obtaining patent protection in all 12 EC countries can be costly. Infringement proceedings are subject to judicial rules of different EC countries. The Strasbourg Patent Convention and the Community Patent Convention, also known as the Luxembourg Convention, were signed in 1963 and became effective 1980. The Strasbourg Convention brings pharmaceuticals, chemicals, etc., under the European Patent System.

**European Payments Union (EPU).**    A union established in 1950 as a facility to settle official European Economic Community (EEC) accounts. EEC countries contributed fixed capital shares to the EPU. The United States was the largest external subscriber, and the EPU's artificial currency unit, the European unit of account, was the equivalent of one U.S. dollar. The EPU was dissolved in 1958 and replaced by the European Monetary Cooperation Fund.

**European Quality System.**    See *Communauté Européenne.*

**European Recovery Program.**    See *Marshall Plan.*

**European Social Charter.**    See *Community Charter of the Fundamental Rights of Workers.*

**European standards.**    See *Communauté Européenne.*

**European System of Central Banks.**    See *European Central Bank.*

**European Telecommunications Standards Institute.**    See *Communauté Européenne.*

**European terms.**    In currency markets, the ratio between a foreign currency and equivalent U.S. dollars. At any given time, European terms reflect the difference between the exchange value of one foreign currency unit and one U.S. dollar.

**European Trade Area.**    See *European Economic Area.*

**European unit of account (EUA).**    1. The official monetary unit of the European Payments Union. One unit of account was equal to the gold content of one U.S. dollar. The official EUA was superseded by the European currency unit (ECU) with the implementation of the European monetary system in 1979. 2. An unofficial unit of account used to denominate some bond issues, primarily because of its stability. Although some flexibility exists, the value of the EUA changes only if the relative values of all currencies in the basket also change, reflecting a realignment of two-thirds of its currency basket. See also *European Payments Union.*

**Europort.**    A European port, particularly Rotterdam.

**Euros.**   The European Community ship registry.

**Euro-SDR.**   A commercial accounting unit based on the official special drawing right (SDR). International bankers developed the Euro-SDR to peg exchange rates in private settlements to SDR-basket currencies. The value of a Euro-SDR fluctuates with changes in the value of official SDRs. Compare *European composite unit, flexible SDR, and frozen special drawing right.*

**Eurotunnel.**   The tunnel beneath the English Channel connecting Britain to the European continent by way of France. The tunnel is also called the Channel Tunnel and the Chunnel.

**Euroyen.**   Japanese yen on deposit outside Japan, especially in a Euro-lending center. See also *Eurocurrency.*

**E.U.S.C.**   The abbreviation for effective United States control.

**evergreen fund.**   A start-up investment in a new company. Unlike venture capital, evergreen funds are injected periodically after the initial investment during a company's early growth years.

**evergreen loan.**   A revolving line of credit without a periodic payoff requirement. Evergreen loans are usually made for a specific length of time, subject to renewal or cancellation.

**ex (xd).**   Latin: without. 1. In securities, a quoted limitation on benefits gained from a purchase; e.g., ex-dividend denotes a share issued without a dividend right, while ex-coupon indicates a bond issued without a right to interest payments. Similarly, ex-bonus, ex-capitalization (ex-cap), and ex-rights mean the seller retains the benefit. The opposite of ex is cum, meaning a right transfers to the buyer with the purchase. 2. In a sales contract, as in ex warehouse or ex works, the seller only bears the costs of making goods available at a named site.

**examination station.**   A customs area for shipment inspections.

**ex aequo et bono.**   Latin: equity and fairness. *Ex aequo et bono* is a principle of civil law that permits a court to decide a case based on notions of justice rather than a strict reading of the law.

**exception.**   A rejection of a proposal in international trade negotiations. The party taking the exception often objects to a proposal's potential impact on its national economy. See also *derogation.*

**exception rating.**   A carrier's basis for levying a hazardous cargo handling fee. The fee is charged in addition to general freight. See also *dangerous goods.*

**excess capacity.**   Underutilized plants, processes, or labor that, if put to use, would reduce the cost of a product or service. Reduced output increases the average per-unit cost of servicing a customer. As excess capacity diminishes, per-unit costs fall.

**excess foreign currencies.**   In the United States, foreign currencies dedicated by the U.S. Department of Treasury to settling overseas accounts. Often, excess reserves develop when the United States is paid in foreign currencies for commodities sold under PL 480, the U.S. foreign agricultural assistance programs. Excess reserves are supplies of foreign currency units held in excess of the U.S. government's needs.

**exch.**   The abbreviation for exchange.

**exchange (exch.).**   1. In finance, the process of trading one currency for another or the currency traded, i.e., foreign exchange. 2. In commerce, the settlement of a debt by payment, often through a clearinghouse. 3. A market for trading commodities or securities. See also *commodity exchange* and *stock exchange.*

**exchange control.**   Limits placed on the use of foreign exchange. Exchange controls are often imposed by a government faced with balance-of-payments deficits or a currency not easily convertible into other currencies. The central bank or ministry of finance regulates foreign currency trading and determines how foreign exchange is spent, usually by issuing exchange permits for foreign purchases. An exchange control system may, but need not, employ a differential exchange rate system. See also *controlled currency rate* and *secondary exchange market.*

**exchange equalization account.**   An account that holds some of a country's official gold reserves, foreign currencies, and artificial currency units. When a government intervenes in world currency markets to stabilize exchange rates, purchases or sales from these accounts are arranged through foreign exchange brokers. The transactions are made through the international swap network, a reciprocal short-term credit facility for central banks. By using swap facilities, central banks buy or sell one currency for another, reversing the transaction at a later date and thus controlling the amount of currency available for speculation. Exchange equalization accounts are managed by a country's central bank. In the United States, the account is called the Exchange Stabilization Fund. It holds U.S. Treasury reserves and is administered by the Federal Reserve Bank of New York.

**exchange license.**  See *exchange permit.*

**exchange offer.**  An offer to acquire stock in one corporation in exchange for those of another. As distinguished from a tender offer, an exchange offer is a technique for acquiring a company without cash expenditures.

**exchange permit.**  A government license to convert local currency into a foreign currency. Exchange permits are required to purchase imports or finance other transactions in countries with exchange controls.

**exchange rate.**  The value of a national currency in relation to foreign currencies.

**exchange rate mechanism.**  See *European monetary system.*

**exchange rate protection arrangement.**  A government's financial guarantee to domestic exporters to avert exchange rate losses. The guarantee covers disparities when a manufacturer's product is priced in a foreign currency and production costs are denominated in the domestic currency. A General Agreement on Tariffs and Trade (GATT) panel found a similar arrangement concerning the European Airbus in violation of the GATT Subsidies Code. In 1992, the European Community and the United States concluded an Airbus Agreement limiting subsidies.

**Exchange Stabilization Fund.**  See *exchange equalization account.*

**Exchequer.**  The ministry of finance of the United Kingdom.

**Exchequer stock.**  See *gilt-edged security.*

**excise tax.**  A sales tax, often collected by a customs agency. Excise taxes are charged against all goods of a given class, irrespective of a product's origin. In the United States, excise taxes are internal revenue taxes, collected by federal, state, and local agencies. When levied on manufactured products, the excise tax is equal to a percentage of a product's sale price and packaging costs, exclusive of insurance and transportation costs. Excise taxes on goods entering foreign trade zones or bonded warehouses are not collected until the goods are released, and are forgiven when goods are exported by manufacturers or their agents. Merchandise purchased by government or foreign diplomatic agencies is exempt from excise taxes. In the United States, an importer delays paying excise taxes by filing a tax deferment bond. See also *value apportionment process.*

**exclusive agency.**  See *agency.*

**exclusive dealing contract.**  An exclusive agency agreement.

**exclusive economic zone (EEZ).**  An area beyond a country's coastline reserved by agreement solely for its economic exploitation. Ocean resources, including fish and the seabed, fall under the sovereign ownership of the coastal state. See also *territorial waters.*

**exclusive patronage contract.**  An exclusive agreement between a shipper and a maritime conference. These agreements are also called merchant's freight agreements, shipper's rate agreements, and merchant's contracts. An exporter executing the agreement is known as a contract shipper and receives a lower freight rate in consideration for signing the agreement. In the United States, shipping agreements are permitted under the Shipping Act of 1916.

**exclusive use.**  1. A licensing arrangement prohibiting the use of goods, processes, or services for reasons other than those specified in an agreement. 2. In transportation, a carrier's agreement to reserve containers or other shipping equipment for the exclusive use of a named shipper. The shipper contracts for a minimum shipment or pays an extra surcharge.

**executive order (EO).**  In the United States, an order issued by the President, giving administrative effect to a law, policy, or treaty. A president's authority to act under executive orders can be delegated to executive departments or administrative agencies. Notices of executive orders are published in the *Federal Register.*

**executor.**   A person or firm named in a will to administer a decedent's estate. An executor's authority is prescribed by the will and by letters testamentary issued by the court. The feminine form of executor is executrix. Compare *administrator.*

**exemplary damages.**   See *damages.*

**exempt company.**   In international commerce, a company excused from tax liability or certain regulations. The exemption may arise from a tax benefit created by a double-taxation treaty or from regulatory incentives adopted to encourage investment.

**exempt de douane.**   French: duty free.

**exempt gilts.**   See *gilt-edged security.*

**exempt securities.**   In the United States, securities exempt from Federal Reserve System margin requirements and Securities and Exchange Commission registration and reporting regulations. These issues include commercial paper, municipal bonds, private placements, some issues of banks and savings and loans, and debt obligations of federal agencies.

**exercise notice.**   A notice from the holder of a call option (a buy option) or a put option (a sell option) who intends to buy or sell at the exercise price. The exercise price, also called the strike price or the striking price, is the per-share price specified in an option.

**exercise price.**   See *exercise notice.*

**ex factory.**   See ex works.

**Eximbank.**   The acronym for the Export-Import Bank of the United States.

**ex int.**   The abbreviation for excepting interest.

**exit bond.**   A debt-reduction security issued by a commercial bank on behalf of a sovereign debtor. Issuing the bond enables the lender to write off a country's loans, frequently as a means of reducing reserves held against uncollectible debts. See also *debt conversion program.*

**exonerated cargo.**   Otherwise dutiable cargo on which duties are eliminated. Usually, exonerated cargo consists of manufacturing components or raw materials used to produce locally finished

goods. Exonerated cargo is often transported only by domestic-flagged carriers.

**Exon-Florio Act of 1988.**   In the United States, a law requiring the U.S. Department of Treasury to block unauthorized takeovers of domestic firms in defense-related industries. Exon-Florio prohibits mergers and acquisitions between U.S. and foreign firms when a national security interest is deemed threatened by external ownership. Amendments extending Exon-Florio to economically strategic industries have been considered but not adopted.

**exotic currency.**   In foreign exchange markets, a currency for which a large international market has not developed, e.g., the Ethiopian birr or the Nicaraguan cordoba. See also *Singapore dollar market.*

**exp.**   The abbreviation for expense and export.

**expenditure tax.**   Also known as an outlay tax, a tax on income expended by a taxpayer. An outlay tax reaches income outflows, but not income earned. Sales taxes and value-added taxes are expenditure taxes.

**expense (exp.).**   A sum of money expended by a business or individual for goods or services. In business accounting, expenses are usually treated as a charge against earnings and displayed on the profit and loss statement.

**expiration date.**   1. The latest date on which an option can be exercised. American options are exercised at any time up to the expiration date. European options are exercised only on the expiration date. 2. The date on which an agreement or obligation expires.

**expiry date.**   A synonym for expiration date.

**explosions clause.**   In marine insurance, a provision that protects a shipper for losses from accidental fires or explosions. The clause does not cover fires or explosions arising from war or civil disorder.

**export (exp.).**   A good or service sold in a foreign market. In balance-of-payments calculations, goods (i.e., merchandise or commodities) are visibles. Services (i.e., banking, insurance, etc.) are invisibles.

**Export Administration Act (EAA) of 1979.**   In the United States, the act of Congress that supersedes the Export Control Act of 1949. Section 4(a) of the act mandates issuance of validated export licenses for items covered by the act. Section 5(a) specifies the terms and conditions under which the President may impose foreign policy controls on U.S. goods and services in international commerce. The act also authorizes the Export Control Program under which the Bureau of Export Administration issues Export Administration Regulations and export licenses. See also *export privilege* and *individual validated license*. Compare *general license*.

**export bar.**   A gold bar transferred between central banks or multilateral institutions.

**export broker.**   An agent who arranges contacts between sellers and importers. Export brokers are compensated on a commission basis.

**export club.**   An association of companies formed to share export information and services. In the United States, the Federation of International Trade Associations acts as a national information clearinghouse for domestic export clubs. See also *Webb-Pomerane Act of 1918*.

**export commission house.**   A local agent for foreign buyers.

**Export Contact List Service (ECLS).**   In the United States, a service provided by the U.S. Department of Commerce. ECLS supplies domestic exporters with mailing lists of foreign buyers based on automated files, which identify foreign agents, importers, wholesalers, and government agencies. The lists include specific data, including a foreign firm's address, year established, product specialities, and contact names.

**Export Control Act of 1949.**   In the United States, a statute governing domestic export licensing. The act introduced selective controls to prevent diversions of strategic weapons to the Warsaw Pact and prohibited most direct U.S. shipments to communist countries. It authorized the President to implement export control regulations, a power subsequently delegated to the secretary of commerce. The Export Control Act was superseded by the Export Administration Act of 1979.

**export control commodity number (ECCN).**   In the United States, a product identification number displayed on a Shipper's Export Declaration.

**Export Control Program.**   In the United States, a program authorized by the Export Administration Act of 1979 and administered by the U.S. Department of Commerce. The program was designed to thwart trade with unfriendly countries (principally Cuba) and restrict exporting by private firms known to have violated domestic export laws. Since 1991, the program's Commerce Control List has been streamlined, but controls on some pharmaceuticals and most weapons and dual-use items remain in place. See also *individual validated license*.

**export credit.**   Subsidized financing provided by one government to another for import purchases, usually farm commodities. In the United States, the Export Credit Guarantee Program sponsored by the U.S. Department of Agriculture extends short-term credits to foreign governments for purchases of U.S. farm commodities. Export credit terms are monitored by the Organization for Economic Cooperation and Development (OECD). The OECD information-sharing system enables member governments to compare country risks for export lending and insurance programs.

**Export Credit Enhanced Leverage (Excel).**   A program organized in 1989 by the Berne Union and the World Bank to finance exports from the Organization for Economic Cooperation and Development countries to developing countries. Under Excel, national export financing agencies (e.g., the Export-Import Bank of the United States) and the World Bank cofinance export loans or loan guarantees. Multilateral development banks manage and distribute Excel funds. The multilateral lenders also assume the credit risks of these transactions.

**export credit insurance.**   Government-subsidized insurance that protects domestic exporters from default by foreign buyers.The Organization for Economic Cooperation and Development (OECD) attempts to bring uniformity and transparency to export credit insurance programs, since some OECD countries provide easier insurance terms to local exporters than other exporters can obtain. The OECD information-sharing system enables member governments to compare country risks when setting export credit insurance premiums. The European Commission has proposed limiting official insurance to medium- to long-term investments, i.e., up to 8 years, while permitting private insurers to underwrite short-term contracts. OECD export credit insurers are *Compagnie Française d'Assurance pour le Commerce Extérieure* in France, *Eksportkreditradet* in Denmark, Export Credits Guarantee Department in the United Kingdom, Export Development Corporation in Canada, Export Insurance Division of the Ministry of International Trade and Industry in Japan, *Exportkreditnamnden* in Sweden, Foreign Credit Insurance Association in the United States, *Hermes Kreditversicherungs-Aktiengesellschaft* in Germany, *Office National du Ducroire (OND)* in Belgium, *Österreichische Kontrollbank AG.* in Austria, and *Sezione Speciale per l'Assicurazione dei Crediti all'Esportazione* in Italy. See also *Berne Union*.

**Export Credits Guarantee Department (ECGD).** The export credit insurance agency in the United Kingdom. ECGD was established in 1919 to insure foreign receivables and promote British exports. The agency is currently authorized under the Export Guarantees and Overseas Investment Act of 1978. ECGD provides export credit insurance, loan guarantees, and overseas investment insurance. The short-term credit insurance arm of ECGD is administered by a private insurer.

**export declaration.**   A shipper's export declaration submitted to a customs agency. The form contains a description and other details of a shipment.

**Export Development Corporation (EDC).**   In Canada, the national export financing and export credit insurance agency. EDC provides export credit insurance under the Loan Pre-Disbursement Insurance (LPI) program; export loan guarantees under the Loan Guarantees program; and financing for consulting, engineering, and feasibility studies under the Loan Support for Services program. Overseas investment insurance is provided by the Foreign Investment Insurance program. EDC also manages the Canada Account.

**export drop shipper.**   A purchasing agent for merchandise produced in foreign countries. The export drop shipper is essentially a conduit for the transfer of documents of title to an end purchaser.

**export duty.**   A tax levied against exports in some countries, primarily on commodity exports.

Export duties are not levied in industrialized countries and are prohibited in the United States by Article 1, Section 9, of the U.S. Constitution.

**Export Enhancement Program (EEP).**   In the United States, a farm price-support program offered by the U.S. Department of Agriculture. U.S. agricultural exporters post performance bonds in exchange for cash bonuses, which represent the difference between the domestic cost of production and a foreign market price. Designed to enable U.S. farmers to compete in foreign subsidized markets, EEP price supports are viewed as illegal export subsidies by some U.S. trading partners, notably Australia.

**Exporter Assistance Division.**   An agency of the U.S. Department of Commerce, which advises exporters on Export Administration Regulations.

**exporter's certificate of origin.**   See *certificate of origin*.

**Export-Import Bank of the United States (Eximbank, EX-IM).**   In the United States, a national export financing agency created by executive order in 1934. Eximbank was chartered by Congress as an independent agency in the Export-Import Bank Act of 1945. The bank provides loans, working capital guarantees, and export insurance. Eximbank also offers export promotion programs and information services, including the City/State Program, a commercial bank referral list, and export briefing programs. U.S. exports financed by the bank must have at least 50 percent domestic content and not adversely affect the domestic economy. The bank does not finance military sales, except in support of selected antinarcotics programs. Country risk is a factor in Eximbank lending. The bank is funded through loan repayments, fees, and financing extended by the U.S. Treasury and the Federal Financing Bank. See also *commercial interest reference rates*.

**export incentive.**   A benefit granted to exporters by a government. Export incentives include bonuses, concessional credit, subsidies, tax benefits, and so on. Although most export incentives constitute illegal subsidies under the GATT Subsidies Code, governments nevertheless provide them under a variety of guises. See also *General Agreement on Tariffs and Trade: Tokyo Round, Subsidies (and Countervailing Measures) Code*.

**export jobber.**  See *export drop shipper.*

**Export Legal Assistance Network (ELAN).**  In the United States, a service sponsored jointly in the United States by the American Bar Association, the U.S. Department of Commerce, and the U.S. Small Business Administration. Established in 1983, ELAN provides free legal consultations to U.S. exporters. The program is available in most major cities in the United States.

**export license.**  A government permit to export. Export licenses are often used in countries that depend on exports of primary commodities for foreign exchange. Licensing enables the exporting government to ration scarce commodities, particularly nonrenewable resources, such as petroleum. In developed countries, export licenses are required mainly for controlled arms and munitions, chemicals, some pharmaceuticals, and dual-use items. An export license may be a general license or a special license. Export permits are universally required for foreign sales of valuable antiques and art. See also *Bureau of Export Administration* and *individual validated license.*

**Export Licensing Application Information Network (ELAIN).**  In the United States, the electronic data interchange system used by the Bureau of Export Administration to process export licenses.

**Export Licensing Voice Information System (ELVIS).**  In the United States, the automated voice information service for export licensing. A service of the Bureau of Export Administration, ELVIS counsels exporters on export licensing procedures, commodity classifications, and emergency handling. See also *System for Tracking Export License Applications.*

**export management company (EMC).**  A company that specializes in arranging foreign sales for manufacturing companies. Export management companies are usually compensated on a commission basis. The commissions may be computed as a straight percentage of the merchandise selling price or as a percentage of the foreign resale price.

**Export Opportunities.**  See *U.S. Agency for International Development.*

**export privilege.**  The doctrine under which a government licenses exports. An export license can

be general or special. It is revocable at the discretion of the licensing government. In the United States, exports licenses are withdrawn from persons or firms found in violation of U.S. export control laws. See also *Export Administration Act of 1979.*

**export processing zone (EPZ).**  A foreign trade zone that provides special benefits to export-oriented manufacturing industries. Incentives include tax forgiveness, reduced or zero import duties on raw materials used to manufacture exports, relaxed regulations, special allowances, and so forth. In some countries, EPZs are known as enterprise zones, industrial free zones, or special economic zones.

**Export Product Review Program (EPR).**  In the United States, a program of the U.S. Department of Agriculture for domestic exporters of prepackaged foods. Program officers advise exporters of international regulatory standards for prepackaged foods. EPR also provides information on foreign national labeling regulations, food ingredient restrictions, product standards, and certification procedures.

**export promotion fund tax.**  In some countries, notably Argentina, a tax imposed on imports to finance exports. Normally, the tax is equal to a fixed percentage of the cost, insurance, and freight value of the import.

**export quota.**  A restriction on domestic exports. Export quotas are used primarily in developing countries. They are imposed unilaterally to control the outflow of scarce commodities or arise from obligations incurred under international commodity agreements.

**export quota agreement.**  A price-stabilization mechanism in some international commodity agreements. Normally, exporting countries belonging to an international commodity group agree to product quota allocations. Importing countries restrict imports from nonsignatory commodity producers in exchange for a continuous supply from signatory countries. See also *buffer stock.* Compare *import quota.*

**Export Revolving Line of Credit Program (ERLC).**  In the United States, a working capital guarantee program for U.S. small-business exporters sponsored by the Small Business Administration. Loans under $200,000 are guaranteed by the SBA. Financing above $200,000 is coguaranteed by the Export-Import Bank of the United States.

**export sales agent.**    A foreign firm that buys a foreign manufacturer's product for its own account to sell in local markets. Manufacturers' mandatory minimum stocking orders (MSO) require export sales agents to maintain preset inventories. An MSO is expressed in terms of specific product quantities or minimum financial value. Compare *manufacturer's export agent*.

**export subsidy.**    A financial incentive provided by a government to stimulate local export production. International trading rules generally impose specific sanctions to control the use of subsidies as inducements to export. See also *countervailing duty action* and *General Agreement on Tariffs and Trade: Tokyo Round, Subsidies (and Countervailing Measures) Code*.

**export tariff.**    See *export duty*.

**export trade certificate of review.**    In the United States, a certificate issued jointly by the Office of Export Trading Company Affairs of the U.S. Department of Commerce and the U.S. Department of Justice. The certificates protect U.S. firms from antitrust prosecution by authorizing certain international trade transactions involving business combinations. Generally, holders of these certificates are immune from prosecution unless their conduct adversely impacts the U.S. domestic economy. See also *business review procedure* and *Export Trading Company Act of 1982*.

**export trading company.**    See *Export Trading Company Act of 1982*.

**Export Trading Company Act (ETCA) of 1982.** In the United States, a law enacted to promote exports of U.S. goods and services. The act enlarged export financing programs and created immunity from prosecution under antitrust laws for certain export transactions. Title I authorizes the U.S. Department of Commerce to provide technical and business assistance to domestic export trading companies. Title II, also known as the Bank Export Services Act, permits U.S. commercial banks to purchase equity in export trading companies and allows federally chartered banks to lend to export trading companies under prescribed circumstances. Title III relaxes the applica-

tion of antitrust laws to companies engaged in external trade, subject to an export trade certificate of review issued by the U.S. Department of Commerce and the U.S. Department of Justice. The section also restricts private antitrust prosecutions of firms engaged in export trade, reduces potential liability, and imposes court costs on unsuccessful plaintiffs. Title IV, known as the Foreign Trade Antitrust Improvements Act, limits the impact of the Sherman Act of 1890 and the Federal Trade Commission Act of 1914 on U.S. external trade unless foreign transactions injure domestic commercial interests.

**Export Yellow Pages.**    In the United States, a directory of domestic companies engaged in international trade. The *Export Yellow Pages* are issued by the Office of Export Trading Company Affairs, an agency of the U.S. Department of Commerce.

**exposure.**    1. In international finance, the total amount of external debt permitted or credit extended to a single country. 2. In trading, the potential loss from fluctuations in market prices. See also *currency exposure*.

**exposure fee.**    A lender's surcharge for assuming a loan risk. Usually, exposure fees amount to a percentage of the loan's face value, but they vary according to the degree of risk.

**expropriation.**    The seizure of private property by a foreign government without just or reasonable compensation. Expropriations normally occur in times of internal political turmoil, insurrection, or war. In rare instances, arbitrary seizures result from political disputes between governments. Compare *eminent domain*.

**ex quay.**    A term of sale. The seller pays all delivery costs, including the cost of loading goods onto a ground carrier at the destination port. The buyer pays all subsequent charges.

**ex ship.**    A term of sale. Also called free overboard or free overside, the seller pays all delivery costs, including the cost of unloading goods from the ship. The buyer pays all subsequent charges.

**Extended Fund Facility (EFF).**    An International Monetary Fund (IMF) program that provides loans for balance-of-payments deficits and medium-term structural adjustment programs. To qualify for IMF lending, countries are required to submit detailed programs of policies, economic objectives, and measures to implement objectives. See also *conditionality*.

**external audit.**   See *customs audit*.

**extraordinary general meeting (EGM).**   In the United Kingdom, a shareholders' meeting other than the annual general meeting. An auditor, directors, shareholders, or a court may require an extraordinary general meeting. Shareholders are notified within 14 to 21 days of the meeting. EGMs are mandatory when a company suffers serious financial losses.

**extraterritorial.**   The description of a government's action, decree, or order that has effect beyond its legal jurisdiction. International law generally frowns on extraterritorial actions, and host countries typically enforce their own laws against foreign nationals and subsidiaries. For example, when Canada's laws conflict with those of another country, the Canadian Foreign Extraterritorial Measures Act requires foreign subsidiaries to comply with the laws of Canada.

**extrinsic value.**   See *time value*.

**EXW.**   The abbreviation for ex works.

**ex warehouse.**   A term of sale. The seller pays to load goods at the warehouse, but the buyer pays delivery costs to a destination point.

**ex works.**   An international commercial term (INCOTERM). The seller pays for loading at the factory. The buyer takes delivery and pays the costs from the factory to a destination point.

# F

**F.** An abbreviation for franc.

**Fa.** The abbreviation for *Firma.*

**FAA.** The abbreviation for Federal Aviation Administration.

**fabriqué aux États-Unis d'Amérique.** The French marking for products originating in the United States.

**fac.** The abbreviation for fast as can.

**FAC.** The abbreviation for Foreign Assets Control. See also *Foreign Assets Control regulations.*

**face value.** 1. The principal payable on a contract, loan agreement, or financial instrument. Face value does not include interest, fees, or surcharges. 2. In securities, the par value displayed on a security. By contrast, market value is the selling price. The difference between a security's par value and market value is the discount or premium paid when it is sold.

**Facilities Information and Resources Management System (FIRMS).** In the United States, the electronic system used by the U.S. Customs Service to track the flow of goods through customs facilities. FIRMS codes in the Automated Commercial System (ACS) identify the customs facility where goods are located.

**facility fee.** A lender's fee for opening a credit facility on behalf of a borrower.

**FACS.** The abbreviation for Federation of American Controlled Shipping. See *effective United States control.*

**factorage.** See *factors.*

**factoring.** Short-term financing provided by factors, usually banks or finance companies, which pay cash for bulk accounts receivables. 1. In discount factoring, the seller receives the discounted price of receivables before they mature. 2. In maturity factoring, the seller receives the face value of the receivables at maturity, less factor's fees. 3. In nonrecourse factoring, also called without recourse financing, the factor assumes all credit risks on the sale and has no resort against the seller if the debtor defaults. However, the risk of a prod-

uct liability suit does not pass to a nonrecourse factor. 4. In recourse factoring, also called accounts receivable financing, the factor recovers from the seller if the buyer defaults. 5. In undisclosed factoring, the factor buys the goods, and the seller, acting as the factor's agent, collects the debt from the buyer. Undisclosed factoring is used when the seller prefers to camouflage the source of financing. 6. In with-service factoring, the factor collects from a buyer and remits the sales proceeds to the seller. 7. In with-service-plus-finance factoring, the factor pays the seller 80 to 90 percent of the invoice price after the merchandise is sold. The balance is paid when the debt is collected from the buyer.

**factors.** 1. Firms that specialize in factoring. 2. Mercantile agents who sell inventory in their own names. Factors receive a commission, called factorage, based on the value of sales represented by a given transaction. See also *factoring.*

**Factors Chain International (FCI).** A worldwide organization created in 1968 to provide a correspondent network for factoring companies. FCI offers factoring services in roughly 35 countries and manages better than 50 percent of all global factoring. The organization is based in Amsterdam.

**factura.** Spanish: invoice.

**facture.** French: invoice.

**facultative reinsurance.** See *reinsurer.*

**fail.** A trade in which securities are not transferred as stipulated in a purchase order. A fail-to-deliver means the seller does not deliver the securities. A fail-to-receive means the buyer fails to pay, usually because securities were not delivered as ordered.

**fair average quality (FAQ).** 1. A description of commodities sold as medium-grade goods and not sampled or tested. FAQ goods are represented as equal in quality to identical goods recently sold from the same source and known to pass without objection in the trade. Compare *sale by sample.* 2. In the United States, an implied warranty of merchantability imposed on the seller of fungible goods under §2-314 of the Uniform Commercial Code.

**fair market value.** The price accepted by a willing seller and an informed buyer, frequently in the home market. Importing countries that require certifications of import prices normally accept fair market value to verify the fairness of an export price. Fair market value is also a factor in antidumping investigations.

**fair trade.**   See *fair trade law.*

**Fair Trade Commission (FTC).**   In Japan, the agency that administers Japanese competition laws and fair business policies. The FTC has limited enforcement powers, primarily because criminal indictments are rarely sought in unfair competition cases in Japan. Under the Anti-Monopoly Law of 1947, the FTC investigates price fixing and other monopolistic practices, but its powers are largely limited to issuing directives similar to cease and desist orders in the United States.

**fair trade law.**   1. In Japan, the equivalent of European competition law and U.S. antitrust law. 2. In the United Kingdom, consumer protection and competition laws.

**Fair Trading Act.**   See *Monopolies and Mergers Commission.*

**fait accompli.**   French: an accomplished fact, i.e., an irreversible act or situation.

**FAK.**   The abbreviation for freight all kinds.

**Faktura.**   German: invoice.

**FAL.**   The acronym for Convention on Facilitation of International Maritime Traffic. See *International Maritime Organization.*

**Fälligkeitstag.**   German: due date; maturity date of a bill of exchange.

**FAM.**   The abbreviation for free at mill.

**familiar drawing techniques.**   The borrowing sequence followed by member countries to obtain balance-of-payments financing from the International Monetary Fund (IMF). A country first borrows to the limit of its reserve tranche, formerly known as the gold tranche. This facility allows unrestricted borrowing up to the prescribed amount of a country's reserves deposited with the IMF. When the reserve tranche is depleted, a country has access to IMF credit tranches.

**F&A.**   The abbreviation for February and August, i.e., semiannual payments of dividends and interest.

**F&D.**   The abbreviation for freight and demurrage.

**Fannie Mae.**   See *Federal National Mortgage Association.*

**FAO.**   The abbreviation for Food and Agricultural Organization of the United Nations.

**FAQ.**   The abbreviation for fair average quality.

**Farm Credit System.**   See *land bank.*

**FAS.**   The abbreviation for Compact of Free Association, Foreign Agricultural Service, and free alongside ship.

**FASB.**   The abbreviation for Financial Accounting Standards Board.

**fast track.**   In the United States, an expedited procedure for legislative approval of international trade agreements. The U.S. Constitution authorizes a President to make treaties with foreign nations (Article II, Section 2). The power to authorize trade negotiations and approve trade agreements is vested in Congress (Article I, Section 8). Fast-track procedures, enacted in the Trade Act of 1974 and the Omnibus Trade Act of 1988, require that Congress approve or reject a trade agreement without amendment within a fixed period of time. Under the acts, the President submits fast-track requests to the Congress by way of the Committee on Ways and Means in the House of Representatives and the Senate Committee on Finance. The Congress affirms or withdraws a President's negotiating authority within 60 days of receiving written notice of pending negotiations. If the negotiating authority is affirmed, the agreement is concluded and presented for a vote. Within 90 legislative days after an agreement is presented, Congress approves or rejects it. The President may receive an extension of negotiating authority if the request is approved within a 90-day period. Fast-track authority is usually extended for 2 years.

**fate.**   See *advisement.*

**FB.**   The abbreviation for freight bill.

**FBH.**   The abbreviation for free on board at harbor.

**fbm.**   The abbreviation for foot-board measure.

**FBT.**   The abbreviation for full berth terms.

**FCA.**   The acronym for free carrier.

**F.C.&S.**   The abbreviation for free of capture and seizure.

**FCC.**   The abbreviation for Federal Communication Commission.

**FCI.**   The abbreviation for Factors Chain International.

**FCIA.**   The abbreviation for Foreign Credit Insurance Association.

**FCN.**   The abbreviation for friendship, commerce, and navigation.

**FCPA.**   The abbreviation for Foreign Corrupt Practices Act.

**FCPA review procedure.**   In the United States, a process under which the U.S. Department of Justice and the Securities and Exchange Commission jointly review proposed international transactions for potential violations of the Foreign Corrupt Practices Act of 1977. A review is based on information submitted by a company concerning a proposed foreign transaction. Like the business review procedure used to evaluate mergers and acquisitions in the United States, an opinion issued under an FCPA review is limited to the facts at issue and does not apply in all cases.

**FC&S.**   The abbreviation for free of capture and seizure.

**FCS.**   The abbreviation for Farm Credit System and (U.S. and) Foreign Commercial Service

**FD.**   The abbreviation for free (at) dock and free discharge.

**FDA.**   The abbreviation for Food and Drug Administration.

**f.desp.**   The abbreviation for free despatch.

**FDI.**   The abbreviation for foreign direct investment.

**f.dis.**   An abbreviation for free discharge.

**f. disp.**   The abbreviation for free dispatch.

**FEACR.**   The acronym for Federal Acquisition Regulations.

**FECOM.**   See *European Monetary Cooperation Fund.*

**Fed.**   The abbreviation for Federal Reserve System.

**Federal Acquisition Regulations (FEACR).**   In the United States, rules governing federal procurement policies. FEACR are available through the U.S. Government Printing Office. See *Office of Management and Budget.*

**Federal Aviation Administration (FAA).**   In the United States, the federal agency that regulates civil aviation. Established in 1958, the FAA became an agency of the U.S. Department of Transportation in 1966. The FAA sets air safety standards, oversees the construction and maintenance of airports, and administers U.S. laws involving international air traffic.

**Federal Bill of Lading Act of 1915.**   See *bill of lading.*

**Federal Communications Commission (FCC).**   In the United States, an independent agency established to administer the Federal Communications Act of 1934. The FCC regulates domestic and foreign radio, telegraph, telephone, and television communications. It also approves rates and accounting procedures for licensed telecommunications operators. In addition to assigning broadcast frequencies, the FCC also approves standards for electronic equipment and oversees communications systems used by seagoing vessels.

**Federal Communications Commission Declaration (FCC 740).**   In the United States, a certificate issued by the Federal Communications Commission (FCC) for imports of radios and television receivers. The declaration verifies that an import conforms to domestic radio emission standards and FCC rules for radio frequencies.

**Federal Deposit Insurance Corporation (FDIC).**   In the United States, an agency created in 1933 to guarantee commercial bank deposits. The FDIC is funded by contributions from federally insured banks and its own investment income. It insures deposits held by commercial banks and savings and loan associations for up to $100,000. The FDIC also administers the Savings Association Insurance Fund, established after the collapse of the U.S. savings and loan industry in the 1980s. The FDIC is managed by a five-member board of directors, which includes the comptroller of the currency.

**federal funds rate.**   The rate at which commercial banks in the United States make interbank short-term loans from reserve funds. The amount loaned may not exceed regulatory reserve limits. Unlike the Federal Reserve discount rate, determined in advance by the Federal Reserve, the funds rate is fixed for each transaction. Interbank loans are arranged by federal funds dealers, i.e., financial institutions authorized to serve as federal funds agents.

**Federal Home Loan Mortgage Corporation (FHLMC).**   In the United States, a secondary-market agent for home mortgages originally authorized by Congress in 1970. Also known as Freddie Mac, FHLMC purchases and resells residential mortgages to insurance companies, pension funds, savings and loan associations, trust funds, etc. Restructured by the Financial Institutions Reform, Recovery, and Enforcement Act of 1989, Freddie Mac is exempt from state blue sky laws. Freddie Mac's participation certificates and mortgage-backed securities are issued by the Government National Mortgage Association, and its repayment obligations are guaranteed by the federal government. Freddie Mac is a quasi-public corporation, and its governing board is selected jointly by its shareholders and the President of the United States. Compare *Federal National Mortgage Association.*

**federalist.**   1. In the United States, a proponent of shared state and federal powers. 2. In Europe, an advocate of European economic and political integration. Jean Monnet and Robert Schuman, both of France, were the most prominent early federalists. Monnet and Schuman were instrumental in creating the European Communities in the 1950s.

**Federal Maritime Commission (FMC).**   In the United States, an independent federal agency that replaced the U.S. Maritime Board. The FMC regulates ocean carriers within the United States and in domestic offshore trade. It administers maritime laws, reviews tariffs, licenses carriers and freight forwarders, and hears maritime disputes. The FMC also loosely regulates shipping conferences, which are exempt from U.S. antitrust laws when approved by the FMC. Conference rate agreements, filed with the FMC, take effect unless the commission requests additional information or raises an objection within a specified period of time, normally within 45 days. The FMC objects to a rate agreement by filing suit in federal court. See also *Shipping Act of 1916.*

**Federal Maritime Lien Act of 1910.**   In the United States, the statute that superseded state laws and established federal jurisdiction over maritime liens. Under federal law, maritime liens attach in inverse order, i.e., a later claim has priority over an earlier one. Claimants who delay in filing claims lose legal rights to subsequent lienholders. See also *laches.*

**Federal National Mortgage Association (FNMA).**   In the United States, a private corporation, also known as Fannie Mae, that purchases conventional and federally guaranteed residential mortgages. Authorized as a government agency in 1938, Fannie Mae was reorganized as a federally chartered shareholder corporation in 1968 to purchase mortgage-backed securities in the secondary market. Its activities are funded from sales of its own securities, mostly debentures, notes, and stock, and from commitment and insurance fees. Compare *Federal Home Loan Mortgage Corporation.*

**Federal Open Market Committee (FOMC).**   In the United States, a committee of the Federal Reserve System that determines interest rate policy, primarily through open-market operations. To set long-term interest rates, the FOMC instructs the Federal Reserve Bank of New York to buy or sell U.S. government securities. Securities trades are made by the Open Market Desk from the Open Market Account. When the FOMC buys securities, it loosens the money supply and makes more credit available. When it sells securities, reserves are reduced and the money supply is tightened. Short-term adjustments are made through repurchase agreements arranged through securities dealers. An FOMC sale for repurchase is called a matched sale-repurchase agreement. When the FOMC buys for resale, the purchase is known simply as a repurchase agreement. The Open Market Committee has thirteen members, including seven governors of the Federal Reserve Board and the presidents of six Federal Reserve Banks. The six bank FOMC seats rotate among the presidents of eleven of the regional Federal Reserve Banks. The president of the Federal Reserve Bank of New York has a permanent seat on the committee.

**Federal Register (FR).**   In the United States, an official publication of the federal government issued on federal working days. First published May 14, 1936, the *Federal Register* contains administrative rules and regulations, executive orders and presidential proclamations, general and special orders, and notices of hearings scheduled by executive departments and federal agencies. The *Federal Register* is available in book form or can be accessed by computer. It is published by the Office of the Federal Register, a unit of the National Archives and Records Service of the General Services Administration.

**Federal Reserve Act of 1913.** See *Federal Reserve System.*

**Federal Reserve Bank of New York.** The Federal Reserve Bank that executes Federal Open Market Committee operations and settles foreign transaction accounts. The bank also certifies exchange rates for U.S. federal agencies based on prevailing market rates quoted in New York. Major international currency rates are certified daily. Others are verified at the request of a federal agency, usually the U.S. Customs Service. For customs purposes, the certified foreign currency rate is the market rate on the export date. See also *Tariff Act of 1930.*

**Federal Reserve Banks (FRBs).** In the United States, the 12 district banks in the Federal Reserve System. The banks are owned by commercial banks in their districts and provide central banking services, including advances, discount window services, check collection, and Fed Wire services for interbank loans. FRBs also determine U.S. interest rate policy by participating in Federal Open Market Committee operations. The banks are located in Atlanta, Boston, Chicago, Cleveland, Dallas, Kansas City, Minneapolis, New York, Philadelphia, Richmond, San Francisco, and St. Louis.

**Federal Reserve Board (FRB) of Governors.** In the United States, the governing body of the Federal Reserve System. The board has seven members, who are appointed by the President to 14-year terms and are confirmed by the Senate. The board sets reserve requirements for commercial banks, implements federal banking laws, and determines interest rate policy through its majority on the Federal Open Market Committee.

**Federal Reserve discount rate.** In the United States, the interest rate at which member banks borrow short-term funds from the Federal Reserve System. The discount rate is set at 2-week intervals and partially determines commercial interest rates and credit terms in the United States. See also *interest rate policy.* Compare *federal funds rate.*

**Federal Reserve note.** The official paper currency of the United States. The bank notes are issued in denominations of $1 to $100. Each bears a letter code identifying the issuing Federal Reserve Bank.

**Federal Reserve Regulation A.** In the United States, a rule defining access to the Federal Reserve discount window. Financial institutions that accept transaction and nonpersonal time deposits have access to temporary and extended credit. Emergency credit is available to nondepository institutions when financing will prevent damage to the domestic economy. The rule also defines the terms of eligibility for banker's acceptances, which must mature within 180 days, except for days of grace, and covers domestic warehoused merchandise secured by a trust receipt. When goods are warehoused, a negotiable receipt must have been issued. The goods must be liquid, i.e., regularly traded on spot markets and unlikely to spoil or lose value during the life of the draft.

**Federal Reserve Regulation G.** In the United States, a rule covering creditors, other than banks, brokers, or dealers, who lend on margin. The regulation requires that lenders register margin loans secured by stock in amounts of $200,000 or more. Nonmargin loans of $500,000 or more must also be registered.

**Federal Reserve Regulation K.** In the United States, a rule regulating international banking services. It authorizes U.S. banking Edge corporations to provide international banking facilities and allows U.S. banks to own 100 percent of foreign nonfinancial companies. Regulation K also restricts the interstate operations of foreign banks.

**Federal Reserve Regulation T.** In the United States, a rule regulating margin loans extended to customers by brokers or dealers. The loans must be secured by securities. The percentage of value required for margin loans, known as the margin requirement, is determined periodically by the Federal Reserve Board. See also *general account* and *maintenance requirement.*

**Federal Reserve Regulation U.** In the United States, a rule controlling bank lending for securities purchases. The regulation requires that a borrower execute a purpose statement detailing the reasons for obtaining a margin loan. See also *maintenance requirements.*

**Federal Reserve Regulation X.** In the United States, a rule applying Regulation G, Regulation T, and Regulation U to credit purchases of federal Treasury securities by foreign borrowers.

**Federal Reserve System (FED).** The central bank of the United States. Created by the Federal Reserve Act of 1913, the Fed is composed of the Federal Reserve Board, the Federal Open Market Committee, the 12 district Federal Reserve Banks, member commercial banks, and an advisory council of commercial bankers. In addition to setting U.S. interest rate policy, the FED supervises bank holding companies, interstate banking activities, and international banking operations.

**Federal Reserve Wire Network.** Commonly called the Federal Wire or the Fed Wire, an electronic network that serves the Federal Reserve System, federal agencies, and commercial banks in the United States. The Fed Wire is used by the central bank system for funds transfers and book entries of U.S. Treasury securities transactions. Wire transfers are final payments when credited to a financial institution's reserve account. See also *Automated Clearing House, Clearing House Interbank Payments System,* and Society for Worldwide Interbank Financial Telecommunications. Compare *Bankwire.*

**Federal Savings and Loan Insurance Corporation (FSLIC).** In the United States, a federal agency established in 1934 to insure deposits in savings and loan associations (S&L). The FSLIC became insolvent in the 1980s after several large S&Ls failed. The Financial Institutions Reform, Recovery, and Enforcement Act of 1989 created the Resolution Trust Corporation to liquidate failed S&Ls. The FSLIC's assets were also transferred by the act to the Federal Deposit Insurance Corporation.

**Federal Tort Claims Act of 1946.** In the United States, a statute authorizing legal actions against the federal government for certain classes of torts. The act waives sovereign immunity for negligent or wrongful acts or omissions by employees or agencies of the U.S. government. The statute applies to torts for which the federal government would be liable if it were a private party.

**Federal Trade Commission (FTC).** In the United States, an independent federal agency established by the Federal Trade Commission Act of 1914. The FTC was created to promote fair competition and prevent price fixing and similar monopolistic practices. Corporate mergers, exclusive agency agreements, deceptive advertising, interlocking directorates, and tying arrangements fall within the FTC's purview. When it enforces antitrust laws, the FTC shares jurisdiction with the Antitrust Division of the U.S. Department of Justice.

**Federal Wire.** See *Federal Reserve Wire Network.*

**Fédération internationale des ingénieurs conseils (FIDIC).** Also known as the Inter-national Federation of Consulting Engineers, an association of civil engineers that frequently writes standards used in international project financing. FIDIC's standards are officially known as Conditions for Works of Civil Engineering Construction.

**Federation of International Trade Associations (FITA).** In the United States, an umbrella organization composed of state and local trade associations, export clubs, and councils. FITA offers member discounts for export-related services and schedules regular export competitiveness seminars to inform members of international trade opportunities. The organization also publishes directories of export company, shipping and transportation, and foreign trade associations. FITA is headquartered in Reston, Virginia.

**fed funds.** See *federal funds rate.*

**Fed Wire.** See *Federal Reserve Wire Network.*

**fee.** A sum of money charged for services provided or for use of an asset. 2. In real property law, an inheritable right to land. See also *freehold.*

**feeder vessel.** A barge or other light craft used to transport cargo between ports and ocean carriers.

**fee simple.** See freehold.

**FEFC.** The abbreviation for Far Eastern Freight Conference. See *conference.*

**felines.** See *certificate of accrual on Treasury securities.*

**feng shui.** Cantonese: wind and water. In China, the art of influencing events by physical positioning. Geomancy is often a factor in choosing office sites or seats for business meetings. Ostensibly, the effects of a poor location can be countered by placing red and black objects at strategic places at a given site.

**FERC.** The abbreviation for Federal Energy Regulatory Commission.

**FET.** The abbreviation for Foreign Economic Trends.

**FEU.** The abbreviation for 40-foot equivalent unit. See *container*.

**FFA.** The abbreviation for free from alongside. See *free alongside ship*.

**FFO.** The abbreviation for free out.

**F.G.A.** The abbreviation for free of general average.

**FHLMC.** The abbreviation for Federal Home Loan Mortgage Corporation.

**FI.** The abbreviation for free in.

**FIA.** The abbreviation for full interest admitted and Futures Industry Association.

**fiat money.** Inconvertible paper money. Fiat money cannot be exchanged for gold or hard currency since it is backed only by a decree of the government issuing it. See also *inconvertible currency*.

**FIB.** The abbreviation for free in bundles, free into barge, and free into bunker.

**fiber constraints.** Quotas on textile imports. In the United States, cotton, wool, and artificial fiber imports are subject to quotas set by the Committee for the Implementation of Textile Agreements. Textile import quotas are imposed unilaterally or negotiated under bilateral agreements authorized by the MultiFiber Arrangement Regarding International Trade in Textiles. See *bilateral restraint agreement* and *Section 204 agreement*.

**FICA.** The abbreviation for Federal Insurance Contributions Act. See *social security*.

**FIDIC.** The abbreviation for *Fédération internationale des ingenieurs conseils*.

**fiduciary.** A person or firm that administers assets in trust for the benefit of another. Fiduciaries are constrained by law from wasting or expropriating trust assets for their own benefit.

**fiduciary currency.** Money backed by government-issued securities, and not by gold. Most con-

temporary currencies are fiduciary issues. Compare *fiat money*.

**fiduciary deposit.** Funds managed by a bank for the benefit of a depositor. Banks exercise considerable discretion when managing and investing fiduciary deposits. In Switzerland, fiduciary management is a common source of banking business.

**field warehouse.** A bonded warehouse.

**field warehousing.** Inventory financing secured by a warehouse receipt. Negotiable warehouse receipts are issued by the warehouseman as collateral for loans obtained by the consignee. The loans are repaid from sales proceeds when the warehoused goods are sold.

**FIFO.** The abbreviation for first in/first out.

**50-mile rule.** A rule established by agreement between the International Longshoremen's Association and steamship operators. The agreement prevents nonunion labor from handling most less-than-containerload shipments. Shippers located within 50 miles of the pier who own the cargo being handled are exempted from the rule. In the United States, the 50-mile rule has been challenged in federal court, but it has not been overturned.

**filer.** See *filer code*.

**filer code.** In the United States, a three-digit electronic code assigned to large-volume exporters by the U.S. Customs Service. A filer code identifies the party filing customs documents through the Automated Commercial System.

**fill or kill.** An instruction from a customer to a stockbroker to fill a securities order immediately or cancel it.

**FIMBRA.** The abbreviation for Financial Intermediaries, Managers and Brokers Regulatory Association Ltd. See *self-regulating organization*.

**final good.** A completely finished product is ready for sale. Compare *intermediate product*.

**final invoice.** A document submitted by a seller once merchandise has arrived at its destination site. The final invoice verifies or corrects tentative information provided in a preliminary invoice. Essentially, it describes the value and quantity of goods and other particulars of a sale.

**Final List.**   In the United States, a customs valuation schedule no longer in use. Before 1979, the Final List determined whether an import duty was based on export value or foreign fair market value. Final Lists were abandoned when transaction value was officially adopted for customs valuation in the Trade Agreements Act of 1979.

**finance bill.**   In the United States, a bill of exchange used to provide working capital. Also known as banker's bills or working capital acceptances, finance bills must qualify for acceptance by a bank. These bills are not eligible for rediscount at the Federal Reserve.

**finance company.**   A nonbank lender, usually affiliated with a manufacturer or a bank holding company. Some finance companies specialize in consumer lending. Others, known as commercial finance or commercial credit companies, lend primarily to manufacturers and wholesalers. Commercial finance companies specialize in lease financing and asset-based lending. They raise funds in the capital markets by selling short-term debt and commercial paper.

**finance house.**   Outside the United States, a finance company.

**Financial Accounting Standards Board (FASB).** In the United States, a nonprofit organization that sets public accounting standards. Corporate public disclosure documents and registrations filed with the Securities and Exchange Commission must conform to FASB accounting standards. In published form, the standards are known as Statements of Financial Accounting Standards. Generally accepted accounting principles, used to prepare financial statements and similar documents in the United States, are based on FASB statements.

**Financial Accounting Standards Board Statement No. 52 (FASB 52).**   In the United States, a 1981 statement of accounting standards for reporting offshore and multicurrency transactions. FASB 52 became mandatory under Securities and Exchange Commission (SEC) rules in 1984 and supplants Financial Accounting Standards Board Statement No. 8 (FASB 8), an earlier statement devoted to foreign currency accounting. FASB 52 differs from FASB 8 by treating foreign exchange as a variable-value asset.

Exchange rate gains or losses are reported in a firm's capital account. FASB 52 also requires that futures contracts be reported as hedges. Transactions denominated in inflation-prone currencies are reported in U.S. dollars. In the United Kingdom, equivalent standards are published in Statement of Standard Accounting Practice No. 20.

**financial daily.**   A daily newspaper in a financial center that reports business news and carries next-day reports on the movements of commodity, currency, and securities markets. The major international financial dailies are *The Financial Times* (London), *The Globe and Mail* (Toronto), *Nihon Keizai Shimbun* (Tokyo), and the *Wall Street Journal* (New York).

**financial documents.**   A term employed by the International Chamber of Commerce to denote checks, bills of exchange, payments receipts, promissory notes, and similar instruments used to obtain payment.

**financial futures.**   Contracts used to hedge against changes in an underlying financial instrument's exchange rate or interest rate. Financial futures are traded for government-issued bills, notes, bonds, and other securities. Futures contracts are also available for stock indexes. See also *futures market.*

**financial guarantee.**   Bond insurance that guarantees principal and interest owed on a security. Financial guarantees are issued by insurance companies to protect securities holders from default by an issuer. In the United States, insurance companies underwriting bond insurance may not directly own property or casualty insurance companies.

**financial institution.**   An organization that collects, invests, and pays out funds to individuals or other institutions. A financial institution may be owned by a government or a private business entity. Broadly, financial institutions are depository institutions or nondepository institutions, although the line has faded in recent years. Depository institutions are commercial banks, credit unions, building societies, savings and loan associations, and savings banks, which accept deposits from the public for lending to borrowers. Funds placed with depository institutions are normally insured by a government. Nondepository institutions include brokerage firms, investment banks, merchant banks, life insurance companies, and pension funds. These organizations invest their own funds and those of the general public for profit.

**Financial Intermediaries, Managers and Brokers Regulatory Association, Ltd.**   See *self-regulating organization.*

**financial intermediary.**   A financial institution.

**Financial Management Service (FMS).**   In the United States, an agency of the U.S. Department of the Treasury that pays suppliers of the federal government. See also *vendor express.*

**financial ombudsman.**   In the United Kingdom, an official who investigates customer complaints for financial service industries. Ombudsmen are intermediaries for the banking, building society, insurance, and trust management industries.

**financial solidarity.**   See *Common Agricultural Policy.*

**financial statement.**   A summary of a borrower's financial condition. A financial statement may include (1) a balance sheet summarizing assets, liabilities, and net worth; (2) an income statement showing income and debts; and (3) a statement of retained earnings for a corporation or a statement of capital accounts for a partnership.

**Financial Statistics.**   In the United Kingdom, monthly financial data published by the Central Statistical Office.

**Financial Times Share Indexes.**   In the United Kingdom, indexes of shares traded on the London Stock Exchange and published in the London *Financial Times.* The indexes are published daily, except Sundays and Mondays. The Financial Times Actuaries Share Indexes reflect weighted-average prices in various industry sectors. There are 54 actuary share indexes. The Financial Times Ordinary Share Index gives unweighted-average prices for 30 industrial stocks. The Financial Times Stock Exchange 100 Index (the FTSE 100 Index), known as FOOTSIE, reflects average prices of 100 securities.

**financial year.**   1. The 12-month accounting period identified by a company for filing financial reports. A financial year may differ from a calendar year or a fiscal year. 2. In the United Kingdom, the period specified by the British government for corporate tax accounting. A financial year begins April 1.

**financing statement.**   See *security interest.*

**Findley Amendment.**   See *PL 480 programs.*

**fine trade bill.**   In the United Kingdom, a bill of exchange eligible for rediscount by the Bank of England. These are prime trade bills arising from the sale of goods. The bills are originally discounted by banks or finance houses.

**FIO.**   The abbreviation for free in and out.

**FIOS.**   The abbreviation for free in and out/ stowed.

**FIOT.**   The abbreviation for free in and out/ trimmed.

**firkin.**   A barrel used to store dairy commodities. A firkin is roughly equal to a quarter of a barrel, 9 gallons, or 56 pounds avoirdupois.

**Firma.**   German: firm.

**firm commitment.**   1. In securities underwriting, the agreement of an underwriting group to purchase all or any portion of an offering not sold to other investors. When a firm commitment is given, the underwriting group assumes the financial risk associated with a securities offering. Compare *best effort.* 2. In banking, any agreement by a bank to fund a transaction or act as an agent according to prearranged terms for a specific period of time.

**firm indication.**   See *indication.*

**firm offer.**   An offer to sell goods or services for a stipulated period. If the buyer accepts the offer within the stated time, the seller is bound to sell on the terms offered. Conversely, if the buyer makes a counteroffer, the seller's offer is invalid.

**firm order.**   An order placed with a broker that remains in effect for a specified period. An order not executed within the stipulated time becomes invalid.

**FIRMS.**   The abbreviation for Facilities Information and Resources Management System.

**FIRMS code.**   See *Facilities Information and Resources Management System.*

**first-class paper.**   Also known as fine paper, a check or bill of exchange drawn on a major bank or finance house.

**first-day notice.**  In futures trading, the first day on which an exchange authorizes delivery notices for settling a particular futures transaction.

**First Enlargement.**  See *enlargement*.

**first-flag carrier.**  A carrier transporting goods under the flag of the country of origin.

**first in/first out (FIFO).**  A method of import inventory management whereby products are sold or used in the order in which they are stocked. See also *inventory control*. Compare *last in /first out*.

**first of exchange.**  See *bill of exchange*.

**fiscal policy.**  The use of taxation and public spending to influence economic trends. Countercyclical policies, or deficit spending to sustain high employment, were common fiscal tools in Western countries for most of the post-World War II period. In the 1980s and early 1990s, the trends in Western countries shifted toward the use of monetary policy to achieve similar economic goals. See also *Keynesian economics*.

**fiscal year.**  Any accounting period designated by a government for official budgets and tax collection. 1. In the United Kingdom, the fiscal year begins April 6 and ends April 5. The period designated for the fiscal year is identical to the tax year. 2. In the United States, the federal fiscal year begins October 1 and ends September 30. The tax year begins April 15, although tax reporting is based on income and losses attributable to the calendar year.

**Fish and Wildlife Service.**  See *Convention on International Trade in Endangered Species of Wild Fauna and Flora*.

**FITA.**  The abbreviation for Federation of International Trade Associations.

**Five Tigers.**  See *Four Tigers*.

**fixed capital.**  See *capital asset*.

**fixed cost.**  See *overhead*.

**fixed exchange rate.**  A rate of exchange established in fixed relation to a commodity. See also *Bretton Woods Conference*. Compare *floating exchange rate*.

**fixing.**  In shipping, concluding a contract containing the negotiated terms for chartering a vessel. The contract is negotiated by a shipowner and a charterer, or the charterer's broker. The act of concluding a charter party is known as *fixture*. 2. In some international banking centers, the setting of exchange rates at daily meetings between financiers and central bankers. Rates are adjusted based on offers to buy and sell currency made during the meetings. See also *gold fixing*.

**flagging out.**  See *flag of convenience*.

**flag of convenience.**  The flag of the country where a ship is registered when its owner is of a different nationality. Transferring a ship's registration is known as flagging out. A shipowner flags out to pay lower taxes and registration fees, benefit from relaxed safety regulations, or both. See also *PANLIBHON*.

**flash.**  A barge-on-board system combined with a feeder. A lighter-aboard ship is placed atop a barge that can be discharged and towed to a port. Flash systems are frequently used in Asia.

**flat tax.**  A tax levied in proportion to a given tax base, usually at a single rate. Ability to pay is not usually a factor in assessing a flat tax, although some flat tax plans contain features of the progressive tax.

**fleet rating.**  A special insurance rate for owners of several ships. The premium is based on the entire fleet's insurance history, and not on a policyholder's claims involving a single ship. The number of ships required for a fleet varies with different underwriters.

**flexible SDR.**  A mechanism for fixing the financial value of a transaction. The special drawing right (SDR) provides a universally accepted means of determining an international contract's worth. When a contract is fixed in flexible SDRs, its proceeds equal the value of the same number of SDRs at a stipulated future date, e.g., the date on which payment is due. Conversely, when a contract is fixed in frozen SDRs, its proceeds are equal to the value of equivalent SDR units at the time the contract was made.

**flexible tariff.**  A duty alterable by executive decision. Nearly all countries have legislative guidelines for setting tariffs, but authorize an executive officer to reduce, raise, or eliminate duties in response to policy changes or the actions of trading partners. Flexible tariffs are usually temporary and reversible by the national legislature. In the United States, the President is authorized to alter tariffs by the Reciprocal Trade Agreements Act of 1934 and the Trade Expansion Act of 1962.

**floating debt.**    Short-term fixed-rate debt issued by a government. Floating debt is current debt. It differs from funded debt, which is composed of bonds or other long-term public debt obligations. See also *Treasury bill*.

**floating exchange rate.**    An exchange rate based primarily on market price. A currency is said to "float" when its price relative to other currencies reflects minimal government intervention. Some countries with dual-exchange-rate systems employ both fixed rates, known as controlled currency rates, and floating free rates, which value some transactions at the local currency's market rate. See also *clean float* and *managed float*. Compare *fixed exchange rate*.

**floating free rate.**    See *floating exchange rate*.

**floating interest rate.**    An interest rate linked to an index rate, or base rate. Floating interest rates can be tied to the London interbank offered rate (LIBOR), the U.S. prime rate, or a similar reference rate. The floating rate moves up or down when the index rate changes in response to the market demand for money. Variable-rate bonds, also called floating-rate notes (FRNs) or floaters, have interest rates tied to the LIBOR. FRNs are major sources of credit in Eurocurrency financing.

**floating lien.**    A loan secured by the borrower's current and future assets, usually inventory, receivables, or cash sales proceeds. The loan agreement gives the lender a security interest in assets acquired by the borrower after the date of the agreement. See also *asset-based lending* and *inventory financing*.

**floating policy.**    A type of open insurance policy with a maximum payout unrelated to the specific items insured. The coverage is not revised when the policyholder adds or deletes an item. Floating policies can, for example, be used to cover inventory, so long as the insured value remains constant.

**floating-rate loan.**    See *floating interest rate*.

**floating-rate note.**    See *floating interest rate*.

**floating supply.**    A commodity or inventory reserve sold in response to market changes. For example, buffer stocks are held as floating supplies to be sold when demand increases.

**floor.**    1. A minimum price or interest rate. Producers normally set floor prices, or the lowest price at which they are willing to sell. Governments use similar price guidelines to trigger producer-price subsidy payments, particularly for farm commodities. The floor price includes a producer's profit. Compare *price ceiling*. 2. On trading exchanges, the area where face-to-face sales are executed.

**floor broker.**    In commodities trading, an exchange member authorized to trade in the pit or the trading ring.

**floor trader.**    In commodities trading, an exchange member who has access to the floor where meetings with brokers and dealers take place and who executes trades for a personal or customer account.

**flotation.**    See *initial public offering*.

**flotsam.**    1. Wreckage from a ship left floating at sea. Flotsam within a sovereign's territorial waters is reclaimable by the ship's owner within a fixed period of time, usually a year. Thereafter, flotsam is owned by the sovereign. 2. In marine insurance, rights forfeited when a policyholder breaches a warranty in an insurance contract. The breach entitles the insurer to deny a policyholder's claim.

**FMC.**    The abbreviation for Federal Maritime Commission.

**FMCG.**    The abbreviation for fast-moving consumer goods.

**FNMA.**    The abbreviation for Federal National Mortgage Association.

**F.O.**    The abbreviation for Foreign Office and free out.

**FOB.**    See *free on board*.

**FOB/FAS sales coverage.**    Insurance coverage for cargo in transit from a warehouse to a port. In a free-on-board (FOB) or free-along-side (FAS) sale, the seller pays carriage and insurance to the port, and FOB/FAS coverage insures the seller against losses during carriage to the port.

**FOC.**    The abbreviation for free of charge.

**FOD.**    The abbreviation for free of damage.

**FOGS.**   The abbreviation for Functioning of the GATT System. See *GATT Standing Committees.*

**FOIA.**   The abbreviation for Freedom of Information Act.

**fonds.**   French: capital.

**fonds de roulement.**   French: working capital.

**Food, Agriculture, Conservation, and Trade Act (FACT) of 1990.**   In the United States, a law enacted to promote exports of domestic farm products. FACT authorizes the Dairy Export Incentive Program and the Export Enhancement Program through 1995. It replaces the prior farm export assistance program with the Market Promotion Program, designed to finance and coordinate export promotion initiatives. FACT also increased funding levels for other export support programs administered by the Commodity Credit Corporation.

**Food and Agriculture Organization of the United Nations (FAO).**   A specialized agency of the United Nations. The FAO was established by conference agreement at Quebec in 1945 to administer UN international rural development and emergency food programs. The organization promotes agricultural investment and conservation and provides technical assistance to national governments for agricultural development and land reform. The FAO is headquartered in Rome. See also *Food Security Assistance Scheme* and *World Food Programme.*

**Food and Drug Administration (FDA).**   In the United States, a division of the U.S. Department of Health and Human Services. The FDA regulates dairy imports and most other products imported for human consumption. The agency is authorized jointly with the U.S. Customs Service to inspect, detain, and seize adulterated and misbranded products at U.S. ports. An adulterated product is defined as one that is defective or unsafe or is produced under unsanitary conditions. A misbranded product carries a false label, a misleading label, or a label failing fully to disclose the product's nature or content. FDA regulations detail procedures for bringing nonconforming imports into compliance with U.S. health standards. The Import Support and Information System is FDA's automated document processing system.

**Food for Development.**   See *PL 480 programs.*

**Food for Peace Program.**   See *PL 480 programs.*

**food manufacturer's/food ingredient certificate.**   1. A health certificate verifying the content of packaged-food imports. 2. In the Middle East, a document required in countries that observe religious dietary restrictions. The certificate must usually be authenticated by a local consulate of the importing country.

**Food Security Assistance Scheme.**   An international agricultural aid program administered by the FAO. The program helps developing countries establish and maintain national food reserves.

**footloose industry.**   A manufacturing sector in which plants are not located near raw materials or components. A footloose industry can be profitable when the cost of transporting inputs is negligible compared with sales revenues.

**FOOTSIE.**   See *Financial Times Share Indexes.*

**FOQ.**   The abbreviation for free on quay.

**FOR.**   The abbreviation for free on rail.

**forced sale.**   A liquidation sale, usually ordered following a bankruptcy. Forced sales bring below-market prices for goods because transactions are not negotiated between buyers and willing sellers.

**force majeure.**   1. Literally, a superior force. A *force majeure* clause in a contract excuses a party from fulfilling a contractual obligation. The clause covers natural disasters, riots, wars, or imponderable and unforeseen circumstances. *Force majeure* clauses typically provide for arbitration when another party challenges the claim. 2. An act of nature that exempts a signatory nation from a treaty obligation.

**foreclosure.**   A legal proceeding initiated by a creditor to reclaim collateral when a debtor defaults. In some cases, the court sets a repayment schedule under an order called a foreclosure nisi. In most instances, however, the creditor files suit and obtains a judgment to seize and sell the debtor's property. Often, a debtor may redeem the property by paying the unretired debt and the creditor's collection expenses.

**foreign access zone.**   See *foreign trade zone.*

**foreign agent.**   In the United States, a lawyer or lobbyist who represents foreign clients on political matters. A foreign agent registers with the Registration Unit of the U.S. Department of Justice, as required by the Foreign Agents Registration Act of 1938. Lawyers who represent foreign clients on purely legal matters, not involving lobbying, are not required to register as foreign agents.

**Foreign Assemblers Declaration and Certification (Form 3317).** See *HTS Item 9802* and *Special Access Program CBI Export Declaration.*

**Foreign Assets Control Regulations.** In the United States, rules issued by the federal government to enforce embargoes or trade sanctions. The regulations are authorized by the Trading with the Enemy Act of 1917 and issued by the Office of Foreign Assets Control in the U.S. Department of the Treasury. The rules prohibit U.S. exports or imports of goods to or from specified countries unless exemptions are authorized by the Treasury Department. Violations of assets control regulations incur civil and criminal penalties.

**Foreign Assistance Act of 1961.** In the United States, the statute that originally authorized official development assistance to developing countries. The act also created the U.S. Trade and Development Program.

**foreign banking corporation.** See *Edge corporation.*

**foreign base company income.** See *Subpart F.*

**foreign bill.** See *bill of exchange.*

**foreign bond.** A bond issued in a country other than the domicile of the borrower. See also *Eurobond.*

**Foreign Business Practices Division.** See *U.S. Department of Commerce.*

**Foreign Buyer Program.** In the United States, a matchmaking and trade show promotion program sponsored by the U.S. Department of Commerce. The program helps U.S. firms and trade show promoters establish contact with foreign buyers, primarily through U.S. & Foreign Commercial Service officers stationed abroad.

**Foreign Claims Settlement Commission.** See *U.S. Department of Justice.*

**foreign corporation.** See *corporation.*

**Foreign Corrupt Practices Act (FCPA) of 1977.** In the United States, an amendment to the Securities Exchange Act of 1934. The FCPA prohibits U.S. corporations from offering or paying bribes to foreign officials or their agents. Gratuities given to a public official to obtain, retain, or direct business to any person are prohibited. The act also applies to contributions to foreign political candidates and parties. The FCPA requires domestic public corporations to maintain internal accounting and record-keeping controls, whether or not a company has international operations. See also *FCPA review procedure.*

**Foreign Credit Insurance Association (FCIA).** The insurance agent for the Export-Import Bank of the United States (Eximbank). The association's members are commercial insurers who insure exporters against default on short- to medium-term loans. Special policies cover bank letters of credit, financial institutions, commercial leases, and trade associations. The Multibuyer Policy insures short- to medium-term export receivables. Its discretionary credit limits permit an exporter to extend open-account credit to foreign buyers up to a prescribed amount without prior Eximbank approval. Most FCIA policies cover 90 to 95 percent of a commercial risk and 95 to 100 percent of a country risk. FCIA provides three basic policies:

*master policy.* Insurance purchased from the FCIA by commercial banks to insure loans to exporters. The banks charge exporters a nominal fee for the insurance, about 1 percent of the amount insured.

*umbrella policy.* Insurance purchased by export trading companies, freight forwarders, and local economic development agencies to insure their clients. These policies, backed by the FCIA and Eximbank, carry lower premiums than individual clients are able to obtain.

*new-to-export policy.* Insurance provided to exporters with minimum export experience. To qualify for coverage, exporters must be first-time export credit insurance purchasers and meet the FCIA's credit standards. See also *export credit insurance.*

**foreign currency transaction.** 1. In accounting, a transaction stated in terms of a currency other than a firm's principal currency. 2. In finance, a purchase or sale priced in a foreign currency, or lending or borrowing in a foreign currency. See also *Financial Accounting Standards Board Statement No. 52.*

**foreign deposit.**   An account owned by an overseas depositor. In the United States, deposits placed with foreign branches of domestic banks are unregulated and are exempt from domestic deposit insurance and reserve requirements. Most U.S. foreign deposits are kept in offshore banking centers in the Bahamas and Cayman Islands. See also *international banking facility* and *offshore banking unit.*

**foreign direct investment (FDI).**   Also called direct foreign investment, funds committed to a foreign enterprise. The investor may gain partial or total control of the enterprise. An investor who buys 10 percent or more of the controlling shares of a foreign enterprise makes a direct investment. Compare *portfolio investment.*

**foreign domicile bill.**   In one country, a bill of exchange drawn and accepted in another.

**Foreign Economic Assistance Act of 1950.**   See *U.S. Agency for International Development.*

**Foreign Economic Trends (FET).**   In the United States, data published by the International Trade Administration (ITA). FETs provide business and economic information about foreign countries based on information compiled by U.S. embassies abroad. Data available in FETs include analyses of current market conditions, growth prospects, and incentives for U.S. trade and investment. FETs are published annually or semiannually, depending on the country.

**foreign entity.**   In accounting, a branch or subsidiary where financial statements are reported in a currency other than its parent's domicile. See also *Financial Accounting Standards Board Statement No. 52.*

**foreign exchange (FOREX, FX).**   In one country, the currency of another. Foreign exchange is used to settle transactions between countries and between nationals of different countries. Currency exchange values are determined by markets or by reference to a commodity, such as gold. In some instances, exchange values are declared by a government or fixed by multilateral agreement, as in the European monetary system. The international foreign exchange market consists of brokers, dealers, central banks, commercial banks, customers, futures traders, and over-the-counter traders.

**foreign exchange broker.**   An agent who arranges purchases and sales of currency on foreign exchange markets, usually between central banks and commercial banks. The fee paid to a foreign exchange broker is called brokerage. Compare *foreign exchange dealer.*

**foreign exchange contract.**   A hedge device against foreign exchange losses. The term is synonymous with forward exchange contract.

**foreign exchange dealer.**   A trader who buys and sells currency on foreign exchange markets. Foreign exchange dealers are usually employees of commercial banks. Compare *foreign exchange broker.*

**foreign exchange market.**   The global currency market, which largely determines the value of national currencies. Foreign exchange dealers buy and sell currencies through foreign exchange brokers. The market consists of a spot market for immediate delivery, a forward exchange market for delivery at a future date, and an options market for hedges on future prices. When dealers buy large amounts of a currency, its price increases. When they sell, the price decreases. If speculation drives prices beyond tolerable levels, one or more central banks intervene attempting to restore equilibrium among currency prices. The size, diversity, and volatility of contemporary currency markets may, however, defeat a single government's efforts to reverse market trends. See also *exchange equalization account.*

**Foreign Extraterritorial Measures Act (FEMA) of 1984.**   In Canada, a statute restricting the extraterritorial reach of foreign laws. When differences in national laws arise, FEMA requires foreign subsidiaries to comply with Canadian laws. FEMA is enforced by the attorney general of Canada. The statute was originally enacted after the United States attempted to block trade with Cuba by restricting the activities of foreign branches of U.S. companies.

**foreign freight forwarder.**   See *freight forwarder.*

**foreign international sales corporation.**   In the United States, before 1984, an offshore tax haven controlled by a domestic international sales corporation (DISC). Offshore DISC subsidiaries were required to meet the following conditions: (1) the parent DISC had to own directly, on each day of the taxable year, more than 50 percent of the voting stock of the foreign subsidiary; (2) 95 percent of the foreign subsidiary's gross receipts had to derive from certain export receipts and interest; and (3) export assets had to account for 95 percent or more of the adjusted basis of the corporation's assets. Foreign international sales corporations and DISCs were replaced by the foreign sales corporation enacted in the Tax Reform Act of 1984.

**foreign investment.**    See *foreign direct investment.*

**foreign investment law.**    A statute that governs foreign direct investment. Typically, foreign investment laws specify the type and amount of foreign participation allowed. The laws also govern profit repatriation and intellectual and industrial property rights. As a part of the trend toward liberalized trade, most developing countries, particularly in Latin America, repealed the most onerous limits on foreign investment by the early 1990s. Several African countries also loosened foreign investment rules, although currency inconvertibility in many African countries makes liberalized investment more difficult to achieve.

**Foreign Investment Review Act (FIRA) of 1974.** In Canada, the investment law repealed by the Investment Canada Act of 1984. FIRA created the Foreign Investment Review Agency to limit foreign investment and takeovers of domestic firms with gross assets greater than $2 million Canadian dollars and more than 100 employees. After the United States requested a General Agreement on Tariffs and Trade review of FIRA, the Foreign Investment Review Agency was supplanted by Investment Canada. Nevertheless, FIRA restrictions on foreign investment in domestic cultural industries were substantially approved in the Canada-U.S. Free Trade Agreement. See also *cultural derogation.*

**Foreign Labor Trends.**    In the United States, a series of annual reports analyzing labor indicators in a number of countries. The reports describe wage regulations, employee benefits, labor relations, and conformity with international labor standards. *Foreign Labor Trends* is published by U.S. Department of Labor.

**foreign personal holding company income.**    See *Subpart F.*

**foreign policy controls.**    Government restraints on trade imposed for noncommercial reasons. The restraints include embargoes, sanctions, and export bans. In Western countries, principally in the United States, trade controls became a permanent fixture of foreign policy after World War II to limit the flow of strategic weapons and dual-use items to communist countries. More recently, foreign policy controls have been employed to disarm international terrorists. Governments use foreign policy controls to protect a national security interest or, in the case of universal sanctions, to avert a threat to global peace. Except in the case of United Nations sanctions imposed against South Africa in the 1980s, multilateral foreign policy controls are rarely used to change the domestic social policies in other countries. In the United States foreign policy controls are governed by the Export Administration Act of 1979.

**foreign processing.**    1. Also known as outward processing, altering the nature or composition of an export in a foreign market. Foreign processing occurs, for example, when parts are shipped abroad and remade into components for finished products. In services trade, transmitting data offshore for reformatting is known as foreign processing. 2. In insurance, a clause that protects a policyholder from financial loss when goods are reassembled or processed abroad or in a foreign trade zone.

**foreign sales agent (FSA).**    An agent in a foreign country who sells imported goods on a commission basis.

**foreign sales corporation (FSC).**    In the United States, an offshore company eligible for a tax rate of 15 to 32 percent. The FSC must have a main office in a U.S. possession or qualified foreign country, as well as one director who is not a resident of the United States. FSCs are established principally in American Samoa, Barbados, Bermuda, Guam, the Marianas, or the U.S. Virgin Islands. An FSC can be organized by a manufacturer or service business. It can act as a principal, buying and selling for its own account, or as a commission agent. FSCs receive the maximum tax deduction when buying from independent suppliers or meeting Internal Revenue Service arm's-length pricing rules. Architectural and engineering services acquired for foreign construction projects, as well as certain export management services purchased from unrelated FSCs, are the only pure service-related costs that FSCs can deduct. FSCs are authorized by the Foreign Sales Corporation Act (FSCA), a statute contained in the Tax Reform Act of 1984. The FSCA became effective after December 31, 1984. See also *interest-charge DISC*. Compare *domestic international sales corporation*.

**Foreign Sales Corporation Act.**    See *foreign sales corporation*.

**Foreign Securities Act of 1934.**    In the United States, a law prohibiting further lending to defaulters on U.S. obligations. Also called the Debt Default Act and the Johnson Act, the statute bars persons or firms in the United States from lending to foreign governments in default on U.S. loans. In 1945, amendments to the act exempted International Monetary Fund members and Export-Import Bank of the United States transactions from the lending bar, effectively leaving few countries subject to its terms.

**foreign subsidiary.**    A branch operating in a country other than the domicile of its parent.

**foreign tax credit.**    See *double taxation*.

**Foreign Trade Antitrust Improvements Act.**    See *Export Trading Company Act of 1982*.

**foreign trade bank.**    A government-owned bank that manages foreign exchange disbursements arising from external transactions. In some countries, foreign trade banks issue letters of credit, authorize other banks to issue credits, and make payments to foreign creditors. When a country has controlled foreign exchange, the foreign trade bank may be the only agency authorized to approve commercial foreign exchange expenditures.

**Foreign Trade Barriers Report.**    See *Omnibus Trade Act of 1988*.

**foreign trade credit system.**    In some countries, a tax benefit permitting local companies to offset the costs of foreign operations. A foreign trade credit system permits a local firm to reduce its domestic income tax liability by taking a credit equal to income taxes paid in another country. Payroll

taxes or value-added taxes are not usually creditable, unless paid in lieu of income taxes. Compare *double taxation*.

**foreign trade organization (FTO).**    In some countries, the authorized agent for external trade where the government monopolizes foreign trade. FTOs buy and sell in international markets for government accounts, often as the sole agents for arranging foreign sales transactions. Despite the global trend toward deregulation, many FTOs retain a monopoly on external trade. Although all companies in a country may be legally authorized to engage in trade, an FTO may, in fact, be the sole party capable of closing a sale.

**Foreign Trade Report (FT ).**    In the United States, a publication of the U.S. Bureau of the Census that records monthly U.S. merchandise exports, including quantity and dollar values. The reports also contain cumulative U.S. merchandise export statistics for a current calendar year.

**foreign trade zone (FTZ).**    A special zone outside a nation's customs territory designated to attract external investment and operated as a public utility. FTZs earn profits from user fees paid by businesses operating in the zone. Also known as free trade areas, FTZs are located in industrial parks or near ports and bonded warehouses where goods are held, exhibited, or manipulated. Duties, taxes, and customs procedures are modified or streamlined for FTZs. Depending on the country, foreign trade zones are called foreign access zones (Japan), industrial free zones (India), special economic zones (China), etc. See also *subzone*.

**Foreign Trade Zones Act.**    See *Foreign Trade Zones Board*.

**Foreign Trade Zones Board.**    In the United States, an office of the U.S. Department of Commerce authorized by the Foreign Trade Zones Act of 1934. The board reviews and approves applications for domestic foreign trade zones.

**FOREX.**    An abbreviation for foreign exchange.

**forfaiting.**    A form of without-recourse financing whereby a third party discounts debt instruments based on a guarantee from a foreign bank and pays the exporter.

**forint.**    The currency of Hungary.

**Form 8K.**   In the United States, a document filed by a registered corporation with the Securities and Exchange Commission, reflecting the anticipated effect of a major event on its financial position and securities values. The 8K discloses the possible impact of a charge against earnings, a charter amendment, or similar event. The document gives notice of the nature of the event and its anticipated effect within 30 days of its occurrence.

**Form 8300.**   In the United States, a form filed with the Internal Revenue Service (IRS) by businesses reporting large cash transactions. Form 8300 is used to identify the source of cash payments of $10,000 or more ascribed to a single transaction or a series of related transactions. The IRS defines cash as cashier's checks, coins, currency, bank drafts, money orders, or traveler's checks. Failure to file is a criminal offense.

**Form TD F 90-22.**   In the United States, a document used by taxpayers to disclose income from foreign accounts and foreign trusts. Form TD F 90-22 is submitted to the U.S. Department of the Treasury in addition to Form 1040/1041 filed with the Internal Revenue Service (IRS). TD F is used by taxpayers who own or have signature control over funds in bank, securities, or other financial accounts located outside the United States. Commercial bank and corporate employees without a direct ownership interest in the foreign accounts, majority shareholders in multinational corporations, and depositors in U.S. military banking facilities are exempt from filing TD F.

**Form 10K.**   In the United States, a financial statement filed annually by a registered corporation with the Securities and Exchange Commission (SEC). Form 10Ks are audited reports disclosing net income, reserves dedicated for tax payments and losses, and financial statements for two previous years. The reports are required of corporations listed on stock exchanges and companies with assets of $2 million or more and 500 or more shareholders. Summaries of 10Ks are published in annual reports and maintained by the SEC for public inspection. Compare *Form 8K* and *Form 10Q*.

**Form 10Q.**   In the United States, a quarterly report filed by registered corporations with the Securities and Exchange Commission. Quarterlies are required in addition to the Form 10K. They summarize current income and expenses and measure present business performance in relation to information disclosed during the same period in the preceding year. A 10Q may, but need not, be audited.

**Form 1040/1041.**   In the United States, the standard individual federal income tax return filed annually with the Internal Revenue Service. Taxable income is adjusted gross income from all sources, i.e., income less exemptions and deductions. For taxpayers using other than the standard deduction, Form 1040 is accompanied by Schedule A (itemized deductions) and, in appropriate instances, by Schedule C (profit or loss from business, including rents and royalties), Schedule D (capital gains and losses), Schedule E (supplemental income or losses), Schedule F (farm profits or losses), and/or Form 4835 (farm rental income or losses). Form 1065 is used to report income from partnerships and joint ventures, Form 2555 to disclose income from foreign sources, and Form 4868 to obtain automatic extensions for filing returns. See also *Form TD F 90-22.*

**Form 1065.**   See *Form 1040/1041.*

**Form 1099.**   In the United States, a document issued annually to depositors and investors by banks or other financial institutions disclosing interest (Form 1099-INT) and dividends (Form 1099-DIV) earned during the year. Form 1099s are required by the Internal Revenue Service and filed by taxpayers with income tax returns. Form 1099-B is used to report gains and losses from transactions involving barter. See also *backup withholding.*

**Form 13D.**   In the United States, a form filed with the Securities and Exchange Commission, when a single investor or a group of associated investors own more than 5 percent of the equity in a publicly held company. The 13D discloses the size of individual holdings and the investor's reasons for purchasing a sizable share of a company's stock.

**formal entry.**   See *customs entry.*

**forty-forty–twenty.**   See *Convention on a Code of Conduct for Liner Conferences.*

**forum shopping.**   In law, a technique used to obtain venue in the most favorable jurisdiction. Parties to lawsuits forum-shop to enhance their chances of winning or to obtain larger damage awards.

**forward contract.**   See *forward exchange contract*.

**forward dealing.**   Purchasing futures contracts for later delivery at a stipulated price. Futures contracts are tied to the price of commodities, currencies, freight, securities, and so on. By contracting in the present for a price payable at a future date, the dealer obtains a hedge against later price changes.

**forwarder.**   See *freight forwarder*.

**forward exchange.**   Foreign currency bought or sold for later delivery. The forward exchange rate is the rate at which currency can be obtained for future delivery. See also *forward margin*.

**forward exchange contract.**   A futures contract between two parties, usually banks or their customers, to eliminate the risk of foreign exchange fluctuations. The contract specifies delivery of a specific amount of currency at a future date. The price of the currency is the current market price. Forward exchange contracts can be changed only with the consent of the parties. The interest rate is called the forward outright rate. Compare *forward rate agreement*.

**forward margin.**   The difference between the current (spot) price and the future price of a currency. The margin reflects a premium if the buyer pays a higher price than the current price. Conversely, the buyer receives a discount if the spot price is higher than the quoted future price.

**forward outright rate.**   See *foreign exchange contract*.

**forward rate agreement (FRA).**   A contract whereby a buyer agrees to pay the seller a fixed rate of interest on a set sum of money at a future date. FRAs are futures contracts covering interest paid on time deposits. The settlement price is the difference between the purchase price and a market index rate at maturity, usually the London interbank offered rate. Compare *forward exchange contract*.

**FOS.**   The abbreviation for free on steamer.

**FOT.**   The abbreviation for free on truck.

**foul bill of lading.**   Also called a claused bill, a dirty bill, or an unclean bill, a bill of lading with a notation that damaged or apparently damaged goods were delivered to a carrier. The seller who presents a foul bill of lading cannot collect payment against a letter of credit. Compare *clean bill of lading*.

**Four Tigers.**   Hong Kong, Singapore, Taiwan, and South Korea, the newly industrialized economies of the 1980s. In 1990, exports accounted for roughly 69 percent of these countries' gross domestic product. When Thailand is included, the countries are known as the Five Tigers. See also *Sino-British Joint Declaration and Basic Law*.

**FOW.**   The abbreviation for first open water and free on wagon.

**FPA.**   The abbreviation for free of particular average.

**FPAAC.**   The abbreviation for free of particular average—American conditions. See *average*.

**FPAEC.**   The abbreviation for free of particular average—English conditions. See *average*.

**F/R.**   The abbreviation for freight release.

**F.R.**   The abbreviation for fully registered.

**fr.**   An abbreviation for franc.

**Frachtbrief.**   German: bill of lading.

**framework agreement.**   The working document used as the basis for international trade negotiations.

**franc (fr., F.).**   The currency of Andorra, Belgium, Burundi, Comoros, Djibouti, France, Guinea, Liechtenstein, Luxembourg, Madagascar, Monaco, Rwanda, and Switzerland.

**franchise.**   1. A license to sell a product or service in a given region for a limited period of time in exchange for a royalty, often paid as a percentage of sales revenues. The party granting the license is the franchiser, and the licensee is the franchisee. Franchisers usually provide financing and technical assistance, while requiring franchisees to maintain predetermined quality-control standards. 2. In commercial insurance, a clause entitling a policyholder to recover losses that exceed a specific percentage of the overall value of a shipment.

**franco.**   French: free. Also called *rendu*, a term of sale denoting that the seller pays carriage and insurance costs to the buyer's warehouse, wherever located. Compare *landed price*.

**Francophone.**   Term used to describe French-speaking countries in Africa. Francophone countries adhere largely to language and civil-law traditions inherited from nineteenth-century French colonialism. The countries constitute a part of the French Economic Community, known as the Franc Zone, and generally follow France's lead on global economic and political issues. Relations between Anglophone countries and Britain are more distant.

**Franc Zone.**   A group of countries and territories mostly encompassing former French colonies whose currencies are supported by the Banque de France. The African countries are Benin, Burkina Faso, Cameroon, Central African Republic, Chad, the Comoros, Congo, Côte d'Ivoire, Equatorial Guinea, Gabon, Mali, Niger, Senegal, and Togo. CFA stands for *Communauté financière africaine* in West Africa and *Coopération financière en Afrique centrale* in Central Africa. The CFP franc (*Comptoirs français du Pacifique*) is the currency of New Caledonia, French Polynesia, Futura Islands, and Wallis Islands. CFA francs and CFP francs are freely convertible at a fixed rate of exchange into French francs in France and in neighboring African countries. The French franc is the principal currency of Monaco and the French West Indies. Along with the Spanish peseta, the French franc is also one of two official currencies of Andorra. See also *French community.*

**fr&cc.**   The abbreviation for free of riot and civil commotions.

**franked investment income.**   See *franked payment.*

**franked payment.**   Gross dividends, i.e., earnings plus the tax on earnings. In European tax systems, corporations pay an initial tax on dividends and other corporate distributions. In the United Kingdom, the tax on dividends is called an advance corporation tax (ACT). A franked payment is a dividend increased by the ACT. Companies earning dividends receive tax credits against dividend payments, making earnings tax exempt to recipients. These dividends are known as franked investment income because they can be passed on to other companies without additional taxes. The ACT is paid on gross dividends minus franked investment income.

**Frankfürter Wertpapierbörse Aktiengesellschaft.** The Frankfurt Stock Exchange founded in 1585. The exchange has four markets: the *Amtlicher Handel* (the primary official market), *Geregelter Markt* ( an official market with lower listing requirements), *Geregelter Freiverkehr* (a semi-official, over-the-counter market), and the *Ungeregelter Freiverkehr* ( the over-the-counter market). Prices are quoted in Deutsche marks and published in the *Amtlich Kursblatt* (the official list) and the *Börsen-Zeitung*. The exchange's index is the DAX (*Deutsche Aktien Indexe*), a weighted average of 30 stocks. Transactions are settled through the *Frankfürter Kassenverein,* an electronic central depository system. In Germany, dealers and brokers are known as *Börsenmakler, Freimakler, Kursmakler,* or *Makler.*

**fraud.**   The intentional misrepresentation of a material fact causing injury to another. Fraud may arise by conduct or omission. In the United States, fraudulent contracts are voidable under the statute of frauds. The Uniform Commercial Code protects parties to sales contracts when a contract is written, signed by the debtor, and valued at $500 or more.

**fraudulent customs entry.**   The use (or attempted use) of misrepresentation to clear imports through customs. The misstated fact may involve an import's character, classification, composition, or value.

**FRB.**   Abbreviation for Federal Reserve Bank and Federal Reserve Board.

**Freddie Mac.**   See *Federal Home Loan Mortgage Corporation.*

**free alongside ship (FAS).**   An international commercial term (INCOTERMS). The seller pays all costs, including the cost of placing goods at the disposal of a carrier. The buyer pays the loading cost and subsequent expenses. In an FAS sale, the seller's obligation is fulfilled when goods are placed near the carrier at the dock or in a light craft at the port. FAS is often called free on quay. See also *FOB/FAS sales coverage.*

**free astray.**   A common carrier term. The carrier provides free carriage to the original destination when cargo has been delivered to the wrong destination. The misdelivery must have been caused by the carrier's error.

**free carrier (FCA).**   An international commercial term. The seller delivers goods to the initial carrier. Unless otherwise specified, the buyer bears all costs after delivery to the carrier.

**free despatch/dispatch.**    A charter party provision excusing a carrier from paying dispatch money. Dispatch money is a bonus paid to a shipper who unloads cargo before the time specified in the contract. See also *lay time*.

**free dock.**    A term of sale. The seller arranges and pays to deliver goods to the dock. The buyer pays all other costs.

**Freedom of Information Act (FOIA) of 1966.**    In the United States, a federal statute, amended in 1974 and 1976, according individuals and organizations the right to disclosure of most information collected and held by federal agencies. FOIA applications are filed with the agency where the information is maintained. Restricted national security information and the business proprietary information of others are exempt from FOIA.

**free economic zone.**    See *free trade zone*.

**freehold.**    In real property law, a fee estate or a life estate. 1. An estate held in fee simple or in fee simple absolute is freely transferable by the owner. The transfer may be by deed (sale) or by will or intestacy (inheritance). 2. A contingent fee is conditional and terminates after the occurrence of a specified event. 3. A fee tail is inheritable among a limited and specified group of heirs. 4. A life estate is measured by the life of the person owning it or by the life of another in whose name the life estate is granted. See also *estate* and compare *leasehold*.

**free import list.**    A list of imports not subject to prior licensing. Usually, the list reflects liberalized trade, whereby imports are removed from the restricted list and regulated by tariffs.

**free in (FI).**    A term of sale. The shipper pays the cost of loading cargo at the origination port.

**free in and out (FIO).**    A term of carriage. The shipper or consignee, and not the carrier, bears the cost of loading and unloading cargo.

**free list.**    An enumeration of imports authorized for duty-free customs entry. The free list is contained in a country's tariff schedule.

**free market economy.**    See *market economy*.

**free market rate.**    See *floating exchange rate*.

**free of address.**    A charter party provision that eliminates the address commission. The owner of a ship is excused from paying the customary percentage bonus to the agent who arranges the charter.

**free of all averages.**    See *average*.

**free of capture and seizure (FC&S).**    In marine insurance, a provision that excludes losses from capture, seizure, and war. Insurance coverage for risks arising from war or civil disorder is normally provided by export credit insurance agencies or overseas investment agencies, e.g., the Overseas Private Investment Corporation. See also *country risk*.

**free of particular average.**    See *average*.

**free of turn.**    A charter party provision that fixes the beginning of lay time from the time the shipper is notified of the ship's port arrival. When a free-of-turn provision is included in a charter contract, the period for unloading begins when the ship arrives, even though a berth is not available.

**free on board (FOB).**    An international commercial term (INCOTERM). The seller pays transportation and insurance, including the cost of loading cargo at a named point. FOB, the preferred term of sale in the United States, is used for import valuations by the U.S. Customs Service. Cost, insurance, and freight is preferred elsewhere. See also *FOB/FAS sales coverage* and *guarantee of collectibility*.

Standard FOB price terms are:

**FOB airport (FOBA).**    The seller arranges and pays for the transport of goods to a carrier at a named airport.

**FOB freight allowed.**    The seller's invoice price is reduced by the amount the buyer pays in freight charges.

**FOB freight prepaid.**    The seller arranges and pays for inland transport to the departure port. The buyer pays all other charges.

**FOB named inland carrier.**    The seller arranges for inland transport to the departure port. The buyer pays all charges.

**FOB named inland port of origin.**    The seller arranges and pays the cost of transport to a named domestic inland port. The buyer pays all other charges.

*FOB named port of exportation.*    The seller arranges to deliver cargo to a named exportation port. The buyer pays all freight charges. Outside the United States, these quotes are often confused with FOB vessel.

*FOB vessel.*    The seller arranges shipment, prepares documentation, and pays all costs, including the costs of loading cargo aboard the vessel. The seller also pays insurance to the loading point. Costs pass to the buyer once goods have been loaded.

**free on board and trimmed.**    A term of sale in FOB contracts for delivery of coal. The seller arranges and pays for loading and stowing coal aboard the ship.

**free on quay.**    See *free alongside ship.*

**free on rail (FOR).**    A synonym for FOB vessel.

**free out (FFO).**    A term of sale. The seller pays all costs, including the cost of unloading cargo at the destination port.

**free overboard.**    See *ex.*

**free perimeter.**    An inland free trade zone where duties, taxes, and certain regulations are suspended for manufacturing, assembly operations, storage, and so on.    Compare *free port.*

**free port.**    A port near a free trade zone where imported goods are held or processed for reexport without the need to pay duties. Compare *free perimeter.*

**free pratique.**    A bill of health, permitting a ship to depart a port. The certificate of free pratique verifies a ship's compliance with the health and sanitation laws of the country it is leaving. In the United States, certificates of free pratique are issued by the U.S. Public Health Service.

**free rider.**    An unintended beneficiary of an international trade agreement. Free-rider problems arise in a number of contexts. For example, a third-party country may benefit from an agreement to which it is not a party when its nationals locate assembly plants in a beneficiary country or when goods are transshipped through its ports. Country-of-origin rules and regional content requirements in preferential trade agreements are intended to thwart free riders. See also *tariff factory.*

**free ships/free goods.**    In customary international law, a neutral ship and cargo that cannot be interdicted or seized by wartime belligerents on the high seas. A contrary view accords belligerents the right to interdict neutral ships in search of implements of war.

**free time.**    See *lay time.*

**free trade.**    International commerce without trade barriers. See also *comparative advantage.*

**free trade agreement.**    See *free trade area.*

**free trade area (FTA).**    A trade area created by treaty between two or more nations, eliminating tariffs and nontariff barriers, usually over a period of years. Countries entering FTAs often agree to harmonize customs regulations and product standards, but need not adopt a common external tariff or eliminate all restrictions on the movement of capital, labor, or technology. See also *ASEAN Free Trade Area, Canada-U.S. Free Trade Agreement, European Economic Area, European Free Trade Association,* and *North American Free Trade Agreement.*

**free trade zone.**    See *foreign trade zone.*

**freight.**    1. Goods transported by a carrier. 2. The cost of shipping goods. Freight is based on weight or measure, i.e, the space used. 3. The cost of a charter.

**freight all kinds (FAK).**    Cargo composed of mixed goods and eligible for a discounted tariff if shipped as a part of a container-load shipment. The rate is less than the usual rate charged for a given class of goods. FAK discounts offered by non-vessel-operating common carriers are frequently larger than similar discounts offered by conferences.

**freight-allowed pricing.**    See *zone-delivered pricing.*

**freight broker.**    See *cargo broker.*

**freight forwarder.**    Also called a forwarder or a foreign freight forwarder, a firm that books cargo space for manufacturers. Forwarders arrange cargo deliveries, prepare shipping documents, and insure shipments under open insurance policies. In the United States, forwarders are licensed by (and required to file periodic freight tariffs with) the Federal Maritime Commission. Forwarders are paid handling fees by shippers and brokerage fees by carriers. See also *non-vessel-operating common carrier.*

**freight note.**   A carrier's invoice for freight owed for a shipment.

**freight release.**   A receipt provided by a carrier when an invoice is paid. The receipt may be noted on the bill of lading or may constitute a separate document.

**freight tariff.**   A carrier's notice of carriage terms. The tariff discloses a carrier's shipping rates, routes, rules of carriage, and limits on liability. Freight is usually based on a class or commodity rate and calculated in standard units of measure (e.g., ton or board foot.). Tariffs may be published by a carrier, conference, or freight forwarder. National laws usually require that tariffs be filed with a regulatory agency.

**French Community.**   1. An economic union formed in 1958 between France and its colonies encompassing the Central African Republic, Chad, the Congo, Gabon, Madagascar, and Senegal. 2. Broadly, France, Francophone Africa, and various French-speaking countries and territories including the French West Indies. See also *domaines et territoires d'outre-mer* and *France zone.*

**French West Indies (FWI).**   The three Caribbean Overseas Departments of France, i.e., Guadeloupe (and the dependencies of St. Martin and St. Barthélemy), Martinique, and French Guiana. The FWI are external extensions of Metropolitan France and do not participate, for example, in the Caribbean Basin Initiative, the trade preference program for Caribbean countries sponsored by the United States.

**friendly society.**   In the United Kingdom, a mutual insurance society. Some large insurance companies in the UK are registered as friendly societies. The societies offer investment plans regulated by the British government.

**friendship, navigation, and commerce (FNC) treaty.**   Also called a freedom of commerce and navigation treaty, a bilateral agreement covering commercial matters. FNCs guarantee signatory countries access to airspace, territorial waters, and inland transportation and telecommunications networks. The treaties also obligate signatories to accord national treatment in taxation and law, including intellectual property rights. Signatories to FNC treaties acquire reciprocal most-favored-nation status. Compare *bilateral investment treaty.*

**front-end load.**   1. Fees paid by an investor in mutual funds. Also called a load, the front-end fees are charged in addition to management fees. 2. In construction loans, a disbursement schedule that pays more in early years and less in later years.

**frozen assets.**   Accounts held by legal order. 1. Assets placed in escrow by a local court when property ownership is to be resolved by legal order. 2. In international commerce, foreign-owned assets blocked from distribution or repatriation by one government when ownership is contested as a consequence of a political dispute with another. 3. In securities industries, assets seized under a court order when trading violations are alleged. Compare *blocked account.*

**frozen special drawing right.**   See *flexible SDR.*

**FSC.**   The abbreviation for foreign sales corporation.

**FSCA.**   The abbreviation for Foreign Sales Corporation Act. See *foreign sales corporation.*

**ft.**   The abbreviation for foot.

**FT.**   The abbreviation for full terms.

**FTA.**   The abbreviation for free trade agreement and free trade area.

**FTA Commission.**   A bilateral commission created by the Canada-U.S. Free Trade Agreement (FTA). The commission is chaired jointly by the Canadian Minister of International Trade and the U.S. Trade Representative. The commission oversees the implementation of the FTA and supervises the work of the Binational Secretariat, the FTA dispute-settlement agency.

**FTA Select Panel.**   Also called the Auto Panel, a committee of industry experts that advises the governments of Canada and the United States regarding the Automotive Products Trade Agreement (the Auto Pact) of 1965. The committee recommends initiatives to improve the international performance of the North American automotive industry.

**ft. bm.** The abbreviation for foot-board measure.

**FTC.** The abbreviation for Fair Trade Commission and Federal Trade Commission.

**FTO.** The abbreviation for foreign trade organization.

**FTW.** The abbreviation for free trade wharf.

**FTZ.** The abbreviation for free trade zone.

**FUA.** The abbreviation for fund unit of account.

**full and down.** A ship loaded to the extent of its cargo-carrying capacity.

**full berth terms.** See *full terms.*

**full interest admitted.** In insurance, the unconditional declaration by an underwriter of a policyholder's insurable interest in goods. The policyholder is relieved of any further obligation to prove ownership, and the underwriter is barred from contesting insurance claims on the grounds of uninsurable interest.

**full tax credit/exemption.** See *double taxation.*

**full terms (FT).** A term of carriage, also known as full berth terms. The charterer is responsible for all costs, including loading and unloading cargo.

**fully paid share capital.** See *share capital.*

**functional currency.** A firm's principal currency. Functional currency is the money or legal tender issued in a company's domicile or place of incorporation. Foreign exchange transactions are normally reported in a company's functional currency.

**fundamental term.** A term without which a contract cannot be enforced. Consideration, price, and the identities of the parties are fundamental terms, although a contract may provide for a future determination of consideration and price. Conversely, conditions or warranties are not fundamental terms, and their omission from a contract does not render it unenforceable.

**funded debt.** A country's long-term debt, as represented by various debt instruments, namely bonds and debentures. Funded debt differs from current (short-term) debt, which is also known as floating debt.

**Fund for International Development.** See *Organization of Petroleum Exporting Countries.*

**fund manager.** See *investment manager.*

**fund of funds.** In the United Kingdom, funds invested in several unit trusts to give small investors access to diversified investment portfolios. A single investment is protected by reinvesting funds in a number of unit trusts managed by the same institution. Unit trusts are known as mutual funds in the United States.

**Fund Unit of Account (FUA).** The artificial currency unit of the African Development Fund. An FUA is equal to a fractional value of one special drawing right. See also *African Development Bank Group.*

**further processing price.** The customs price used to assess duties on goods imported for manufacturing. Also known as the superdeductive, the further processing price is the unit price of a product reduced by the value added in the importing country. Normally, to qualify for the superdeductive, imports must undergo substantial transformation in the importing country. In the United States, a qualified import must also be sold from 90 to 180 days of the importation date. Compare *duty drawback.*

**futs.** The abbreviation for futures.

**futures (futs.).** A contract for the purchase of a commodity for delivery at a future date. See also *futures contract.*

**futures commission merchant (FCM).** In the United States, an agent licensed to trade futures by the Commodities Futures Trading Commission (CFTC). An FCM accepts customer orders for futures contracts, which are purchased with cash or secured margin loans. In 1980, CFTC expanded the definition of an FCM to include any agent for a foreign broker or trader, or any broker managing accounts on behalf of a foreign broker.

**futures contract.** Also known as a forward contract, an agreement to buy or sell a stipulated quantity of a commodity or financial instrument on a specified future date at a fixed price. Futures contracts are traded in regulated exchange markets. Sellers of futures contracts (called shorts) notify exchanges of their intent to deliver contracts to buyers (called longs) before the contract delivery date. Actual delivery rarely occurs. Usually, a buyer and seller agree to a new contract before the old contract expires. Unlike option contracts, futures contracts are risky purchases, but are used to hedge against price changes or interest rate fluctuations. See also *futures options* and *variation margin*.

**futures market.** Exchanges where bond indexes, commodities, and financial futures contracts are traded. Brokers, but not dealers, trade on all exchanges. Transactions are settled through clearinghouses. In international markets, futures are traded on numerous exchanges, including the Baltic Exchange (London), Chicago Board of Trade, Chicago Mercantile Exchange-International Monetary Market, Commodity Exchange of New York, Financial Futures Market (Montreal), Gold Exchange of Singapore, Hong Kong Commodity Exchange, International Futures Exchange (Bermuda), International Petroleum Exchange (London), London Futures and Options Exchange, London International Financial Futures Exchange, London Metal Exchange, Marché à Terme International de France, New York Futures Exchange, Osaka Securities Exchange, Singapore International Monetary Exchange, Sydney Futures Exchange, Tokyo International Financial Futures Exchange, Toronto Stock Exchange Futures Market, and Winnipeg Commodity Exchange. See also *Wiener Edelmetallwarenbörse*.

**futures option.** See *option*.

**fwd.** The abbreviation for forward.

**f.w.d.** The abbreviation for fresh water damage.

**FWI.** The abbreviation for French West Indies.

**FX.** The abbreviation for foreign exchange.

# G

**g.** The abbreviation for gold, grain, and gram.

**G-3, G-5, G-7, G-10, G-24.** The abbreviations for Group of Three, Group of Five, Group of Seven, Group of Ten, and Group of Twenty-Four.

**G/A.** The abbreviation for general average.

**GAB.** The abbreviation for General Arrangements to Borrow.

**gal.** The abbreviation for gallon.

**GALs.** The abbreviation for guaranteed access levels.

**gamma.** See *delta*.

**gamma stocks.** See *SEAQ*.

**GAO.** The abbreviation for General Accounting Office.

**garage.** In finance, a place for storing assets, usually money. Funds are parked to avoid reporting for tax purposes or until reinvestment can yield more favorable returns. See also *offshore banking unit*.

**garment-on-hanger trailer (GOH).** A trailer used to transport apparel products.

**garnishment.** A court order barring payments to a debtor until a creditor's claim is satisfied.

**gate price.** Also known as the lock-gate price and the sluice-gate price, the minimum European Community (EC) import price for pork, poultry, and eggs. The gate price is computed by adjusting input and productions costs to world market prices. Under the Common Agricultural Policy, EC countries impose supplementary duties when the import price of covered commodities falls below the gate price.

**gateway.** The pick-up or drop-off point for in-transit shipments between different customs jurisdictions.

**Gateway to China.** Singapore. The idea of Singapore as the most convenient entry point into mainland China is actively promoted by the Singapore Trade Development Board to attract foreign investment. See also *Five Tigers* and *Growth Triangle*.

**GATT.** The abbreviation for General Agreement on Tariffs and Trade.

**GATT Standing Committees.** Permanent committees of the General Agreement on Tariffs and Trade (GATT) established to supervise the organization's staff work. The principal GATT committee is the Trade Negotiations Committee, which oversees major working groups on goods and services. The permanent committees are the 13 standing committees, or negotiating groups, for agriculture, dispute settlement, the functioning of the GATT System, GATT Articles, multilateral trade negotiation agreements, natural resources, nontariff measures, safeguards, subsidies, textiles and clothing, trade-related intellectual property, trade-related investment measures, and tropical products.

**GCBS.** The abbreviation for General Council of British Shipping.

**GCC.** The abbreviation for Gulf Cooperation Council.

**GDP.** The abbreviation for gross domestic product.

**gearing.** See *leverage*.

**Geldschein.** German: bank note.

**Geldwesen.** German: finance.

**GEMSU.** The abbreviation for German Economic, Monetary, and Social Union, the compact between the former Federal Republic of (West) Germany and the (East) German Democratic Republic adopted in 1990, ending a process begun in 1989. The agreement concluded the reunification of Germany, which was officially divided in 1961 when East Germany constructed the Berlin Wall.

**general account.** In securities and commodities trading, a brokerage account from which margin loans are made. General accounts are maintained by brokers and dealers, particularly those trading on stock exchanges. In the United States, the accounts are subject to Federal Reserve Regulation T.

**General Accounting Office (GAO).** In the United States, the independent auditor of the federal government. Established in 1921, the GAO prescribes accounting procedures for federal agencies and settles financial claims when the United States is a creditor or a debtor. The GAO is also the investigative agency of the U.S. Congress.

**General Agreement on Tariffs and Trade (GATT).** A global trade organization established by the Havana Charter of 1947, which became effective January 1, 1948. GATT was founded as an interim agreement, pending creation of a permanent United Nations agency to have been known as the International Trade Organization (ITO). After the Senate of the United States and the UN General Assembly failed to approve the ITO, GATT became the permanent forum for global trade negotiations. GATT is structured to liberalize international trade in merchandise, primarily through negotiated reductions in tariff and nontariff barriers. Nondiscrimination, low and transparent tariffs, binding contractual commitments, and conciliation between member countries are basic GATT tenets. Generally, the GATT adopts decisions by consensus rather than by vote. When votes do occur, each nation has one vote. Majority votes are sufficient on most issues, although a two-thirds majority is required when a vote involves deviation from an existing GATT obligation. Policies are made during annual Sessions of the Contracting Parties (GATT member states) or interim meetings of the Council of Representatives. GATT standing committees and working parties handle most GATT issues; conciliation panels arbitrate disputes between member states. Multilateral trade negotiations (MTNs) are supervised by the Trade Negotiations Committee (TNC). GATT is headquartered in Geneva.

There have been eight rounds of MTNs. The first five rounds reduced tariffs on a per-product basis. Those were Geneva (1947), also called the Geneva Trade Conference; Annecy (France, 1949); Torquay (United Kingdom, 1950); Geneva (1956); and Geneva (1962), also called the Dillon Round. Subsequent rounds achieved relatively more innovation:

*Kennedy Round (Geneva, 1963–1967).* The Kennedy Round developed a single formula for reducing tariffs. Duties were cut by product categories, with an average 35 percent cut in duties on

some industrial products. The round also adopted the first GATT Antidumping Code and the principle of non-reciprocal trade concessions for developing countries. See also *Generalized System of Preferences.*

*Tokyo Round (Tokyo/Geneva, 1973–1979).* The Tokyo Round improved on the single tariff-cut formula of the Kennedy Round, principally by addressing nontariff barriers for the first time in GATT negotiations and adopting the following multilateral trade negotiations codes:

*Aircraft Agreement (Agreement on Trade in Civil Aircraft).* The Agreement requires that contracting parties apply competitive commercial criteria when purchasing civil aircraft. It also eliminates duties on civil aircraft and parts, and it liberalizes aircraft procurement procedures.

*Antidumping Code (Agreement on Antidumping Practices).* A revised agreement that supplanted the Kennedy Round Antidumping code. The new code defines dumped goods as imports sold at prices below those in the producer's home country. It contains an arbitration procedure for dispute settlement, although arbitration rulings are not binding on the parties or enforceable by the GATT. See also *antidumping action* and *duty.*

*Beef Agreement (Arrangement Regarding Bovine Meat).* The Beef Agreement liberalizes trade in beef products. National restraints on beef trade are monitored by the International Meat Council.

*Customs Valuation Code (Agreement on Customs Valuation).* This code sets uniform rules for determining *ad valorem* duties. It adopts transaction value, or the arm's-length sales price, as the basis for import valuation. The Customs Valuation Code also authorizes alternative valuation methods when transaction value cannot be determined. Duties are levied on an import's FOB or CIF invoice price. See also *Harmonized Commodity Description and Coding System.*

*Developing Countries.* The Tokyo Round reaffirmed the principle of nonreciprocal concessions to developing countries accepted by the Kennedy Round. See also *Generalized System of Preferences.*

*Government Procurement Code (Agreement on Government Procurement).* The Government Procurement Code requires public display of government tender offers and national treatment of foreign bidders for government contracts. National security procurements and contracts valued under 150,000 special drawing rights are exempt from the code. A 1988 Protocol of Amendments further reduced the contract value for nondiscriminatory bidding to 130,000 special drawing rights.

*International Dairy Arrangement.* The Dairy Arrangement fixes floor prices for dairy products, including butter, most cheeses, and various milk products. The International Dairy Products Council supervises the implementation of the agreement.

*Licensing Code (Agreement on Import Licensing).* The Licensing Code attempts to establish transparent procedures for import licensing. Discriminatory licensing unrelated to an importing country's national interest is prohibited. A member country may require special licensing for certain types of imports, except when licensing is employed to raise nontariff barriers to trade. Intellectual property rights are not covered by the code. See also *Uruguay Round,* which follows.

*Standards Code (Agreement on Technical Barriers to Trade).* This code prohibits the use of regulatory standards to impede trade. Technical product standards enforced to advance legitimate domestic goals, including environmental, health, national security, and safety protections, are permitted. The code also commits GATT members to work toward adopting uniform product standards developed by international standards organizations.

*Subsidies (and Countervailing Measures) Code (Agreement on the Interpretation and Application of Articles VI, XVI, and XXIII of the General Agreement on Tariffs and Trade).* The code generally prohibits payment of government bounties to local producers solely to stimulate exports. But it contains limited exemptions for developing countries and permits certain other subsidies to advance purely domestic economic objectives. A contracting party enforces the Subsidies Code by imposing countervailing duties after a GATT panel rules affirmatively on a complaint. It also creates arbitration procedures for resolving subsidy disputes. Mediation panels, composed of GATT members,

are authorized to impose multinational retaliation to enforce a settlement in subsidy cases.

*Tariff reductions.* The Tokyo Round cut tariffs on most imports by 34 percent over 10 years, beginning January 1, 1980, and ending January 1, 1987.

***Uruguay Round.*** The Uruguay Round commenced at Punta del Este in 1986 and, as of mid-1993, had not been concluded. The negotiations covered agricultural subsidies, gradual phaseouts of the MultiFiber Arrangement (MFA) quotas, intellectual property, investment, market access, services, and tariff reductions. The complexity of applying uniform rules to intangibles, such as services and intellectual property, raised modest problems in the negotiations. However, the contracting parties deadlocked over agricultural subsidies. Following 5 years of inconclusive negotiations, Arthur Dunkel, the director-general of the GATT, submitted a draft treaty, known as the Dunkel Text, in December 1991. The draft treaty was not approved after the European Community and the United States failed to agree on reductions in agricultural subsidies. A 1992 agreement between the EC and the United States, known as the Blair House Accord, did not end the stalemate, largely because heavily subsidized French farmers objected to its terms. In mid-1993, however, Canada, the EC, Japan, and the United States agreed to a limited number of merchandise tariff cuts as a preliminary step toward resurrecting the round. The most contentious issues (i.e., those related to agricultural subsidies, textiles, and services) remained unresolved.

**General Arrangements to Borrow (GAB).** An accord between members of the Group of Ten (G-10) to lend to the International Monetary Fund (IMF) in G-10 currencies. Under the original GAB of 1962, the G-10 pledged up to $6 billion U.S. dollars over a 4-year period to finance loans to other G-10 members. The GAB now lends to IMF members with balance-of-payments deficits. See also *Basel Concordat.*

**General Assembly (GA).** The parliamentary body of the United Nations. All United Nations states are represented in the General Assembly. Delegates are chosen by their national governments, and each country is accorded one vote.

Depending on the issue, matters pending before the GA are decided by a simple majority or a two-thirds majority.

**general average.**   See *average.*

**general average security.**   A bond, cash deposit, or other surety posted as a shipper's contribution to general average.

**general endorsement.**   See *endorsement.*

**Generalized System of Preferences (GSP).**   A global trade preference program authorized by the General Agreement on Tariffs and Trade (GATT). Premised on the concept of special and differential treatment, universal preferences were approved by the United Nations Conference on Trade and Development (UNCTAD II) at New Delhi in 1968 and implemented in 1971. Beneficiary countries and eligible products are noted in national or regional customs tariff schedules. Quotas frequently apply to GSP imports. UNCTAD Form A is submitted for goods entering under the GSP. The U.S.-Generalized System of Preferences (US-GSP) was created by the Trade Act of 1974 and extended until July 4, 1993 by the Trade and Tariff Act of 1984.

**general ledger.**   A company's primary accounting record for a given period. Financial statements and financial disclosures required by regulatory agencies are based on general ledgers. Compare *nominal ledger.*

**general license.**   Also called the general export license, a permit to export certain commodities for which a formal or written request is not required. In the United States, products covered by general license are published by the U.S. Department of Commerce in the Comprehensive Export Schedules. Other exports require a validated export license.

**generally accepted accounting principles (GAAP).**   Uniform rules used to prepare financial statements. In the United States, GAAPs are followed by auditors and certified public accountants. See also *Financial Accounting Standards Board.*

**general obligation bond.**   Also known as a G-O bond, a security supported by the credit of the issuing government unit. In the United States, G-O bonds are issued by state and local govern-

ments, usually for nonrevenue-yielding public works projects, such as road and school construction. The borrowings are secured by the taxing authority of the issuing state or municipality. Compare *revenue bond.*

**general order (GO).**   1. The status of unclaimed goods held for customs entry. 2. Premises owned or leased by a customs service for goods stored for customs examination, or held pending seizure or release from customs custody.

**general order merchandise.**   See *general order.*

**general partner.**   See *partnership.*

**general superintendence.**   Cargo inspections conducted by the *Société Générale de Surveillance* (SGS), a Swiss inspection firm, or its affiliates. SGS inspects cargoes and shipping documents prior to shipment, usually at factories, piers, or warehouses. Shipments are inspected for quantity and discrepancies in the terms of sale agreed to by an importer. In some countries, foreign exchange to purchase imports is not released unless SGS issues a clean report of findings.

**general tariff.**   See *customs tariff.*

**general technical data available (GTDA)/ restricted (GTDR).**   In the United States, a term used to determine the export status of certain technical data. 1. General technical data available denotes publicly available information, such as unpublished research, textbooks, course materials, professional periodicals, etc. GTDA may be exported to any country without a validated export license, including countries on the Commerce Control List. 2. General technical data restricted without written assurances can be exported to all countries without a validated export license, except those specifically identified. 3. GTDR with a letter of assurance bans unauthorized reexport by the importing country. It requires a validated license for export to any country, exclusive of proscribed countries. 4. General technical data unrestricted (GTDU), a new category, has been proposed to replace GTDR without written assurances. The change would eliminate confusion over GTDR with assurance and without assurance.

**general term bond.**   A customs bond provided by an importer as surety for import duties. General term bonds are issued by approved bonding firms. A single bond usually covers an importer's shipments to several ports in the same country.

**general trading partner.**   A nation without most-favored-nation trading status. Imports from general trading partners are dutiable at the highest customs tariff rates.

**Generaltullstyrelsen.**   Swedish: customs agency.

**general turnover tax.**   See *value-added tax.*

**generic.**   1. Any undifferentiated item indistinguishable from others of its class. 2. A product without a manufacturer's brand name. Unbranded products resemble branded products in their composition, but are sold at lower prices because expensive advertising and packaging expenses are not included. Compare *differentiated product line.*

**gen-saki.**   Called the *gen-saki* market, the short-term money market in Japan. Bonds and bank debentures with maturities of roughly 2 to 3 months are sold under repurchase agreements. Unlike the call money market, the *gen-saki* market is open to corporate borrowers. It is also the only Japanese secondary market for medium- to long-term securities issued by corporate borrowers and by the Bank of Japan.

**German reunification.**   See *GEMSU.*

**germinal franc.**   A gold franc defined originally in terms of a gram of gold of 0.900 fineness, but now valued in terms of the special drawing right. Also known as the Latin Union franc, the germinal franc is used to determine the financial value of obligations and damages under international postal and telecommunications conventions.

**Ges.**   The abbreviation for *Gesellschaft.*

**Gesellschaft (Ges).**   German: company.

**Gesellschaft mit beschränkter Haftung (GmbH).** In Germany, a small limited-liability company. A GmbH is registered with the appropriate agency in the place of incorporation. The board of directors is optional. The letters "GmbH" appear after the company's name.

**gift tax.**   See *inter vivos gift.*

**gilt-edged security.**   1. Also called a gilt, a fixed-rate security issued by the Bank of England in the form of an Exchequer or Treasury stock.

Irredeemable gilts are called consols. Redeemable gilts may be long-dated (longs) with maturities of 15 years or more, medium-dated (mediums) with 5- to 15-year maturities, or short-dated (shorts) with maturities under 5 years. Index-linked gilts provide inflation protection. 2. Tap stocks, or undersubscribed gilts, sold on the open market. Tap stocks can be short-dated (short taps) or long-dated (long taps). 3. AAA-rated corporate bonds issued in the United States. See also *bond rating.*

**gilts primary dealers.**   A small number of dealers authorized to trade gilt-edged securities on behalf of the Bank of England.

**Ginnie Mae.**   See *Government National Mortgage Association.*

**giro.**   The electronic funds transfer system in Europe and Japan. In a giro system, funds are automatically transferred from the payer's account to a creditor's account. The credit transfer is made by a payment order and recorded when the transfer is complete. Originally created for consumers without bank accounts, the giro system is now widely used by businesses for direct collections.

**Glass-Steagall Act of 1933.**   In the United States, a statute that bars domestic commercial banks from securities underwriting and dealing. Since 1980, the Federal Reserve Board has somewhat deregulated banking, permitting commercial banks to underwrite limited securities issues, primarily through affiliates of bank holding companies. Commercial banks may also offer discount brokerage services and manage mutual funds issues. Also known as the Banking Act of 1933, Glass-Steagall created the Federal Deposit Insurance Corporation.

**global bond.**   A temporary bond circulated until documents representing a Eurobond offering are printed and issued. Global bonds are traded in international markets at a value equal to the face amount of the Eurobond borrowing. See also *lock-up.*

**Global System of Trade Preferences.**   See *Generalized System of Preferences.*

**Globex.**   In the United States, an after-hours electronic trading system, the product of a joint venture between the Chicago Board of Trade (CBT), the Chicago Mercantile Exchange (CME), and Reuters Holdings plc. Globex uses electronic terminals in Chicago, London, New York, and Paris, primarily for currency trading between 6 p.m. and 6 a.m. (U.S.A. Central Standard Time). The system permits brokers to access a menu of trading options and market data. Globex also creates an electronic audit trail for policing trades. As of 1992, the system was dedicated to CBT, CME, and *Marché à Terme International de France* financial futures contracts. Globex will be fully implemented in 1995.

**GmbH.**   The abbreviation for *Gesellschaft mit beschränkter Haftung.*

**GNMA.**   The abbreviation for Government National Mortgage Association.

**GNP.**   The abbreviation for gross national product.

**GO.**   The abbreviation for general order.

**G-O bond.**   See *general obligation bond.*

**godfather offer.**   In an corporate takeover, a lucrative tender offer that shareholders accept over the protest of the target company's board of directors.

**godown.**   A waterfront warehouse in the Far East.

**GOH.**   The abbreviation for garments on hangers.

**going long.**   Buying a security for long-term investment.

**going short.**   The sale by a dealer of uncovered securities. Short sellers do not own the securities sold in a short sale. The sale creates an open position, which is covered if the dealer can buy at or below the selling price. The dealer profits if the purchase price is lower than the selling price.

**Gold Act of 1934.**   See *gold standard.*

**gold certificates.**   In the United States, bearer instruments issued by the U.S. Department of the Treasury and circulated within the Federal Reserve System. Gold certificates are convertible into gold at a fixed rate set by the Federal Reserve, but actual paper certificates are never issued. Held in a fund known as the Interdistrict Settlement Fund, gold certificates are accounting credits used by Federal Reserve Banks to settle accounts within the Federal Reserve System.

**gold clause.**   A clause in loan agreements, usually between governments, stipulating repayment in gold. A gold clause is included in a loan agreement when the value of a sovereign debtor's currency is determined by a high inflation rate or otherwise prone to depreciation.

**golden share.**   Equity that entitles an owner to 51 percent or more of a corporation's voting shares.

**gold fixing.**   The daily ritual for setting spot gold prices in the international gold market. The spot-market price is the average price paid for large gold orders. It is influenced by gold traders in London, Paris, Zurich, New York, and Hong Kong, although the key fixing occurs at Rothschild's in London. Fixing occurs on business days between 10:30 a.m. and 3:30 p.m. (London time). See also *fixing.*

**gold franc.**   Any one of several units of exchange used to settle international transactions, primarily between governments or under terms established by an international agreement. There are several types of gold franc, including the germinal franc and the Poincaré franc. The gold franc, used by the Bank for International Settlements to pay, among others, accounts between member central banks, contains 0.2903 gram of pure gold, the composition of the original Swiss gold franc.

**gold-indexed investment.**   An investment linked to the market price of gold. These investments include bank certificates of deposit, gold futures, gold mutual funds, gold options, etc.

**Gold Key Service.**   In the United States, a service offered by the U.S. Department of Commerce to domestic firms conducting business tours abroad. The service provides market information, joint-venture matching services, interpreters, and investment planning.

**gold standard.**   A monetary system that values a national currency unit in terms of a fixed amount of gold. Under a pure gold standard, bank notes are freely convertible into gold. The United Kingdom adopted the gold standard in 1821, but abandoned it in 1931. The United States remained on the gold standard until 1971, although the Gold Act of 1934 barred private citizens from converting dollars into gold. See also *Bretton Woods Conference* and *Smithsonian Agreement.*

**gold stock.** A portion of a nation's gold reserves. Gold stock consists of gold bullion and monetized gold, or paper certificates issued against gold bullion. In the United States, gold reserved for specific purposes is not gold stock. For example, gold stock does not include gold reserves that are in the custody of the Exchange Stabilization Fund, that are on deposit with the International Monetary Fund, or that are held by the Federal Reserve Bank of New York for international payments.

**gold tranche.** One of two basic lending facilities originally available to members of the International Monetary Fund (IMF). Before 1978, a country joining the IMF subscribed by placing a specified amount of gold on deposit with the Fund. Under IMF rules, a country could borrow up to the limit of its gold subscription without complying with conditionality or incurring a repayment obligation. In 1978, the gold tranche was replaced by the reserve tranche to which a member country also has unlimited access. A country joining the IMF may now contribute 25 percent of its quota in gold, special drawing rights, or hard currency. The balance may be contributed in a local currency.

**good.** 1. In economics, any product *or* service that has worth or value because of its utility in the course of human affairs. Economic goods are those for which scarcity creates a market price. Free goods are those in sufficient supply to eliminate a selling market. Capital goods, also known as producer goods, are used to produce products for consumer markets; raw commodities, industrial equipment, etc., are capital goods. Consumer goods are composed of durable goods (e.g., automobiles and washing machines) and disposable (nondurable) goods (e.g., soaps and paper) purchased for use by the general public. 2. In commerce and law, a product, merchandise, or ware as distinguished from a service. For example, as of 1992, the General Agreement on Tariffs and Trade applied to goods (i.e., products) but not to services.

**good delivery.** In the securities industry, a stock certificate transferred to a buyer and bearing an appropriate endorsement and signature. A buyer is obligated to accept a good delivery.

**good delivery bar.** The international standard for solid gold. The minimum gold content of a good delivery bar is 99.5 percent pure gold with a weight of 350 to 430 troy ounces. The shapes of good delivery bars vary. Brick-shaped bars are used in the United States. Trapezoidal bars are common elsewhere.

**goods and services tax.** See value-added tax.

**good ship.** Also commonly referred to as good vessel, a phrase that warrants a seaworthy ship. The warranty appears in marine insurance policies and shipping contracts.

**goods in free circulation.** Any product circulated outside a customs territory. Freely circulating goods include domestic products and imports cleared by the national customs agency.

**goods-in-transit insurance.** In commercial insurance, a policy covering products transported by means other than water. The cargo is insured while in transit from an origin point to a destination point. An insurer often specifies the mode of carriage. Compare *marine insurance.*

**good title.** See *marketable title.*

**goodwill.** An intangible asset that, when combined with tangible assets, partially determines the financial value of a business. Goodwill can be sold and purchased. When a business is sold, the buyer can normally amortize goodwill, usually within a year of the purchase.

**go public.** Also called taking a company public, the process of converting a private company to a publicly owned company. In the United States, for example, a company "goes public" when it meets the listing requirements of a stock exchange and registers its initial public offering with the Securities and Exchange Commission.

**gourde.** The currency of Haiti.

**government broker.** A broker appointed by the Bank of England to sell government securities on the London Stock Exchange.

**Government National Mortgage Association (GNMA).** In the United States, an agency of the federal Department of Housing and Urban Development created by the Housing and Urban Development Act of 1968. Known popularly as Ginnie Mae, GNMA issues securities collateralized by federally backed residential mortgages. Guaranteed by the U.S. government, GNMA securities are known as modified pass-throughs because they pay principal and interest, less the issuer's fees, directly to secondary-market investors. See also *Federal Home Loan Mortgage Corporation*.

**government procurement.**   See *procurement*.

**Government Procurement Initiative.**   In the United States, a program implemented to comply with the Government Procurement Code adopted by the Tokyo Round of the General Agreement on Tariffs and Trade. Under the Government Procurement Initiative, foreign firms may bid for 10 to 20 percent of U.S. federal procurement contracts when reciprocal procurement opportunities are available to U.S. contractors. Caribbean Basin Initiative countries are exempt from the reciprocity requirement. Procurement contracts are subject to minimum values established by the GATT Procurement Code.

**governments.**   In the United States, a colloquial term for negotiable securities issued by the U.S. Department of Treasury. Governments include bonds, notes, and Treasury bills, as well as securities issued on behalf of U.S. federal agencies.

**government security.**   A bond, bill, note, or stock issued and backed by a country's national treasury.

**GPO.**   The abbreviation for General Post Office.

**GPT.**   The abbreviation for General Preferential Tariff. See *Generalized System of Preferences*.

**gr.**   The abbreviation for grade, grain, and gram.

**grace period.**   A time period permitted for a payment after a due date has passed. Grace periods are usually allowed for payments of bills of exchange and insurance premiums.

**graduation.**   Losing eligibility for concessional lending or trade preferences. A developing country that obtains a significant export market share, particularly in high value-added manufactured products, typically loses Generalized System of Preferences (GSP) benefits. GSP preferences can be withdrawn for specific imports or for all classes of imports. A country with a balance-of-payments surplus also loses access to International Monetary Fund lending.

**grainspace.**   The total capacity of a ship to transport pulverized solid products in its hold.

**grandfather clause.**   A provision in a law or treaty that exempts a party from a new obligation and instead permits the party to continue an existing practice. For example, a taxpayer receiving a tax benefit under a prior law continues to receive it, even though the benefit is withdrawn under a new tax law.

**gray knight.**   In a corporate takeover, a suitor whose motives and intentions are unknown to the owners of the target company. The black knight is the unfriendly bidder, and the white knight is the purportedly friendly suitor. As the unknown quantity, the gray knight complicates negotiations and is not favored by either side.

**gray market.**   1. Originally, a hidden distribution channel, often encountered in countries under economic sanctions or embargo. In these markets, goods are routed through unofficial channels, usually in major trading centers, and buyers pay a premium above the market price based on the scarcity factor and degree of risk to the seller. Recently, gray-market goods have also come to mean brand-named goods purchased at a low price in foreign markets and resold through discount stores in the domestic market. 2. A market for dealing in securities that have not been issued. Some investors bid on unissued shares with the expectation of receiving an allotment after the issue.

**Green Book.**   Officially entitled *Unlisted Securities Market*, a book of regulations issued by the London Stock Exchange. The *Green Book* contains rules for trading unlisted securities in the over-the-counter market, known in London as the unlisted securities market.

**green card system.**   1. An international automobile insurance verification system. The card does not guarantee that other countries will accept the coverage; rather, it serves as proof of insurance. The extent of insurance coverage is explained in various languages on the card. 2. In the United States, an identification system for documented foreign workers.

**green clause letter of credit (L/C).**   A letter of credit instructing a bank to pay an exporter after shipping documents have been presented. The advancing bank collects the advance and fees when the letter is presented for payment. Compare *red clause credit.*

**green currencies.**   See *green rate.*

**greenmail.**   Buying a large block of shares and selling them back to the target company. In exchange for a premium price, the greenmailer promises not to launch a takeover bid.

**green product.**   A nonpolluting product. See also *green technology.*

**green rate.**   A special rate of exchange used by the European Community (EC) to compute agricultural prices under the Common Agricultural Policy (CAP). Prices are expressed in European currency units. Revised periodically, the green rate is used to convert prices from ECUs into EC national currencies, but it does not correspond to currency market prices. For primary agricultural products, the EC resolves the disparity between the green rate and currency prices by paying the difference in monetary compensatory amounts.

**green technology.**   A product or process developed to preserve the environment and natural resources. Green technologies include biotechnologies, environmental consulting services, oil-spill-control equipment, pollution-control equipment, and resource-conserving processes, as well as new forms of contraception. See also *environmental* and *sustainable development.*

**gross charter.**   A maritime phrase, sometimes referred to as gross terms. A gross charter is a contract in which the shipowner pays all charter expenses, including pilotage to or from a primary carrier.

**gross domestic product (GDP).**   One measure of a country's wealth. GDP calculations are usually based on a country's annual production (i.e., the aggregate market value of all goods and services it produces). However, GDP can also be estimated from annual national income (i.e., salaries and wages, self-employment income, profits and rents, interest, royalties, etc.) or annual national expenditures (i.e., investment, consumption, exports less imports, etc.). Compare *gross national product.*

**gross domestic purchases.**   A country's annual expenditures. Gross domestic purchases are com-

puted by adding imports to gross national product and subtracting exports.

**gross income.**   The income of a person or organization before expenses and taxes have been deducted. Income and expenditures are attributed to a given accounting period, usually one quarter or one year. Compare *adjusted gross income.*

**gross interest.**   Interest earned before taxes are deducted.

**gross margin.**   The spread or yield, i.e., the difference between the cost of a transaction and its gross earnings. In banking, the spread is the difference between the lender's borrowing cost and interest earned plus fees paid by the borrower. In the securities industry, the margin is the difference between the underwriter's selling cost, including fees and discounts, and the price paid by investors.

**gross national product (GNP).**   One measure of a country's wealth. GNP is the aggregate value of the goods and services produced within a country plus its net foreign income, usually for 1 year. Net foreign income is the total value of external earnings (including labor remittances, dividends, and interest) less the aggregate sum owed to external sources. Compare *gross domestic product.*

**gross receipts.**   The total amount earned by a business before costs, expenses, and taxes are deducted.

**gross register ton.**   See *gross ton.*

**gross spread.**   See *gross margin.*

**gross terms.**   See *gross charter.*

**gross ton (gr.t., gt).**   A ship's unit of measure. A ton is roughly equal to 100 cubic feet. Gross tonnage is the internal cubic footage of a ship divided by 100.

**gross weight (gwt).**   The total weight of a cargo, including packing and shipping containers.

**gross yield.**   The yield on a security before taxes are deducted. See also *gross margin.*

**grounded container.**   A flat ocean container that can be laid on a ship's bottom. Grounded containers are loaded and unloaded with cranelike devices and transported by truck or rail.

**grounded vessel.**   A ship stuck in the water. Grounded ships are towed to navigable waters.

**group of companies.**   In the United Kingdom, parent companies and their subsidiaries, which are required to file group accounts with the Department of Trade and Industry (DTI). Group accounts combine consolidated balance sheets, as well as combined profit and loss statements. DTI may grant exemptions permitting companies to file separate accounts.

**Group of Five (G-5).**   The countries whose currencies make up the special drawing right basket, i.e., France, Germany, Japan, the United Kingdom, and the United States. See also *basket of currencies.*

**Group of Four (G-4).**   Four countries in the Southern Cone of Latin America, i.e., Argentina, Brazil, Paraguay, and Uruguay. See also *Mercosur.*

**Group of Seven (G-7).**   A group formed in 1986 and composed of the seven major industrialized nations, i.e., Canada, France, Germany, Japan, Italy, the United Kingdom, and the United States. Because of their combined economic power and voting shares in multilateral financial institutions, the G-7 determine official international economic policy when they act in concert. G-7 heads of state hold annual summer meetings, often called world economic summits. Since the advent of European economic integration, participants at the summits are known as the Quad, which includes Canada, the European Community, Japan, and the United States. Russia is also a participant at G-7 summits, although on an as yet undefined basis.

**Group of Seventy-Seven (G-77).**   A group of African, Asian, and Latin American countries formed following the first United Nations Conference on Trade and Development in 1964. The G-77's Joint Declaration called for reallocating 45 percent of International Monetary Fund (IMF) voting quotas to developing countries. As of mid-1993, IMF voting quotas had not been changed.

**Group of Ten (G-10).**   Also known as the Paris Club, the world's 10 principal creditor nations, which grew to 11 when Switzerland joined in 1984. Created in 1962 in connection with the General Arrangements to Borrow (GAB), the G-10 collaborates on international financial issues, including central bank policies and official debt restructurings. G-10 members are Belgium, Canada, France, Germany, Italy, Japan, the Netherlands, Sweden, Switzerland, the United Kingdom, and the United States. Most G-10 discussions are conducted within the frameworks of the Bank for International Settlements and the Organization for Economic Cooperation and Development. See also *Basel Concordat.*

**Group of Thirteen (G-13).**   A group of developing countries formed in 1989 to improve their bargaining position in multilateral financial and trade organizations. G-13 members are Algeria, Argentina, Egypt, India, Indonesia, Jamaica, Malaysia, Nigeria, Peru, Senegal, Venezuela, and Zimbabwe. The former country of Yugoslavia was an original member.

**Group of Three (G-3).**   1. The economic powers of the 1990s, i.e., Germany, Japan, and the United States. 2. Latin American oil-exporting countries that consitute a free trade-linked energy basin. The G-3 includes Colombia, Mexico, and Venezuela, which are to sign a free trade agreement in 1993. Chile is also expected to join the free trade area. The G-3 plan to liberalize internal trade and remove internal tariffs on manufactured goods by the beginning of 1994.

**Group of Twenty (G-20).**   Also called the Committee of Twenty, a body authorized by the International Monetary Fund (IMF) in 1972 to study the global system of payments. The G-20 delegates, known as the Committee on Reform of the International Monetary System and Related Issues, were elected by IMF members. On balance, the committee approved the floating exchange-rate system and rejected the use of trade regulation to correct balance-of-payments deficits. It recommended that the IMF adopt mechanisms for stabilizing exchange rates and that it use the special drawing right to increase global liquidity.

**Group of Twenty-Four (G-24).**   A group of developing countries organized at Lima, Peru, in 1972. Officially known as the Intergovernmental Group of 24 on International Monetary Affairs, the G-24 advises the International Monetary Fund (IMF) on developing country issues. In 1985, the G-24 published the *Revised Plan for Immediate Action* to advance the interests of developing countries within the IMF.

**Groups of Negotiations on Goods and on Services.** See *GATT Standing Committees.*

**growth company.** A company with a record of expansion. Growth companies typically plan greater investments in research and development, employee training, state-of-the-art plant and equipment, and other assets to spur expansion.

**growth industry.** An industry poised to grow at a faster rate than others. Economic resources, an emerging market, location, or new technologies may contribute to expectations of an industry's growth.

**growth stock.** Equities expected to produce capital gains. A growth stock is the common stock of a well-managed company with increasing earnings. Companies issuing growth stocks usually also make substantial investments in equipment, new plants, and research and development. Compare *income stock.*

**Growth Triangle.** The flourishing trade centers of Singapore, Johor (Malaysia), and Riau Province (Indonesia). The phrase was coined in Singapore, the center of trading activity on the Malay Peninsula. See also *Gateway to China.*

**gr.t.** An abbreviation for gross ton.

**gr. wt.** The abbreviation for gross weight.

**GSA.** The abbreviation for General Services Administration.

**GSM-102 (Export Credit Guarantee Program).** In the United States, an agricultural export program that guarantees commercial bank loans. The loans are made at commercial rates and are guaranteed for up to 3 years by the Commodity Credit Corporation. Successful applicants demonstrate that export financing is needed to gain or sustain external market share. Compare *GSM-103.*

**GSM-103 (Intermediate Export Credit Guarantee Program).** In the United States, an agricultural export program that guarantees commercial bank loans. The loans are made at commercial rates and are guaranteed for up to 10 years by the Commodity Credit Corporation. Successful applicants demonstrate that export financing is needed to gain or sustain foreign market share. Compare *GSM-102.*

**GSP.** The abbreviation for Generalized System of Preferences.

**GSP Form A.** See *UNCTAD Certificate of Origin Form A.*

**GST.** The abbreviation for goods and services tax. See *value-added tax.*

**gt.** An abbreviation for gross ton.

**GTB.** The abbreviation for general term bond.

**GTC.** The abbreviation for (order) good till canceled.

**gtd.** An abbreviation for guaranteed.

**GTDA.** The abbreviation for general technical data available.

**GTDR.** The abbreviation for general technical data restricted.

**GTDU.** The abbreviation for general technical data unrestricted.

**GTM.** The abbreviation for (order) good this month.

**GTT.** The abbreviation for general turnover tax. See *value-added tax.*

**GTW.** The abbreviation for (order) good this week.

**guar.** An abbreviation for guaranteed.

**guaraní** The currency of Paraguay.

**guaranteed access levels (GALS).** In the United States, quotas applied to apparel imports from Caribbean Basin Initiative countries. Imports entering under GALS require special certification. More liberal than other U.S. textile quotas, GAL entry is available only for apparels assembled in the Caribbean Basin from fabric formed and cut in the United States. A GAL increase requested by a CBI country is effective immediately, unless expressly rejected by the United States within 30 days. Duty reductions available under HTS 9802 also apply to GAL imports.

**guaranteed stocks.** Equities issued by a government-owned industry. Income earned from the stocks is guaranteed by the issuing government.

**guarantee of collectibility.** In commercial insurance, a clause that protects a policyholder when goods are sold on free-on-board (FOB) terms.

Normally, FOB goods are insured by the seller until loaded aboard a vessel, but the consignee's insurance may not take effect until title is transferred. In the interim, a guarantee of collectibility insures a policyholder's cargo up to the amount of the consignee's coverage.

**guarantor.**    Also known as a surety, a party who guarantees payment on behalf of another. Corporations often back loans to subsidiaries by issuing a letter of credit or a written statement of intent to guarantee an obligation. The guarantor is fully liable if the debtor defaults, though the guarantor's liability is contingent.

**guest currency.**    A currency that is not the domicile currency of one or both parties to a transaction. Bonds or other financial obligations are often denominated in a guest currency.

**guest workers.**    Foreign labor admitted to a country to perform specific tasks for a limited period of time. Guest workers require entry and work permits.

**guia de importação.**    Portuguese: import license.

**guide price.**    Also known as the orientation price, the target price for cattle and calf imports under the European Community's Common Agricultural Policy.

**Guide to Financing Exports.**    In the United States, a list of export financing sources published by the U.S. & Foreign Commercial Service. The publication is available from the U.S. Department of Commerce.

**guilder.**    The currency of the Netherlands, the Netherlands Antilles, and Surinam.

**Gulf Cooperation Council (GCC).**    A common market of Middle Eastern Gulf states created at Abu Dhabi, United Arab Emirates, in 1982. The GCC agreement anticipates a common external tariff, monetary union, and uniform industrial and investment policies. Interregional imports enter duty-free if 40 percent of a product's value is added by companies controlled by GCC nationals. Bahrain, Kuwait, Oman, Qatar, Saudi Arabia, and the United Arab Emirates are GCC members. The council has headquarters in Riyadh, Saudi Arabia.

**gulf riyal.**    The currency of Dubai and Qatar.

**gwt.**    The abbreviation for gross weight.

**gyosei-shido.**    Japanese: administrative guidance, principally inside information. *Gyosei-shido* are formal or informal government statements indicating how laws and regulations are enforced. A government statement may take the form of a written opinion, but it need not. Foreign executives complain that the often casual nature of *gyosei-shido* is a major barrier to market penetration by foreign businesses in Japan.

# H

**h.** The abbreviation for harbor.

**habatsu.** In Japan, the political elite. *Habatsu* consists of both career bureaucrats, known as *gikan* (technicians), *jimukan* (administrators), and *kanryoha* (former bureaucrats), and influential politicians, known as *amakudari* (former politicians) and *toginha* (current politicians).

**Hague Agreement.** See *Hague-Visby Rules*.

**Hague Agreement Concerning the International Deposit of Industrial Designs.** Commonly known as the Hague Act of 1960, an international agreement protecting industrial designs. The original agreement was adopted at The Hague in 1825 and revised at London in 1934, The Hague in 1960, Monaco in 1961, and Stockholm in 1967. A protocol was added at Geneva in 1975. Industrial designs are protected in some adhering countries when a single application is filed with the World Intellectual Property Organization. Other adherents require that applicants also file with national agencies. In most instances, designs may be submitted under open cover or sealed cover, although some countries only protect designs registered under open cover. An open cover submission is one generally available for public inspection; a sealed cover submission is open to public view subject to the owner's permission. Designs are usually protected for a minimum of 5 years, but national laws vary. The act itself protects designs for 15 years, but it requires that they be opened for public inspection after 5 years. The Hague Act is open to signatories of the Paris Convention for the Protection of Industrial Property.

**Hague Convention Abolishing the Requirement of Legalization for Foreign Public Documents.** See *apostille sheet*.

**Hague Convention on the Carriage of Goods by Sea.** See *Hague-Visby Rules* and *Hamburg Rules*.

**Hague Formation Convention.** See *United Nations Convention on Contracts for the International Sale of Goods*.

**Hague Sales Convention.** See *United Nations Convention on Contracts for the International Sale of Goods*.

**Hague-Visby Rules.** A product of the Hague Convention on the Carriage of Goods by Sea sponsored by the International Chamber of Commerce in 1924. The Hague Rules are the basis of national maritime laws governing the liability of ocean carriers for damaged or lost cargo. The convention limits carrier liability to 100 pounds sterling, or roughly $500 U.S. dollars per package or customary freight unit, even when a carrier is negligent. The Visby Amendment of 1968, also known as the Visby Protocol, effective in 1977, raises the liability limit from 500 U.S. dollars to 1,000 U.S. dollars per package. A 1978 protocol converts the limit from U.S. dollars to 667 special drawing rights. The Hague Rules were not constructed to account for containerization, and the Visby Rules do not resolve the liability issues raised by containers and consolidated shipments. The United States adopted the Hague Rules on the Carriage of Goods by Sea Act of 1936, but has not adopted the Visby Amendment. See also *Hamburg Rules*.

**half-commission man.** An agent who receives a fee for introducing stockbrokers to prospective customers.

**hallmark.** In the United Kingdom, an official mark stamped on gold, platinum, or silver articles. The mark is issued by a government assay office, known as a hall. Each hall, located in various UK cities, has a distinctive mark that identifies metal quality and the stamping date. In the UK, hallmarks are protected trademarks, and forging a hallmark is a legal offense.

**Hamburg Rules.** Rules adopted by the United Nations Convention on the Carriage of Goods by Sea held at Hamburg in 1978, effective in 1992. The Hamburg Rules were drafted to correct deficiencies in the Hague-Visby Rules that limit ocean carrier liability. The Hamburg Rules apply to cargoes covered by bills of lading issued in an adhering state, entering or departing an adhering state, or subject to a contract that incorporates them by reference. Cargoes transported under a charter party are not governed by the rules, unless the bill of lading is subject to them on other grounds. The

Hamburg Rules accept electronic codes, facsimiles, stamps, symbols, etc., as alternatives to handwritten endorsements on negotiable bills of lading. They also contain other innovations: (1) a carrier is liable for negligent cargo losses, unless a shipper acts with intentional or reckless disregard; (2) maximum carrier liability is the greater of 835 units of account (UA) or 2.5 UA per kilogram. One UA equals one special drawing right; (3) the statute of limitations on shipper claims is 2 years; (4) a shipping container is a package, unless the shipper identifies the number of units or cartons on the bill of lading. Then each carton or unit constitutes a package.

**hammering.**    In the United Kingdom, the procedure for announcing that a trader on the London Stock Exchange cannot meet financial obligations to customers.

**Handelskammer.**    German: chamber of commerce, also known as *Industrie und Handelskammer.*

**Hangelsorganisation (HO).**    German: state retail store in the former East Germany.

**Hang Seng Index.**    See *Stock Exchange of Hong Kong Limited.*

**hara gei.**    Japanese: belly art, i.e., indirect communication skills that enable a business manager to obtain favorable outcomes in negotiations without direct mention of terms and conditions.

**harbor dues.**    Also called harbor maintenance fees, user fees paid to a port authority for the cost of operating a harbor. The fees are paid by carriers and passed on to shippers as surcharges. In the United States, the harbor maintenance fee is authorized by the Water Resources Development Act of 1986.

**hard currency.**    A currency that is freely convertible into another. Hard currencies are convertible because their exchange values are stable relative to those of other currencies. See also *Big Eight.*

**harmonization.**    The process of eliminating disparities in laws or regulations, particularly when countries enter into trading accords. The degree of harmonization depends on the nature of the agreement. Customs rules conform to a single standard in a customs union. In common markets and free trade agreements, some degree of uniformity in customs, environmental, labor, and investment rules and product standards is required. In an economic union, the harmonization is more complete, including the adoption of common fiscal and monetary policies.

**Harmonized Commodity Description and Coding System (HS).**    Also called the Harmonized System and the Harmonized System of Tariffs, a numerical product classification system developed by the Customs Cooperation Council (CCC). Derived from the Customs Cooperation Council Nomenclature, the HS is a flexible classification system with 96 chapters designed to permit users to customize tariffs to accommodate different customs or product requirements. Approximately five thousand items are identified in the HS under headings or subheadings, which are based on a six-digit code. A four-digit number is assigned to each heading; the first two digits indicate the chapter where the item is located; the next two digits show the subchapter where the item is found. Items are assigned two more digits under each subheading, and a country may add additional digits beyond the six-number code. CCC's Harmonized System Committee reviews proposals submitted by official agencies to modify the Harmonized System. Since 1988, the HS has gradually begun to replace the Brussels Tariff Nomenclature, the first international system for import classification. See also *Harmonized Tariff Schedule of the United States.*

**Harmonized Tariff (HT).**    A tariff schedule that conforms to the Harmonized Commodity Description and Coding System.

**Harmonized System of Tariffs.**    See *Harmonized Commodity Description and Coding System.*

**Harmonized Tariff Schedule of the United States (HTS).**    An abstract of the Harmonized Tariff Schedule of the United States, Annotated. The abstract is published by the U.S. International Trade Commission. HTS is also the computer code entered into the Automated Broker Interface system to indicate the use of the Harmonized Schedule.

**Harmonized Tariff Schedule of the United States, Annotated (HTSUSA).**    The import classifications and rates of duty for the United States.

Published by the Bureau of the Census, HTSUSA lists concessional and statutory rates by product category. Concessional rates include reduced duties for the Canada-U.S. Free Trade Agreement (FTA), Caribbean Basin Initiative (CBI), Israel-U.S. Free Trade Agreement (FTA), most favored nations, and U.S. Generalized System of Preferences (US-GSP). Imports entering under the Canadian FTA are identified by "CA," the CBI by "E," the Israeli FTA by "I," and the US-GSP by "A." Conditional duty-free entry is noted in the special column. Countries eligible for various U.S. trade preferences are identified in HTSUSA General Notes.

**Harter Act of 1893.**    In the United States, the law that governed ocean carrier liability before the enactment of the Carriage of Goods at Sea Act (COGSA) in 1936. The Harter Act reflected a compromise between unlimited loss liability imposed on ocean carriers by customary international law and disclaimers of liability added to ocean bills of lading. The act was supplanted by COGSA. See also *Hague-Visby Rules* and *Hamburg Rules*.

**haulage.**    The charge for transporting goods, primarily by road.

**Havana Charter.**    See *General Agreement on Tariffs and Trade*.

**hazardous cargo.**    A shipment that requires special handling but which need not be inherently dangerous. Hazards can arise from a combination of factors, including the conditions under which cargo is transported. The transport of hazardous cargoes is regulated by international convention and by national laws. In the United States, the Hazardous Materials Transportation Act of 1974, contained in the Transportation Safety Act and the Hazardous Materials Transportation Uniform Safety Act of 1990, regulates the handling of hazardous cargo. Recent regulations issued under the 1990 act require, among other things, that employers train employees to handle dangerous cargoes. Packaging and documentation rules are found in the Code of Federal Regulations (Title 49), effective July 1, 1976, also known as CFR 49. Cargo moving in U.S. domestic commerce defined as hazardous includes combustibles, compressed gases, corrosives, etiologic agents, explosives, flammables, poisons, radioactive substances, etc. When properly marked, certain substances used to manufacture consumer products are exempt from CFR 49. In the case of a conflict with international regulations, CFR 49 applies in the United States. The regulations are issued by the Office of Hazardous Materials Transportation in the U.S. Department of Transportation (DOT). DOT Regulation 181 revising U.S. hazardous cargo rules is scheduled for full implementation in 1996; however, a regulation requiring the posting of hazardous warnings on trucks carrying dangerous articles took effect October 1, 1991. See also *dangerous goods*.

**Hazardous Materials Transportation Act of 1974.** See *hazardous cargo*.

**Hazardous Materials Transportation Uniform Safety Act of 1990.**    See *hazardous cargo*.

**head lease.**    A primary lease.

**heavy cargo.**    A massive shipment that weighs a ship down to its water marks. A heavy cargo need not fill the cargo capacity of a ship in terms of its length or width. See also *load line*.

**heavy grain.**    A shipment of solid pulverized products with a density of 48 to 50 cubic feet per ton.

**hedge.**    Any device, including a contract, used to reduce the risk of a venture. The odds are narrowed by balancing a risky investment with a relatively safer one. Buying foreign currencies or forward exchange contracts to sell at a future date is a common hedge used to protect against exchange rate changes. In a foreign exchange hedge, a contract or a currency is purchased at the spot price prevailing on the date of purchase. In theory, interest earned on the purchase by the settlement date, also called the value date, offsets losses from any decline in the value of a currency. In an interest rate hedge, an investor normally purchases a futures contract to lock in a prevailing or anticipated interest rate. The investor selling a forward contract takes a long hedge. The investor buying a forward contract takes a short hedge. See also *forward outright rate, futures, futures option, option,* and *warrant*.

**hedge ratio.**    The proportion of options to futures contracts that a buyer purchases to eliminate the risks of a transaction. The ratio is based on an option's delta. For example, if a $1 change in the futures contract price alters the option premium by $0.50, the ratio is two options for each futures contract.

**hell-or-high-water charter.** A vessel charter where the charterer pays all costs without deductions or setoffs.

**Hermes Kreditversicherungs-Aktiengeschellshaft (AG).** In Germany, one of two private insurers authorized by the German government to manage official export credit insurance. A regulated company, Hermes insures most country risks and commercial risks when commercial financing is otherwise unavailable.

**High Authority.** The executive agency for the European Coal and Steel Community. The High Authority was dissolved when the European Economic Community was formed in 1961.

**high cube.** A container taller than that recognized as standard by the International Standards Organization (ISO). High cubes are 40 feet long and 9 feet to 9 feet 6 inches in height. Super-high cubes exceed 40 feet in length. High and super-high containers are not used in international trade. See *container.*

**higher rate.** See *marginal rate.*

**highest original statutory rate.** A provision in a tariff schedule stipulating that the highest duty rate be imposed when an import matches more than one product classification. Where required, the highest rate is applied, even though a lower concessional rate is available. See also *duty.*

**high-grade bond.** In the United States, an AAA-rated or AA-rated bond. The debt rating of a bond can be enhanced. A bank letter of credit is the most common form of enhancement. See also *bond rating.*

**high seas.** Generally, the unenclosed portion of waters unbounded by the territory of any nation. The most common view accepts the English rule, which defines the high seas as beginning 3 miles from a nation's coastline. The American rule is contrary and denotes the high seas as any unenclosed water beyond the low-water mark.

**high yielder.** A speculative stock.

**Himalaya clause.** A clause in an ocean bill of lading that permits employees to raise a carrier's defenses against claims for damaged or lost cargo.

The clause takes its name from the ship *Himalaya,* which was the subject of the British court case *Adler v. Dickson.*

**hire.** In a charter party, revenue earned by a ship during a voyage.

**hire purchase (HP).** A sales transaction in which a buyer makes a deposit toward the purchase of goods and becomes the owner when the balance is paid. Unlike purchasers on a credit sale where ownership passes at the time a sales contract is signed, the buyer in a hire purchase does not own the goods until the full price has been paid.

**HM 181.** The abbreviation for Hazardous Materials, Regulation 181. See *hazardous cargo.*

**HMC.** The abbreviation for Her (His) Majesty's Customs, the British customs authority.

**HMF.** The abbreviation for harbor maintenance fee. See *harbor dues.*

**holder in due course.** A party who receives a financial instrument or document of title in exchange for legal consideration. The instrument can be in bearer or blank form, or it can be endorsed and made to the order of the holder. A bona fide holder acquires an instrument without notice or knowledge that it has been dishonored or that another party has a claim against proceeds owed on it. Holders with recourse can compel a prior endorser to pay the value of an instrument dishonored by its maker, drawee, or acceptor. A holder without recourse cannot force a prior endorser to pay a dishonored instrument's value and absorbs the loss.

**hold harmless clause.** A contract clause that excuses one or both parties from performing contractual obligations when unforeseen events interfere with performance.

**holding company.** A company that owns enough voting shares to control one or more companies. Holding companies permit businesses to engage in activities otherwise prohibited by law or regulation. In the United States, for example, bank holding companies are allowed to engage in certain nonbank activities, such as consumer financing and securities underwriting.

**hold on dock.** The temporary stowage of cargo on the dock at a port. Temporary stowage permits a seller to release cargo from a warehouse before the cargo is sold or shipped. Prices are quoted as free-alongside-ship pier (FAS) or free-on-board pier (FOB). In some jurisdictions, the offer by a carrier of a hold-on-dock arrangement is considered an improper inducement and disallowed under local regulations.

**holiday.**   In a charter party, an exemption excusing cargo handling during local holidays. A holiday is determined by customs of the port.

**home credit.**   A subsidy from a government to domestic shipowners to encourage the purchase of ships built in local shipyards.

**home port.**   The place where a vessel is registered or the place of a shipowner's domicile.

**Hong Kong Stock Exchange.**   See *Stock Exchange of Hong Kong Limited*.

**honor.**   Payment of the amount shown on a draft or bill of exchange when it is presented to a bank.

**hook and haul.**   A phrase excusing a ground carrier from loading and unloading cargo. The carrier is responsible for hooking up equipment and hauling the cargo. The shipper or consignee loads and unloads it.

**horizontal integration.**   A business combination between firms engaged in the same level of production, i.e., one parts supplier that owns another. Compare *vertical integration*.

**horizontal spread.**   See *calendar spread*.

**hostile embargo.**   See *embargo*.

**hot money.**   1. Funds held for speculative purposes. Hot money is composed of short-term deposits that can be quickly transferred when exchange rates or interest rates change. 2. Funds transferred between banks for overnight or short-term loans. 3. In the United States, uninsured deposits that exceed the federal deposit insurance limit.

**hots.**   In the United Kingdom, a colloquial term for Treasury bills on the day of issue.

**house air waybill.**   See *airbill*.

**house bill number.**   The computer code entered in the Automated Commercial System to identify a single shipment transported under a master bill of lading.

**house paper.**   A bill of exchange drawn by a parent or subsidiary and accepted by an affiliated company.

**HP.**   The abbreviation for hire purchase.

**HS.**   The abbreviation for Harmonized System. See *Harmonized Commodity Description and Coding System*.

**HT.**   The abbreviation for Harmonized Tariff.

**HTS.**   The abbreviation for Harmonized Tariff Schedule of the United States.

**HTS Item 9802.**   In the United States, an item in the Harmonized Tariff Schedule of the United States, Annotated, that reduces duties on U.S. imports assembled or processed abroad from U.S. exports. To gain favorable treatment, an import's value added in the beneficiary country must have been incidental (rather than central) to the main industrial process creating the product. Duties on these imports, formerly known as 807 imports, are paid to the extent of nonincidental foreign values. The import entry form used for 9802 imports is the Special Access Program CBI Export Declaration (Form ITA-370P).

**HTS number.**   The eight- or ten-digit code in the Automated Commercial System used to identify commodities listed in the Harmonized Tariff Schedule of the United States.

**HTSUSA.**   The abbreviation for Harmonized Tariff Schedule of the United States, Annotated.

**hull insurance.**   A policy that protects a shipowner from losses caused by damage to the structure or body of a ship or aircraft.

**human capital.**   A nation's intangible income-producing assets that derive from the intellectual and inventive capacity of its labor force. Human capital denotes creativity and problem-solving skills, developed through education and training, which add value to a country's gross national product.

**hundredweight.**   A unit of measure that varies depending on the jurisdiction. In the United States, a hundredweight is equal to 100 pounds, or one-twentieth of a short ton. In the United Kingdom, the measure is equal to 122 pounds, or one-twentieth of a long ton.

**husbanding agent.**   An ocean carrier's representative at a particular port. The husbanding agent supervises the maintenance of a carrier's ships anchored at port.

**hyperinflation.**   A state of rapidly increasing prices with corresponding declines in consumer purchasing power. Prices rising at rates exceeding 50 percent per month are indicative of hyperinflation.

**hypothec.**   A lien or claim on property not owned or in possession of the claimant.

**hypothecation.**   1. In banking, the pledging of documents of title as collateral for a loan. Hypothecation agreements require the borrower to deposit a warehouse receipt or bill of lading with the lender until the debt is paid. The agreements often include provisions for rehypothecation, whereby a lender is able to borrow against repledged collateral. 2. In maritime usage, the use of a ship or cargo as collateral for a loan. When a ship is pledged, with or without its cargo, a bottomry bond or bottomry bill secures the loan. If the cargo alone is pledged, the hypothecation is called respondentia, which is secured by a respondentia bond. Bottomry and respondentia bonds create maritime liens. Lenders do not recover on maritime liens when collateral covered by a bond is lost at sea.

**hypothecation certificate.**   A letter of hypothecation. The certificate entitles the holder of a bill of exchange to sell the underlying goods if the bill is dishonored.

# I

**I.** The mark of origin for imports entering the United States from Israel under the U.S.-Israel Free Trade Agreement. See also *Harmonized Tariff Schedule of the United States, Annotated.*

**i.A.** The abbreviation for *im Auftrag.*

**IA.** The abbreviation for Import Administration.

**IAC.** The abbreviation for import allocation certificate.

**IADA.** The abbreviation for Intra-Asia Discussion Agreement. See *conference.*

**IaDB.** An informal abbreviation for Inter-American Development Bank.

**IAEA.** The abbreviation for International Atomic Energy Agency.

**IAIGC.** The abbreviation for Inter-Arab Investment Guarantee Corporation.

**IAP.** The abbreviation for Import Administration Program.

**IAPH.** The abbreviation for International Association of Ports and Harbors.

**IATA.** The abbreviation for International Air Transport Association.

**IBA.** The abbreviation for International Bauxite Association. See *international commodity agreement.*

**IBC.** The abbreviation for international banking center.

**IBF.** The abbreviation for international banking facility.

**IBLC.** The abbreviation for *Institut Belgo-Luxembourgeois du Change.*

**IBOS.** The abbreviation for International Business Opportunities Services.

**IBRD.** The abbreviation for International Bank for Reconstruction and Development.

**IC.** The abbreviation for import certificate.

**ICAC.** The abbreviation for International Cotton Advisory Committee. See *international commodity agreement.*

**ICAO.** The abbreviation for International Civil Aviation Organization.

**ICC.** The abbreviation for International Chamber of Commerce and Interstate Commerce Commission.

**ICCEC.** The abbreviation for Intergovernmental Council of Copper Exporting Countries. See *Conseil Inter-gouvernemental des Pays Exportateurs de Cuivre.*

**ICCH.** The abbreviation for International Commodities Clearing House.

**ICCO.** The acronym for International Cocoa Organization. See *international commodity agreement.*

**ICFTU.** The abbreviation for International Confederation of Free Trade Unions.

**ICI.** The abbreviation for independent commercial importer.

**ICIA.** The abbreviation for Import Certificate Issuing Authority. See *import certificate.*

**ICM.** The abbreviation for *imposto sobre circulação de mercadoria.*

**ICO.** The abbreviation for International Coffee Organization and international commodity organization. See *international commodity agreement.*

**ICS.** The abbreviation for International Chamber of Shipping and International Coordinating Secretariat.

**ICSID.** The abbreviation for International Centre for the Settlement of Investment Disputes.

**ID.** The abbreviation for immediate delivery.

**IDA.** The abbreviation for International Development Association.

**IDB.** The abbreviation for International Data Base, Islamic Development Bank, and Inter-American Development Bank.

**IDC.** the abbreviation for industrial development certificate.

**identical or similar merchandise.** A product whose economic value is established by reference to an import. Identical merchandise is a like product originating with the same producer. Similar merchandise is an equivalent product produced by a competitor in the same country or region. The value of identical or similar merchandise is used by customs officials to determine import value when the invoice price is inconsistent with other evidence of value.

**identical treatment.**   See *national treatment.*

**ID/entry.**   See *immediate delivery entry.*

**IDF.**   The abbreviation for import declaration form.

**IDR.**   The abbreviation for international depositary receipt.

**IE.**   The abbreviation for immediate export.

**I/E.**   The abbreviation for informal entry. See *customs entry.*

**IEA.**   The abbreviation for International Energy Agency.

**IEP.**   The abbreviation for International Economic Policy. See *International Trade Administration.*

**IFAD.**   The abbreviation for International Fund for Agricultural Development.

**IFC.**   The abbreviation for International Finance Corporation.

**IFZ.**   The abbreviation for industrial free zone. See *export processing zone.*

**IHVS.**   The abbreviation for intelligent highway vehicle systems.

**IIB.**   The abbreviation for International Investment Bank.

**IIEDS.**   The abbreviation for Individual Investor Express Delivery Service. See *New York Stock Exchange, Inc.*

**IJO.**   The abbreviation for International Jute Organization. See *international commodity agreement.*

**ILA.**   The abbreviation for International Longshoremen's Association.

**ILG.**   The abbreviation for Import Licensing Group.

**illegal contract.**   A contract covering an activity prohibited by common law or statute. For example, a loan agreement promising a usurious rate of return is illegal and void. An illegal contract can only be enforced against one party when the other is without culpability in the unlawful conduct and unaware of the illegality underlying the agreement.

**illiquid asset.**   An asset not easily converted to cash, despite its intrinsic value. Assets are illiquid when there is no market for them or when they are overvalued in terms of current prices.

**ILO.**   The abbreviation for International Labour Organisation.

**ILU.**   The abbreviation for Institute of London Underwriters.

**ILWU.**   The abbreviation for International Longshoremen Workers Union.

**IMAO.**   The abbreviation for International Maritime Arbitration Organization. See *International Maritime Organization.*

**im Auftrag (i.A.).**   German: on behalf of.

**IMB.**   The abbreviation for International Moscow Bank.

**IMF.**   The abbreviation for International Monetary Fund.

**IMM.**   The abbreviation for International Money Market. See *Chicago Mercantile Exchange–International Money Market.*

**immediate delivery (ID) entry.**   In the United States, a customs code permitting cargo clearance before duties are paid, usually for up to 10 days. The code is assigned to fresh fruits, vegetables, and similar produce imported from Canada and Mexico.

**immediate order.**   See *fill or kill.*

**immediate transportation (IT) entry.**   In the United States, a code assigned to in-bond shipments at a customs entry port. The code permits cargo to be moved by a bonded carrier to an inland destination without formal customs entry or payment of duties.

**immigrant remittances.**   Also called worker remittances, money earned abroad and sent to families in the home country. Remittances are foreign exchange earnings for the recipient country.

**immunization.**   Investment strategies used to minimize portfolio risks, e.g., an interest rate swap. For example, an investor's risk is minimized when earnings match outflows. Bondholders are immunized when payments of principal and interest are received during the holding period.

**IMO.**    The abbreviation for International Maritime Organization.

**imp.**    The abbreviation for import.

**IMP.**    The abbreviation for International Marketing Profiles.

**impact day.**    In financial markets, the day on which public notice of a new securities issue is given.

**imperfect competition.**    See *perfect competition.*

**imperial preference.**    See *commonwealth preference.*

**import (imp.).**    1. A good or a service originating in one country or territory for sale in another. 2. The act of moving a product or service from one sovereign jurisdiction into the commerce of another.

**Import Administration (IA).**    In the United States, a division of the International Trade Administration (ITA) of the U.S. Department of Commerce. The ITA regulates U.S. imports, and the IA administers most domestic nonagricultural import quotas.

**import allocation certificate (IAC).**    An import license issued by a central monetary agency authorizing foreign exchange for imports. The certificates enable a government to regulate foreign exchange expenditures. In Japan, for example, an import allocation certificate is required for imports valued above 1 million yen. In some countries, IACs are called import registration certificates. See also *mark sheet.*

**import authorization and therapeutic license.**    An import license required in some countries for imports of pharmaceuticals.

**import budget.**    The means of administering import quotas in some countries. For example, in Yemen, the Ministry of Economy, Supply, and Trade determines the type and quantity of goods eligible for importation. The annual findings are contained in the government's import budget. The budget breakdown is not made public.

**import certificate (IC).**    In India, an import license for U.S. exports entering under the memorandum of understanding reached between India and the United States in the 1980s. The certificates are provided by Import Certificate Issuing Authorities, which are Indian government agencies responsible for regulating various industries. The certificates substantiate the Indian government's assurances that U.S. exports will not be diverted or reexported without ICIA approval.

**import certificate/delivery verification.**    See *COCOM Lists.*

**import declaration form (IDF).**    An application for foreign exchange used in countries with foreign exchange controls. For example, an IDF is presented to the Bank of Ghana prior to weekly foreign exchange auctions. If the application is approved, the importer submits the IDF to a government-approved bank for a line of credit. In some countries, IDFs are presented to exchange bureaus for conversion at market rates.

**import duty.**    See *duty.*

**importé des États-Unis d' Amérique.**    French: imported from the United States of America.

**import entry form.**    A form used to assess duties. When its representations are accepted by a customs agency, an import entry form becomes a receipt, also called a warrant, authorizing the release of cargo to an importer.

**import-export passbook scheme.**    In India, a licensing system for facilitating foreign trade. The passbook scheme is employed to reduce duplication in import license processing, particularly for goods used to manufacture exports.

**import house.**    A private firm that represents foreign producers and imports for its own account. Encountered primarily in Latin America, import houses assume the credit risks of importing. Some import houses sell exclusively to government agencies in response to tender offers; others also operate general merchandise outlets through branches and subsidiaries.

**import license.**    A permit granted by a country allowing fixed quantities of specified goods to enter its customs territory. Licenses are used to enforce import quotas, protect domestic markets from import competition, ration foreign exchange, and restrict imports from certain exporting countries. See also *COCOM Lists.* Compare *export license.*

**Import Licensing Group (ILG).**    In the United States, an office of the Foreign Agricultural Service of the U.S. Department of Agriculture. The office determines annual quotas for dairy products imported under license. The quotas are enforced by the U.S. Customs Service.

**import permit.**    Also known as a clearance permit, any authorization issued by a government permitting goods or services originating in a foreign jurisdiction to enter its territory.

**import quota.**    A limit on the number of imports admitted by a country. Also called quantitative restraints, import quotas are authorized by legislation, directive, executive order, or proclamation. 1. Absolute quotas restrict the quantity of a class of imports during a given quota period. These quotas may be global (i.e., limiting a class of imports irrespective of country of origin) or specific (i.e., allocating a predetermined number of imports among designated countries). Imports exceeding absolute quotas are reexported or warehoused for entry in another quota period. 2. Tariff rate quotas permit a specified quantity of imports to enter at reduced duty rates during a quota period. There are no limits on the number of imports allowed to enter, but quantities exceeding the quota are subject to higher duties.

**import registration certificate (IRC).**    An import license required for closely regulated products. Import registration certificates are often needed for goods entering under import quotas or restricted for national security reasons, as, for example, in the international import certificate/delivery verification system.

**import restriction.**    A trade barrier, mainly tariffs, quotas, or regulations.

**import-sensitive industry.**    An economic sector vulnerable to low-cost imports, usually because cheaper manufactures substitute adequately for its products. Import-sensitive industries employ mostly unskilled labor for whom there are few alternative jobs. For example, the textiles, clothing, and footwear industries are import-sensitive.

Such import-sensitive industries are prone to seek government protection.

**import specialist.**    In the United States, an employee of the U.S. Customs Service who examines and classifies imports.

**import statement.**    See *American manufacturing clause.*

**import substitution.**    A policy of replacing imports with domestic products. Import substitution involves charging higher import duties and/or restricting imports through quotas or outright bans.

**Import Support and Information System.**    See *Food and Drug Administration.*

**import surcharge.**    An extra tax added to import duties. Import surcharges are used by governments to collect additional foreign trade revenues without breaching bound tariffs agreed to in international agreements. The surcharges are usually temporary.

**import trade control order notice.**    A directive identifying imports subject to quotas. In Japan, import control notices are issued by the Ministry of International Trade and Industry.

**impost.**    Duties, taxes, or fees imposed by a country to raise revenue or regulate trade.

**imposto sobre circulação de mercadoria (ICM).**    Portuguese: merchandise circulation tax, i.e., a value-added tax.

**imposto sobre produtos industrializados (IPI).**    Portuguese: industrial products tax.

**imprest account.**    An accounting method for controlling petty-cash expenditures. Vouchers are submitted in exchange for cash to verify disbursements and identify the persons receiving them. Reimbursed cash is similarly noted.

**imprevision.**    In civil law, a doctrine that permits a court to alter a contract's terms if enforcing them would create inequities. When changed, but unforeseen, circumstances intervene, a court may act to restore fairness to a transaction. The rule is sometimes invoked when abnormal exchange rate fluctuations alter the nature of a contractual obligation. See also *laesio enormis.*

**imprimes.**    A French marking for printed matter.

**improper inducement.**    A bonus offered in violation of law or industry practice. It may consist of a cash payment, rebate, service, or entertainment. Improper inducements are generally illegal, subjecting the parties involved to civil and/or criminal penalties.

**imputation tax system.**    A system of corporate taxation common in Europe and other tax jurisdictions. The corporation pays taxes on its own revenues, as well as earnings distributed to shareholders; i.e., a stockholder's tax liability is imputed to the corporation. At the end of a tax accounting period, both the corporation and shareholder receive credit against taxes payable. The United Kingdom adopted the imputation system in 1972 by enacting the advance corporation tax. Australia enacted a similar system in 1987. See also *avoir fiscal* and *crédit d'impôt.*

**imputed cost.**    An accounting method used to value the financial cost of holding an asset as opposed to selling it. Imputed cost is derived by adding the interest that could be earned on proceeds from the sale of the asset to its resale price.

**in-bond shipment.**    Cargo temporarily exempt from customs clearance and duties. In-bond shipments are transported under a surety from one port to another. The goods are held, often in a bonded warehouse, until examined and cleared at a second port .

**inc., incl.**    The abbreviation for inclusive.

**Inc.**    The abbreviation for incorporated. See *corporation.*

**inchmaree clause.**    In marine insurance, a provision protecting a policyholder from losses caused by defects in a vessel's construction, equipment, maintenance, or management.

**income.**    Money and financial benefits earned from work or investments. Gross income is total earnings. Net income is gross earnings less expenses incurred in earning income and taxes. In some jurisdictions, employer-paid benefits, such as insurance premiums or private club memberships, are counted as income to the recipient.

**income bond.**    A savings bond issued by a government agency or an insurance company. Income bonds yield monthly minimum interest. Guaranteed-income bonds repay principal at the end of the term plus fixed interest.

**income distribution.**    The return paid to an investor in a mutual fund or unit trust. Income is distributed in proportion to owned shares from total earnings less management fees and taxes.

**income effect.**    The impact of price changes on a consumer's purchasing power. When the price of one product decreases, a consumer with stable income has more to spend on other products. While income effects cause growth in some sectors, an industry receiving lower prices is less profitable. Compare *substitution effect.*

**incomes policy.**    A structure implemented to control wage and price inflation when a government pursues an active fiscal policy. Incomes policies are intended to maintain employment by restraining inflation through a prudent balance between wage and price increases.

**income statement.**    See *financial statement.*

**income stock.**    A blue-chip stock purchased for steady, long-lasting returns. Compare *high yielder.*

**income tax.**    A direct tax on earnings. Income tax is based on gross income less deductible expenses. Most income tax systems consider a taxpayer's ability to pay, although the flat taxation structure has many advocates. Ability-to-pay taxes are called progressive because income earned in excess of a prescribed amount is taxed at a higher rate above the basic rate. Conversely, flat taxes are often called regressive because roughly the same percentage of income is taxed, irrespective of a taxpayer's actual income.

**income tax allowance.**    A tax deduction.

**inconvertible currency.**    A currency that cannot be freely exchanged for other currencies or for gold, usually because of the issuing country's balance-of-payments position. See also *exchange control.* Compare *convertible.*

**incorporated trustee.**    A bank or trust company appointed to act as a fiduciary. Incorporated trustees manage trust accounts for the benefit of individuals, nonprofit organizations, and other corporations.

**incorporation.**    The process of obtaining a government charter to operate a corporation.

Incorporation requires filing the requisite documents with the appropriate government agency. In the United States, articles of incorporation are submitted to the secretary of state in the state granting the charter. Incorporated companies are identified by the abbreviation "Inc." Outside the United States, incorporated companies are known as limited-liability companies and are identified by "Limited" or "Ltd." In the United Kingdom, the registering agency is the Registrar of Companies.

**INCOTERMS.**    See *International Commercial Terms*.

**ind.**    The abbreviation for index and industry.

**indemnity.**    Insurance covering restoration of a damaged or lost item. Fire insurance, marine insurance, and automobile insurance are indemnities because insured items are replaceable. Life insurance is not an indemnity because a life cannot be restored.

**indent.**    To place a purchase order (for goods) with an agent. A closed indent specifies the manufacturer of the goods being purchased while an open indent does not.

**indent agent.**    A local agent who arranges foreign sales. Import regulations in some countries require that indent agents register imports with a local government agency. Usually, the agents must themselves be registered with a local indenting association. The associations issue indenting registration certificates to authorized importers.

**indenture.**    An agreement stipulating the terms and conditions for issuing bonds. The indenture specifies the type of bond issued and states the maturity date, the interest payable, and the repayment schedule. Indentures also detail call provisions, covenants, payment dates, and obligations of the issuer and trustee. The bond trustee oversees the payment of interest to bondholders. In the United States, bond indentures are regulated under the Trust Indenture Act of 1939.

**independent action.**    A pricing option that permits an independent carrier to offer its own freight rate for a specific contract. The independent rate need not be the same as rates published in the common tariff with a shipping conference and need not be filed with a regulatory agency.

**independent carrier.**    A carrier that shares business with a shipping conference on a given trade route but does not itself belong to a conference.

**independent commercial importer (ICI).**    In the United States, a dealer certified by the Environmental Protection Agency (EPA) to adapt automobile imports and equipment to meet domestic emissions standards. Nonconforming vehicles imported after July 1, 1988 are imported through an ICI. Some vehicles entered temporarily for sports or research are exempt from emissions standards with prior EPA approval.

**index clause.**    Also known as a maintenance-of-value clause, a provision in an international contract that protects parties from exchange rate fluctuations. The clause provides for specified adjustments in contract prices in the event of unanticipated rate changes.

**index fleet valuation.**    A composite of the nominal resale market prices of bulk carriers and tankers. Prices shown on the index reflect the estimated value of world shipping fleets at a given period of time.

**indexing.**    The upward or downward adjustment of wages, taxes, or benefits in response to price inflation.

**indication.**    1. In securities, an investor's stated interest in buying securities from an underwriter. See also *book*. 2. A document presented by a principal in charter party negotiations. The indication is a negotiating text, containing proposed terms and conditions for a contract. The indication is nonbinding on the parties, but it may be accepted, in whole or in part, as the basis for a charter party.

**indicative price.**    Also called the norm price, the target price for olive oil under the European Community's Common Agricultural Policy. The norm price is lower than the market price, reflecting the difference between olive oil prices and the prices of competing substitutes.

**indirect controls.**    See *direct controls*.

**indirect costs.**    See *overhead costs*.

**indirect exporting.**    A technique used in international trade to conceal the identity of the ultimate purchaser. For example, goods may be routed through an intermediary engaged by an exporter to sell to a third party, often an anonymous buyer. Also known as gray-market sales, indirect means of exporting are frequently used when economic sanctions are in force against a country involved in the transaction. Compare *direct export.*

**indirect offset.**    The cost of an import reduced by the value of local inputs or peripherals. Local inputs enhance the overall market value of a product by reducing its foreign exchange cost.

**indirect subsidy.**    See *subsidy.*

**indirect tax.**    A tax reported by taxpayers other than those who ultimately pay it. Value-added taxes (VATs) are indirect taxes, paid by sellers on behalf of buyers. The costs of VATs are passed through producers and collected from consumers.

**Individual Investor Express Delivery Service.** See *New York Stock Exchange, Inc.*

**individual retirement account (IRA).**    In the United States, a personal savings account offering annual income tax deferments authorized by the Economic Recovery Tax Act of 1981. IRA principal and interest are not taxed until withdrawn. Individuals may deduct between $2000 and $2250 in annual contributions to the account from adjusted gross income when reporting federal taxes. Unpenalized withdrawals are begun when contributors are between the ages of 59 1/2 and 70 1/2. Below age 59 1/2, a taxpayer may withdraw and roll over funds from one IRA account to another without a tax penalty. Ordinary tax rates apply to IRA withdrawals. Since 1987, IRA tax benefits have been restricted by the Tax Reform Act of 1986. The 1986 act limits, for example, the full IRA deduction to individuals reporting $25,000 or less ($40,000 or less for married couples) and eliminates the tax deduction entirely for taxpayers covered by business pension, profit-sharing, or employee savings plans. Compare *Keogh Plan.*

**individual validated license.**    A validated export license. See also *periodic requirements license.*

**inducement.**    In maritime usage, a lucrative diversion warranting a stop at an unscheduled port. A shipowner makes unscheduled stops when shipments to a given port yield sufficient profits.

**Industrial and Technological Cooperation Accord.**    An agreement between the People's Republic of China (PRC) and the United States

regarding sharing of commercial information and technical data. In 1984, the Office of PRC was created in the U.S. Department of Commerce to implement the agreement.

**industrial bank.**    A bank that lends for specific projects or purchases. In the United Kingdom, industrial banks are finance companies that lend for installment purchases. The banks finance their lending primarily by accepting long-term consumer deposits.

**industrial competitiveness index.**    The measure of a nation's industrial strength. The index measures annual national industrial output compared with the aggregated manufacturing export income earned by trading partners. Export values are reported in terms of national currency values derived by comparing currency prices adjusted for inflation and exchange rate differences.

**industrial espionage.**    Spying to gain unfair advantage by uncovering competitors' trade secrets. Most industrial espionage is conduced by electronic means, primarily through the use of telephones and computers. The espionage targets are new manufacturing techniques, marketing plans, and technologies developed by competitors.

**industrial free zone.**    See *export processing zone.*

**industrial incentives.**    See *investment incentive.*

**industrialized country.**    A group of countries characterized by a relatively high gross national product, substantial manufacturing enterprises, industry diversification, and adequate reserves of financial, human, and physical capital. By most estimates, the industrialized countries are Australia, Austria, Canada, European Community countries, Finland, Iceland, Japan, New Zealand, Norway, Sweden, Switzerland, and the United States. See also *Organisation for Economic Cooperation and Development.*

**industrial park.**    An area designated for manufacturing companies and related firms. Land is acquired cheaply from a local government, and rents are often subsidized. Most industrial parks have better than average infrastructure and support services. In the United Kingdom, industrial parks are known as trading estates.

**industrial policy.**    Also called targeting or "picking winners and losers," the basis of government programs that select specific industries for public investment and support. Industrial policies are designed to exploit limited national resources for maximum economic effect. Programs implementing these policies provide subsidies (direct and indirect), sponsor research and development, train or retrain workers, etc. Industrial policies are common in Asia and Europe but are controversial in the United States.

**Industrial Price Index.**   See *Journal of Commerce Industrial Price Index.*

**industrial property.**   See *intellectual property.*

**industrial relations.**   Known as labor relations in the United States, work relationships between business owners, managers, and other employees. Some aspects of these relations are governed by national fair labor laws. The quality of labor relations depends more often, however, on the attitudes of owners, their managers, and workers. As a rule, employees who own shares in a company or participate in decision making tend to avoid strikes, work slowdowns, and other indications of labor discontent.

**Industrial Revolution.**   In England, a shift in the eigthteenth century from small family-based enterprises to large-scale factories brought about by the mechanization of production. The revolution's economic changes also produced other changes, such as demands for political democracy and social mobility.

**Industrie und Handelskammer.**   See *Handelskammer.*

**industry.**   An organization that combines capital and labor to produce goods or services. A manufacturing sector is considered an industry. Providers of a given service constitute a service industry.

**Industry, Science and Technology Canada (ISTC).**   In Canada, the successor to the defunct Department of Industry, Trade, and Commerce. ISTC is an executive agency that sponsors national economic development and trade programs. The agency was established in 1989. See also *Department of External Affairs.*

**Industry Sector Advisory Committee.**   See *Advisory Committee on Trade Policy Negotiations.*

**ineligible banker's acceptance.**   See *ineligible for discount.*

**ineligible for discount.**   In the United States, a banker's acceptance that cannot be rediscounted at a Federal Reserve discount window, often because its maturity date is longer than the 180 days required for eligible paper. Some ineligible acceptances, payable within 270 days, are purchased and resold by the Federal Open Market Committee. Eligibility for discount is determined by Federal Reserve Regulation A.

**inf.**   An abbreviation for information.

**infant industry.**   An underdeveloped industry especially vulnerable to foreign competition. In some countries, infant industries are given government subsidies, relaxed regulatory oversight, and import protection.

**inflation.**   An economic environment in which average levels of prices and/or wages rise steeply and quickly. Inflation diminishes consumer purchasing power and lowers national savings rates. Depending on the government, tight money policies, wage and price controls, reduced government spending, or a combination thereof may be implemented to reduce inflation. See also *hyperinflation.*

**informal entry (Customs Form 5119A).**   In the United States, imports entered without extensive customs examination, classification, or appraisement. Imports eligible for informal entry include items entered for personal use, certain textile imports valued at $250 or less, and some commercial shipments having a value of $1250 or less.

**informales.**   Spanish: sellers engaged in informal trade.

**informal trade.**   Commerce in an entrepreneurial market structured to evade regulatory and tax requirements. Also known as the underground economy, informal trade is common in countries where the government controls most economic activity. The informal sector is known to, but often unacknowledged by, governmental authorities.

**informatics.**   See *information technology.*

**information letter.**   In the United States, a document issued by the U.S. Customs Service setting forth its interpretation of a domestic customs law.

Information letters do not address a particular set of facts.

**information statement.**   See *proxy statement.*

**information technology.**   Computers and other electronic devices used to transfer information. Information technology includes cables, databases, electronic mail systems, satellite links, telephone links, etc. Merchandise and services linked to information technologies are known as informatics.

**infrastructure.**   The principal goods and services vital to a well-organized economy, the development of which requires substantial capital investments. Physical infrastructure includes bridges, communications systems, roads, and utilities that enable producers to deliver products efficiently and at relatively low costs. Industrial infrastructure covers factories, plants, equipment, and state-of-the-art technology. Human and information infrastructures include a skilled work force, occupational training and development, and information systems capable of transmitting up-to-date data and knowledge.

**inherent vice.**   In insurance, an intrinsically dangerous product. The product must be defective or composed of properties susceptible to explosion, implosion, or similar accidents. Inherent vices create uninsurable risks.

**inheritance tax.**   Also known as an estate tax, a tax on a decedent's estate after allowable deductions.

**initial public offering (IPO).**   The initial sale of securities to the public, usually by an underwriting syndicate according to the terms of an underwriting agreement. Also known as flotations, IPOs can take several forms. For example, a broker may purchase shares to offer to clients (introduction) or may ask clients to bid for shares (issue by tender). Issuers make IPOs through investment banks or merchant banks (offer for sale), by prospectus (offer by prospectus), or through advertisements in the press (public issue). Alternatively, the issuer may offer shares to a select group of investors through the process known as placement. In the United States, IPOs must meet Securities and Exchange Commission registration requirements.

**injunction.**   A court order that can be preventive, restraining a course of conduct, or can be mandatory, commanding it. Injunctions are interlocutory when issued while a suit is pending and permanent when issued after a case has been decided. Failure to obey an injunction is punishable by a fine or imprisonment.

**injury.**   In law, the violation of a legal right causing damage to the person, property, or reputation of another. A party causing injury is not liable unless guilty of a legal injury. In common-law countries, statutes or judicial decisions arising from a specific set of facts define injury.

**inland bill.**   See *bill of lading.*

**Inland Revenue.**   See *Board of Inland Revenue.*

**inland shipping document.**   See *bill of lading.*

**INM.**   The abbreviation for international nautical mile.

**INMARSAT.**   See *International Maritime Organization.*

**innocent passage.**   Under international law, the right of free navigation permitting a ship registered in one nation to transit the territorial waters of another, so long as its passage is peaceful. The right of innocent passage is contingent and limited, since coastal nations are entitled to regulate domestic traffic and trade. Except when it enjoys sovereign immunity, a ship violating the rules and regulations of a coastal state may be lawfully detained and seized. See also *maritime passport.*

**innovation.**   A novel design, method, product, process, or service that increases the competitive advantage of an organization. The novelty may reside in a product itself or in the manner in which it is sold. Copyrights, patents, and other forms of proprietary protection can secure an owner's profits from innovations, although often for a limited period of time.

**input tax.**   See *value-added tax.*

**INRA.**   The abbreviation for the International Natural Rubber Agreement. See *international commodity agreement.*

**in regular turn.**   See *berth clause.*

**INRO.**   The abbreviation for International Natural Rubber Organization.   See *international commodity agreement.*

**ins.**   The abbreviation for inches and insurance.

**inscribed stock.**   A registered stock.

**inside director.**   A director who is also an employee of the organization.

**insider information.**   Privileged knowledge of a corporation's internal operations exploited for profit at the expense of outside investors. Insiders include accountants, brokers, directors, employees, confidants and family members of directors and employees, and lawyers. In the United States, the Securities and Exchange Commission requires insiders owning 10 percent or more of a company's stocks to report trades in its shares. Securities exchanges also monitor insider trading through computer systems capable of creating electronic audit trails. In the United Kingdom, insider dealing is prohibited by the Companies Securities Act of 1985. See also *Intermarket Surveillance Information System*.

**insolvency.**   A debtor's inability to meet obligations as they fall due. See also *bankruptcy*.

**insp.**   The abbreviation for inspected and inspector.

**inspection firm.**   See *Société Générale de Surveillance, S.A.* and *National Cargo Bureau, Inc.*

**inst.**   The abbreviation for instant.

**installed base.**   A facility operating with pirated foreign equipment and domestic clones. The pirated equipment usually consists of export-controlled computers and software, often obtained from COCOM countries with relaxed export authorization procedures. In the United States, the Department of Commerce authorizes domestic exporters to repair or sell specified "upgrade" equipment to installed base facilities under limited conditions. The upgrades must be decontrolled or covered by a validated export license.

**installment shipments.**   Cargo shipped in consecutive installments from one consignor to a single consignee. In the United States, installment shipments may be moved under a single invoice, provided the shipments are delivered to a domestic entry port within 10 days of the first installment's arrival. Compare *assembled shipment*.

**instant (inst.).**   In the present. For example, the 10th instant (or 10th inst.) denotes the 10th day of the current month. Compare *proximo* and *ultimo*.

**Institut Belgo-Luxembourgeois du Change.**   See *Belgium-Luxembourg Economic Union*.

**Institute cargo clause.**   See *Institute of London Underwriters*.

**Institute of London Underwriters (ILU).**   An association of aviation and marine insurers formed to establish global standards for air and water transportation insurance. Institute cargo clauses approved by the ILU set industry standards for flexible cargo coverage, depending on the needs of a given policyholder. The association cooperates with Lloyd's and Liverpool underwriters. Its Joint Hull Committee established an innovative system for setting premiums based on prior insurance claims.

**institutional investor.**   A bank, insurance company, mutual fund, or pension fund that invests substantial sums in stocks. Institutional funds are managed by professional investment advisors, who trade large blocks of stock for commissions. Block trades occasionally cause sharp fluctuations on stock exchanges. Known as program trading, block trades are made with the aid of computer programs. See also *limit*.

**instituto de salud pública.**   Spanish: institute of public health. In some Latin countries, imports of pharmaceuticals and cosmetics, as well as biological and biochemical agents, must be registered with the *instituto de salud pública* prior to customs entry.

**instructing bank.**   A bank that makes a payment requested by a customer. In letter-of-credit financing, the instructing bank, also known as the ordering party, notifies the advising bank that credit has been opened on behalf of a seller.

**instrument.**   In finance, an enforceable contract obligating one party to pay money or transfer property to another. Credit documents (e.g., drafts, bonds, etc.) are instruments, as are documents of title, such as deeds or stock certificates.

**instruments of international traffic.**   Shipping equipment, including reusable containers, pallets, tanks, vans, etc. Whether full or empty, reusable shipping equipment is not subject to customs entry or duties. In the United States, the test for reusability is whether the equipment is suitable for successive uses.

**insular possessions.**    In the United States, offshore possessions beyond its domestic customs territory. U.S. insular possessions are American Samoa, Guam, Johnson Island, Kingman Reef, the Midway Islands, the U.S. Virgin Islands, and Wake Island. Exports produced in insular possessions enter U.S. customs territory duty-free, providing the imports' other foreign components do not exceed 50 percent of the value of the finished article. U.S. components, as well items otherwise eligible for duty-free entry, are not counted in the 50 percent limitation. Puerto Rico, which is within U.S. customs territory, is not an insular possession. Compare *U.S. territories.*

**insurable interest.**    A legal claim to property or an interest in the life of a person entitling a policyholder to enter into an insurance contract. The test for insurable interest is whether the party obtaining insurance faces financial injury if the insured dies or if the property is damaged or lost. In the case of property, insurance protection is limited to the value of the item insured. In the case of persons, insurance claims are paid against the face value of the policy.

**insurable risk.**    See *risk.*

**insurance agent.**    A person or firm, also called an insurance broker, authorized to sell insurance in exchange for a commission paid by the underwriter. Agents often sell for several insurance companies. In the United States, an insurance agent is approved by the underwriter and licensed by a state regulatory agency. In most countries, the sale of insurance is regulated by national statute.

**insurance policy.**    An insurer's contract promising to pay for losses suffered by the policyholder in exchange for a premium. The policyholder must have an insurable interest in the insured subject, and the insurance risk must be discernible and acceptable. See also *reinsurance.*

**insurance tied agent.**    An insurance agent under exclusive contract to a single insurer.

**int.**    The abbreviation for interest.

**intangible asset.**    Also called a balance-sheet asset, an accounting entry representing an economic benefit. Income-generating copyrights, franchises, patents, or trademarks, as well as goodwill that contributes to sales revenues, are intangible assets.

**Integrated Programme for Commodities.**    A program sponsored by the United Nations Conference on Trade and Development (UNCTAD) to secure fair prices for commodity producers and stable supplies for consumers. UNCTAD supervises negotiations of fixed-term commodity agreements between producing and consuming nations, e.g., natural rubber (1987), cocoa (1986), olive oil (1986), tin (1981), jute (1982), and tropical timber (1983). The rubber and tin agreements negotiated by UNCTAD set precedents for joint buffer stock financing by producers and consumers. See also *Common Fund for Commodities.*

**integrated tug/barge.**    A barge propelled by an internal propulsion unit.

**intellectual property.**    See *intellectual property right.*

**intellectual property right (IPR).**    Ownership of intangible property covered by copyrights, patents, and trademarks. Intangible property includes designs and inventions protected by patents and trademarks, as well as artistic, literary, and musical works, computer software, and designs subject to copyrights. Intellectual property rights are protected by statute, court decision, and international convention. Trade-related intellectual property rights (TRIPs) were a subject of the Uruguay Round of the General Agreement on Tariffs and Trade negotiations.

**intelligent highway vehicles system (IHVS).**    An electronic system for managing road traffic. IHVS systems collect tolls, purchase gas, pay repair expenses, weigh trucks in motion, and record shipping manifests, local permits, and other documentation.

**INTELSAT.**    The acronym for International Telecommunications Satellite Organization.

**Inter-African Coffee Organization.**    See *Organisation Inter-Africaine de Café.*

**Interagency Country Exposure Review Committee.**    See *Country Exposure Lending Survey.*

**inter alia.**   Latin: among other things.

**Inter-American Convention on Inventions, Patents, Designs, and Industrial Models.**   An international convention protecting industrial property rights adopted at Buenos Aires in 1910. Although it is adhered to principally in Latin America, the United States is also a member. Similar in scope to the Paris Convention for the Protection of Industrial Property, the Inter-American Convention requires national treatment of protected inventions and recognizes priority rights granted in other signatory states.

**Inter-American Development Bank (IaDB, IDB).**   A multinational development bank organized in 1959 to promote economic development in the Americas. The IDB arranges project funding and operates the Fund for Special Operations, a soft-loan window, for less developed countries. In addition to providing equity financing, primarily through the Inter-American Investment Corporation, the bank also manages several special-purpose trust funds, including the Social Progress Trust Fund and the Venezuelan Investment Fund (VIF). The VIF, established in 1974, is the single largest financier of regional projects in Latin America. The IDB has 26 Latin American members, who own a majority of the IDB's shares, and 16 nonregional members. Its accounts are settled in U.S. dollars. IDB is based in Washington, D.C.

**Inter-American Investment Corporation (IIC).**   An affiliate of the Inter-American Development Bank. Organized in 1986, the IIC finances private-sector enterprises and privatization projects in the Caribbean and Latin America. As of 1992, the IIC had 33 members.

**Inter-American Treaty of Reciprocal Assistance.** See *Organization of American States.*

**Inter-Arab Investment Guarantee Corporation (IAIGC).**   A multinational public corporation created by several Arab countries in 1972 to facilitate capital transfers within the region and provide overseas investment insurance for Arab investors. IAIGC members are Algeria, Egypt, Iraq, Jordan, Kuwait, Lebanon, Libya, Mauritania, Morocco, Qatar, Saudi Arabia, Sudan, Syria, Tunisia, United Arab Emirate, and Yemen. Its headquarters are located in Kuwait City.

**interbank offered rate.**   The rate at which commercial banks within a given national system lend to one another. Interbank rates are frequently used as reference rates for other commercial loans. In international finance, the London interbank offered rate (LIBOR) is the most frequently used reference rate. There are, however, numerous others, e.g., the Abu Dhabi interbank offered rate (AIBOR), the Luxembourg interbank offered rate (LUXIBOR), the Singapore interbank offered rate (SIBOR), etc.

**INTERCARGO.**   The acronym for International Association of Dry Cargo Shipowners.

**interchange agreement.**   An equipment-sharing contract between transportation firms. Frequently used by ocean carriers and trucking firms, interchange agreements facilitate intermodal carriage by setting terms for the transfer of shipping containers and equipment between carriers, including specifications for their use, repair, and redelivery to the owner. Interchange receipts and safety inspection reports indicate the condition of equipment at delivery.

**interdealer broker.**   A stockbroker who arranges trades between market makers but does not handle transactions for the general public.

**interdependence.**   In contemporary usage, the condition of nations and individuals in an industrialized global economy. Since the 1970s, technological advances have progressively reduced the costs of communicating and the time required to travel across distances. These innovations have increased cross-border flows of capital, data, goods, and services, while also reducing the importance of national boundaries and, by implication, sovereignty. Thus, in the 1990s, national economies, as well as individuals, are said to be interdependent.

**interdiction.**   The seizure of property by a police agency from a party who holds or possesses it in violation of law.

**interest (int.).**   The cost of money over a specific period of time. Interest is expressed as a percentage of the principal amount of a loan or deposit, usually at an annual rate. Simple interest is paid on principal. Compound interest is paid on principal plus accrued interest. See also *true interest cost.*

**interest arbitrage.** The process of moving capital between accounts in anticipation of earning higher rates of interest. See also *arbitrage.*

**interest-charge DISC.** In the United States, a variant of the domestic international sales corporation (DISC). The interest-charge DISC, authorized by the Tax Reform Act of 1984, allows shareholders to defer tax payments on 90 percent or more of export earnings and pay annual interest on the deferred taxes. Interest payable on taxes deferred after December 31, 1984, is also tax deductible.

**interest rate cap.** A ceiling on interest payable on a loan. The borrower pays an up-front fee (a cap fee) in exchange for a ceiling fixed in advance. Cap fees are common in Eurocurrency lending when the London interbank offered rate (LIBOR) is the reference interest rate. If the rate rises above the cap, the lender pays the borrower the difference between the cap and the LIBOR.

**interest rate futures.** A hedge in the form of a contract obligating a party to buy or sell a financial instrument on a future date at a preset price. Futures minimize the risks of falling or rising interest rates. In the United States, interest rate futures are linked to commercial paper, bonds, notes, and Treasury bills. Compare *interest rate option.*

**interest rate option.** Also called a debt option or fixed-income option, a contract traded on a securities exchange or commodity exchange entitling the holder to buy or sell a financial instrument on a future date at a preset price. The option price is known as the strike price or exercise price. Interest rate options are traded through brokers or arranged in over-the-counter markets. Financial futures often also contain interest rate options. Compare *interest rate futures.*

**interest rate policy.** The collective measures adopted by a country's central monetary authority to regulate the money supply, usually involving the raising or lowering of short-term interest rates. Examples of mechanisms used to implement interest rate policies in five major countries* are:

---

*Adapted from International Monetary Fund, "Five Major Industrial Countries: Official and Key Money Market Interest Rates," reprinted at *IMF Survey*, vol. 19, no. 15, 1990, p. 246.

*France*

*taux des pensions sur appels d'offres.* The interest rate on tenders for repurchase agreements, i.e., the discretionary rate offered by the Bank of France for lending to financial institutions. The *taux des pensions sur appels d'offres* is typically the lower band for short-term market rates.

*rate on 5 to 10-day repurchase agreements.* The rate set by the Bank of France for emergency funding and accepted at the discretion of financial institutions. The repurchase rate is often higher than short-term interest rates and generally serves as the upper band for market rates.

*Germany*

*discount rate.* The rate charged by the Bundesbank for rediscounting eligible assets of financial institutions. The rate is typically the lower band for short-term market rates.

*Lombard rate.* The interest rate charged by the Bundesbank for collateralized short-term loans designed to cover a financial institution's temporary reserve shortages. The Lombard rate is typically higher than short-term market interest rates and generally serves as an upper band for market rates.

*repurchase rate.* The interest rate charged by the Bundesbank for periodic securities repurchase agreements.

*Japan*

*official discount rate.* The interest rate charged by the Bank of Japan when lending to financial institutions.

*call money rate.* The interest rate charged on short-term loans in the interbank market. Maturities range from overnight to 1 week on collateralized call loans and from overnight to 6 months on uncollateralized call loans.

*bill discount rate.* The interest rate charged in the interbank market for rediscounting private bills with maturities ranging from 7 to 180 days.

*United Kingdom.*

*Bank of England dealing rates.* The interest rates at which the Bank of England lends to discount houses or rediscounts bills of exchange of different maturities. See also *back door/front door.*

*United States*

*discount rate.*    The interest rate charged by the Federal Reserve on its short-term lending to depository institutions.

*federal funds rate.*    The interest rate charged in the interbank market where depository institutions borrow from other institutions to cover reserve deficiencies.

**Inter-governmental Council of Copper Exporting Countries.**    See *Conseil Inter-gouvernemental des Pays Exportateurs de Cuivre.*

**Intergovernmental Working Group of Experts on International Standards of Accounting and Reporting.**    See *United Nations Centre on Transnational Corporations.*

**Interim Committee.**    Formally known as the Interim Committee of the Board of Governors of the International Monetary Fund on the International Monetary System, a committee established by the IMF in 1974. The committee advises the IMF Board of Governors on the operations of the international monetary system. The Interim Committee is composed of IMF governors and officials holding ministerial rank in their home countries.

**interline.**    The transfer of cargo between ground carriers, usually under a single bill of lading. Interline is the inland equivalent of transshipment.

**Intermarket Surveillance Information System (ISIS).**    In the United States, the electronic tracking system used by the New York Stock Exchange to police insider trading. ISIS is a database that enables the exchange to reconstruct the details of a transaction. A component of ISIS, Automated Search and Match, contains names of accountants, directors, officers, lawyers, and other corporate insiders. The system performs an audit to identify irregular transactions and the parties involved in them.

**intermediate consignee.**    The party designated in shipping documents to receive cargo for transfer to an end buyer.

**intermediate product.**    An input used to produce a final good, i.e., a finished product.

Intermediate products are also known as current account purchases.

**intermediation.**    See *disintermediation.*

**intermodal service.**    The seamless transfer of cargo between different modes of carriage. Intermodal service involves moving cargo by water, air, road, or rail in the same shipping containers, often under a through bill of lading. The development of multimodal containers and electronic data interchange contributed to the growth of intermodal shipping services.

**internal audit.**    In international trade, a firm's internal controls to prevent violations of customs and tax laws, sometimes revealed during audits. In the case of customs compliance, internal audits are designed to uncover duplicated invoices and record-keeping errors, particularly those related to the costs of assists, commissions, discounts, freight, insurance, and packing.

**Internal Revenue Service (IRS).**    In the United States, a division of the U.S. Department of the Treasury. The IRS collects income and excise taxes and enforces U.S. laws prohibiting tax fraud. Depending on the issue, adverse IRS decisions are appealed to the Tax Court of the United States, the U.S. Claims Court, or a U.S. District Court.

**International Air Transport Association (IATA).**    A global trade association of airline owners organized in 1945. Member airlines are registered in countries belonging to the International Civil Aviation Organization. IATA members cooperate to improve passenger and air cargo transport services. The association is based in Montreal.

**International Atomic Energy Agency (IAEA).**    An agency created by the United Nations in 1956. IAEA administers the 1968 Treaty of the Nonproliferation of Nuclear Weapons, promotes the peaceful uses of atomic energy, and sets international safety standards for nuclear facilities. In 1964, the agency created the International Centre for Theoretical Physics at Trieste, Italy, for research on nuclear energy issues. In 1970, it established the International Nuclear Information System for the international exchange of nuclear energy information. IAEA is headquartered in Vienna. See also *United Nations Industrial Development Organization.*

**International Bank for Economic Cooperation (IBEC).** The clearinghouse for international settlements established by the former Soviet Union and its allies. Created at Moscow in 1963, IBEC was formed to process accounts in transferable rubles. IBEC also offered short-term credit facilities to promote internal trade. The transferable ruble was never convertible. See also *International Investment Bank.*

**International Bank for Reconstruction and Development (IBRD).** Popularly known as the World Bank and a facility of the World Bank Group, an international lending institution founded at the Bretton Woods Conference in 1944. The IBRD was originally created to finance the post-World War II reconstruction of Europe. Since the 1950s, the IBRD has concentrated on providing long-term, low-interest funding to developing countries when commercial financing is unavailable. Recently, the bank has attempted to enhance the value of private capital in developing countries by supplementing private investment with public financing. The IBRD is headquartered in Washington, D.C.

**international banking center (IBC).** A city where international financial markets and international banking facilities are located. Among others, Brussels, Chicago, Frankfurt, London, New York, and Paris are international banking centers. Foreign banks and other financial institutions doing business in IBCs are regulated by the jurisdiction in which they operate, usually in the same manner as domestic banks and financial institutions. Compare offshore banking center.

**international banking facility (IBF).** In the United States, a local office of a national bank or the domestic branch of a nonresident bank that maintains separate accounts for Eurocurrency deposits and lending. IBFs were originally authorized by the Federal Reserve Board in 1981 to enable U.S. banks to participate in offshore financing and operate largely beyond domestic banking regulation. IBFs lend to (and accept deposits from) non-U.S. residents, other IBFs, and IBF parent companies. IBFs are exempt from some taxes, are free of domestic reserve requirements, and do not participate in the Federal Deposit Insurance Corporation system. U.S. banking regulations permit U.S. depository institutions to establish IBFs upon notice to the Federal Reserve. Compare *offshore banking unit.*

**International Bauxite Association.** See *international commodity agreement.*

**international bond.** A foreign bond or a Eurobond.

**international boycott factor.** In the United States, an accounting measure prescribed by Section 999 of the Internal Revenue Code to strengthen U.S. antiboycott regulations. The factor is used to compute tax penalties against firms complying with illegal international boycotts. The numerator is based on a firm's earnings in boycotting countries; the denominator reflects the firm's total earnings from all sources. Regulations governing the boycott factor are issued by the secretary of the treasury. See also *Tax Reform Act of 1976.*

**International Bureau of Weights and Measurements.** See *Bureau International Poids et Mesures.*

**international cartel.** See *cartel.*

**International Centre for Science and High Technology.** See *United Nations Industrial Development Organization.*

**International Centre for the Settlement of Investment Disputes (ICSID).** An independent affiliate of the World Bank Group established to conduct arbitrations in commercial disputes between private parties. The center was created by the Convention on the Settlement of Investment Disputes between States and Nationals of Other States. The founding convention was opened for signature by World Bank members in 1965 and became effective in 1966. Countries belonging to the convention recognize ICSID arbitral awards as binding, and the local courts of adhering states are obliged to enforce them. The ICSID is governed by an administrative council composed of officers representing convention signatories. The president of the World Bank is the council's nonvoting chair.

**International Chamber of Commerce (ICC).** A business service organization formed in 1919. Since its formation, the ICC has sponsored several international carnet conventions and, in 1940, codified the Uniform Customs and Practice for

Documentary Credits setting uniform standards for letters of credit. The ICC also developed the International Commercial Terms, widely used in international trade, and issued Uniform Rules for Collections of Non-Documentary Credits in 1978. The ICC is based in Paris.

**International Civil Aviation Organization (ICAO).**  A United Nations specialized agency, which oversees the orderly operation of international civil aviation. The ICAO was created in 1947, following the 1944 Chicago International Civil Aviation Conference. The ICAO attempts to reduce redundancy in civil aviation procedures and provides technical assistance to developing countries. The ICAO is headquartered in Montreal. See also *International Air Transport Association.*

**International Clearing Union.**  An international credit institution proposed in the 1940s by John Maynard Keynes, the British economist, as a vehicle for resolving payments imbalances. Under the Keynes proposal, the clearing union would have used an international settlement unit, known as the bancor, to guarantee international credit. The World Bank and International Monetary Fund were created at the 1944 Bretton Woods Conference in lieu of the International Clearing Union.

**International Cocoa Organization.**  See *international commodity agreement.*

**International Coffee Organization.**  See *international commodity agreement.*

**International Commercial Terms (INCOTERMS).** Uniform terms of delivery codified by the International Chamber of Commerce in 1936 to provide a global standard for commercial discourse and documentation. The 13 INCOTERMS, which were revised in 1990, are carriage and insurance paid to (CIP); carriage paid to (CPT); cost and freight (CFR); cost, insurance, and freight (CIF); delivered at frontier (DAF); delivered duty paid (DDP); delivered duty unpaid (DDU); delivered ex quay/duty paid (DEQ); delivered ex ship (DES); ex works (EXW); free alongside ship (FAS); free carrier (FCA); and free on board (FOB). INCOTERMS are incorporated by reference into most international commercial contracts, especially those appearing in contracts governed by the United Nations Convention on Contracts for the International Sale of Goods. INCOTERMS are recognized by courts in virtually all jurisdictions.

**International Commodities Clearing House.**  In the United Kingdom, a clearing facility for contracts traded on the London International Financial Futures Exchange and various commodity markets in London. Contracts traded on, among others, the Australian Options Market, the Hong Kong Commodity Exchange, and the Sydney Futures Exchange are also cleared through the system. The facility is owned by British banks.

**international commodity agreement (ICA).**  A multilateral trade agreement to promote demand and price stability for a given commodity. The agreements are negotiated between producing and consuming countries, known as international commodity groups (ICGs) or international commodity organizations (ICOs). Councils established to oversee implementation of commodity agreements set prices, approve the building of buffer stocks, and fix terms of sale. Most recent commodity agreements have been negotiated under the auspices of the United Nations Conference on Trade and Development (UNCTAD). Major commodity groups are the International Bauxite Association, International Cocoa Organization, International Coffee Organization, International Cotton Advisory Committee, International Jute Organization, International Natural Rubber Organization, International Olive Oil Council, International Sugar Organization, International Tin Council, and International Wheat Council.

**international commodity group.**  See *international commodity agreement.*

**International Commodity Index.**  In the United States, a weighted index of prices, consisting of 18 commodity futures contracts listed on domestic and foreign exchanges. The list covers agriculture, energy, livestock, and metals. The index is published by the Commodity Research Bureau, a division of Knight-Ridder, Inc.

**international commodity organization.**  See *international commodity agreement.*

**International Convention for Safe Containers (CSC).**  An international convention adopted in

1972 requiring safety approval of shipping containers. The convention specifies procedures for container inspections and requires that safety-approval plates be affixed to containers moving in international water commerce. The convention does not apply to, among others, containers designed only for air carriers. The agreement is administered by the International Maritime Organization. See also *data plate* and *manufacturer's particulars.*

**International Convention for the Prevention of Pollution from Ships (MARPOL).** An international convention adopted in 1973 to control ocean pollution. MARPOL incorporates provisions of the International Convention for the Prevention of Pollution of the Sea by Oil. The convention and its annexes cover pollution by oil, noxious liquid substances, harmful packaged substances transported in containers or tanks, sewage, and garbage. Amendments adopted in 1989 and 1991 granted special protection to the North Sea and Wider Caribbean areas. The convention is administered by the International Maritime Organization.

**International Convention for the Prevention of Pollution of the Sea by Oil (OILPOL).** An international convention adopted in 1954 to control ocean oil pollution. The convention banned all discharges of oil from most ships and tankers in areas known as prohibited zones. The zones include waters 50 miles beyond land in most areas and extending at least 100 miles into the Adriatic, the Mediterranean Sea, the Red Sea, the Persian Gulf, etc. The convention and its 1969 and 1971 amendments were incorporated into the International Convention for the Prevention of Pollution from Ships.

**International Convention for the Protection of Industrial Property.** See *Paris Convention for the Protection of Industrial Property.*

**International Convention for the Safety of Life at Sea.** See *International Maritime Organization.*

**International Convention on Civil Liability for Oil Pollution Damage.** See *International Maritime Organization.*

**International Convention on the Establishment of an International Convention on Load Lines.** See *International Maritime Organization.*

**International Cotton Advisory Committee.** See *international commodity agreement.*

**International Court of Justice.** Also known as the World Court, the judicial branch of the United Nations established as the Permanent Court of International Justice by the League of Nations in 1920 and reorganized by the United Nations Charter in 1945. The World Court has jurisdiction over issues arising under the UN Charter, international treaties, or conventions. Any UN member may raise an issue before the court, which has no enforcement powers. Although UN members are bound to accept its decisions, in reality countries voluntarily submit to it jurisdiction, usually on an ad hoc basis. The court decides cases in accord with Article 38 of its founding statute. Its legal rules are derived from international conventions, customary international law, accepted rules of law, judicial decisions, and treatises published by recognized legal experts. The court's 15 judges are chosen by the General Assembly and Security Council for 9-year terms. No two judges from the same country may serve concurrently on the court. The court's headquarters are at The Hague.

**International Criminal Police Organization (INTERPOL).** An international organization that cooperates with various national police agencies around the world to investigate criminal activity and assist in enforcing national criminal laws. INTERPOL specializes in coordinating investigations of counterfeiting, drug trafficking, international kidnapping and terrorism, smuggling, and so on. The organization is headquartered in Paris. Compare *International Maritime Bureau.*

**International Dairy Arrangement.** See *General Agreement on Tariffs and Trade: Tokyo Round.*

**International Data Base (IDB).** In the United States, demographic data on various countries available in electronic and print formats. The information in the database is regularly updated. The IDB is published by the U.S. Bureau of the Census.

**international depositary receipt (IDR).** A negotiable certificate issued by a bank reflecting ownership of foreign securities. The bank issuing the receipt retains custody of the securities. The American depositary receipt and European depositary receipt are the U.S. and European equivalents of IDRs.

**International Development Association (IDA).** A member of the World Bank Group created in 1960 as a soft-loan window for concessional lending to poor countries. Members of the IDA are divided into two groups. Part I countries are developed countries, which contribute to the IDA in convertible currencies; all Part I funds may be used for lending. Part II countries are all other members, who contribute 10 percent of their commitments in convertible currencies and the balance in local currencies. Part II funds may be used for lending only with the contributing country's consent.

**International Development Information Network (IDIN).** An information-sharing system coordinated by the Development Centre of the Organisation for Economic Cooperation and Development. IDIN and its regional associations sponsor research projects and training institutes in Africa, the Middle East, Asia, Europe, and Latin America. The network also disseminates economic development data.

**International Economic Policy.** See *International Trade Administration.*

**International Electrotechnical Commission.** See *International Standards Organization.*

**International Energy Agency (IEA).** An agency of the Organisation for Economic Cooperation and Development. The IEA was organized in 1974 in response to the 1973 embargo on oil exports imposed on Western nations by the Organization of Petroleum Exporting Countries. IEA advises governments on energy conservation, alternative energy sources, and negotiated quotas on oil imports. IEA was instrumental in creating an international system of emergency sharing, called the Emergency Oil Allocation System.

**International Federation of Consulting Engineers.** See *Fédération internationale des ingénieurs conseils.*

**International Finance Corporation (IFC).** An affiliate of the World Bank Group created in 1956. The IFC promotes and invests in private enterprises in member countries. The agency's activities are financed through the capital subscriptions of its members and from its own accumulated earnings. IFC investments in member countries do not require national government guarantees.

**International Fund for Agricultural Development (IFAD).** An organization founded by the United Nations in 1977, following the 1974 UN World Food Conference. The IFAD was created to finance improved food production and distribution in developing countries. Contributors to the IFAD are members of the Organisation for Economic Cooperation and Development and the Organization of Petroleum Exporting Countries. Other IFAD members are developing-country recipients of its resources. IFAD lends on concessional terms for food production and distribution projects. Its headquarters are in Rome.

**International Fund for Compensation for Oil Pollution Damage.** See *International Maritime Organization.*

**International Import Certificate/Delivery Verification System.** See *COCOM Lists.*

**International Investment Bank (IIB).** The multinational development bank of the former Soviet Union and its allies. The IIB was established in 1970, following the adoption of the Agreement on Multilateral Payments in Transferable Rubles in Moscow in 1963. The International Bank for Economic Cooperation (IBEC) was created by the same agreement. The IIB's medium- to long-term credit facilities (2 to 15 years) are intended to complement the short-term lending (1 year or less) of the IBEC. The IIB is designed to fund agricultural projects, heavy industries, infrastructure development, and research and development. The bank is based in Moscow.

**International Joint Commission (IJC).** A body created in 1911 by the 1909 Boundary Waters Treaty between Canada and the United States. The commission arbitrates disputes over pollution, fishing and navigation rights, etc., along the Great Lakes and other water boundaries shared by Canada and the United States. The commission exercises quasi-judicial authority over cases involving boundary waters.

**International Jute Organization.** See *international commodity agreement.*

**International Labor Organisation (ILO).** An agency created in 1919 by the Treaty of Versailles.

The ILO became a specialized agency of the United Nations in 1946. The agency formulates international labor standards and provides technical assistance to governments developing labor regulations. It also sponsors training programs for government and labor officials, primarily through the International Institute for Labour Studies in Geneva (Switzerland) and the International Centre for Advanced Technical and Vocational Training in Turin (Italy). The ILO is headquartered in Geneva.

**International Law Commission.** A commission created by the United Nation General Assembly in 1947 to harmonize international law and various legal codes. Draft articles prepared by the commission frequently lead to international conferences convened by the General Assembly. The articles are later adopted by convention and opened for signature to UN member states. Commission members are elected to 5-year terms by the General Assembly and serve as individuals, and not as representatives of their national governments.

**International Lead and Zinc Study Group.** See *study group.*

**International Maritime Bureau (IMB).** The investigative arm of the International Chamber of Commerce. The organization was established to investigate fraud, piracy, and theft in international commerce. The IMB is based in Paris. Compare *International Criminal Police Organization.*

**International Maritime Dangerous Goods Code.** See *dangerous goods.*

**International Maritime Organization (IMO).** A United Nations specialized agency created in 1958 by the 1948 Geneva Maritime Conference. Formerly called the Inter-Governmental Maritime Consultative Organization, the IMO formulates maritime safety and marine environment rules. Among others, the IMO administers the following agreements: *on maritime safety,* the 1972 Convention on the International Regulations for Preventing Collisions at Sea, the 1976 Convention on the International Maritime Satellite Organization, the 1960 and 1974 International Conventions for the Safety of Life at Sea, the 1966 International Convention on Load Lines, and the 1979 International Convention on

Maritime Search and Rescue (SAR); *on marine pollution,* the 1972 Convention on the Prevention of Marine Pollution by Dumping of Wastes and Other Matter, the 1973 International Convention for the Prevention of Pollution from Ships, and the 1969 International Convention relating to Intervention on the High Seas in Cases of Oil Pollution; *on liability,* the 1974 Athens Convention Relating to the Carriage of Passengers and Their Luggage by Sea, the 1976 Convention on Limitation of Liability for Maritime Claims, the 1971 Convention Relating to Civil Liability in the Field of Maritime Carriage of Nuclear Materials, the 1969 International Convention on Civil Liability for Oil Pollution Damage, and the 1971 International Convention on the Establishment of an International Fund for Compensation for Oil Pollution Damage. The IMO is governed by an assembly, with each member having one vote. The IMO is based in London.

**International Maritime Satellite Organization (INMARSAT).** An international organization created by the 1976 Convention on the International Maritime Satellite Organization to improve maritime communications through the use of space technology. In 1985 and 1989, the convention was amended to extend INMARSAT services to aircraft and land-based vehicles. In operation since 1982, INMARSAT manages a global electronic communications network, which provides emergency services and logistical support to the maritime industry. The organization is owned by national communications agencies. INMARSAT is based in London. See also *International Maritime Organization.*

**International Meat Council (IMC).** See *General Agreement on Tariffs and Trade: Tokyo Round, Beef Agreement.*

**International Monetary Fund (IMF).** A multilateral lending institution created at the 1944 Bretton Woods Conference and established in 1945. The IMF lends to member countries to cure balance-of-payments deficits and expand international trade. A country joins the IMF by applying for membership and contributing a quota subscription based on the size of its economy. Twenty-five percent of a quota is subscribed in gold, hard currency, or IMF special drawing rights. The balance is usually paid in a local currency. IMF subscriptions do not require direct outlays, but may be handled through bookkeeping transactions. The IMF finances its lending primarily through subscriptions and loan repayments, known as repurchases. It borrows from the Group of Ten under the General Arrangement to Borrow and has credit arrangements with the Bank for International Settlements, Japan, and the Saudi Arabian Monetary Agency. The IMF is governed by a board of governors appointed by member countries, an executive board, and a managing director. The United States is the largest IMF subscriber, and the Maldives is the smallest. The IMF is based in Washington, D.C.

IMF lending is available through the following programs:

*Reserve Tranche.*    A country may borrow up to 25 percent of its quota subscription. The loan is unconditional and need not be repaid. See also *gold tranche.*

*Credit Tranches.*    Loans in this category are repaid over $3^{1}/_{4}$ to 5 years. Under the first credit tranche, a country is required to adjust policies to overcome balance-of-payment difficulties, but no specific criteria apply. The second facility, called the upper credit tranche, is a standby arrangement that requires the borrower to meet IMF performance criteria and draw in installments.

*Extended Fund Facility (EFF).*    A loan facility combined with a structural adjustment program of 3 to 4 years duration. The IMF must approve the borrower's economic reform program. Loans are drawn in installments, and performance criteria must be met. Repayments are made over $4^{1}/_{2}$ to 10 years.

*Enlarged Access Policy (EAP).*    A loan facility that supplements lending under standby and extended credit arrangements. Like most other IMF lending, conditionality applies to EAP borrowing. Performance requirements must be met, and loans are drawn in installments.

*Structural Adjustment Facility (SAF).*    A medium-term loan coupled with a structural adjustment program for low-income countries. Borrowers submit a policy framework paper, which describes a 3-year economic reform program, drafted in cooperation with the World Bank. Installments are disbursed annually after a revised program is submitted. SAF borrowers must meet quarterly benchmarks. SAF loans are concessional and are repaid over $5^{1}/_{2}$ to 10 years.

*Enhanced Structural Adjustment Facility (ESAF).* An adjustment program that requires the borrower to submit to periodic IMF surveillance. The criteria are nearly identical to the requirements for the SAF, except ESAF borrowers must adopt rigorous adjustment programs and meet semiannual performance criteria. ESAF loans are repaid over $5^{1}/_{2}$ to 10 years.

*Compensatory and Contingency Financing Facility (CCFF).*    A lending program that replaced the Compensatory Financing Facility in 1989. The CCFF is designed for commodity-exporting countries whose payments deficits arise from low export prices or increased cereal import prices. CCFF lending helps borrowing countries maintain adjustment programs when adverse external conditions (e.g., natural disasters) threaten economic reforms undertaken at the IMF's direction. CCFF loans are repaid over $3^{1}/_{3}$ to 5 years.

*Buffer Stock Financing Facility.*    A lending program for countries belonging to international commodity agreements. The facility finances buffer-stock purchases. The loans are repaid over $3^{1}/_{4}$ to 5 years.

**International Moscow Bank (IMB).**    In Russia, an investment bank originally formed to facilitate joint ventures in the former Soviet Union. Sixty percent of the bank's shares are owned by European banks and another forty percent by Russian banks. IMB is expected to evolve into a commercial retail banking network. Compare *Vnesheconombank.*

**International Natural Rubber Organization.** See *international commodity agreement.*

**International Olive Oil Council.**    See *international commodity agreement.*

**International Options Clearing Corporation (IOCC).**    A 24-hour clearing center for international trading in options contracts. The IOCC is jointly owned by the Association of Australian Exchanges (Sydney), the European Options

Exchange (Amsterdam), the *Bourse de Montréal,* and the Vancouver Stock Exchange. The market is known as the International Options Market.

**International Organization for Standardization.** See *International Standards Organization.*

**International Patent Classification (IPC) Agreement.** An agreement adopted in 1971, which authorized the international patent classification system and facilitated searches of patent filings. The agreement is designed to promote uniformity in patent classifications through the International Patent Classification System, which divides patentable inventions into eight categories. The IPC System has more than 50,000 subdivisions, each consisting of Roman letters and Arabic numerals. The agreement is administered by the World Intellectual Property Organization and is open to states belonging to the Paris Convention for the Protection of Industrial Property. See also *Patent Cooperation Treaty.*

**International Petroleum Exchange (IPE).** In the United Kingdom, an exchange for trading oil and gas futures and options. Futures contracts can be exchanged for actual commodities on the IPE. The exchange was established in 1980 and is based in London.

**International Preliminary Examining Authority (IPEA).** Any one of eight national patent offices designated to conduct patent investigations under the Patent Cooperation Treaty. The agencies are the Australian Patent Office, Austrian Patent Office, European Patent Office, Japanese Patent Office, Russian Soyuzpatent, Swedish Royal Patent & Registration Office, United Kingdom Patent Office, and United States Patent and Trademark Office.

**International Price Index.** In the United States, a price index that measures global inflation. The index is based on the cost, insurance, and freight value of industrial country exports to developing countries. The index is priced in U.S. dollars and published by the Bureau of Labor Statistics, Department of Labor.

**International Quality Systems Standard.** The product quality audit and certification process approved by the International Standards Organization (ISO). The ISO standard has been adopted by the European Community. See also *American National Standards Institute.*

**international reserves.** Financial commodities used for interbank settlements between central banks, i.e., gold, special drawing rights, and hard currencies.

**International Rubber Agreement.** See *International commodity agreement.*

**International Rubber Study Group.** See *study group.*

**International Standards Organization (ISO).** An organization established in 1946 to coordinate industry technical standards. The ISO develops uniform standards for products and for quality audit procedures used in international commerce. It approves standards drafted largely by private standards-writing organizations covering most products traded in global markets. The ISO is headquartered in Geneva. See also *ISO 9000.*

**International Sugar Organization.** See *international commodity agreement.*

**International System (of measurement).** See *Système Internationale.*

**International Tanker Nominal Freight Scale.** See *Worldscale.*

**International Telecommunications Satellite Organization (INTELSAT).** An organization formed in 1964 to manage the global communications satellite system. INTELSAT's satellite links are used to transmit financial and commercial data between multilateral financial institutions and private users, such as stock and commodity exchanges. INTELSAT is based in Washington.

**International Telecommunication Union (ITU).** The successor to the International Telegraph Union founded at Paris in 1865 to harmonize global telecommunications systems. The ITU was reorganized in 1934 following the International Telecommunication Convention held at Madrid in 1932 and became a United Nations specialized agency in 1947. In addition to proposing international telecommunications standards, the organization oversees allocations and registrations of radio frequencies. The ITU is based in Geneva.

**International Trade Administration (ITA).** In the United States, a division of the U.S.

Department of Commerce. The ITA promotes U.S. exports and administers international trade agreements and domestic trade legislation. Dumping and subsidy actions originate in the ITA, which shares jurisdiction over unfair trade cases with the International Trade Commission. The ITA includes the following:

*Import Administration (IA).*   Oversees the implementation of trade laws and treaties.

*International Economic Policy (IEP).*   Oversees foreign commercial relations and advances the interest of U.S. industries abroad. Organized on a country and regional basis, IEP country desk officers provide information on foreign economies, trade policies, and political conditions.

*Trade Development.*   Promotes trade and develops trade expansion policies. The Trade Advisory Center provides information on foreign trade regulations, including the implementation of trade treaties.

*U.S. & Foreign Commercial Service (US&FCS).* Gathers and disseminates business information at home and abroad.

**International Trade Advisory Committee (ITAC).**   In Canada, a private trade advisory group established in 1989. The ITAC advises the Canadian government on international trade issues and reflects the views of business, consumers, labor, etc. The ITAC is aided by sectoral advisory groups on international trade, which represent 13 domestic economic sectors, including agriculture, the arts, financial services, and textiles. ITAC opinions are sought by the Canadian government during bilateral and multilateral trade negotiations.

**International Trade Centres (ITCs).**   1. Offices established around the world in 1964 by the General Agreement on Tariffs and Trade (GATT) to promote external trade by developing countries. Primarily providers of advisory and information services, the centers have been operated jointly by the GATT and the United Nations Conference on Trade and Development since 1968. 2. In Canada, regional offices of Industry, Science and Technology Canada, which provide trade and financing information to Canadian exporters.

**International Trade Commission (ITC).**   In the United States, an independent agency originally established in 1916 as the U.S. Tariff Commission and reorganized in 1974. The ITC shares jurisdiction with the International Trade Administration over antidumping and subsidy cases. Most ITC functions are mandated by the Tariff Act of 1930. It advises the President on trade negotiations, collects trade data, investigates injury in import relief cases, sets import quotas, and issues tariff schedules. The ITC also publishes *Summaries of Trade and Tariff Information* and its annual reports to Congress. Tariff classifications issued by the ITC are authorized by the Tariff Classification Act of 1962. See also *International Trade Administration* and *U.S. Court of International Trade.*

**International Trade Organization (ITO).**   A proposed agency of the United Nations.   The ITO's charter was drafted at Geneva in 1947, but was never approved. The General Agreement on Tariffs and Trade (GATT) evolved in its place as an interim organization. The proposal to authorize the ITO was revived by the United Nations Conference on Trade and Development in 1956. A similar recommendation was advanced in 1992 during the Uruguay Round of GATT negotiations by the United States. The organization proposed by the United States would be known as the Multilateral Trade Organization.

**International Traffic in Arms Regulations (ITAR).**   National rules designed to control international trade in military weapons and materials. In the United States, the regulations are issued under the Arms Export Control Act of 1976 by the secretaries of state and the treasury (after consultations with the secretary of defense). ITAR items are enumerated in the U.S. Munitions Lists.

**International Transport of Goods under Cover of TIR Carnet.**   See *carnet.*

**International Trusteeship System.**   See *Trusteeship Council.*

**International Union of Credit and Investment Insurers.**   See *Berne Union.*

**International Vine and Wine Study Group.** See *study group: Office Internationale de la Vigne et du Vin.*

**International Wheat Council.** See *international commodity agreement.*

**International Wool Study Group.** See *study group.*

**INTERPOL.** The acronym for International Criminal Police Organization.

**interrogatories.** Written questions submitted to witnesses to uncover evidence for a legal proceeding. Interrogatories are presented by an attorney to an opposing party or to a person not a party to the legal action. Answers to interrogatories are submitted in writing and sworn under oath.

**Interstate Commerce Commission (ICC).** In the United States, an independent commission established in 1887 by the Interstate Commerce Commission Act. The ICC regulates non-air carriers in U.S. domestic commerce, including carriers operating in inland waterways within the contiguous 48 states. Compare *Federal Maritime Commission.*

**INTERTANKO.** The acronym for International Association of Independent Tanker Owners.

**intervention.** A measure undertaken by a central monetary institution to stabilize or maintain prices in commercial or financial markets. A government intervenes when it buys or sells a commodity to reduce or expand the supply in private markets. A forward exchange intervention occurs when a central bank buys or sells in the forward market to change the value of its currency in the spot market.

**intervention currency.** A Big Eight currency used by a central monetary authority when buying or selling in the international money market to stabilize the exchange value of a national currency. See also *managed float.*

**intervention price.** See *Common Agricultural Policy.*

**inter vivos gift.** Also known as a lifetime transfer, an irrevocable gift made by a living person. Depending on the jurisdiction, the value of a lifetime transfer may be taxed as a gift during the life of the donor or as an inheritance after the donor dies. In the United States, donors pay a graduated federal tax on the value of lifetime gifts under a unified gift estate tax system. State gift tax laws

vary. The federal tax is based on a gift's fair market value. In the United Kingdom, the capital-transfer tax on lifetime gifts was supplanted by an inheritance tax in 1986. Compare *inheritance tax.*

**intestacy.** The condition of dying without a will. The decedent may not have made a will, an existing will may have been revoked by the deceased, or the will may be otherwise legally invalid. All jurisdictions have statutes governing the passing of an intestate's property. Normally, a surviving spouse receives a life estate in half of the property, with the remainder passed to the intestate's children. When there is no surviving spouse or linear descendants, the property passes to lateral survivors. When there are no survivors, the property is transferred to the state under the legal doctrine of *bona vacantia.* See also *administrator.*

**in the money.** In options trading, an option on which the futures price is less than a put option's strike price but greater than the strike price of the call option. Compare *at the money* and *out of the money.*

**intra vires.** Latin: within its powers. An act of an agent or corporation that is within its delegated authority. An agent's principal or a corporation cannot avoid liability for *intra vires* actions. Compare *ultra vires.*

**intrinsic value.** In options trading, an in-the-money option. The intrinsic value of a call option is the amount by which the market price of the underlying commodity exceeds the strike price. The intrinsic value of a put option is the difference between the lower price of the commodity and the strike price.

**introduction.** 1. A technique used by securities issuers to sell a small lot of shares to clients through brokers. See also *placement.* 2. Listing a security on a stock exchange without issuing shares to raise capital. Companies usually obtain listing by introduction to gain recognition in a new market. Foreign listings on stock exchanges are often accomplished by introduction when applicants meet the exchange's listing requirements. 3. The arranging of money-market loans by a broker for banks, discount houses, etc.

**introduction patent.** Also known as an importation patent or a revalidation patent, a form of protection granted primarily to holders of foreign patents. Introduction patents permit the local use of inventions, which are protected elsewhere. Where national laws authorize the award of introduction patents to local residents, usually after a period of exclusive protection, original holders lose the sole right to exploit their inventions for the duration of the underlying patent.

**inv.**   The abbreviation for invoice.

**inventor's certificate.**   In the former Soviet Union and other Warsaw Pact countries, a form of protection available to inventors in addition to patents. The inventor's certificate entitled an inventor to cash payment upon assigning the ownership and exclusive use rights in an invention to the state. As of 1993, the status of intellectual property law in the former Eastern bloc is unsettled. Normally, however, nationals sought inventor's certificates, while nonnationals preferred patent protection.

**inventory (invt.).**   Also called stock-in-trade, a company's store of components, raw materials, and finished products.

**inventory control.**   A procedure used to track inflows and outflows of materials consumed in a business. Ideally, inventory control ensures that needed materials are available, but not in oversupply. Most large firms use computerized systems to reorder goods consumed or sold. See also *first in/first out*, *last in/first out*, and *just-in-time*.

**inventory financing.**   A loan obtained to buy inventory. The loan is repaid as inventory is sold. Inventory financing is also called floor financing or warehouse financing.

**inventory investment.**   The sum total of inventory held by a nation's private sector.

**investment.**   A purchase made in anticipation of gain or an investment return. For example, purchasing plant and equipment to produce future income is a capital investment, while buying securities or antiques is a financial investment. Selling investment assets results in capital gains or losses.

**investment advisor.**   In the United States, a person or firm registered with the Securities and Exchange Commission under the Investment Advisors Act of 1940. Any person or firm giving market information and advice to the public is required to register with the SEC. Investment advisors stand in fiduciary relation to their clients and are bound by duties of care, full disclosure, and adequate accounting.

**investment bank.**   The American variant of the British merchant bank. Investment banks underwrite securities issues, advise clients on mergers and acquisitions, and sell divisible lots of shares to investors. The process of buying and selling securities to investors is known as underwriting. The investment banker who manages an underwriting is known as the lead manager or the managing underwriter. Investment banks are called broker-dealers because, apart from their roles as intermediaries, investment banks may also buy and sell as principals. See also *Glass-Steagall Act of 1933*.

**Investment Canada.**   In Canada, a federal agency that regulates foreign direct investment, as well as mergers and acquisitions. Created by the Investment Canada Act of 1984, Investment Canada supplanted the Canadian Foreign Investment Review Agency in 1985. See also *Foreign Investment Review Act*.

**investment company.**   A firm that pools securities and sells shares to individual investors. In the United States, investment companies are registered with the Securities and Exchange Commission and regulated by the Investment Company Act of 1940. The act applies to firms selling shares in certificates of deposit, mutual funds, and unit investment trusts. Investment companies are required to disclose the distribution of investment funds, prices requested for shares, and fees charged for services. Shareholders are entitled to approve changes in the company's policies and to have an accounting of its financial position. See also *investment advisor* and *subchapter M*.

**investment credit.**   Also called the investment tax credit (ITC), a credit to compensate consumers of capital equipment and/or research and development for their investment expenditures. The credit is taken in the tax year the asset is first used. In the United States, the ITC was repealed by the Tax Reform Act of 1986, although limited exceptions were left in place. As of 1993, new investment tax credits have been recommended by some experts, but they have not been enacted.

**Investment Edge.**   See *Edge corporation.*

**investment-grade bond.**   A bond issued by a high-quality borrower, usually a government or a multinational corporation. A low credit risk is associated with investment-grade securities. In the United States, these bonds are assigned an AAA to BBB rating by bond-rating services.

**investment incentive.**   A financial grant, tax benefit, or regulatory exemption intended to encourage investment, especially foreign direct investment. In external trade, countries usually give foreign investors incentives to establish manufacturing plants, which increase export income. With the exception of tourism, few incentives, if any, are given to service industries, which consume more local capital than they provide.

**investment income.**   Passive earnings. Investment income is earned from capital invested rather than produced through work.

**investment letter.**   A letter of intent fixing the terms of sale for privately placed securities. The seller promises that the securities will not be offered for public sale for a specified period; buyers promise that the securities will not be resold, usually for 2 years. An investment letter sets forth conditions for an agreement, but it cannot be enforced as a contract. Securities sold in this manner are called letter bonds or letter stocks. In the United States, letter securities are exempt from Securities and Exchange Commission registration. See also *placement.*

**investment manager.**   Also called a fund manager, an agent who manages an investment fund, such as a pension fund or mutual fund. The manager determines the criteria for investing, e.g., high yields or steady growth. See also *institutional investor.*

**investment performance requirements (IPRs).** Conditions placed on foreign direct investment. A country may require a foreign investor to agree in advance to make a minimum hard-currency investment, comply with domestic content rules, or provide a fixed percentage of local jobs. IPRs are viewed as a country's return on capital invested in infrastructure and business facilities.

IPRs are nontariff barriers to international trade, but are used by many countries.

**investment portfolio.**   See *portfolio investment.*

**investment service center (ISC).**   Also known as an investment center, an agency established in a developing country to process applications for foreign investment in local facilities or projects. In some countries, ISCs may issue import and investment permits, but their authority is often limited to responding to routine requests.

**investment trust.**   Outside the United States, a closed-end mutual fund. The investment trust invests capital and issues a fixed number of shares to outside shareholders. Investment trust shares represent investments in specific companies and a limited number of assets.

**invisible asset.**   See *intangible asset.*

**invisible hand.**   A basic concept in classical economics pioneered by Adam Smith, the eighteenth-century Scottish economist. The invisible hand theory explains the socially beneficial effects of free markets operating in perfect competition. According to Smith, the pursuit of rational self-interest creates a neutral factor, i.e., an invisible hand, which allocates resources for the common public good. See also *neoclassical economics.*

**invisibles.**   Income reflected in a country's balance of payments from trade in intangible goods. Invisibles are intellectual property rights and services, including accounting, banking, interest-earning credit arrangements, legal services, and tourism. Compare *visibles.*

**invitation to treat.**   See *offer.*

**invoice (inv.).**   A document stating charges or fees and provided by a seller to a buyer as the basis of billings. Depending on customary practices in the trade, invoices vary from detailed charges to more general statements of date, merchandise and/or service delivered, and charge incurred. 1. A certified invoice specifies that certain required conditions of sale have been met. 2. A commercial invoice describes goods or services sold, the price and quality, and details of shipment. 3. A pro forma invoice solicits an order and describes the price of goods and other sales terms.

**invt.**   The abbreviation for inventory.

**inward processing.**   Adding value to foreign goods in the country of importation. See also *duty drawback.*

**inward processing relief.**   See *duty drawback.*

**I/O.**   The abbreviation for input and output.

**IOC.**   The abbreviation for immediate order of cancellation, Indian Ocean Commission, Intergovernmental Oceanographic Commission, International Olympic Committee, and International Ozone Commission.

**IOCC.**   The abbrevation for *International Options Clearing Corporation.*

**IOM.**   The abbreviation for International Options Market. See *International Options Clearing Corporation.*

**IOOC.**   The abbreviation for International Olive Oil Council.   See *international commodity agreement.*

**IOU.**   The abbreviation for "I owe you." An IOU is a written promise by one party to pay a debt. IOUs are not promissory notes, but are admissible as legal evidence of a prior promise to pay a debt.

**IP.**   The abbreviation for import permit.

**IPA.**   The abbreviation for including particular average. See *average.*

**IPC.**   The abbreviation for International Patent Classification. See *International Patent Classification Agreement.*

**IPE.**   The abbreviation for International Petroleum Exchange.

**IPI.**   The abbreviation for *imposto sobre produtos industrializados.*

**IPO.**   The abbreviation for initial public offering.

**IPR.**   The abbreviation for intellectual property rights and inward processing relief.

**I.R.**   The abbreviation for Inland Revenue.

**IRC.**   The abbreviation for import registration certificate and indenting registration certificate.

**I.R.C.**   The abbreviation for Internal Revenue Code. See *Internal Revenue Service.*

**irredeemable security.**   A government bond or debenture without a redemption date. These are fixed-rate securities that vary in value with interest rate changes.

**irrevocable documentary credit.**   An importer's instruction to a bank to pay a seller against the issuing bank's irrevocable promise to accept or pay a bill of exchange. The credit is paid when shipping documents are presented if conditions of payment have been satisfied.

**irrevocable documentary payment order.**   An importer's order instructing a bank to pay a seller a percentage of the total cost of a shipment. The importer pays the balance when shipping documents conforming to the order are delivered. Documentary payment orders offer lower financing costs than letters of credit.

**irrevocable letter of credit (L/C).**   A letter of credit that a buyer cannot revoke if the seller delivers goods or performs services specified in the credit. Conversely, a revocable letter of credit can be revoked by a buyer, even though the conditions for payment are fulfilled.

**irrevocable trust.**   See *trust.*

**IRS.**   The abbreviation for Internal Revenue Service.

**IRT.**   The abbreviation for internal revenue tax.

**IRTU.**   The abbreviation for International Road Transport Union.

**ISF.**   The abbreviation for International Shipping Federation.

**Islamic Development Bank (IDB).**   A multilateral bank created in 1974 by the Organization of the Islamic Conference. IDB lending is controlled by Shari'a, which prohibits the charging of interest. The bank makes interest-free loans or assumes an equity position in projects. The IDB funds development and infrastructure projects, primarily in Moslem countries. Its unit of account is the Islamic dinar, equal to one special drawing right. The bank is headquartered in Jidda, Saudi Arabia.

**Islamic dinar.**   See *Islamic Development Bank.*

**ISO.**   The abbreviation for the International Standards Organization and the International Sugar Organization. See *international commodity agreement.*

**ISO 668.**   See *container.*

**ISO 9000.**   A series of international quality standards for products and services issued in 1987 by the International Standards Organization (ISO).

Firms engaged in international trade often comply with ISO standards by undergoing internal and external quality assurance audits. ISO 9001-9004 contains specific standards for product design, production, installation, inspection, testing, and quality system management. In Europe, ISO 9000 is known as EN 29000. See *American National Standards Institute, Communauté Européenne,* and *National Institute of Standards and Technology.*

**ISO codes.**   Uniform industrial and technical identification codes developed by the International Standards Organization (ISO). Two-letter codes identify countries, and three-letter codes identify currencies. Electronic data interchange systems employ these codes.

**issue by tender.**   See *initial public offering.*

**issued share capital.**   See *share capital.*

**issue price.**   The price asked for a securities issue. It is fixed by the issuer, the highest bidder, or the party who accepts a negotiated price. The market price may be greater or less than the issue price.

**issuing bank.**   See *instructing bank.*

**issuing house.**   A financial institution, usually an investment bank or a merchant bank, that specializes in underwriting initial public offerings of securities. The issuing house may purchase the entire offering or arrange a public sale. See also *managing underwriter.*

**Istituto Centrale per Credito a Medio Termine.** In Italy, a government agency that subsidizes export credits, primarily through refinancing or rebating interest on export loans.   Created in 1952, the agency is financed by the Italian government and its own borrowings in financial markets.

**IT.**   The abbreviation for immediate transportation entry and in- transit/entry. See *customs entry.*

**ITA.**   The abbreviation for International Trade Administration.

**ITAR.**   The abbreviation for International Traffic in Arms Regulations.

**item-by-item tariff reductions.**   Specific cuts in duties on particular products rather than an across-the-board reduction in tariffs on a broad range of goods. Since the Kennedy Round of General Agreement on Tariffs and Trade negotiations of the 1960s, the negotiating goal of multilateral trade negotiations has been straight negotiated percentage reductions in duties on traded goods.

**ITC.**   The abbreviation for International Tin Council and International Trade Commission.

**ITO.**   The abbreviation for International Trade Organization.

**ITU.**   The abbreviation for International Telecommunication Union.

**IUMI.**   The abbreviation for International Union of Marine Insurers.

**IVL.**   The abbreviation for individual validated license.

# J

**J/A.** The abbreviation for joint account.

**Jackson-Vanik Amendment.** In the United States, a 1975 amendment to the Trade Reform Act of 1973 denying most-favored-nation (MFN) status to the former Union of Soviet Socialist Republics (U.S.S.R.). MFN status was denied to protest Soviet bans on emigration by religious minorities. As of 1992, Jackson-Vanik had not been repealed despite the transformation of the U.S.S.R. into the Commonwealth of Independent States.

**Jamaica Agreement.** A 1976 accord among members of the Interim Committee of the International Monetary Fund (IMF) to sever the price of gold from the value of the U.S. dollar. The accord modified the IMF's Articles of Agreement to abolish the par-value system created at the Bretton Woods Conference in 1944 and authorized floating exchange rates. The Bretton Woods system was effectively ended with the Smithsonian Agreement in the early 1970s. By abolishing the official price of gold, the Jamaica Agreement created the global gold-fixing market.

**Japan Agricultural Standards.** See *Japan Industrial Standards.*

**Japanese long-term prime rate (JLTPR).** The interest rate extended to the most creditworthy customers by Japanese banks for loans maturing in more than one year. The JLTPR, usually somewhat higher than the short-time prime rate, is sometimes used to price yen-denominated loans borrowed in Euromarkets. See also *interest rate policy.*

**Japan Export Information Center (JEIC).** In the United States, an office of the U.S. Department of Commerce that provides information on Japanese customs procedures, import regulations, and commercial markets.

**Japan Fair Trade Commission.** See *Anti-Monopoly Law of 1947.*

**Japan Inc.** A colloquial term in the West for intertwining government and business relation-

ships in Japan. Although Japan's industrial and export policies have generally succeeded, the Western image of a perfectly coordinated Japanese corporate culture is probably misleading. While Japan clearly pursues industrial policies and qualifies as a state-trading nation, the influence of its government agencies on domestic business decision making, including the powerful Ministry of International Trade and Industry, appears exaggerated.

**Japan Industrial Standards (JIS).** In Japan, a semiprivate organization that writes technical standards for industrial products. The Japan Agricultural Standards determines standards for farm and processed-food products. The Standards Information Service in the Ministry of Foreign Affairs and the Japan External Trade Organization issue product standards guidelines. English translations of most Japanese standards are available through the American National Standards Institute.

**Japan Ministry of International Trade and Industry (MITI).** The national agency responsible for formulating commercial policies and regulating industry in Japan. MITI is known outside Japan primarily for implementing industrial policies and export strategies. See also *Japan Inc.*

**Java tobacco survey clause.** In marine insurance, a clause requiring third-party inspection of bulk tobacco products before claims for damage or reduced bulk are paid.

**J-curve effect.** In economics, the impact of currency devaluation on a country's balance of trade. When a currency is devalued, import prices usually rise, while export earnings decline. Presumably, after a period of worsening trade deficits (reflected by the bottom of the J), exports and foreign currency inflows grow as the impact of devaluation takes hold. The improved balance of payments is symbolized by the upturn of the J.

**JDB.** The abbreviation for Japan Development Bank.

**JEIC.** The abbreviation for Japan Export Information Center.

**jeopardy clause.** In Eurocurrency lending, a clause permitting revised repayment terms as conditions change in the Euromarket. Also known as disaster clauses, jeopardy clauses permit interest rate revisions when rates fluctuate greatly or renegotiations when other circumstances change. Compare *break clause*.

**jerquer note.**    A certificate issued by a customs official after inspecting a ship's contents. The jerquer note verifies the quantity of cargo entered on a ship's manifest.

**JETRO.**    The abbreviation for Japan External Trade Organization.

**jetsam.**    Cargo thrown overboard that sinks below water. Compare *flotsam*.

**jettisons.**    Items tossed overboard to save a ship endangered by its load. Jettisons are a general average loss if insured. See also *average*.

**JEXIM.**    The acronym for Export-Import Bank of Japan.

**JICA.**    The abbreviation for Japan International Cooperation Agency. See *official development assistance*.

**jinmyaku.**    Japanese: personal vein. *Jinmyaku* denotes a business network based on personal and professional ties.

**J-List.**    In the United States, a list of products exempt from country-of-origin markings under Section 704 of the Tariff Act of 1930. Flowers, newsprint, pulp wood, and similar items are included in the list. Revised J-Lists are issued periodically by the U.S. Department of Treasury.

**JLTPR.**    The abbreviation for Japanese long-term prime rate.

**jobbers.**    Dealers who buy and sell for their own accounts, as opposed to dealing on behalf of a customer or client. Compare *broker*.

**job costing.**    Determining the value of a contract to deliver a product or service. When a product or service is not already priced in the market, the value of each contract is assessed separately. Job costing enables a business to evaluate the financial value of a contract in terms of the costs of completing a project.

**Johnson Act of 1934.**    See *Foreign Securities Act of 1934*.

**joint account.**    See *joint tenants*.

**joint and several liability.**    The legal liability of two or more parties for the same debt. Parties jointly and severally liable can be sued individually and collectively.

**Joint Belgium-Luxembourg Administrative Commission.**    See *Belgium-Luxembourg Economic Union*.

**Joint Council of the European Free Trade Area and Finland.**    See *European Free Trade Association*.

**joint investment.**    An asset purchased by two or more investors where the degree of ownership is proportional and determined by agreement between the parties. In finance, certificates for jointly owned securities are issued in the name of each investor. When the securities are sold, both owners sign a transfer deed.

**joint note.**    A promissory note signed by two borrowers. The lender has legal recourse against both borrowers if the loan is not repaid.

**Joint Research Centre.**    See *European Community of Research and Technology*.

**joint-stock company.**    See *company*.

**joint tenants.**    Two or more parties with equal ownership rights in property. Most assets held by married couples are owned in joint tenancy. When one owner dies, property is inherited by right of survivorship and passed without probate.

**joint venture (JV).**    An agreement between parties to share costs, profits, and losses from a commercial venture. In the United States, domestic joint ventures are subject to antitrust regulation. Antitrust laws do not apply, however, to foreign joint ventures.

**Jones Act of 1920.**    In the United States, the maritime cabotage law contained in the Merchant Marine Act of 1920. The act requires the use of U.S.-built ships to transport cargoes moved in domestic coastal and offshore trade. The act also permits seamen injured in the course of employment to recover damages from shipowners. The U.S. Virgin Islands are not covered by the Jones Act. See also *Cargo Preference Act of 1954*.

**Journal of Commerce (JofC) Industrial Price Index.**    In the United States, a weighted index of prices for 18 industrial commodities published by the *Journal of Commerce*. The index reflects daily, monthly, and annual price changes using 1980 as the base year. The *JofC* Index covers textiles, base metals, and miscellaneous products, including crude petroleum, hides, rubber, and some wood products. See also *commodity price index*.

**judgment creditor.**   A party who wins a court judgment ordering a debtor to pay a debt.

**judgment currency clause.**   A loan agreement clause under which a debtor who does not repay a loan bears the exchange rate cost. These clauses are common in Eurocurrency lending agreements. If a foreign court orders payment in its local currency, the debtor pays the difference between the value of the judgment currency and the currency in which the loan was made.

**jumbo certificate of deposit (CD).**   In the United States, a high-yield certificate of deposit with a face value above $100,000 and a variable interest rate. The yield is high because jumbo CDs exceed the amount guaranteed by Federal Deposit Insurance Corporation protection. Jumbo CDs can be negotiable or nonnegotiable.

**junk bond.**   Also called a high-yield bond, a security issued by a company with an insubstantial credit rating. The ratings of junk bonds are low because the issuing company is new or highly leveraged. Usually issued to finance leveraged buyouts, junk bonds pay a higher interest rate than investment-grade bonds because of the higher risk of default. The bonds are retired from earnings or from proceeds of company asset sales.

**just-in-time (JIT).**   A method of inventory management. Just-in-time requires that production and distribution be coordinated, so that inventory on hand is used efficiently. The goal is to maintain low levels of stocks, while ensuring a steady flow of products. Just-in-time was pioneered in Japan. See also *inventory control*.

# K

**K.**  The abbreviation for *Konzern*.

**kabushiki kaisha (KK).**  In Japan, a form of limited-liability company. A *kabushiki kaisha* requires a minimum of seven incorporators and a managing director. There are no nationality or capital requirements, although a prescribed percentage of share capital must be subscribed.

**kaffirs.**  A British colloquial term for South African gold-mining shares.

**kamer van koophandel en fabrieken.**  Dutch: chamber of commerce.

**kangaroos.**  A British term for shares in Australian companies.

**Kashrut.**  The proper name for Israeli dietary laws. See also *Talmud* and *Uniform Standard of Weights and Volumes*.

**Kassenobligation.**  In Germany, a medium-term debt security resembling a certificate of deposit issued by a bank or government agency. Usually in bearer form, *Kassenobligationen* are traded on stock exchanges.

**Kassenverein.**  In Germany, a depositary for securities' deliveries. Once a transaction is completed, securities are delivered at the exchange or deposited at a *Kassenverein* or at similar facilities known as *Wertpapiersammelbanken*.

**Keefe Bank Index.**  In the United States, an index of the stocks of banks and bank holding companies used by analysts to monitor the prices and performance of bank stocks. The unweighted index of 24 stocks is published in New York by Keefe Bruyette & Woods.

**keelage.**  A dock fee paid by the owner of a ship.

**keibatsu.**  Japanese: family relations, i.e., networks that generate business contacts.

**Keidanren.**  In Japan, the Federation of Economic Organizations, an arm of Japan's business elite, also known as *zaikai*. The Automobile Manufacturers' Association, the Japan Foreign Trade Council, and the Shipbuilders' Association are *Keidanren* members.

**keiretsu.**  Japanese: conglomerate. *Keiretsu* are interlocking business groups that supplanted the zaibatsu in the 1950s. These are vertically integrated monopolies made up of banks, manufacturers, suppliers, and distributors. *Keiretsu* determine pricing, distribution channels, and delivery times. Because they tend to avoid business dealings with outsiders, *keiretsu* are viewed as barriers to trade outside Japan. See also *Anti-Monopoly Law of 1947* and *Structural Impediments Initiative*.

**keizai doyukai.**  Japanese: economic development committee.

**kengen.**  Japanese: authority.

**ken'i.**  Japanese: personal influence.

**Kennedy Round.**  See *General Agreement on Tariffs and Trade*.

**Keogh plan.**  In the United States, an individual retirement plan for employees of businesses and the self-employed. The taxpayer makes up to $30,000 (or 15 percent of net profits) in tax-deferred contributions to a pension trust. Withdrawals begun when plan participants are between the ages of 59 1/2 and 70 1/2 are not penalized. Ordinary tax rates apply to Keogh withdrawals. Participants in Keogh Plans are also eligible for individual retirement account tax-deferred savings.

**kerb market.**  A British variant of curb trading, or an informal commodity dealer's market, usually used to denote trading by telephone or after the official close of an exchange. Dealing in unlisted securities is also called kerb trading.

**key currency.**  See *Big Eight*.

**Keynesian economics.**  A theory of economics adapted from the work of John Maynard Keynes, a twentieth-century British economist, from whom an influential school of economists is named. In *The General Theory of Employment, Interest and Money* (1935), written at the height of the Great Depression of the 1930s, Keynes argued that government deficits cure depressions by generating increased revenues. Concerned primarily with avoiding high levels of involuntary unemployment, Keynesians advocate coordinated government spending (i.e., fiscal) policies to avoid deep economic slumps. Keynesian theory dominated economic policymaking for most of the post-

World War II period. With the ascendancy of conservative governments in the 1980s in most Group of Seven countries, Keynesianism fell into disfavor during the decade. See also *macroeconomics*. Compare *monetarism, Pigou effect,* and *supply-side economics*.

**key rate.**    See *interest rate policy*.

**KFAED.**    The abbreviation for Kuwait Fund for Arab Economic Development.

**KfW.**    The abbreviation for Kreditanstalt für Wiederaufbau.

**kg.**    The abbreviation for kilogram.

**Kg.**    The abbreviation for *Kommanditgesellschaft*.

**kilogram (kg).**    In the metric system of measures, a unit of mass equal to 2.2046 pounds. See also *Systéme Internationale*.

**kilometer (km).**    In the metric system of measures, a unit of length equal to 0.62137 mile. See *Systéme Internationale*.

**km.**    The abbreviation for kilometer.

**knock-off goods.**    Counterfeit goods, including unauthorized copies of brand-named, trademarked, and copyrighted merchandise. In the United States, the Trade Act of 1974 authorizes trade retaliation against trading partners that fail to police exports of counterfeit goods. See also *Section 301*.

**Kommanditgesellschaft.**    German: limited partnership.

**Kondratieff cycle.**    A cyclical theory advanced by the twentieth-century Russian economist Kondratieff. The theory presumes the existence of inevitable periods of expansive economic growth and deep depression. Also known as Kondratieff waves, the cycles lasts for roughly 40 years. Under the Kondratieff theory, the most recent severe downturn occurred during the Great Depression of the 1930s.

**Konto (kto).**    German: account.

**Konzern.**    German: conglomerate. *Konzernen* are affiliated companies owned or controlled by a single parent. The term is used in Germany and elsewhere in Europe.

**Korea Stock Exchange (KSE).**    A securities exchange established in Seoul in 1956 and recently reorganized in 1988. Bonds, investment trust certificates, and stock are traded on the exchange. Prices are quoted in Korean won and published daily in *The Securities Market,* as well as in *Stocks* and the *Monthly Review*. Special restrictions apply to foreign investments in shares of listed companies. Regulations governing the exchange are administered by the Ministry of Finance.

**koruna.**    The currency of the Czech Republic and Slovakia.

**Kreditanstalt für Wiederaufbau (KfW).**    In Germany, an agency that provides financial capital to developing countries. Created in 1948, KfW was originally established as an export finance agency. Its activities are financed by the German government and its borrowings in money markets.

**Kreditbrief.**    German: letter of credit.

**krona.**    The currency of Iceland and Sweden.

**krone.**    The currency of Denmark and Norway.

**Krugerrand.**    In South Africa, a coin containing one troy ounce of gold minted and sold since 1967. In the United States, Krugerrands were popular forms of investment until economic sanctions were imposed on South Africa by the Comprehensive Anti-Apartheid Act of 1986. The British Britannia and Canadian Maple Leaf are competing investment coins.

**KSE.**    The abbreviation for Korea Stock Exchange.

**kto.**    The abbreviation for Konto.

**Kuponsteuer.**    German: coupon (bond) tax.

**Kursmakler.**    In Germany, an official stockbroker roughly equivalent to a market maker. *Kursmakler* trade for banks and for their own accounts under restricted circumstances. Compare *Makler*.

**Kurspflege.**    In Germany, a term denoting the entry of the *Bundesbank* and other financial institutions into the domestic bond market to stabilize prices.

**Kuwait Fund for Arab Economic Development (KFAED).**    An official development assistance agency operated by the government of Kuwait. Created in 1961 to assist Arab countries, KFAED now provides aid to non-Arab developing countries. KFAED is headquartered in Kuwait City.

**kwacha.**   The currency of Malawi and Zambia.

**kwanza.**   The currency of Angola.

**kyat.**   The currency of Myanmar, formerly known as Burma.

**Kyoto Convention on the Simplification and Harmonization of Customs Procedures.**   A 1973 agreement sponsored by the Customs Cooperation Council to harmonize national customs procedures. The convention contains uniform rules for customs agencies handling cargoes and documents. It requires signatories to review national practices that conflict with its terms. The convention contains 30 optional annexes clarifying rules for customs procedures.

# L

**£.** The symbol for British pound sterling.

**l.** The abbreviation for length and liter.

**L/A.** The abbreviation for letter of authorization.

**LAAI.** The abbreviation for the Latin American Association for Integration. See *Asociación Latinoamericana de Integración.*

**LAAITC.** The abbreviation for Latin American Association of International Trading Companies, also known as *Asociación Latinoamericano de Traficantes.* See *Asociación Latinoamericana de Integración.*

**labor intensive.** A task or industry requiring a higher investment in employees than in capital goods or raw materials. When the reverse is true, a task or industry is said to be capital intensive. For example, the telecommunications industry is capital intensive, while the fishing industry is labor intensive. Capital-intensive industries usually have few entrants because of their high start-up costs.

**labor theory of value.** See *classical economics.*

**labor union.** An association organized to bargain for wages and benefits on behalf of workers. Relations between employers and labor unions are governed by national laws and regulations in almost all countries. 1. A craft union consists of workers skilled in a given craft. 2. A government employees union represents workers employed by a national or local government. 3. An industrial union is composed of workers in a given industry.

**LACBDC.** The abbreviation for Latin America and Caribbean Business Development Center.

**laches.** In law, a negligent delay by a party entitled to pursue a legal claim resulting in the forfeiture of the right. For example, maritime liens have priority in inverse order. A claimant who delays in filing a claim may be barred from recovery under the laches principle.

**ladder.** In finance, a technique used by banks to measure foreign exchange and money-market risks. Maturities of forward foreign exchange contracts and money-market deposits are recorded

and tracked to minimize the risk of mismatched maturities.

**Ladebrief/Ladeschein.** German: bill of lading.

**l'AELE.** The abbreviation for *Association Européenne de Libre Échange.*

**laesio enormis.** Latin: extraordinary injury. In civil law, a court may rescind a contract if the price charged for goods or services is deemed unfair or unreasonable in light of other evidence. See also *imprevision.*

**LAFTA.** The abbreviation for Latin American Free Trade Area. See *Asociación Latinoamericana de Integración.*

**lagan.** A seafaring term for jettisoned goods. When goods are jettisoned to save a ship, buoys mark the location of lagan, indicating the owner's intent to retrieve the goods.

**lagging indicator.** See *leading indicator.*

**LAIA.** The abbreviation for Latin American Integration Association. See *Asociación Latinoamericana de Integración.*

**laissez-faire.** French: let people act as they wish. Associated with the eighteenth-century merchant Gourlay, laissez-faire denotes an economic philosophy advocating minimum government intervention in the marketplace. See also *comparative advantage.*

**laker.** A vessel transporting cargo along the Great Lakes.

**lakh.** In South Asia, 100,000 of any commodity, but usually rupees.

**land bank.** Also known as an agricultural bank, any government-sponsored financial institution that extends credit to farmers and agricultural enterprises. In the United States, the equivalent lender is the Farm Credit System. Agricultural loans are insured through the Farm Credit System Insurance Corporation. The secondary market for agricultural loans is managed by the Federal Agricultural Mortgage Corporation, or Farmer Mac. Federally guaranteed bonds are issued by the Farm Credit Financial Assistance Corporation. See also *agricultural paper.*

**landbridge.** Multimodal cargo transport combining overland and ocean carriage covered by a single through bill of lading. In pure landbridge, goods are carried from ocean by land to ocean. In minilandbrige, goods cross a continent over land before *or* after carriage by water. In microland-bridge, goods travel inland before *or* after carriage by water. See also *multimodal shipping*. Compare *seabridge*.

**L&D.**   The abbreviation for lost and damaged.

**landed price.**   Often simply called landed, a delivery term whereby the shipper pays the cost to a destination port, including landing charges. The buyer pays docking fees and all other costs. Compare *franco*.

**Landeszentralbank.**   German: land (provincial) central bank. *Landeszentralbanken* are regional affiliates of the *Bundesbank,* which provide settlement facilities analogous to those offered within the U.S. Federal Reserve System by regional Federal Reserve Banks.

**landing account.**   A warehouse invoice given to an importer when cargo is received for warehousing.

**landing certificate.**   A document issued by an importing country for imports entered under bond for reexport.

**landing charges.**   Fees charged for unloading cargo from a ship.

**landing order.**   A customs document entitling an importer to remove cargo to a warehouse until duties are paid or the goods are reexported.

**large-scale industrial transfer (LSIT).**   The relocation of an industrial plant to a low-cost area. Typically, LSITs also involve technology transfers.

**largest hatch principle.**   In a charter party, terms specifying lay time for shipments of unpackaged grain cargoes. Under a largest hatch clause, lay time can mean the time required to handle the largest amount of cargo, or it can mean the maximum number of hatches that can be worked per day.

**Lash.**   The acronym for lighter aboard ship.

**last in/first out (LIFO).**   A method of import inventory management, whereby the last products received are the first products sold or used. See also *inventory control*. Compare *first in/first out*.

**last trading day.**   In commodities trading, the date by which a futures contract or options contract scheduled for a specific delivery month must be delivered. In most futures markets, open contracts can only be settled by actual delivery after the last trading day.

**latent defect.**   An imperfection in the nature, manufacture, or construction of a product that is not discernible through reasonably diligent inspection.

**Latin America/Caribbean Business Development Center (LACBDC).**   In the United States, an office of the U.S. Commerce Department that includes the Caribbean Basin Division. The center provides information and support services for the Caribbean Basin Initiative and publishes the *LA/C Business Bulletin,* a monthly newsletter of trade and investment information in the Caribbean region.

**Latin American Association of International Trading Companies (LAAITC).**   The *Asociación Latinoamericano de Traficantes.* See *Asociación Latinoamericana de Integración.*

**Latin American Country Profiles.**   In the United States, business guides to Latin America published annually by the Association of American Chambers of Commerce. The profiles contain regional economic, investment, political, and trade data.

**Latin American Economic System.**   See *Sistema Económico Latinoamericano.*

**Latin American Free Trade Association.**   See *Asociación Latinoamericana de Integración.*

**Latin American Integration Association.**   See *Asociación Latinoamericana de Integración.*

**Latin dollars.**   U.S. dollars deposited in Latin American banks.

**Latin Union franc.**   See *germinal franc.*

**laundered money.**   Money gained by illicit means, but with traces of its source erased. Money is usually laundered by transferring cash from one country or financial activity to another. In the United States, the Bank Secrecy Act of 1970 requires banks to file currency transaction reports (CTRs) with the Internal Revenue Service for cash deposits of $10,000 or more. International transactions are reported to the U.S. Customs Service. The Money Laundering Control Act of 1986 further requires domestic financial institutions to monitor cash transactions involving less than $10,000.

**Laurentian Pilotage Authority (LPA).** In Canada, the federal agency that oversees pilotage on the St. Lawrence River. The LPA issues pilotage certificates and collects fees for pilot services. Ships transiting the St. Lawrence River are required to use LPA licensed pilots' services.

**law of one price.** An economic theory holding that competition equalizes prices of identical products sold in different countries when trade barriers and transportation costs are eliminated. The law of one price is a basic premise of free trade theory. See also *comparative advantage*.

**Law of the Sea Treaty.** See *United Nations Convention on the Law of the Sea*.

**lay days.** See *lay time*.

**lay time.** Sometimes referred to as lay days, the period of time stipulated in an ocean shipping contract for loading and unloading cargo. When lay time is expressed as running days, cargo can be handled on any day. A working-days clause excludes Sundays and holidays observed according to customs of the port. Weather working days exclude Sundays, holidays, and bad weather days. Lay-time clauses are also called free-time provisions. See also *demurrage* and *dispatch*.

**lb.** The abbreviation for pound.

**LBO.** The abbreviation for leveraged buyout.

**LC, L/C.** The abbreviations for letter of credit.

**LCA.** The abbreviation for letter of credit authorization.

**LCAF.** The abbreviation for letter of credit authorization form.

**LCL.** The abbreviation for less than a carload or less than a containerload.

**lcr.** The abbreviation for less than current rate.

**LCV.** The abbreviation for longer-combination vehicle.

**LDC.** The abbreviation for least developed country or less developed country.

**LDMA.** The abbreviation for London Discount Market Association.

**LDT.** The abbreviation for loss during transit.

**lead bank.** 1. A managing underwriter in the Eurobond market. 2. A bank managing a banking syndicate. Banking syndicates are formed to permit several banks to purchase shares of a large loan, known as participations, spreading the risks of financing expensive projects. The lead bank administers drawdowns and advances against the loan and notifies member banks of changes in interest rates and exchange rates. In the case of default, the lead bank forms a committee of member banks to negotiate write-downs or other recaptures of the debt. See also *investment bank* and *syndicate agreement*.

**leading indicator.** Any one of several indexes used by economists to predict stages of a business cycle. In the United States, for example, consumer spending, durable goods orders, and residential housing starts over a fiscal quarter are viewed as leading indicators for forecasting recovery. On the other hand, since employers are slow to hire after recessions, improved employment statistics are viewed as a lagging indicator.

**lead manager.** See *lead bank* and *managing underwriter*.

**leads and lags.** Contract terms that permit a company to accelerate (lead) or delay (lag) payments to foreign partners or overseas branches. The clause protects a company against exchange rate changes. If a payment is denominated in revalued currency, the company attempts to delay payment. Conversely, if the payment currency is devaluated, the company tries to accelerate payments.

**League of Arab States.** See *Arab League*.

**lease.** A contract giving an exclusive right to possess property for a specified term. 1. In real property, the tenant (lessee) surrenders the property at the end of the term. The landlord (lessor) may retake it earlier if the tenant breaches the terms of the lease, e.g., fails to pay the rent. A sublease is a subordinate property right given by a tenant to another party. Usually, the landlord must approve the sublease, and the tenant remains liable for property damage attributed to the sublessee. 2. In equipment leasing, a contract financing the use of one or more pieces of equipment. A master lease covers several pieces of equipment. In the United States, a true lease, also called a tax-oriented lease, permits the lessee to claim tax benefits as the owner of equipment. The tax benefits result in lower net rental costs. A finance lease is a conditional sales contract by which the purchaser acquires title to property at the end of the lease term.

**leaseback.**  A means of raising business capital. A company sells physical assets to an investor, who leases the property back to the company for a fixed term at a specified rental. A leaseback adds to a company's reserves by converting an asset to cash or providing an account receivable. In the United States, a leaseback may result in the loss of tax benefits attributable to depreciation under a tax-oriented lease.

**leasehold.**  A temporary right to possess land, which reverts to the owner at the end of a lease. In business property leases, the lessor possesses common areas and executes separate leases for office suites. A leasehold not fixed for a specific duration is known as a tenancy at will. Compare *freehold.*

**least developed country (LDC).**  A very poor less developed country, usually measured by a per capita income of 100 U.S. dollars or less. In addition to meager physical and financial resources, LDCs have low literacy rates and high infant mortality rates. Most LDCs are in Africa. Haiti is the only LDC in the Western Hemisphere.

**legalization.**  The process of officially verifying a document. For example, import documents stamped by a consular official are said to be legalized; e.g., a commercial invoice stamped at an embassy is a legalized invoice. As a form of verification, legalization is required almost exclusively by developing countries. See also *consular documents.*

**legal list.**  In the United States, securities accepted by state banking regulators as approved investments for fiduciary institutions. Generally, only high-quality investments, such as AAA-rated bonds or blue-chip stock, appear on a legal list.

**Legal Precedent (Binding Rulings) Index.**  In the United States, a list of import classifications published by the Office of Regulations and Rulings, a division of the U.S. Customs Service. Once a product classification has been published in the index, an importer of like goods must obtain a product redefinition to avoid quotas or obtain more favorable customs tariff rates.

**legal presence.**  The fictional persona adopted by a business to arrange loans and negotiate contracts in its own name. A legal entity can assume the form of a corporation, partnership, or sole proprietorship. Expedited registration may be sufficient to establish a presence in a foreign jurisdiction. In some jurisdictions, foreign firms create a legal presence by acquiring a local partner.

**legal rate of interest.**  Also called the usury rate, the highest rate a lender can charge in a given jurisdiction. The usury rate is set by statute in most jurisdictions, and excessive rates are subject to forfeiture or penalties. Usury rates may not apply to business loans.

**legal reserves.**  See *reserves.*

**legal tender.**  Bank notes and coins authorized by a legally constituted government that must be accepted to settle debts within its jurisdiction, except when a contract requires a different settlement medium. In the United States, all money issued by the Federal Reserve is legal tender. Outside the United States, unlimited legal tender may differ from limited legal tender. For example, in the United Kingdom, bank notes and certain coins in large denominations are accepted in settlement of any debt, but smaller coins (e.g., 5-pence and 10-pence coins) may only be used to settle debts of a prescribed amount.

**legal weight.**  The total weight of a commercial article, e.g. , a coffee tin *and* the coffee. Exterior wrappings or packaging are not included in legal weight.

**legging out.**  In a hedge, selling one side of a dual option, e.g., the short side or long side, before liquidating the other. In futures and money markets, legging out is also called lifting a leg.

**Lehman Brothers Daily Treasury Bond Index.** A price index that measures movements in U.S. Treasury issues with maturities of a year or longer. The index is published in New York.

**lek.**  The currency of Albania.

**lempira.**  The currency of Honduras.

**lender of last resort.**  A country's ultimate lender, especially when it provides credit or guarantees to its national banking system. In the United States, the Federal Reserve System, acting principally through the regional Federal Reserve Banks, is the lender of last resort. In most other countries, similar functions are provided by the ministry of finance. Eurocurrency lending markets are without lenders of last resort.

**leone.**    The currency of Sierra Leone.

**less developed country (LDC).**    A country that is characterized by endemic underdevelopment, meager natural resources, and inadequate reserves of skilled labor and physical capital and that is dependent on primary commodity exports for income. Known collectively as the Third World, most LDCs are located in the Southern Hemisphere. Because their economies are commodity sensitive, LDCs suffer extremes of poverty when droughts or drastic drops in the price of a commodity occur. The International Monetary Fund offers special programs to compensate for the effects of weather and price changes on LDC economies.

**less developed country (LDC) corporation.**    In the United States, a company that earns 80 percent or more of its income in less developed countries. Eighty percent of its assets must also be located in the LDC. Earned income from these sources, if reinvested in an LDC corporation, is excluded from a company's taxable earnings. However, the Tax Reform Act of 1976 disallows deductions for income earned from trading in LDC stocks when it is not reinvested.

**less than containerload.**    A quantity of cargo too small to fill a shipping container. A carrier's freight tariff specifies the minimum load requirement. Shippers may be charged a higher rate for unused capacity or a flat rate unrelated to the amount of space used.

**less than fair value (LTFV).**    The basis of an antidumping complaint. In a less-than-fair-value sale, the export price is significantly below the home market price for the same product. Often, an antidumping action succeeds when an exporter sells at or near the cost of production because the export price does not include a profit. The duty assessed on the dumping margin is designed to enable local producers to compete at a price that includes profit. See also *General Agreement on Tariffs and Trade.*

**less-than-prime-quality goods.**    Used or slightly damaged goods. In customs, less-than-prime-quality goods are valued at a fixed discount off the price of identical new goods. Reconditioned products upgraded to meet original manufacturer's specifications are not less-than-prime-quality goods.

**less-than-trailerload truck (LTL).**    A truck carrying a smaller than normal shipment. Depending on the nature and density of the product, an LTL shipment weighs 10,000 to 24,000 pounds.

**letra de cambio.**    Spanish: bill of exchange.

**letter of advice.**    See *advisement.*

**letter of allotment.**    See *allotment.*

**letter of comfort.**    A letter from a bank or corporation verifying the creditworthiness and reputation of a client, subsidiary, or supplier. A comfort letter does not offer legal guarantees and may expressly disclaim a future obligation to repay or provide surety for a debt.

**letter of comment.**    In the United States, a document issued by the Food and Drug Administration in lieu of the certificate of free sale. A letter of comment clarifies whether and how a product complies with U.S. health standards.

**letter of conditional reimbursement.**    In the United States, a letter of commitment from the U.S. Department of Agriculture guaranteeing payment under a PL 480 program. The letters are issued when a formal aid agreement has not been signed. The guarantee is limited to the percentage of the purchase price specified in the financing agreement.

**letter of correction.**    A letter that corrects errors in a ship's manifest, usually resulting from mistakes in a bill of lading. Issued mainly in Latin America, the letter of correction is certified by a carrier's agent at the origin port. The importing country may also require that the letter be authenticated by the carrier's agent at the destination port.

**letter of credit (L/C).**    A bank's letter instructing payment to a named beneficiary. The payment is made when conditions stipulated in the letter are fulfilled, including the presentation of conforming documentation. In the United States, a bank paying the exporter is usually the advising bank, although that need not be the case. In the United Kingdom, the paying bank is known as the negotiating bank. The amount paid is the face value of the credit less deductions for bank fees and charges. Costs include, among others, the charges for examining documentation and processing and negotiating the letter of credit. Rules governing the form and uses of letters of credit are codified in the Uniform Customs and Practices for Documentary Credits published by the International Chamber of Commerce in Paris. See also *advised letter of credit, back-to-back letter of credit, circular letter of credit, confirmed letter of credit, documentary credit, green clause letter of credit, irrevocable documentary payment order, irrevocable letter of credit, operative instrument, red clause credit, standby letter of credit, time letter of credit, and usance letter of credit.*

**letter-of-credit authorization (LCA).**    A letter from a central bank instructing a bank or agent to release foreign exchange to pay for imports. Importers apply for foreign exchange using a letter-of-credit authorization form. The letter authorizing the credit specifies the rate of exchange. Importers of goods for industrial consumption usually receive a more favorable rate than importers of commercial goods.

**letter-of-credit clause.**    In insurance, a clause that protects a policyholder from delays in payment of letters of credit. The shipper reimburses the insurer when payment is received.

**letter of exchange.**    A synonym for bill of exchange.

**letter of hypothecation.**    A variant of the hypothecation certificate, which entitles a bank to sell pledged collateral when the owner's draft is dishonored. If the goods have been shipped, the bank's foreign agent sells them upon arrival.

**letter of indemnity.**    1. A letter requesting replacement of a lost stock certificate. It indemnifies the issuer against losses arising from a reissue. 2. A letter given by a shipper to a carrier in exchange for a clean bill of lading when the dock receipt reveals damaged cargo. Normally, a bank paying a letter of credit will not accept a foul bill of lading. The letter indemnifies the carrier who issues a clean bill against claims by subsequent holders of the bill of lading. A letter of indemnity is also called a back letter.

**letter of indication.**    Also called a letter of identification, a letter issued by a bank identifying the holder of a letter of credit. Letters of indication were common when circular letters of credit were used by foreign travelers to obtain cash, but have been largely supplanted by traveler's checks.

**letter of intent.**    1. Also known as a letter of moral intent, a letter of comfort. 2. An investment letter.

**letter of license.**    In the United Kingdom, a creditor's letter to a debtor setting a deadline for paying a debt. The letter states the time when legal action will be commenced.

**letters of administration.**    A document issued by a court appointing the administrator of an intestate decedent's estate. The assets of the estate are disposed of under laws of intestacy. Compare *letters testamentary.*

**letters patent.**    A letter bestowing an exclusive right to own and use a patent. The right is of limited duration and passes to the patent owner's heirs and assigns. Letters patent originated in monarchical regimes, where sovereigns conferred titles and rights to land and other property.

**letters testamentary.**    A document issued by a court appointing an executor named in a will to administer the decedent's estate. Letters testamentary authorize an executor to distribute the assets of the estate according to the terms of the decedent's will. Compare *letters of administration.*

**lettre de crédit.**    French: letter of credit.

**level playing field.**    In international trade, a condition arising from national treatment. An economic playing field is level when nationals and nonnationals compete in commercial arenas without government interference, preferences, or subsidies.

**leverage.**    1. The use of borrowed money to increase the value of an investment. 2. A company's ratio of debt or preferred stock to capital invested in common stock. When the ratio of debt exceeds invested capital, a company is said to be highly leveraged. Outside the United States, leveraging is called gearing or capital gearing.

**leveraged buyout (LBO).**    A corporate takeover financed with the assets of the acquired company. LBOs use debt, usually junk bonds, backed by the acquired company's assets to purchase all or a majority of its outstanding shares. The debt is repaid with future earnings, sales of assets, or spin-offs (sales) of one or more subsidiaries.

**liability.**    A debt or obligation giving rise to a legally enforceable claim on a debtor's personal or business assets. If a business is incorporated, the owners' liability is limited to the extent of their invested capital or corporate guarantees. If the business is a partnership, general partners are personally liable for the debts of the business. Limited partners are liable to the extent of the capital they invest in the partnership. Liability can be current (payable within a year or less) or deferred (contingent on a future event). Liabilities appear on the right side of a balance sheet.

**liability insurance.**    A policy that compensates the policyholder for sums paid to compensate others for personal injury or property damage.

**libel.**    1. A written defamation. 2. In admiralty, the legal complaint filed by a plaintiff, called a libelant. The legal action itself is known as a libel in rem.

**liberalization.**    The objective of international trade negotiations. Liberalized trade requires reduced tariff and nontariff barriers to the free movement of goods, investment, and labor.

**LIBOR.**    The abbreviation for London interbank offered rate.

**license.**    An official permit to perform an act or enter a business, subject to supervision by the licenser. Activities licensed by a government are illegal without the license. Private licenses involve an agreement by a licensee to pay royalties or fees in exchange for the right to profit from the licenser's product or service. See also *franchise.*

**licensed deposit taker.**    In the United Kingdom, a commercial bank or building society. The Banking Acts of 1979 and 1987 regulate depository institutions in the UK.

**lien.**    1. A creditor's claim to secured property or its proceeds. A blanket or general lien covers goods held for a debtor's total debts, while a specific or particular lien secures a specific obligation. An equitable lien is imposed by a court to protect an injured party without other recourse against the party causing the injury. A possessory lien attaches to goods over which the creditor has

actual or nominal possession. 2. In admiralty, a maritime lien for salvage costs in average, or from bottomry or respondentia debts.

**LIFFE.**    The abbreviation for London International Financial Futures Exchange.

**LIFO.**    The abbreviation for last in/first out.

**lifting a leg.**    See *legging out.*

**lift-on/lift-off (LOLO).**    A ship designed to accommodate cranes or other mechanical "lift" devices used to handle heavy cargo.

**light cargo.**    A shipment too light to weigh a ship down to its water marks. See also *load line.*

**light dues.**    See *light money.*

**lighter.**    A flat-bottomed barge. A lighter may be motorized or towed by a tug. Cargo is carried aboard lighters from shallow inland ports to ships anchored at deep-water ports or to waterfront warehouses.

**lighter aboard ship (Lash).**    A ship designed to accommodate barges. The barges are lifted on and off the ship by cranes attached to it. Compare *barge-on-board.*

**lighterage.**    1. The transport of cargo by a lighter. 2. The charge for using a lighter.

**light money.**    In the United States, a tax imposed on undocumented ships entering domestic harbors. The tax is based on a predetermined per-ton rate. See also *tonnage tax.*

**like perils.**    In insurance, a provision that extends coverage to accidents similar to those specifically enumerated in a policy.

**Limean.**    In finance, the mean between lending rate bids and offers when London banks borrow from one another. Compare *London interbank offered rate.*

**limit.**    1. The maximum daily price change in the value of stock allowed by some stock exchanges. When a market is volatile, the exchange sets trading limits on the upward or downward fluctuation of the market during a given trading day. Limits were imposed by the New York Stock Exchange in 1987 to control volatility caused by computerized program trading. 2. On commodity exchanges, the maximum fluctuations in futures prices or the minimum fluctuations in futures prices or option premiums permitted on any given trading day. 3. An investor's order to a broker to buy or sell at a stated price.

**limitation.**  See *statute of limitations.*

**limited carrier.**  See *carrier.*

**limited company.**  See *company.*

**limited partner.**  See *partnership.*

**limit order.**  An order placed with a broker by a customer specifying a maximum or minimum price to be paid or received for a transaction. Unless executed at the specified price or at a better price, a limit order is canceled. Compare *market order* and *stop order.*

**LIMNET.**  The abbreviation for London Insurance Market Network.

**linear tariff cut.**  See *across-the-board tariff reduction.*

**liner.**  A ship making regularly scheduled stops along a trade route. By contrast, a tramp steamer stops at unscheduled ports.

**liner shipment.**  A shipment transported in a vessel equipped to haul shipping containers. Compare *break-bulk shipment.*

**liner terms.**  A charter party clause stipulating the handling charges to be borne by the ship's owner.

**lingua franca.**  Italian: the language of commerce.

**LIQ.**  The acronym for liquidated. See *liquidation.*

**liquid assets.**  Also called liquid capital or realizable assets, cash holdings or assets readily converted to cash. Liquid assets include marketable common stock, commercial paper, and government Treasury bills. The ratio of an organization's liquid assets to debts is a measure of its solvency.

**liquidated damages.**  See *damages.*

**liquidation.**  1. The distribution of a company's assets before it is dissolved. The company's owners may liquidate voluntarily or be compelled to do so by court order. See also *bankruptcy* and *voluntary liquidation*. 2. In commodity trading, the closing out of open positions. 3. In customs, the process of satisfying customs entry requirements after an import has been classified and duties

determined. Liquidation is largely a matter of paying taxes and fees. In the United States, notices of liquidation are posted at the customhouse where an import is entered. When entry documents are amended, usually to claim a refund for overpayment, the process is known as reliquidation.

**liquidation committee.**  A committee of creditors in a bankruptcy proceeding.

**liquidation date.**  The date on which a customs entry is completed and duties are paid.

**liquidator.**  A person appointed to supervise the distribution of assets and payment of debts before a business enterprise is dissolved. When the dissolution is voluntary, the liquidator may be appointed by the firm's owners or by its creditors. In an involuntary bankruptcy, the liquidator is appointed by the court and may be subject to terms established by the court or by a liquidation committee, which may consist of creditors and shareholders. The liquidator assembles assets, pays debts and liquidation expenses, and distributes any remaining assets among owners according to the firm's articles of incorporation or partnership. See also *receiver.*

**liquidity.**  See *liquid assets.*

**lira.**  The currency of Italy, Malta, and Turkey.

**Lirma.**  The abbreviation for London Insurance and Reinsurance Market Association.

**Lisbon Agreement for the Protection of Appellations of Origin and Their International Registration.**  An international agreement adopted at Lisbon in 1958 and amended at Stockholm in 1967 protecting appellations of origin. An appellation identifies a product whose essential nature and quality are associated with a place of origin. Applications for local brand-name protection are submitted by a signatory country to the World Intellectual Property Organization (WIPO). If another signatory country objects within 1 year, the appellation is nonetheless protected in other countries as long as protection continues in the country of origin. The Lisbon Agreement is administered by the WIPO.

**lis pendens.**  Latin term: suit pending, or a notice in the press that property interests may be affected by the outcome of a lawsuit.

**listed company.**  See *company.*

**listed security.**   A security whose price is quoted on a stock exchange.

**listing requirements.**   Regulations established by a stock exchange governing companies selling securities in its facilities. Listing requirements vary depending on the market in which a security trades. Generally, a company must hold assets of a prescribed value, sign a listing agreement with the exchange requiring regular public financial disclosures, and have prices of its shares quoted at specified intervals. Normally reserved for the largest companies, an exchange's main market has the most rigorous listing requirements. The lowest requirements are applied to unlisted securities traded in the over-the-counter markets.

**liter/litre (l).**   In the metric system of weights and measures, a unit of volume equal to 0.908 dry quart and 1.056 liquid quarts. See also *Système Internationale.*

**LL.**   The abbreviation for International Convention on Load Lines. See *International Maritime Organization.*

**Lloyd's.**   Often called Lloyd's of London, the world's premier insurer. Lloyd's is not an insurance company, but an insurance market composed of individuals, underwriting syndicates, and brokers. Individual investors are known as Lloyd's Names. Underwriters receive a share of premiums paid on a given venture and spread risks, either through internal syndicates or by retaining outside underwriters. The Corporation of Lloyd's was chartered by an act of the British Parliament in 1871. Lloyd's has a long tradition of insuring otherwise uninsurable commercial ventures.

**Lloyd's agent.**   An employee of Lloyd's of London stationed at a local port. Lloyd's agents arrange ship surveys, investigate accidents, and settle claims.

**Lloyd's List and Shipping Gazette.**   A shipping industry trade daily published in London by Lloyd's Register of British Shipping, which covers, inter alia, aircraft and ship schedules. Once known as *Lloyd's List*, the daily was founded in 1734. Its weekly companion is *Lloyd's Loading List*, which details ship loadings at European ports and carries insurance news.

**Lloyd's Names.**   Individuals who deposit substantial sums with Lloyd's and share in the profits and losses from policies underwritten by the Corporation of Lloyd's. Names have traditionally assumed unlimited liability for Lloyd's policies, which are secured by their personal wealth. However, underwriting reforms at Lloyd's may alter the practice in the future.

**Lloyd's Register of British and Foreign Shipping.**   An annual publication of Lloyd's Register of Shipping, the British ship classification society formed in 1760, detailing the condition and construction of ships. The *Register* is used to evaluate risks when underwriting marine policies.

**Lloyd's standard policy.**   In the United Kingdom, the marine insurance industry's uniform policy. The format was approved by the British Parliament in the Marine Insurance acts of 1899 and 1906.

**load.**   In mutual funds, the sales commission paid to an investment company. In back-end load funds, the commission is a redemption fee. In front-end load funds, the fee is charged at the time of the sale. No commission is charged by a no-load fund. Some funds also charge a distribution fee, known as a 12b1 fee. The commission is the difference between the selling price of shares and the net asset value of shares.

**loadcenter.**   A pick-up site for cargo transported from inland points. In shipping, loadcenters at major ports enable carriers to avoid calling at outlying ports.

**load fund.**   See *load.*

**loading.**   A bank's addition of a variable-risk premium to discount a bill of exchange. The surcharge is added on top of ordinary interest and acceptance fees. The premium, interest, and other fees are deducted from the face value when a bill is presented for discounting.

**loan.**   1. Money lent to a borrower to be repaid at a later date. The cost of borrowing is interest. A secured loan is guaranteed by collateral, or pledged assets, in which the creditor takes a security interest. A loan may be secured by cash, inventory, personal assets, realty, receivables, and some securities. When a debtor fails to repay according to the loan terms, the creditor can enforce the claim by seizing and selling the collateral. An unsecured loan is based on the borrower's credit history, earning potential, or personal reputation. The borrower's assets may figure in the lending decision, but are not pledged. 2. Lending by the International Bank for Reconstruction and Development as distinguished from International Development Association financing, which is extended in credits.

**load line.**    Also called water marks, lines on a ship showing how far its hull can be immersed in water. Also called Plimsoll lines or marks since the 1870s, load lines are safety markings, such as F for fresh water, W for winter sea water, etc. Heavy penalties are imposed on shipowners and masters who overload a ship, so that it sinks below its load line.

**loan fee.**    The fee assessed by a lender for a loan. Fees are charged to hold open an approved line of credit (annual fee), maintain the unused portion of a line of credit or loan (commitment fee), and service draw-downs against a line of credit (utilization fee).

**loan note.**    A credit dividend paid on loan stock or debenture stock in lieu of cash. Loan notes are usually payable on demand at a variable interest rate and are used to defer tax liability.

**Loan Purchase Program.**    In the United States, a loan program administered by the Private Export Funding Corporation (PEFCO). When a domestic exporter finances a foreign sale with a commercial loan, PEFCO is authorized to buy the debt from the bank if repayment is guaranteed by the Export-Import Bank of the United States. The Loan Purchase Program provides liquidity to expand foreign sales.

**loan receipt.**    A document used by marine underwriters to recapture funds loaned to policyholders awaiting court judgments. The receipts are common in cases involving ocean carrier liability. The underwriter is reimbursed from damages won by the shipper when a judgment is obtained against a carrier in a negligence suit for lost or damaged cargo. See also *benefit-of-insurance clause.*

**loan sales.**    Loans sold to investors in the secondary market directly or indirectly through intermediaries. The sales price depends on the quality of the debt, which may be discounted or sold at or above par value. See also *participation loan.*

**loan stock.**    See *debenture stock.*

**lock-up.**    1. An investment in assets held for a long term, either because they are part of an investment plan or because the assets are illiquid. 2. In the Eurobond market, the condition of unregistered securities in the United States. U.S. securities laws prohibit the sale of bonds until they are registered with the Securities and Exchange Commission. See also *global bond.* 3. In banking, a certificate of deposit held usually by the issuing bank to prevent secondary-market trading in the issue.

**loco.**    Latin: *locus* meaning place. In commodity trading, it denotes the pick-up site for a shipment, e.g., loco Chicago.

**locus sigilli (L.S.).**    Latin: Loosely, the place for affixing a seal.

**logistics support vessel (LSV).**    A military ship with sealift/landing capacity. Roll-on/roll-off cargoes can be handled at sites without docking facilities.

**lolo.**    The abbreviation for lift-on/lift-off.

**Lombard loan.**    In Germany, a short-term loan by the Bundesbank to commercial banks. See also *interest rate policy.*

**Lombard rate.**    See *Lombardsatz.*

**Lombardsatz/Lombardzinsfuss.**    German: Lombard rate. 1. The rate on lending to commercial banks set by the Bundesbank. See also *interest rate policy.* 2. The rate set by German banks for loans backed by pledged securities. Elsewhere in Europe, a loan collateralized by securities. Compare *Luxembourg interbank offered rate.*

**Lombard Street.**    The center of the financial district in the City of London.

**Lomé Conventions.**    The European Community's (EC's) preferential trade and economic assistance program for developing countries. The Treaty of Rome authorized special economic relationships between EC countries and former European colonies. The Six, the original members of the European Economic Community, signed the first Yaoundé Convention with 18 African states and Madagascar in 1964; a second Yaoundé Convention was signed in 1969. Former British colonies were brought into the program when Britain joined the European Common Market in 1973. The first Lomé Convention, known as Lomé I, was signed at Lomé, Togo, in 1975. Lomé I granted duty-free status to imports of agricultural products and ores entering the EC from African, Caribbean, and Pacific (APC) countries. Lomé II, the second convention signed in 1979, created the Stabex and Sysmin mechanisms for currency stabilization. Lomé III was effective from 1986 to 1989. Lomé IV, signed in 1989, expires December 14, 1999. While Lomé IV failed to achieve the APC group's goals of entering more duty-free imports into the EC, the agreement commits the EC to significant contributions toward debt relief and capital investment in APC countries. The EC's contributions are financed by the European Investment Bank and the European Development Fund.

**London Club.**  See *debt conversion program.*

**London Commodity Exchange.**  See *London Futures and Options Exchange.*

**London discount market.**  The market composed of London discount houses that specialize in trading commercial and short-term government debt. The discount market is financed by London clearing banks. Local discount houses are members of the London Discount Market Association, which facilitates contacts between the houses and the Bank of England.

**London Dumping Convention.**  See *Convention on the Prevention of Marine Pollution by Dumping of Wastes and Other Matter.*

**London Futures and Options Exchange (FOX).** In the United Kingdom, the exchange that replaced the London Commodity Exchange in 1987. FOX brokers deal in cocoa, coffee, and sugar futures and options. The exchange shares quarters with the International Petroleum Exchange.

**London Grain Futures Market.**  See *Baltic Exchange.*

**London interbank offered rate (LIBOR).**  1. Also known as the London interbank offer/offering rate, the LIBOR is the rate at which one London bank lends surplus Eurocurrency and sterling deposits to another. LIBOR loans are made overnight or for periods of up to 5 years. Compare *Bank of England dealing rate.* 2. In commercial lending, the international benchmark for short-term loans. LIBOR rates are fixed-term rates quoted daily by five London banks. The quotes are announced at 11 a.m. (London time) for specific maturities. The actual commercial lending rate varies, depending on the reference bank used to determine the LIBOR for a given loan. For syndicated loans, the rate is quoted as a spread above the LIBOR, or the difference between the cost of Eurofunds and the interest earned on Eurodeposits. See also *interbank offered rate.*

**London International Financial Futures Exchange (LIFFE).**  In the United Kingdom, a financial futures market that began dealing in 1982. LIFFE trades futures and options contracts for foreign currencies, government bonds, interest rates, and stock indexes, including a contract based on the Financial Times–Stock Exchange Index. LIFFE transactions are cleared through the International Commodities Clearing House.

**London Metal Exchange (LME).**  The central international market for dealing in nonferrous metals. The LME was established in 1877 and deals in minimum lots of aluminum, copper, lead, nickel, tin, and zinc, as well as metal-based futures contracts and options contracts. Official prices set by the LME are used worldwide as reference prices for long-term metals contracts. The LME also arranges storage facilities for shipments of metals. LME transactions are cleared through the International Commodities Clearing House.

**London Stock Exchange (LSE).**  The securities market in London, formally established in 1802. Known as the International Stock Exchange of the United Kingdom and Republic of Ireland Ltd., the exchange has several markets: a main market for listed companies; the unlisted securities market; the third market for riskier unlisted securities; and the London Traded Options Market, a subsidiary which deals exclusively in option contracts. Securities traded on the main market are noted on the LSE's *Official List.* The list, which is published daily, notes prices, dividends, and new issues recorded during a trading day. Prices are also quoted on the Stock Exchange Automated Quotations System in the currency in which shares are issued. The LSE is overseen by the Securities and Investment Board of the Department of Trade and Industry.

**London Terminal Sugar Market.**  An international sugar market managed by the United Terminal Sugar Market Association. A part of the London Commodity Exchange, the sugar market trades standardized sugar contracts. The current standard contract is quoted in U.S. dollars rather than pound sterling. The sugar market's transactions are cleared through the International Commodities Clearing House.

**London Traded Options Market.**   See *London Stock Exchange.*

**long bill of exchange.**   A bill of exchange payable after a certain date (e.g., 60 days after sight). A bill drawn in London is called a long sterling, or simply a long. The rate paid for such bills is known as a long rate. Short bills of exchange, known as shorts, differ from longs and are paid near the date of presentation, usually within 10 days.

**long bond.**   See *Treasury bond.*

**long coupon.**   A bond interest payment stretched over a longer period than the normal 6-month intervals.

**longer-combination vehicle.**   A multitrailer truck.

**long position.**   Holdings of commodities, currencies, or securities in excess of sales. A dealer holds an asset (i.e., takes a long position) waiting to sell at a profit when prices increase. 1. In futures trading, the situation of the purchaser of a futures contract with provisions for accepting delivery or liquidating the transaction with an offsetting sale. 2. In options trading, holding a put option or a call option. Compare *short position.*

**Long-Term Agreement on Cotton Textiles.**   See *MultiFiber Arrangement Regarding International Trade in Textiles.*

**long ton.**   See *ton.*

**Lonham Trademark Act of 1946.**   In the United States, a law prohibiting imports of falsely labeled products. False labelings include fraudulent country-of-origin markings and misleading trademarks or symbols. Falsely marked goods or unauthorized imports of trademarked products are subject to forfeiture, seizure, or destruction by the U.S. Customs Service.

**loon.**   A dollar coin issued by the Bank of Canada. Because of its bulk, the loon is discounted at a higher rate in the United States than Canadian bank notes.

**LORCS.**   The abbreviation for League of Red Cross and Red Crescent Societies.

**loro account.**   In accounting, a ledger summary reporting currency transfers or obligations accrued in transactions with others. Derived from the Italian *loro* meaning their, the term is widely used outside the United States to describe foreign exchange transactions.

**loss.**   1. The depreciated resale value of a damaged asset. A badly damaged or destroyed asset represents a loss, since its resale value is reduced to zero. 2. The operating deficit incurred by a business when expenditures exceed revenues for a transaction or accounting period. 3. In insurance, the financial value of damage, injury, or death, giving rise to a payment in settlement of a claim. 4. In sales, the difference between the lower selling price of an asset and its higher acquisition cost *or* fair market value. 5. In finance, the cost of unpaid principal and interest plus collection fees when a loan is uncollectible.

**loss adjuster.**   An independent contractor appointed by an insurer to negotiate an insurance settlement. The adjuster evaluates losses and proposes terms for settling claims.

**loss leader.**   A low-value good advertised to attract sales of higher-priced products or services. Also known as sales bait, loss leaders represent a form of deceptive advertising prohibited by consumer protection regulations in most jurisdictions.

**loss of specie.**   The process by which a product is transformed in some essential characteristic. The transformation occurs as a consequence of some external factor, e.g., a liquid losing volume when overheated or a solid losing mass when pressure is applied. Loss of specie is an insurable risk.

**lot.**   Any quantity of a commodity recognizable in the trade as a standard unit of sale, e.g., *x* bales of cotton or *x* barrels of oil.

**loti.**   The currency of Lesotho.

**Louvre Accord.**   An agreement reached by Canada, France, Germany, Japan, the United Kingdom, and the United States in Paris in 1987 to coordinate intervention in international currency markets to stabilize exchange rate values. The agreement was adopted following several unilateral attempts by central banks to reduce speculation in international currency markets. The speculative environment had been created in part by the rapid globalization of private capital markets and the strong dollar policy implemented in the United States to compensate for its historically high federal budget deficits. See also *Plaza Accord*.

**loyalty agreement.**   A pledge required by a shipping conference binding a shipper to transport a prearranged portion of its goods aboard a conference carrier. The pledge is signed in exchange for a freight discount. In the United States, the discount is limited to 15 percent of the carrier's tariff rate. Elsewhere, conferences may offer rebates in addition to the discount. Compare *exclusive patronage contract*.

**LPA.**   The abbreviation for Laurentian Pilotage Authority.

**l.s.**   The abbreviation for lump sum.

**LSV.**   The abbreviation for logistics support vessel.

**l.t.**   The abbreviation for liner terms and long ton.

**LTA.**   The abbreviation for Long-Term Agreement on Cotton Textiles. See *MultiFiber Arrangement Regarding International Trade in Textiles.*

**Ltd.**   The abbreviation for limited company.

**Ltge.**   The abbreviation for lighterage.

**LTL.**   The abbreviation for less than a trailerload.

**LTOM.**   The abbreviation for London Traded Options Market.

**lump-sum charter.**   A charter arrangement under which the charterer pays a flat fee to conclude an agreement, even though an actual shipment may never occur.

**Luxembourg interbank offered rate (LUXIBOR).** The interest rate at which commercial banks lend to one another in Deutsche marks. The LUXIBOR is also the market rate for deposits denominated in Deutsche marks. See also *interbank offered rate*. Compare *Lombardsatz*.

**Luxembourg Patent Convention.**   See *European Patent System*.

**LUXIBOR.**   The acronym for Luxembourg interbank offered rate.

# M

**m.**   The abbreviation for meter and mile.

**M.**   The abbreviation for thousand.

**M0–M5.**   See *money supply*.

**MA.**   The abbreviation for managing agent.

**macroeconomics.**   The study of the impact of a large economic factor on the direction of an economic variable. For example, a macroeconomic approach might concentrate on the effects of fiscal policy or monetary policy on a particular economic variable, such as consumption, employment, incomes, investment, or productivity. See also *Keynesian economics*. Compare *microeconomics*.

**Madrid Agreement concerning the International Registration of Marks.**   Also known as the Agreement concerning the International Registration of Marks, a global accord signed at Madrid in 1891 covering owners' rights in trademarks and service marks. The agreement grants national treatment in one signatory to marks registered with the World Industrial Property Organization through the registration agency of another signatory. An application not rejected by a signatory within 1 year of the filing date is automatically approved. Applications are submitted in French. Registrations are renewable at 20-year intervals. Cancellation in one signatory country cancels registrations in other signatories. The Madrid Agreement has been revised several times, beginning with the Brussels revision of 1900. The most recent revision was concluded in Stockholm in 1967. The Madrid Agreement is open to member states of the Paris Convention for the Protection of Industrial Property. Compare *Trademark Registration Treaty*.

**Madrid Agreement for the Repression of False or Deceptive Indications of Source on Goods.**   Also known as the Madrid Union, an international agreement to suppress global traffic in falsely labeled goods. Signatory countries are required to seize and/or otherwise prevent the importation of goods bearing false-origin markings of member states. First signed at Madrid in 1891, the agreement was last revised in Stockholm in 1975. The Madrid Union is administered by the World Industrial Property Organization and open to signature by members of the Paris Union.

**Mahgreb Common Market (MCM).**   Officially known as the Arab Mahgreb Union, an agreement between Algeria, Libya, Mauritania, Morocco, and Tunisia to integrate the economies of the North African Mahgreb region. MCM succeeded the Mahgreb Permanent Consultative Committee, also known as the Permanent Consultative Committee of the Mahgreb, established at Tunis in 1964. Created as the predecessor to the Mahgreb Economic Community (or the North African Common Market) to be formed in 1995, the MCM envisions harmonized regulations, a common external tariff, and monetary union. MCM was established by agreement at Marrakesh in 1989.

**mail fee.**   In the United States, the user fee charged by the U.S. Customs Service for documenting imports through the international mail.

**main market.**   The principal equities market on a major stock exchange. A company whose shares are traded on the main market must meet an exchange's most stringent listing requirements.

**mainstream corporation tax (MCT).**   In the United Kingdom, the corporate tax paid by a company after the advance corporation tax on distributions to shareholders has been paid. The MCT is a company's remaining tax liability.

**maintenance-of-value clause.**   See *index clause*.

**maintenance requirements.**   1. In securities trading, a deposit of money or securities maintained by a customer in a brokerage account. In the United States, maintenance requirements, also known as minimum maintenance, are governed by Federal Reserve Regulation T and Federal Reserve Regulation U, which limit margin credit extended by banks and brokerage firms. A customer makes an initial deposit of $2000. Margin loans can be extended to the full value of securities purchased. When an account balance falls below a preset minimum, additional security is required. The current margin requirement is 50 percent of the market value of securities in the account. Brokers often impose higher margin requirements, particularly in the over-the-counter market . 2. In futures markets, a performance bond required of buyers and sellers of futures contracts. The initial margin is the deposit made when a customer places an order. The minimum deposit required for a given account is known as the maintenance margin. See also *margin call*.

**maison de réescompte.**    French: discount house.

**Major Projects Program.**    In the United States, a program sponsored by the U.S. Department of Commerce to assist domestic firms vying for foreign contracts. Directed by the Office of International Major Projects, the program provides technical assistance to construction, engineering, and supplier firms seeking contracts for large infrastructure and industrial development projects.

**make bulk.**    See *consolidation*.

**maker.**    The party who signs a negotiable instrument and assumes primary liability for payment.

**making a price.**    On a securities exchange, quoting a buy or sell price. Market makers make a market price by announcing the prices at which they are willing to buy or sell a specific quantity of securities. The market maker asking or offering a price is bound to deal at the quoted price.

**Makler.**    German and Swiss: broker. Typically, *Makler* deal exclusively with traders, although they may also trade for their own accounts under limited circumstances. Compare *Kursmakler*.

**managed currency.**    See *managed float*.

**managed float.**    An exchange rate value influenced by a government entering currency markets to achieve specific policy objectives. For example, a government may sell quantities of its national currency to reduce its exchange value relative to other currencies, thereby making its domestic exports more competitive in international markets. When a government buys its national currency, the reverse is true. A managed float is also called a dirty float. Compare *clean float*.

**managed trade.**    Import-export regulation implemented to achieve domestic economic objectives. A government manages trade by raising barriers to imports and nourishing export industries. Import barriers arise when duties are set at a higher rate than the administrative costs of processing customs entries require and when product standards are more rigorous than sound health and safety regulations demand. Export industries are regulated largely by protecting and subsidizing infant or favored industries. Recently, the newer trend has been toward setting specific foreign export targets and requiring reciprocity in specified economic sectors. See also *Semiconductor Agreement* and *Structural Impediments Initiative*.

**management agreement.**    A written agreement between a broker or investment advisor and a client. The agreement sets forth earnings objectives and fees charged for advisory services.

**management board.**    In the European Community, the body charged with managing the day-to-day affairs of a European company. The board's chief operating officer is the managing director. Management boards are overseen by supervisory boards. Compare *administrative board*.

**management buy-in.**    The purchase of a company's shares by its managers. Management buy-ins are usually popular with outside investors and creditors, principally on the theory that managers are familiar with the industry and have personal incentives to make the business profitable. Compare *management buyout*.

**management buyout.**    The purchase of the controlling interest in a company by its managers, usually to thwart an unwanted takeover or prevent a breakup and sell-off of its assets. Management buyouts are often financed by outside investors or banks as incentives for managers to return the company to profitability. A buyout will occasionally spark an increase in the value of a company's stock, which managers and other investors are able to sell later at a profit. See also *leveraged buyout*. Compare *management buy-in*.

**management fee.**    1. A fee charged by the managing underwriter of a securities issue or syndicated loan, usually a Eurocurrency loan. 2. The fee charged by an investment company.

**managing agent (MA).**    The local representative of a foreign manufacturer, often operating under an exclusive agency agreement. Managing agents typically represent foreign manufacturers in dealings with governments, particularly when a manufacturer obtains or bids for a procurement contract. Managing agents are compensated on a commissioned or retained basis.

**managing director (MD).**    Also known as a *directeur général* (DG), the corporate officer responsible for the daily operation of a company. The term is not generally used in the United States, where the nearest equivalent is chief executive officer.

**managing underwriter.**    An agent bank for a syndicate underwriting a new securities issue. The managing underwriter organizes the group, files registration papers, allots shares to each member, and represents the group's interests in fixing the price for an offering. The managing underwriter is compensated according to the terms of the syndicate agreement. See also *lead bank*.

**M&A.**    The abbreviation for merger and acquisition.

**Mandate of Cartagena.**    A 1969 agreement between the members of the *Pacto Andino*, the Andean Common Market, creating a regional council, a court of justice, and a common parliament. The agreement was designed to further the goal of full economic and political integration in Latin American. The *Pacto Andino* is composed of Bolivia, Colombia, Ecuador, Peru, and Venezuela. Chile withdrew from the agreement.

**mandatory convertible.**    A redeemable note issued in connection with a bond offering. The note is converted into common stock at maturity or at intervals stated in the bond indenture. Mandatory convertibles enable the issuer to redeem debt with equity rather than cash outlays. Conversions are structured to have a minimum dilution effect on existing shareholder stock values.

**mandatory deletion program.**    In some countries with substantial foreign assembly operations, a program designed to protect market share for local producers of component parts, particularly those used in automobile assembly. Automobiles are exported as completely built-up cars or as completely knocked-down (CKD) kits. The kits are used to assemble automobiles abroad. Under a mandatory deletion program, local components are classified as original manufacturer's equipment and competing imports are deleted from the CKD kit. Mandatory deletion programs are nontariff barriers, but they have not been ruled illegal by the General Agreement on Tariffs and Trade.

**manifest.**    An official inventory of a ship's or aircraft's cargo. The manifest is signed by the vessel's captain and presented to customs at ports of entry.

**manipulation warehouse.**    See *bonded warehouse*.

**Mansholt Plan.**    A comprehensive agricultural plan for the European Economic Community (EEC) proposed in 1968 by EEC Commissioner Sicco Mansholt. The plan recommended a series of programs to maintain and adjust farm income in order to accommodate agricultural differences in EC countries. Programs proposed in the Mansholt Plan were adopted by the European Council in a series of directives. See also *Common Agricultural Policy*.

**manufactured or processed.**    Criteria for duty drawback, i.e., a rebate on imports used to manufacture products for reexport. To qualify for drawback, the import must be transformed into a new product with a distinctive identity, nature, or use; a simple change, such as repackaging, is not sufficient. Unfit imports rehabilitated for the use originally intended and imports destroyed or reexported in the same condition are exempt from the "manufactured or processed" criteria and are eligible for drawback.

**manufacturer's agent.**    An agent who sells a manufacturer's product in a local market, usually under an exclusive franchise. Manufacturer's agents are paid commissions on the volume or value of local sales. Compare *manufacturer's export agent*.

**manufacturer's brand.**    See *brand name*.

**manufacturer's declaration.**    A manufacturer's description of a product's price, nature, and conformity to regulatory standards. The manufacturer is liable for false representations of product quality and safety.

**manufacturer's export agent (MEA).**    A firm that sells the products of several noncompeting foreign manufacturers in a given country or region, usually under an exclusive franchise. The MEA is a commission agent conducting business under its own name rather than as a part of a manufacturer's marketing department. MEAs are paid commissions on the volume or value of foreign sales. Compare *export sales agent*.

**manufacturer's identification code (MID).**    A customs code used to identify manufacturers. The code is an abbreviation of a manufacturer's name and address. In the United States, U.S. Customs Directive 3500-13 (November 24, 1986) contains instructions for obtaining and using a MID.

**manufacturer's particulars.**   A data plate welded to an intermodal container identifying its manufacturer and shipping capacity. The notice is required by the International Convention for Safe Containers.

**manufacturer's recommended price.**   See *recommended retail price.*

**manufacturer's representative (MR).**   A local agent who takes orders for a foreign manufacturer's products. Manufacturer's representatives are extensions of a company's sales force and are compensated on a commission basis.

**manufacturing clause.**   See *American manufacturing clause.*

**maquiladora.**   Spanish: assembly plant, also known as a twin-plant assembly operation. Most *maquiladoras* are located on the Yucátan side of the U.S.-Mexican border and assemble imports for export. *Maquiladoras* are mostly exempt from Mexico's environmental, foreign investment, and labor regulations. Since the late 1980s, Guatemala City has also become a *maquiladora* center. See also *American components assembled abroad* and *North American Free Trade Agreement.*

**MARAD.**   The acronym for Maritime Administration.

**marché à réglement mensuel (RM).**   French: forward market.

**Marché à Terme International de France.**   See *futures market* and *Globex.*

**marché au comptant.**   French: spot market.

**Marché des Options Négociables de Paris (MONEP).**   The Paris Traded Options Market established in 1988. MONEP's primary product is the CAC-40 (*Cotation Assistée en Continue*) stock index option. The short-term contracts are American-style options, permitting exercise at any time up to the maturity date. The long-term option, added in 1991, is a European-style option, allowing exercise only on the maturity date.

**marché des reports.**   French: contango market.

**Mareva injunction.**   In the United Kingdom, a court's order enjoining a defendant in a legal proceeding from removing property from its jurisdiction.

**margin.**   1. The difference between the value of collateral and the loan secured by it. 2. In finance, the spread, or the difference between a bank's borrowing and lending rates. 3. On a trading exchange, the deposit posted as security for a loan obtained to purchase securities or guarantee a commodities contract. See also *maintenance requirements* and *margin call.*

**margin account.**   See *margin loan.*

**marginal cost.**   The difference between the direct cost of producing a product or service and its selling price. Marginal costing enables a producer to calculate a product's economic value in relation to profits and overhead expenses.

**marginal productivity.**   The incremental value of adding new machinery or hiring one employee. Marginal productivity is the degree by which an added factor of production increases output. The increase in earnings gained from an added factor of production is known as marginal revenue.

**marginal rate.**   In the United States, an incremental increase in tax liability above the standard rate. For example, at a standard rate of 20 percent on income up to $20,000, a higher rate of 30 percent on income above $20,000 is the marginal rate. The marginal rate applies to each dollar of net income (i.e., earnings less taxes and allowable deductions) above $20,000. Outside the United States, marginal rates are called higher rates.

**margin call.**   A lender's demand that a customer surrender additional funds or eligible securities to offset losses from a margin loan. The customer is usually given 24 hours to post more security or the lender calls the loan or, in the case of a brokerage house, sells the securities to retire the debt. See also *maintenance requirements.*

**margin fee.**   In maritime insurance, the excise tax levied in some jurisdictions on premiums paid to foreign insurers. The insurers may be primary underwriters or reinsurers who combine to underwrite coverage for a ship or cargo.

**margining system.**   See *original margin.*

**margin loan.**   In commodity, futures, or securities trading, a loan obtained by a customer from a broker to purchase securities, commodities, or futures contracts. Secured by deposits of cash or securities, margin loan funds are held in margin accounts carried in the customer's name. In the United States, trading exchanges and federal regulatory agencies establish margin or maintenance requirements. See also *general account* and *margin call.*

**margin requirement.**   See *maintenance requirements.*

**marine bill of lading.**   See *bill of lading.*

**marine extension clause.**   In maritime insurance, a provision that covers most insurable cargo losses. The provision applies to losses incurred while cargo is in transit and or left at a discharge port for sale or onward transit.

**marine insurance.**   Insurance coverage for a ship and its cargo. Originally restricted to loss or damage at sea, marine insurance now covers cargo in transit overland to and from a port. Marine insurers underwrite all losses caused by accidents or natural disasters. In the United States, when an accident results from carrier negligence or crew misconduct, the insurer is reimbursed for claims paid from judgments obtained by a policyholder against a carrier. See also *loan receipt.*

**marine insurance certificate.**   See *certificate of insurance.*

**marine interest.**   The rate of interest charged for bottomry or respondentia bonds when a ship or cargo is pledged for a loan. Marine interest usually exceeds the commercial lending rate.

**Maritime Administration (MARAD).**   In the United States, the agency established in 1950 to regulate the merchant marine. MARAD is a division of the U.S. Department of Transportation. The agency administers the Merchant Marine Act of 1936 and the Cargo Preference Act of 1954; approves the design and construction of merchant ships; sets construction differential subsidies and operational differential subsidies; directs the National Shipping Authority, which coordinates the merchant marine in national emergencies; and administers a war-risk insurance program for U.S.-flagged vessels when commercial insurance is unavailable. Subsidy applications are reviewed by the Maritime Subsidy Board, a MARAD body. Compare *Federal Maritime Commission.*

**maritime lien.**   In admiralty law, a legal claim that attaches to a ship by statutory mandate or

when a legal action is filed. In the United States, a statutory lien arises when a shipowner defaults on a ship mortgage or similar obligation or is responsible for the injury of a seaman. In an admiralty action, or libel in rem, a maritime lien derives from a tort or similar claim concerning a ship's maintenance, operation, or cargo. Maritime liens have priority in inverse order, so that delay in executing a maritime lien may bar a claim. See also *Federal Maritime Lien Act of 1910,* and *Jones Act of 1920,* and *laches.*

**maritime passport.**   Also called a sea brief, sea letter, or sea pass, a special document asserting a right of innocent passage on the high seas. Maritime passports are issued to ship captains by some neutral countries in times of war. The United States no longer issues maritime passports.

**Maritime Subsidy Board.**   See *Maritime Administration.*

**marked cheque.**   A check approved for payment by the bank on which it is drawn. Marked checks are known as certified checks in the United States.

**market.**   1. A place where willing buyers and sellers gather to decide the market price of a commodity. Market price is determined by supply and demand. 2. A public exchange where market makers buy and sell at quoted prices. The exchange can be an open-outcry market with traders setting prices by hand signals or a securities market where most deals are arranged by telephone or computer. 3. The actual demand for a product, usually determined by sales over a preset period of time.

**marketable title.**   Also known as a good title or clear title, a title to goods or other property that is without legal defects. A marketable title is valid and not subject to litigation concerning its merchantability. In practical terms, title is marketable when a prudent and reasonable person would accept it for the purposes presented. Compare *defective title.*

**market disruption.**   The condition of a domestic economic sector flooded with imports cheaper than local manufacturers can produce. An import surge causes plant shutdowns and increased unemployment. Importing countries have remedies under the escape clause and Antidumping Code of the General Agreement on Tariffs and

Trade. Bilateral trade agreements also contain dispute-settlement mechanisms designed to address market disruption. Most countries have national antidumping or antimarket disruption laws under which unilateral action can be taken when an import surge results from unfair trade practices.

**market economy.**    An economy where commercial transactions are managed largely by private interests. Ideally, capital, labor, raw materials, etc., are allocated mainly according to supply and demand, and government intervention in pricing and other market activity is kept to a minimum. In practice, however, government intervention in commercial markets is a matter of degree. At a minimum, all governments set environmental, health, and labor standards and regulate some prices in the public interest. Compare *nonmarket economy*.

**market-exchange method.**    A technique used to measure the size of one national economy in relation to another. The method involves converting the gross domestic product of several nations into U.S. dollars and ranking countries in terms of the relative dollar values of their economies. Fluctuating exchange rates and purchasing mixes in different countries have largely rendered the market-exchange technique obsolete. It has been substantially supplanted by another method, known as purchasing-power parity.

**market forces.**    Supply and demand in a market economy. As demand increases, prices and supply also increase. When supply exceeds demand, prices decrease.

**marketing.**    The process of developing and implementing plans to create or maintain a market for a product, process, or service. Marketing usually requires research to identify a market and assess customer needs, preferences, and purchasing power. Marketing plans are developed to promote sales, determine pricing, and advertise quality and postsales service. Marketing strategies differ, depending on the nature, size, capital base, and target customers of a given business. Media advertising, direct mail, telemarketing, and cold calls are marketing devices.

**marketing mix.**    The combination of business factors that enables a firm to develop a market for its product and determines the profitability of sales. Known collectively as the four Ps, the marketing mix includes the product (suitability, quality, packaging, etc.), its price (retail price, volume discounts, etc.), promotion (advertising, telemarketing, etc.), and place (local distributors, retail outlets, etc.). Marketing strategies are developed to enhance the attractiveness of a firm's marketing mix.

**Market Intelligence Reports (MINTEL).**    In the United Kingdom, consumer market analyses published by Mintel Publications Ltd. The reports provide detailed information on new and existing consumer markets in the UK.

**market leader.**    A company with the largest market share in a given industry. Market leaders often determine industry prices and service standards by setting an example for an industry. Compare *price leader*.

**market maker.**    A dealer in a market, usually licensed by a trading exchange or a regulatory agency. Market makers buy for their own accounts (as dealers) or for customers (as commission agents). When acting as agents, market makers buy at publicly quoted prices. When buying as principals, market makers determine the price and absorb the personal risk of dealing. Dealing is also known as making a market.

**market order.**    An instruction from a customer to a broker to buy commodities, futures contracts, or securities at the best asked price. Most securities sales are executed through market orders. In slow trading, the purchase price is frequently at or close to the price prevailing when the order was placed. In fast trading, the purchase price may differ substantially from an earlier market price. Compare *limit order* and *stop order*.

**market price.**    The price at which a product or service is bought and sold by informed and willing buyers and sellers. In organized exchange markets (e.g., on commodity or stock exchanges), the market buying price and the market selling price differ. The quoted price is the mean price between the buying price and the selling price.

**Market Promotion Program (MPP).**    In the United States, a program of the U.S. Department of Agriculture developed to promote export sales of domestic farm products. The MPP provides partial funding for sales promotions, market research, technical assistance projects, etc., through the Commodity Credit Corporation. Private firms and trade associations are eligible MPP recipients.

**market rate.**   The rate of interest paid on deposits and debt obligations. Market rates are determined by the supply and demand for money at any given time.

**market risk.**   The chance that an asset will depreciate in value and be sold at a loss. Risks may arise from the general economic environment, price declines or increases, problems in a given economic sector, and so on. Hedges are used to reduce market risks. Compare *commercial risk* and *country risk.*

**Market Share Reports.**   In the United States, international trade trend reports published by the U.S. Department of Commerce. *Market Share Reports* contain data for evaluating foreign markets. The data measure changes in the demand for specific products and compare U.S export performance to foreign competition.

**market value.**   Also called fair market value, the highest price an asset can command from a willing and informed buyer in an open market. Securities and futures are adjusted daily to reflect changes in market value. Other assets, such as bank loans, are revalued when a borrower's credit deteriorates or collateral depreciates. The process of revaluing financial assets is known as marking to the market. Compare *appraised value* and *less than fair value.*

**marking duty.**   See *duty.*

**marking name.**   In the United Kingdom, the name of a London bank, broker, or jobber approved by the London Stock Exchange in which foreign shares are registered for trading. Bearer certificates issued for marking-name shares are held in trust by an authorized depositary to which dividends are paid. Compare *nominee* and *street name.*

**markings, marks.**   1. Symbols affixed to cargo and bills of lading. Marks must be of sufficient clarity and permanence to identify the country of origin and a shipment's destination port. 2. The official number of transactions completed during a business day on a stock exchange. 3. A trademark.

**marking to the market.**   See *market value.*

**markka.**   The currency of Finland.

**mark sheet.**   In Japan, the equivalent of an import declaration form. Mark sheets are submitted to the Bank of Japan for imports valued in excess of 1 million yen.

**markup.**   See *gross margin.*

**MARPOL.**   The abbreviation for International Convention for the Prevention of Pollution from Ships.

**marques.**   French: marks or markings.

**marques de produits.**   French: trademarks.

**Marshall Plan.**   Also known as the European Recovery Program, a plan proposed in 1947 by George Marshall, the secretary of state of the United States. The plan called for the infusion of substantial U.S. capital to rebuild post-World War II Europe, largely on the theory that a modern and prosperous Europe would spurn radical political ideologies and contribute to global economic development. Funding for the Marshall Plan was authorized by the Economic Cooperation Act of 1948.

**mart and countermark.**   Documents, sometimes called letters patent, issued by a government authorizing the seizure of enemy ships. The practice, also known as marque and reprisal, is approved by the U.S. Constitution. The Treaty of London of 1851 commits adhering countries to eliminate marts and countermarks.

**MAS.**   The abbreviation for Monetary Authority of Singapore.

**mask work.**   A form of intellectual property that evolved from electronic technologies. Mask work includes electrical circuit designs and processes used to implant circuits in computer semiconductor chips.

**masse monétaire.**   French: money supply.

**master.**   A merchant ship's captain.

**master air waybill.**   See *airbill.*

**master's protest.**   Also called captain's protest, a log of the events surrounding a maritime accident or other disaster. In admiralty suits, the master's log is admissible as evidence in settling liability claims.

**matched bargain.**   A transaction managed by a broker, who matches buyers and sellers, coordinating sales involving similar quantities of the same stock.

**matched book.**    An investment portfolio in which assets and liabilities have equal maturities. When maturities differ, the portfolio is known as a mismatched book.

**matched sale-repurchase agreement.**    See *repurchase agreement*.

**material fact.**    1. Any information that has a direct bearing on the outcome of a transaction or legal dispute. A contract is voidable when made without knowledge of a material fact, which, had it been known, might have prevented the agreement. In most jurisdictions, a party who conceals a material fact is subject to contempt of court or other legal penalties. 2. In insurance, a fact alleged in an application that would influence the insurer's decision to write a policy or determine the size of the premium. Compare *misrepresentation*.

**mate's receipt.**    A document of title issued by an ocean carrier verifying that cargo has been loaded for onward transit. The mate's receipt is proof of ownership and entitles the recipient to a bill of lading issued by the carrier.

**MATIF.**    See *Marché à Terme International de France*.

**matrix.**    The set of export credit interest rates approved as OECD consensus rates.

**maturity date.**    The date on which the proceeds from a financial instrument are payable. In the case of redeemable bonds, the maturity date is called the redemption date.

**max.**    The abbreviation for maximum.

**maximum price fluctuation.**    See *limit*.

**m.b.**    The abbreviation for merchant's broker.

**MBA.**    The abbreviation for Master of Business Administration.

**M. bd. ft.**    The abbreviation for thousand board feet.

**Mbm.**    The abbreviation for thousand-foot-board measure.

**mc.**    The abbreviation for millicurie.

**MCA.**    The abbreviation for monetary compensation amount and Monetary Control Act.

**McFadden Act of 1927.**    In the United States, a federal statute authorizing states to regulate branch banking. The act bans interstate banking by national banks when branch banking by locally chartered banks is prohibited by state law. Where state law allows, exemptions from branch banking restrictions are available to national banks through the comptroller of the currency and to state bank members of the Federal Reserve System through the Federal Reserve Board of Governors. See also *bank holding company*.

**MCT.**    The abbreviation for mainstream corporation tax.

**MD.**    The abbreviation for managing director.

**MDB.**    The abbreviation for multilateral development bank.

**mdse.**    The abbreviation for merchandise.

**MEA.**    The abbreviation for manufacturer's export agent.

**mean price.**    In currency, commodities, and securities markets, the middle price between the bid price and the offer price. See also *market price*.

**measurement ton.**    A measurement equal to 40 cubic feet. In a metric system, a measurement ton is roughly equivalent to a cubic meter. Vessel space and freight charges are calculated in measurement tons.

**MEC.**    The abbreviation for marine extension clause.

**med.**    The abbreviation for median and medium.

**Med.**    The abbreviation for Mediterranean.

**medium-dated gilt.**    See *gilt-edged security*.

**medium of exchange.**    A commodity, usually money, that can be used to settle a debt.

**mediums.**    See *gilt-edged security*.

**medium-term debt.**    A debt payable in fewer than 10 years. Compare *short-term capital*.

**Meech Lake Agreement.**    In Canada, a 1987 internal agreement to protect the French language and culture in Quebec. The agreement was subject to ratification by Canada's Parliament and provincial legislatures, but it was rejected by the provinces of Newfoundland and Manitoba, largely on the grounds that similar protections were not extended to other provinces.

**meeting of creditors.**    See *bankruptcy*.

**Mehrwertsteuer.**    German: value-added tax.

**meishi.**    Japanese: business cards, which are exchanged extensively in Japan.

**members' voluntary liquidation.**    See *voluntary liquidation*.

**memorandum invoice.**    A seller's notice to a buyer regarding the quantity, value, details of shipment, etc. Memorandum invoices can become the conclusive statement of a transaction's terms.

**memorandum of association.**    See *articles of incorporation*.

**memorandum of understanding (MOU).**    1. A document setting forth the terms of an agreement. Memoranda of understanding are exchanged between governments (or between a government and a foreign national). An MOU is not enforceable as a contract, unless a government voluntarily submits to the jurisdiction of a court. 2. In the United States, a statement by a private party to a federal agency agreeing to refrain from a course of conduct. The memorandum can be introduced in a legal proceeding as evidence of a prior commitment made and broken, but not necessarily as an admission of prior misconduct.

**memorandum tariff.**    A published summary of a carrier's tariff.

**Merc.**    The popular acronym for the Chicago Mercantile Exchange.

**Mercado Común Centroamericano (MCC).**    Also known as the Central American Common Market, a regional economic association created at Managua, Nicaragua, in 1960. MCC was originally established by the Treaty of Central American Economic Integration, revised in 1976, which authorizes the creation of the Economic and Social Community of Central America by 1994. The common market encompasses Costa Rica, El Salvador, Guatemala, and Nicaragua. Honduras withdrew in 1970. MCC's development bank is *Banco Centroamericano de Integración Económica*. The organization also operates the Central American Clearing House, a multilateral clearing facility for member central banks. MCC is headquartered in Guatemala. See also *Nomenclatura Arancelaria Uniforme Centroamericana II*.

**mercantile law.**    Commercial law, including the law of banking, contracts, the formation and dissolution of companies, insurance, intellectual property, sales, transportation, and warehousing.

**mercantile paper.**    A merchant's short-term debt obligations, mainly acceptances and notes.

**mercantilism.**    A theory of political economy that emerged in Europe, primarily in England and France, following the decline of feudalism. Mercantilism was based on the notion that exports enrich a nation, while imports impoverish it. National policies were developed to increase exports, accumulate bullion, create a merchant marine, and establish foreign colonies to supply cheap commodities for domestic enterprises. Free trade theory espoused by Adam Smith (1723–1790) supplanted mercantilism by the nineteenth century.

**merchandise concerned.**    A term used broadly to refer to merchandise subject to customs valuation under the deductive value method. Merchandise concerned includes the import itself, as well as identical merchandise or similar merchandise.

**merchandise of the same class or kind.**    In customs valuation, a factor in finding an import's computed value or deductive value. For computed value, the import and merchandise of the same class or kind are manufactured by similar producers in the same country. For deductive value, merchandise of the same class or kind originates in a country other than the import's country of origin.

**merchandise processing fee.**    In customs, a fee based on the entry value of an import.

**merchantability.**    The description of an implied warranty that arises from the sale of goods by a merchant who customarily sells the same type of goods. In the United States, §2-314 of the Uniform Commercial Code creates an obligation in the seller to sell goods that are, among other things, acceptable according to practices of the trade, fit for the purposes intended, adequately packaged and fairly labeled, and, in the case of fungible goods, of fair average quality. See also *merchantable quality*.

**merchantable quality.**    In common law and buyer protection statutes, an implied warranty provided by a merchant that a product offered for sale is without hidden defects. Implied warranties do not extend to defects of which the buyer was notified or should have noticed before goods were accepted. See also *merchantability*.

**merchant bank.**    A bank that specializes in arranging commercial financing but does not hold loans to maturity. Originally established in Britain to finance international trade transactions, contemporary merchant banks also manage portfolio investments and invest in acquisitions and corporate restructurings for their own accounts. Unlike investment banks in the United States, British merchant banks also engage in retail banking activities. French *banques d'affaires* more nearly resemble investment banks.

**merchant marine.**    The ships registered under a nation's flag, including passenger ships and commercial cargo carriers. In most nations, the merchant marine fleets are owned by private interests, although a few governments are the sole owners of national merchant marines. Merchant marine fleets can be requisitioned and deployed during periods of national emergency.

**Merchant Marine Act of 1920.**    See *Jones Act of 1920*.

**Merchant Marine Act of 1936.**    In the United States, a law that authorizes U.S. ship construction differential subsidies and operating differential subsidies. Section 804 of the act also bars owners of ships constructed with U.S. government subsidies from operating foreign-registered ships in competition with U.S.-flagged carriers essential to the foreign commerce of the United States. The limitation on foreign competition has been protested by U.S. trading partners before the General Agreement on Tariffs and Trade, but it has been maintained by the United States on national security grounds. The act is administered by the Maritime Administration. See also *Jones Act of 1920*.

**merchant marine fund tax.**    A tax imposed on imports, primarily in Latin America. The taxes are often used to subsidize local shipbuilding industries.

**merchant's contract.**    See *exclusive patronage contract*.

**merchant's freight agreement.**    See *exclusive patronage contract*.

**Mercosur (Southern Cone Market).**    A trading association encompassing Argentina, Brazil, Paraguay, Uruguay, and possibly Chile. Mercosur was formed in 1991 by the Treaty of Asunción to create a regional common market. The first bilateral agreement leading to a Southern Cone Market was negotiated between Argentina and Brazil in 1986. Officially known as the Program for Cooperation, the bilateral agreement eliminates duties on capital goods. It also contemplates harmonization of the *Nomenclatura Arancelaria y Derechos de Importación*, Argentina's tariff classification system, based on the Brussels Tariff Nomenclature, and the *Nomenclatura Brasileira de Mercadoria*, the Brazilian tariff system, based on the Harmonized Commodity Description and Coding System. Beginning in 1995, the Argentina-Brazil agreement creates an internal free market in goods, investment, services, and labor. Uruguay and Paraguay are scheduled to join the common market in 1996. See also *Asociación Latinoamericana de Integración*.

**merger and acquisition (M&A).**    The combination of two or more business firms, known as an acquisition when a larger organization absorbs a smaller one. Mergers involve pooling common stock or redeeming stock, often at a premium. In the United States, M&As are regulated under antitrust laws by the Antitrust Division of the U.S. Department of Justice. In the United Kingdom, M&As are subject to regulation by the Department of Trade and Industry and the Mergers and Monopolies Commission. In Canada, takeovers of publicly held companies are generally approved by the stock exchange where a targeted company's shares are traded. In France, takeover bids are channeled for approval through banks to the *Chambre Syndicale*. Notification statements of takeover bids are filed with the Ministry of Finance in Japan, but most mergers are not negated by a failure to file. In Germany, there are no enforced guidelines on mergers and acquisitions.

**meter (m).**    In the metric system of weights and measures, the basic unit of length equivalent to 39.37 inches. See also *Système Internationale*.

**metical.**    The currency of Mozambique.

**Metric Conversion Act of 1975.**    In the United States, a law mandating conversion from the U.S. Customary System to the *Système Internationale*

(SI). Although the metric system was first approved by Congress in 1866 and adopted for scientific use by the U.S. National Bureau of Standards in 1964, metric units of measure are still not widely used in the United States.

**metric system.**   See *Système Internationale.*

**Mexican-U.S. Free Trade Agreement.**   See *North American Free Trade Agreement.*

**mezzanine bracket.**   The status of an underwriter who subscribes to the second-largest share of a securities issue. The managing underwriter subscribes to the largest share.

**mezzanine financing.**   1. Intermediate financing obtained by a company between its start-up financing and an initial public offering. 2. In an acquisition or financial restructuring, financing obtained through issues of convertible debentures, preferred stock, or other types of subordinated debt. Mezzanine financing increases equity rather than debt.

**mf.**   The abbreviation for machine (or mill) finish.

**MFA.**   The abbreviation for MultiFiber Arrangement Regarding International Trade in Textiles.

**mfd.**   The abbreviation for manufactured.

**mfg.**   The abbreviation for manufacturing.

**MFN.**   The abbreviation for most favored nation.

**mfr.**   The abbreviation for manufacture and manufacturer.

**MFTA.**   The abbreviation for Mexican-U.S. Free Trade Agreement. See *North American Free Trade Agreement.*

**MFZ.**   The abbreviation for Miami Free Zone.

**mg.**   The abbreviation for margin and machine (or mill) glazed.

**mgr.**   The abbreviation for manager.

**m.h.**   The abbreviation for main hatch.

**mi.**   The abbreviation for mile and mill.

**microbridge.**   The transport of cargo from a foreign port to an inland discharge point by way of another port. The cargo is transported under a single through bill of lading. See also *landbridge.*

**microeconomics.**   The analysis of one factor (e.g., employment or consumer prices) in measur-

ing the direction of an economy and the allocation of resources. See also *monetarism.* Compare *macroeconomics.*

**MID.**   The abbreviation for manufacturer identification code.

**Middle East Development Bank (MEDB).**   A multilateral development bank for the Middle East proposed by the United States following the Gulf War of 1991. As of 1992, the bank has not been established. In all probability, the creation of the MEDB depends on the outcome of the 1993 political settlement reducing conflict between Arab countries and Israel.

**middle price.**   See *mean price.*

**midstream operation.**   The process of hauling cargo from a barge to a heavy seagoing vessel. The midstream transfer is made while the ocean vessel rests at anchor in midchannel.

**MIGA.**   The abbreviation for Multilateral Investment Guarantee Agency.

**milliard.**   In Europe, 1000 million, or 1 billion.

**min.**   The abbreviation for minimum and minute.

**Mincing Lane.**   The commodity trading center in the City of London. The main office building in the center is called Plantation House.

**minibridge.**   The transport of cargo from a foreign port to an inland point by way of intermediate and destination ports. The cargo is transported under a single through bill of lading. See also *landbridge.*

**minilandbridge service.**   Carrier service whereby merchandise is transported by land and sea to a destination point. See also *intermodal service, landbridge,* and *multimodal shipping.*

**minimum import price.**   The gate, or import entry, price under the European Community's Common Agricultural Policy.

**minimum lending rate (MLR).**   See *competition and credit control.*

**minimum price fluctuation.**   See *limit.*

**minimum stocking order.**   See *export sales agent.*

**minimum subscription.**   In the prospectus for a securities issue, the minimum capital investment sought by the owners of a company from investors.

**minimum wage.**   The lowest sum an employer must pay to compensate an employee for labor or services. Minimum wages are set by national law or by an authorized agency.

**Ministère de l'Économie des Finances et du Budget.**   In France, the Ministry of Finance. In Belgium, the finance ministry is known as the *Ministère des Finances.*

**ministerie van financien.**   Dutch: ministry of finance.

**ministério das finanças.**   Portuguese: ministry of finance.

**ministerio de finanzas.**   Spanish: ministry of finance.

**ministerio de hacienda.**   In some Spanish-speaking countries, the ministry of finance.

**ministry of finance (MOF).**   A central monetary authority responsible for managing a nation's finances. Among other things, an MOF oversees the collection of revenues, the printing of money, the implementation of tax and credit policies, and the government's participation in international lending and borrowing. The ministry of finance is known as the Department of Treasury in the United States and the Exchequer in the United Kingdom.

**Ministry of International Trade and Industry.** See *Japan Ministry of International Trade and Industry.*

**minority interest.**   Equity owned in a company entitling a shareholder to fewer than 51 percent of the company's voting shares. In most jurisdictions, the rights of minority shareholders are protected by statute or judicial decisions. Minority shareholders are entitled to dividends and a fair distribution of liquidated assets when a company is dissolved. Although permitted to bring derivative legal actions to inspect a company's books or dislodge directors and officers who abuse trust, minority shareholders do not own enough equity to determine company policy.

**minority protection.**   1. Antidiscrimination laws protecting ethnic, gender, racial, and religious minorities. 2. Legal rights accorded minority shareholders in a company. See also *minority interest.*

**MINTEL.**   The acronym for *Market Intelligence Reports.*

**min. wt.**   The abbreviation for minimum weight.

**MIP.**   The abbreviation for marine insurance policy, maximum investment plan, minimum insurance policy, and monthly investment plan.

**MIS.**   The abbreviation for management information system.

**misc.**   The abbreviation for miscellaneous.

**misfeasance.**   A breach of duty or trust, particularly by a company officer entrusted with the care of assets belonging to others. Owners suffering financial losses caused by a breach of trust have legal recourse to obtain fair restitution.

**misrepresentation.**   A conscious and willful misstatement of fact. A person who states a misguided opinion or makes an unwitting misstatement is not guilty of misrepresentation. To have legal effect, a misrepresentation must be relied on by another party and cause injury to the person who hears or reads it. A contract arising from a fraudulent or negligent misrepresentation can be rescinded, and the injured party can sue for damages. A contract based on an innocent misrepresentation is merely rescinded. See also *material fact.*

**missionary rate.**   A dedicated transportation rate for infant or emerging industries.

**mistake.**   An error involving an issue of fact or a matter of law. A mistake of law does not void an agreement, but a mistake of fact may make it void or voidable. When both parties share a common mistake, a contract is not void unless the mistake is vital to the agreement's meaning. When the mistake is mutual, a contract is void if both parties could have been correct in different views of the contract's meaning. If a unilateral mistake is made regarding the offer to contract, the contract is void if the mistake might have been corrected by the other party.

**Mitbestimmung.**   German: codetermination. In Germany, *Mitbestimmung* is reflected in the practice of having employees represented on corporate boards when a company has 500 or more employees. The concept of coparticipation has been adopted by the European Community. See also *Community Charter of Fundamental Social Rights of Workers.*

**MITI.**   The abbreviation for Ministry of International Trade and Industry. See *Japan Ministry of International Trade and Industry.*

**mitigation of damage.**  At common law, an obligation imposed on an injured party. A party seeking legal damages is required to take reasonable steps to minimize a prospective defendant's losses. Courts deny claims that might have been avoided.

**mixed credit.**  See *crédit mixte.*

**mixed economy.**  An economy in which both the public sector and the private sector offer goods and services. Most modern market economies are mixed, with governments providing some critical products and services, while private interests provide others. Although most countries combine features of public and private ownership, global trends in the 1980s and early 1990s favor private interests. See also *social market.*

**mixed regulations.**  Government regulations requiring domestic content in foreign imports.

**mkt.**  The abbreviation for market.

**MLR.**  The abbreviation for minimum lending rate.

**MMC.**  The abbreviation for Monopolies and Mergers Commission.

**MMDA.**  The abbreviation for money-market deposit account.

**MMP.**  The abbreviation for masters, mates, and pilots.

**MNC.**  The abbreviation for multinational corporation.

**MNE.**  The abbreviation for multinational enterprise.

**mo.**  The abbreviation for month.

**m.o.**  The abbreviation for mail order and money order.

**MOA.**  The abbreviation for memorandum of agreement.

**mobilisation.**  French: discounting (financial) paper, usually by Banque de France.

**Model Law on International Commercial Arbitration.**  See *United Nations Commission on International Trade Law.*

**MOF.**  The abbreviation for ministry of finance.

**MOLCO.**  The abbreviation for more or less—charterer's option.

**MOLOO.**  The abbreviation for more or less—owner's option.

**MONEP.**  See *Marché des Options Négociables de Paris.*

**monetarism.**  The use of the money supply to influence economic growth rates. Monetarists, led by Milton Friedman, an American economist, advocate loosening and tightening monetary aggregates to produce stable growth with low inflation. The application of monetarist theories in the United States in the early 1990s kept inflation low but failed to yield satisfactory economic growth rates. Compare *Keynesian economics.*

**monetary aggregates.**  See *money supply.*

**Monetary Authority of Singapore (MAS).**  The central bank of Singapore.

**monetary compensation amount.**  See *Common Agricultural Policy.*

**monetary economy.**  An economy where money, and not bartered goods, is used to settle debts.

**monetary policy.**  Measures taken by a central monetary authority to influence the rate at which credit flows through an economy. Monetary policies are designed to sustain reasonable levels of employment, stabilize prices, and maintain balanced trade with other countries. The cost and availability of credit are determined by interest rate policy. Compare *fiscal policy.*

**monetary reserves.**  A country's stock of precious metals and hard currency.

**monetary system.**  A system used to distribute money for internal use, influence its flow through the internal economy, and establish the value of a national currency unit relative to others. A nation's monetary system is managed by a central monetary authority.

**monetary union.**  A formal agreement between countries to reduce internal transaction costs by creating a common central bank and a single currency. Monetary union is an element of economic union, which entails eliminating internal barriers to trade and investment, as well as harmonizing product standards and fiscal and tax policies. Ultimately, monetary union is a step toward political union. See also *European Community.*

**monetary unit.**  An artificial currency unit or unit of account authorized by law as a settlement medium for a nation's official accounts.

**monetize.**    The mechanism by which a nation covers its national debt, often by printing additional money. Various sorts of paper certificates collateralized by assets, such as gold, may also be issued for conversion to cash.

**money.**    A commodity accepted as legal tender or a settlement medium to balance accounts and purchase goods and services. Money is a unit of account with a measurable purchasing value, i.e., a unit of exchange for payments. To qualify as money, a commodity must retain predictable economic value for future transactions. Money can be paper currency, metal coins, or accounting debits and credits. In the United States, the Uniform Commercial Code adopts the definition of money accepted by Section 6 (5) of the Uniform Negotiable Instruments Law, i.e., any medium of exchange authorized as currency by a government.

**money at call.**    See *call money*.

**money broker.**    A firm that arranges deposits or short-term loans between banks, discount houses, and other financial institutions. Money brokers operate in national markets and in Euromarkets. The fee charged by a money broker for an introduction is called a commission.

**money-center bank.**    A bank located in a major financial center that offers national and international banking services. Money-center banks provide depository, foreign exchange, and trust facilities.

**money laundering.**    See *laundered money*.

**money market.**    An informal network of dealers and investors where short-term debt securities are traded. Money-market securities are debt obligations issued by highly rated firms for short periods, usually under 90 days. The largely unregulated Euromarket is the world's largest money market, where numerous currencies are also actively traded.

**money-market deposit account (MMDA).**    In the United States, a deposit account without interest rate controls. MMDAs were authorized in 1982 as a part of a program of financial deregulation.

**money-market fund.**    A mutual fund that invests in short-term debt instruments, usually of investment grade. Shares in money-market funds are offered by prospectus and pay regular interest. In the United States, money-market fund managers are registered with the Securities and Exchange Commission. See also *unit trust*.

**money-market instruments.**    High-quality debt instruments, usually with maturities of 1 year or less. These instruments include banker's acceptances, commercial paper, short-term local government securities, and Treasury bills. Money-market instruments and futures are actively traded in major financial centers and on financial futures markets.

**money-market rates.**    Interest paid on money-market instruments. Rates on banker's acceptances, broker call loans, and Eurocurrency time deposits are quoted in financial dailies, as are the London interbank offered rate, the U.S. federal funds rate, the U.S. prime rate, and the U.S. Treasury bill rate.

**money supply.**    Also known as the money stock, the measure of liquidity in a country's economy. The money supply is defined in terms of aggregated liquid assets, or short-term assets immediately available for transactions and investment. Central banks use interest rate policy and bank reserve requirements to expand or restrict the money supply. When the money supply is too loose, inflation increases. When money is too tight, recessions deepen. The money supply is measured in monetary aggregates, but countries measure monetary aggregates differently. Two examples follow:

*United Kingdom*

*M0.*    Circulating notes and coins plus bank till money and Bank of England balances.

*M1.*    Circulating notes and coins plus private current accounts and deposit checking accounts.

*M2.*    Circulating notes and coins plus non-interest-bearing bank deposits and savings accounts.

*M3.*    M1 plus certificates of deposit plus other bank deposits from private sources.

*M3c.*    M3 plus foreign currency bank deposits.

*M4.*    M1 plus bank deposits from private sources and money-market instruments.

*M5.*    M4 plus certain savings deposits.

*United States*

*M1.*    Currency and traveler's checks held by the general public, demand deposits, ready withdrawal accounts, and credit union share drafts.

*M2.*    M1 plus small time deposits, savings accounts, money-market mutual fund shares owned by individuals, money-market withdrawal accounts, certain Eurodollar deposits, and overnight repurchase agreements.

*M3.*    M2 plus money-market mutual fund shares owned by institutional investors, large time deposits and term repurchase agreements, and certain Eurodollar deposits.

*L.*    M3 plus other long-term liquid assets, banker's acceptances, commercial paper, short-term government securities, and nonbank investments in U.S. savings bonds.

**monobank.**    The banking system in a centrally planned economy. In a monobank system, supplies of money and credit are determined directly, rather than indirectly, by a central bank. The other banks, which are branches of the government bank, do not compete on credit or service terms.

**Monopolies and Mergers Commission (MMC).** In the United Kingdom, the national agency that investigates mergers and acquisitions under the Fair Trading Act of 1973. The MMC also administers the Competition Act of 1980, which governs public-sector monopolies. Anticompetitive labor practices are within the MMC's jurisdiction.

**monopoly.**    A market with a single supplier of a good or service for which there is no adequate substitute. In theory, consumers suffer when a monopoly controls a market because there is no competition. Except for public utilities and exempt industries, monopolies are prohibited by the antitrust laws of the United States. Elsewhere, antimonopoly laws and competition laws regulate monopolies. Compare *monopsony.*

**monopsony.**    A market with a single buyer. Defense industries in most countries are monopsonies. Compare *monopoly.*

**montant forfaitaire.**    Also known as *abattement forfaitaire,* the amount by which European Community (EC) countries reduce internal duties and taxes on products imported from other EC countries. The *montant forfaitaire* ensures a local price advantage to EC products over external imports.

**Monthly Digest of Statistics.**    In the United Kingdom, a monthly digest of economic data published by the Central Statistical Office detailing with information on local industries and national income.

**Moody's Investors Service.**    See *Dun & Bradstreet.*

**moorsom ton.**    A ship unit of measure equal to 100 cubic feet.

**moratorium.**    An official suspension of a service or benefit, normally by a government, during periods of national emergency or fiscal crisis.

**mordida.**    In Latin America, a gratuity paid to a government official or business agent to facilitate a transaction.

**mortgage.**    A loan agreement secured by the asset financed. A mortgage gives the purchaser conditional equity in an asset. The lender's lien is removed when the debt is paid.

**mortgage debenture.**    A business loan secured by the real property of the borrower.

**most favored nation (MFN).**    A country granted access to a foreign market on equal terms with similarly situated trading partners. Except for items entering under trade preferences for developing countries, MFN status provides MFN-country exporters the lowest available rate of duty on a product. MFN status is routinely granted to all but a handful of trading partners, known as general trading partners. The loss of MFN status can mean substantial increases in import tariffs.

**MOT.**    The abbreviation for Ministry of Transport.

**mother ship.**    A ship that makes regular calls at major ports.

**MOU.**    The abbreviation for memorandum of understanding.

**MPF.**    The abbreviation for merchandise processing fee.

**MPP.**    The abbreviation for Market Promotion Program.

**M/R.**    The abbreviation for mate's receipt.

**MRP.**    The abbreviation for manufacturer's recommended price.

**MSA.**    The abbreviation for Multilateral Steel Agreement.

**MS-DOS.**    The abbreviation for MicroSoft Disk Operation System, a trademark owned by

Microsoft Corporation, a U.S. corporation. DOS is the most widely used software system for personal computers.

**MSO.**   The abbreviation for marine staff officer.

**M/T.**   The abbreviation for mail transfer and metric ton.

**MTN Codes.**   See *Multilateral Trade Negotiations Codes.*

**MTO.**   The abbreviation for Multilateral Trade Organization and multimodal transport operator. See *multimodal bill of lading.*

**muestras sin valor.**   Spanish: samples without value, a customs marking for sample goods entered for display, demonstration, professional use, or order solicitations. The marking is required in Latin American countries that do not belong to carnet conventions.

**MultiFiber Arrangement regarding International Trade in Textiles (MFA).**   Also known as the MultiFiber Arrangement, an international agreement setting rules for orderly trade in textiles. Negotiated by the General Agreement on Tariffs and Trade (GATT) and concluded on December 30, 1973, effective January 1, 1974, the MFA supplanted the 1962 Long-Term Arrangement regarding International Trade in Cotton Textiles (LTA). Although the LTA covered only cotton products, the MFA also applies to most fibers and apparel. Countries are permitted to negotiate bilateral quotas, called import restraints, to minimize market disruption caused by import surges. The MFA contains a consultation mechanism for dispute settlement and allows for reasonable growth in textile import levels. In the United States, negotiated textile restraints are authorized by Section 204 of the Agricultural Act of 1956 and administered by the Committee on the Implementation of Textile Agreements. Internationally, the MFA is managed by the Textile Surveillance Board (TSB), which issues rulings on tariff schedule reclassifications and arbitrates disputes between signatories.The European Community, Japan, and the United States are permanent TSB members; other members are selected annually by member states. The MFA has been extended by two protocols, the last ending in 1986. Bringing textiles within the framework in order to replace

MFA quotas with tariffs was a primary objective of the Uruguay Round.

**MultiFiber Textile Surveillance Board.**   See *MultiFiber Arrangement regarding International Trade in Textiles.*

**multilateral development bank.**   See *development bank.*

**Multilateral Investment Guarantee Agency (MIGA).**   An agency of the World Bank Group established in 1987 that began operations in 1988. MIGA provides country risk insurance to foreign firms investing in developing countries. Its insurance covers breach of contract, civil strife, currency inconvertibility, expropriation, and war. MIGA is based in Washington, D.C.

**multilateral netting.**   A method of financial management used by companies with subsidiaries in several countries. Credits and debits attributed to different subsidiaries are equalized, or netted out, which reduces the need to settle balances in several foreign currencies.

**multilateral trade agreement.**   An agreement among several countries to reduce or abolish barriers to trade.

**multilateral trade negotiation (MTN).**   1. International trade negotiations involving several countries. Compare *bilateral* and *trilateral trade.* 2. Negotiations conducted by the General Agreement on Tariffs and Trade or the United Nations Conference on Trade and Development.

**Multilateral Trade Negotiations (MTN) Codes.** International trade rules reached during the Tokyo Round of the General Agreement on Tariffs and Trade negotiations. The codes were negotiated between 1973 and 1979; most became effective on January 1, 1980. The codes cover agriculture, antidumping, civil aircraft, customs valuation, government procurement, import licensing, product standards, and subsidies.

**Multilateral Trade Organization (MTO).**   A successor to the General Agreement on Tariffs and Trade (GATT) proposed by the United States during the Uruguay Round of global negotiations. The MTO would replace the GATT, an ad hoc interim agreement created after the International Trade Organization failed to win approval following World War II. Among other things, the MTO would provide a permanent legal structure for international trade, bring services and investment under the multilateral regime, and establish a dispute-settlement system under which an MTO finding would be binding unless overturned by contracting parties.

**multimodal bill of lading.** A bill of lading issued for different modes of carriage (e.g., water, air, and land). Each carrier moving goods under a multimodal bill is liable to the shipper for damage to cargo during its phase of carriage. A combined transport bill of lading covers multimodal shipments issued by a combined transport operator. It resembles a multimodal bill, except the carrier issuing a combined transport bill is solely responsible for the shipment. See also *division*.

**multimodal shipping.** A shipping transaction that combines several modes of carriage for a single shipment, e.g., by ship, truck, and rail. Multimodal shipping achieves faster delivery time at a lower cost to the shipper than separate shipping arrangements. A single through bill of lading or multimodal bill of lading covers the goods to a final destination point. Carriage charges are combined in a single freight tariff. See also *intermodal service* and *landbridge*.

**multinational corporation (MNC).** A firm with branches or subsidiaries in several countries from which it derives at least 25 percent of its annual sales income. Corporations become multinational to avoid barriers to entry in target markets, benefit from lower cost labor, and secure sources of cheap raw materials. Multinational companies are also known as transnational corporations and multinational enterprises.

**multiple.** See *price-earnings ratio*.

**multiple application.** The submission of several applications to subscribe to a new securities issue. Multiple applications are used when an issue is likely to be oversubscribed. In some countries, multiple applications filed in the same name are illegal. All countries prohibit the use of false names to file multiple applications.

**multiple-consignee container.** A shipping container loaded with cargo destined for more than one consignee.

**multiple green rate.** See *Common Agricultural Policy*.

**multiple taxation.** Taxes paid on the same income in more than two countries. If all countries involved have double-taxation treaties, multiple taxation can possibly be avoided.

**multiplier effect.** See *ratchet effect*.

**multitank container.** A shipping container designed to transport different kinds of liquid cargoes. The container contains coils or other heating devices to liquefy certain substances.

**muni.** The popular name for a municipal bond.

**municipal bond.** A debt instrument issued by a local government agency. In the United States, municipal bonds are general obligation bonds or revenue bonds that yield tax-exempt earnings.

**municipal law.** 1. The local law of a political subdivision. 2. In international law, the law of a nation.

**Munitions List.** In the United States, a list of defense articles maintained by the Office of Munitions Control (OMC) of the U.S. Department of State. Manufacturers of items named in the Munitions List file Form DSP-9 to register with OMC. The office also issues transaction licenses for each export shipment of items on the Munitions List.

**mutual fund.** Money assembled and pooled by an investment company. Mutual funds invest in stocks, bonds, futures, options, etc.; and investors in a mutual fund own proportional shares of its holdings. When the number of its outstanding shares varies, a mutual fund in known as an open-end fund, or, outside the United States, a unit trust. When its outstanding shares are fixed in number, the fund is called a closed-end fund in the United States and an investment trust elsewhere. Mutual fund shares are usually redeemable at net asset value, although some funds also deduct management fees (called a back-end load) when shares are redeemed. Distributions are taxable, often at the time shares are redeemed. 1. Balanced funds, also known as total-return funds, invest in stocks and bonds. 2. Growth funds concentrate investments in stocks with high growth potential. 3. Income funds invest in safe, modest-yield securities. 4. Index funds invest in a broad range of stocks to reduce the risks of holding individual stocks. 5. Preferred funds hold priority securities, i.e., bonds, convertibles, preferred stock, and high-quality common stock. 6. Sector or speciality funds concentrate holdings in specific sectors, e.g., money-markets or metals.

**mutuality of benefits.** See *reciprocity*.

**mutual mistake.** See *mistake*.

**MV.** The abbreviation for market value, motor vehicle, and motor vessel.

**MW.** The abbreviation for minimum weight.

**MwSt.** The abbreviation for *Mehrwertsteuer*.

**Myanmar.** The name adopted in 1989 by the country formerly known as Burma.

# N

**Naamloze Vennootschap (NV).** Dutch: limited-liability company. See *corporation*.

**NABANDINA.** The tariff nomenclature of the *Pacto Andino*. NABANDINA is based on the Brussels Tariff Nomenclature and consists of an eight-digit sequence covering roughly 5042 product classifications.

**Nachteil.** German: drawback. See *duty drawback*.

**naira.** The currency of Nigeria.

**naked debenture.** An unsecured debenture.

**naked option.** See *option*.

**naked position.** The position of a holder of an unhedged futures or option contract. Hedges protect holders against market price changes.

**Names.** See *Lloyd's*.

**NAO.** The abbreviation for National Administrative Office.

**Narodny Bank.** See *Vneshekonombank*.

**narrow money.** The most liquid aggregates in a country's money supply. Different countries use different measures of liquidity, but narrow money generally ranges from M0 through M1. Compare *broad money*.

**narrow-range security.** In the United Kingdom, a fixed-interest debt security. The Trustees Investment Act of 1961 specifies the nature of investments made by trustees managing assets for the benefit of others. Under the act, roughly one-half of trustee investments are required to be bond investments.

**narrow sea.** A body of water, such as the Persian Gulf, that lies between two narrowly aligned coasts.

**NASD.** The abbreviation for National Association of Securities Dealers.

**NASDAQ.** The abbreviation for National Association of Securities Dealers Automated Quotations. See *National Association of Securities Dealers*.

**National Association of Securities Dealers (NASD).** In the United States, a dealers' association authorized to regulate over-the-counter trading in unlisted stocks. The association licenses broker-dealers and operates as a self-regulating organization (SRO) under the Securities Act of 1934 and the Maloney Act of 1938. NASD members include securities brokers-dealers and non-commercial bank securities underwriters. NASD operates the NASDAQ, the National Association of Securities Dealers Automated Quotations system, which provides bid and offer quotes for unlisted securities. Created in 1971, NASDAQ offers Level 1 quotations to NASD members' sales personnel, Level 2 quotations to retail traders, and Level 3 quotations to market makers. NASD is based in New York.

**National Association of Securities Dealers Automated Quotations.** See *National Association of Securities Dealers*.

**National Automated Clearing House Association (NACHA).** A trade association that sets uniform rules and standards for the Automated Clearing House system in the United States. NACHA is based in Herndon, Virginia.

**National Bank Surveillance System.** See *comptroller of the currency*.

**National Cargo Bureau, Inc.** (NCB). In the United States, a nonprofit corporation created in 1952 and headquartered in New York City. NCB inspects and surveys cargo-handling services and equipment for insurance underwriters and regulatory agencies. Its certificates and deadweight (or draft) surveys are accepted by the International Labor Organisation (ILO) as evidence of compliance with ILO safety standards.

**National Chamber of Trade (NCT).** In the United Kingdom, a business association representing private business interests, including local chambers of commerce and trade associations. NCT reviews legislation and lobbies the British Parliament and European Community agencies on behalf of UK companies. NCT has headquarters in London.

**National Cooperative Research Act of 1984.** In the United States, a law designed to improve the competitiveness of domestic companies. Among other things, the act limits the impact of antitrust laws on domestic companies forming joint ventures for research and development (R&D) by reducing antitrust liability from treble to single damages. It also specifically authorizes the business justification defense for R&D joint ventures. Federal agencies and courts are required to decide whether a joint venture is reasonable in business terms before finding an antitrust violation.

**National Council for International Trade Documentation.**    See *NCITD*.

**national currency.**    See *legal tender*.

**national debt.**    A country's official obligations, including principal and interest owed to external sources. National debt adversely affects a nation's balance of payments and reduces the resources available for investment in an economy. Debt is managed by a country's central monetary authority.

**National Entry Processing (NEP).**    In the United States, an electronic data interchange system for customs brokers operated by the U.S. Customs Service. The NEP system permits electronic filings of customs entry documents, inspection of cargoes, and payments of customs duties. See also *Automated Commercial System* and *customs entry*.

**national exports.**    Goods manufactured or processed for export in a nation's domestic market, local free trade zones, or similar facilities dedicated to export trade.

**national flag carrier.**    A common carrier registered within a national jurisdiction and bearing the registering country's flag.

**National Girobank.**    See *giro*.

**national importer liquidation.**    See *Automated Commercial System*.

**national income accounts.**    Balance sheets that reflect the flow of money through a nation's economy. Income accounts show annual capital inflows and outflows. The accounts are stated in terms of consumption, investment, and other macroeconomic variables. A uniform standard for reporting national income has been established by the United Nations.

**National Institute of Standards and Technology (NIST).**    In the United States, a division of the

Technology Administration of the U.S. Department of Commerce that coordinates the work of private standards-writing associations, principally the American National Standards Institute, and provides information on international product and quality certification standards. NIST operates electronic message services that provide information on European Community directives and General Agreement on Tariffs and Trade regulations. A Conformity Assessment Systems Evaluation Program has been proposed by NIST to evaluate the competence of registrars who certify U.S. products and services for conformity to international quality standards.

**nationalization.**    The conversion of private assets into public property. In some instances, a government nationalizes an insolvent privately held natural monopoly, such as a public utility, to prevent disruptions in the delivery of essential services. More frequently, nationalizations are undertaken for political reasons and rationalized on national security or equity grounds. During the 1980s, denationalizing state-owned industries, ranging from mining to food-processing plants, became a global trend. Denationalization is also known as privatization.

**nationalized industries.**    See *nationalization*.

**National Labor Relations Board (NLRB).**    In the United States, an independent agency established by the National Labor Relations Act of 1935. The NLRB certifies unions for collective bargaining, supervises union elections, and hears labor complaints. The board is authorized to issue cease and desist orders when employers violate U.S. labor laws. To enforce its orders, the NLRB petitions the federal courts.

**National Mediation Board (NMB).**    In the United States, a labor relations board created in 1934 by amendment to the Railway Labor Act of 1926. The NMB certifies unions for collective bargaining and hears labor disputes involving airlines and railroads.

**national plan.**    A government's economic blueprint. National plans are prominent features of centrally planned economies. The plans allocate resources to certain industries with targets for agricultural and industrial output, usually for a 5- to 10-year period.

**National Price Commission (NPC).** A government body authorized to establish maximum prices to control inflation. In Ireland, the NPC requires firms sheltered from price competition to obtain advance permission for price increases. Other firms, known as undominant, nonprotected firms, may implement price increases upon notice to the NPC, usually within 60 days. The price controls are limited to products sold in retail trade.

**National Savings Bank.** See *Department of National Savings.*

**National Savings Stock Register.** See *Department of National Savings.*

**National Securities Clearing Corporation (NSCC).** In the United States, a company founded in 1977 that clears stock transfers. Jointly owned by the American Stock Exchange, the National Association of Securities Dealers, and the New York Stock Exchange, NSCC determines settlement balances and places securities with the Depository Trust Company or oversees their transfer to authorized agents. The Securities Industry Automation Corporation, NSCC's processing agent, provides electronic records of transactions once trades are completed on member exchanges.

**National Trade Data Bank (NTDB).** In the United States, a database containing international trade information compiled by 15 U.S. government agencies and maintained by the U.S. Department of Commerce. The NTDB carries regular updates of market research and foreign buyer data, compiled from information published by the Bureau of the Census and the U.S. & Foreign Commercial Service. Sources for NTDB data include the *Foreign Traders Index* and the *CIA World Factbook.*

**national treatment.** A nondiscriminatory international trade policy that accepts foreign imports and investment on equivalent terms with local products and investment. The concept was developed by the Organisation for Economic Cooperation and Development (OECD) in the National Treatment Instrument of 1976. The instrument commits OECD members, on a best-efforts basis, to accord equal treatment to trading partners' imports. National treatment is also a basic tenet of the General Agreement on Tariffs and Trade. Compare *reciprocity.*

**natural monopoly.** An industry in which substantial economies of scale and minimum production are required to satisfy demand. Public utilities, such as electric companies, are natural monopolies. Usually, natural monopolies are overseen by a national government. In the United States, public utilities are largely regulated by state agencies.

**NAUCA II.** The abbreviation for *Nomenclatura Arancelaria Uniforme Centroamericana II.*

**NAV.** The abbreviation for net asset value.

**navigable waters.** Bodies of water over which the public has rights of innocent passage. Navigable waters include oceans, rivers, and some lakes. Except for open seas, an owner, including a coastal state, retains title to the land beneath navigable waters. The United Nations has declared the lands beneath the open seas to be the "common heritage of mankind." See also *United Nations Convention on the Law of the Sea.*

**navigation certificate.** A document issued by a wartime belligerent verifying that a liner and its cargo have been searched, enabling it to proceed to a neutral port.

**Navtex.** The first phase of a comprehensive global maritime distress and safety system. The product of a joint venture between the Singapore Telecommunications Agency and Marine Department, Navtex uses radio and satellite technology to improve maritime safety. The system reduces errors caused by poor reception from voice radio and Morse code transmissions.

**NBV.** The abbreviation for net book value.

**NCITD.** Known variously as the National Council for International Trade Documentation and NCITD-The International Trade Facilitation Council, a nonprofit association dedicated to improving the operation of international trade. NCITD is composed of banks, brokers, carriers, forwarders, and exporters and importers. The association is recognized as a trade facilitation organization by the United Nations Working Party on Trade Facilitation. NCITD is headquartered in Alexandria, Virginia.

**NCT.** The abbreviation for National Chamber of Trade.

**NDP.** The abbreviation for net domestic product.

**NEA.**   The abbreviation for Nuclear Energy Agency. See *Organisation for Economic Cooperation and Development.*

**near money.**   Semiliquid assets convertible into cash on relatively short notice, e.g., short-term government securities and bills of exchange. Although readily transferable, near-money assets cannot be liquidated as quickly as bank notes or coins. Because it cannot be immediately converted to pay debts, near money is not included in national money-supply aggregates.

**Nederlands Normalisatie Instituut (NNI).**   In the Netherlands, the product standards agency.

**negative cashflow.**   The condition of an account where outflows exceed inflows.

**negative income tax (NIT).**   A sum of money paid to some taxpayers by a revenue agency. In a NIT system, personal allowances reduce tax liability to the standard income tax rate, which, in the case of low-income taxpayers, is zero. The difference is paid by the revenue agency as income maintenance.

**negative yield curve.**   Also called an inverted yield curve, a measure used to anticipate investor behavior in periods of high inflation. When interest rates are inflated, investors use short-term instruments to increase immediate returns on investments. The negative yield curve reflects the higher short-term interest rates compared with lower long-term rates.

**negligence.**   A failure to use ordinary care. Negligence creates civil tort liability if the negligent party owes a duty of care to the party injured by a negligent act. When a negligent act amounts to recklessness causing injury or death, the conduct may constitute a criminal offense.

**negotiable bill of lading.**   A bill of lading used to transfer the ownership of cargo from one holder to another. If the bill of lading is a bearer document, title to goods is transferred by the bill's delivery. If it is an order bill of lading, title is transferred by an endorsement and delivery of the bill.

**negotiable certificate of deposit (CD).**   A time-deposit instrument issued in the United States, primarily by the 25 largest U.S. banks, to institutional investors for minimum investments of $100,000 or more. Negotiable CDs can be sold before the maturity date and are actively traded in the secondary market, usually in lots of $1 million to $5 million. They are also issued in discount form. The average maturity of a negotiable CD is 3 to 12 months.

**negotiable instrument.**   Also know as negotiable paper, a negotiable instrument can be a bill of exchange, bill of lading, bond, check, draft, note, or warehouse receipt. An instrument is negotiable when title to the instrument, or to the merchandise underlying the instrument, can be transferred by an endorsement and/or delivery. To be negotiable, an instrument must contain a written unconditional promise to pay a holder or bearer a stated amount of money on demand or at a future date. See also *negotiation.*

**negotiable order of withdrawal (NOW) account.**   A checking account that pays interest to nonbusiness depositors, usually at the rate of a passbook savings account. In the United States, NOW accounts were authorized nationwide by the Monetary Control Act of 1980. Super NOW accounts pay interest at prevailing money-market rates, but unlike NOW accounts, they often require prior notice for withdrawals.

**negotiated underwriting.**   A sale of securities by means other than competitive bidding. Negotiated bids are the usual method of underwriting corporate bonds, common-stock offerings, and, where allowed by law, municipal revenue bonds. In a negotiated bid, the issuer and the lead underwriter fix the spread, or the difference between the initial public offering price and the purchase price paid by investors.

**negotiating bank.**   A bank that pays the holder of a negotiable instrument.

**negotiation.**   The transfer of title or a right to payment. A document can be negotiated by endorsement and/or by delivery. The negotiation entitles the recipient, i.e., the holder, to rights of ownership in drafts, notes, commercial paper, or documents of title. An instrument made payable to bearer or endorsed in blank (i.e., without a named transferee) is negotiated by delivery. An instrument made payable to order (i.e., to a named transferee) is known as an order instrument and negotiated by endorsement and delivery.

**neibu.**   In the People's Republic of China, unpublished government regulations.

**neoclassical economics.**    In Britain and the United States, economic theories deriving from the work of Alfred Marshall in the *Principles of Economics* (1890). Neoclassical economists describe the effects of profit seeking and product utility on economic output and consumption. Originally used only in the study of microeconomics, Marshall's theories are also influential in macroeconomic studies. See also *classical economics.*

**net assets.**    Working capital, or liquid assets, minus current liabilities. Compare *net worth.*

**net asset value (NAV).**    Also called tangible book value, the net worth of a company's securities. NAV is the book value of securities minus liabilities, including bond debt and preferred stock. The NAV of a mutual fund is cash, accrued earnings, and the value of portfolio securities divided by the number of outstanding shares. The result is the per-share value of a fund's assets.

**net avails.**    The balance available for advances against a financial instrument after it has been discounted and associated charges have been deducted.

**netback.**    A pricing term for commodities denoting the net free-on-board price when a product is offered on a cost, insurance, and freight basis. Netback is equal to the landed price less shipment costs.

**net book value (NBV).**    The value of an asset recorded at the end of an accounting period, usually quarterly. The asset's value is based on its purchase price or the last revaluation price less subsequent depreciation.

**net capacity.**    See *deadweight tonnage.*

**net charter.**    A vessel hire under which the charterer bears all costs incurred after the ship arrives at the first port of call.

**net-cost value.**    Also known as the net-cost method, a customs valuation method whereby royalties, sales promotion costs, allowable interest, and packing and shipping costs are deducted from the total cost of an import. The North American Free Trade Agreement permits the alternative use of transaction value, except in the case of certain products, such as automobiles. See also *valuation.*

**Netherlands Antilles.**    The self-governing territories of the Kingdom of the Netherlands, i.e.,

Curaçao, St. Maarten, Bonaire, St. Eustatius, and Saba. The territories are internally autonomous but are subordinate to the Netherlands in foreign policy and defense matters. Aruba, granted separate status in 1986, manages its own internal and external affairs.

**net income.**    Earnings after expenses and taxes.

**net landed weights.**    A seller's term of sale indicating that the selling price will be reduced by losses in value caused by product shrinkage or deterioration.

**net position.**    In commodity trading, the spread between an open long position and short position.

**net present value (NPV).**    The current economic worth of a project. The NPV is calculated by adding the revenues projected over the life of a proposed project and deducting the sum of its cost over the same period. Both revenue and cost projections are discounted to present value. NPV calculations are rarely precise because future interest rates cannot be accurately predicted.

**net price.**    The purchase price of goods or services less deductions for discounts.

**net profit.**    Before taxes, gross profit less expenses. After taxes, gross profit reduced by expenses and taxes.

**net realizable value (NRV).**    The profit anticipated from the sale of an asset. NRV is the selling price less the cost of presale repairs and expenses associated with completing the sale.

**net receipts.**    Gross earnings less costs and taxes.

**net register ton.**    The per-unit accounting value of a ship's cargo capacity. A net register ton, or net tonnage, is a gross ton's storage capacity minus space occupied by the engine, fuel containers, crew quarters, etc.

**net return.**    The profit earned on an investment less expenses. Net returns are calculated before or after deductions for capital-gains taxes.

**net tangible assets.**    See *tangible assets.*

**net tare weight.**    See *net weight.*

**net tonnage.**    See *net register ton.*

**net weight.**    Sometimes referred to as actual net weight, the weight of packaged goods less the weight of external wrappings in which goods are packaged.

**net worth.** The economic value of all assets, tangible and intangible, less liabilities. The accounting measures used to calculate net worth are imprecise, primarily because balance sheets reflect asset book value rather than actual market value. Goodwill, a valuable intangible asset, is also not reflected on balance sheets. Compare *net assets*.

**net yield.** 1. The gain or loss on a financial investment. 2. Earnings on debt instruments less the purchase price and time value to maturity.

**neutral margins.** See also *Common Agricultural Policy*.

**New Asian Industrial Development Plan.** See *ASEAN-Japan Development Fund*.

**New Community Instrument (NCI).** A European Community (EC) credit facility created in 1979 and managed by the European Investment Bank. The NCI finances energy, infrastructure, and other job-creating projects in the EC.

**New Delhi Declaration.** A 1980 proposal advanced by developing countries at the New Delhi conference sponsored by the United Nations Industrial Development Organization. The declaration proposed a North-South Global Fund for increased aid transfers from industrialized countries to developing countries. The New Delhi Declaration also reiterated the goal of the 1975 Lima Declaration that developing countries control 25 percent of the world's industrial production by the year 2000.

**new economic mechanism.** A management technique adopted in Eastern Europe in the early 1990s, especially in Hungary. Under the new mechanism, Western consulting firms are hired to operate state-owned industries, formerly managed by state planning agencies. The new economic mechanism attempts to improve domestic industrial productivity and efficiency.

**new entrant.** A firm entering an industry or an export market for the first time.

**new international economic order (NIEO).** A policy proclaimed in 1974 by the United Nations General Assembly. The sixth special session of the General Assembly adopted the Declaration and Programme of Action on the Establishment of a New International Economic Order, expressing the General Assembly's sense that income dispari-

ties between nations should be eliminated. NIEO principles were also incorporated into the United Nations Charter of Economic Rights and Duties of States in 1974. Implementing mechanisms were never adopted by the United Nations.

**new issue.** An initial public offering of securities on a stock exchange. See also *initial public offering*.

**New Jason clause.** In the United States, a clause incorporated into ocean bills of lading subject to the Carriage of Goods by Sea Act. Under a *New Jason* clause, the shipper shares in general average liability, including the cost of salvage, when the loss is not caused by a carrier's negligence. The clause is named after a ship, the subject of a U.S. Supreme Court decision in 1912.

**newly industrialized country (NIC).** A developing country in which industrial exports exceed exports of primary commodities. Also known as newly industrialized economies, the NICs of the 1980s were Hong Kong, Singapore, Taiwan, and South Korea, where annual growth rates approached or exceeded 5 percent. In the 1990s, Argentina, Brazil, Malaysia, Mexico, and Thailand are also classified as newly industrialized countries.

**newly industrialized economy (NIE).** See *newly industrialized country*.

**new time.** The description of a stock transaction completed during the last two dealing days of an account. New-time transactions are settled in the next account period. When the broker or market maker is not notified of an investor's intention to defer settlement, the investor is expected to settle during the current account.

**new-to-export company.** A business entity having limited or no prior export experience.

**New York Clearing House Association.** In the United States, a trade association that operates the Clearing House Interbank Payments System (CHIPS) and the New York Automated Clearing House. Founded in 1853, the association is owned by major U.S. money-center banks. CHIPS processes roughly 90 percent of all international payments in the United States.

**New York Convention.** See *United Nations Convention on the Recognition and Enforcement of Foreign Arbitral Awards*.

**New York dollars.** Funds drawn by a foreign correspondent bank against a U.S. bank's funds on deposit in New York. Interest computed according to the exact number of days in a month is known as New York interest, as distinguished from ordinary interest.

**New York Futures Exchange.** See *New York Stock Exchange, Inc.*

**New York Mercantile Exchange.** See *futures market.*

**New York Stock Exchange, Inc. (NYSE).** Also known as the Big Board, the oldest stock exchange in the United States, founded in 1792. The NYSE is a nonprofit corporation that lists securities of the largest U.S. companies, including those constituting the Dow Jones Industrial Average of 30 blue-chip industrial companies and the Standard and Poor's 500 Stock Index. The NYSE trades bank bonds, common and preferred stocks, corporate bonds, equity and index options, rights, warrants, and U.S. and foreign government bonds. The New York Stock Exchange Composite Index is the weighted average of all stocks traded on the exchange. Subindexes measure market values for financial, industrial, transportation, and utility stocks. The New York Futures Exchange, an NYSE subsidiary, opened in 1980. Prices are quoted in U.S. dollars and published in electronic and print formats. Orders are executed by brokers or through the electronic SuperDot System, which routes orders and notifies participants when transactions are completed. The Individual Investor Express Delivery Service, implemented in the late 1980s, processes individual investors' orders before institutional investors' orders are executed. The NYSE is a self-regulating organization subject to oversight by the Securities and Exchange Commission. NYSE brokers-dealers are known as assigned dealers or specialists.

**NGO.** The abbreviation for nongovernmental organization.

**ngultrum.** The currency of Bhutan.

**Nice Agreement concerning the International Classification of Goods and Services for the Purposes of Registration of Marks.** Also known as the Nice Agreement or the Geneva Act of the Nice Agreement, an accord adopted in 1957 to establish a global trademark classification system.

The Nice International Classification System consists of 34 product and 7 service classes for registering trademarks. The Nice System is administered by the World Intellectual Property Organization.

**niche market.** A segment of a consumer or business market, usually a maturing one. Entry costs increase as markets mature, and finding a niche in a speciality product or service line enables new entrants to obtain market share at relatively lower costs. Niche markets are typically found at the high end of a consumer market and among experienced users of a product or service.

**NIF.** The abbreviation for note issuance facility.

**Nihon Keizai Shimbun.** See *financial daily.*

**Nikkei.** See *Tokyo Stock Exchange.*

**Nikkeiren.** In Japan, the Federation of Employers' Associations, the employer bargaining unit for major Japanese companies.

**nil issue.** A notification by an importing country prohibiting imports of specified products.

**NIMEXE.** The statistical classification system of the European Economic Community (EEC) devised in 1966 and modified in 1969. The NIMEXE, used to classify products for the EEC's Common Customs Tariff, was supplanted by the Harmonized Commodity Description and Coding System in the late 1980s. It was based on the four-digit system of the Brussels Tariff Nomenclature, but it used two additional digits to permit further statistical subdivisions. EEC members were also allowed to develop additional subdivisions beyond those provided in NIMEXE. The NIMEXE system incorporated the Harmonized Coal and Steel Nomenclature for Foreign Trade in force since 1964.

**Nippon Kaiji Kyokai.** See *classification society.*

**NIT.** The abbreviation for negative income tax.

**NL.** The abbreviation for no liability.

**NNP.** The abbreviation for net national product.

**no-action letter.** In the United States, a letter issued by the Securities and Exchange Commission (SEC) reviewing the legality of a proposed venture, such as a merger and acquisition, involving shares of publicly held companies. No-action letters are issued when the SEC declines to take legal action if a proposed venture proceeds. The findings of no-action letters are limited to the factual case presented and do not bind the SEC on a different set of facts. Compare *business review procedure.*

**no arrival, no sale.**   A sales contract provision excusing a buyer from payment until goods have been received. The provision enables the buyer to avoid liability for cargo damaged or lost between the origin port and the destination port.

**no-load fund.**   A mutual fund without a sales commission, or load. Investors in a no-load fund may nevertheless be required to pay a 12b-1 fee, i.e., a distribution fee at the time the investment is made.

**Nomenclatura Arancelaria Uniforme Centro-americana II (NAUCA II).**   The uniform tariff classification system of *Mercado Común Centroamericano* (MCC), the Central American Common Market. MCC imposes a single ad valorem duty, called the *derechos arancelarios de importacion* (DAI), based on an import's cost, insurance, and freight value. Depending on the import, the DAI may range from 1 percent to 100 percent. There are no specific duties on weights and measures. The Uniform Central American Customs Code prescribes the information contained in bills of lading covering shipments to MCC.

**Nomenclatura Arancelaria y Derechos de Importación.**   See *Mercosur.*

**Nomenclatura Brasileira de Mercadoria.**   See *Mercosur.*

**nomenklatura.**   In the former Union of Soviet Socialist Republics, top-level communists and government bureaucrats.

**nominal capital.**   See *share capital.*

**nominal damages.**   See *damages.*

**nominal ledger.**   An accounting ledger containing accounts summarized by category, e.g., bad debts or investment accounts. Nominal ledgers reflect a company's earnings and liabilities but do not identify customers and suppliers. Compare *general ledger.*

**nominal price.**   1. The price or par value attributed to a security on the date of issue. Par value differs from market value, which is determined when a security is sold. The buyer of a security cannot be asked to pay more than its par value. 2. A price stated as consideration to legalize a transaction. A nominal price is a minimal price, often the equivalent of $1.

**nominal rate of protection.**   A customs tariff rate providing minimal protection to domestic producers, e.g., a low ad valorem duty. A nominal rate differs from the actual rate of protection, which cannot be determined unless the real cost of producing an import is known.

**nominal value.**   See *nominal price.*

**nominal yield.**   See *yield.*

**nominee.**   Outside the United States, a registered holder of securities purchased on behalf of a beneficial owner. A nominee is authorized to trade securities held in trust for another. In the United States, securities registered in the name of a party other than the beneficial owner are called street-name securities. See also *Transfer Accounting Lodgement for Investors and Stock Management.*

**nonacceptance.**   The refusal of a drawee to accept a bill of exchange presented for payment.

**nonassented stock.**   See *assented stock.*

**nonbank.**   A financial institution that provides credit and loans, such as consumer credit and financing. Although licensed to operate in a given jurisdiction, nonbanks are not bound by reserve regulations and, in most countries, are free of domestic capital-adequacy requirements.

**nonbank bank.**   A bank which is chartered to accept deposits or make loans but which may not do both at the same time. In the United States, the Competitive Equality Banking Act disallowed charters for nonbank banks after 1987. Previously chartered nonbank banks may continue existing operations, provided they comply with growth restrictions and limitations on marketing. The deposits of nonbank banks are insured by the Federal Deposit Insurance Corporation.

**noncallable.**   A straight bond or preferred stock that is not redeemable before maturity or a call date.   Most corporate indentures guarantee that bonds will not be called for 5 years after issue. In the United States, Treasury bonds are usually not called for a longer period.

**noncompetition agreement.**    In the United States, an agreement with an employer prohibiting an employee from competing for customers or clients. Depending on the circumstances, enforceable noncompetition agreements usually bind employees for a limited period after the business relationship is severed and within a limited geographical area. Subcontractors may also be bound by these agreements. Compare *restraint of trade.*

**noncompetitive bid.**    1. A bid for a contract to supply a product or service in response to an exclusive tender. 2. In securities dealing, an offer of government securities based on the weighted average price of competitive bids. For example, in auctions of U.S. Treasury securities, noncompetitive tenders allow small investors to offer bids from $10,000 to $1 million without competing with institutional investors, who have access to substantially larger capital resources.

**nonconference carrier.**    A carrier that is not a member of a shipping conference or does not have a sharing agreement with a conference on a given trade route.

**noncontract rate.**    A tariff rate granted to a shipper not covered by an exclusive patronage contract.

**noncontract shipper.**    A firm that has not executed an exclusive patronage contract.

**noncumulative letter of credit.**    A revolving letter of credit.

**nondumping certificate.**    A document issued in an exporting country verifying the home market price of goods. These certificates are used by sellers to avoid allegations of dumping in a foreign market.

**nondurables.**    See *consumer good.*

**nongovernmental organization (NGO).**    A private nonprofit organization dedicated to a public purpose. For example, the Red Cross and Care are NGOs, which fund their activities largely through private contributions.

**nonimportation.**    The status of goods sufficiently damaged or wasted to be of no commercial value. Goods without commercial value are not dutiable and are, therefore, not technically importable.

**nonmarketable securities.**    Government-issued securities that cannot be traded on a securities exchange. Most government savings bonds and certificates are nonmarketable securities and must be purchased from a government agency.

**nonmarket economy (NME).**    Also known as a centrally planned economy, a national economy in which resources and investment are managed by the government. Compare *market economy.*

**nonnegotiable instruments.**    See *negotiable instrument.*

**nonperforming asset.**    An uncollectible debt written off, in whole or in part, by the lender.

**nonprice competition.**    Methods of vying for market share involving factors other than price. Advertising, product quality, service, improved packaging, etc., enable producers of like products to compete on terms other than price.

**nonprivileged domestic status.**    See *status of merchandise.*

**nonprivileged foreign status.**    See *status of merchandise.*

**nonprofit organization.**    An organization that routinely provides a service for reasons other than profit. Nonprofits, such as libraries and museums, are subsidized by government or charitable contributions to furnish services in the public interest. These institutions receive government subsidies in the form of direct grants or tax-deductible contributions because they offer services at a lower cost than for-profit enterprises would provide.

**nonrecourse.**    See *without recourse.*

**nonrecourse loan.**    Also known as without-recourse financing, a loan secured by accounts receivables, agricultural crops, commodities, or other collateral. A borrower who defaults on a nonrecourse loan is not personally liable for the debt. The lender recovers by seizing and selling the collateral.

**nonresident.**    A person employed abroad who spends most of a calendar year outside the country of domicile. Tax policies vary in different countries, but nonresidents are generally not taxed in the country of domicile when they reside abroad for most of the year. Compare *resident.*

**non-self-governing territory.**    A territory administered by an external power and not under the protection of the International Trusteeship System operated by the United Nations Trusteeship Council. Non-self-governing territories are managed according to the Declaration on Decolonization. Administering powers furnish the United Nations with regular statistical data on the social and economic progress of non-self-governing territories. In 1986, roughly 19 territories were non-self-governing. As of 1992, British dependent territories include Anguilla, Bermuda, British Virgin Islands, Cayman Islands, Falkland Islands, Gibraltar, Montserrat, Pitcairn, St. Helena, and the Turks and Caicos Islands. The U.S. territories are American Samoa, Guam, and U.S. Virgin Islands. France administers New Caledonia, designated as a non-self-governing territory by the UN General Assembly in 1986. See also *overseas countries and territories*.

**nontariff barrier (NTB).**    Any impediment to trade other than a tariff barrier. Common NTBs include conditional import authorizations, domestic or local content rules, "buy-national" procurement policies, import licensing, internal network distribution systems, nonautomatic licenses, opaque product standards, performance requirements, undue certification requirements, unpublished regulations, and voluntary export restraints. Some NTBs are addressed by codes agreed to during the Tokyo Round of the General Agreement on Tariffs and Trade (GATT). Trade-related investment measures were the subject of GATT negotiations in the Uruguay Round. Reductions in NTBs are difficult to achieve because many are tied to local business customs or affect industries, such as telecommunications, closely associated with sovereignty and national security.

**nontaxable income.**    Income that cannot be taxed by law. For example, a certain portion of Social Security is nontaxable under current law in the United States. In the United Kingdom, the interest on certain National Savings bonds cannot be taxed.

**nonvessel-operating common carrier (NVOCC).** A private freight forwarder that consolidates and brokers cargo space for small shippers and exporters but that does not own or operate a carrier. In the United States, NVOCCs must file tariffs with the Federal Maritime Commission because they issue bills of lading.

**nonvoting shares.**    Common stock that does not entitle the owner to fixed dividends or the right to vote on company policy. Nonvoting shares are issued to raise capital without diluting the voting rights of existing shareholders.

**no-par value (NPV).**    Shares issued without a nominal price. No-par-value shares are legal in Canada and the United States, but they are illegal in the United Kingdom.

**norazi agent.**    A middleman engaged in illegal trade. A norazi agent traffics in contraband or diverts otherwise legal products to illegal channels.

**Nordic Council.**    A body formed in 1952 by Denmark, Finland, Norway, and Sweden to facilitate cooperation on economic and social matters. Partly under the council's direction, the countries removed border controls regulating internal travel and developed complementary social welfare systems.

**Nordisk Andelsforbund.**    The Scandinavian Cooperative Wholesale Society, a joint purchasing agency for business cooperatives in Denmark, Sweden, Norway, Finland, and Iceland. *Nordisk Andelsforbund* buys overseas provisions and raw materials for manufacturing plants. The society is headquartered in Copenhagen.

**normal price.**    The theoretical price for determining import duties using the Brussels definition of value. The normal price is an import's market price in the ordinary course of trade at the time and place of importation, including transportation and associated costs paid to bring the import to the entry port. Adjustments to the normal price are made for costs not included in the purchase price (e.g., patent royalties). In 1980, the transaction value adopted by the General Agreement on Tariffs and Trade in the Customs Valuation Code supplanted the normal price for most customs valuations.

**normal trade loss.**    The residue lost from bulk shipment during the ordinary course of carriage. Unless substantially greater than might be expected from routine carriage, normal trade losses are not covered by cargo insurance policies.

**normative economics.**    An approach to the study of economics that factors social or political policies into analysis. Proponents of the normative approach view economics as an impure science and recommend the use of government policies to test and verify theories. Compare *positive economics*.

**norm price.**    See *indicative price*.

**North African Common Market.**    See *Mahgreb Common Market*.

**North American currency unit (NACU).**    A currency unit proposed for a free trade area to be created by the North American Free Trade Agreement. The proposal has been advanced by academics, but it has not been adopted by the governments of Canada, Mexico, or the United States, the parties to the accord.

**North American Free Trade Agreement (NAFTA).**    A trilateral treaty concluded on August 12, 1992, creating a free trade area between Canada, Mexico, and the United States. NAFTA is envisioned as the precursor to a hemispheric trading area proposed by the Enterprise for the Americas Initiative. NAFTA gradually phases out barriers to most internal trade and investment, includes safeguards against import surges, imposes strict domestic content and origin rules, creates a mechanism for trilateral dispute settlement, and mandates enforcement of intellectual property rights. Although the treaty provides for the gradual harmonization of environmental, health, and labor standards, the United States proposed a series of supplemental agreements, including additional provisions covering import surges. NAFTA is scheduled for ratification by the countries' national legislatures in 1993. See also *North American currency unit*.

**North Atlantic Treaty Organization (NATO).**    A mutual defense organization established by the North Atlantic Treaty signed at Washington in 1949. NATO was created to protect the western half of Europe, following the division of Europe into American and Soviet spheres of influence after World War II. The Soviet counterpart of NATO, known as the Warsaw Pact, dissolved in 1990. The members of NATO are Belgium, Canada, Denmark, Germany, Greece, Iceland, Italy, Luxembourg, the Netherlands, Norway, Portugal, Turkey, Spain, the United Kingdom, and the United States. France, an original signatory,

withdrew from the alliance in the 1960s. NATO's headquarters are in Brussels. See also *Conference on Security and Cooperation in Europe*.

**Northern Corridor Transit Agreement (NCTA).**    A security treaty signed in 1985 by Burundi, Kenya, Rwanda, Tanzania, and Uganda, and joined by Zaire in 1987. The NCTA's purpose is to safeguard transportation links to the Kenyan port of Mombasa, and it removes some impediments to regional trade by modifying rigid border controls. The NCTA commits signatories to improve road and rail service, while also easing travel restrictions from landlocked countries to Mombasa on the Indian Ocean.

**North/South.**    A dichotomy used to describe relations between the industrialized countries of the Northern Hemisphere and the relatively poorer developing countries in the Southern Hemisphere. The contrast is used primarily to illustrate disparities in financial resources, industrial development, and technology. On the other hand, mutual cooperation between countries in the Southern Hemisphere is said to derive from South/South dialogue. Compare *East-West trade*.

**Northwest Atlantic Fisheries Organization (NAFO).**    A multilateral organization formed in 1979 to manage fisheries in the Northwest Atlantic Ocean. NAFO sets catch quotas, or total allowable catches, for commercial fishing on the high seas. Catch quotas are reviewed annually. All Atlantic countries are members of NAFO, including the European Community.

**nostro account.**    Literally, "our" account, or an account denominated in the local currency of the country where funds are held. Conversely, a vostro account ("your" account) holds foreign currency on hand. Nostro and vostro accounts are used to manage foreign exchange transactions.

**nota bene (NB).**    Latin: note well.

**notary public.**    An officer licensed by the government to administer oaths and authenticate legal documents, usually by affixing a signature and a seal. A notary verifies an attestor's signature on affidavits, on deeds, and on protest notices issued when a negotiable instrument is dishonored by a bank. In the United Kingdom, notaries are mainly solicitors.

**note.**   A written promise to pay a debt, i.e., a promissory note.

**note issuance facility (NIF).**   A revolving credit facility that permits a short-term borrower to issue Euronotes, i.e., promissory notes with maturities of less than 1 year. An NIF is managed by a single bank, which sells participations to a syndicate of underwriting banks. The syndicate establishes a standby line of credit or purchases unsold notes at specified dates. See also *revolving underwriting facility.*

**notice in lieu of distringas.**   See *stop notice.*

**notice of abandonment.**   See *abandonment.*

**notice of arrival.**   A notice required before some imports can be cleared through customs. For example, in the United States, a notice announcing the arrival of pesticides is forwarded to the U.S. Customs Service by the Office of Pesticides and Toxic Substances before pesticide imports are cleared for customs entry.

**notice of dishonor.**   A written notice signed by a notary public that a bill of exchange, check, or draft has been dishonored when presented for payment.

**notice of readiness.**   See *berth–no-berth.*

**noting.**   A procedure for collecting a dishonored bill of exchange. The bill is presented by the holder to a notary public on the business day after dishonor. Once the dishonor has been noted, the bill is again presented for payment. If the instrument is not accepted or paid within a prescribed period of time, the notary records the transaction in a register and on a notarial ticket attached to it. A protest can then be lodged against the drawer.

**notional valuation.**   The theoretical basis for accepting a normal price in customs valuation. The theory holds that import duties should be based on the price an import would bring under similar circumstances. The contrary view, called the positive concept of valuation, holds that customs value should be determined by an import's actual transaction costs. The positive valuation concept underlies transaction value adopted by the Customs Valuation Code. See also *General Agreement on Tariffs and Trade: Tokyo Round, Customs Valuation Code.*

**not negotiable.**   A phrase inscribed on the face of a bill of exchange to avert theft. The instrument is still negotiable, but a subsequent holder cannot obtain better title to it than adhered in the immediate prior holder.

**novation.**   A change in a contractual obligation, whereby new terms are substituted for existing ones. A novation requires the mutual assent of the parties to the original contract.

**NOW.**   The abbreviation for negotiable order of withdrawal.

**NPD.**   The abbreviation for new product development.

**NPV.**   The abbreviation for net present value and no-par value.

**NTB.**   The abbreviation for nontariff barrier.

**nudum pactum.**   Latin: nude contract, or a contract that is unenforceable for lack of consideration.

**numbered account.**   A bank account identified by number. Numbered accounts are havens for illegal funds because the name of the depositor is not disclosed.

**numeraire system.**   A method of measuring the value of goods or services in terms of money. In international business, a numeraire is the currency used to measure the financial worth of a transaction. It can be the Deutsche mark, the U.S. dollar, gold, or an artificial currency unit (ACU), such as the special drawing right. When the numeraire is an ACU, the standard of measurement is determined by a basket of currencies of weighted values. Each currency within a numeraire system is assigned a specific value, or central rate, and a margin of fluctuation in relation to the other basket currencies. Fluctuations exceeding the fixed margin, whether above or below the assigned value, trigger official government intervention to restore stability to the system.

**numeric.**   An electronic code composed exclusively of numbers. Compare *alphanumeric.*

**NV.**   The abbreviation for *Naamloze Venootschap.*

# O

**O.** The abbreviation for order.

**OA.** The abbreviation for on account.

**OAC.** The abbreviation for Office of Antiboycott Compliance.

**OAMPI.** The abbreviation for *Office Africain et Malgache de la Propriété Industrielle.*

**O&M.** The abbreviation for operations and maintenance and organization and methods.

**OAPEC.** The abbreviation for Organization of Arab Petroleum Exporting Countries.

**OAS.** The abbreviation for Organization of American States.

**OAU.** The abbreviation for Organization of African Unity.

**OBC.** The abbreviation for offshore banking center.

**OBL.** The abbreviation for Office of Business Liaison.

**obligor.** Also known as the obligator, a party obligated to pay a debt on demand or by a fixed date. The creditor is the obligee.

**OBO.** The abbreviation for oil/bulk ore combination vessel.

**OBR.** The abbreviation for *Overseas Business Report.*

**observer status.** Official recognition given by an international organization to guests invited to observe deliberations or negotiations. Observer status is reserved for representatives of governments or nongovernmental organizations. Observers are not participants at the table in negotiations.

**obsolescence.** The condition of an asset of limited use due to its depreciated value. An asset becomes obsolete because it is too old or because technology outpaces its capability. Planned or built-in obsolescence occurs when a product is made less durable than available technology necessitates. If obsolescence is built in, consumers buy replacements sooner than they might otherwise.

**OBU.** The abbreviation for offshore banking unit.

**O/C.** The abbreviation for open charter.

**OCC.** The abbreviation for Options Clearing Corporation.

**ocean bill of lading.** See *bill of lading.*

**ocean freight differential.** The sum of money paid by a government to transport official cargoes by domestic carriers, i.e., the difference between higher domestic and lower foreign freight costs.

**Ocean Shipping Act of 1978.** In the United States, a law that amended the Shipping Act of 1916. Also known as the Controlled Carrier Act, the amendment was enacted to prohibit predatory pricing by foreign subsidized carriers, particularly the merchant marine of the former Soviet Union. The act requires that freight rates be reasonable based on carrier cost and a profit margin. When true cost cannot be determined, the law provides that reasonable cost be constructed from freight charged by noncontrolled carriers on the same trade route.

**OCT.** The abbreviation for overseas countries and territories.

**O/D.** The abbreviation for on demand.

**ODA.** The abbreviation for official development assistance and Overseas Development Administration.

**odd lot.** See *round lot.*

**ODL.** The abbreviation for overdimensional load.

**ODS.** The abbreviation for operating differential subsidy.

**OEA.** The abbreviation for Office of Export Administration.

**OECD.** The abbreviation for Organisation for Economic Cooperation and Development.

**OECD Codes.** Formally known as the OECD Codes of Liberalization, advisory statements adopted in 1961 by the Organisation for Economic Cooperation and Development. The codes govern capital investment and trade in services between OECD countries, but do not contain enforcement mechanisms. The OECD codes are not applicable to non-OECD countries. See also *Capital Movements Code* and *national treatment.*

**OECD consensus rates.**   Also known as OECD consensus guidelines, interest rates for official loans established by the Organisation for Economic Cooperation and Development. The OECD rate is adjusted semiannually to reflect changes in global interest rates. For concessional lending, the OECD classifies developing countries as relatively rich, intermediate, and relatively poor. See also *commercial interest reference rates* and *crédit mixte.*

**OECF.**   The abbreviation for Overseas Economic Cooperation Fund.

**OEEC.**   The abbreviation for Organization for European Economic Cooperation.

**OEM.**   The abbreviation for original equipment manufacturer.

**OER.**   The abbreviation for official exchange rate.

**OFAC.**   The abbreviation for Office of Foreign Assets Control.

**off-charter.**   A vessel not under charter. When a charterer fails to abide by the terms of a charter party, the shipowner is free to pursue other charter business. Compare *off-hire clause.*

**offene Handelsgesellschaft (OHG).**   German: general partnership.

**offer.**   1. Also called the offered or asked price, the price asked by a seller. The bid price is the price offered by a buyer. The actual selling price is the difference between the asked price and the bid price. 2. In maritime transactions, a firm offer.

**offer by prospectus.**   See *initial public offering.*

**offer document.**   A notice to shareholders containing the details of a takeover bid. The notice specifies the per-share price and explains how the proposed takeover benefits shareholders.

**offer for sale.**   See *initial public offering.*

**offering circular.**   See *prospectus.*

**offer list.**   In international trade negotiations, a list of products not subject to negotiation *or* a list of products on which tariffs can be reduced or eliminated.

**off-hire clause.**   Also known as the breakdown clause, a charter party provision that excuses a

charterer from paying charter fees when a ship is retired for repairs. The repair period is called off-hire time.

**Office Africain et Malgache de la Propriété Industrielle (OAMPI).**   Also know as the African and Malagasy Intellectual Property Organization, an organization established to harmonize intellectual property rules for 12 African nations. The OAMPI uses a common system for patent and trademark registration. OAMPI should not be confused with OMPI, the *Office Marocain de la Propriété Industrielle*, the intellectual property agency of Morocco. The OAMPI is headquartered in Yaoundé, Cameroon.

**Office of Antiboycott.**   See *antiboycott regulations.*

**Office of Business Liaison.**   In the United States, an agency of the U.S. Department of Commerce that administers the Business Assistance Program and Business Outreach Program. The programs are designed to provide information on domestic government assistance and improve opportunities for domestic businesses.

**Office of Commercial Operations.**   In the United States, a U.S. Customs Service agency that contains the Office of Regulatory Audit, which monitors compliance with customs regulations. The agency also supervises the work of the customs attaché, who manages U.S. relations with the Customs Cooperation Council in Brussels.

**Office of the Comptroller of the Currency.**   See *comptroller of the currency.*

**Office of Consumer Affairs.**   See *U.S. Department of Commerce.*

**Office of Defense Trade Controls (DTC).**   In the United States, an agency of the U.S. Department of State with jurisdiction over most international trade in defense items. Exports of goods and services classified as defense articles are registered with DTC.

**Office of Enforcement.**   See *Offices of Enforcement and Inspection & Control.*

**Office of Export Control.**   See *Bureau of Export Administration.*

**Office of Export Licensing.**   See *Bureau of Export Administration.*

**Office of Export Trading Company Affairs.**   In the United States, the federal clearinghouse for export trading company information. An agency of the U.S. Department of Commerce, the office publishes *Export Yellow Pages* and issues export trade certificates of review.

**Office of Fair Trading.**    In the United Kingdom, the consumer protection agency. Created in 1973 under the director general of fair trading, the agency administers the Competition Act of 1980, the Consumer Credit Act of 1974, the Fair Trading Act of 1973, the Restrictive Trade Practices Act of 1976, and the Control of Misleading Advertisements Regulations of 1988.

**Office of Federal Procurement Policy.**    See *Office of Management and Budget.*

**Office of Foreign Assets Control.**    See *Foreign Assets Control Regulations.*

**Office of Hazardous Materials Transportation.** See *U.S. Department of Transportation.*

**Office of Inspection & Contorl.**    See *Offices of Enforcement and Inspection Control.*

**Office of Management and Budget (OMB).**    In the United States, an agency of the executive branch that advises the President on federal budget issues. The Office of Federal Procurement Policy, which determines federal purchasing policies, is a unit of the OMB.

**Office of Maritime Standards.**    See *U.S. Department of Commerce.*

**Office of Munitions Control.**    See *Munitions List.*

**Office of Regulations and Rulings.**    See *U.S. Customs Service.*

**Office of Regulatory Audit.**    In the United States, an agency of the U.S. Customs Service Office of Commercial Operations that conducts external customs audits to ensure compliance with U.S. customs laws. The agency audits U.S. firms active in international trade to determine the accuracy of representations in customs documents.

**Office of the U.S.Trade Representative (USTR).** In the United States, an executive agency responsible for negotiating international trade agreements. The office was created during the Kennedy Round of the General Agreement on Tariffs and Trade (GATT) Negotiations as the Office of the Special Trade Representative. It was authorized as an executive agency by the Trade Act of 1974 and reorganized by Executive Order 12188, effective January 2, 1980. Headed by the U.S. trade representative, the USTR's office negotiates agreements, pursues U.S. interests before the GATT and other international trade forums, and initiates complaints against unfair trade practices under Section 201 and Section 301 of the 1974 Trade Act.

**Office of Trade Finance.**    See *U.S. Department of Commerce.*

**Office of Trade Operation.**    See *U.S. Customs Service.*

**officer.**    A senior corporate official. In the United States, the highest-ranking corporate officer is the chairman of the board of directors. The chief executive officer (CEO) manages the daily affairs of a company. The CEO is often also a company's chairman of the board or president of the corporation. Compare *managing director.*

**Offices of Enforcement and Inspection & Control.**    In the United States, U.S. Customs Service offices that regulate trade at U.S. borders and international airports. The offices are responsible for customs inspections and investigations, subject to oversight by assistant regional commissioners for enforcement stationed at regional headquarters.

**official development assistance (ODA).** Financial and technical assistance provided by industrialized countries to developing countries. Most ODA is offered through national agencies and coordinated by the Development Assistance Committee (DAC) of the Organisation for Economic Cooperation and Development (OECD). The DAC was created in 1961 to implement the OECD Resolution on the Common Aid Effort. Multilateral ODA is available through, among others, the World Bank Group, United Nations specialized agencies, and regional development banks and special funds, such as the Organization of Petroleum Exporting Countries' Fund for International Development. National ODA agencies include the Australian Development Assistance Bureau, Belgian *Administration Générale pour la Coopération au Développement,* Canadian International Development Agency, French *Caisse Centrale de Coopération Économique,* German *Bundesministerium für Wirtschaftliche Zusammenarbeit,* Japan International Cooperation Agency, Netherlands Ministry of Development Cooperation, Norwegian Agency for International

Development, Sweden International Development Authority, United Kingdom Overseas Development Administration, and United States Agency for International Development.

**official exchange rate (OER/OR).** 1. In a floating-exchange-rate system, the rate set by government policy. When the official rate differs from the market rate, a government attempts to realign rates by buying or selling its currency in international currency markets. 2. In a dual-rate exchange system, the higher rate for local currency, reserved mainly for favored transactions, i.e., government procurements, industrial imports, etc. See also *secondary exchange market.*

**Official Gazette.** See *U.S. Patent and Trademark Office.*

**official list.** On a stock exchange, a list of securities traded on the primary securities market, also known as the main market. The official list is usually published daily with notice of transactions concluded during the business day. It also includes securities prices, new issues, dividend dates, etc. See also *listing requirements.*

**official rate.** See *official exchange rate.*

**official settlements balance.** See *balance of payments.*

**official value.** The dutiable value ascribed by a customs agency to a given import. Ad valorem duties are based on official value, which may differ from the import's invoice price.

**offset.** In futures and options dealing, closing an open position by buying an equal number of contracts for the same delivery month. By offsetting an existing contract, the dealer cancels the obligation to accept or deliver a commodity or instrument covered by the original contract.

**offset trade.** See *countertrade.*

**offshore banking center (OBC).** An international banking market approved for nonresident depositories and lending facilities. Offshore banking centers offer foreign branch banks, or offshore banking units, liberal regulatory and tax treatment, including favorable reserve requirements, and less stringent exchange controls. Invented in the 1970s, offshore banking centers are found in Asia, the Caribbean, Europe, and the Middle East. Prominent offshore centers are the Bahamas, Bahrain, the Cayman Islands, Hong Kong, Luxembourg, Panama, Singapore, and the United Arab Emirates. Compare *international banking center.*

**offshore banking unit (OBU).** A branch office established by a foreign bank in an offshore banking center to conduct business with nonresidents. OBUs specialize in Eurocurrency financing, do not accept domestic deposits, and are concentrated in countries with lenient licensing rules for offshore banking. For example, the Monetary Authority of Singapore rarely licenses full-service branches of nonresident commercial banks, but it has liberal licensing rules for OBUs dealing in Asian dollar markets. In the United States, international banking facilities, authorized by the Federal Reserve Board in 1981, enable domestic banks to perform the functions of OBUs without going offshore.

**offshore funds.** Funds on deposit in a country other than the domicile or resident country of the owner. Cash or negotiable instruments are deposited offshore to avoid taxes in the domicile or resident country or to benefit from higher interest rates See also *offshore banking unit.*

**OGIL.** The abbreviation for open general import license.

**OGL.** The abbreviation for open general license.

**OHG.** The abbreviation for *offene Handelgesellschaft.*

**OIC.** The abbreviation for Organization of the Islamic Conference.

**OIEC.** The abbreviation for Organization for International Economic Cooperation. See *Council for Mutual Economic Assistance.*

**OILPOL.** The acronym for International Convention for the Prevention of Pollution of the Sea by Oil.

**Oil Pollution Act (OPA) of 1990.** In the United States, a federal law that increased carrier liability for damage caused by oil spills and forced major changes in tanker design and equipment. The act defers to state laws regulating spills and spill cleanups, which are often stricter than federal policy. Prospective liability contemplated by the act exceeds the insurance coverage available to most carriers through commercial marine insurers. See also *protection & indemnity club.*

**OIMP.** The abbreviation for Office of International Major Projects. See *Major Projects Program*.

**oligopoly.** A market with few sellers and many buyers. Oligopolistic firms often agree to avoid price competition. In theory, the structure of an oligopolistic market guarantees excessive profits to noncompeting firms. In a global economy, however, other factors also influence prices, e.g., market size, the value of a national currency, the rate of tariff protection, etc. See also *antitrust laws*.

**OMB.** The abbreviation for Office of Management and Budget.

**OME.** See *original equipment manufacturer*.

**Omnibus Trade Act of 1988.** Known officially as the Omnibus Trade and Competitiveness Act, a law enacted in the United States to enhance domestic competitiveness and improve enforcement of U.S. trade laws. Title VII of the act establishes formal procedures for monitoring foreign import barriers, including a requirement that the U.S. trade representative (USTR) issue annual Foreign Trade Barriers Reports listing countries with broadly restrictive trade policies. The act also provides for domestic export enhancement and authorizes retaliation for violations of U.S. intellectual property laws, and it extended congressional fast-track procedures through June 1, 1993 and barred foreign takeovers of domestic companies in strategically vital sections. The most controversial provisions of the Omnibus Trade Act, contained in a section known as Super 301, expired in 1990. Super 301 required the USTR to develop a priority watch list naming countries presumed to distort U.S. trade, primarily by failing to negotiate reduced trade barriers in good faith. Negotiations leading to market openings were conducted for 1 year. Thereafter, the USTR was authorized to retaliate by imposing tariffs or other import restrictions and to suspend or withdraw from bilateral trade agreements. As of 1993, Super 301 had not been revived. See also *Exon-Florio Act of 1988, Section 301*, and *Special 301*.

**O/N.** The abbreviation for order/notify.

**on-board bill of lading.** Also called a shipped bill of lading, a description by a carrier of cargo loaded aboard the ship. An on-board bill is not released to the exporter until a ship has departed port.

**on consignment.** See *consignment*.

**on-deck bill of lading.** A bill of lading describing cargo stowed on the deck of the ship. On-deck bills cover cargo too bulky or dangerous to place in the hold of a ship. When sales are financed by letters of credit, the paying bank must agree in advance to accept an on-deck bill. Insurers usually limit coverage of cargo transported under on-deck bills.

**on-deck cargo.** See *on-deck bill of lading*.

**on demand.** A draft or bill of exchange that is payable when presented.

**O/O.** The abbreviation for order of.

**OO.** The abbreviation for oil/ore.

**OP.** The abbreviation for open policy.

**OPA.** The abbreviation for Oil Pollution Act.

**OPEC.** The abbreviation for Organization of Petroleum Exporting Countries.

**OPEC basket price.** See *Organization of Petroleum Exporting Countries*.

**OPEC Fund for International Development.** See *Organization of Petroleum Exporting Countries*.

**open account.** Any of a variety of credit methods for financing trade transactions. Under the usual arrangement, a seller carries a transaction account, typically for 30 to 90 days. Interest is not charged if the debt is settled within the agreed time. The purchase price may be discounted if the debt is paid before the due date.

**open charter.** See *charter*.

**open check.** In some banking jurisdictions, a check without restrictions on its negotiability when cashed at the bank that originally issued it to the maker. Compare *crossed check*.

**open contract.** An unliquidated futures contract. Futures contracts are liquidated when the underlying commodity or financial instrument is sold, bought, or delivered.

**open cover.** See *open insurance policy*.

**open door.** A country that imports products from other countries on equal terms, usually with low or zero import duties. A significant amount of an open-door country's income derives from international trade. The trade must be two-way, since a country that relies on exports but restricts imports is not an open door.

**open-end fund.**   See *mutual fund.*

**open-end trust.**   See *mutual fund.*

**open general license.**   See *general license.*

**open indent.**   See *indent.*

**opening bank.**   See *instructing bank.*

**opening prices.**   The morning bid and offer prices on a trading exchange. Opening prices may differ from the previous day's closing prices, depending on intervening events.

**open insurance policy.**   1. Also known as an open policy (OP), marine insurance covering more than one export shipment. The policyholder reports specific transactions weekly, monthly, or quarterly on a declaration form supplied by the insurer. Premiums are based on the information provided in the declaration forms. Exports not declared when shipped are covered if the insurance value of the policy is not exceeded. See also *bordereaux.* 2. A floating policy. Compare *special cargo policy.*

**open-market operations.**   In the United States, transactions in which the Federal Open Market Committee instructs the Open Market desk at the Federal Reserve Bank of New York to buy and sell U.S. government securities. Sales of securities remove money from circulation; conversely, purchases increase the supply of available money. Open-market operations, adjusting commercial bank reserves, are indicators of U.S. interest rate policy. See also *back door/front door.*

**open-market rates.**   Unregulated interest rates determined by supply and demand. Open-market rates are rates on banker's acceptances, Eurocurrency deposits, and negotiable certificates of deposit.

**open outcry.**   In commodity exchanges, an auction method whereby brokers in trading pits make verbal bids and offers supplemented by hand signals.

**open policy.**   See *open insurance policy.*

**open position.**   1. A dealer's position when holding uncovered or unhedged securities. See also *open contract.* 2. The status of an account when foreign currency is bought or sold. The account is open until an equivalent amount of the same currency is bought or sold.

**open-pricing agreement.**   See *oligopoly.*

**open rates.**   In ocean shipping, negotiable freight rates not set by a conference.

**open registry shipping.**   The policy of a government that permits foreign-owned ships to register under its nation's flag. See also *PANLIBHON.*

**open skies policy.**   A liberal cabotage policy in one nation granting relatively free access and landing rights to foreign-registered civil aircraft transiting its airspace. Open skies are not covered by the Agreement on Trade in Civil Aircraft adopted by the Tokyo Round of the General Agreements on Tariffs and Trade. Air cabotage remains one of the most difficult areas for liberalizing trade, primarily because civil aviation is a traditional government monopoly in most countries and is heavily regulated in others. For example, open skies have been the subject of continuing negotiations between Canada and the United States since a modest bilateral agreement was reached in 1966. On the other hand, the European Community (EC) has adopted a civil aviation regime removing most internal cabotage restrictions by 1993. New EC rules permit carriers to obtain regional licenses and operate along previously closed air routes.

**open trading system.**   An international trading system characterized by low import duties and transparent customs entry procedures.

**OPEP.**   The abbreviation for *Organisation des Pays Exportateurs de Pétrole.*

**operating costs.**   See *overhead costs.*

**operating differential subsidy (ODS).**   In the United States, a federal subsidy provided to carriers operating U.S.-built ships along subsidized trade routes also plied by foreign carriers and deemed essential to domestic commerce. The subsidy reduces the net operating costs to U.S. carriers, enabling them to compete with lower-cost foreign shipping lines. Authorized by Title VI of the Merchant Marine Act of 1936, the subsidies are administered by the Maritime Administration. Compare *construction differential subsidy.*

**operational headquarters (OHQ).**   In Singapore, a name given to foreign companies eligible for special tax incentives. An OHQ must be incorporated in Singapore by a foreign company to provide management services to its local branches and subsidiaries. OHQ regulations exclude letterbox businesses, or companies without a substantial presence.

**operations and maintenance (O&M).**   The broad characterization of a relatively new business sector, which includes sales and management consulting services. O&M often involves the export of services in connection with maintaining high-technology equipment and managing foreign business or government operations.

**operative instrument.**   A telexed instruction from an importer's bank to pay an exporter. If the telex describes credit terms in detail, it constitutes an electronic letter of credit. When the telex notes "mail confirmation to follow" (or a similar limitation), the cable is an advisement rather than a firm statement of credit terms. However, to qualify as a letter of credit, a telex need not state that it is a substitute for a mailed letter of credit.

**OPIC.**   The abbreviation for Overseas Private Investment Corporation.

**opportunity cost.**   Profit lost when an asset is not put to profitable use. For example, investing in blue-chip stocks rather than junk bonds may yield lower short-term profits. The opportunity cost is the difference between earnings from a blue-chip security and potential earnings from the junk bond. Opportunity costs figure in investment decisions along with other factors, i.e., in this case, the junk bond risk factor.

**optimization.**   In business, maximizing efficiency and productivity, thereby increasing profits.

**optimum cube.**   A shipping container or trailer whose interior is designed for maximum cargo stowage.

**optimum tariff.**   The most favorable rate of duty available. A duty rate is favorable when it improves a country's terms of trade; i.e., the country pays a lower duty on exports than it remits for imports. For an exporter, an optimum rate is obtained when an export is imported on concessional terms or reclassified to qualify for a lower rate.

**option.**   A contract giving a purchaser the right to buy or sell assets on a certain date at an exercise or strike price. The purchase price of the option itself is called a premium or option money. The premium is fixed by various factors, including the price of the underlying asset, its maturity, etc. Option contracts are traded on securities and commodity exchanges and purchased as hedges in commodity, currency, and futures transactions. An option does not create a contract obligation. Most are never exercised; rather, they are sold before the expiration date. There are several types of option contracts:

*American option.*   A holder is permitted to exercise the option at any time up to the expiration date.

*call option.*   A holder is entitled to buy a specified quantity at a stated price. If the commodity's market value is lower than the exercise price, the holder is said to be out of the money; if it is higher, the holder is in the money.

*call-of-more option.*   A holder is entitled to buy double the quantity specified in the original call option.

*European option.*   A holder is permitted to exercise the option only on the expiration date.

*futures option.*   A holder is entitled to purchase a stipulated quantity of a commodity for a fixed price at a specified time in the future.

*naked option.*   A holder receives an option from a party who does not own the underlying asset. Also called uncovered options, naked options carry high risks for option writers because the asset's acquisition price may not rise or fall as expected. The option writer's risk is limited to the life of the option.

*put option.*   A holder is permitted to sell a specified quantity at a stated price. If the commodity's market value is higher than the strike price, the holder is out of the money; if it is lower, the holder is in the money.

*put-of-more option.*   A holder is entitled to sell double the quantity specified in the original put option.

*strap (option).*   A holder has two call options and one put option with the same exercise date and strike price.

*strip (option).*  A holder has one call option and two put options with the same exercise date and strike price.

*swaption.*  A holder is entitled to a fixed interest rate at a future date. The seller of an interest rate swap option bears the risk of interest rate changes in exchange for the premium paid by the purchaser.

*traditional option.*  A holder cannot resell the option, which expires if not exercised.

*uncovered option.*  See *naked option* above.

**Options Clearing Corporation (OCC).**  In the United States, a corporation established to clear transactions, eliminate credit risks to option holders by guaranteeing option contracts, and issue standardized options contracts. The OCC publishes the *Directory of Exchange Listed Options*, listing options traded on the basis of stocks, and the *Characteristics and Risks of Standardized Options*. The corporation is located in Chicago. Compare *International Options Clearing Corporation.*

**Optionsschein.**  German: warrant.

**OR.**  The abbreviation for official rate and owner's risk.

**ORB.**  The abbreviation for owner's risk of breakage.

**ORC.**  The abbreviation for owner's risk of chaffing.

**ORD.**  The abbreviation for owner's risk of damage.

**order.**  1. A check or draft ordering payment to a third party. See also *payable to order.* 2. A customer's instructions to a broker or dealer. Types of customer orders are:

*good-for-one-day-order.*  The order is automatically canceled at the end of the trading day.

*good-until-canceled order.*  The broker attempts to fill the order according to the customer's original instructions until the order is canceled.

*limit order.*  The order cannot be executed unless the market price is at or better than the price noted in the order.

*market order.*  The order must be executed within a specific month.

*open order.*  The order can be executed or canceled for an indefinite time period.

*stop order.*  The order must be executed at a stated price, which may be above or below the market price when the order was given. See also *stop order.*

**ordering party.**  See *instructing bank.*

**orderly marketing agreement (OMA).**  A bilateral restraint agreement. In the United States, OMAs are authorized by the Trade Act of 1974. The act permits the President to negotiate an OMA of 5 years' duration. It can be reduced after 3 years unless the national interest requires the contrary, in which event the agreement can be extended for 3 additional years.

**OR. DET.**  The abbreviation for owner's risk of deterioration.

**ordinary course of trade.**  Sales made through customary channels of distribution. Ordinary course of trade is applied in customs valuation, mainly under the Brussels definition of value. The dutiable value of an import is the normal price it would command if sold in the ordinary course of trade. For example, if a product is normally sold to an end user, a duty is placed on the manufacturer's selling price. Countries belonging to the Customs Valuation Code negotiated during the Tokyo Round of the General Agreement on Tariffs and Trade largely avoid valuations based on the ordinary course of trade by applying transaction value.

**ordinary interest.**  An interest rate based on a 360-day year rather than a 365-day year, as compared with interest priced in New York dollars.

**ordinary share.**  The international term for common stock.

**ordre public.**  In international law, public policy. The term is used frequently in international agreements.

**ORF.**  The abbreviation for owner's risk of fire / freezing.

**org.**  The abbreviation for organization.

**Organisation Commune Africaine et Mauricienne (OCAM).** Also known as the African and Mauritian Common Organization, a Francophone subgroup of the Organization for African Unity. Since adopting its charter at Tananarive, Madagascar, in 1966, OCAM has undergone several transformations, emphasizing economic development on some occasions and political reform on others. In its present form, OCAM is a free trade area organized to reduce internal trade and investment barriers. OCAM members are Benin, Burkina Faso, Central African Republic, Côte d'Ivoire, Gabon, Mauritius, Niger, Rwanda, Senegal, and Togo. Madagascar and Cameroon have withdrawn. OCAM's headquarters are in Bangui, Central African Republic.

**Organisation for Economic Cooperation and Development (OECD).** An organization of 24 industrialized countries formed to coordinate multilateral economic and social polices. Originally established in 1948 as the Organization for European Economic Cooperation, the OECD was formed in 1961. Never given supranational authority, the organization is primarily a data-gathering and advisory body. It publishes the biannual *OECD Economic Outlook* and periodic *OECD Economic Surveys*, providing economic performance data on member countries, and issues OECD consensus rates for official lending. The OECD has also enacted the OECD Codes, established rules for official development assistance and export credit insurance, and developed the concept of national treatment in international trade and investment. In 1957, the organization created the Nuclear Energy Agency to promote peaceful and safe uses of nuclear energy. OECD operations are overseen by a secretariat headquartered in Paris.

**Organisation Interafricaine du Café (OICAFE).** Also known as the Inter-African Coffee Organization, a group of African coffee-producing countries organized in 1960. OICAFE coordinates domestic commodity policies to improve production and maintain price stability. The organization has 22 members. OICAFE has headquarters in Abidjan, Côte d'Ivoire.

**Organización de Estados Centroamericanos (OECA).** Also known as the Organization of Central American States, a regional organization created at Panama City in 1962. Originally formed to promote political unity, OECA's recent efforts to lead the region's economic integration have been frustrated by the growing authority of *Mercado Común Centroamericano*. OECA members are Costa Rica, El Salvador, Guatemala, Honduras, and Nicaragua. Its headquarters are in San Salvador.

**Organization for European Economic Cooperation (OEEC).** The organization established in 1948 to implement the Marshall Plan. In 1950, the OEEC created the European Payments Union, the first quasi-integrated monetary facility for European states. Although the organization was originally intended as the precursor to a European federal union, the OEEC was quickly supplanted by the Organisation for Economic Cooperation and Development (OECD). Non-European states are also OECD members.

**Organization of the Islamic Conference (OIC).** A multilateral organization established to promote cooperation between Moslem countries. Primarily a political association, OIC was created at Jidda, Saudi Arabia, in 1971. It is composed of all members of the Arab League plus non-Arab African and Asian countries with substantial Moslem populations. The Palestine Liberation Organization is an OIC member. See also *Islamic Development Bank*.

**Organization of African Unity (OAU).** A continental organization established at Addis Ababa, Ethiopia, in 1963. The OAU was originally formed to encourage political cooperation among African states. More recently, it has worked for trade reform and debt relief for developing countries. All African countries are OAU members, except South Africa.

**Organization of American States (OAS).** A mutual defense association and economic association, which originated with the International Union of American Republics in 1890. The Inter-American Treaty of Reciprocal Assistance, known as the Rio Treaty or Rio Pact, was signed at Rio de Janeiro in 1947. The OAS Charter was signed at Bogotá in 1948. All countries in the Americas, except Canada, were founding OAS members;

Cuba was expelled in 1962. Canada became an official observer in 1972 and a member in 1989. The original administrative agency of the OAS, the Pan-American Union, was replaced in 1970 with the General Secretariat. The Inter-American Development Bank is the OAS multilateral development bank. The OAS has headquarters in Washington, D.C.

**Organization of Arab Petroleum Exporting Countries (OAPEC).**   A regional subgroup of the Organization of Petroleum Exporting Countries (OPEC). Established in 1968, OAPEC often votes as a bloc in OPEC and played a major role in wresting control of the global petroleum industry from Western oil companies. Since the 1970s, OAPEC has largely controlled the international market price of petroleum products. OAPEC members are Algeria, Bahrain, Egypt, Iraq, Libya, Kuwait, Qatar, Syria, Tunisia, Saudi Arabia, and the United Arab Emirates. Its headquarters are in Kuwait City.

**Organization of Central American States.**   See *Organización de Estados Centroamericanos.*

**Organization for International Economic Cooperation.**   See *Council for Mutual Economic Assistance.*

**Organization of Petroleum Exporting Countries (OPEC).**   Also known as the *Organisation des Pays Exportateurs de Pétrole*, a commodity cartel conceived at Baghdad in 1960 to coordinate the export policies of petroleum-producing countries. OPEC was officially organized at Caracas, Venezuela, in 1961. In 1973, OPEC launched an oil embargo against the United States (for its support of Israel during the 1973 Arab-Israeli war) and the Netherlands, effectively ending the flow of oil through Rotterdam, the European Common Market's largest refinery and transshipment port. The embargo established OPEC as the world's most successful commodity cartel. After the 1973 embargo, oil supplies were relatively plentiful, but the structure of the international petroleum industry was also changed. By some estimates, global oil prices rose tenfold between 1973 and 1990. The international market price for petroleum products is determined primarily by the OPEC basket price, a composite price for crude petroleum originating in seven member countries of the Organization of Arab Petroleum Exporting Countries. In 1976, OPEC established the OPEC Fund for International Development for concessional lending to non-oil-producing developing countries to compensate for petroleum purchases. OPEC members are Algeria, Gabon, Indonesia, Iran, Iraq, Kuwait, Libya, Nigeria, Qatar, Saudi Arabia, United Arab Emirates, and Venezuela. Ecuador withdrew in 1992. OPEC's headquarters are in Vienna.

**orientation price.**   In the European Community, the target price for cattle and calves under the Common Agricultural Policy. The orientation price is also known as the guide price.

**orig.**   The abbreviation for original.

**original bill of exchange.**   See *bill of exchange.*

**original equipment manufacturer (OEM).**   A firm that produces inputs or peripherals by order or under subcontract for a larger manufacturing company. Known as original manufacturer's equipment, inputs or peripherals are sold under the brand name of the company ordering the product. See also *bundling.*

**original manufacturer's equipment.**   See *original equipment manufacturer.*

**original margin.**   In commodity exchanges, an initial deposit placed with an exchange by a trader to guarantee the fulfillment of contract obligations. See also *margin.*

**original maturity.**   In bond issues, the difference between the issue date and the maturity date. A bond's current maturity is the difference between the present date and the maturity date.

**origination fee.**   A lender's charge for reviewing a loan application and credit report.

**ORL.**   The abbreviation for owner's risk of leakage.

**ORS.**   The abbreviation for owner's risk of shifting.

**ORM.**   The abbreviation for other restricted material.

**ORW.**   The abbreviation for owner's risk of water damage.

**O/S.**   The abbreviation for out of stock.

**OS&D.**   The abbreviation for over, short, and damaged.

**Österreichische Kontrollbank AG.**   See *export credit insurance.*

**OT.**   The abbreviation for on truck.

**OTC market.**   The abbreviation for over-the-counter market.

**OTE.**   The abbreviation for on-target earnings.

**OTEXA.**   The abbreviation for Office of Textile and Apparel. See *U.S. Department of Commerce.*

**other holders.**   See *prescribed holders.*

**other-than-prime-quality goods.**   See *less-than-prime-quality goods.*

**ouguiya.**   The currency of Mauritania.

**out of the money.**   In options trading, an option for which the strike price is lower than the underlying futures price. Compare *at the money* and *in the money.*

**output tax.**   See *value-added tax.*

**outside broker.**   A stockbroker who is not a member of an established stock exchange.

**outside director.**   A director who is not employed by an organization, but serves on its board of directors.

**outsider.**   A nonconference carrier, i.e., one not a member of a shipping conference.

**outsourcing.**   The process of letting work out to independent contractors or consultants. In some contemporary industry downsizings, former workers are rehired as contractors to perform the same tasks they performed as employees, but the company no longer pays insurance and pension benefits. In other instances, work is let out to firms established by former employers or others at negotiated rates. See also *piece rate.*

**out-turn report.**   A document issued by a carrier following the discharge of cargo at the destination port. Out-turn reports are used by carriers to defend against claims of negligent cargo handling.

**outward processing.**   Exporting components from one country for assembly or further processing in another. When outward processing is com-pleted in a developing country, finished products are often re-imported free of duty under preferential trade programs. Dutiable products, later reexported, are usually eligible for duty drawback. See also *foreign processing.*

**outworking payments.**   See *piece rate.*

**overbought.**   1. The description of a stock market that rapidly increases in value because of the number of shares purchased in a given period. Overbought markets often fall as rapidly as they rise. 2. A brokerage account where the customer's purchases exceed margin funds on deposit. When the market falls, an account becomes overbought if the value of the commodity falls below the unpaid loan balance.

**overcapitalization.**   A company with more debt or invested capital than its business justifies. An overcapitalized company usually pays off long-term debt to reduce interest charges or buys back equity to avoid excessive dividend payments.

**overcarried cargo.**   Cargo transported to a discharge port other than the destination port.

**overdraft.**   The amount by which a check exceeds funds available in a bank account. Banks normally extend overdraft protection, or an automatic loan, to cover checks of customers in good standing. The amount and conditions of overdraft protection vary, depending on the customer and a bank's lending policies.

**overentry certificate.**   A document issued by a customs agency entitling the importer to reclaim excess duties paid. A postentry claim is issued when too little duty has been paid.

**overhead costs.**   Also called indirect costs and operating costs, the expenses of producing goods or services not paid for labor and materials. Fixed overhead does not change (e.g., office rent, most insurance, equipment maintenance, etc.). Variable overhead changes with the demands of production (e.g., telephone expenses, fuel, etc.).

**overinvestment.**   An investment made in anticipation of increased future demand. Investments based on optimistic assumptions can leave a producer with excess capacity, a critical shortage of capital, or both.

**overlap.**  In a charter party, the period during which a charterer breaches the agreement by not returning the ship to its owner.

**Overseas Business Reports (OBRs).**  In the United States, foreign country economic data published by the International Trade Administration. OBRs contain background analysis, commercial profiles, and overviews of U.S. trade prospects in a given country.

**overseas company.**  A foreign parent of a local branch or subsidiary. Overseas companies are usually required to provide incorporation information, annual balance sheets, and profit and loss accounts in countries where branches and subsidiaries operate.

**overseas countries and territories (OCTs).** Former colonies of European Community (EC) countries. The association between the EC and the OCTs was formalized by the Treaty of Rome, but relations between OCTs and the EC are complex. For example, known collectively as *domaines et territoires d'outre-mer*, French *territoires d'outre-mer* are autonomous, while *collectivités territoriales* are dependencies. Other OCTs include British dependent territories, the Netherlands Antilles, and Greenland, an autonomous region of Denmark. See also *non-self-governing territory.*

**Overseas Development Administration.**  See *official development assistance.*

**Overseas Economic Cooperation Fund (OECF).** In Japan, an agency that provides concessional loans, development project grants, and equity investments for foreign enterprises. OECF usually procures from recipient countries, although some independent procurement agencies, including the United Nations Development Programme, are authorized to manage untied aid. OECF is based in Tokyo.

**overseas-income tax.**  See *double taxation.*

**overseas investment.**  See *foreign direct investment.*

**Overseas Private Investment Corporation (OPIC).**  In the United States, a corporation created by the Foreign Assistance Act of 1969 to finance and insure U.S. overseas investment. In 1979, OPIC became a unit of the U.S. International Development Cooperation Agency. A for-profit corporation, OPIC does not receive federal funds, although its insurance and guarantee commitments are backed by the full faith and credit of the U.S. government. The corporation provides medium- to long-term direct loans and guarantees for overseas investments in roughly 120 developing countries. It also manages a capital investment program, which buys stock or convertible debentures in eligible Caribbean, Eastern European, Latin American, and sub-Saharan African companies. OPIC insurance programs cover country risks, principally currency and political risks. OPIC also offers a number of private-investor matchmaking and advisory services, including investment missions to sub-Saharan Africa. Compare *Multilateral Investment Guarantee Agency.*

**over, short, and damaged (OS&D).**  Descriptions used by a carrier's port agent to report the condition of discharged cargo. Cargo is over or short when an inspection conflicts with quantities noted on the shipping manifest. Damaged cargo arrives in poor condition.

**overside delivery clause.**  Also known as a tackle clause, a charter provision that authorizes the transfer of cargo to a lighter. When cargo is moved to a lighter approved by the buyer, the insurance risk passes from the shipper.

**oversold.**  Also known as overheated, a market rapidly decreasing in value because of increased sales volumes. In cyclical fashion, oversold markets rise and increase in value. Compare *overbought.*

**overspill.**  Taxes paid by a foreign firm that are subject to rebate or reduction in the domicile country. Overspills are reduced by tax credits or exemptions available under double-taxation treaties.

**oversubscribed issue.**  A securities issue in which the number of applications exceeds the available shares. Shares of oversubscribed issues are allotted by the issuer. When an issue is undersubscribed, the underwriter usually buys the excess shares.

**over-the-counter (OTC) market.**  A market for securities not subject to a listing agreement. The OTC market is also called the third market and the unlisted securities market. OTC prices are fixed by negotiations between brokers rather than by floor bidding. Asset-backed securities, corporate bonds, and some government securities are traded in the over-the-counter market. In the United States, the OTC market, known as the NASDAQ, is regulated by the National Association of Securities Dealers. OTC stock prices are published in financial dailies and in weekly publications known as *Pink Sheets*. Margin requirements for the U.S. OTC market are governed by Federal Reserve Regulation T.

**overtonnaged.** The description of a trade route plied by more ships than the volume of cargo justifies.

**own brand.** See *private brand*.

**owner's account.** Any item identified in a charter agreement as payable by the vessel's owner.

**owner's broker.** An agent who negotiates a vessel charter on behalf of its owner.

**owner's charter party.** A charter agreement with terms advantageous to the vessel's owner.

# P

**p.a.** The abbreviation for per annum.

**PA.** The abbreviation for particular average and personal account.

**pa'anga.** The currency of the Tonga Islands.

**Pacific Economic Cooperation Council (PECC).** Known previously as the Pacific Economic Cooperation Conference, a regional association created at Canberra, Australia, in 1980 to pursue mutual trade interests. PECC members are the Association of Southeast Asian Nations countries, Argentina, Australia, Canada, Commonwealth of Independent States, Hong Kong, Japan, Mexico, New Zealand, Pacific Island Nations, People's Republic of China, Peru, South Korea, Taiwan, and the United States. Colombia is an associate member. PECC's secretariat is located in Singapore.

**package.** A unit of cargo wrapped or otherwise encased in exterior packing. See also *Carriage of Goods by Sea Act of 1936.*

**packing list.** An inventory of items to be shipped.

**paid-in capital.** See paid-up capital.

**paid-up capital.** Also called fully paid capital, the total amount of money invested by shareholders in a company's equity. Paid-in capital is the difference between the par value and market value of outstanding common stock. Uncalled capital is the amount by which capital authorized by shareholders exceeds paid-up capital. Callable capital is the amount of capital not paid up, which can be called for payment by a company's board of directors. See also *share capital.*

**paid-up policy.** See *surrender value.*

**paid-up value.** Equity in a company for which the full par value has been paid.

**paipu.** Japanese: entree, i.e., access to people of influence.

**PAL.** The acronym for Athens Convention Relating to the Carriage of Passengers and Their Luggage by Sea.

**pallet.** A wooden or metal frame on which cartons are stacked for lifting by pallet trucks or forklifts. Ocean carriers provide discounts for pallet shipments. The pallet allowance is based on a cargo's total cubic measurement less the cubic measurement of a standard pallet. Pallet dimensions are noted on bills of lading.

**Panama Canal Commission.** See *Panama Canal Zone.*

**Panama Canal Zone (CZ).** A canal linking Central America and South America. The canal was started by a French company in 1883, but construction was taken over by the United States under the 1903 Hay–Bunau-Varilla Treaty. In exchange, the United States received a perpetual lease covering roughly 370 square miles, and extending 5 miles on either side of the Panama Canal, but excluding Colón and Panama City. The canal was completed in 1915. Under the 1977 Canal Treaty between Panama and the United States, first proposed by the United States in 1964, the Canal Zone reverts to Panama on December 31, 1999. The zone is administered by the Panama Canal Commission, which supervises its operations and sets rates for ships transiting the canal.

**Panama in Transit.** The marking for goods transshipped through the Panama Canal Zone.

**Pan-American Copyright Convention.** Also known as the Buenos Aires Convention, an international accord protecting copyrights adopted at Buenos Aires in 1910. The convention is adhered to principally in Latin America, but the United States is also a member. The agreement requires national treatment of copyrights recognized in signatory states when the protected material contains a "statement" reserving the property right.

**Pan-American Union.** See *Organization of American States.*

**P&I.** The abbreviation for protection and indemnity club.

**PANLIBHON.** Panama, Liberia, and Honduras, also known as flag-of-convenience countries. See *effective United States control.*

**paper.** See *short-term paper.*

**paper profits/losses.** The difference between the market price of a financial asset and its purchase price. A gain or loss is realized when the asset is sold. If capital is invested in futures or options contracts, gains or losses are realized when the contracts are sold or traded.

**paper rate.**    A rate that is published in a carrier's freight tariff but that is rarely used. Paper rates usually apply to stops at ports where cargo is seldom delivered.

**parallel financing.**    A four-party loan made to a multinational parent and its foreign subsidiary. The parent uses its share of the loan to secure financing for the subsidiary. Although similar to back-to-back loans, parallel financing leaves a lender without recourse against the parent if the subsidiary defaults.

**parallel market.**    See *underground economy.*

**parallel trade.**    Also known as parallel exporting and importing, international trading outside normal channels of distribution. Parallel trading occurs when an authorized distributor services products sold by competing distributors. For example, a competing supplier obtains access to the product through a third-country supplier and undercuts the authorized distributor by selling to discount stores. The authorized distributor is often forced to service the discounted products to retain the exclusive distribution contract. In most instances, parallel trading is not illegal.

**parastatal.**    A quasi-official company, such as a public utility or nationalized industry, in which a government owns 50 percent or more of the equity.

**parcel post receipt.**    A document signed by a postal authority attesting to the receipt of a parcel for onward shipment.

**parcel receipt.**    A small package transported by an ocean carrier at a reduced rate. A parcel receipt is issued in lieu of a bill of lading. The freight rate and conditions of carriage for parcel receipts are published in the carrier's freight tariff.

**parcel tanker.**    A specially constructed bulk carrier equipped with multiple tanks for transporting liquid cargoes.

**parent company.**    A company that owns branches or subsidiaries, often in one or more countries. See also *corporation.*

**Pareto optimum.**    A concept developed by Vilfredo Pareto, a twentieth-century economist, to analyze economic efficiency. Goods and services are said to be Pareto optimal, i.e., allocated or distributed most efficiently, when the existing system does not harm the interests of one individual and an alternative system would not improve the lot of any other. Thus, equilibrium between economic forces is Pareto efficient. Several important economic theories derive from complementary views of equilibria. For example, Say's law recognizes a natural equilibrium between supply and demand, and Walras's law finds a similar balance between the values of goods offered for sale and those purchased.

**par exchange rate.**    See *par of exchange.*

**par grade.**    See *basis grade.*

**pari passu.**    Latin: with equal ranking. 1. In lending, a debtor gives a lender a priority right to collateral, thereby denying a subsequent creditor rights superior to those of the original lender. 2. In securities, shares in a new issue with the same dividend and liquidation rights as existing shares.

**Paris Charter.**    Officially, the Paris Charter for a New Europe, a multilateral agreement between members of the Conference on Security and Cooperation in Europe (CSCE) following the fall of the Warsaw Pact. The charter commits CSCE members to seek nonmilitary solutions to conflicts and the restoration of human rights in Europe. Although the agreement was signed at Paris in 1990, CSCE members were unable to bring an early conclusion to the war between the former republics of Yugoslavia that erupted 2 years later.

**Paris Club.**    An informal association of Group of Ten creditor governments that establishes rules for rescheduling official debts of indebted countries. The Paris Club was organized in 1956 to renegotiate Argentina's official debt. It meets regularly with representatives of indebted countries and conducted most sovereign renegotiations in the 1980s. Recent reschedulings reflect the Toronto Terms agreed to at the Toronto Group of Seven summit in 1988, although some countries are granted longer repayment periods under the Venice Terms. In the 1980s, African countries were the major beneficiaries of Paris Club reschedulings. Commercial debts are renegotiated by the London Club.

**Paris Convention for the Protection of Industrial Property.** Also known as the Paris Union Convention, an international agreement reached at Paris in 1883 covering patents for industrial designs, inventions, and utility models, as well as trademarks and trade names. The convention was revised at Stockholm in 1967. The agreement accords national treatment to patents and trademarks registered in signatory countries and adopts the first-to-file principle. The expiration or revocation of a patent in one country does not affect its validity in another country. The Paris Convention also does not mandate reciprocal treatment of foreign patents or harmony between the laws of signatory countries. A patent challenge is governed by the law of the country in which a legal action is brought. The convention is administered by the Paris Union and World Intellectual Property Organization. Compare *Patent Cooperation Treaty*.

**Paris Pact.** See *Louvre Accord*.

**Paris Union.** See *Paris Convention for the Protection of Industrial Property*.

**parity.** 1. A state of equivalence, usually in the cost or value of similar items. 2. The status of currencies trading at the same price. In foreign exchange trades, dealers trade at par when no price difference exists between bids and offers. 3. A price level for agricultural commodities set and maintained by a government. 4. In negotiations, an agreement between the parties to accept reciprocal obligations.

**par of exchange.** 1. A hypothetical exchange rate where currencies are equal in supply and demand. The par value is the market mean between currency buying and selling prices. 2. The equivalent gold content in two currencies.

**partial loss.** See *average*.

**participating preference share.** See *preference share*.

**participation loan.** Also called participation financing, a loan risk shared by a group of banks to reduce the risk to a single bank. Participations in large loans may involve 50 to 100 banks. A participation is orchestrated by a lead bank, which organizes a network of correspondent banks to contribute to the loan in exchange for a share of the profits. Small banks participate by buying shares of loan packages from correspondent network banks. A participation enables small banks, known as respondents, to earn fees from interest paid on a loan, while avoiding regulatory lending limits. Participations are usually sold at a discount below current market rates. Unlike those involved in a syndication, banks lending in a participation are not necessarily known to the borrower. See also *loan sales*.

**particular average.** See *average*.

**partly paid shares.** Shares for which the par value has been partially paid. Partially paid shares are used primarily in privatizations of large-scale industries. Investors pay a portion of par value for equity and make subsequent payments on call dates.

**partnership.** An unincorporated business association of two or more people. Partners share in profits to the extent of their investments. General partners are fully liable for the debts of the partnership, while limited partners (i.e., passive investors) are liable only to the extent of invested capital. A partnership at will is terminated when one partner gives notice of the intention to withdraw. The operation of a partnership is determined by a partnership agreement, which specifies the way profits are to be distributed and the terms of withdrawal, retirement, and liquidation. See also *articles of incorporation/partnership* and *Uniform Partnership Acts*.

**par value.** The face value of a stock or financial instrument on the issue date. Par value is different from market value, which is current price or yield when an asset is sold. The par value of a stock is fixed by a company's charter. The par value of a bond or note is the amount promised to a holder at maturity. A bond's coupon rate is based on the percentage of par value paid, usually annually or semiannually. Dividends paid on preferred shares may also be stated as a percentage of par value, but are usually priced at auctions. A financial instrument is said to be revalued when the issuer alters its par value.

**pase libre.** Spanish: free permit. In countries not members of carnet conventions, primarily in Latin America, an imported sample of commercial value is entered temporarily under a *pase libre*. A customs bond is posted for the amount of the duty. Normally, free-permit imports are reexported within 3 months of entry.

**passing a name.** In securities trading, the disclosure by a broker of a principal's name. Usually, when principals' names are not disclosed, the broker guarantees their solvency.

**passive investor.** See *partnership*.

**password.** An identification code providing access to the Automated Commercial System.

**pataca.** The currency of Macao.

**patent.** 1. The grant of a privilege by a sovereign, usually in relation to the use or ownership of property. 2. An exclusive right to exploit an invention for a limited period of time. The limited right is granted by a government in exchange for future disclosure of the invention. Patents are approved for new, nonobvious processes and products with industrial uses. Ideas, thought processes, and copyrightable materials are not patentable. Eligibility for patent protection is based on a novelty examination, which establishes the newness of the invention. The opposition period permits a third party to contest a patent application or seek cancellation of a previously granted patent. When a party opposing a patent grant establishes prejudicial conditions (i.e., prior publication, knowledge, or use), the novelty of the invention is rebutted and patent protection denied. In some countries, compulsory licensing of patents may be required after a specified period of time. In other countries, patents must meet what are known as "working" requirements; i.e., an invention must be exploited or the protection lapses. In most jurisdictions, patent protection is awarded on a first-to-file basis, i.e., to the first party who files a patent application. However, merely filing an application in some jurisdictions may result in inadvertent disclosures of inventions, and the technique of cluster filing is used by some inventors to minimize the risk of unintended revelation. In the United States, patent protection is based on the first to invent, i.e., the first applicant to demonstrate the invention of a new and different product or process. Proposed changes in U.S. patent law would adopt the international first-to-file standard. See also *confirmation patent; introduction patent; Inter-American Convention on Inventions,*

*Patents, Designs and Industrial Models; inventor's certificate; letters patent; Paris Convention for the Protection of Industrial Property;* and *Patent Cooperation Treaty.*

**Patent & Trademark Office.** In the United States, an agency of the U.S. Department of Commerce that administers patent and trademark laws. Administrative decisions of the Patent & Trademark Office are appealed to the U.S. Court for the Federal Circuit.

**Patent Cooperation Treaty (PCT).** A multilateral agreement that created the international patent application system. The agreement was signed at Geneva in 1970 under the auspices of the World Intellectual Property Organization. The PCT creates a priority period of 18 months. It adopted a standardized application format and centralized system for filing multiple applications. National patent offices, known as International Searching Authorities, conduct worldwide patent searches when an application is filed. If the novelty of an invention is challenged, an international preliminary examination is conducted by an International Preliminary Examining Authority (IPEA). A favorable finding by an IPEA establishes the patentability of an invention in other PCT countries. An applicant pays patent fees and translation costs in each country where an application is filed. See also *International Patent Classification Agreement.* Compare *Paris Convention for the Protection of Industrial Property.*

**patent law.** A statute or decree governing the granting and duration of patent rights in a given legal jurisdiction.

**patent piracy.** See *piracy.*

**patent rolls.** The official records of a government's grant of patent rights. Patent rolls identify patentholders by name and summarize the inventions for which patents were awarded.

**paternalistic finance.** A system of finance that grants preferential access to capital to a favored group of beneficiaries, usually through subsidized or low-interest lending facilities and extended repayment terms.

**pat. off.** The abbreviation for patent office.

**pat. pend.** The abbreviation for patent pending.

**payable to bearer.**    See *bearer.*

**payable to order.**    A negotiable instrument payable to a third party by endorsement and delivery. Proceeds from the instrument are paid only after it is endorsed by the holder.

**payable with exchange.**    A notice affixed to a draft or bill of exchange. The notice provides that the cost of converting the instrument into another currency will be borne by the payee or maker.

**pay as you earn (PAYE).**    A tax system in which the employer collects taxes from employees when wages or salaries are paid. The employer remits taxes to the national revenue agency.

**pay as you go (PAYG).**    An immediate payment system. Accounts are settled at the time of purchase or when outlays are made.

**payback.**    The recovery of initial capital outlays used to finance a project. Paybacks are based on the value of a project over a fixed period of time. Earnings in excess of payback are treated as profit. See also *discounted cashflow* and *net present value.*

**paydown.**    The partial repayment of a debt.

**PAYE.**    The abbreviation for pay as you earn.

**payee.**    The beneficiary of proceeds from a negotiable instrument. The payee may be the drawer or holder of a draft.

**payer.**    The party obligated to make payment on a negotiable instrument. The maker is the party on whom a draft is drawn.

**PAYG.**    The abbreviation for pay as you go.

**paying agent.**    An agent for a securities issuer who makes principal and interest payments to bondholders. The paying agent is usually a commercial bank, although some issuers assign this role to their treasurer.

**paying bank.**    A bank that pays a draft, bill of exchange, or letter of credit.

**payload.**    The portion of a ship's cargo that yields revenue for the carrier.

**payment (payt., pmt., pymt.).**    The transfer of funds to settle a debt. 1. A payment in advance is a prepayment made before goods or services have been delivered. 2. A payment in due course is a payment made when a financial instrument matures. 3. A payment in kind is a payment made with goods or services, and not cash. 4. A payment on account is made before a final bill is received.

**payment date.**    Also called the record date, the date for principal and interest payments specified in a bond indenture.

**payment for honor.**    See *acceptance supra protest.*

**payment in advance.**    Also known as a prepayment, a sum paid for a product or service before it is delivered. For example, rents and utility rates are often collected in advance of the month in which payment falls due.

**payment on account.**    1. An installment payment on an outstanding debt. The payments are usually made at regular intervals until the debt is retired. 2. A deposit credited against the purchase price of a product or service.

**payment on arrival.**    A timing term requiring a seller to permit inspection of goods before payment is received. When goods are lost or destroyed in transit and the insurance risk has passed to the buyer, payment is due at the time the goods should have arrived.

**payment order.**    Also known as a negotiable order of withdrawal or a payment order of withdrawal, an instruction to a bank to pay a stated sum to a third party. A payment order is not a demand instrument, since the drawee bank may refuse to honor the instruction.

**payment supra protest.**    See *acceptance supra protest.*

**payment terms.**    Conditions on which a seller agrees to sell goods or services. The most common payment terms are acceptance, cash against documents, cash in X days from invoice (e.g., 30, 60, or 90 days), cash on delivery, cash with order, or prompt cash (e.g., within 2 weeks of delivery). Other common terms are documentary payment orders and various forms of letters of credit.

**payroll tax.**    See *pay as you earn.*

**payt.**    An abbreviation for payment.

**PB.**    The abbreviation for permanent bunkers.

**PBX.**    The abbreviation for private branch exchange.

**pc.**    The abbreviation for percent, petty cash, piece, and price.

**PCA.**    The abbreviation for Panama Canal Authority and Permanent Court of Arbitration.

**pct.**    The abbreviation for percent.

**PCT.**    The abbreviation for Patent Cooperation Treaty.

**pd.**    The abbreviation for paid and pound.

**p.d.**    The abbreviation for per diem.

**PDR.**    The abbreviation for price-dividend ratio.

**péage dues.**    A special form of harbor dues charged by some North African ports for bulk phosphate cargoes.

**PECC.**    The abbreviation for Pacific Economic Cooperation Council.

**pecuniary exchange.**    A term of sale requiring that a debt be settled with money, and not with goods or services.

**pedimento.**    See *permiso de importación.*

**PEFCO.**    The abbreviation for Private Export Funding Corporation.

**pegged exchange rate.**    A currency value tied to an index currency or basket of currencies. Adjustable pegged rates, called pegs, are altered periodically to maintain values against the index basket or currency. When rates are adjusted frequently, often daily, the rate is known as a crawling peg. See also *floating exchange rate.* Compare *fixed exchange rate.*

**penalty.**    1. A sum of money or right forfeited as a consequence of undesirable or illegal conduct. 2. In contract law, an amount of money specified in an agreement as payable for a breach of contract. Courts often disregard penalty provisions as requiring payment of arbitrary sums unrelated to the actual loss sustained from a breach. See also *damages.*

**penny shares.**    Stocks sold at a very low price. Penny stocks are usually only issued by insolvent or nearly insolvent companies.

**pension.**    1. A regular payment to retired persons or their spouses. Pensions are paid from the retirement date until the pensioner dies, although some pensions continue as survivors benefits to the heirs of a deceased pensioner. 2. In France, money-market lending collateralized by securities held in trust (*en pension*) by the lender. The analogous term in German is *Pensionsgeschäft.*

**pension fund.**    A fund managed by a fiduciary for the benefit of an organization's employees. The employer makes regular tax-free contributions to the fund. In the United States, pension fund investments are exempt from capital-gains taxes and holding requirements.

**P/E ratio.**    See *price-earnings ratio.*

**per capita income.**    The sum of income earned by a group divided by the number of members in the group.

**per diem.**    1. A daily stipend, usually paid as a fee for time and expenses. 2. In shipping, the daily fee charged for the use of transportation equipment.

**perestroika.**    Russian: restructuring. Economic restructuring was adopted as the policy of the Union of Soviet Socialist Republics in the mid-1980s to improving its lagging economy. Intended as a progressive phase-in of market prices and other economic reforms, perestroika failed and was replaced in the early 1990s in some former U.S.S.R. republics, particularly in Russia, by a relatively free market. See also *Commonwealth of Independent States.*

**perfect competition.**    The condition of a market characterized by willing sellers and a sizable number of well-informed buyers, so that the market price of a good is determined by the invisible hand of the marketplace. The prerequisites for perfect competition are several: (1) rational and self-interested sellers in pursuit of maximum profits, (2) fully knowledgeable buyers, (3) identical products offered by sellers, (4) free access to the market, (5) equivalent and mobile factors of production, and (6) no government intervention. In theory, the price of a good is its true market price, reflecting efficiency in its production and delivery rather than the pricing decisions of one individual, group, or government. In reality, markets are rarely perfect. Imperfect competition in which firms benefit from government intervention or the incomplete knowledge of buyers is more common. See also *classical economics* and *neo-classical economics.*

**perfected lien.**    A lien, filed with the appropriate government agency, creating a creditor's security interest in collateral guaranteeing a debt. In the United States, a lien of realty is perfected by filing a deed of trust with a municipal agency. Liens on personal property, including stocks and bonds, are perfected under the Uniform Commercial Code (UCC) by filing a financing statement (UCC-1) with a county records office or the secretary of state. After 5 years, the creditor files a continuation statement, as required by the state in which the collateral is located. See also *termination statement*.

**performance bond.**    See *standby letter of credit* and *surety*.

**performance bonus.**    See *bonus*.

**performance requirement.**    A mandatory production quota imposed by a country as a condition of investment. Some countries require foreign manufacturers to agree to preset employment, export, or output quotas before foreign investment is approved. See also *nontariff barrier*.

**peril.**    A risk of loss, normally covered by an insurance policy. Uninsurable risks are known as excepted perils.

**peril of the sea.**    A natural agent that causes losses not attributable to a carrier's negligence. In maritime usage, a peril is an elemental force distinguishable from the normal hazards of an ocean voyage. A carrier is not liable for losses arising from perils of the sea.

**peril-point provision.**    A reservation in a country's trade laws that prevents negotiated tariff concessions when a domestic industry might be imperiled. See also *market disruption*.

**period and trading limits.**    A charter party phrase describing limitations on the use of a vessel during the course of a charter. A common limitation restricts carriage of hazardous cargoes.

**period charter.**    See *time charter*.

**periodic requirements license.**    In the United States, a special individual validated license authorizing exports of items covered by the Commodity Control List. The license is valid for 1 year and names authorized consignees in specified countries.

**Permanent Court of Arbitration (PCA).**    An international forum established at The Hague in 1899 to resolve disputes between nations.

Countries who are parties to an arbitration select the mediators and determine ground rules for arbitral settlements, which are based on compromises proposed by the parties.

**permanent establishment.**    A plant, branch, subsidiary, or office owned by a foreign company. A multinational parent is liable for taxes in jurisdictions where it maintains permanent establishments. A storage facility may qualify as a permanent establishment, since the term covers any fixed site where work is performed. See also *double taxation*.

**permiso de importación.**    Spanish: permission for importation. Also known as pedimento, an import document issued in Mexico verifying that a buyer has paid import taxes.

**perpetual debenture.**    A security that cannot be redeemed on demand. See also *irredeemable security*.

**perpetual inventory.**    A method of continuous inventory control whereby each item is logged when received and identified when issued for sale or use. Perpetual accounting allows a company to maintain accurate records of the quantity and value of inventory. Continuous inventory control is usually used only by large companies because of attendant record-keeping expenses.

**per pro./per proc.**    The abbreviation for *per procurationem*.

**per procurationem (P/P).**    Latin: by procuration. A notice that an agent is acting on behalf of a principal. The notice, affixed to a contract or financial instrument, renders the principal liable for the acts of the agent. See also *agency*.

**persistent dumping.**    See *dumping*.

**personal account.**    A bank account or trade account carried in the name of an individual.

**personal allowance.**    An amount deductible from gross income for personal expenses. Allowances vary depending on the jurisdiction, but generally include a blanket deduction covering expenditures for which a taxpayer need not account.

**personal effects.**    1. In customs, items acquired by a traveler during a journey and eligible for expedited customs entry. Commercial samples and contraband are not personal effects. 2. In insurance, personal property, usually of an intimate nature, which can be worn or carried on the person of the insured.

**personal identification number (PIN).**   A numbered security code used by bank or credit card customers to withdraw funds by electronic transfer. The PIN is also called an access code.

**personal loan.**   A consumer loan. Personal loans are given for family and household uses. Although a cosigner may be required, personal loans usually are unsecured or are secured by consumer purchases.

**personal property.**   Also called personalty, movable intangible or tangible goods, but not real estate. Personal property can be pledged as collateral for loans. See also *personal effects.*

**personal surety.**   See *surety.*

**peseta.**   The currency of Andorra, the Balearic Islands, the Canary Islands, and Spain.

**peso.**   The currency of Argentina, Chile, Colombia, Cuba, the Dominican Republic, Guinea Bissau, Mexico, the Philippines, and Uruguay.

**PET.**   The abbreviation for potentially exempt transfer.

**petrocurrency/petrodollars.**   Remittances to oil-producing countries arising from the sale of petroleum products in international markets. Petrocurrency is frequently recycled in the form of bank deposits or direct investment in Western industrialized countries.

**petroleum revenue tax.**   See *windfall profits tax.*

**petty average.**   See *primage and average.*

**p.f.**   The abbreviation for pro forma.

**pfd.**   The abbreviation for preferred.

**P/F.**   The abbreviation for pro forma invoice. See *invoice.*

**Pfandbriefe.**   German: a mortgage bond with an original maturity of up to 30 years.

**PFP.**   The abbreviation for policy framework paper.

**Phillips curve.**   A technique for measuring the impact of inflation on unemployment. Developed by A. Phillips, a twentieth-century British economist, the Phillips curve was used to demonstrate a link between low inflation and high unemployment, and vice versa. Applied to Keynesian economics, the constancy of the curve suggests governments that coordinate fiscal and monetary policies can keep unemployment low. However, some economists accept the contrary view of a natural rate of unemployment on which government policy has little substantial effect. See also *stagflation.*

**physical capital.**   Capital facilities and equipment, such as buildings, land, and machinery, used to produce goods and services. Physical capital differs from financial capital and human capital.

**physicals.**   See *actuals.*

**phytosanitary inspection certificate.**   A certificate of health issued in the exporting country verifying that a commodity passed inspection. Sanitary certificates are required for grain, livestock, and other commodity imports. They attest to the import's freedom from disease and pests.

**PIB.**   The abbreviation for *produit intérieur brut.* See *gross domestic product.*

**piece rate.**   A wage or payment based on the unit of work produced. Also known as outworking payments and payment by results, piece rates are normally paid for outsourcing. Although once associated with low-wage industries, such as apparel manufacturing and subsistence farming, outsourcing is used by all types of companies to compensate for downsizing and other changes in corporate hiring practices. Piece-rate earnings are determined largely by productivity and access to business.

**pig/piggyback.**   A railroad trailer transported atop a railway flatcar. Shipping services using pigs are known as piggyback plans. Devices used to move trailers to and from railcars are known as piggybackers.

**piggybacking.**   In stock markets, purchasing existing shares and newly issued shares at the same time.

**Pigou effect.**   Also known as the wealth effect, an economic theory that price changes affect the value of assets. Keynesian economics holds that falling prices create unemployment by reducing overall demand. By contrast, proponents of the

Pigou effect argue that falling prices enhance the intrinsic value of money and increase aggregate demand with no apparent impact on employment rates.

**pilferage.**  A partial theft of cargo.

**pilotage.**  The fee charged by a pilot to lead a ship to and from a harbor. The costs of pilot services are based per pilotage units. A pilotage unit is derived by multiplying a ship's width by its length and depth and dividing the resulting product by 10,000.

**pilot program.**  A small-scale test run of a new program or product. Pilot programs are used to improve new products or test a product's market appeal. Government agencies often use pilots to verify the efficacy of a program before implementing it on a large scale.

**PIN.**  The abbreviation for personal identification number.

**Pink Book.**  In the United Kingdom, the *UK Balance of Payments* that provides national accounts data for a given year. The *Pink Book* is published annually by the Central Statistical Office. See also *Blue Book.*

**Pink Sheets.**  See *over-the-counter market.*

**pioneer status (PS).**  A status conferred on new foreign enterprises in developing countries, usually as an inducement to bring high-value industries to the country. The incentives typically include tax forgiveness for a specified period and relaxed regulations.

**pip.**  In foreign exchange dealing, a minimum change in the price of floating rates. An example of a pip is the difference between a quoted price of 1.8514 and 1.8513.

**piracy.**  1.The process of stealing a marine vessel and/or its contents. To qualify as piracy, an act at sea must be sufficiently serious to constitute a felony had it occurred on land. Piracy on the high seas is a grave violation of customary international law, subjecting the bounty to forfeiture, the act to suppression, and the perpetrator to capture and punishment in the nation discovering it. 2. Paper piracy involves presenting false or forged documents, such as a fraudulent bill of lading, in order to obtain payment under a letter of credit. 3.

Rogue piracy occurs when an unscrupulous shipowner or captain sells cargo destined for a named purchaser or consignee. 4. Rust-bucket piracy occurs when fraudulent insurance claims are filed following the intentional sinking of a ship. 5. The theft of a copyrighted, patented, or trademarked design, product, or work.

**pit.**  An area on the floor of a commodity exchange where face-to-face trading takes place. Brokers who trade in these areas are called pit brokers.

**pivot charge.**  A surcharge levied by air carriers for the use of shipping containers or unit load devices. The surcharge is based on the device's pivot weight, or the minimum ratable weight plus a flat rate for excess weight.

**pk.**  The abbreviation for pack.

**pkg.**  The abbreviation for package.

**pl.**  The abbreviation for plate.

**PL.**  The abbreviation for partial loss and public law.

**PL 480 programs.**  In the United States, the popular name for domestic foreign-food-aid programs authorized by the Agricultural Trade Development and Assistance Act of 1954. Title I of the act authorizes long-term, low-interest government loans to developing countries to purchase U.S. commodities. Recipient governments are permitted to resell the commodities in local consumer markets. Title II permits the U.S. Department of Agriculture (USDA) to procure and donate agricultural commodities in the event of foreign natural or civil disasters and for nutritional feeding programs. Title III, also known as Food for Development, authorizes the USDA to forgive debts incurred by recipient countries when proceeds from Title I resales are used to support agricultural development. The Findley Amendment to the act prohibits commodity sales to unfriendly countries.

**placement.**  Also known as private placement or direct placement, the private sale of a securities issue. In the United States, the Securities Act of 1933 exempts private placements involving up to 35 investors from Securities and Exchange Commission (SEC) registration requirements. However, the Deficit Reduction Act of 1984 mandates that privately placed securities eligible for tax shelters be registered with the SEC. See also *bought deal* and *investment letter.*

**planned economy.**   See *nonmarket economy.*

**planned obsolescence.**   See *obsolescence.*

**plant.**   A facility where products are produced. The term also covers equipment and machinery used in the normal course of business.

**Plantation House.**   In Britain, an office block in the City of London where many commodities traders are located.

**Plaza Accord.**   A 1985 agreement reached by the Group of Seven (G-7) to stabilize international exchange rates and improve the competitiveness of U.S. exports. Under the agreement, the exchange value of the U.S. dollar was reduced to lower the cost of U.S. goods in foreign markets, while the yen was revalued upward to make Japanese exports more expensive. The agreement is named for the Plaza Hotel in New York, where G-7 finance ministers met. At the 1988 Toronto economic summit, G-7 heads of state and finance ministers agreed to maintain the devalued U.S. dollar near 1987 levels. See also *Louvre Accord.*

**plc.**   The abbreviation for public limited company.

**pledge.**   The use of an asset to secure a loan by assigning a lender a security interest in it. When the pledged assets are securities, the lender normally takes possession of them. See also *hypothecation.*

**Plimsoll line.**   See *load line.*

**PLR.**   The abbreviation for public lending right.

**plutocracy.**   A government controlled by a few wealthy financiers, industrialists, and landowners.

**pluvial insurance.**   Coverage against lost profits caused by weather. Pluvial insurance is purchased primarily by organizers of for-profit summer events, such as concerts or sporting matches.

**pm.**   The abbreviation for premium.

**P.M.**   The abbreviation for paymaster, postmaster, and prime minister.

**pmkd.**   The abbreviation for postmarked.

**pmt.**   An abbreviation for payment.

**pn.**   The abbreviation for promissory note.

**PNB.**   The abbreviation for *produit national brut.* See *gross national product.*

**P/O.**   The abbreviation for postal order, post office, and purchase order.

**POB.**   The abbreviation for post office box.

**POC.**   The abbreviation for port of call.

**POD.**   The abbreviation for pay on delivery.

**Poincaré franc.**   A gold franc first issued in France in 1928 and named for Raymond Poincaré, a former prime minister and president of France. The Poincaré franc was originally equal to 65.5 milligrams of gold of 0.900 fineness, but its value is now fixed in terms of the special drawing right. It is used to value financial obligations and liabilities incurred under international shipping conventions.

**point.**   The smallest unit used to measure price in a given transaction. 1. In finance, a discount point equal to 1 percent of the principal of a loan. A basis point is equal to $1/100$ of 1 percent. 2. In interest rate futures, a point, also called a tick, is the smallest minimum price change, or $1/32$ of a percentage point. 3. In foreign exchange prices, a point is the last digit in a quoted price. For example, if 1 U.S. dollar = 2.9456 pounds sterling, a fluctuation to 1 U.S. dollar = 2.9457 pounds is a 1-point change. 4. In securities, a point is equal to one currency unit in stock prices (e.g., 1 U.S. dollar) or 1 percent of a bond's value.

**point forecast.**   The expected rate of exchange for a particular national currency at a fixed time in the future.

**Point Four Program.**   See *U.S. Agency for International Development.*

**point of sale.**   See *electronic funds transfer.*

**poison pills.**   Also called shark repellents, strategies adopted by a company faced with an unwanted takeover. A poison pill is any component in a scorched earth defense intended to dilute the value of the target company. Poison pill strategies include acquiring large debts or issuing convertible securities to reduce the value of the acquirer's equity. Staggered directorships are another poison pill. When directors' terms of office are staggered, the unwanted suitor cannot gain immediate control of a company unless existing directors are dismissed with compensation, often in the form of share options.

**policy.** See *insurance policy.*

**policy proof of interest (PPI).** In marine insurance, a provision in which the insurer stipulates a policyholder's insurable interest in cargo. The stipulation guarantees that a claim will be paid if the other terms of the policy are met.

**political risk.** See *country risk.* Compare *commercial risk.*

**political union.** An agreement between countries to subordinate national sovereignty to a supranational body, often a regional parliament or executive agency.

**poll tax.** A lump-sum tax paid by each adult in a country. The poll tax is a flat tax assessed without regard to income, except for personal allowances. Poll taxes are said to be regressive because a taxpayer's ability to pay is not taken into account in determining the assessment rate.

**Polski Registr.** See *classification society.*

**polycentric pricing.** A pricing policy adopted by a multinational firm that permits foreign subsidiaries to price like products differently, mainly to suit diverse local market conditions.

**pool.** 1. In finance, any combination, merger, or joining of funds, stocks, or other assets for the common benefit of parties to a transaction, e.g., a mutual fund or unit trust. 2. In transportation, a shared supply of shipping containers. 3. Parties combining assets for mutual benefit.

**pooling of interests.** In mergers and acquisitions, the exchange of equivalent amounts of voting stock. A pooling transaction is an accounting method whereby equity is acquired without cash payment. When at least 10 percent of an acquired company's equity is purchased with cash, bonds, debt paper, or preferred shares, the accounting method is known as a purchase acquisition. In a purchase acquisition, the acquired company's assets and liabilities are stated at fair market value. Conversely, in a pooling transaction, the company's assets and liabilities are merged and stated without adjustments for fair market value.

**Poor Four.** In the European Community, Greece, Ireland, Portugal, and Spain, which all require financial assistance from other EC countries. The need to equalize incomes of EC countries is called the cohesion question. The Treaty of Maastricht pledges to address income equalization in future EC budgets.

**POP.** The abbreviation for point of purchase.

**POR.** The abbreviation for pay on receipt, pay on return, and price on request.

**port (pt.).** Also known as a port of call, an area within which vessels regularly load or discharge cargo and passengers, including places where vessels await berthing.

**port authority.** A government agency that oversees the operations of a seaport. Autorité portuaire is the French term for port authority.

**port autonome.** French: *autonomous port.*

**port charge.** A surcharge paid by a ship to enter or leave a harbor. Port charges include harbor dues, any extra port dues, and pilotage paid for pilots and tugs.

**port congestion surcharge.** An extra charge imposed by ocean carriers to deliver goods to ports known to be inefficient in handling cargo. The surcharge is usually based on a fixed percentage of the carriage rate.

**port dues.** Administrative charges or tolls levied against a vessel for the privilege of docking at a port.

**portfolio investment.** An investment too small to give an investor partial or total control of a company, i.e., under 51 percent. See also *foreign direct investment.*

**port mark.** Any marking inscribed on cargo indicating its origin and destination ports.

**port of call.** See *port.*

**port of departure.** The port from which a journey begins. Health, sanitation, and other exit regulations are enforced at the departure port.

**port of destination.** Depending on a vessel's routing, the destination port may be the port of unlading, the pick-up point for cargo, the final port for a specific voyage, or the home port.

**port of entry.**   A port designated to inspect and clear imports. Officials at an entry port process customs entries and collect duties and taxes. Entry port officials also supervise bonded warehouses, seize contraband, and hear protests of valuations and duty-drawback claims. Entry ports may be ocean ports, inland border areas, or interior in-bond transshipping points.

**port of unlading.**   Also known as the port of discharge, the port where goods are unloaded or otherwise discharged from a vessel. Compare *release port*.

**port reeve.**   See *port warden*.

**port warden.**   In some jurisdictions, the principal official who enforces regulations of the port.

**POS.**   The abbreviation for point of sale.

**position.**   The extent of a dealer's or an investor's exposure in the market. See also *long position, open position*, and *short position*.

**position audit.**   A review of an organization's financial standing, organizational structure, market position, and efficiency. The review enables the organization to assess its strengths, weaknesses, and capacity for adjustment to changed circumstances. Conducted by an internal committee or by outside consultants, audits are often used to improve productivity and plan future projects.

**positive concept of valuation.**   The theory underlying the transaction value method of customs valuation. It holds that duties should be imposed on the value of the transaction, as defined by the buyer and seller. The price paid for a product is the basis on which duties are assessed. Compare *notional valuation*.

**positive economics.**   An empirical approach to the study of economics, which rejects social and moral judgments as factors in economic analysis. The most prominent proponent of positive economics in the United States is Milton Friedman, a Nobel laureate. Friedman was instrumental in developing what has come to be known as the Chicago school of economics, named from conservative theorists associated with the University of Chicago. See also *monetarism*. Compare *normative economics*.

**positive spread.**   The profit earned by an investor when the cost of purchasing an asset is lower than its market value. Alternatively, a bond issuer benefits from a positive spread when the cost of issuing debt is lower than the payout to bondholders.

**possession.**   Physical control of tangible assets, such as land or movable property. Possession is usually actual; i.e., the holder is in legal possession of property. It may also be constructive (imposed by law), apparent (an heir's future right of possession), or naked (i.e., actual, but illegal, possession).

**possum belly.**   A trailer designed to transport bulk goods. The possum belly differs from more conventional trailers in that its floor is close to the ground.

**post.**   To record a bookkeeping entry.

**postdated.**   A negotiable instrument dated for future payment. However, some financial instruments, such as time drafts, are always payable at a future date.

**postentry.**   A partial customs entry after the original shipment has been liquidated. When duties are underpaid, a postentry duty is charged if payments do not cover the partial shipment. Compare *overentry certificate*.

**poste restante.**   French: general delivery, i.e., a mail service where letters or parcels are forwarded to a post office to be retrieved by the addressee.

**postindustrial society.**   A theory of political economy advanced in the 1970s by Daniel Bell, a U.S. sociologist. Broadly, the theory holds that a shift from manufacturing to service-based economies is a natural progression in advanced societies. In the late 1980s, more than 50 percent of the gross domestic product of developed countries derived from services rather than manufacturing. By the early 1990s, however, developed countries competed to increase industrial production on the theory that a pure service economy, devoid of a strong industrial base, could probably not be sustained.

**potential entrant.**   A company seeking an opportunity to enter a new market, usually after entry barriers have fallen or market prices have increased. The presence of potential entrants is believed by most theorists to prevent price gouging by monopolies.

**potentially exempt transfer (PET).** A gift on which no tax is paid when it is made. The gift may become subject to inheritance tax after the donor dies.

**pound.** The currency of Bermuda, Cyprus, Egypt, Ireland, Lebanon, Sudan, and Syria.

**pound sterling.** The currency of the United Kingdom.

**power of attorney.** A written document witnessed by a notary public authorizing one party to act on behalf of another. Power of attorney is a form of agency, which can be a general or limited grant of authority.

**P/P.** The abbreviation for parcel post, *per procurationem,* point of purchase, and postage paid.

**ppd.** The abbreviation for prepaid.

**PPI.** The abbreviation for policy proof of interest and producer price index.

**PPP.** The abbreviation for purchasing power parity.

**pr.** The abbreviation for pair, preferred, and price.

**PR.** The abbreviation for public relations.

**praecipium/praecipuum.** In Eurocurrency lending, the portion of the management fee retained by the lead manager. The praecipium is deducted before fees are remitted to other members of the lending group.

**Prämie.** German: premium.

**PRC.** The abbreviation for the People's Republic of China.

**precious metals.** Gold, platinum, and silver. Compare *base metals.*

**preclassification.** In the United States, a procedure used to obtain import classifications prior to customs entry. A customs inspector undertakes on-site examinations of product samples and notifies an importer of import classifications in advance of actual entry of shipped goods. See also *binding tariff classification ruling.*

**preclusive buying.** The wholesale purchase of commodities to reduce the supply of goods available to other purchasers.

**precommercial research and development (R&D).** The process of developing new technologies at the earliest stages. The term denotes the phase after basic research is complete but before a product is developed for commercial exploitation.

**précompte mobilier.** French: tax withheld from payments of dividends and interest.

**predatory dumping.** See *dumping.*

**predatory pricing.** A practice of pricing goods or services below the level needed to earn a profit. Predatory pricing is intended to drive competitors from the market by depriving them of profit.

**predatory rate.** In transportation, a low freight rate offered by a common carrier intended to undercut competitors and gain a monopoly share of a given market. See also *Ocean Shipping Act of 1978.*

**preemption.** 1. A right of first refusal, i.e., an option to enter into a contract at a stated price, usually for a limited period of time. 2. In international trade, the prerogative of a customs authority to seize and sell imports that are undervalued on customs documents.

**preemptive right.** A right of existing shareholders to purchase a new issue of shares before an initial public offering. Preemptive rights protect existing shareholders against future dilution of their equity. Compare *shareholder's derivative rights.*

**preexport financing.** Short-term lending based on a purchase order or other evidence that a foreign sale has been made. The loan is granted for the purpose of financing goods or services needed to complete the sale.

**preference.** In international trade, a concession, usually in the form of reduced tariffs. See also *Generalized System of Preferences.*

**preference share.** Preferred stock that pays a fixed rate of interest rather than dividends.

**preferential creditor.** A creditor whose lien is given preference over other creditors when a company is dissolved. Government revenue agencies are usually first in line, followed by other government agencies, pension funds, employees owed salaries or wages, secured creditors, and ordinary creditors.

**preferential duty.** See *preference.*

**preferential trade area (PTA).**   A regional trading association whereby member states lower barriers, including duties and border regulations, to stimulate internal trade.

**Preferential Trade Area for Eastern and Southern African States (PTA).**   A cross-border agreement between African countries adopted in 1982. The PTA contemplates eliminating all internal trade barriers by the year 2000, but with provisions to accelerate or delay tariff reductions, depending on future economic circumstances. The PTA is the successor to the East African Economic Community, which dissolved in 1978. Its members are Angola, Burundi, the Comoros, Djibouti, Ethiopia, Kenya, Lesotho, Malawi, Mauritius, Mozambique, Namibia, Rwanda, Somalia, Sudan, Swaziland, Tanzania, Uganda, Zaire, Zambia, and Zimbabwe. Its development bank is the Eastern and Southern African Trade and Development Bank, a subregional bank of the African Development Bank Group. The PTA bank's currency unit is the unit of account–preferential trade area (UAPTA). The bank is located in Bujumbura, Burundi. The PTA's secretariat is based in Lusaka, Zambia.

**preferential trade program (PTP).**   A program by one country reducing or eliminating tariffs on imports from another.

**preferred dividend.**   Fixed dividends paid to holders of preferred stock. Preferred dividends have priority to the full extent of their value over dividends paid to holders of common stock.

**preferred ordinary share.**   An equity with dividend rights ranking between preferred stock and common stock.

**preferred stock.**   Also called preference stock, equity paying a fixed dividend. Preferred stock carries no voting rights, but may be convertible into common stock. When a company is liquidated, the claims of holders of preferred stock have priority over the claims of holders of common stock, but lesser claims than holders of bonds or debentures. Preferred shares can have a limited life with a stated maturity date, or they can be perpetual with no redemption date. See also *senior security.*

**preliminary invoice.**   A statement forwarded by a seller to a buyer proposing terms of sale in the early stages of a transaction. The preliminary invoice can be the basis for future negotiations, or it may be accepted by the buyer as the definitive statement of the terms of sale.

**premium (PM).**   1. A description of high-quality goods and services. 2. A free gift or low-cost incentive for purchasing goods or services. 3. The amount paid to an underwriter for insurance coverage. Premiums are paid annually, semiannually, quarterly, or monthly. 4. In finance, the spread between the face value and above-par value of a bond. Compare *discount.* 5. In foreign exchange, the *agio,* or fee paid to an exchange dealer to cover the risk of exchange rate changes. 6. In options trading, the price of an option reached by competitive bidding on the floor of a trading exchange. 7. The exchange value paid for gold or silver coins above that paid for equivalent units of paper currency.

**prepayment.**   See *payment in advance.*

**prescribed holders.**   The 16 official agencies authorized by the International Monetary Fund to hold special drawing rights. Some holders use the SDR as a unit of account, while others use it to settle all international accounts. The holders are the African Development Bank, African Development Fund, Andean Reserve Fund, Arab Monetary Fund, Asian Development Bank, Bank for International Settlements, Bank of Central African States, Central Bank of Western African States, East African Development Bank, Eastern Caribbean Central Bank, International Development Association, International Fund for Agricultural Development, Islamic Development Bank, Nordic Investment Bank, Swiss National Bank, and World Bank.

**presentment.**   A demand for payment by a holder of a negotiable instrument. Presentment is made to an acceptor, drawee, or maker.

**present value.**   See *time value.*

**president.**   In the United States, a corporate officer ranked below the chairman of the board of directors. The president is often the company's chief executive officer. Elsewhere, an honorary title sometimes given to a retired chairman of the board or managing director.

**pretax profit.**   Net earnings before taxes paid.

**price cartel.**  See *cartel*.

**price ceiling.**  The upper-limit price charged by a producer of goods or services. In most jurisdictions, usury laws limit the amount of interest lenders may charge for consumer loans. Some jurisdictions also impose price controls on utilities and producers of consumer goods. As a practical matter, price ceilings are set by competition in most sectors in market economies, since consumers comparison-shop and buy cheaper substitutes when the price exceeds the utility of a product.

**price controls.**  Government restraints on price increases. Price controls are implemented to control inflation or to lower the costs of raw materials (or manufacturing inputs) used to produce goods. While developed countries may institute them on a temporary basis, permanent price restraints are more common in developing countries. Where enforced controls are in place, a producer applies to an office of price control, usually in the ministry of finance or the ministry of commerce, for approval of proposed increases. See also *wage and price controls*.

**price discrimination.**  The sale of a product at different prices to different classes of consumers. Price discrimination is difficult to maintain, unless the higher price is charged for enhanced services (e.g., first class air travel). When unrelated to discounts or additional costs, egregious price discrimination is illegal under the competition laws of most developed countries.

**price-dividend (P/D) ratio.**  The market price of a stock divided by the previous year's per-share dividend. P/D ratio determines the asset value of a given stock in an investor's portfolio.

**price-earnings ratio.**  Also known as P/E ratio or P/E multiple, the market price of a stock divided by a company's per-share earnings. The P/E ratio determines the value of a share in terms of its market price. A high P/E reflects a company that has better than average growth potential but carries greater risks to investors. See also *price–net tangible assets ratio*.

**price escalation.**  An increase in price above that normally charged for a product or service. Often, the increase is attributable to added costs. For example, an export sale is more costly than a domestic sale, largely because of added transportation and financing cost. Higher labor wages or component costs also cause price escalation.

**price fixing.**  In the United States, an agreement between two or more firms to set prices. A violation of antitrust laws, price fixing may involve a conspiracy to drive others from the market, but it need not. Any agreement to lower, raise, or attempt to stabilize prices constitutes price fixing, even through there may be no effect on actual prices. The test is whether other producers are restrained by the agreement from exercising independent judgment in setting their prices. See also *restraint of trade*.

**price index.**  An index of average retail and wholesale prices paid for goods or services. Used to measure inflation, an index is expressed as a percentage of average prices calculated from a base year. Consumer indexes are often called the retail price index (RPI) or the consumer price index (CPI). Wholesale indexes are generally called the producer price index (PPI) or the wholesale price index (WPI).

**price leader.**  A firm with enough market power in a given industry to thwart price competition. The price leader sets prices in an oligopoly and competitors follow to avoid price wars. Price setting is not illegal per se. But when competitors conspire to set minimum prices, a price ring develops. Price rings are illegal in most countries. See also *antitrust laws*. Compare *market leader*.

**price list.**  In international trade, a list submitted to an importing country, often notarized, certifying that the price charged for an import is consistent with home market prices. See also *chamber of commerce certificate*.

**price method.**  See *piece rate*.

**price–net tangible assets ratio.**  The market price of a share divided by its net tangible assets, i.e., tangible assets less liabilities. A company with a high ratio of assets to share price is a sound investment. See also *price-earnings ratio*.

**price policy.**  A course of action adopted by a business or government setting the price of a product or service. Government price policies are evidenced by rate setting for public utilities or price controls on sellers of goods and services. Companies formulate policies for achieving the optimum price for a product or service. Factors in pricing include the cost of producing a product or service, its nature and quality, the size and elasticity of the market, and competitor pricing. Patents, copyrights, and product differentiation may also be factors in business pricing policies.

**price ring.**   See *price leader.*

**prices and incomes policy.**   See *wage and price controls.*

**price support.**   A government program created to increase or maintain prices of local commodities, usually agricultural products, above the level dictated by the market. Price supports normally include some combination of low-cost, long-term financing, direct cash payments, and surplus stocks maintained to reduce supply in commercial markets.

**price suppression.**   In dumping and countervailing duty actions, domestic sales prices lowered by import competition. In theory, free trade reduces consumer prices by forcing domestic producers to compete with foreign producers in terms of price and quality. In unfair trade proceedings, however, reduced sales prices are entered as evidence of injury to a domestic industry caused by price suppression.

**price war.**   Vigorous competition between firms seeking to increase market share by cutting prices for competing products. Over time, selling at a loss imperils an industry. Most firms avoid price wars and compete on nonprice terms, such as service, packaging, and advertising.

**prima facie.**   Latin: first appearance. In a legal action, *prima facie* evidence appears certain at first glance. It creates a presumption in favor of a given conclusion, but it can be rebutted or overcome by proof of a contrary set of facts.

**primage and average.**   Formerly, a fee paid to ship masters in excess of freight charges. In modern usage, primage and average is a levy included in a carrier's carriage rate. Also known as petty average, the levy is based on the value of a particular shipment and charged for wharfage, pilotage, and other expenses specifically related to the cost of transporting a given shipment.

**primary dealer.**   In the United States, a market maker in U.S. Treasury auctions. The Federal Reserve System sets capital reserve requirements for primary dealers, who report portfolio positions and trading volumes to the Federal Reserve Bank of New York. Primary dealers are also known as reporting dealers.

**primary market.**   1. Generally, any market where the first sale of a category of goods takes place. 2. In securities trading, a market where original issues of securities are offered for sale. 3. In lending, a market where loans are made directly to a borrower. Compare *secondary market* and *terminal market.*

**primary product.**   An agricultural product or mineral extract containing the minimum value added that is required to adapt it for sale in a commercial market.

**prime.**   A description of a financial instrument indicating the maker's extraordinary creditworthiness.

**prime banker's acceptance.**   A high-quality acceptance. See also *eligible paper.*

**prime bill of exchange.**   A bill of exchange that arises from the sale of goods. See also *eligible paper.*

**prime maker.**   A party drawing a draft or bill of exchange, as well as an issuer of negotiable paper. The prime maker is the party bearing ultimate responsibility for paying the debt represented by the instrument.

**prime rate.**   In the United States, the base percentage rate at which commercial banks make short-term loans to their most creditworthy borrowers, usually corporations. Since many corporations borrow on the capital markets, the prime rate is no longer the only U.S. benchmark interest rate. A lender's borrowing costs, the London interbank offered rate, or a similar index rate may determine a commercial borrower's rate, which is often lower than the prime rate.

**prime underwriting facility (PUF).**   A revolving underwriting facility pegged to the prime rate.

**princ.**   The abbreviation for principal.

**principal (princ.).**   1. A person who makes a contract or takes equity in a business or joint venture. 2. In finance, a party primarily liable on a loan, as distinguished from a comaker or guarantor, who is secondarily liable. 3. The face amount of a debt, excluding charges for interest and fees.

**principal-exchange-rate-linked security (PERL).** A bond whose yield is pegged to foreign exchange rates. PERLs pay semiannual interest. A bond denominated in one currency that pays interest in another is called a reverse PERL.

**principal market.** The primary place where goods are sold. A principal market is often different from the place where goods are produced.

**principal supplier.** The primary supply source for goods or services, usually a local enterprise.

**principles of international trade (PIT).** The basic tenets of the General Agreement on Tariffs and Trade, i.e., national treatment, nondiscrimination, reduced barriers to imports, reciprocity, and transparency.

**principles of taxation.** The concepts underlying tax systems in relatively free economies, i.e., equitable and predictable rates, minimal effects on economic choice, and minimal collection costs. In the view of some economists, a national tax system should also guarantee social equity by redistributing some degree of wealth to the poor.

**prior import deposit.** In some countries, a sum deposited by an importer with a central bank to obtain an import license. The deposit may equal 100 percent of an import's value and is refundable. It constitutes a non-interest loan to the central bank.

**priority date.** 1. The date on which a patent or trademark application is filed when intellectual property protection is accorded on a first-to-file basis. 2. The date on which chattel paper is filed creating a priority lien.

**priority lien.** A creditor's lien paid ahead of other liens when assets are liquidated. In the United States, the Uniform Commercial Code places secured creditors ahead of unsecured creditors. Priority among secured creditors is determined by the first to file a chattel paper with the appropriate government agency.

**priority percentage.** The profit owed to holders of bonds, debentures, and preferred stock. The priority percentage determines the value of a common stock after priority holders have been paid.

**priority practices.** See *Omnibus Trade Act of 1988*.

**priority watch list.** See *Omnibus Trade Act of 1988*.

**prior or subsequent movement by water.** In transportation, a condition for discounted ground carriage. Most domestic carriers offer lower shipping rates for goods moving in international trade. The discount is available when cargo is transported by an ocean liner at some point during carriage. Depending on whether the transaction involves importing or exporting, the consignee or the exporter informs the ground carrier of water carriage and receives a discount.

**Privatdiskont AG.** In Germany, a private firm owned by a banking consortium through which the *Bundesbank* deals in its open-market operations. *Privatdiskont* is the sole official market maker for banker's acceptances in Germany.

**private bill of exchange.** A bill of exchange arising from an international trade transaction and drawn or accepted by a nonbank institution, usually a multinational corporation or finance house.

**private branch exchange (PBX).** An internal telephone network that routes inside and outside calls through a single exchange. Private automated branch exchanges (PABXs) are the automatic exchanges used by most large organizations.

**private brand.** A specially made product carrying a distributor's label and sold in its outlets. Also known as own brands or house brands, private-label goods are advertised as the distributor's products rather than the manufacturer's. Compare *brand name*.

**private carrier.** See *carrier*.

**private enterprise.** Also called free enterprise, an economic system that operates with minimal government intervention. Individuals or private groups are permitted to own capital and property and manage resources with little official direction.

**Private Export Funding Corporation (PEFCO).** In the United States, an international trade finance corporation established in 1970. PEFCO finances purchases of U.S. capital goods and services by foreign buyers. Its direct loans and debt purchases are guaranteed by the Export-Import Bank of the United States (Eximbank) or insured by the

Foreign Credit Insurance Association. PEFCO is owned by a consortium of U.S. banks and corporations. Its activities are financed through credit from the Eximbank, U.S. commercial banks, and the sale of debt securities on capital markets.

**private international law.**    The branch of international law devoted to the conduct of private parties. Legal actions involving private parties are decided by municipal courts. In international law, a municipal court is any court sitting in the country where a case is heard. Compare *public international law.*

**private limited company.**    See *company.*

**private placement.**    See *placement.*

**private-purpose bond.**    A government-issued bond repaid from revenues earned by a private business. In the United States, private-purpose bonds are issued for waste disposal and treatment plants, airports and other public transportation facilities, educational institutions, etc. Although the Tax Reform Act of 1986 exempts earnings on private bonds issued for rural development from federal taxes, most bond interest is taxable in the United States. Compare *public-purpose bond.*

**private risk insurance.**    An insurance policy protecting an exporter or investor from losses on foreign accounts or investments. Private risk insurance may not cover political or sovereign risks. See also *commercial risk* and *country risk.*

**private sector.**    The sector in a market economy composed of commercial and industrial firms. The firms can be private (i.e., owned by individuals or partnerships), or they can be publicly held (i.e., owned by purchasers of shares on an organized exchange). Some segments of the private sector are regulated, though not owned or controlled, by government agencies. For example, privately owned utilities are subject to regulation in the public interest.

**private treaty.**    A commercial contract between buyers and sellers.

**privatization.**    The sale of government-owned industries to private investors in a reverse takeover. Also known as denationalization, industries are privatized to increase efficiency and reduce costs. In theory, the need to earn a profit makes private firms more responsive to consumer demands, thereby improving productivity and efficiency.

**privilege money.**    See *discount house.*

**probate.**    The authentication of a will by a probate court. Once a will has been declared valid, the court appoints an administrator or executor to distribute assets of the estate.

**proc.**    The abbreviation for proceedings.

**processing tax.**    In some countries, a special duty imposed on products imported for inward processing. The tax is levied on imports processed for consumption or reexport.

**proctor in admiralty.**    A lawyer who specializes in maritime law.

**procurement.**    The purchase of goods and services by a government agency or multilateral institution. In national procurements, governments have traditionally favored domestic suppliers when purchasing for national agencies. The Government Procurement Code adopted by the Tokyo Round of the General Agreement on Tariffs and Trade commits signatories to open tender procedures to external suppliers. A 1988 amendment to the code also reduces the value of procurement contracts reserved for domestic bids. Nevertheless, open and competitive bidding in national procurement remains difficult to achieve.

**prod.**    The abbreviation for produce.

**produce.**    See *commodity.*

**producer price index.**    See *price index.*

**producer surplus.**    1. A commodity for which supply exceeds demand. 2. The amount by which the market price for goods exceeds the selling price a producer is willing to accept.

**product.**    A good made, grown, processed, or distributed for sale.

**product cycle.**    See *product life cycle.*

**product differentiation.**    The process by which producers distinguish their products or services from like products and services. Quality, novel forms of packaging and advertising, sales promotions, and pricing are forms of differentiation. In an oligopoly where firms sell highly similar products (e.g., automobiles), successful product differentiation leads to increased sales, often at higher prices than those commanded by close substitutes. In oligopolies where firms sell identical products (e.g., paper products), grades are differentiated, but equivalent grades usually are indistinguishable. See also *differentiated product line*. Compare *generic*.

**product guarantee insurance.** An insurance policy that indemnifies a manufacturer against financial losses when damaged or defective products are withdrawn from the market and sales are lost. Product guarantee policies also cover manufacturer costs when recalled products are repaired. The policies do not, however, compensate victims for injuries proved in product liability cases.

**production.** The process of transforming raw materials or components into salable assets. Producers consume capital, labor, and raw materials to manufacture products for profit.

**production effect of tariff.** See *tariff effect*.

**production sharing.** See *outward processing*.

**productive expenditure.** A current investment for a future benefit. Business investments in physical facilities, machinery and equipment, or skilled labor are productive expenditures. Public investments in education, infrastructure, communications systems, etc., are also generally deemed to be productive expenditures.

**productivity.** The extent of resources and work time needed to convert an idea or component into a product. The speed with which labor can accomplish a task is the primary measure of productivity, although the efficiency with which capital, machinery, inputs, etc., are used is also an index of productivity. In modern industry, productivity is enhanced by human skill and advanced technology.

**product liability.** The penalty imposed on a producer for the sale of defective products. In most jurisdictions, product liability is determined by statute, though the nature of proof and penalties vary. In common-law jurisdictions, the purchaser of a defective product may also bring a legal action in tort or for breach of contract. Under rules adopted by the European Community, manufacturers of defective products are strictly liable without regard to fault. In the United States, depend-ing on the circumstances, a manufacturer may be permitted to raise a plaintiff's contributory negligence and the absence of proximate cause as defenses. However, in nearly all jurisdictions, defendants face some level of liability when an uninformed consumer uses a defective product for the purposes and in the manner prescribed by the seller. When the injured party is an innocent bystander, a manufacturer may also face criminal prosecution. Parties liable for death or injury from defective products include manufacturers, producers of raw commodities, importers, and some suppliers. Product liability insurance pays victims compensation and legal damages. Compare *product guarantee insurance*.

**product liability insurance.** See *product liability*.

**product life cycle.** A marketing concept for measuring the sales of a product over its useful life. The development or prelaunch (pioneering) stage is the research and development phase for designing a product, testing and improving prototypes, assessing competition, and evaluating the market. The introduction or growth phase is a low-sales phase, as distributors and consumers inspect and test a new product. Sales increase in the mature phase as the product develops brand identity and market share. During the saturation phase, sales stabilize as brand familiarity attracts new buyers and brand loyalty creates repeat buyers. In the decline phase, a new and improved product competes for market share and sales decline. In the abandonment phase, the manufacturer withdraws the product from the market.

**product line.** A group of similar products sold by the same company.

**product manager.** A marketing executive responsible for a company's planning. Product managers specialize in product differentiation, promotion, pricing, and distribution.

**product standards.** See *standards*.

**product testing.** An evaluation of a product's performance, usually by an independent third-party firm. Products are tested for defects and marketability. Test results are often used in product promotions.

**produit national brut (PNB).** French: gross national product.

**professional liability insurance.** Also called professional indemnity insurance, a policy that protects professionals, such as physicians and lawyers, against negligence claims. Although these policies cover specialists in a number of areas, they are commonly purchased by members of licensed professions.

**profit.** The return on capital or an investment. Profit is the amount earned after costs are deducted. It is sometimes expressed as a return on assets, i.e., net income divided by total assets, or a return on equity, i.e., net income divided by total equity.

**profit and loss statement.** See *financial statement.*

**profit à prendre.** The right to remove a fixture from the land of another. The object removed must be corporal, e.g., plants, minerals, animals, but not water.

**profit center.** A business unit that produces revenues and expenditures. The income and expenses of a profit center are ultimately factored into the parent company's financial statement and balance sheet. Compare *cost center.*

**profiteer.** A person who earns excessive profits by selling scarce commodities. Profiteers flourish when commodities are rationed due to natural disasters or wars.

**profit forecast.** A prediction by corporate officers of future profits for a certain period. Profit forecasts are made by companies issuing stock or bonds, usually as a part of an initial public offering.

**profit maximizing.** A company's adoption of policies designed to increase profits. Efforts to maximize profits may be reflected by new investments in plants and equipment, changing suppliers or distribution channels, or downsizing, i.e., laying off workers and seeking increased productivity from remaining workers.

**profit motive.** The objective of an investor who supplies capital and/or time in anticipation of increased earnings.

**profit sharing.** Distributing a share of a company's profits to employees, often as cash bonuses or equity. Profit sharing is an incentive intended to induce higher employee productivity.

**profits tax.** A tax imposed on a company's profits, usually in the form of a corporate or corporation tax.

**pro forma (P/F) invoice.** A document provided by an exporter to a buyer in advance of shipment describing the quantity and value of goods to be shipped. Pro forma invoices are used to apply for import licenses, letters of credit, and foreign exchange permits. In the United States, pro forma invoices are accepted for customs entries, so long as a commercial invoice or customs invoice is presented within 180 days of the original filing.

**pro forma statement.** A statement reflecting unrealized gains and losses. Pro forma statements are hypothetical financial statements, often requested by banks reviewing business loan applications. The statement is used to illustrate the impact of a loan or projected earnings on current assets and liabilities.

**program trading.** Computerized trading on a stock exchange. Computer programs are used to buy or sell blocks of stock when differences in futures and share prices indicate a probable loss or gain. See also *institutional investor* and *limit.*

**progressive tax.** A tax that increases with the taxpayer's ability to pay. The income tax, inheritance tax, and some property taxes are often progressive. The opposite of progressive tax is regressive tax, where the same rate is applied to all taxpayers without regard to income or assets.

**progress payment.** One of multiple installment payments to a contractor. Also known as stage payments, progress payments enable a contractor to collect payments at regular intervals. The buyer also has the advantage of approving work in stages before paying the total contract price.

**prohibitive duty.** See *duty.*

**Project A.** See *Chicago Board of Trade.*

**project finance.** Funding obtained to purchase plant, equipment, technology, etc., for a specific project. Repayments of project loans are repaid funds earned by the project.

**project license.** In the United States, a special validated export license authorizing exports of COCOM-controlled items for a specific purpose. A project license is also issued for some exports of noncontrolled items to controlled destinations. A project license is normally valid for 1 year or less.

**promissory note (pn).** A written promise to pay a bearer or a named payee. A promissory note must be unconditional, signed by the maker, and delivered to the bearer or payee. Promissory notes are negotiable instruments not widely used outside the United States.

**prompt cash.**    A term of sale when the seller expects payment within a short time after a product or service is delivered. Payment on a prompt cash sale is usually due within 2 weeks.

**prompt day.**    1. The day on which a commodity contract matures. 2. The day payments are due and goods delivered on some commodity spot markets.

**prompt ship.**    A ship available for immediate or timely loading.

**pro number.**    A term used by rail and motor carriers to describe the numerical code affixed to a freight bill. Pro numbers are assigned to keep track of shipments.

**prop.**    The abbreviation for property, proprietary, proprietor, and proper.

**property.**    An asset that can be owned. Property may be tangible, i.e., a boat or house, or intangible, i.e., a contract right.

**property bond.**    A bond issued by an insurance company, which reinvests premiums paid by the bondholder in asset-based funds.

**property insurance.**    An insurance policy covering the loss of tangible property, whether personal, business, or real property. The policy usually specifies a maximum coverage, which may permit the policyholder to recover the property's appreciated value, depreciated value property, or replacement cost.

**property tax.**    A tax assessed on the value of tangible property. In some jurisdictions, both real and personal property are taxed.

**proportional rate.**    In transportation, a composite freight rate applied to one shipment transported before or after another covered by a tariff rate. Compare *combination rate.*

**proportional tax.**    See *flat tax.*

**proprietary company (Pty).**    A private limited company in Australia, New Zealand, and South Africa. The abbreviation "Pty" follows the name of the company.

**pro rata.**    Latin: in proportion. A pro rata share is a fraction of any quantity in proportion to a known factor. For example, the pro rata share of a

project's cost is total cost divided by the number participants in the project.

**prospective damages.**    See *damages.*

**prospectus.**    A written offer to sell securities to the general public. Also called an offering circular, a prospectus describes the nature of an issue, the business and financial condition of the issuer, the terms of sale, redemption rights, and dividends paid on the issue. It also identifies the principal officers of the issuing company. An introductory statement, known as a red herring or preliminary prospectus, forms the first page of the prospectus. The red herring, printed in red, contains public disclosure notices to prospective purchasers. In the United States, the prospectus is a summary of the registration statement filed with the Securities and Exchange Commission. A prospectus is obtained from the underwriter or issuer.

**protected market.**    See *protectionism.*

**protection & indemnity club (P&I).**    A self-insurance pool created by shipowners covering risks uninsurable through commercial underwriters. P&I clubs issue most certificates of insurance required in the United States by the Oil Pollution Act of 1990, although some multinational corporations provide their own self-insurance. P&I clubs do not guarantee a member shipowner's solvency.

**protection effect of tariff.**    See *tariff effect.*

**protectionism.**    The product of a government's decision to shield domestic producers from foreign competition. Protectionist policies encompass excessive tariffs, import surcharges, quotas, exchange controls, and nontariff barriers. The arguments for and against protectionism are complex. Some industries are protected to guarantee national security, e.g., defense and shipbuilding industries. Others are protected to preserve employment in sectors with large numbers of unskilled workers, e.g., agriculture and textile industries. On balance, however, protected markets are less efficient and more costly to consumers than unprotected ones.

**protectionist trading practices (PTP).**    Restraints on trade, including protective duties and nontariff barriers.

**protective duty.**    See *duty.*

**protest.**    1. An express reservation by a person performing an act to avoid admitting liability, e.g., a payment made under protest. 2. A formal notice that a draft, check, or bill of exchange has been dishonored by a bank. The notice, signed by a notary public, is legal evidence that the instrument had been presented for payment. 3. The formal objection by an importer to an import classification, or an importer's claim for a refund or adjustment of duties. In the United States, the right of protest commences when a notice of customs entry liquidation is posted. Most protests are filed on Customs Form 19 within 90 days of the entry date. If the party filing the protest is not a customs broker or attorney, the protest is submitted on Customs Form 5291. Under the Tariff Act of 1930, appeals from unfavorable rulings by the U.S. Customs Service are filed with the U.S. Court of International Trade. 4. A sworn statement by a ship's master attesting to cargo damage and the circumstances under which the damage occurred.

**protocol.**   1. Any set of formalities generally expected in a business, trade, proceeding, setting, or course of conduct. Protocol is strictly observed in diplomatic circles. 2. A set of preliminary rules adopted by international agreement.

**provision.**   An accounting procedure for setting aside a sum of money to pay for anticipated losses, usually bad debts and depreciation. The sum is credited to an account and deducted from balance-sheet entries.

**provisional invoice.**   A synonym for preliminary invoice.

**provisional liquidator.**   A person appointed in a bankruptcy proceeding to protect the interests of creditors until a final bankruptcy order is issued.

**prox.**   The abbreviation for *proximo*.

**proximate cause.**   An act or omission without which an event (or chain of events) would not have occurred. In common-law tort actions, a plaintiff must demonstrate that the defendant's negligence bore a causal and provable relationship to the injury suffered. To collect insurance claims, policyholders must demonstrate the relationship between the losses claimed, their insurable interests, and insurable risks covered by the policy.

**proximo (prox.).**   Latin: in the next (month). For example, the 10th proximo denotes the 10th day of the next month. Compare *instant* and *ultimo*.

**proxy.**   One person acting in the place of another. A proxy votes on behalf of an absent director or shareholder at corporate meetings. A proxy may be special, i.e., authorized for one meeting, or general, i.e., authorized for all meetings.

**proxy statement.**   In the United States, a document filed by publicly traded companies with the Securities and Exchange Commission (SEC) under Schedule Rule 14(a). The proxy statement includes, among other things, notice of the time of shareholder meetings, the place, and provisions for proxy revocations. When new directors are recommended, their names, principal occupations, prior transactions with the company, and remuneration are included in proxy statements. SEC Regulation 14(c) requires that an information statement be filed for shareholder meetings when proxies are not mandatory, e.g., when insiders own more than 51 percent of a company's voting shares. Apart from SEC rules, proxy requirements in the United States are also governed by state law and stock exchange regulations.

**prs.**   The abbreviation for pairs.

**PRT.**   The abbreviation for petroleum revenue tax.

**PS.**   The abbreviation for pioneer status.

**PSBR.**   The abbreviation for public-sector borrowing requirement.

**PSC.**   The abbreviation for production sharing contract.

**PSL.**   The abbreviation for private-sector liquidity.

**pt.**   The abbreviation for part and port.

**PTA.**   The abbreviation for Preferential Trade Area for Eastern and Southern Africa.

**PTE.**   The abbreviation for private trading entity.

**PTP.**   The abbreviation for preferential trade program.

**Pty.**   The abbreviation for proprietary company.

**pub.**   The abbreviation for public.

**public company.**   See *company*.

**public corporation.**   See *corporation*.

**public finance.**   Money raised and expended for a public purpose. Goods and services furnished to the general public by a government are financed with funds raised through taxes, fees, or public debt issues.

**public finance accountant.**   In some countries, an accounting firm authorized to prepare the financial statements of national government agencies, municipalities, public corporations, and other public bodies. Special procedures exist for certifying public finance accountants.

**public international law.**   The body of law that governs relations between nations. Public international law derives from custom, treaties, and the judicial decisions of multinational courts, such as the International Court of Justice,i.e., the World Court. Compare *private international law.*

**public issue.**   See *initial public offering.*

**Public Law 480.**   See *PL 480 programs.*

**public lending rate (PLR).**   In some countries, a feature of copyright law that compensates authors for royalties lost when books are loaned by libraries. In the United Kingdom, an author receives a fee, not to exceed 5000 pounds, based on the number of times a book is borrowed from a representative sample of libraries. U.S. copyright law does not contain similar provisions, but it grants library patrons a general public-use exemption for limited copying of copyrighted materials for research and educational purposes.

**public limited company.**   See *company.*

**publicly held corporation.**   See *corporation.*

**public offering.**   An initial public offering (IPO) or a secondary sale of securities issued previously as an IPO.

**public policy.**   An imprecise term meaning a policy adopted to protect the collective rights of a community. Public policy is expressed in statutes, regulations, court decisions, edicts, and decrees. In all countries, acts or contracts in violation of a perceived public policy can be punished or set aside by a legally constituted court or tribunal.

**public-purpose bond.**   A general obligation bond or bond anticipation note. Compare *private-purpose bond.*

**public relations.**   The use of advertising, media, and community service projects to enhance one's public image. Most companies attempt to increase profitability through public relations strategies designed to cast their business and community activities in a favorable light.

**public sector.**   The government sector in a market economy composed of the central government, regional and municipal authorities, and public companies. Local services, including education, police services, etc., are provided by the public sector.

**public store.**   See *public warehouse.*

**public warehouse.**   In the United States, a storage facility operated by the U.S. Customs Service where unentered imports are held. Imports not entered within a specific period of time, usually within 5 working days, are placed in a public warehouse and stored at the expense and risk of the owner. Goods seized or held for examination are sent to a general-order warehouse, which is privately owned and licensed by the U.S. Customs Service.

**public works.**   Construction projects financed with government funds, usually to improve infrastructure. Public works projects are also used to increase employment during depressions or recessions. Large-scale government investments in public works are called pump priming—creating a government budget deficit to stimulate economic activity.

**published accounts.**   Business accounts that must be disclosed by law when a company raises money from the public. Most jurisdictions require that balance sheets, profit and loss statements, annual reports, and auditors' reports be opened for inspection. Disclosure is made by filing published accounts with the appropriate regulatory agency.

**puerto autonomo de...**   Spanish: autonomous port.

**pula.**   The currency of Botswana.

**pump priming.**   See *public works.*

**punitive duty.**   See *duty: countervailing duty.*

**punt.**   The currency of the Republic of Ireland.

**punter.**   A person who speculates in stocks or commodities, usually in anticipation of a quick profit.

**purchase acquisition.**   See *pooling of interests.*

**purchase price.**   The price paid for a product or service. In international trade, the purchase price is the price of an import prior to exportation. The import's purchase price is usually the ex factory price in the exporting country.

**purchasing agent.**   An intermediary, often a private firm, that purchases inventories or supplies for an organization. Some purchasing agents specialize in buying imports.

**purchasing officer.**   A company employee who purchases components, raw materials, or supplies for a business.

**purchasing power parity (PPP).**   1. Relatively equivalent prices or currency values. Equivalences are relative when the only price disparity arises from different exchange rates. A modest difference in exchange rates does not, in itself, affect parity. Thus, consumers in Canada and the United States can be said to have equal power to purchase a given automobile if the only price disparity is the difference in the exchange value of the Canadian dollar and the U.S. dollar. 2. A method used to measure the size of one national economy in relation to another. PPP involves collecting data on the prices of goods and services. Prices in one country are adjusted for exchange rate fluctuations and compared with prices of goods and services in other countries. By factoring out exchange-rate differences and permitting analysts to take different buying patterns into account (e.g., more services than goods or more manufactures than commodities), purchasing-power parity is said to yield a fairly accurate measure of the relative size of a nation's economy. Compare *market-exchange method.*

**purpose statement.**   In the United States, an affidavit signed by a borrower, who obtains a margin loan collateralized by securities, explaining the reasons for the loan. Federal Reserve Regulation U requires persons borrowing on margin from commercial banks to complete Federal Reserve Form U-1.

**put bond.**   Also called an option bond, a debt instrument with a specific redemption right. A bondholder may resell the bond to the issuer at stated times and prices after the issue date. Redemption prices are fixed by the original issue.

**put-of-more option.**   See *option.*

**put option.**   See *option.*

**put through.**   Simultaneous trades concluded by a dealer on a stock exchange. In a put through sale, one client sells and another buys a block of stock.

**pvt.**   The abbreviation for private.

**pw.**   The abbreviation for packed weight.

**pwt.**   The abbreviation for pennyweight.

**pymt.**   An abbreviation for payment.

**pyramid scheme.**   A selling method whereby one distributor sells franchises to regional distributors, who recruit local distributors. Distributors at each level of the pyramid take a smaller share of the inventory and attempt to sell to a dwindling number of buyers. Pyramid schemes are illegal in most places because of the opportunities for fraud.

# Q

**q.** An abbreviation for query.

**QPSII.** The abbreviation for qualified possession source investment income.

**qt.** The abbreviation for quantity.

**Quad.** See *Group of Seven.*

**quadrilateral trade agreement.** A cross-border trade agreement among four countries.

**qualified acceptance.** A limitation on the terms of acceptance by the holder of a bill of exchange. Drawers and prior endorsers are released from liability when an acceptance is qualified unless previously notified of a holder's refusal to accept it.

**qualified endorsement.** An endorser's written disavowal of secondary liability on a financial instrument. When without recourse or a similar limitation is affixed to an instrument, the endorser is not liable if it is not paid or accepted.

**qualified opinion.** An opinion issued by a certified auditor who refuses to verify a company's accounts. Qualified opinions are sometimes issued following audits of small companies, often because of poor internal record keeping. For large corporations, qualified opinions raise more serious questions about a company's financial management.

**qualified possession source investment income (QPSII).** Income earned in Puerto Rico by companies incorporated in the United States. Retained earnings repatriated to the United States are subject to a Puerto Rican toll gate tax, imposed at a maximum rate of 10 percent and an average rate of 4 percent. Earnings not removed are exempt from the toll gate tax and from U.S. federal taxation under Section 936 of the Internal Revenue Code. Section 936 permits the Caribbean Basin Projects Financing Authority (CARIFA) to loan QPSII (QUIPSY) funds for economic and private-sector development projects in Caribbean Basin Initiative (CBI) countries. To be eligible for QUIPSY financing, a CBI country must have signed a Tax Information Exchange Agreement with the United States. See also *Caribbean Basin Initiative II.*

**qualified report.** See *qualified opinion.*

**qualitative market research.** The use of consumer interviews and focus groups to determine if or why a given product has market appeal. The accuracy of the results depends on the size and nature of the sample. Qualitative research is often used to test new product concepts. Compare *quantitative market research.*

**quality assurance.** See *ISO 9000.*

**quality audit.** A process for certifying the quality of a product. See also *American National Standards Institute* and *ISO 9000.*

**quality circle.** A company management technique pioneered in Japan. Quality circles consist of groups of employees who work together to locate problems, manage quality control, and improve productivity.

**quality control.** A systematic procedure designed to maintain the quality of a product. Units of the product may be inspected during production or in postproduction tests, often using random samples. For mass-produced products, quality control is monitored by reviewing charts to plot the percentage of defective products in relation to samples over an extended period of time. A sustained increase in the number of defective samples signals problems in the production process.

**quango.** The acronym for quasi-autonomous government organization.

**quantitative export restraint.** See *bilateral restraint agreement.*

**quantitative market research.** The use of questionnaires, usually mailed, to determine the number of consumers of a product. Samples are divided into categories, such as income or age, to measure the product's appeal to selected demographic groups. Product or advertising strategies may be redesigned based on market research data. Quantitative research is used primarily for existing products. Compare *qualitative market research.*

**quantitative quota.** See *quota.*

**quantity restriction.** See *quota.*

**quantity theory of money.** An economic theory first advanced in the eighteenth-century by David Hume, the Scottish philosopher, correlating prices to the quantity of money circulating in an economy. In a somewhat modified version, the theory was popularized in the United States by Milton Friedman, a twentieth-century economist, who advocates the use of the money supply to control inflation. Friedman's theories underlie much of the shift toward monetarism that influenced U.S. economic policymaking in the 1980s and early 1990s. See also *positive economics.*

**quantum meruit.**   Latin: as much as was earned. *Quantum meruit* underlies an equitable quasi-contract theory for recovering damages when a written contract does not support a legal claim. The plaintiff sues, not for the amount promised in the contract, but for a judicial settlement for the value of goods or services delivered. *Quantum meruit* may permit recovery of damages, even though one party performed an obligation before the contract price was agreed to.

**quarantine certificate.**   In some countries, a sanitation certificate required for livestock and plant imports in addition to a health certificate. In the United States, the Quarantine Division of the Centers for Disease Control determines quarantine requirements, which usually apply to imported birds, cats, dogs, monkeys, and turtles.

**quarterlies.**   In the United States, Form 10Qs, or financial reports issued each quarter by publicly held corporations.

**quasi-autonomous government organization (quango).**   A semiofficial body organized by a government agency to perform a public mandate. Quangos are usually commissions appointed to undertake tasks of limited duration. The commissions are often formed to make unpopular policy recommendations, which elected officials are then free to implement. The expenses of quangos are paid by the public.

**quasi-contract.**   A contract implied from the conduct of the parties, although an agreement has not been concluded. See also *quantum meruit.*

**quasi-money.**   See *broad money.*

**quasi-public corporation.**   See *corporation.*

**quay.**   A wharf constructed for berthing on one side. Fees paid for berthing are called quayage or quay dues.

**Queen's warehouse.**   In Canada and the United Kingdom, a government customs warehouse.

**quetzal.**   The currency of Guatemala.

**quick assets.**   See *liquid assets.*

**quid pro quo.**   Latin: something for something. A compensated exchange, e.g., consideration for a contract or a fee for services.

**quintal.**   One-tenth of a metric ton.

**quintal bag.**   The standard packing unit of a granular commodity, such as bagged coffee. A quintal bag is equivalent to 60 kilograms.

**QUIPSY.**   See *qualified possession source investment income.*

**quitclaim deed.**   A document that passes the title in property to a purchaser but that does not warrant its validity. The seller is not required to defend the title passed to a subsequent buyer. Compare *warranty deed.*

**quoin.**   A wedge-shaped device made of wood or metal and used to secure casks during an ocean voyage.

**quot.**   The abbreviation for quotation.

**quota.**   Also called a quantity restriction (QR), a government-imposed limit on items of trade. Import quotas are enforced to protect domestic industries from competition. Export quotas are used, often by countries belonging to commodity cartels, to control the outflow of a product and maintain prices or to verify the identity of an import's end user. A quota may be global, i.e., applied equally to all other countries, or allocated, i.e., divided among several countries. If a quota is absolute, a quantitative limit is fixed for a set period of time. If a quota is flexible, quantitative limits can be adjusted as circumstances change. When an import tariff rate quota is imposed, unlimited units of a quota item may enter an import market, but a higher duty is assessed on units in excess of a preset number.

**quota cartel.**   A market-division arrangement between members of a cartel, usually international commodity producers. A quota, or a strict limit on the commodity's availability, is the essential component in fulfilling a cartel's purpose. When a commodity derives from a renewable resource, the cartel hopes to maintain prices at a level acceptable to its members. In the case of a nonrenewable resource (e.g., oil), the cartel also hopes to reduce exploitation of the resource and preserve the asset for future generations.

**quota-class merchandise.** Goods subject to quota.

**quota proration.** A means of adjusting imports entered in excess of a quota limit. The adjustment is made at the port of entry; excess imports may be temporarily stored. When goods are allowed to enter, the allocation in a future quota period is reduced.

**quota-share treaty.** A reinsurance contract. The quota-share agreement determines the percentage of risk assumed by a reinsurer.

**quotation.** 1. On a securities exchange, a broker's indication of a security's price, including the highest bid price (i.e., the buying price) and the lowest asked price (i.e., the selling price). 2. In the sales of goods, a seller's statement of a possible selling price. A quotation is not a firm offer to sell.

**quoted company.** A publicly held corporation or listed company.

**quoted price.** The price displayed for a commodity or security in an organized market. Quoted prices are also published in newspapers and financial dailies.

**qy.** An abbreviation for query.

# R

**rack car.** A railroad flatcar.

**rag top.** A canvas-topped trailer or container.

**raider.** An investor who specializes in takeovers of companies with undervalued assets.

**rail plan.** See *pig/piggyback*.

**rainmaker.** A person who has the contacts and influence to conclude an important business deal. See also *agents of influence* and *habatsu*.

**rally.** A surge in market prices following a decline, often based on expectations of higher profits. A technical rally occurs when a market has more buyers than sellers, irrespective of market sentiment. Compare *correction*.

**RAN.** The abbreviation for revenue anticipation note.

**rand.** The currency of South Africa.

**R&CC.** The abbreviation for riot and civil commotion.

**R&D.** The abbreviation for research and development.

**R&E.** The abbreviation for research and expenditure. See *research and development*.

**range forward.** A foreign exchange contract to buy a specific quantity of currency in order to limit losses from falling exchange rates. A range forward contains both futures and options provisions, permitting the holder to buy at the strike price on rising exchange rates.

**ratchet effect.** A change in an economic variable, such as prices, made irreversible because of parallel changes in other variables. For example, a temporary wage increase in one sector can cause price increases in other sectors. The multiplier effect ripples through the entire economy, resulting in sustained inflation.

**rate of drawback.** See *duty drawback*.

**rate of exchange.** See *exchange rate*.

**rate of return.** 1. Also called return on assets and return on equity, the annual net income from an investment. Rates of return are after-tax yields expressed as a percentage of the original investment. 2. In equity finance, a company's earnings per share. 3. The gross annual yield on a time deposit or a certificate of deposit. Gross annual yield is the effective annual yield, including accrued or compounded interest.

**rating.** A quality rating given to borrowers, certificates of deposits, commercial paper, corporate bonds, and other financial instruments. The evaluations issued by rating services indicate the degree of lender or investor risk. See also *Standard and Poor's*.

**rationalization.** The process of restructuring a business to increase efficiency and reduce costs. Restructuring can involve downsizing, i.e., closing plants, merging with another business, sharing costs, etc. See also *capacity stabilization agreement*.

**rationing by price.** Increasing prices to reduce consumption, often on necessary commodities. Although luxury goods are rationed by price, the term is most often applied to commodities in short supply. See also *scarcity*.

**rationing of exchange.** A procedure for controlling the outflow of foreign exchange. In a controlled regime, foreign exchange is issued first for official or priority purposes. Normally, preference is given to foreign exchange earners and low priority to consumer imports. Exchange is issued by a government or its authorized agents.

**readily marketable staples.** See *Federal Reserve Regulation A*.

**real estate.** See *real property*.

**real estate investment trust (REIT).** In the United States, a private corporation or trust that earns income from profit-generating realty. An equity REIT owns and manages income-producing properties, such as office buildings or shopping centers. A mortgage REIT provides mortgage-backed lending to real estate developers. Although shareholder dividends are taxable, a REIT distributing 90 percent of its earnings as dividends is exempt from federal taxation.

**real investment.** An investment in capital goods (e.g., plants or equipment) or human development (e.g., schools or health services), as opposed to paper assets (e.g., securities).

**realized gain/loss.**    The profit or loss from the sale of an asset. Compare *paper gain/loss*.

**real property.**    Also called real estate, land or immovable property, such as buildings or houses.

**real rate of interest.**    See *real rate of return*.

**real rate of return.**    The real rate of interest earned on an investment less the inflation rate. When inflation rises above the real interest rate, an investment becomes unprofitable. Real rates of interest are true rates, determined by the rate of inflation in the country where capital is invested. See also *real value*.

**realtor.**    A commission agent who sells real property.

**real value.**    The economic value of an asset adjusted for inflation.    The adjustment is based on a price index, using a base year to calculate increases in market prices.

**real wages.**    The economic value of wages adjusted for inflation. If wages increase faster than prices, a wage earner's standard of living also improves. If wages decrease relative to prices, a wage earner's living standard falls.

**reasonable dispatch.**    In transportation, the implied duty of a common carrier to transport goods with reasonable speed. Reasonable dispatch does not create carrier liability for economic losses suffered by a shipper from nonnegligent delays in delivering goods.

**rebate.**    1. The return of all or a portion of money paid. 2. A discount for a cash or credit purchase. 3. An ocean carrier's refund of a portion of the freight paid by a shipper. Conference contracts often provide for rebates when shippers agree to exclusive carriage arrangements. In the United States, however, carrier rebates are prohibited by the Shipping Act of 1916.

**receivables financing.**    Short-term lending secured by accounts receivables. In most instances, lenders prefer receivables to inventory as collateral because receivables are usually easier to convert to cash.

**receiver.**    In a bankruptcy proceeding, a person appointed to collect and manage a bankrupt's assets until debts have been discharged. The receiver is obligated to hold property in trust for the benefit of creditors and beneficial owners. In business insolvencies, the receiver may be charged with reorganizing a company or liquidating it when obligations to creditors cannot otherwise be satisfied. See also *liquidator*.

**recession.**    An economic downturn, usually defined as two consecutive quarters of decline in real gross national product preceded by a sudden increase in the unemployment rate. After World War II, countercyclical policies were often used to avert or soften the impact of recessions. Between 1980 and 1992, monetary policy was the favored tool for stimulating economic expansion.

**Reciprocal Trade Agreements (RTA) Act of 1934.** In the United States, an amendment to the Tariff Act of 1930 establishing reciprocity in trade relations as official U.S. policy and approving the use of flexible duties to adjust tariff rates in response to trading partners' actions. The act also created the Reciprocal Trade Agreements Program under which the President negotiates bilateral agreements granting unconditional most-favored-nation status to trading partners. The RTA program has been superseded by obligations incurred under the General Agreement on Tariffs and Trade and authorized by the Trade Expansion Act of 1962.

**Reciprocal Trade Agreements Program.**    See *Reciprocal Trade Agreements Act of 1934*.

**reciprocity.**    In international trade negotiations, the mutual exchange of benefits between participants. Also known as mutuality of benefits, reciprocal concessions may involve equivalent duty reductions or more complicated issues, such as equal access to markets. When mutual concessions are granted in specific sectors, the exchange of benefits is known as sectoral reciprocity. Compare *balance of concessions*.

**reclamation.**    In securities trading, the right of one party to reclaim money or securities from another when a transaction proves irregular. Fraud and theft are the usual bases for reclamation.

**recommended retail price (RRP).**    Also called manufacturer's retail price, the selling price for a product suggested by its manufacturer. Many countries prohibit recommended retail prices unless price maintenance is in the public interest.

**reconsignment.**    A change in a bill of lading at the shipper's request when goods are in transit.

The cargo may be reassigned to a different destination or to a different consignee.

**record.**   1. A memorial of an event or proceeding. 2. A unit of information in a database or computer file. Records are usually separated by fields for each category of information.

**record date.**   1. In equity financing, the date on which declared dividends are payable or when shareholders are entitled to vote on corporate matters. 2. In bond financing, the payment date when bondholders are entitled to collect principal and interest.

**recourse.**   See *holder in due course* and *with recourse.*

**red clause credit.**   A method of intermediate financing that allows an exporter to obtain an advance against the proceeds of a letter of credit. The advance is used to purchase goods or services needed to manufacture a product for export. Compare *green clause letter of credit.*

**redeemable share.**   See *redemption.*

**redelivery.**   The return of a vessel to its owner by a charterer.

**redemption.**   1. The repayment of principal by the issuer of a bond or preferred stock. Debt securities are redeemed on the redemption date, which can be later than the maturity date or the call date. The issuer pays a premium if a bond is called before maturity or a specified call date. See also *refunding.* 2. The resale of mutual fund shares to the fund's manager. The liquidation price is the net asset value price. 3. In bankruptcy, a debtor's payment of market value to reclaim personal property.

**redemption date.**   See *redemption.*

**redemption yield.**   See *yield.*

**red herring.**   See *prospectus.*

**rediscount.**   The process of discounting a previously discounted banker's acceptance, bill of exchange, or promissory note. When an instrument is rediscounted, funds are advanced to the creditor who originally discounted it. In the United Kingdom, commercial paper is rediscounted at discount houses.   In the United States, Federal Reserve Banks rediscount debt paper previously discounted by commercial banks. See also *discount window.*

**redraft.**   The drawing of a subsequent draft or bill of exchange by the holder of a previously dishonored instrument. The redrafted instrument has a face value equal to, or greater than, that of the original instrument. Penalties are added, including the cost of exchange rate losses and protest fees. The holder may draw the new draft on the maker or endorser (s) of the original instrument.

**reefer service.**   Refrigerated shipping service for perishable break-bulk cargoes.

**reexports.**   Goods imported for the entrepôt trade and subsequently shipped to a foreign destination. Reexports are usually eligible for duty drawbacks. In balance-of-payments accounts, earnings from reexports are distinguished from domestic export earnings. Compare *reimports.*

**reference price.**   Under the European Community's (EC's) Common Agricultural Policy, the trigger price for certain vegetables, fruits, fish, and wine. The EC suspends imports or imposes a levy when import prices fall below the reference price.

**reference rate.**   See *base rate.*

**refer to drawer.**   In some countries, a bank's notice that a draft is dishonored. The notice can mean the maker's account is overdrawn, the check is incorrectly written, or a garnishee order is outstanding. In the United States, banks stamp "insufficient funds" on unpaid checks when an account is overdrawn.

**refinance credit.**   A loan facility opened on behalf of a foreign importer when an exporter will not extend credit. A local branch of a foreign bank discounts a bill of exchange drawn on the buyer. The exporter receives the proceeds from the branch in the exporting country.

**refinancing.**   A new loan that alters the terms of an existing loan and adds to the amount of the debt owed. Loans are often refinanced at lower interest rates. See also *restructured loan.*

**reflation.**   A government program to stimulate economic growth. See also *Keynesian economics.*

**refugee capital.**   Also known as hot money, funds invested offshore in anticipation of high profit.

**refunding.**   Repayment of the principal owed on a corporate or government bond. Bonds are redeemable when the indenture provides for redemption before maturity. Some redemption provisions permit refundings only from sinking funds, while others allow the issuer to finance refunding with lower-rate issues. When interest rates fall, issuers benefit from lower costs when high-rate bonds are redeemed with proceeds from a new issue.

**regional development banks.**    See *development bank*.

**regional information kits.**    See *country information kits*.

**registered agent.**    See *foreign agent*.

**registered bond.**    A bond whose owner is identified in the records of the issuer or its transfer agent. A bond is fully registered when both principal and interest are registered in the name of the owner. When only principal, and not interest, is registered in the name of the owner, a bond is partially registered. Interest and principal for fully registered bonds are paid by checks issued by the transfer agent. Partially registered bonds are negotiated by the holder's endorsement. Compare *bearer bond*.

**registered company.**    See *company*.

**registered name.**    In the United Kingdom, the name used to incorporate a business. The use of names already registered or deemed offensive is prohibited by law. Registered names are exhibited at the place of business, on business stationery, and on bills of exchange.

**registered office.**    In the United Kingdom, a business address listed with the Registrar of Companies, which must be notified of address changes within 2 weeks. The notice is published in the *London Gazette*. Registers containing names of company directors, secretaries, and members are kept at the registered office.

**registered stock.**    Convertible debentures or debenture stock owned by holders whose names are inscribed in a register.

**register ton.**    A unit of measure used to determine the cubic capacity of a ship. A register ton is equal to 100 cubic feet.

**Registrar of Companies.**    In the United Kingdom, the agency responsible for regulating companies. England, Scotland, and Wales each

have registrars. Among others, a registrar's duties include maintaining records and issuing certificates of incorporation. See also *Companies House*.

**registration.**    1. In most countries, the process by which a company informs the appropriate agency of its intention to operate a public business and meets regulatory disclosure requirements. 2. In the United States, the process of filing a registration statement with the Securities and Exchange Commission.

**registration statement.**    In the United States, a statement filed for most public securities offerings and required by the Securities Act of 1933. Offerings valued under $500,000 are exempt from registration. A registration statement is placed with the Securities and Exchange Commission, disclosing the issuer's financial position, identifying its management, and describing the use to be made of the proceeds. The statement also discloses the number of shares issued and the offering price. A waiting period between the time the statement is filed and a public offering is mandatory. Since 1982, the registration requirement can be satisfied by shelf registration.

**règlement.**    French: regulation.

**règlement de compte.**    French: settlement of account.

**regressive tax.**    A tax with uniform rates applied irrespective of a taxpayer's income. The taxpayer's burden decreases as income rises. Excise taxes, flat taxes, and value-added taxes are regressive taxes. Compare *progressive tax*.

**regular tonnage tax.**    See *tonnage tax*.

**regulation.**    1. An administrative rule made by a government agency and usually authorized by statute. 2. A government program designed to control the conduct of private enterprises. For example, governments regulate private industries that provide necessary public services, e.g., telecommunications, transportation, and other utilities.

**Regulation 181.**    See *hazardous cargo*.

**regulatory accounting principles (RAPs).**    In the United States, special accounting rules authorized for savings and loan associations (S&Ls). RAPs were adopted following the collapse of the U.S. savings and loan industry in the 1980s. Among other things, RAPs permit an S&L to defer write-offs of liabilities and accelerate reported income. See also *Resolution Trust Corporation.* Compare *generally accepted accounting principles.*

**rehypothecation.**   A method used by banks to obtain loans secured by negotiable instruments in their possession. The instruments represent outstanding obligations payable by commercial customers. The loans are obtained from a central bank. Compare *hypothecation.*

**reimports.**   1. Products exported for outward processing and returned to the original manufacturer for sale in the home market. 2. Locally-manufactured products purchased abroad for sale in the domestic retail market. When domestic goods can be purchased at lower prices in foreign markets, sellers profit from buying the same goods abroad and selling them at a discount in local retail markets. See also *gray market.* Compare *reexports.*

**reinsurance.**   A form of insurance protection whereby primary insurers pass the risks of an existing insurance contract on to secondary insurers. Reinsurers are secondary underwriters who share insurance risks with primary insurers. They are paid from premiums received by the primary insurer, although policyholders are not notified when risks are reinsured. A facultative agreement, creating facultative reinsurance, is an agreement between a single reinsurer and an underwriter covering a specified category of risk. Conversely, a treaty arrangement is an agreement among several reinsurers to accept specific types of risk within a limited dollar amount. Compare *coinsurance.*

**reintermediation.**   The inflow of funds to depository financial institutions, principally banks, from equities and money-market funds. Investors move funds into bank time deposits and similar instruments, to benefit from deposit insurance. See also *disintermediation.*

**REIT.**   The abbreviation for real estate investment trust.

**rejected merchandise.**   Nonconforming imported goods, which are eligible for duty drawback. Rejected merchandise deviates in some manner from the importer's expectations based on specifications or previously inspected samples. Rejected goods are returned to the customs agency for reexportation.

**related-party transaction.**   In customs, a factor in determining transaction value when a sale involves closely related parties (e.g., subsidiaries and parent companies). In the United States, a related-party importer must establish the arm's-length nature of an import price. Otherwise duties are based on the market value of the import rather than the declared transaction value. See also *test value.*

**related specificity.**   In customs, a rule used to select tariff classifications. An import fitting descriptions in two or more classifications is placed in the tariff category that most nearly describes it.

**released valuation rate.**   A lower freight rate offered by a ground carrier when shippers agree to limit damage claims. In the United States, valuation rate agreements are approved by the Interstate Commerce Commission.

**release on minimum documentation (RMD).**   In Canada, a procedure for expedited import release. RMD information identifies the importer, describes the import, and contains an entry transaction number in bar-code form. Within 5 working days of an RMD, full import documentation is presented and duties and fees are paid.

**release port.**   The port at which goods are freed from customs custody.

**relief consignments.**   In customs, emergency relief supplies destined for victims of natural disasters. Customs jurisdictions have special procedures for accelerated release of relief consignments.

**reliquidation.**   See *liquidation.*

**remainder.**   In real property law, the right to own land once another's temporary right to possess it has expired. A remainder becomes effective when the owner of the remainder, known as the remainderman, has an unconditional right to possess land. For example, a remainderman's claim becomes unconditional when another person's life estate expires, provided title to the property has not reverted to the grantor or the grantor's heirs. See also *freehold.*

**remainderman.**   See *remainder.*

**remittance.**   A payment on a debt. An installment payment is a partial remittance, leaving a balance remaining on the debt. A full remittance pays off a debt.

**remitting bank.**    A bank that acts as the forwarding agent for documents of title or payments.

**renegotiated loan.**    See *restructured loan*.

**renounceable documents.**    An allotment letter or other written evidence of temporary stock ownership. Renounceable documents are documents of title transferable to others.

**rent.**    The amount paid for the use of another's real property, usually in monthly installments over a lease term of 1 year.

**rentes.**    French: bonds issued by a European government, often in France. The bonds are irredeemable, and their annual interest is called *rente*.

**rentier.**    French: A person who lives on *rentes*, or unearned income, rather than a salary.

**renunciation.**    The surrender of ownership rights in an asset to another.

**reorganization.**    1. A corporate restructuring, usually involving the combination of related firms. 2. In the United States, a corporate restructuring in bankruptcy. Reorganizations are governed by Chapter 11 of the Bankruptcy Code.

**reparation.**    1. In international law, a government payment to foreign nationals as compensation for injury caused by improper official conduct. Compensation is owed foreign nationals who are victims of war or unlawful detention or whose property is confiscated or expropriated. 2. In ground transportation, a carrier's refund of illegal charges. In the United States, reparations are fixed by the Interstate Commerce Commission.

**repatriation.**    1. The removal of a financial asset, including capital or investment proceeds, from a foreign country to the country of domicile. 2. The return of a person to the country of origin.

**replacement cost.**    In accounting, the current cost of replacing an asset with one suited to similar uses. Original purchase price and depreciation are not factors in calculating replacement cost.

**replenishment.**    1. In official finance, the refunding of a multilateral financial institution. 2. In India, a special import license for imports designated for reexport.

**reply time.**    In shipping, the duration of a charter offer. When the recipient accepts offered terms during the reply time, the offerer is bound by the original offer. If the reply time expires without acceptance, an offer can be renegotiated.

**repo.**    See *repurchase agreement*.

**réport.**    French: premium.

**reporting currency.**    Also called a functional currency, the currency in which a multinational firm's financial statements are reported to lenders, regulatory agencies, and shareholders.

**reporting day.**    The day a vessel charterer is authorized to begin loading cargo.

**repossession.**    The seizure by a creditor of collateral when a debtor defaults on a loan.

**representation.**    In law, a statement made by a party to a contract, especially concerning a material fact. Compare *misrepresentation*.

**repudiation.**    1. A suggestion by one party that a contract will be breached. See also *breach of contract*. 2. A refusal to pay a debt, often by a government for a debt incurred by a previous government. Compare *default*.

**repurchase agreement (repo, RP).**    1. In finance, an agreement to sell and repurchase a stated number of financial instruments on a fixed date at a prearranged price. Repurchase agreements with maturities of more than 1 day are known as term repurchase agreements. 2. In banking, an agreement by a central bank to purchase government securities from a dealer, who agrees to buy them back at a stated price on a specified date. When the transaction is reversed, the agreement is known as a reverse repurchase agreement or a matched sale-repurchase agreement. Repurchase agreements are used by central banks, primarily in France, Germany, and the United States, to make temporary adjustments in the reserves of commercial banks. Outright sales or purchases of securities have longer-term effects. When a central bank sells securities, commercial bank reserves are reduced, leaving less money for lending and investment. When a central bank purchases securities, commercial bank reserves are increased. U.S. open-market operations agreements generally last 1 day and never more than 15 days. In France, the usual period is 10 to 20 days, while agreements spanning 28 to 35 days are customary in Germany. Repurchase agreements are not factors in reserve regulation in Japan or the United Kingdom. See also *discount window* and *interest rate policy.*

**request for information and inspection form.** A form sent from an inspection firm to a shipper requesting information about cargo. The request is forwarded when an import license is issued. Requests for inspection are noted on bills of lading and air waybills. See also *Société Générale de Surveillance, S.A.*

**resale price maintenance (RPM).** An agreement between a manufacturer and wholesalers (or retailers) to sell at an agreed price. Most RPMs are illegal in the United States and several other countries.

**rescheduling.** Debt service reduction, often replacing an existing loan with a new one. Usually, the new loan carries a reduced interest rate, longer maturity, or deferred payments of principal. Reschedulings of a developing country's debts are undertaken in connection with structural adjustment programs approved by the International Monetary Fund and the World Bank. Official debts (i.e., debts owed to governments or multilateral financial institutions) are restructured through the Paris Club. Country commercial debt is restructured through the London Club. Ideally, a rescheduling improves an indebted country's debt service ratio. See also *debt conversion program.*

**rescission.** Setting a contract aside by mutual agreement between the parties or by a unilateral court order to restore one party to a prior position. Material mistakes, misrepresentations, unconscionable bargains, and undue influence are grounds for rescinding a contract. Rescission is an equitable remedy available at the discretion of a court.

**research and development (R&D).** Broadly, inquiry undertaken by an organization to enhance the state of technical knowledge or to develop a new process or product. R&D encompasses pure research, pursued primarily to further knowledge, and applied research, intended to produce a specific result. Tax laws in most countries permit companies to deduct or amortize R&D expenses,

also known as research and expenditure, through investment tax credits.

**reservation price.** A floor price set by a seller of goods or services.

**reserve assets.** Hard currency or precious metals, usually gold, held as reserves by a national government. Reserve assets are maintained by central banks as security for their national currencies.

**reserve bank.** See *central bank.*

**reserve capital.** Also known as uncalled capital, funds held by a company as reserves to pay expenses, finance investments, and retire debts, especially in the event of restructuring or dissolution.

**reserve currency.** The currency portion of a nation's central bank reserve assets. Reserve currencies are held to secure the value of private holdings, are used as intervention media to preserve financial liquidity, are quoted in commodity and stock markets as standards of value, and are adopted as pegs to which weaker, less stable currencies are linked. The principal reserve currencies of the early 1990s are the Japanese yen and the Deutsche mark, although the U.S. dollar remains the international safe-haven currency. Also called strong currencies, reserve currencies trade at a premium in foreign exchange markets. See also *hard currency.*

**reserve regulation.** Rules set by a central bank requiring commercial banks to segregate certain financial assets. Open-market operations are major instruments of reserve management. In France, Germany, and the United States, central banks use repurchase agreements to regulate commercial bank reserves. See also *interest rate policy.*

**reserves.** Funds reserved for future payments. 1. In accounting, an allowance for future obligations set aside from retained earnings. 2. In banking, reserves can be primary or secondary. Primary (or legal) reserves are funds segregated to meet a bank's operational expenses and comply with central bank reserve regulations. Secondary reserves are funds invested in liquid assets, such as Treasury securities. Bank reserve accounts are non-interest-bearing deposits maintained with a central bank or a correspondent bank. See also *repurchase agreement.*

**reserve tranche.**   See *International Monetary Fund*.

**resident legal.**   A legal term of art denoting a person or firm with a permanent abode or business address in a given jurisdiction. Not to be confused with domicile, residence is any locality where a person resides or a firm does business. Thus, a party may have more than one residence, but only one domicile. Compare *nonresident*.

**residuary legatee.**   An heir to the portion of a decedent's estate not specifically willed to others.

**Resolution Trust Corporation (RTC).**   In the United States, a government corporation created by the Financial Institutions Reform, Recovery and Enforcement Act of 1989 to liquidate problem savings and loan associations (S&Ls). Operated by the Federal Deposit Insurance Corporation, the RTC transfers assets from insolvent to solvent financial institutions. The RTC is scheduled to be dissolved in 1996. Its assets will be deposited with the Savings Association Insurance Fund.

**respondent.**   1. In civil and criminal law, a party responding to a legal claim. 2. In admiralty law, a defendant against whom a claim is lodged.

**respondentia.**   See *hypothecation*.

**restitution.**   1. The restoration of a right of which a person has been unfairly deprived. Restitution derives from the legal principle that one party should not be unjustly enriched at the expense of another. See also *quantum meruit*. 2. A subsidy paid to a farmer under the European Community's Common Agricultural Policy.

**restraint of trade.**   1. An illegal contract preventing one or more parties from engaging in lawful commerce. Unreasonable restraints on trade are illegal per se, e.g., an agreement involving price fixing, restricting a party's right to enter a different trade, barring another from selling a dissimilar product or service, etc. Compare *noncompetition agreement*. 2. An unreasonable act by a government banning imports for reasons unrelated to national security or public health.

**restricted asset.**   An asset that cannot be freely used or transferred by the owner. Assets may be restricted by creditors, government directive, or court order.

**restrictive covenant.**   A contract clause that limits the conduct of one party to a transaction.

In the United States, restrictive covenants are unenforceable when their purpose is illegal discrimination based on race, religion, national origin, or, in some instances, gender. However, a noncompetition covenant limiting the right of an employee to compete with a former employer may be enforceable unless it constitutes an unreasonable restraint of trade, e.g., prohibiting a former employee from entering a related, but different, type of business or the same business in a different location. See also *restrictive trade practice*.

**restrictive endorsement.**   See *endorsement*.

**restrictive list.**   A list of prohibited imports barred for public health, safety, or cultural reasons. In the Middle East, for example, restrictive lists prohibit imports of foods deemed unclean under various religious dietary laws.

**restrictive trade practice.**   1. A government policy or business agreement that limits the free sale of goods or services. 2. In the United Kingdom, an agreement prohibited by the Restrictive Trade Practices Acts of 1956, 1968, and 1976, as well as the Fair Trading Act of 1973. For example, restrictive covenants in supplier contracts are registered with the director general of fair trading and, in some instances, investigated by the Restrictive Practices Court. These agreements are presumed to injure the public interest.

**restructured loan.**   Also called a renegotiated loan, a debt with payment terms other than those originally agreed to. Debts are restructured when a debtor's financial condition deteriorates. Restructuring enables the lender to avoid foreclosure on collateral or a charge-off of the debt. Normally, the loan's maturity is extended or the interest rate reduced. See also *rescheduling*.

**retail cooperative society.**   A nonprofit organization engaged in retail trade. Cooperative buying societies are owned by individuals, who pay a small subscription fee and receive periodic dividends from surplus profits. Dividends are usually apportioned according to the value of members' purchases.

**retail trade.**   The sale of products or services directly to consumers. Retail sales are made through distributors known as retailers. Compare *wholesale trade*.

**retained earnings.** Profits not distributed to a company's shareholders or placed in a surplus account. Also called retentions, retained earnings are included in a company's capital reserves.

**retained profits.** Annual earnings reinvested by a company. Retained profits are a primary source of expansion capital, also called ploughed-back profits.

**retaliation.** A measure imposed in response to unfair trade practices. Retaliation usually takes the form of a 100 percent duty on imports from the offending country. If the unfair practice involves a given class of exports, retaliation is often directed against the same class of imports. See also *cross retaliation* and *retorsion*.

**retiring a bill.** The act of redeeming the obligation arising from a bill of exchange. Normally, a bill of exchange is discounted and paid in an amount less than its face value at maturity.

**retorsion.** 1. Retaliation. 2. In international law, one government's reprisal against the citizens of another for misconduct toward its own citizens. Retorsion is not illegal under international law, although a government that treats nonnationals harshly, even for seemingly just cause, faces universal public condemnation.

**retractable bond.** A bond with a redemption option. The bond is redeemable upon exercise of the option on a prescribed date.

**returned and refused shipment.** An insurance provision that covers returned cargo. When goods are refused by a buyer, the policyholder is reimbursed for costs.

**returned check.** A check returned unpaid by the maker's bank. In the United States, returned checks are stamped with an insufficient-funds notice. Returned checks are usually presented twice for payment before the maker is notified of the insufficiency. See also *refer to drawer*.

**returned without action.** In the United States, a stamped notice on a validated export license application that the license is not needed. The U.S. Customs Service honors returned-without-action notices and frees cargo for export.

**return on assets (ROA).** The measure of a company's efficiency in exploiting its assets. ROA is a company's net income divided by the market value of its assets. Pricing assets at book value usually undervalues a company's holdings.

**return on equity (ROE).** The measure of an investment portfolio's profitability. ROE is net income divided by total equity. Comparing ROEs enables an investor to judge the relative performance of a company's or industrial sector's stock.

**return shipment rate.** The rate charged by a common carrier to return empty packaging or shipping containers to a shipper.

**returns to scale.** See *economies of scale*.

**revalidation patent.** See *introduction patent*.

**revalorization.** The process of replacing one currency unit with another. Currency that has been substantially depreciated by frequent devaluations is usually revalorized. Compare *revaluation*.

**revaluation.** 1. In finance, the process used by a central monetary authority to increase the nominal value of its currency in relation to gold or foreign currencies. Countries with extended balance-of-payments surpluses may revalue a currency to, among other things, increase consumers' purchasing power. Conversely, a country with balance-of-payments deficits may devalue its currency. In the contemporary floating-exchange-rate system, money markets effectively revalue and devalue currencies on an ad hoc basis. Compare *devaluation* and *revalorization*. 2. In international trade, a customs adjustment in the declared value of an import. In some countries, customs agents regularly revalue imports on the theory that most shippers undervalue exports to lower import duties. Importers attempt to protect against revaluations by having prices certified in the exporting country. See also *chamber of commerce certificate*.

**revenue account.** The segment of an accounting ledger devoted to earned income and related expenses.

**revenue anticipation note (RAN).** In the United States, a short-term, tax-exempt note issued by a municipality. Revenue notes resemble general obligation bonds and are backed by the issuer's credit. RANs are repaid from tax revenues. See also *tax anticipation note*. Compare *bond anticipation note*.

**revenue bond.** A bond issued by a government agency to finance the construction of a public facility, e.g., a stadium or toll bridge. Principal and interest are repaid from income earned through user fees. In the United States, revenue bonds are not backed by the taxing authority of the issuing government agency, but they are tax exempt in the issuing jurisdiction. Compare *general obligation bond*.

**revenue tariff.** A duty designed to increase an importing country's revenue.

**revenue ton.** The measure used by a carrier to calculate freight charges based on a measurement ton or a weight ton. Ordinarily, a revenue ton is computed using a base rate, which excludes surcharges and accessorial fees, such as wharfage or pilotage.

**reverse repurchase agreement.** See *repurchase agreement*.

**reverse swap.** A transaction used to realize a gain on interest rate or exchange rate changes by trading an existing swap agreement for a new contract in the secondary market. Depending on the circumstances, a swap can be reversed with the original coparty or with a new coparty.

**reverse takeover.** The takeover of a public company by a private firm when a government privatizes a state-owned industry. Public companies are purchased, often at a discount and usually by firms in the process of expanding. When reverse takeovers involve publicly traded companies, privatization is ordinarily subject to stock exchange regulation.

**reversible lay days.** A charter party clause that assigns loading and unloading times to one unit. The shipper is credited for unused loading time and in recompense is given additional unloading time.

**Revised American Foreign Trade Definitions— 1941.** In the United States, international trade definitions published in 1919 and reissued in 1941 by the U.S. Chamber of Commerce in cooperation with the National Council of American Importers and the National Foreign Trade Council. The revised definitions have been largely supplanted by international commercial terms, but still have limited legal standing when incorporated into commercial contracts.

**revocable letter of credit.** See *irrevocable letter of credit*.

**revocable trust.** See *trust*.

**revolving line of credit.** A credit facility that is automatically renewed, unless canceled. A revolving credit does not have fixed repayment terms, although it does have an upper limit. The credit may be drawn against or paid off without a penalty at any time. A commitment fee is charged by banks to establish credit lines.

**revolving underwriting facility (RUF).** A medium-term lending facility for Euronotes issued in overseas markets, usually of 3 to 7 years' duration. Euronotes typically have maturities under 6 months and are offered through tender panels composed of commercial and investment banks. The notes are priced at a spread above the London interbank offered rate. The revolving credit is arranged by a bank, known as an arranger, and managed by the original underwriter, known as a project manager. When the project manager is authorized to transfer management to another bank, the arrangement is called a transferable revolving underwriting facility. See also *note issuance facility*.

**rial.** The currency of Iran, Oman, and Yemen.

**rider.** Any amendment to a contract or insurance policy. The parties acknowledge a rider as a clarification of the agreement.

**riel.** The currency of Cambodia.

**rigging a market.** An effort to corner a commodity or securities market in order to influence prices. The holder of a strong market position can maintain or depress prices by buying or selling.

**right of establishment.** In international trade, an aspect of national treatment, whereby a country treats foreign investors equally with domestic investors. Rights of establishment are crucial to liberalized trade in services where a market presence is required to deliver the product. Establishment rights include equivalent rights before administrative and legal bodies.

**right of redemption.** See *redemption*.

**right of resale.** The right of a seller to resell goods under contract when the buyer fails to pay the purchase price. When a contract covers perishable goods, or when the seller is notified of the buyer's inability to pay, goods can be resold and damages recovered from the buyer.

**right of survivorship.**   A spouse's claim to jointly owned marital property in assets held in joint tenancy.

**rights letter.**   See *rights offering*.

**rights offering.**   A written offer from a corporation to sell newly issued or additional shares to existing shareholders. Also called a rights issue, rights offerings are used to raise new capital without diluting existing shareholders' holdings and usually involve the sale of common stock. The rights letter containing the offer states the date on which the purchase option must be exercised. Shares sold under a rights offering are priced lower than public-issue shares. Compare *bought deal* and *vendor placing*.

**Rio Accords.**   See *United Nations Conference on Environment and Development*.

**riot and civil commotion (R&CC).**   An event requiring a special clause for insurance coverage. Normally, losses arising from civil disorders are not covered by commercial insurance. See also *country risk*.

**Rio Treaty.**   See *Organization of American States*.

**risk.**   1. The possibility that a loss will be realized on a loan or an investment. The risk may arise from the financial condition of the borrower or from circumstances beyond the borrower's control. See also *commercial risk* and *country risk*. 2. In insurance, an assessment of the probability that an event will occur. A measurable probability is called an insurable risk, largely because a premium can be calculated. Accidents, fires, floods, etc., are insurable risks. An improbable event is an uninsurable risk. See also *warranted free*.

**risk capital.**   Also known as venture capital, money invested in a new or expanding company, usually at considerable risk. Venture capital is often provided in exchange for stock in a newly emerging company. Depending on the tax jurisdiction, investors in limited partnerships may realize tax benefits from deductible losses attributable to some risky investments.

**risk distribution.**   Risk sharing, or spreading the risks inherent in a given venture, to diminish the prospect of serious economic loss to a single investor. See also *syndication*.

**risk management.**   Also known as risk minimization, procedures adopted by an organization to reduce its exposure to potential losses. Banks sell commercial risk management services, including credit risk analyses, interest rate and exchange rate hedges, and business loan caps. In international trade and transactions, banks and other firms determine country risk based on evaluations of a specific transaction or the aggregate exposure in a particular country. Among others, risk minimization strategies include purchasing export credit insurance or overseas investment insurance, entering into barter arrangements, and requiring irrevocable letters of credit.

**risk retention.**   See *self-insurance*.

**River Plate Basin System.**   See *Sistema de la Cuenca del Plata*.

**riyal.**   The currency of Qatar and Saudi Arabia.

**RM.**   The abbreviation for *marché à règlement mensuel*.

**RMD.**   The abbreviation for release on minimum documentation.

**ROA.**   The abbreviation for return on assets.

**roadstead.**   The site near a harbor where ocean vessels anchor before entering a berth.

**Robinson-Patman Act of 1936.**   In the United States, an amendment to the Clayton Act of 1914 barring anticompetitive pricing. The law prohibits special discounts or other price discrimination that might affect a company's market share and create a monopoly. See also *antitrust laws*.

**ROE.**   The abbreviation for return on equity.

**roll-back.**   In international trade, a safeguard measure permitting an importing country to suspend import privileges or reduce negotiated quota levels to avert injury to a domestic industry. See also *escape clause*. Compare *standstill*.

**roll-on, roll-off (RO-RO) service.**   A ferry service with ramps that can be dropped to accommodate cargo loading and unloading. RO-RO service improves cargo handling at congested or inefficient seaports. The service is also used to transport road vehicles by water, for example, the ferry service for automobiles crossing the English Channel.

**rollover.**   1. In banking, the renewal of a loan or an extension of its maturity. 2. In currency dealing, a sale and purchase of currency in one day. In an overnight rollover, delivery is made the day after sale. Compare *spot next, swap,* and *tomorrow next.* 3. A Eurocurrency loan with an interest repricing provision. The interest rate is recomputed at specified intervals at a spread above the London interbank offered rate or another index rate.

**rollover ratio.** The measure of a nation's liquidity as reflected by the average maturity of its external debt.

**rollover relief.** A feature of the capital-gains tax that defers tax payments when gains on an existing asset are deducted from the cost of a newly acquired asset. When the second asset is sold, the taxable gains are increased by profits attributable to the first sale.

**roll trailer.** A trailer used for roll-on, roll-off service when cargoes are transported between piers. Roll trailers are also called MAFI trailers, named for the original German manufacturer.

**roly-poly certificate of deposit (CD).** A series of 6-month debt instruments issued as a unit. The debts have different maturities, although the certificate is held to final maturity. In the United States, roly-poly CDs usually require minimum $5000 investments.

**RO-RO.** The abbreviation for roll-on, roll-off.

**Rosvneshtorgbank.** In Russia, the apparent successor to *Vneshekonombank,* the foreign trade bank of the former Union of Soviet Socialist Republics. As of 1993, most export credit guarantees provided to Russia by the United States required a coguarantee by *Rosvneshtorgbank.* The bank is based is Moscow.

**rough lumber.** Lumber that is sometimes trimmed but not dressed.

**round lot.** In securities trading, an even-numbered block of stock offered for sale. When sold intact, round lots often bring better prices than odd-lots orders, which contain lesser quantities than are usually traded on an exchange.

**round turn.** In commodity trading, the completed purchase and sale of a futures contract.

**routing order.** An instruction to a supplier to route merchandise through a designated freight forwarder.

**royalty.** A fee paid to profit from the property of another. Royalties are granted for the use of intellectual property or for the privilege of extracting and selling minerals from land.

**RPM.** The abbreviation for resale price maintenance.

**RRP.** The abbreviation for recommended retail price.

**RTA.** The abbreviation for Reciprocal Trade Agreements Act of 1934.

**RTC.** The abbreviation for Resolution Trust Corporation.

**ruble.** The national currency of former Soviet Republics, including Georgia, Kazakhstan, Russia, Ukraine, and Uzbekistan. See also *Commonwealth of Independent States.*

**RUF.** The abbreviation for revolving underwriting facility.

**rule.** A regulation or standard adopted by an official body. The process of establishing a standard is known as rule making. In the United States, procedures followed by federal administrative agencies when adopting rules are contained in the Administrative Procedure Act of 1946 (APA). Statutes regulating the conduct of state agencies are substantially patterned after the APA.

**Rule 10(b)-18.** See *safe harbor.*

**Rule 14(a).** See *proxy statement.*

**Rule 415.** See *shelf registration.*

**rule making.** See *rule.*

**Rule of 72.** A formula used to compute the time needed for money to double its value. The number 72 is divided by a given interest rate. For example, a certificate of deposit with a 5 percent rate of interest will double in $14\,^1/_4$ years.

**rules of origin.** In international trade, rules used by an importing country to ascertain country of origin, i.e., the original source of an import. Origin determines the rate of duty paid on an import. It also enables a country to interdict imports from countries under trade sanctions and honor trade commitments, including obligations to protect appellations of origin.

**rummage.** A search by customs agents for contraband, illegal drugs, or weapons.

**running broker.**  A commission agent for the owners or discounters of bills of exchange.

**running-down clause.**  A provision in a hull insurance policy protecting a shipowner from liability resulting from a collision with another ship.

**running time.**  The means of calculating the duration of a ship charter. Running time is expressed in consecutive days, which include weekends and holidays, rather than working days.

**rupee.**  The currency of India, Mauritius, Nepal, Pakistan, the Seychelles, and Sri Lanka.

**rupiah.**  The currency of Indonesia.

**rust bucket.**  A ship in poor condition.

**rye terms.**  In contracts for the sale of bulk granular products, a warranty of quantity and quality. Allowance is made for the reasonable loss of product during transit. See also *fair average quality* and *tale quale*.

# S

**$.** A currency symbol used to represent, among others, the dollar and the yuan.

**s.** The abbreviation for stere.

**SA.** The abbreviation for *sociedad anónima, sociedade anônima, and société anonyme.*

**SAARC.** The abbreviation for South Asian Association for Regional Cooperation.

**sacrifice.** Economic losses arising from rescue actions covered by average.

**SACU.** The abbreviation for Southern African Customs Union.

**SACUA.** The abbreviation for Southern African Customs Union Agreement.

**SAD.** The abbreviation for single administrative document.

**SADCC.** The abbreviation for Southern African Development Coordination Conference.

**SAF.** The abbreviation for structural adjustment facility. See *structural adjustment program.*

**safe custody.** See *safekeeping.*

**safeguards.** Unilateral, temporary restrictions on imports implemented to halt injury to a domestic industry. Escape clause measures authorized by the General Agreement on Tariffs and Trade (GATT) permit a signatory country to exclude imports under standstill arrangements or rollback programs when import surges threaten domestic industries. Safeguards are monitored by the GATT Surveillance Body to prevent their becoming permanent trade barriers. See also *Trade Act of 1974.* Compare *retaliation.*

**safe harbor.** In the United States, Securities and Exchange Commission Rule 10b-18. Known as the safe harbor rule, 10b-18 permits a publicly held company to buy back its stock without facing charges of stock manipulation.

**safekeeping.** A service allowing customers to deposit securities in a bank vault. The bank issues receipts, known as safekeeping certificates, and maintains records for the securities it holds. American depositary receipts and international depositary receipts are examples of safekeeping certificates.

**safe port.** A well-operated port. Safe ports are known in the shipping trade for good facilities, efficient labor, and well-managed traffic.

**safety deposit box.** A small locked box in a bank's vault area rented to customers for storing personal property. Signature cards identify persons authorized to use the box. Entry is controlled with matching keys, one kept by the bank and the other by authorized users. Banks disavow knowledge of a safety deposit box's contents and disclaim liability for lost items placed ostensibly therein.

**Saints' days.** In Christian cultures, holidays honoring venerated persons. The most widely observed is All Saints' Day, a festival dedicated to the Virgin Mary and Christian martyrs. The holiday is observed on or near November 1st in several Christian countries, but it is not uniformly recognized as a bank or public holiday. In Ireland, St. Patrick's Day (March 17) is a bank holiday.

**salary.** An employee's monthly compensation, exclusive of benefits. Executives, professionals, and managerial staff earn salaries. Unlike wages, which are calculated by the hour or week, salaries are stated in annual terms.

**sale and leaseback.** See *leaseback.*

**sale as seen.** A transaction based on a buyer's inspection of goods without the seller's warranty of condition or quality. A buyer takes sold-as-seen cargo free of guarantees or implied warranties.

**sale by sample.** A sale based on a tested sample, often by an independent inspection firm. Contracts for bulk sales contain specific testing terms and include a seller's warranty that the shipment equals the sample in quality. Sale-by-sample contracts stipulate buyers' remedies when inferior goods are delivered. Compare *fair average quality.*

**sale or return.** A conditional sale giving a buyer the option of returning goods by a stated date. Retail distribution contracts often contain sale-or-return provisions.

**sales tax.** A tax on the price of a product or service. Sales taxes are said to be regressive because the tax burden is greatest on low-income taxpayers. When taxes on the sale of components used to produce goods are not deductible by producers, the ratchet effect of sales taxes can be inflationary.

**salvage.**   Wreckage from an accident. In marine insurance, a total-loss-only claim entitles the insurer to sell scrap for salvage value. When general average claims are filed, the salvor, or person who helps rescue a ship, is paid salvage money. A maritime lien arises when salvage money is owed.

**same-condition drawback.**   See *duty drawback.*

**samurai bond.**   In Japan, a bond issued by a foreign corporation. Samurai bonds are unsecured yen-denominated bonds, usually with minimum 5-year maturities.

**sanctions.**   See *economic sanctions.*

**S&IOGA.**   The abbreviation for State & Industry-Organized Government-Approved Trade Mission.

**sanitary certificate.**   See *phytosanitary inspection certificate.*

**sans recours.**   See *without recourse.*

**SAP.**   The abbreviation for structural adjustment program.

**SAR.**   The abbreviation for International Convention on Maritime Search and Rescue. See *International Maritime Organization.*

**SaR/Sarl.**   The abbreviation for *società a responsabilità limitata.*

**Sarl/S.á.R.L**   The abbreviation for société à responsabilité limitée.

**SATCC.**   The abbreviation for Southern African Transport and Communications Commission.

**savings account.**   An account for personal savings deposited with a bank or savings and loan association.

**savings and loan (S&L) association.**   In the United States, a government-chartered financial institution. Also known as thrift institutions, savings and loans were originally voluntary lending associations formed to finance real property purchases. Contemporary S&Ls also make consumer loans and issue credit cards. Although technically owned by depositors, many S&Ls are actually owned by shareholders. S&Ls are regulated by the Federal Home Loan Bank Board created by the Home Owners Loan Act of 1933. Deposit insur-

ance is provided by the Savings Association Insurance Fund, operated by the Federal Deposit Insurance Corporation. S&Ls are known as building societies in the United Kingdom.

**savings bond.**   In the United States, a bond issued by the Federal Reserve. Savings bonds are sold in denominations from $50 to $10,000. Series EE bonds, issued at a discount, pay interest at average market rates. Series HH bonds are income bonds, which pay interest semiannually. Earnings from some savings bonds are fully tax exempt if used for educational purposes. Interest earned from other savings bonds is only exempt from state and local taxes.

**savings certificate.**   A nonnegotiable certificate of deposit issued by a bank for fixed-rate time deposits of $500 or more.

**savings ratio.**   The proportion of a country's savings retained from disposable income. Domestic savings by individuals and business are reflected in national income accounts. A high national savings ratio provides capital for industrial development and economic growth.

**Say's law.**   An economic theory devised in nineteenth-century France by J. B. Say purporting to demonstrate that demand is created by supply. The law implies that unemployment is unnecessary, since an infinite supply of workers stimulates an infinite demand for their labor. See also *Pareto optimum.*

**SB.**   The abbreviation for southbound.

**SBA.**   The abbreviation for Small Business Administration.

**SBDC.**   The abbreviation for Small Business Development Center. See *Small Business Administration.*

**SBI.**   The abbreviation for Small Business Institute. See *Small Business Administration.*

**SBU.**   The abbreviation for strategic business unit.

**sc.**   The abbreviation for scale.

**scale.**   See *economies of scale.*

**S.C.&S.**   The abbreviation for strapped, corded, and sealed.

**scarcity.**   The absence of a sufficient supply of a product or service to satisfy demand. Finite resources require allocation, which often means rationing. In market economies, most products and services are allocated by price. In nonmarket economies, they are allocated by government directive. See also *rationing by price.*

**Schatzwechsel.**   German: A short-term Treasury bill. *Schatzwechsel* are issued to banks on an as-needed basis by the *Bundesbank,* normally for 90 days or for earlier resale to the *Bundesbank.*

**schedule.**   A list of information classified to clarify an administrative procedure. Loan repayment dates and amounts are often provided in a schedule. Most revenue jurisdictions publish schedules of tax rates by income. Customs agencies classify products to regulate trade and collect duties.

**Schedule B number.**   In the United States, a seven-digit code assigned to exports under the Harmonized Tariff System of the United States. Known as the Statistical Classification of Domestic and Foreign Commodities Exported from the United States, Schedule B is published by the Bureau of the Census. A Schedule B number is displayed on the Shipper's Export Declaration. See also *Commerce Control List.*

**schedule tare.**   In the United States, an amount deducted from the declared weight of certain products in order to calculate specific duties determined by per-unit weight. Schedule tares are provided in U.S. Customs Regulations at 19 *Code of Federal Regulations* 159.22.

**Schengen Agreement.**   A 1985 accord concluded by Belgium, France, Germany, Luxembourg, and the Netherlands eliminating internal border controls. Signed in 1990, the agreement became effective in 1992. Italy joined the accord in 1990. Spain and Portugal are scheduled to join the agreement subject to revisions in their visa laws regulating entry of foreign nationals.

**schilling.**   The currency of Austria.

**Schuldschein.**   German: a marketable debt instrument issued against a borrower's note.

**Schuldverschreibung.**   German: bond, debenture, or promissory note.

**Schuman Plan.**   A series of proposals advanced by Robert Schuman of France leading to the creation of the European Coal and Steel Community (ECSC). The Schuman Plan proposed a coal and steel union to advance the industrial reconstruction of Europe following World War II. The proposals were accepted by Belgium, Luxembourg, Netherlands, Italy, France, and the former West Germany, and the ECSC was established in 1951.

**SCI.**   The abbreviation for Special Customs Invoice.

**scorched earth defense.**   The use of poison pills to reduce the value of a company to an unwanted raider. Scorched earth policies are rarely implemented, but they are frequently threatened to thwart hostile takeovers.

**SCORE.**   The abbreviation for Service Corps of Retired Executives.

**SCOUT.**   The abbreviation for shared currency option under tender.

**scrip.**   1. A stock certificate or bond coupon with a nominal value. 2. In the United Kingdom, a certificate representing a scrip issue.

**scrip issue.**   See *stock split.*

**s.d.**   The abbreviation for *sine die.*

**S.D.**   The abbreviation for short delivery.

**S/D.**   The abbreviation for sight draft.

**SD/BL.**   The abbreviation for sight draft/bill of lading (attached).

**SDR.**   The abbreviation for special drawing right.

**SE.**   The abbreviation for single (customs) entry and *Societas Europaea.* See *European company.*

**SEA.**   The abbreviation for Single European Act.

**Sea-Automated Manifest System (AMS).**   In the United States, an electronic warning system informing carriers of the status of import shipments following preentry customs audits. Carriers are notified whether cargo has been cleared through customs or requires further customs examination. The Automated Manifest System protects a carrier from fines attributable to moving shipments when customs audits identify goods subject to customs inspection. See also *Automated Commercial System.*

**seabee.**   A jumbo barge hoisted aboard a larger vessel with lifting devices. Seabee barges are larger than barges used in lash systems. Compare *barge-on-board.*

**seabridge.** In maritime transport, the water carriage version of landbridge. In seabridge, goods are transported entirely by water through different types of waterways under a single through bill of lading. Seabridge is offered primarily for cargo transiting the United States between destinations in Europe and East Asia.

**sea brief.** Also known as a sea letter and sea pass, a maritime passport.

**SEAF.** The abbreviation for Stock Exchange Automatic Exchange Facility.

**seaport authority.** See *port authority.*

**SEAQ.** The abbreviation for Stock Exchange Automated Quotations System.

**sea shed.** A detachable section inside the hold of a container ship designed to facilitate the loading and discharge of heavy cargoes.

**seasonal credit.** In banking, a business loan, usually a line of credit, used to finance cyclical inventory costs and operating expenses.

**seasonal port.** A port open for business for a limited number of days per year.

**seasoned security.** A security whose value is enhanced because of its reputation among investors. Seasoned securities are traded frequently in secondary markets.

**SEATO.** The abbreviation for South-East Asia Treaty Organization.

**seavan.** An ocean shipping container constructed to transport dry cargoes.

**seaworthy.** A term used to indicate properly constructed and well-equipped vessel manned by a competent crew and adequately documented in its country of registration. Seaworthiness also implies a vessel's suitability to undertake a given voyage.

**SEC.** The abbreviation for Securities and Exchange Commission.

**SEC Financial Reporting Release No. 1, Section 101.** In the United States, an official statement of the Securities and Exchange Commission (SEC) accepting Financial Accounting Standards Board standards for financial statements and other reporting by companies subject to SEC regulation. The Securities and Exchange Act of 1933 autho-

rizes the SEC to devise accounting standards for regulations issued under federal securities laws.

**Secofi.** The acronym for *Secretaría de Comercio y Fomento Industrial.*

**secondary exchange market (SEM).** The unofficial market for foreign exchange in a country with a dual-exchange-rate system. The SEM is a legal market with less favorable rates for low-priority transactions than the official exchange rates for preferred transactions. In developing countries, workers' remittances from foreign sources are usually converted on the SEM.

**secondary liability.** Contingent legal liability, e.g., the liability of an endorser when a draft is dishonored or the maker defaults on a debt.

**secondary market.** A market where investors purchase existing securities, including mortgages and other loans, repackaged for sale to parties other than the original investors. A secondary market differs from the primary market where securities are offered for the first time. Secondary markets strengthen original markets by increasing liquidity and reducing risks to initial investors. Money markets are secondary markets. See also *securitization* and *servicing agreement.*

**secondary reserves.** Short-term marketable securities held as reserves by commercial banks, especially short-term government securities. Unlike primary reserves, secondary reserves are composed of interest-earning assets, which are quickly convertible to cash.

**Second Enlargement.** See *enlargement.*

**second-flag carriage.** Transporting cargo aboard a ship registered in the importing country.

**second mortgage.** A new mortgage on property with an existing mortgage, often used to finance home improvements. The total obligation of first and second mortgages may not exceed the overall value of the property. In the United States, home equity loans permit homeowners to borrow to the extent of their equity in residential property for purposes other than home repairs.

**second of exchange.** See *bill of exchange.*

**Secretaría de Comercio y Fomento Industrial (Secofi).** In Mexico, an executive government department that regulates domestic and foreign commerce. Although roughly equivalent to the

U.S. Department of Commerce, Secofi also includes the Mexican external trade ministry.

**secretaría de educación.**    Spanish: education ministry. In some Latin countries, copyrights are registered with the education ministry.

**secretaría de estado de salud pública.**    Spanish: public health ministry. Health certificates and certificates of free sale are registered with the public health ministry.

**Secretaría de Hacienda y Credito Público.**    In Mexico, the ministry of finance.

**secretaría de industria y comercio.**    Spanish: ministry of industry and commerce. Patent and trademark offices are sometimes located in commerce ministries.

**secretariat.**    1. A government ministry. 2. The executive office of an international organization.

**secretaríat d'état du commerce et de l'industrie.**    French: ministry of commerce and industry.

**Section 15 agreement.**    In the United States, an agreement authorized by the Shipping Act of 1916 restraining price competition between ocean carriers. When approved by the Federal Maritime Commission, Section 15 agreements immunize shipping conferences from antitrust prosecution.

**Section 201.**    See *Trade Act of 1974.*

**Section 204 agreement.**    In the United States, a bilateral restraint agreement authorized by the Agricultural Act of 1956 restricting textile and apparel imports.

**Section 301.**    In the United States, a provision of the Trade Act of 1974 authorizing broad unilateral retaliation against trading partners who engage in unfair trade practices and raise nontariff barriers to U.S. imports. Section 301 covers, among other things, discriminatory government procurements, restrictive market access practices, and special taxes implemented solely to restrain trade. Under Section 301, the President may retaliate within 6 months from the start of a 301 review, initiated by the U.S. trade representative when issues in dispute are not resolved by negotiation. Retaliation may be in the form of 100 percent tariffs or a ban on offending imports. The Section 301 Committee, composed of staff of the Office of the U.S. Trade Representative, investigates complaints, holds hearings, and reports its findings to the President.

Special 301 targets infringement of intellectual property rights (IPRs) and foreign barriers to IPR protection. Super 301 reaches unfair procurement practices and market access restrictions in service sectors, as well as more traditional trade barriers on goods. Super 301 was enacted in the Omnibus Trade Act of 1988 and expired in 1990. As of 1993, Super 301 has not been revived.

More generally, U.S. trading partners condemn Section 301 as a violation of the General Agreement on Tariffs and Trade. The unilateral measures permitted under Section 301 contravene the obligation accepted by GATT members to resolve disputes through negotiated settlement, especially those unrelated to trade-induced economic emergencies. In particular, GATT disfavors unilateral measures taken by one member state to induce changes in the trade policies of other member states. Nevertheless, the U.S. Congress is unlikely to repeal or weaken Section 301 in 1993 or soon thereafter.

**Section 337.**    In the United States, a provision of the Tariff Act of 1930 that bans imports resulting from unfair competition. Section 337 complaints, most often filed in cases of patent-infringing imports, are lodged with the International Trade Commission (ITC). An ITC order banning an offending import becomes permanent after 60 days if not revoked by the President. Imports subject to ITC orders may be imported under special bonds during the 60-day waiting period but are re-exported when orders become final.

**Section 482.**    In the United States, provisions contained in the Internal Revenue Code that govern taxes in related-company transactions. Under Section 482, the Internal Revenue Service is authorized to determine whether a foreign corporation has been created to avoid full payment of taxes in the United States. When related companies do not deal at arm's-length, underpayments are imputed as taxable income to the U.S. parent company. See also *Subpart F.*

**Section 806-807.**    See *HTS Item 9802.*

**Section 931 corporation.**    In the United States, a corporation with operations in a U.S. offshore possession. In most instances, Section 931 income was tax exempt unless distributed as dividends in the United States. Tax benefits for Section 931 corporations were repealed by the Tax Reform Act of 1976.

**Section 936 funds.**   See *qualified possession source investment income*.

**Section 951-64.**   See *Subpart F*.

**Sectoral Advisory Group on International Trade.** See *International Trade Advisory Committee*.

**sectoral reciprocity.**   See *reciprocity*.

**sectoral trade agreement.**   A trade accord limited to a specific industry, e.g., the Canada-U.S. Automotive Products Trade Agreement.

**secured credit.**   See *secured loan*.

**secured creditor.**   A lender whose risk is protected by collateral. The creditor holds a security interest in a debtor's personal property or a mortgage on real property.

**secured debenture.**   A debenture secured by the issuer's property. The rights of debenture holders, stipulated in a trust deed, are enforceable when an issuer fails to repay principal or interest.

**secured loan.**   A loan collateralized by personal or real property. Mortgages are loans secured by real property. Other forms of collateral are accounts receivables, cash, inventory, marketable securities, etc. When a borrower defaults on a secured loan, the creditor is entitled to sue for legal authority to seize and sell collateral.

**Securities Act of 1933.**   In the United States, a statute requiring the registration of securities offered to the general public, including offers made by mail or other means. Registration statements are filed with the Securities and Exchange Commission (SEC). An issuer's prospectus discloses information contained in the registration statement. The antifraud provisions of the act ban fraudulent or misleading statements in all public securities offerings, including issues otherwise exempt from SEC regulation. See also *Trust Indenture Act of 1939*.

**Securities and Exchange Act of 1934.**   In the United States, a statute that created the Securities and Exchange Commission. The act applies registration and disclosure rules mandated by the Securities Act of 1933 to companies with more than 500 shareholders and assets over $1 million when securities are traded on a national stock exchange. It also requires the registration of over-the-counter brokers and dealers and authorizes

the Federal Reserve Board of Governors to regulate credit for margin lending. In addition, the act grants enforcement powers of the SEC, while also authorizing criminal prosecutions for securities violations by the U.S. Department of Justice.

**Securities and Exchange Commission (SEC).**   In the United States, an independent agency established by the Securities and Exchange Act of 1934 to administer federal securities laws. The SEC regulates most securities trading, primarily by requiring publicly owned companies to disclose financial information. Company books and records can be subpoenaed to facilitate SEC investigations. The agency is authorized to bar brokers and dealers found guilty of securities violations from further trading on national exchanges. The SEC is composed of five commissioners appointed by the President to 5-year terms.

**Securities and Investment Board (SIB).**   In the United Kingdom, a regulatory body created by the Financial Services Act of 1986. The SIB oversees self-regulating organizations, which include the London Stock Exchange, life insurance companies, and mutual funds. SIB members are appointed by the head of the Bank of England and the secretary of state for trade and industry.

**Securities Industry Automation Corporation.** See *National Securities Clearing Corporation*.

**securities loan.**   A loan collaterized by marketable securities. In the United States, securities loans are regulated by Federal Reserve Regulation G, Federal Reserve Regulation T, and Federal Reserve Regulation U. 2. A broker's call loan.

**securitization.**   A method of bank financing whereby outstanding loans are converted to securities for sale in secondary markets, passing loan credit risks to secondary-market investors. Securitization has altered loan underwriting standards, primarily because banks now grant loans based less on a borrower's repayment ability than on the marketability of repackaged loans in capital markets.

**security.**   1. Assets pledged by a borrower as collateral for a loan or a cosigner's debt guarantee. A lender has recourse against collateral or the cosigner when a primary maker defaults. 2. Financial asset evidencing the right to collect money from a debtor. Technically, only bonds, debentures, and certificates of deposit are properly called securities, but the term is also used to mean stocks and mutual fund shares.

**security agreement.**    See *security interest.*

**Security Council.**    The principal policymaking body of the United Nations (UN) on issues of international security. The Security Council's five permanent members are China, France, Russia (as the successor to the former Union of Soviet Socialist Republics), the United Kingdom, and the United States. Ten additional members are selected by the General Assembly for rotating 2-year terms. Of the various UN bodies, only the Security Council has enforcement powers, which derive from its ability to organize armed forces and dispatch troops to troubled regions around the world.

**security interest.**    A creditor's claim on a debtor's pledged assets. A security interest is created by a security agreement signed by the borrower. The security agreement describes collateral, identifies its location, and assigns creditors the right to dispose of it if a borrower defaults. A perfected lien gives a creditor priority on the proceeds of a forced sale of assets.

**SED.**    The abbreviation for Shipper's Export Declaration.

**seed money.**    Funds used to pay for preliminary research and expenses before a new company is created. Seed money is sometimes expended to finance market studies or develop business plans. Compare *risk capital.*

**segregation.**    1. In banking, the separation of trust accounts from other bank assets. 2. In finance, the separation of customer margin accounts from other assets of the firm.

**seigniorage.**    1.The difference between the assay value of a coin and its face value. Assay value is the cost of metals used to mint a coin. 2. The financial value accruing to a government when it partially appropriates privately held assets through reserve regulation and interest rate policy and through the issuance of non-interest-bearing government securities.

**SELA.**    The abbreviation for *Sistema Económico Latinoamericano.*

**selective safeguard.**    See *bilateral restraint agreement.*

**self-insurance.**    Financing insurance from internal funds without purchasing costly commercial insurance. Most multinational companies deposit self-insurance funds with offshore subsidiaries. For smaller businesses, pooling arrangements are available through trade and industry associations. Directors and officers insurance, employee health plans, liability insurance, worker's compensation, etc., can be financed internally. Self-insurance has the advantage of providing risk coverage that either is not available through commercial insurers or is available only at a high premium.

**self-liquidating loan.**    A short-term loan repaid with proceeds from liquidated inventories. Self-liquidating loans are usually obtained by seasonal enterprises as working capital to acquire equipment and supplies.

**self-regulating organization (SRO).**    A trade or professional organization that establishes a code of conduct, issues licenses, and disciplines errant members, often under the auspices of a government agency. In the United States, stock exchanges and commodity exchanges are SROs, subject to oversight by the Securities and Exchange Commission and the Commodities Futures Trading Commission. In the United Kingdom, SROs are known as self-regulatory organizations, denoting groups authorized by the Financial Services Act of 1986 to enforce professional codes regulating investment firms. UK SROs are overseen by the Securities and Investment Board and include the Association of Futures Brokers and Dealers; the Financial Intermediaries, Managers and Brokers Regulatory Association; the Investment Management Regulatory Organization; the Life Assurance and Unit Trust Regulatory Organization; and The Securities Association (TSA).

**self-tender.**    A company's offer to buy back its stock from shareholders. Self-tenders are made to avoid hostile takeovers or to increase a company's profitability by reducing the number of shareholders entitled to dividends.

**sell-downs.**    1. In banking, loan participations sold to respondent banks that are not members of the underwriting group. 2. In securities underwriting, the offer of a portion of a syndicated underwriting to the general public. Securities sell-downs are offered through selling groups, which distribute new offerings for commissions or concession fees.

**sellers' market.**  A market in which demand exceeds supply, leaving sellers free to increase prices. When buyers eventually resist price increases, supply exceeds demand. Buyers' markets then develop.

**sellers' over.**  A weak market in which buyers' demands have been fulfilled, leaving too few buyers for profitable sales.

**selling group.**  Any agreement among several sellers to collaborate in marketing and selling a product.

**selling short.**  See *short selling*.

**SEM.**  The abbreviation for secondary exchange market and Single European Market.

**Semiconductor Agreement.**  A 1986 trade agreement, known officially as the Arrangement between the Government of Japan and the United States of America Concerning Trade in Semiconductor Products. Under the agreement, Japan granted foreign companies access to 20 percent of its domestic superconductor market. The terms of the agreement were met by 1992. See also *managed trade*.

**senior security.**  A security with a priority claim on an issuer's assets and earnings. Holders of senior securities are paid before other investors. In priority order, bondholders are paid before preferred-stock shareholders and preferred-stock shareholders before common-stock shareholders.

**senmosha.**  In Japan, a trading firm that specializes in high-value products. *Senmosha* buy for their own accounts and service niche markets. Compare *sogo shosha*.

**SEPON.**  The acronym for Stock Exchange Pooled Nominees. See *Transfer Accounting Lodgement for Investors and Stock Management*.

**sequestration.**  Impoundment, or the process of blocking outflows of funds, by court order or government directive. Courts sequester funds pending the outcome of a legal action. Governments sequester funds to implement budget constraints.

**serial bond.**  A bond issued as one of a series under a single indenture. Each bond in the series has a different maturity date. In the United States, serial bonds are usually issued by local governments. Compare *term bond*.

**service.**  An intangible good that consists primarily of human skill in the form of advice, labor, management, or ideas. Service industries encompass consumer services (e.g., caterers, florists, booksellers), professional services (e.g., accountants, business consultants, doctors, lawyers), and trade services (e.g., banking, insurance, tourism).

**service contract.**  1. In shipping, a pricing option under which an ocean carrier contracts with a shipper for carriage at a nontariff rate. See also *Shipping Act of 1984*. 2. An employment contract, usually involving an independent contractor or senior manager. In the United Kingdom, service contracts are maintained at a company's registered office. The Companies Acts of 1980 and 1985 prohibit service contracts guaranteeing employment for more than 5 years.

**Service Corps of Retired Executives (SCORE).**  In the United States, a private-sector arm of the Small Business Administration (SBA). SCORE provides emerging businesses with marketing assistance, financial planning, and technical advice. SCORE services are available through local SBA offices in most cities in the United States.

**service des douanes.**  French: customs agency.

**service industry.**  See *service*.

**service supply license.**  In the United States, a validated export license issued to a domestic or foreign firm. Service supply licenses authorize exports of spare or replacement parts to controlled foreign purchasers. The consignee must have been the original purchaser of controlled equipment under a prior validated export license.

**servicing agreement.**  An agreement between financial institutions covering the sale of securities in secondary markets. The seller becomes the purchaser's trustee for proceeds from secondary-market sales. Sellers under servicing agreements normally purchase both errors and omissions insurance and fidelity bonds. A servicing agreement entitles a purchaser to audit the seller's books.

**SESDAQ.**    The abbreviation for Stock Exchange of Singapore Dealing and Automated Quotation system. See *Stock Exchange of Singapore Limited.*

**Session of Contracting Parties.**    See *General Agreement on Tariffs and Trade.*

**set-off.**    1. In bankruptcy, a settlement of accounts between an insolvent debtor and a creditor. 2. In banking, the right of a bank to seize a customer's deposits for an unpaid debt.

**settlement.**    1. The payment of an account, usually at the invoice price. 2. The conclusion of a legal action, often by a mutual agreement between the parties. 3. In commodity, financial, or stock markets, the delivery of an asset in exchange for payment. Market settlements are often accounting transfers of credits and debits. See also *settlement date.*

**settlement date.**    The date on which financial accounts are reconciled. 1. In securities trading, when a transaction is concluded by regular-way settlement, securities are delivered and accounts paid within 5 days of the sale. When the transaction is concluded by a seller's-option settlement, ownership is transferred within 60 days of a sale. 2. The trade date. See also *closing date.*

**settlement price.**    1. In futures, the prices used to calculate gains, losses, delivery invoice prices, margin calls, etc. 2. In options, the exercise price.

**settlor.**    See *trustor.*

**Seusa.**    The abbreviation for South Europe/USA Rate Conference. See *conference.*

**severance.**    1. The division of a contract to remove provisions rendered void by common law or statute. Severance saves the valid portions of a contract. 2. Final compensation paid to an employee who leaves a firm.

**SEZ.**    The abbreviation for special economic zone.

**SFTC.**    The abbreviation for Standard Foreign Trade Classification.

**sgd.**    The abbreviation for signed.

**SGS.**    The abbreviation for *Société Générale de Surveillance S.A..*

**sh.**    The abbreviation for share.

**shadow director.**    An unofficial advisor to a company's board of directors. In the United States, a shadow director is an insider for purposes of insider trading regulation. In the United Kingdom, a shadow director can be charged with wrongful trading.

**share.**    1. An equity, or ownership, interest in a business. 2. A stock.

**share capital.**    Money earned by a company from a stock issue. 1. Minimum share capital is invested capital declared when a company incorporates. 2. Authorized capital (nominal capital) is capital to be raised from sales of equity to investors, as specified in a company's articles of incorporation. 3. Subscribed capital, or issued share capital, is the amount paid by investors for outstanding shares. A stock issue is not fully subscribed until the full par value of authorized shares is paid. 4. Fully paid-in capital is the amount equal to par value actually paid by investors. 5. Partially paid capital, also known as called-up capital, is the amount less than par value paid by investors.

**share certificate.**    A stock certificate.

**share currency option under tender (SCOUT).**    In the United Kingdom, a currency option available to certain exporters. SCOUT permits companies bidding for foreign contracts to purchase a single currency hedge, thereby reducing the cost of foreign exchange to individual bidders.

**shareholder.**    An owner of equity in a limited liability company or corporation. A shareholder's ownership interest is evidenced by a stock certificate or by an electronic accounting entry. In the United States, shareholders are often called stockholders. In the United Kingdom, a limited partner is also known as a shareholder. See also *shareholders' derivative rights* and *annual general meeting.*

**shareholders' derivative rights.**    In law, the perogatives that accrue to shareholders who file legal actions against companies in which they own equity. In most jurisdictions, shareholders are entitled to sue corporate managers and directors who fail to protect the value of a company's equity. Known as derivative actions, these suits are brought for breach of fiduciary duty and are said to be derivative because the shareholders sue on behalf of the company. Some jurisdictions attempt to deter the filing of frivolous suits by requiring small shareholders to post security in an amount equal to the costs incurred by a company forced to defend against a derivative action. Compare *preemptive right*.

**shareholders' meeting.**   See *annual general meeting*.

**share index.**   See *stock index*.

**share register.**   A written record of a company's shareholders, listing names, addresses, and the number and class of shares owned by each. When stock certificates are lost, ownership can be verified by the registry and shares reissued. Since most contemporary share registries are electronic, stock certificates are rarely issued to establish equity ownership.

**share split.**   The splitting of a company's shares into smaller units. Shares are split when their quoted price exceeds the market price purchasers are willing to pay. See also *stock split*.

**Shari'a.**   In Moslem countries, Islamic law. Business relations are regulated primarily by code law (*mu'amalat*) interpreted by religious *Shari'a* courts. Islamic codes define the obligations of one person to another, and certain business practices are strictly forbidden. Nevertheless, the *Shari'a* courts can usually be avoided. For example, the Islamic ban against usury prohibits the charging of interest, so banks typically assess fees or purchase equity in lieu of interest. Most other commercial matters, especially involving foreign nationals, are placed by government edict beyond the religious courts' jurisdiction. Agency is frequently governed by contract, and business liability is often settled by arbitration.

**shark repellent.**   Any device used by a company to thwart an unwelcome takeover, e.g., a poison pill.

**shekel.**   The currency of Israel.

**shelf registration.**   In the United States, the popular name for Securities and Exchange Commission Rule 415. Adopted in 1982, the rule permits a securities' issuer to file a registration statement well in advance of a public stock offering. Shelf registration enables the issuer to delay a stock offering (i.e., leave the registration on the shelf) until market conditions are favorable. Filed registration statements are later amended as disclosed information changes.

**shell branch.**   In the United States, a commercial bank's offshore booking office, used primarily for trading in Eurocurrency markets. U.S. banks can maintain offshore banking units and domestic international banking facilities.

**shell company.**   1. Also called a mailbox or paper company, an overseas tax haven managed by a local agent. Bermuda, the Cayman Islands, and Liechtenstein are traditional tax havens, although tax havens are common around the world. 2. An inactive company maintained for future use, such as subsequent expansion or overseas investment.

**Sherman Antitrust Act of 1890.**   In the United States, the principal antitrust law. The Sherman Act prohibits all contracts, combinations, conspiracies in restraint of trade, monopolies, and attempts to monopolize. Penalties imposed under the act include confiscation, criminal prosecution, injunction, and triple damages. The Sherman Act is enforced by the Antitrust Division of the U.S. Department of Justice.

**SHEX.**   The abbreviation for Sundays—holidays excluded.

**shibosai.**   Japanese: private placement market.

**shilling.**   The currency of Kenya, Somalia, Tanzania, and Uganda.

**SHINC.**   The abbreviation for Sundays—holidays included.

**shipbroker.**   A commission agent who books charters, cargo space, and passenger seats for air travel. See also *Baltic Exchange*.

**shipowner's lien.**   See *lien*.

**shipped bill.**   See *on-board bill of lading*.

**shipper.**   1. A firm that exports products to a foreign country. 2. A local seller who pays freight for transporting goods to an inland port.

**shipper's association.**   A group of companies organized to negotiate transportation rates with common carriers. Also called transportation associations, these groups consist of multinational corporations that use collective economic power to obtain more favorable shipping rates. Although shipper's associations are common in Canada and elsewhere, similar combinations operating in the United States must be authorized by the Antitrust

Division of the U.S. Department of Justice. See also *business review procedure.*

**shippers' cooperative.**   A nonprofit membership organization that acts as the freight forwarder for exporters in a given industry. Members share in the cooperative's profits.

**shipper's credit agreement.**   A credit agreement between a shipper and an ocean conference. The conference finances shipments transported by conference carriers.

**shipper's declaration of origin.**   A shipper's statement verifying an import's country of origin. See also *declaration.*

**Shipper's Export Declaration (SED).**   In the United States, a statement provided to a carrier for filing at the exit port, as mandated by the Export Administration Act of 1979. SEDs are required for most commercial shipments to any foreign destination, including U.S. territories and U.S.-associated Pacific Islands under the Compact of Freely Associated States. The declarations are mandatory for all export shipments valued in excess of $250 or covered by a validated export license, except exports of technical data. SEDs disclose the identities of shippers and consignees and the destination, value, and weight of shipments. The older SED form is Customs Form 7525-V. The newer Customs Form 7525-V-ALT is designed for use with international trade master sets, which permit the simultaneous preparation of several trade documents. SEDs are available in electronic data interchange formats.

**shipper's rate agreement.**   See *exclusive patronage contract.*

**Shipping Act of 1916.**   In the United States, the statute authorizing Federal Maritime Commission oversight of shipping conferences. The act also approves exclusive patronage contracts between shippers and ocean conferences. See also *Section 15 agreement.*

**Shipping Act of 1984.**   In the United States, a statute authorizing service contracts between shippers and ocean carriers based on volume-discounted pricing. The contracts are filed with the Federal Maritime Commission (FMC). Before 1992, once filed, a service contract could usually not be amended. Recent regulations issued by the FMC permit parties to agree to changes in the terms of service contracts.

**shipping and forwarding agent.**   See *freight forwarder.*

**shipping association.**   See *shipper's association.*

**shipping bill.**   In some countries, a document required for imports and/or exports. Shipping bills may also be required to claim duty drawbacks when goods are removed from a bonded warehouse.

**shipping conference.**   See *conference.*

**shipping documents.**   Documents presented to a local bank to receive payment for exports. Shipping documents consist of a bill of lading (or air waybill), certificate of origin, commercial invoice, insurance policy or certificate, customs or consular invoice, dock receipt, quality inspection certificate, weight certificate, and, if required, an export license. Shipping documents are always required when the exporter is paid based on a letter of credit.

**shipping permit.**   A document issued by a common carrier authorizing a receiving clerk to accept cargo for shipment.

**shipping ton.**   See *ton.*

**ship's certificate of registry.**   See *ship's papers.*

**ship's papers.**   The documents a ship's master maintains for inspection, including the ship's certificate of registry, indicating the country of registration; a bill of health; bills of lading; and a manifest. The papers also include the charter party when a ship is chartered and a passenger manifest if passengers are aboard. When ships arrive at port, masters submit ship reports, identifying the ship, crew, passengers, and cargo.

**shogun bond.**   In Japan, a bond denominated in a foreign currency.

**shore clause.**   In maritime insurance, a provision covering cargo in transit over land. The policyholder is protected from losses arising from accidents or natural disasters.

**short bill.**   See *long bill of exchange.*

**short covering.**   See *short selling.*

**short-dated security.**   See *gilt-edged security.*

**short delivery.**    Delivery of goods fewer in number or lower in weight than the commercial invoice describes. A disparity can arise from shrinkage, accidental loss, or seller's fraud. Contracts for bulk commodity shipments usually provide for settlement when shrinkage causes short delivery. When an accident causes the loss, the shipper or buyer files an insurance claim. Seller fraud gives rise to a legal action, although the judgment may not be enforceable in a foreign jurisdiction.

**shorting.**    See *short selling*.

**short interest.**    In marine insurance, the excess in a cargo's insured value over its market value. The premium paid by a policyholder for coverage in excess of market value is refunded.

**short position.**    1. In futures trading, the situation of a seller who is obligated to deliver a commodity or liquidate a contract. 2. In options trading, the position of a holder of a call or put option.

**shorts.**    See *gilt-edged security* and *short selling*.

**short selling.**    A speculative sale of a commodity, currency, or security not owned by the trader. Dealers are said to be in a short position when their sales volumes exceed holdings. A short seller attempts to sell on rising prices and buy on falling prices. The profit is the difference between the selling price and the purchase price paid before delivery to a buyer. Short sellers cover their positions, called short covering, when a substitute contract is executed or the underlying commodity is purchased at a price lower than the selling price. See also *bear spread*.

**short-term capital.**    A loan repayable in 1 year or less. Short-term loans are used to cover costs and operating expenses.

**short-term capital transactions.**    A ledger entry in balance-of-payments accounting. The account identifies foreign receivables and external debt obligations payable in 1 year or less.

**short-term gain (loss).**    A profit (or loss) for purposes of computing the capital-gains tax. Depending on the jurisdiction, a short-term gain (or loss) is profit (or loss) from an investment held between 6 months and 1 year. A long-term gain (or loss) is realized on investments held longer than a year.

**short-term interest rate.**    The rate of interest on loans made for a short time, usually for 3 months. Short-term rates are set by central banks when loans are advanced to financial institutions. Changes in these rates signal changes in a country's monetary policy. See also *interest rate policy*.

**short-term loss.**    See *short-term gain* (*loss*).

**short-term paper.**    1. Bills of exchange, drafts, or notes payable within 1 year. 2. Commercial paper (e.g., a promissory note) payable in under 270 days. 3. An installment loan payable within 1 year.

**short ton.**    See *ton*.

**shpt., shpmt.**    The abbreviation for shipment.

**shtg.**    The abbreviation for shortage.

**shunto.**    Japanese: spring offensive, i.e., the annual wage negotiations by Japanese workers. The negotiations are often conducted amid noisy demonstrations, but strikes in Japan are rare.

**shutout.**    In marine shipping, postponing a shipment when a ship is overbooked. The cargo is held for loading on a ship scheduled to sail at a later time.

**SI.**    The abbreviation for *Système Internationale*.

**SIB.**    The abbreviation for Securities and Investment Board.

**SIBOR.**    The abbreviation for Singapore interbank offered rate.

**SIC.**    The abbreviation for Standard Industrial Code.

**SICAV.**    The abbreviation for *société d'investissement à capital variable*.

**Sicherheit.**    German: security, i.e., collateral.

**side deal.**    A transaction in which one party agrees to influence a corporate or government decision in exchange for personal profit. The line between legal and illegal conduct is not always clear in these cases. In many countries, allegations of side deals involving public officials are usually thoroughly investigated by a regulatory agency, particularly after details are publicized in the press.

**sig.**    The symbol for mark, label, sign, and signature.

**sight bill of exchange.**    A bill of exchange paid after presentation.

**sight draft.** A draft or bill of exchange payable on sight, i.e., when the draft or shipping documents are presented.

**sight draft endorsement.** In marine insurance, a provision designed to protect a policyholder when merchandise is detained at a foreign port. The coverage can be for an indefinite or limited period of time, depending on the terms of the policy and the premium paid.

**sighting.** Presenting a sight draft or bill of exchange for payment.

**sight letter of credit.** A letter of credit instructing a bank to pay a seller when drafts are presented.

**sight rate.** The rate of exchange when a sight bill of exchange or draft is denominated in a foreign currency.

**signature loan.** An unsecured loan granted on the basis of the borrower's credit standing and signature on a promissory note.

**SII.** The abbreviation for Structural Impediments Initiative.

**silent partner.** A partner with invested capital who takes no active interest in managing the partnership's business. A silent partner's share of profits and losses is determined by the partnership agreement.

**silver certificate.** Paper currency formerly issued in the United States. The certificates were redeemable for equivalent amounts of silver. Silver certificates were replaced by Federal Reserve notes in 1967.

**similar merchandise.** In customs, a product with an established economic value that resembles an unvalued import. Similar merchandise determines transaction value when the invoice price or appraised price is inconsistent with other evidence of value. In the United States, similar merchandise must have originated in the import's country of origin, been produced by the same or a similar producer, and consist of like components, ingredients, or materials.

**similitude.** In customs, a precondition for classifying an import not already identified in a country's tariff schedules. When there are several comparable items, the import is placed in the category it or its component materials most nearly resemble.

**SIMIS.** The abbreviation for Single Internal Market Information Service.

**simple interest.** An interest rate based on principal and not compounded. Finance charges are determined by the unpaid principal.

**sine die (s.d.).** Latin: without a date.

**sing.** The abbreviation for singular.

**Singapore dollar market.** The primary market for offshore Eurodollars deposited in Asia. The Singapore dollar is a unit of currency introduced in 1967. It has floated freely against other world currencies since 1973. In 1975, Singapore dollar CDs were introduced with minimum denominations of 100,000 Singapore dollars and maximum denominations of 1 million Singapore dollars. Maturities range from 3 months to 3 years. There is also a brisk exotic currency market in Singapore dollars operated by licensed private money changers from small family-owned businesses. In 1992, the estimated foreign exchange turnover in Singapore averaged roughly 80 billion U.S. dollars daily. Compare *Asian dollar market*.

**Singapore interbank offered rate (SIBOR).** The interest rate at which Asian currency units are loaned to the highest-rated banks in Singapore. See also *interbank offered rate*.

**Single Administrative Document (SAD).** In the European Community (EC), a uniform customs document in use since 1988. The SAD is an export declaration, transit permit, and import declaration for internal EC shipments. The document has also been adopted by the European Free Trade Association. The SAD is officially known as the D.V.1, or the Declaration of Particulars Relating to Customs Value.

**Single European Act (SEA).** Also known as the Single Act, a law enacted in 1986 to create the 1993 Single Market in the European Community. The SEA amended the Treaty of Rome, thereby authorizing the policymaking body to adopt integration decisions by majority vote, and established 1992 as the deadline for a union treaty. The Treaty of Maastricht creating the Single Market was signed in 1992.

**Single Internal Market Information Service (SIMIS).** In the United States, a database maintained by the U.S. Department of Commerce containing market and regulatory information on the European Community (EC). SIMIS also publishes *Europe Now,* a quarterly newsletter of commercial and official information for trade and investment in the EC.

**Single Market, 1993.** The unified market in the European Community (EC) approved by the Single European Act and created by the 1992 Treaty of Maastricht. The agreement gradually eliminates regional barriers to the free movement of goods, services, and people, beginning in 1993. Environmental, product, and labor standards are to be harmonized, and cabotage restrictions are to be reduced. The Single Market plan envisions monetary union, including a single European currency and central bank, to be implemented before the year 2000. See also *subsidiarity.*

**single-rate tariff.** See *conference.*

**single-tax system.** A tax system where all government revenue derives from a uniform tax, usually a comprehensive income tax. A single-tax system eliminates capital-gains taxes, sales taxes, property taxes, etc. Uniform tax systems create procedures that are easy to administer and difficult to evade, but are also less flexible than other tax systems for targeting multiple sources of revenue.

**sinking fund.** Money segregated in a mandatory account to redeem bonds. Bond issuers pay into sinking funds before debt obligations mature. Some bond indentures create pro rata sinking funds, whereby a formula prescribes amounts of debt redeemed by the issuer. Other issues are redeemed on the open market at current market prices, often below the call price. Sinking fund requirements for revenue bonds are met with revenues from user fees or other taxes.

**Sino-British Joint Declaration and Basic Law.** A 1984 agreement between the United Kingdom and the People's Republic of China (PRC) concerning the British Crown Colony of Hong Kong. The British gained sovereignty over Hong Kong Island by the 1842 Treaty of Nanking, following the Chinese opium wars of the nineteenth century. The Kowloon Peninsula was ceded to Britain in 1860. Britain leased the New Territories from China in 1898. Under the Joint Declaration, sovereignty over Hong Kong will be transferred to the PRC in 1997. Hong Kong will be classified as a special administrative region for 50 years.

**Sistema de la Cuenca del Plata (SICDEP).** Also known as the River Plate Basin System (RPBS), an organization established at Brasilia in 1969 to promote the development of regional river basin resources. A number of the region's development projects are financed by FONPLATA, the organization's economic assistance fund, in cooperation with the Inter-American Development Bank. SICDEP members are Argentina, Bolivia, Brazil, Paraguay, and Uruguay. The organization is based in Buenos Aires.

**Sistema Económico Latinoamericano (SELA).** Also known as the Latin American Economic System, an association of Caribbean and Latin American countries created in Panama in 1975 to promote internal economic growth. The primary business of SELA is conducted by action committees, or *Comites de Accion,* which organize cooperative ventures in specific industrial sectors. SELA members are organized to attract foreign investment, reduce external debt, stabilize local currencies, dismantle internal trade barriers, and develop common policies for future international trade negotiations. SELA is headquartered in Caracas, Venezuela.

**sister ship.** In marine insurance, a policy provision covering accidents involving two or more ships owned by the same policyholder. The provision is made because the policyholder may have no legal recourse against another party.

**S.I.T.** The abbreviation for stop in transit.

**SITC.** The abbreviation for Standard International Trade Classification.

**SITC-3.** The abbreviation for Standard International Trade Classification, Revision 3. See *Standard International Trade Classification.*

**SIU.** The abbreviation for Seafarers International Union.

**SL.** The abbreviation for specific limit.

**SL&C.** The abbreviation for shipper's load and count.

**SL&T.** The abbreviation for shipper's load and tally.

**S/LC.** The abbreviation for sue and labor clause.

**sld.** The abbreviation for sold.

**sleeping partner.** See *silent partner.*

**sleep insurance.** Export credit insurance protecting an exporter against unanticipated country risks. See also *WRAP policy.*

**sliding peg.** See *crawling peg.*

**sliding-scale tariff.** A customs tariff with variable rates of duty, depending on the invoice price of a given import. As the price of an item declines, so does the duty. Under a sliding scale, duties may be assessed on an ad valorem or specific basis.

**slops.** Liquid discharged from a ship's hold. Slops are residues of bulk cargoes, mostly crude petroleum, mixed with water and cleansing agents.

**slot.** The space taken up by a container loaded on a ship's deck or deposited in its hold.

**slot ship.** See *cellularized vessel.*

**sluice-gate price.** See *Common Agricultural Policy.*

**slump.** See *recession.*

**slush fund.** An account maintained by an organization to entertain or otherwise ingratiate itself to influential people. Slush funds are used to gain information, recognition, or profit. Anti-corruption policies vary. As a rule, however, financing a politician's weekend golfing trip with slush fund money is not a bribe, although an equivalent cash payment might be.

**small business.** In the United States, an imprecise term, but generally a business with 500 or fewer employees. A microbusiness employs 20 or fewer workers. Growth companies, also known as dynamic businesses, employ between 20 and 500 employees. Small businesses are also known as small- to medium-sized enterprises. See also *small company.*

**Small Business Administration (SBA).** In the United States, an independent federal agency created in 1953 to finance small-business development. The SBA extends direct loans and loan guarantees to companies otherwise unable to obtain financing and licenses. It also regulates and subsidizes small-business investment companies, which are private venture capital firms investing equity capital and extending long-term loans to small businesses. The Small Business Credit Program, administered jointly by SBA and the Export-Import Bank (Eximbank) of the United

States, guarantees loans to domestic small-business exporters. Under the export financing program, SBA and Eximbank offer medium-term, fixed-rate loans at the lowest rate permitted by OECD consensus guidelines. SBA Small Business Development Centers and Small Business Institutes provide business counseling services for college and university students.

**small claims.** A civil action to recover a small loss, the amount of which varies, but is usually less $1000. Small claims are handled by municipal (or county) courts or, in some jurisdictions, by arbitration.

**small company.** In the United Kingdom, a company with, among other things, 50 or fewer employees and gross assets of under 1 million British pounds. The rules applied to small companies are set forth in the Companies Act of 1981. See also *small business.*

**SME.** The abbreviation for small- to medium-sized enterprise. See *small business.*

**Smithsonian Agreement.** An agreement reached among the Group of Ten (G-10) in 1971 following the collapse of the Bretton Woods Conference agreement. At a meeting at the Smithsonian Institution in Washington, D.C., the G-10 agreed to implement a floating-exchange-rate system when the United States abandoned the gold standard. The European Economic Community (EEC) subsequently adopted the European currency snake, pegging EEC currencies to the strongest national currency in the group.

**smokestack industry.** A heavy manufacturing industry, such as steel smelting, named for the factory smokestacks that emit the pollution produced during the manufacturing process. Green technologies are gradually reducing the number of industries that rely on polluting production processes.

**Smoot-Hawley Tariff Act of 1930.** In the United States, the law that established statutory duty rates. Because it imposed excessively high import duties, Smoot-Hawley is said to have caused the Great Depression of the 1930s. The law was modified by the Reciprocal Trade Agreements Act of 1934, but many of its provisions survive as the Tariff Act of 1930. See also *statutory rate of duty.*

**smuff.** A colloquial term for laundered *money.*

344    smuggling

**smuggling.** 1. Unlawful trafficking in international commerce. 2. Theft of government revenue by failing to pay customs duties.

**snake.** See *European currency snake.*

**SO.** The abbreviation for seller's option.

**SOAP.** The abbreviation for Sunflowerseed Oil Assistance Program.

**sobretasa.** An import surcharge encountered in Latin America. The surcharge is levied in addition to customs duties based on the cost, insurance, and freight value of imports.

**Social Charter.** See *Community Charter of the Fundamental Rights of Workers.*

**social democracy.** See *social market.*

**socialism.** An economic system in which the production and distribution of goods and services are directed by the government. In socialist systems, the political sector allocates resources, which are managed by government agencies, ostensibly to prevent the exploitation of workers and concentrations of vast private wealth. Compare *capitalism* and *social market.*

**socially responsible investing.** Selecting investments based on social, as well as economic, criteria. In the United States, some investment advisory firms specialize in steering investors toward companies whose corporate policies are congenial to certain social values, e.g., companies that have nondiscriminatory hiring and promotion policies or companies that create nonpolluting products.

**social market.** A market economy that places a high priority on human development. While the price mechanism allocates most resources, vital economic sectors are operated by the government in the public interest. Canada and the European Community are social markets. Compare *socialism.*

**social responsibility.** In business, the concept that a company deriving profits from a community should act in the public interest. Public and business expectations vary widely, depending on the community and the nature of an industry. Generally, however, companies are expected to adopt ecologically sound policies, engage in fair labor practices, and contribute employee time, company expertise, or some share of their profits to charitable or socially beneficial causes.

**social security.** A government program that provides health and financial benefits to designated classes of recipients. In the United States, the national insurance program was enacted in the Social Security Act of 1935 to provide retirement income, disability benefits, unemployment insurance, and public assistance to the aged, the blind, and dependent children. Retirement benefits are combined with medical insurance for the aged, known as Medicare. The retirement insurance is financed from employment, or Federal Insurance Contributions Act (FICA), taxes. Elsewhere, national social security programs guarantee health care, pensions, unemployment benefits, and welfare subsidies. In Europe, uniform social security standards were originally adopted in the European Code of Social Security approved by the Council of Europe. In 1989, the European Community approved the Community Charter of the Fundamental Rights of Workers, which, inter alia, guarantees a minimum employment age and equitable remuneration to the young and a "decent standard of living" to the aged.

**sociedad anónima (SA).** Spanish: a public limited company.

**sociedade anônima (SA).** Portuguese: a public limited company.

**società a responsabilità limitata (SaR/Sarl).** Italian: a private limited-liability company.

**Societas Europaea.** See *European company.*

**société.** French: company.

**société anonyme (SA).** French: a public limited company.

**société à responsabilité limitée (Sarl/S.à.R.L.).** French: a private limited-liability company.

**société d'investissement à capital variable (SICAV).** French: unit trust.

**Société Générale de Surveillance, S.A.** (SGS). A private firm designated by a number of countries as the authorized import inspection agent. SGS verifies the condition, quantity, and prices of imports, often before foreign exchange is authorized. A favorable inspection report is called a clean report of findings. A negative report is called advice of nonconformity. SGS is based in Geneva. Its New York office is known as SGS Control Services, Inc. See also *request for information* and *inspection form.*

**sociétés d'économie mixte.**     French: joint venture.

**Society for Worldwide Interbank Financial Telecommunications (SWIFT).**     A global banking network financed by participating financial institutions to process notices of remittances and collections. SWIFT has operating centers in Belgium, the Netherlands, and the United States. Member banks are connected through regional centers in more than 50 countries. Established in 1977, SWIFT is based in Brussels. See also *wire transfer.*

**soft commodities.**     Nonmetal commodities traded in futures markets. Soft commodities include cocoa, coffee, grain, sugar, etc.

**soft currency.**     A currency not freely convertible into gold or a foreign currency because of the issuing country's balance-of-payments situation. Official soft-currency values are fixed by government directive at a rate of exchange unrelated to true market value.

**soft goods.**     Nondurable goods. Compare *durable good.*

**soft-loan window.**     The special lending facility of a development bank. Soft loans are generally repayable in hard currency, but priced below market rates and amortized over extended periods of time with lengthy grace periods before repayment begins. Soft-loan windows are only available to developing countries. See also *African Development Bank Group* and *Asian Development Bank.*

**Software for Market Analysis and Restrictions on Trade (SMART).**     An electronic system developed jointly by the United Nations Conference on Trade and Development and the World Bank. The system provides developing countries with trade statistics needed to formulate negotiating strategies for multilateral trade negotiations. Technical assistance for SMART is provided by the United Nations Development Program. The system is coordinated in Geneva.

**sogo shosa.**     Japanese: general trading company. *Sogo shosa* are Japan's largest exporters, e.g., Mitsubishi, Mitsui, C. Itoh, Marubeni, Sumitomo, etc. They trade for their own accounts and on behalf of other companies.

**sol.**     The currency of Peru.

**sola/solus.**     See *bill of exchange.*

**SOLAS.**     The abbreviation for International Convention for Safety of Life at Sea. See *International Maritime Organization.*

**solde.**     French: balance.

**sole agency.**     See *agency.*

**sole of exchange.**     See *bill of exchange.*

**sole proprietor.**     An individual who owns a business alone. The business is known as a *sole proprietorship.* In the United States, there are no registration requirements for sole proprietors, who may operate under company or their own names. Sole proprietors are personally liable for debts accrued during the life of the business.

**sole proprietorship.**     See *sole proprietor.*

**solvency.**     1. In banking, the ability of a borrower to repay debt obligations according to schedule or on demand. 2. In finance, the assets of a company over and above its liabilities.

**South Asian Association for Regional Cooperation (SAARC).**     A regional economic cooperation group of seven South Asian nations formed in 1980. SAARC held its first ministerial meeting in 1985. Its members are Bangladesh, Bhutan, India, Maldives, Nepal, Pakistan, and Sri Lanka. SAARC's secretariat is located in Katmandu, Nepal.

**South-East Asia Treaty Organization (SEATO).**     A mutual defense organization created by the Southeast Asia Collective Defense Treaty of 1954. SEATO signatories are Australia, France, New Zealand, the Philippines, Thailand, the United Kingdom, and the United States. Although SEATO dissolved in 1977, the defense treaty remains in force.

**Southern African Customs Union Agreement (SACUA).**     A customs union composed of Botswana, Lesotho, Namibia, South Africa, and Swaziland. Created in 1969, SACUA permits free travel and, in most cases, uninhibited movement of goods between member countries. South Africa fixes customs and excise duties and distributes revenues to other SACUA members based on their relative volumes of trade. SACUA does not have a permanent secretariat.

**Southern African Development Coordination Conference (SADCC).**     An economic association formed in 1979 by southern African states to reduce regional dependence on the Republic of South Africa. SADCC has undertaken major development programs, including projects to integrate regional telecommunications and transportation networks. SADCC members are Angola, Botswana, Lesotho, Malawi, Mozambique, Namibia, Swaziland, Tanzania, Zambia, and Zimbabwe. Its headquarters are located in Gaborone, Botswana.

**Southern Cone Common Market.**   See *Mercosur.*

**South Pacific Bureau for Economic Cooperation (SPEC).**   An organization formed in 1971 to forge closer economic ties between Australia, New Zealand, and the South Pacific island nations of the Cook Islands, Fiji, Nauru, Tonga, and Western Samoa. SPEC grew out of the South Pacific Forum, a discussion group composed of regional heads of state. Other members of SPEC are Kiribati, Niue, Papua New Guinea, Solomon Islands, and Tuvalu. The organization's goals are to reduce internal barriers to trade and harmonize product standards. SPEC is based in Suva, Fiji.

**South Pacific Commission (SPC).**   An association of countries with dependent territories in the South Pacific. SPC members are Australia, France, the Netherlands, New Zealand, the United Kingdom, and the United States. The SPC cooperates on matters of common interest in the South Pacific. The association has headquarters in Noumea, New Caledonia.

**South Pacific Forum.**   See *South Pacific Bureau for Economic Cooperation.*

**South/South.**   See *North/South.*

**sovereign.**   The primary political power within defined borders. Before World War I, most nations achieved sovereignty through war or custom. Rapid decolonialization after World War II created numerous new nations, which gained sovereignty largely through recognition by the United Nations. Under customary international law, a sovereign nation is not accountable to another legal authority.

**sovereign immunity.**   A principle of international law holding a sovereign's territory, property, and officials exempt from the legal processes of another jurisdiction. The exemption extends to arrests of diplomats, civil actions against the sov-

ereign, and seizures of sovereign property. A violation of sovereign immunity constitutes an act of war, although the effect of the doctrine is frequently limited by international agreement and comity among nations.

**space charter.**   A charter agreement specifying the amount of space assigned to a shipper for one or more shipping transactions.

**SPC.**   The abbreviation for state planning committee/commission.

**spd.**   The abbreviation for steamer pays dues.

**spec.**   The abbreviation for special.

**Special 301.**   In the United States, a provision of the Omnibus Trade Act of 1988 designed to curb foreign piracy of U.S. intellectual property. The act enhances Section 301 of the Trade Act of 1974 and requires the U.S. trade representative (USTR) to retaliate against countries failing to protect U.S. copyrights, patents, trademarks, and trade secrets. The USTR identifies offending countries by way of a priority watch list. Following a 30-day review, a 6-month study of unfair trade practices can be undertaken. If negotiations fail to resolve differences within roughly one year, trade sanctions are authorized.

**Special Access Program CBI Export Declaration (Form ITA-370P).**   In the United States, a form used to enter duty-free apparel imports assembled in the Caribbean Basin from U.S.-made and -cut fabric under the Guaranteed Access Level program. A two-part special-access declaration form is required. Form ITA-370P contains the Shipper's Export Declaration, signed by a manager of the U.S. exporting firm, and a Foreign Assemblers Declaration and Certification Form, completed in the Caribbean Basin. See also *HTS Item 9802.*

**special and differential treatment.**   The notion underlying nonreciprocal concessions granted to developing nations in multilateral trade agreements. The concept holds that developing countries require a period of trade adjustment and assistance to compete on a level playing field with developed countries. The idea was institutionalized in the Generalized System of Preferences, substantially agreed to during the Kennedy Round of the General Agreement on Tariffs and

Trade (GATT) and reaffirmed in subsequent GATT negotiations.

**special cargo.**    See *cargo.*

**special cargo policy.**    In maritime insurance, a cargo policy with coverage limited to a specific shipment. Special cargo policies are available for infrequent shippers or extremely valuable cargoes. Compare *open insurance policy.*

**special crossing.**    See *check.*

**Special Customs Invoice (SCI).**    In the United States, a special import form used before March 1, 1982. The SCI was required when imports were valued above $500 or when duties were otherwise based on value. The SIC has been replaced with the Entry Summary (Customs Form 7501) for commercial shipments and the Informal Entry (Customs Form 5119A) for other imports. See also *Special Permit for Immediate Delivery.*

**special deposits.**    In the United Kingdom, funds deposited by commercial banks with the Bank of England at the instruction of the British government. The balances are deposited to reduce the amount of money in circulation. Special deposits are similar to reserve accounts maintained by U.S. commercial banks to meet Federal Reserve Board requirements.

**Special drawing right (SDR).**    A financial unit of account created in 1969 by the International Monetary Fund (IMF) as a universal reserve currency. SDRs are artificial currency units held by the IMF, some central monetary institutions, and prescribed holders. Originally valued at 1/35 ounce of gold, the par value of the U.S. dollar in 1969, the SDR was converted to a value represented by 16 national currencies in 1974. Since 1981, the SDR has represented five basket currencies: the British pound sterling, the Deutsche mark, the French franc, the Japanese yen, and the U.S. dollar. Currently, SDR basket values are adjusted daily by the IMF and weighted in proportion to the market value of goods and services produced by the issuing country. Member countries with balance-of-payments surpluses may convert cash into SDRs. Beginning in 1981, SDRs held in excess of quota earn interest at full market rates. If holdings fall below quota, interest is earned at the rate of 1.5 percent per year. When

used as an index value for commercial contract prices, SDRs are known as flexible SDRs and frozen SDRs. See also *collective reserve unit* and *Triffin Plan.* Compare *Euro-SDR.*

**Special drawing right (SDR) certificates.**    In the United States, instruments issued to Federal Reserve Banks by the Department of Treasury representing U.S. holdings of SDRs. SDR certificates are similar to gold certificates issued by the Treasury.

**special economic zone (SEZ).**    In a nonmarket economy, a foreign trade zone. Local rules of commerce are suspended in SEZs to encourage foreign investment, especially in joint ventures. Taxes and regulations are relaxed for manufacturers producing goods for export. For example, Shenzhen, the largest SEZ in the People's Republic of China, contains special customs declaration agencies to facilitate customs clearance. See also *export processing zone.*

**special endorsement.**    See *endorsement.*

**Special Import Measures Act.**    See *Canadian International Trade Tribunal.*

**special import surcharge.**    See *import surcharge.*

**special initial allowance.**    Any of a variety of schemes offered by a government to attract foreign direct investment. Some countries offer, for example, special allowances permitting up to 100 percent recapture of the cost of plants and equipment.

**specialized agency.**    Any one of the sixteen autonomous agencies operating within the United Nations system, many of which report annually to the United Nations Economic and Social Council. The following international organizations are UN specialized agencies: the Food and Agriculture Organization of the United Nations (FAO), International Bank for Reconstruction and Development (IBRD), International Civil Aviation Organization (ICAO), International Development Association (IDA), International Finance Corporation (IFC), Interna-tional Fund for Agricultural Development (IFAD), International Labor Organization (ILO), International Maritime Organization (IMO), International Monetary Fund (IMF), International Telecommunication Union (ITU), United Nations Educational, Scientific and Cultural Organization (UNESCO), United Nations

Industrial Develop-ment Organization (UNIDO), Universal Postal Union (UPU) World Health Organization (WHO), World Intellectual Property Organization (WIPO), and World Meteorological Organization (WMO).

**specially designated nationals.**  In the United States, a designation by the U.S. Department of the Treasury applied to firms or persons who violate U.S. laws by engaging in commerce with unfriendly countries. As of 1993, the principal targets of the ban are Cuba, Iraq, and Vietnam. Unilateral U.S. embargoes against Cuba and Vietnam have not been lifted, and international sanctions against Iraq remain in place. The bans are administered by the Office of Foreign Assets Control, a Treasury Department agency. The names of specially designated nationals are published in the *Federal Register*.

**Special Permit for Immediate Delivery (Customs Form 3461).**  In the United States, a customs form used to expedite customs entry for certain imports. The form is authorized for approved shipments from Canada and Mexico, imports entering under carnets, and shipments destined for U.S. government agencies. Some reduced-duty and quota imports are also eligible for expedited entry upon application by the importer to the U.S. Customs Service.

**Special Programs Indicator (SPI).**  In the United States, a special code entered in the Automated Commercial System for preferential imports allowed under the Compact of Freely Associated States.

**special tonnage tax.**  See *tonnage tax*.

**Special Trade Relations Bureau.**  See *Department of External Affairs*.

**specie.**  Coins, primarily those composed of gold or silver, but not paper money. Coins are also called hard currency.

**specific duty.**  See *duty*.

**specific limit (SL).**  An absolute quota on a class of imports that increases annually by a fixed percentage. Specific limits are negotiated or imposed unilaterally by an importing nation. Compare *designated consultation level*.

**specific performance.**  In a common-law legal system, a judicial remedy used to prevent injury to one party to a contract when the other party breaches (or threatens to breach) the terms of the agreement. In an action for breach of contract, a court can require the parties to perform according to the original contract terms. An equitable judgment, specific performance is granted only when damages are an inadequate remedy and the original contract terms can be met.

**speculation.**  The act of putting money at risk in anticipation of profit. A speculator faces higher risks of financial loss than conservative investors, who preserve capital in exchange for a reasonable return on investment.

**speculative security.**  A security rated poorly by a rating service. In the United States, securities rated as BB or lower by Standard & Poor's or Ba or lower by Moody's Investors Service are considered substandard investments.

**SPI.**  The abbreviation for Special Programs Indicator.

**split delivery/pick-up.**  A shipment split into smaller loads, usually for shipment to different purchasers or loading at different sites. Common carriers typically charge additional surcharges for handling split shipments.

**sponsor.**  1.The issuer of an initial public offering of securities. 2. A person or organization that helps a person enter a foreign country. In most countries, sponsorship is required for persons seeking residence permits, although some countries require sponsors for foreign nationals entering for any purpose. For example, business visitors are sponsored in Oman, usually by the Omani Chamber of Commerce.

**spot.**  1. The spot market price or the availability of a commodity. 2. In commodity and financial markets, the ability to fill orders for sales or purchases at the current market price within 2 business days. The quoted rate is the spot price. Compare *futures* and *option*.

**spot charter.**  An ocean vessel capable of taking on cargo immediately after a charter agreement is concluded.

**spot exchange.**  A foreign currency sold or purchased at the current market price. See *end-to-end*.

**spot market.**  The market for the cash purchases of commodities, including currencies, available for immediate delivery on the spot date at the actual or adjusted spot price. A spot price is adjusted when the delivery date is more than 2 days from the date the order was executed. Spot prices are usually higher than the forward prices paid on futures contracts, unless the supply of the product exceeds demand.

**spot next.**    The purchase of a currency for delivery after the spot date. A spot-one-week contract means delivery one week after the trade is executed. A spot-fortnight contract means delivery within two weeks of the execution date.

**spot price.**    The price of a commodity scheduled for delivery within 2 days. A price quoted in a spot market usually differs from the actual transaction price when delivery occurs at a later date. Spot prices are composite prices based on current market information provided primarily by suppliers.

**spot rate.**    The interest rate assigned to a financial instrument, or the settlement rate in a financial transaction. The spot rate reflects the market interest rate over a 2-day period from the date of sale.

**SPR.**    The abbreviation for Strategic Petroleum Reserve.

**spread.**    The difference between earnings from an asset and the cost of the asset. 1. On trading exchanges, the difference between the bid price and the offer price. 2. In underwriting, the gross spread, i.e., the difference between the dealer's purchase price and the price paid by an investor. 3. In options trading, buying and selling call or puts options with different expiration dates or strike prices. 4. In futures trading, simultaneously buying and selling different contracts, or buying and selling in different markets or months. 5. In banking, the difference between a bank's borrowing and lending costs.

**spreadsheet.**    1. An accounting worksheet used to prepare balance sheets and income statements. 2. An electronic format for testing investment models. Computerized spreadsheets are used to forecast the effects of exchange rate and interest rate changes on investments.

**SPS.**    The abbreviation for sanitary and phytosanitary (measures).

**SRO.**    The abbreviation for self-regulating organization.

**S.S.**    The abbreviation for steamship.

**ss&c.**    The abbreviation for same sea and country coast.

**Stabex.**    The acronym for *System of Stabilization of Export Earnings,* a program administered by the European Development Fund to aid African, Caribbean, and Pacific (APC) countries. Stabex was negotiated in 1979 during Lomé Convention II. The European Community compensates APC countries when nonmineral export earnings cause balance-of-payments deficits. Compare *Sysmin.*

**stabilization.**    Measures taken to reduce volatility in a market or the impact of market changes on price. Members of international commodity groups buy surplus supplies to stabilize prices. Central banks also enter markets to support currency prices or reduce the effects of market volatility on exchange values.

**stabilization bond.**    A bond denominated in a hard currency and sold as part of a developing country's debt conversion program. Stabilization bonds are swapped for bonds denominated in local currencies. Principal and interest are dedicated to finance local projects, usually economic development or environmental programs. A local bond supported by a stabilization bond has the same maturity date.

**stagflation.**    A condition characteristic of most Western industrialized economies in the 1970s. The combination of recession and high inflation resulted partly from steep and sudden increases in petroleum prices instituted by the Organization of Petroleum Exporting Countries. Declining productivity in Western countries was also a factor. Following the stagflation of the 1970s, Keynesian economics, which had dominated post-World War II economic policymaking, was largely supplanted by monetarism and supply-side economics.

**stag market.**    A securities market in which dealers speculate in new issues to increase the market price before dealing begins. When allocations are made, stags anticipate selling their shares at a profit above the issue price. Compare *bear market* and *bull market.*

**STAGS.**    The abbreviation for sterling transferable a accruing government securities.

**stale check.** A check not presented for payment within 6 months of its making. In the United States and elsewhere, banks need not honor stale checks.

**stale document.** A shipping document, usually a bill of lading, presented after the time customarily allowed for sighting documents related to letter-of-credit transactions. Under the Uniform Customs and Practices for Documentary Credits, a bill of lading dated more than 21 days before presentation is not acceptable unless specifically authorized by a letter of credit.

**stamp duty.** A tax collected for affixing a government stamp to a document of title. In some countries, stamp duties are assessed for transfers of land or securities. The stamp tax is collected by banks in some countries when financial instruments are issued. The tax is equal to a percentage of the face value of negotiable instruments, such as certificates of deposit, drafts, and letters of credit. See also *documentary collection.*

**Stamp tax.** See *Stamp duty.*

**Standard and Poor's (S&P).** An investment-rating service that evaluates securities and commercial paper. The highest S&P bond rating is AAA, given to companies with sufficient liquidity to retire obligations with maturities of up to 40 years. Market-grade commercial paper is rated A1, A2, and A3. AAA indicates the highest-quality certificates of deposit (CDs) with maturities longer than 1 year. A1 is the highest rating for shorter-term CDs. Securities' ratings derived from public information are identified by the letter Q. Standard and Poor's 500 Stock Index measures the performance of 500 major U.S. industrial, transportation, and utility stocks on behalf of the New York Stock Exchange. Standard and Poor's is a subsidiary of McGraw-Hill.

**standard costing.** An accounting system used by an organization to monitor changes in fixed costs. Standard costs for components, equipment, labor, overhead, and raw materials are tracked and recorded. When actual costs differ from standard costs, budgets are controlled by adjusting operating procedures or changing suppliers.

**standard deviation.** A means of measuring the risk inherent in an investment. The higher the deviation of any factor from a given reference point, the greater the risk.

**Standard Industrial Code (SIC).** In the United States, the uniform classification system for identifying goods and services. The SIC applies numeric codes to products and services by category. SIC codes are recorded on a variety of business documents and used to gather international trade statistics. The SIC is published by the U.S. Department of Commerce.

**Standard International Trade Classification (SITC).** A uniform system of codes for collecting international trade data. Originally adopted by the United Nations Economic and Social Council in 1950, the SITC was revised and published in 1960. The SITC-2, or the Standard International Trade Classification, Revision 2, was issued in 1975. The most recent version, the SITC-3, published in 1986, is currently used to report trade statistics to the United Nations. The SITC-3 is correlated to the Harmonized Commodity Description and Coding System by specific product headings or aggregated categories and adapted for use in electronic data interchange systems. The SITC is published by the United Nations Statistical Office.

**standardized product.** An unvariegated product. Standardized products are usually fungible and produced en masse from simple components. Compare *differentiated product line.*

**standard money.** See *legal tender.*

**standard price.** In the European Community, the trigger price for tobacco under the Common Agricultural Policy.

**standard rate.** The base rate used to calculate income taxes in a progressive taxation system. For example, the standard rate may be 30 percent for taxable income between $6000 and $28,000. The tax on the next dollar earned is assessed at the marginal rate. In the United Kingdom, marginal rates are called higher rates.

**standards (stds.).** Criteria used by regulatory agencies to determine a product's fitness for sale. Import standards, prescribed by the importing country, are frequently imposed and raise technical barriers to trade. The International Standards Organization was created to harmonize global product standards and reduce divergencies in national technical standards. See also *American National Standards Institute, Communauté Européenne, General Agreement on Tariffs and Trade: Tokyo Round,* and ISO 9000.

**Standards Code.** See *General Agreement on Tariffs and Trade: Tokyo Round*.

**Standards Council of Canada.** The national product standards authority in Canada, which writes and administers health, safety, and technical standards. The council consults private industry groups before formulating standards. Standards adopted by the council are publicized through the Canadian Standards Information Service.

**standby agreement.** An International Monetary Fund (IMF) facility permitting members to draw down emergency balance-of-payments supplements. The drawdowns are available in addition to other IMF lending facilities.

**standby commitment.** A loan commitment by a bank, often convertible to a line of credit.

**standby letter of credit.** A letter of credit provided as a bid bond or performance bond. Standby credits are used primarily to secure bids on international projects or to guarantee payment when specially manufactured goods are ordered. See also *surety*.

**standby note issuance facility (SNIF).** A lending facility used for project financing, often by insubstantial corporate or sovereign borrowers. Repayment of the debt is guaranteed by a third party, who receives a commission for assuming the credit risk. Compare *revolving underwriting facility*.

**standing order.** A customer's instruction to a bank to remit drafts in specified amounts at regular intervals, usually monthly, to a named payee. Once issued, a standing order remains in effect until revoked by the customer. If the drafts exceed the customer's account or overdraft balance, a bank can revoke the order.

**standstill.** 1. A creditor's agreement to renegotiate a loan when a borrower is near default. Standstill agreements are often preferred to foreclosure when the borrower may recover from financial difficulty. New credit terms usually involve debt rescheduling and refinancing at lower interest rates. 2. In international trade, a safeguard or a temporary suspension of a treaty commitment to reduce tariffs or otherwise liberalize trade. See also *escape clause*. Compare *roll-back*.

**start-up financing.** Funds used to start a business. See also *risk capital* and *seed money*.

**state-controlled trading company.** In nonmarket-economy countries, an authorized trading monopoly, frequently the principal purchasing agent of basic commodities and manufactures.

**state insurance company (SIC).** A government-owned insurer, often the sole underwriter of policies covering government-subsidized imports and exports. In some countries, state insurers underwrite all marine and casualty policies for officially traded products.

**statement of account.** A written statement of purchases, payments, and amounts payable. Statements of account are usually issued monthly, often in invoice form.

**statement of charges.** A document issued by an exporter notifying the importer of sums payable in excess of the quoted selling price. Statements of charges cover actual shipping costs, including packing costs.

**statement of standard accounting practice.** In the United Kingdom, financial accounting standards issued by the Combined Accountancy Bodies. The statements are used by accountants as the best guide to reporting transactions involving acquisitions and mergers, depreciation, securities issues, etc. Financial Accounting Standards Board statements are the equivalent guidelines published in the United States.

**state planning committee (SPC).** The principal government planning agency in a command economy, e.g., the State Planning Commission of the People's Republic of China. Production objectives are set by official directive. The SPC oversees purchasing and manufacturing plans that correspond to political objectives. The plans are designed by the state-owned enterprises to meet official production targets. See also *GOSPLAN*.

**state trading company (STC).** The principal public-sector purchaser of goods and services in some countries. The STC is, for example, the authorized trading agency for the government of India with offices around the world. India's STC office in the United States is located in New York.

**state trading nation (STN).** A country where external trade is controlled by the government. Countries with command economies are clearly STNs, although some mixed-economy countries also qualify, e.g., Japan with its finely tuned external trade programs.

**statistical tax.**  A tax levied in some countries to defray administrative expenses. The tax is usually equal to a fixed percentage (e.g., 2 percent) of the cost, insurance, and freight value of imports. Some exemptions are available for imports of books, commercial samples, etc.

**status of merchandise.**  The dutiable status of products withdrawn from a foreign trade zone (FTZ) for customs entry or reexport. Status is usually determined by a district or regional authority. In the United States, privileged domestic goods have been classified or appraised and taxes paid. Privileged foreign products have not been altered in the FTZ, are dutiable if entered for consumption, and are duty-free when re-exported. Nonprivileged domestic products have not been classified or appraised; unless reclassified as privileged goods, these products may be dutiable if entered for consumption. Nonprivileged foreign goods are dutiable when entered for consumption.

**statutes of frauds.**  In the United States, state laws designed to prevent fraudulent commercial contracts. Statutes of fraud vary, but generally require a written contract for the sale of goods valued at or above $500 and for a lease of 1 year's duration. See also *Uniform Commercial Code.*

**statute of limitations.**  A law setting a time limit for filing a legal action. When the limitation date expires, claimants are barred from suing. In the United States, a contract or tort action must usually be filed within 5 to 6 years. Claims of strict liability in defective product cases must often be filed within 3 years of an event or when the claimant discovers (or should have discovered) the injury. Limitations in criminal cases are set by specific criminal statutes.

**statutory company.**  See *company.*

**statutory damages.**  See *damages.*

**statutory meeting.**  See *Companies Act of 1985.*

**statutory rate of duty.**  Import duties fixed by statute. In the United States, statutory rates are set by the Smoot-Hawley Act of 1930 and apply to imports from countries without most-favored-nation status. The rates are listed in the Harmonized Tariff Schedules of the United States.

**statutory report.**  See *Companies Act of 1985.*

**std(s).**  The abbreviation for standard(s).

**sté.**  The abbreviation for *société.*

**steamship conference.**  See *conference.*

**STELA.**  The abbreviation for System for Tracking Export License Applications. See *Bureau of Export Administration.*

**stemdate.**  See *subject to stem.*

**stere (s).**  In the metric system of weights and measures, a unit of solid volume equal to 35.314 cubic feet. See also *Systeme Internationale.*

**sterling balance.**  Monetary reserves denominated in British pound sterling.

**sterling bill of exchange.**  A bill of exchange drawn in British pound sterling.

**sterling letter of credit.**  A letter of credit instructing a bank to draw a bill of exchange in British pound sterling.

**sterling transferable accruing government security (STAG).**  In the United Kingdom, a deep-discount bond issued by the Bank of England. STAGs are zero-coupon bonds that pay no interest, although holders receive a substantial capital gain. The bonds are backed by British Treasury stock.

**Steuer.**  German: tax.

**stk.**  The abbreviation for stock.

**stock (stk.).**  1. The ownership interest in an incorporated company, often divided into shares and sold to the general public in exchange for certificates representing shares owned. In the United States, stock is common or preferred. Owners of common stock receive regular dividends declared by the board of directors and vote in person or by proxy at shareholder meetings. Owners of preferred stock receive limited dividends, have no voting rights, but are entitled to priority claims on assets when a company dissolves. Outside the United States, a common stock is known as an ordinary share and a preferred stock as a preference share. 2. The inventory consumed or sold by a business. 3. The assets of an organization, including buildings, equipment, and cash and credit reserves. 4. In the United Kingdom, a security issued by a national government, municipality, or corporation with combined features of a bond and a preferred stock. The fixed-interest issues are traded on stock exchanges at variable prices but have a redemption date when the par, or nominal, value is repaid. Stocks are often issued in units of 100 pounds each.

**stockbroker.**    A commission agent who trades securities on behalf of customers. Brokers may also buy and sell for their own accounts. In the United States, stockbrokers in New York, known as specialists, are licensed and regulated by the American Stock Exchange and New York Stock Exchange. The National Association of Securities Dealers licenses brokers for over-the-counter trading. See *self-regulating organization* and *Securities and Exchange Commision.*

**stock control.**    See *inventory control.*

**stock exchange.**    A market where publicly quoted corporate stocks are bought and sold. Government securities are also quoted on some exchanges. The major international stock exchanges are the American Stock Exchange in New York, the Bourse in Paris, the London Stock Exchange, the New York Stock Exchange, and the Tokyo Stock Exchange.

**Stock Exchange Automated Quotations System (SEAQ).**    The electronic price-display system of the London Stock Exchange (LSE). SEAQ securities are divided into four categories of shares, which must meet certain market price and frequent-display criteria. Alpha stocks, the equities of the largest companies listed on the LSE, are the most frequently traded. Beta stocks are equities of moderate-sized companies, which are traded less frequently. Delta and gamma stocks, the equities of smaller companies, are infrequently traded and have few or no price-display criteria.

**Stock Exchange Automatic Exchange Facility (SEAF).**    An automated system used to execute trades on the London Stock Exchange. The system matches buy orders with sellers at the best available price. Like other stock exchange automated systems, the SEAF records transactions for settlement and has virtually eliminated face-to-face floor dealing.

**Stock Exchange Daily Official List.**    See *London Stock Exchange.*

**Stock Exchange of Hong Kong Limited.**    The unified stock exchange of Hong Kong approved in 1981. The exchange began trading in 1986. Listed securities include ordinary shares, preference shares, debt instruments, warrants, and unit trusts. Prices are quoted in Hong Kong dollars and published in the *Daily Quotation Sheet, The Weekly Report,* and *The Securities Bulletin* (monthly). The exchange's index, the Nang Seng Index, measures the weighted value of 33 stocks. There are no nationality requirements for foreign investment, although membership in the exchange is limited by nationality and residency. Corporate takeover proposals are regulated by the Code on Takeovers and Mergers and subject to approval by the exchange. The operations of the Hong Kong securities market are supervised by the Securities Commission.

**Stock Exchange of Singapore Limited.**    A stock exchange incorporated in 1973. Bonds, debentures, loan stocks, and shares are traded on the exchange. Securities of companies meeting the strictest listing requirements are listed in the first trading section. Listings are also available for the second trading section and the second market. Prices are quoted in Singapore dollars on the Stock Exchange of Singapore Dealing and Automated Quotation system, established in 1987, and announced daily in *Financial News* and monthly in the *Journal.* Corporate takeovers are regulated by the Securities Industry Council. Foreign investment in local companies is restricted. The exchange is a self-regulating organization overseen by the Monetary Authority of Singapore.

**Stockholm Convention.**    See *European Free Trade Association.*

**stock market.**    1. A stock exchange. 2. A livestock market.

**stock option.**    See *option.*

**stockpile.**    A commodity purchased in large quantities for storage. Stockpiles are maintained as emergency supplies or as a means of influencing market price. See also *buffer stock* and *strategic stockpile.*

**stock split.**    A change in the number of shares issued to existing shareholders, usually to attract new investors by reducing the proportional price or number of outstanding shares. A split up means the number of shares is increased and the price of a single share is proportionally decreased. Conversely, a split down (or reverse split) means the number of shares is decreased and the price of a single share is increased. Although new stock certificates are issued when stocks are split, the value of a shareholder's equity is unchanged by the split unless the market price of the stock increases. Stock splits require an amendment to a corporation's charter. In the United Kingdom, stock splits are called scrip issues.

**stock watering.** The process of creating more shares in a company than its tangible assets justify. If the company is dissolved, owners of watered stock may not collect on earnings.

**s. ton.** The abbreviation for short ton.

**stop charge.** A surcharge billed by a common carrier for delivering cargo to an intermediate destination along a given delivery route.

**stop-loss order.** An order to a broker to execute a securities or commodities transaction to cover an open position. When the market is volatile, speculators use stop orders to instruct brokers to trade at a stated price to reduce losses.

**stop notice.** Formerly called a notice in lieu of distringas, a legal order barring payments of dividends or transfers of stock unless unregistered owners are notified. The procedure protects owners without share certificates registered in their names.

**stop order.** An order to a broker to buy or sell when a specified market price is reached, usually to liquidate an existing transaction. The current market price may be higher or lower than the price when the original order was placed. If a stop order cannot be executed at the stipulated price, the broker buys or sells at the next best price. Stop orders are also called buy-stop orders, sell-stop orders, stop-out orders, stop-loss orders, and stop-limit orders.

**stop-out price.** In the United States, the lowest price paid for new securities auctioned by the U.S. Department of the Treasury. The Treasury Department fills orders at the highest price and then at progressively lower prices. Securities bought at stop-out prices pay the highest yields.

Often, the percentage of stop-out sales in an auction is reported by the Treasury Department.

**stoppage in transit.** A notice issued to a carrier to return goods that are in transit to an insolvent buyer. When a carrier is notified of a stoppage order, goods are redelivered to the seller. If a stoppage notice is not issued, delivered goods are subject to seizure by the buyer's creditors.

**stop payment.** An instruction to a bank that a check should not be honored. The order is issued by the maker of the check. The order may sometimes be given by telephone, but must usually be in writing.

**storage warehouse.** See *bonded warehouse.*

**store of value.** The characteristic of money that retains most of its purchasing power and exchange value. A currency's value is reduced by inflation, but a low, steady inflation rate creates a predictable store of value. Currencies are convertible when markets perceive them as instruments of predictable tradable value.

**story paper.** A stock or financial instrument without an established trading record, the novelty of which creates risks for an investor. Fraud suits or other legal remedies are available to investors who lose money based on misrepresentations about the value of newly issued financial instruments.

**stowage.** The process of loading cargo into shipping containers or into the hold of a ship.

**stow ton.** See *measurement ton.*

**str.** The abbreviation for steamer.

**STR.** The abbreviation for special trade representative. See *Office of the U.S. Trade Representative.*

**straddle.** 1. In options trades, simultaneous purchases and sales of put options and call options with the same expiration date at the same exercise price. Straddles enable traders to profit from price volatility. By contrast, when call options carry different exercise prices or different expiration dates are bought and sold simultaneously, the trading strategy is called a *butterfly*. Traders profit most from butterflies when underlying commodity price trends are relatively stable. 2. In futures trading, the spread, or the purchase of a commodity in one month to sell in another month in order to benefit from price variations in different months. 3. A vehicle with mechanical lift devices.

**straight bill of lading.**    A bill of lading entitling a consignee to obtain immediate possession of cargo. Compare *negotiable bill of lading.*

**straight bond.**    A noncallable bond, e.g., Eurobonds, Treasury bonds, and savings bonds.

**straight consignment.**    Cargo transported under a straight bill of lading.

**straight letter of credit.**    A letter of credit instructing payment to the beneficiary only at the office of the paying bank. Drafts must be drawn on or before the credit's expiration date.

**straight-line depreciation.**    See *depreciation.*

**stranding.**    In marine insurance, the running aground of a ship, usually to avoid colliding with another object. A stranded ship is one that cannot be refloated.

**strap.**    See *option.*

**Strasbourg Patent Convention.**    See *European Patent System.*

**strategic business unit (SBU).**    A corporate unit responsible for planning marketing strategies for a specific product line.

**strategic petroleum reserve.**    In the United States, a program authorized by the Energy Policy and Conservation Act of 1975. Under the program, the Department of Energy stockpiles petroleum supplies to prevent economic disruption when foreign oil supplies are endangered. The original authority permitted the stockpiling of a 90-day supply in Texas and Louisiana. See also *strategic stockpile.*

**strategic stockpile.**    Also called strategic reserves, any commodity supply maintained by a government for use during national emergencies. Strategic reserves consist of critical minerals, metals, and industrial commodities. In the United States, the building of reserves is authorized by the Strategic and Critical Material Stockpiling Act of 1946. See also *strategic petroleum reserve.*

**street name.**    In the United States, a nominee in whose name a security is registered, as opposed to the beneficial owner. Securities registered in street

names can be transferred without delivering certificates to a broker. Nominees are usually banks or brokerage firms, which hold securities in trust for individuals, corporations, or nonprofit institutions. Street-name stocks are called nominee stocks in the United Kingdom. Compare *marking name.*

**stress of weather.**    A marine insurance term meaning heavy weather, or an elemental force sufficiently grave to constitute a peril of the sea.

**strike.**    A walkout by employees during a labor dispute. Workers strike for better wages or benefits, safer working conditions, etc. Often, national labor laws force a cooling-off period and binding arbitration in critical industries, such as rail and truck transportation.

**strike price.**    1. The exercise price, i.e., the price at which an option can be taken up. 2. The price set by an agent who receives bids for a new securities issue. Normally, only buyers who bid near or above the strike price receive a portion of the issue.

**strip.**    See *option.*

**stripped bond.**    A gilt-edged security that does not entitle the holder to a current dividend. In the United Kingdom, government stocks and bonds carry no dividend rights within 36 days of an interest payment. Stripped bonds can be purchased and later sold, once the dividend right is restored. The holder of stripped bonds avoids receiving taxable earnings, but sells with a tax-free capital gain, a practice known as bond washing. Bond washing is profitable only when interest can be deferred or when accrued interest is taxed at a low rate. See also *ex.*

**stripping.**    In the shipping industry, the process of unloading an intermodal ocean container.

**strong currency.**    See *reserve currency.*

**structural adjustment program (SAP).**    A program adopted by a beneficiary of World Bank lending to cure internal economic problems. The bank operates a medium-term financing facility established in 1979 to grant hard-currency loans when SAPs are implemented. Structural adjustment lending incorporates conditionality, which also underlies International Monetary Fund lending. SAPs require improved national budgeting, managed public debt, and reduced barriers to trade and foreign investment. An SAP loan is usually spread over 5 to 10 years.

**Structural Impediments Initiative (SII).** Bilateral negotiations undertaken in 1990 to reduce Japan's trade surplus with the United States. The discussions were initiated by the United States in 1989. The United States requested that Japan (1) implement a competitive pricing system; (2) reduce the power of *keiretsu* to block market access and financing, particularly in government procurements; (3) eliminate preferences in favor of national ownership and use of prime land; (4) make customs regulations and product standards transparent; (5) simplify its complex internal distribution system; and (6) reduce the national savings rate. Japan requested that the United States reduce its federal budget deficit, increase spending for research and development, and improve its primary and secondary educational system. As of mid-1993, the results of the SSI negotiations were inconclusive, but Japan and the United States agreed on a framework for bilateral trade negotiations. The United States is expected to seek both quantitative and qualitative targets for measuring any negotiated reduction in Japan's persistent trade surplus with the United States. See also *managed trade*.

**study group.** An international commodity association created to conduct studies on a specific commodity market. Unlike international commodity groups, which consist primarily of developing countries, study groups are largely composed of commodity-consuming countries and relatively strong producer countries. While commodity groups are organized to maintain prices through international commodity agreements, study groups attempt to ensure adequate supplies, stable prices, and open markets. The major commodity study groups inclue the following:

*International Lead and Zinc Study Group (ILZSG).* A commodity group created in 1959, primarily to secure the supply of lead and zinc. ILZSG members are mostly European countries dependent on developing countries for supplies of these commodities. The ILZSG is based in London.

*International Rubber Study Group (IRSG).* A commodity group organized in 1944. The IRSG is a group of developed and newly industrialized countries (NICs), mainly concerned with maintaining stable supplies of rubber products. The IRSG has headquarters in London. Compare *Association of Natural Rubber Producing Countries*.

*International Wool Study Group (IWSG).* A commodity group created in 1949 to share information on supplies and prices of wool products. The IWSG is based in London.

*Office Internationale de la Vigne et du Vin (OIVV).* The International Vine and Wine Study Group, a commodity group that shares technical and price information on grape products and wine production. Founded in 1924, OIVV is headquartered in Paris.

**stuffing.** The shipping industry term for the process of loading an intermodal container.

**subagent.** See *agency*.

**subchapter M.** In the United States, a regulated investment company exempt under the Internal Revenue Code from federal taxes on most gains and income earned from investments. Gains and income are tax exempt if 90 percent of the company's net income is distributed to shareholders and earned from securities' sales, falling within specific short-term capital-gains regulations.

**subchapter S.** In the United States, a corporation taxed as a partnership under the Internal Revenue Code, i.e., gains (or losses) are taxable to each individual shareholder. Also known as a small-business corporation, a subchapter S corporation has 35 or fewer shareholders. Unlike other corporations, a subchapter S is permitted to use cash basis accounting.

**subcontractor.** See *contractor*.

**subject offer.** A tentative offer to sell, usually to elicit a buyer's counteroffer.

**subject open.** Also called subject ship being free, a tentative offer to charter a ship. For the duration of the offer, the shipowner is free to commit the ship to another charter.

**subject to stem.** A charter party provision, limited largely to cargoes of coal. Cargo must be received for loading within the stipulated lay time. A stemdate is the day on which loading of the cargo actually begins.

**sublease.** See *lease*.

**subordinated debt.** A secondary claim on the assets of a company in liquidation or bankruptcy. Unsecured claims rank lower than secured claims. Securities holders rank in the following order: bondholders, preferred-stock owners, and common-stock owners.

**subordinated security.** A debenture issued by a bank or other depository institution. In a dissolution, a debenture holder's claim on assets is subordinate to the rights of depositors. In the United Kingdom, these debentures are known as subordinated unsecured loan stocks.

**Subpart F.** In the United States, Sections 951 to 964 of the Internal Revenue Code, which impose taxes on passive income earned by a U.S. shareholder from a controlled foreign corporation. Enacted in the Revenue Act of 1962, the provision treats undistributed income earned abroad, which can be easily transferred between different jurisdictions, as taxable dividends to the shareholder. Subpart F reaches foreign base company income, risk insurance income, sums paid in the form of illegal bribes and questionable payments to foreign officials, amounts subject to the international boycott factor, and income from foreign sources deemed ineligible for foreign tax credits. Foreign-base company income is income from certain foreign transactions, including oil-related sales, services, and shipping investments. It also includes foreign personal holding company income, such as earnings from annuities, commodity and foreign currency transactions, property holdings, interest, rents, and royalties.

**subpoena.** A legal order instructing a person to appear at a specified place to give testimony on a specified date. The *subpoena ad testificandum* compels a witness to appear and give evidence during a deposition or trial; a *subpoena duces tecum* compels a witness to produce documents or similar tangible evidence. A witness must be served personally with a subpoena and is subject to contempt-of-court penalties for failing to appear.

**subrogation.** The substitution of one party's rights for those of another. 1. In insurance, an insurer's right to collect legal damages won by a policyholder when the insurance claim has already been paid. 2. In the secondary market, the rights of a purchaser to recover money based on an obligation made to the original investor.

**subscribed capital.** See *share capital*.

**subscription.** An offer to purchase securities. The offer can be exercised during the prescribed waiting period, usually up to 60 days following the initial public offering.

**subsidiarity.** In the European Community (EC), the principle defining the division of regulatory authority between EC bodies and member states. Regulatory decisions are made at the lowest possible local level, leaving mainly cross-border issues to EC governing bodies. Subsidiarity is intended to acknowledge national differences and preserve diversity in the EC. See also *Treaty of Maastricht*.

**subsidiary.** A company controlled by a parent company owning 51 percent or more of its voting stock. Through its nominal share ownership, the parent controls the subsidiary's board of directors.

**Subsidies (and Countervailing Measures) Code.** See *General Agreement on Tariffs and Trade: Tokyo Round*.

**Subsidies Committee.** See *GATT Standing Committees*.

**subsidized trade routes.** See *operating differential subsidy*.

**subsidy.** A government payment to a producer to compensate for low prices or high costs. Export subsidies distort international trade and are generally prohibited by the Subsidies Code adopted during the Tokyo Round of the General Agreement on Tariffs and Trade (GATT) negotiations. However, under GATT, developing countries exporting manufactured goods to developed countries may provide subsidies if subsidized exports do not significantly harm the economic interests of other GATT members. 1. A direct subsidy is a payment made directly to a producer, usually as a cash grant, tax benefit, or concessional loan. 2. A domestic subsidy is an incentive to produce products for local consumption and is not illegal. Domestic incentives include bonus payments, concessional loans, deductions of direct taxes, etc. 3. An export subsidy is a direct subsidy paid to encourage production for export. 4. An indirect subsidy is a payment to a critical industry, usually in support of research and development that is later adapted for commercial exploitation. See also *countervailing duty action*.

**subsistence crop.**   A product consumed by the producer and also sold as a cash crop.

**substandard loan.**   A loan on which timely payments of principal and interest are doubtful. Inadequate collateral may have been pledged, or the borrower's financial position may have deteriorated. Loans to indebted developing countries are considered substandard when an obligation has not been met or a negotiated rescheduling with creditors has not been completed.

**substantial or essential part doctrine.**   In customs law, a rule used in import classifications. To be placed in the same classification as a finished product, an import must contain the same essential components as the finished product.

**substantial transformation.**   In the United States, a rule used to determine country of origin for preferential imports that contain content from a third country. An import entering under the U.S. Generalized System of Preferences must have been refashioned into a new and different product in a beneficiary country. For example, adding paint to a product does not qualify as substantial transformation, but altering its chemical nature through a simple process may be sufficient. Caribbean Basin Initiative II exports must have been substantially transformed in the region. See also *Canada-U.S. Free Trade Agreement.* Compare *double substantial transformation.*

**substituted expense.**   In maritime shipping, an expense claimed as a general average loss. Under the York-Antwerp Rules, substituted expenses are recoverable on the same basis as other expenses, provided the cost of the substituted expense does not exceed that of a clearly recoverable expense.

**substitution.**   1. In contract law, a novation, or the process of replacing one set of contract terms with another. 2. A subrogation of one creditor's claims to those of another. 3. In banking, the seizure and sale of collateral for a secured loan in default. 4. In finance, a change in collateral securing a broker's call loan. 5. In secondary-market financing, an investor's right of subrogation.

**substitution effect.**   The impact of price changes on demand for a product. The market for cheaper substitutes is enlarged as the price of a primary product increases and the demand for complementary products decreases. Compare *income effect.*

**subzone.**   A special foreign trade zone established for a company's convenience. Subzones are located at the company's facilities.

**sucre.**   The currency of Peru.

**sue and labor clause.**   In marine insurance, a provision under which an insurer reimburses a policyholder who prevents or mitigates losses. In addition to other expenses covered by the claim, costs incurred by the policyholder who prevents or mitigates a loss are paid by the insurer.

**sufferance warehouse.**   In Canada, private warehouses used for customs storage. Sufferance warehouses substitute for free ports and free trade zones in Canada. Compare *Queen's warehouse.*

**sufferance wharf.**   A pier where goods are temporarily stored prior to customs clearance.

**summary sale.**   The sale of another's assets without a judicial proceeding. In most jurisdictions, police and revenue agencies, including customs authorities, are authorized to conduct summary sales of forfeited or seized goods.

**sumptuary tax.**   A tax imposed on luxury imports to discourage consumption.

**Sunflowerseed Oil Assistance Program.**   See *Cottonseed Oil Assistance Program.*

**sup.**   The abbreviation for supply.

**superdeductive.**   In the United States, also known as the further processing method, a customs deduction for the costs of finishing an import locally for sale in the domestic market. The superdeductive is used when import duties are based on deductive value. Processing costs, an allowance for waste, and industry practice determine the value of the deduction. The superdeductive is applied to goods sold within 90 to 180 days of importation, but it is not available when the identity of the import is destroyed by inward processing. See also *further processing price* and *unit price.*

**super-high cube.**   See *high cube.*

**superimposed clause.**   A notice affixed to a foul bill of lading or an on-deck bill of lading warning of damaged or dangerous cargo. Foul or on-deck bills of lading disqualify a shipper seeking payment under a letter of credit, unless the credit specifically authorizes foul documents.

**supervisory board.**    In the European Community (EC), the board of directors of a European company. Under the EC's two-tier corporate structure, the supervisory board oversees the operations of a company's management board. Compare *administrative board.*

**supplementary levy.**    In the European Community, an additional duty imposed on imports of pork, poultry, or eggs when the import price is lower than the Common Agricultural Policy gate price.

**supplier credit.**    In banking, interim financing provided to a supplier. The supplier is paid with drafts secured by an irrevocable letter of credit. See also *red clause credit.*

**supply-side economics.**    An economic theory popularized in the United States in the 1980s by Arthur Laffer, a U.S. economist. Supply-side economists advocate low taxes and reduced government regulation to increase economic growth. The theory holds that higher growth rates overcome national budget deficits, which may result from deep tax cuts. Compare *Keynesian economics.*

**supranational.**    The description of an agency or organization the jurisdiction of which is not limited by a national regulatory authority. The International Monetary Fund, the United Nations, and the World Bank Group are supranational organizations. However, their operations are governed by charter and controlled by member states' voting rights.

**supra protest.**    See *acceptance supra protest.*

**surcharge.**    An extra charge in addition to the quoted duty, price, or rate.

**surety.**    1. A performance bond guaranteeing fulfillment of an obligation. The surety bond can be an insurance policy, standby letter of credit, demand certificate of deposit, or cash on deposit in an escrow account. 2. A guarantee required to obtain release of imports from customs. The surety covers estimated duties, other taxes, and penalties. In the United States, a customs bond or a general term bond is posted when import

release documents are presented. U.S. Customs Regulations require two guarantors for personal sureties. The guarantors must be U.S. citizens or residents owning property in the customs district and having no legal disabilities under the law of the state where a bond is executed.

**surplus.**    1. Also called retained earnings, net profits saved by a company after dividends are distributed. 2. The assets held by a corporation in excess of its liabilities.

**surplus funds.**    Funds earned by a foreign-owned enterprise. In some countries with foreign exchange controls, surplus funds cannot be reinvested or repatriated without government authorization. See also *blocked funds.*

**surplus treaty.**    A reinsurance agreement whereby a secondary underwriter assumes a prearranged insurance risk.

**surrender value.**    The amount of money available to a policyholder before the face value of a policy is paid. 1. The portion of a whole life insurance premium that a policyholder can borrow. If the loan is not repaid, principal and interest are deducted from the amount payable to the beneficiary. 2. The portion of a paid-in premium refunded to a policyholder when an insurance policy is canceled.

**surtax.**    A sum added to taxes payable. Surcharges are often temporary and are imposed by administrative action until permanent rate changes are authorized by a legislature.

**surveillance.**    1. Procedures used by an administering agency to monitor compliance with an international agreement. 2. Measures taken by the International Monetary Fund to monitor the effects of a structural adjustment program on a country's balance-of-payments deficit.

**Surveillance Body.**    See *safeguards.*

**survey.**    The examination of cargo or inspection of a vessel by a third-party inspection agent.

**suspension.**    1. The temporary revocation of a trade obligation incurred by treaty. 2. A forgiveness of duties on products imported for inward processing. Duties are suspended unless an import is entered for sale in the domestic market. See also *superdeductive.*

**sustainable development.**   Economic development that produces long-term economic and soical gains because it enhances the natural environment and the quality of human life. The concept of sustainable development was devised primarily to address problems arising from pollution, deforestation, mounting industrial waste, and other forms of environmental degradation caused by rapid industrialization and technological innovation. In theory, economic development that degrades the natural and social environments may yield short-term profits, but it does not produce long-term prosperity or socially beneficial results. Conversely, the notion of sustainable development presupposes that prolonged economic growth can be sustained if green technologies are employed and quality-of-life issues are factored into economic decision making. See also *United Nations Conference on Environment and Development*.

**sv.**   The abbreviation for sailing vessel.

**swap.**   A financial instrument used by currency brokers and banks to reduce risks when currency market prices fluctuate. In the United States, the Commodities Future Trading Commission exempted swaps from regulation in 1993. 1. A currency swap, or the combined purchase and sale of equal amounts of currency under contracts with different maturity dates. Swaps reduce the exchange risk to one party for a specific period of time before the transaction is reversed. The swap price is the difference in the exchange values of the swapped currencies at maturity. 2. An interest rate swap, or the conversion of fixed-rate debt into a floating-rate obligation. The holder benefits from rising interest rates before the transaction is reversed. When fixed-rate debt in one currency is exchanged for floating-rate debt in another, the transaction is called a cross-currency swap.

**swap arrangement.**   A countertrade in which goods are transferred at designated sites to reduce transportation costs. See also *swap*.

**swap network.**   See *exchange equalization account*.

**swapping.**   See *swap arrangement*.

**swaption.**   See *option*.

**SWIFT.**   The abbreviation for Society for Worldwide Interbank Financial Telecommunications.

**swingline.**   In banking, a backup line of credit. Swinglines are short-term contingency borrowing facilities for issuers of commercial paper. Funds are drawn down when an issue's sales proceeds are insufficient to cover the debt or when older debt paper cannot be rolled over.

**switch.**   In foreign trade, a transshipment through a third country when the importing country has insufficient foreign exchange. The goods are paid for in the third country, which accepts the importing country's local currency. Switch transactions must comply with validated export license regulations. Compare *countertrade*.

**switch trading.**   See *switch*.

**switch transaction.**   A contract to ship goods to a destination country by way of an intermediary country. See also *switch*.

**syndicate.**   1. A group of underwriters formed to spread the risk of underwriting an insurance policy. See also *Lloyd's* and *reinsurance*. 2. A group of banks formed to underwrite a credit facility or a securities issue. See also *syndication*.

**syndicate agreement.**   A contract between members of a banking group created to underwrite and issue a new securities offering. Also known as an agreement among underwriters, the contract names the members of the syndicate and the lead bank, or managing underwriter; the purpose and duration of the agreement; and the portion of the offering allotted to each member. The contract also indicates whether the underwriters will purchase securities or offer them on a best-effort basis. The contract terminates when the transaction has been concluded.

**syndication.**   1. In banking, a group of commercial banks and investment banks organized to finance a loan, usually in the Eurobond or Euronote market. Syndications are arranged by a syndicator, or investment manager. A syndicate member advances a portion of the loan and shares in the interest. Typically, the syndicator earns under 10 percent of the face value of the loan. See also *revolving underwriting facility*. Compare *participation*. 2. In finance, a purchase group of investment banks formed to underwrite a securities issue. The terms of the sale are set forth in a syndicate agreement and arranged by a managing underwriter. Compare *selling group*.

**synthetic security.** A financial instrument with combined features of more familiar instruments, but designed to produce a specific result, e.g., exchange rate protection or enhanced liquidity. Synthetic securities are traded between parties through private placements, usually involving exchange rate or interest rate swaps.

**Sysmin.** A short form for System for Stabilizing Export Earnings in the Mining Sector, a program administered by the European Development Fund to aid African, Caribbean, and Pacific (APC) countries. Sysmin emerged in 1979 from Lomé Convention II to assist APC countries that depend on export earnings from minerals. The system is designed to avert long-term damage to APC mining operations when obsolete equipment or untrained personnel cause serious malfunctions. Sysmin does not replace lost export earnings, but it does finance equipment purchases, repairs, and personnel training. Compare *Stabex*.

**syst.** The abbreviation for system.

**Système Internationale (SI).** Also known as the metric system and the International System, a decimal system of weights and measurements in which all units are composed of multiples of 10. In the metric system, the primary units are the ampere (electric current), candela (luminous intensity), kilometer/meter (length), kelvin (tem-perature), kilogram (mass), liter (liquid volume), second (time), and stere (solid volume). The metric system was proposed by Gabriel Mouton of Lyons, France, in 1670 and was officially adopted in France in 1795. By the 1850s, most other European countries had also adopted the metric system. The British imperial system was officially replaced by the metric system in 1963. The UK Weights and Measures Act of 1985 identifies British imperial units no longer approved for commerce, including the bushel, cubic foot, square mile, and ton. In the United States, the Système Internationale was approved for scientific purposes by the National Bureau of Standards in 1964 and was adopted for official use by the Metric Conversion Act of 1975. As of 1992, the United States Customary System is still widely used in U.S. domestic commerce.

**System for Tracking Export License Applications (STELA).** In the United States, a voice-answering service informing exporters of the status of export licenses. If an exporter's application is approved, STELA authorizes immediate shipment, even before paper authorization is received. STELA is a service of the Bureau of Export Administration.

**system of mineral supports.** See *Sysmin*.

**System of Stabilization of Export Earnings.** See *Stabex*.

# T

**t.** The abbreviation for tare.

**T.** The abbreviation for ton.

**ta.** The abbreviation for trading as.

**TA.** The abbreviation for the Tariff Act of 1930.

**TAA.** The abbreviation for trade adjustment assistance and the acronym for Transatlantic (Rate) Agreement. See *conference*.

**Table of Denial Orders.** In the United States, a list of individuals and firms whose export privileges have been revoked by the U.S. Customs Service. The list is published in the *Federal Register*. Engaging in international trade with parties under denial orders is illegal in the United States.

**tacit acceptance.** A procedure used by the International Maritime Organization (IMO) to adopt technical agreements. Unless member states expressly object, an IMO technical agreement becomes effective on a specified date. The procedure departs from the customary international practice of requiring that a prescribed number of states affirmatively adopt an international convention before its effective date. Tacit acceptance became IMO policy in 1972.

**tackle clause.** See *overside delivery clause*.

**Tagesgeld.** German: a loan repayable on the following day.

**tägliches Geld.** German: call money.

**tail.** 1. In bond pricing, the numbers after the decimal point, e.g., the tail is .4521 in a bond quote of $85.4521. 2. In money markets, the difference in maturities when a financial instrument is partially paid with a repurchase agreement. 3. In a U.S. Treasury auction, the difference between the average competitive bid and the lowest price the Treasury accepts for an issue, i.e., the stop-out price.

**Taiwan Stock Exchange Corporation.** A securities exchange established in Taipei in 1961, which trades bonds and corporate stock. Over-the-counter trading began in 1988. Securities of companies meeting the strictest listing requirements are known as Category A shares; lesser listing criteria are applied to shares of companies falling in Categories B and C. Prices are quoted in Taiwan dollars and announced daily in reports issued by the exchange and the public media. Corporate takeovers are approved by the Security Exchange and Commission. Special rules apply to technology enterprises and foreign investment.

**taka.** The currency of Bangladesh.

**take a position.** The act of speculating in financial instruments. See also *long position* and *short position*.

**take delivery.** 1. The conclusion of a securities transaction on the settlement date. Most buyers take delivery in regular-way settlements, i.e., within 5 days of the transaction date. 2. The act of liquidating a futures transaction by accepting the underlying commodity. Traders rarely liquidate futures contracts, but instead sell them before maturity.

**take-down.** 1. In banking, a draw on funds available under a credit facility. 2. An underwriter's purchase of a portion of a new securities issue at a prearranged price.

**take-out.** 1. Buying out another investor's position. 2. The profit earned when one group of securities is sold and another is purchased at a lower price. Take-out proceeds can be retained as earnings or reinvested.

**take-out loan.** A loan that substitutes permanent financing for bridge financing.

**takeover.** Gaining control of a company by buying shareholders' equity, usually at a premium above market price. A friendly offer is called a merger proposal, while an unfriendly one is called a hostile takeover bid. In a conditional bid, shares are purchased only if the offerer can gain enough stock to control the company. A bid is unconditional when the offerer purchases shares without regard to gaining a controlling interest.

**tala.** The currency of Samoa.

**tale quale.** Literally, as it arrives, i.e., a term of sale indicating that the buyer accepts cargo in the condition in which it is delivered. Tale quale applies to grain contracts when cargo has been inspected and certified by an independent inspection firm. See also *rye terms*.

**TALISMAN.** The abbreviation for Transfer Accounting Lodgement for Investors and Stock Management.

**Talmud.** Jewish civil and religious writings, consisting of the *Mishnah*, the text, and *Gemara*, the commentary. The *Talmud* is a body of code law, including the *Kashrut* prescribing dietary restrictions in Israel.

**talon.** A form used by a bondholder to apply for bearer bond coupons when an existing supply is depleted.

**T&E.** The abbreviation for transportation and exportation entry.

**tangible asset.** An imprecise term, but usually any asset not clearly intangible. Personal property and real property are tangibles, which are depreciated over their useful lives. Accounts receivables, goodwill, and intellectual property are intangibles amortized over a given accounting period. Natural resources (e.g., oil reserves) are intangible wasting assets, which are depreciated though an accounting method known as depletion.

**tanker.** An ocean carrier designed to transport bulk liquids, usually oil or liquefied gases.

**tap stock.** See *gilt-edged security*.

**tare (t).** The weight of packing and shipping containers deducted from gross weight to calculate net weight, i.e., the weight of a shipment's contents.

**target company.** The object of a corporate takeover.

**Targeted Export Assistance Program (TEA).** In the United States, a farm program offered through the U.S. Department of Agriculture (USDA) to help domestic producers compete with subsidized exports in foreign markets. The TEA was replaced in 1990 with USDA's Market Promotion Program.

**target price.** The wholesale price set by a government or an international commodity group as the preferred price for a commodity. Subsidies are provided to guarantee the target price to producers. See also *Common Agricultural Policy*.

**tarif douanier commun.** French: common customs tariff. See *common external tariff*.

**tariff.** 1. A customs tariff. 2. A freight tariff.

**Tariff Act (TA) of 1930.** In the United States, the act that, *inter alia*, established statutory duty rates for U.S. imports, subsequently modified by the Reciprocal Trade Agreements Act of 1934. Section 307 of the act bans imports produced through convict labor or forced labor. Section 311 defines permissible operations when warehoused goods are subject to customs regulations. Section 330 fixes the terms of the International Trade Commission (ITC) commissioners. Section 332 empowers the ITC to implement U.S. customs laws. Section 337 prohibits imports unfairly produced or entered for sale in the United States. Section 402 approves customs valuation methods. Section 484 authorizes the ITC to collect statistical data and publish tariff schedules. Section 514 establishes procedures for protesting import tariff classifications. Section 522 authorizes the Federal Reserve Bank of New York to certify foreign currencies for customs purposes. Section 571 empowers the ITC to reconsider antidumping and countervailing duty orders. Section 592 fixes penalties for violations of U.S. tariff laws. Section 703 (formerly Section 303) grants authority to the ITC to conduct injury reviews of antidumping and subsidy complaints. Section 704 (formerly Section 304) specifies standards for country-of-origin markings and imports exempt from the origin-marking requirements under the J-List. Section 705 (formerly Section 305) bans obscene or seditious imports. Section 751 authorizes the ITC to determine the domestic impact of suspended or revoked trade benefits.

**tariff barrier.** A duty levied in excess of an importing country's revenue needs and the administrative costs of trade. Compare *nontariff barrier*.

**tariff classification.** The process used by a customs agency to determine import duties. Imports are defined by generic type, component materials, or use. A nominal rate is assigned to import classes, but the actual duty rate often depends on the trading status of the country of origin. Most countries provide advance tariff rulings through a tariff classification bureau or department. In the United States, classifications are reviewed by the Office of Regulations and Rulings in the U.S. Customs Service.

**Tariff Classification Act of 1962.** See *International Trade Commission*.

**tariff effect.** The economic impact of a duty. Tariffs have an impact on (1) consumption patterns by influencing the price of a given product, (2) production by making certain investments more or less attractive, and (3) external and internal trade by decreasing or increasing competition.

**tariff escalation.** 1. Raising a duty. 2. A progressive increase in duties as an import's value-added increases. In some developing countries, imports of raw materials carry low or zero duties, while moderate duties are imposed on semiprocessed products and higher duties on finished manufactures. Progressive rates lower the costs of imported goods used in domestic industries and increase the costs of consumer imports, which reduce foreign exchange reserves.

**tariff factory.** An offshore operation established to avoid high import duties. Tariff factories are located in countries with low duties, but which provide preferential access to a target market with substantially higher duties. See also *free rider*.

**tariffication.** The process of replacing opaque trade regulations with transparent tariffs. Duties eliminate hidden forms of protection. Increased tariffication is the objective of most international trade negotiations.

**tariff number.** See *HTS number*.

**tariff preference.** See *trade preference*.

**tariff rate.** 1. The percentage by which a duty increases the per-unit cost of an import. 2. The premium prescribed for a commercial insurance policy by a local regulatory agency. Ordinarily, tariff rate premiums are more expensive than negotiated premiums.

**Tariff Schedules of the United States, Annotated (TSUSA).** The tariff classification codes that governed U.S. imports from 1954 to 1989. Authorized by the Tariff Simplification Act of 1954, TSUSAs also described administrative import entry procedures. TSUSA was revised by authority of the Tariff Classification Act in 1962 and replaced by the Harmonized Tariff Schedule of the United States in 1989.

**tariff values administrator.** In Canada, an agent of Customs and Excise, Revenue Canada, who hears appeals from import tariff classifications

and valuations. An application for appeal from an adverse ruling is filed with Customs and Excise within 90 days of customs entry.

**TATE.** The abbreviation for Technical Assistance to Exporters.

**TAURUS.** The abbreviation for Transfer and Automated Registration of Uncertified Stock.

**taux d' intérêt.** French: interest rate.

**tax.** A sum of money collected from individuals and companies by a taxing authority. Types of taxes levied around the world are the business tax (on imports or net earnings), business-profits tax (on net earnings), capital-gains tax (on profits from asset sales), corporate tax (on a company's gross earnings), consumption tax (on the value of goods or services purchased), defensive tax (on assets to finance military operations), excise tax (on the value of goods and services purchased), export tax (on the value of exports), fiscal tax (on a percentage of export value), income tax (on a percentage of net earnings), industrial and commercial tax (on business earnings), inheritance tax (on the heritable value of a decedent's estate), lump-sum tax (on a percentage of export value), municipal tax (on income expended or government services used), ocean freight tax (on a percentage of a freight charge), processing tax (on a percentage of export value), property tax (on the value of property owned), public housing fund tax (on a percentage of import value), research tax (on a percentage of export value), sales tax (on the value of a purchase), stabilization fund (on a percentage of import value), stamp tax (on a flat fee or transaction basis), statistical tax (on a percentage of export value), support and price stabilization fund tax (on a percentage of import value), tonnage tax (on cargo volume), turnover tax (on a company's sales), user fee (on the cost of providing a facility or service), and value-added tax (on the value of products or services purchased).

**taxable estate.** The portion of a decedent's estate on which estate taxes are payable. Among others, deductions are allowed for funeral expenses, charitable contributions, marital estates, and other taxes payable.

**taxable income.** Income subject to taxation. Taxable income is computed by subtracting allowable deductions from a taxpayer's gross income.

Allowable deductions are abatements for personal expenses.

**tax anticipation bill (TAB).**    In the United States, a method formerly used by the U.S. Department of the Treasury to finance government expenditures before collecting tax receipts. Since 1974, the Department of the Treasury has issued cash management bills, which replaced TABs as short-term U.S. government debt paper.

**tax anticipation note (TAN).**    In the United States, a short-term note issued by a state or local government to finance expenditures before tax receipts are collected. Also called tax anticipation warrants, TANs are discounted notes with priority claims on collected tax payments. TANs mature in 1 year or less.

**taxation.**    A government levy, or tax, on income and assets to finance operations and implement policies. Income taxes are the most common form of taxation, in which taxpayers are divided into tax brackets with wealth taxed at specific rates.

**tax avoidance.**    Using legal means to reduce tax liability. Tax planning and tax shelters are permissible tax avoidance devices. Compare *tax evasion*.

**tax base.**    A source of wealth on which a tax is imposed, e.g., corporate profits, a decedent's estate, income, or property transfers.

**tax bracket.**    See *taxation*.

**tax clearance.**    An advisory opinion from a taxing authority that a specific activity or transaction will not create tax liability.

**tax credit.**    A sum deductible from taxes payable, usually in the form of an income tax credit or investment tax credit. Credits yield more benefits to high-income taxpayers in a graduated system, while deductions benefit low-income taxpayers by reducing the amount of income subject to taxation. Compare *tax deduction*.

**tax credit method.**    See *double taxation*.

**tax deduction.**    An allowance for reducing taxes payable by an amount equal to expenditures for personal or business expenses. Compare *tax credit*.

**tax-deferred savings.**    A savings plan or annuity used to generate retirement income. Taxes on invested funds are deferred until retirement. If the taxpayer's retirement income is lower than earnings in peak years, the deferment yields net tax savings.

**tax deposit certificate.**    In the United Kingdom, a certificate issued by Inland Revenue for a taxpayer's deposit against future or disputed corporation taxes. The deposit earns interest until paid in taxes.

**Taxe.**    German: quotation, i.e., of exchange rates or interest rates. Its plural form is *taxen*.

**Tax Equity and Fiscal Responsibility Act (TEFRA) of 1982.**    In the United States, a statute, which, among other things, created the business finance lease, also known as a financial lease. The provision permits a lessee to exercise a purchase option and recapture 10 percent or more of the original cost of the lease. See also *Economic Recovery Tax Act of 1981*. Compare *Tax Reform Act of 1984* and *Tax Reform Act of 1986*.

**taxe sur la valeur ajoutée (TVA).**    French: value-added tax.

**tax evasion.**    Using illegal means to reduce tax liability. Tax evasion usually involves failing to disclose income and filing false tax returns. Tax evaders are subject to civil and/or criminal penalties. Compare *tax avoidance*.

**tax-exempt bond.**    A municipal bond with tax-free yields. In the United States, most general obligation municipal bonds are exempt from federal, state, and local taxes.

**tax-exemption method.**    See *double taxation*.

**tax haven.**    A country or principality with low tax rates. Foreign companies establish a legal presence to realize tax savings. The Bahamas, the Cayman Islands, Liechtenstein, and Monaco are prominent tax havens.

**tax holiday.**    A limited period of time when tax exemptions are available to pioneering enterprises. Tax holidays are used to attract investment in high-value manufacturing industries. See also *investment incentive*.

**tax invoice.**    An invoice issued by a seller registered to collect value-added taxes (VATs). The invoice, showing the purchase price of goods or services and the VAT levied on them, is used by purchasers to claim input tax deductions from VATs.

**tax lien.**    A charge against real property for unpaid taxes. Tax liens have priority over other liens.

**taxpayer identification number (TIN).** In the United States, a number required to open a bank account. The TIN is an individual's Social Security number. A business association, corporation, nonprofit organization, partnership, or sole proprietor obtains a business tax identification number, or employer identification number (EIN), from the Internal Revenue Service.

**tax planning.** Reducing tax liability through financial planning. Tax-exempt or -deferred investments and sheltering income are legal tax avoidance devices. Compare *tax evasion.*

**tax preference items.** In the United States, accounting items used to calculate the federal alternative minimum tax (AMT) enacted in the Tax Reform Act of 1986. The items include investment tax credits and accelerated depreciation, claimed by corporations, and certain capital gains earned by individuals. The tax due is the greater of the amount after deductions or the AMT.

**Tax Reform Act of 1976.** In the United States, a statute, which, among other things, permits a business to deduct from its tax liability the cost of excess inventory donated to qualified charities. The value of the deduction is equal to the cost of the inventory itself plus one-half of the difference between the amount paid for the inventory and its fair market value. The act also imposes tax penalties on U.S. firms engaged in foreign-directed commercial boycotts in violation of domestic antiboycott regulations. The antiboycott provisions of the act are enforced by the U.S. Department of the Treasury. See also *international boycott factor.*

**Tax Reform Act of 1984.** In the United States, a statute that authorizes tax benefits for domestic companies operating abroad. The act created the foreign sales corporation, which reduces the tax liability of a U.S. company when it does business in a qualified country and meets other specified criteria. The 1984 act also replaced the domestic international sales corporation with the interest-charge DISC, thereby substituting deductible interest for DISC tax deferments. Compare *Tax Reform Act of 1986.*

**Tax Reform Act of 1986.** In the United States, revision of the U.S. Internal Revenue Code. For corporations, the law (1) reduced the top corporate rate from 46 percent, (2) imposed an alternative minimum tax (AMT) on some types of depre-

ciation and municipal bonds, (3) eliminated the investment tax credit, (4) altered the accounting period for accelerated depreciation, (5) prohibited cash basis accounting for most business firms, and (6) restricted tax credits on foreign investments. For individuals, the law (1) reduced the top individual rate from 50 percent, (2) imposed an alternative minimum tax on some high-income tax payers, (3) limited personal interest deductions on home mortgages, (4) lowered deductions for some municipal bonds, (5) exempted from federal taxes interest on rural development private-purpose bonds, (6) reduced tax-free contributions to personal retirement plans, and (7) limited benefits from passive investments and other tax shelters. See also *tax preference items.* Compare *Economic Recovery Tax Act of 1981, Tax Equity and Fiscal Responsibility Act of 1982,* and *Tax Reform Act of 1984.*

**tax return.** A form prepared by a taxpayer itemizing income and certain expenditures for a given tax period. Tax assessments are based on information provided in the form. In the United States, individual returns are filed annually. Business returns are filed quarterly.

**tax shelter.** A device used to reduce tax liability. In the United States, the Tax Reform Act of 1986 limited tax deductions for passive real estate investments and most other devices employed by limited partnerships to avoid taxes on income earned from passive investments. Previously, passive investors deducted all losses from a venture.

**tax sparing.** A type of tax holiday, usually offered by a country as an investment incentive. The duration of a tax holiday may be indefinite, lasting for the entire life of an enterprise or until otherwise revoked.

**TB.** The abbreviation for term bond.

**TBL.** The abbreviation for through bill of lading.

**TC.** The abbreviation for till countermanded.

**TCF.** The abbreviation for textiles, clothing, and footwear.

**T/D.** The abbreviation for time draft.

**tdba.** The abbreviation for trading and doing business as.

**TDI.** The abbreviation for Trade Data Interchange.

**TDP.** The abbreviation for Trade and Development Program.

**TDW.** The abbreviation for tons deadweight.

**TE.** The abbreviation for trade expense.

**T/E.** The abbreviation for transportation and exportation entry.

**TEA.** The abbreviation for Targeted Export Assistance Program.

**technical analysis.** Financial forecasting based on charting patterns in a market. Technical analyses are used to predict price movements in commodities, foreign exchange, financial futures, and stocks. Forecasts are based on estimates of price trends, supply and demand, trading volume, etc. Since markets are often more volatile than orderly, technical analyses are not always reliable. Moreover, true patterns, even if recognized, may be misleading indicators of future trends.

**Technical Assistance to Exporters.** See *Underwriter's Laboratories.*

**technical barrier to trade.** A regulatory impediment to trade. Technical standards raise complex issues in international trade negotiations because nations have different customs and regulatory preferences, often reflected in technical standards. In trade negotiations, participants attempt to distinguish technical trade barriers from technical standards supported by authentic local customs and legitimate health and safety concerns. See also *General Agreement on Tariffs and Trade:Tokyo Round, nontariff barrier,* and *standards.*

**technical correction.** See *correction.*

**technical data (TD).** In the United States, information regulated for export by the Bureau of Export Administration. Technical data consist of any information employed in the design, manufacture, repair, or use of tangible objects. TD include blueprints, models, operating manuals, and prototypes. See also *general technical data available/restricted.*

**technical rally.** See *rally.*

**technology management.** Procedures instituted by an organization to gain maximum efficiency by using newly invented products and processes, particularly automated equipment. Effective management requires assessing the costs of new technologies, the correlation between employee skill and the degree of difficulty faced when using a new product or process, and the investment in training time. Other factors include pricing and the size of the consumer market for an enhanced product or service. For example, the investment required of a manufacturer to purchase a state-of-the-art computer system in order to reduce delivery time may not be reasonable in terms of the price a customer will pay for quicker shipment.

**technology transfer.** The process of sharing technical knowledge and skill gained from research and development, usually through the licensing of patents or through joint-venture agreements. In external trade, transfers of technology are arguably more valuable than foreign capital investment, since, once acquired, technologies cannot be unlearned.

**technopolis.** In Asia, the popular name for government-operated research and development facilities. A technopolis often also contains private high-technology research institutes.

**TEFRA.** The abbreviation for Tax Equity and Fiscal Responsibility Act.

**TEI.** The abbreviation for Trade Enhancement Initiative for Central and Eastern Europe.

**telegraphic transfer.** See *wire transfer.*

**telemarketing.** Selling a product by telephone.

**teletext.** A subscription information service through which data are transmitted from a central database to a computer terminal. For example, the London Stock Exchange system, TOPIC (for teletext output price information computer), carries stock market data from the LSE to brokers' and market makers' computer terminals.

**telex for authority to pay.** A request to waive a discrepancy in a letter of credit. The importer is notified of the discrepancy by the advising or negotiating bank. Discrepancies are corrected by amendment or waived by the importer's bank before the exporter is paid.

**temporary duty rates.** See *flexible tariff.*

**temporary importation under bond (TIB).** Imports admitted for 1 year or less, with extensions of up to 3 years, and not sold in the importing country. TIB covers articles, equipment, and samples imported for testing, repair, solicitation of sales orders, or reexport. It also applies to items that are imported for temporary use in special events, such as fashion shows or sports activities. A TIB bond is equal to twice the estimated duties payable on an import. Compare *carnet.*

**temporary loan.** A working capital loan, usually obtained to finance accounts receivables or inventory. Temporary loans are granted on secured or unsecured promissory notes or warrants, typically with maturities of less than a year, and are repaid as merchants convert inventory or receivables to cash.

**temporary tariff surcharge.** A charge imposed on imports, usually to correct a short-term balance-of-trade deficit. See also *balance of payments.*

**tenancy by the entirety.** At common law, jointly owned marital property when the entire estate is heritable by a surviving spouse. Unlike assets owned by joint tenants or in a tenancy in common, creditors cannot seize property owned in the entirety to settle a deceased spouse's debts. Both spouses enjoy equal rights of possession and survivorship.

**tenancy in common.** At common law, jointly owned property where each party has an indivisible share without a right of survivorship. The owners of property in common pass shares to their heirs, but not to other joint tenants. Tenancy-in-common arrangements are the usual way in which business partnerships hold property. See also *joint tenants* and *tenancy by the entirety.*

**tender.** 1. An offer to sell to the highest bidder. 2. An offer or bid to contract for the lowest offered price or best service. 3. An offer to buy stock from shareholders at the offered price for a specific period of time. The tenderer proposes a takeover by paying a cash premium above the stock's market price. Compare *exchange offer.* 4. A notice that the holder of a futures contract intends to deliver the underlying commodity. 5. In the United Kingdom, a Treasury bill auction.

**tender document.** 1. A formal offer by a company or government to purchase goods or services. Specifications, qualifications, procedures, and the designated purchasing agent are noted in tender documents. 2. A corporate offer to sell securities. Securities tenders request bids above a specified minimum selling price.

**tender offer.** An offer to pay cash or sell shares in exchange for a specific quantity of securities. The offer price is usually quoted at a premium above a security's current market price.

**tender panel.** In Eurocurrency financing, a panel of agents representing a syndicate arranging project financing under a revolving underwriting facility. The tender panel finds buyers for medium-term Euronotes (promissory notes) of 5- to 7-year maturities and solicits bids on a best-effort basis.

**tenor.** A sight draft payable when delivered or a time draft payable at a future date.

**ter., ty.** The abbreviation for territory.

**term.** 1. A stipulation in a contract or a condition on which a loan is made. 2. A time limit, e.g., the length of a loan's maturity.

**term.** The abbreviation for terminal and termination.

**termaillage.** French: leads and lags.

**term bill.** See *usance.*

**term bond.** A bond with a single maturity date. Term bonds are redeemed from sinking funds. Compare *serial bond.*

**term clause two.** See *berth clause.*

**terme.** French: period (of maturity).

**termes de l'échange.** French: terms of trade.

**terminal bonus.** In insurance, a cash payment made in addition to the proceeds of a policy when the policy matures or the insured dies. Terminal bonuses are paid from net profits earned from investments covered by a policy at the discretion of the insurer. Compare *bonus payment.*

**terminal market.** A commodity market located in a major trading center, such as Chicago or London. Transactions in terminal markets are mainly centered on futures, although spot-market commodities may also be traded. Nonterminal markets are found in producing centers, such as Calcutta, India, or Kaula Lumpur, Malaysia.

**terminal operator.** A private firm, usually regulated by a maritime authority, which provides warehousing and container facilities at major ports. In the United States, terminal operators are regulated by the Federal Maritime Commission.

**termination statement.**   A written statement releasing a creditor's lien on a borrower's assets when a debt is paid. In the United States, a creditor signs Form UCC-3 (Uniform Commercial Code) to terminate a security interest claimed in a publicly filed financing statement.

**Termingeld.**   In Germany, money market operations of more than 1 month in duration. Terminiertes Tagesgeld denotes shorter-term money-market operations.

**Termingeschäfte.**   German: futures.

**term loan.**   A fixed-term working capital loan provided to a business, often to acquire plant, equipment, or inventory. Term loans may be secured or unsecured and have varying maturities, typically 1 to 5 years. The interest rate may be fixed by the U.S. federal funds rate, the London interbank offered rate, the U.S. prime rate, or a similar index rate. Repayments are amortized over a fixed schedule. Syndications are used to finance large term loans. Compare *time loan.*

**term repurchase agreement.**   See *repurchase agreement.*

**term share.**   A financial unit that cannot be cashed on demand, e.g., a share in a credit union or savings and loan association.

**terms of delivery.**   A sales contract term indicating the point at which title to an asset passes to the buyer. Delivery terms are fixed by industry practice or negotiations between the parties. They are usually expressed in International Commercial Terms.

**terms of sale.**   A seller's conditions for selling to a given buyer. Also known as trade terms, terms of sale specify price, quantity, delivery, insurance obligations, and means of payment. See also *International Commercial Terms.*

**terms of trade.**   Also known as trade terms, one measure of a nation's economic performance as determined by the value of its exports when compared with its imports. A country with favorable terms of trade receives more in export receipts than it remits for imports, or the value-added of its exports is greater than that of its imports. Conversely, a country with unfavorable terms of trade remits more for imports than it receives for exports.

**territorial content questionnaire.**   In Canada, a document required by Customs and Excise to verify an import's country of origin. Import duties are determined by the trading status of the country where an import originates or where content is added to the import. Like other unilateral preferential trade programs, the Caribbean-Canadian Economic Trade Development Assistance Program and the Canadian Generalized System of Preferences impose content requirements as a condition of receiving reduced or zero duties on imports. Various negotiated agreements, including the Canada-U.S. Free Trade Agreement and the proposed North American Free Trade Agreement also specify local content for preferential imports.

**territorial waters.**   The nautical distance from its shoreline over which a country claims sovereign jurisdiction. Customary international law recognizes a 3-mile limit, although national claims of sovereignty over contiguous waterways vary. Most nations claim sovereignty over waters from between 10 and 15 miles beyond their coastlines. Many also claim fishing rights in waters extending up to 200 miles; e.g., the United Nations recognizes 200-mile zones as exclusive economic zones (EEZs) consistent, for example, with the Common Fisheries Policy adopted by the European Community. All marine resources within an EEZ fall under a contiguous country's sovereignty. The United Kingdom and the United States assert sovereignty over 12 nautical miles. See also *United Nations Convention on the Law of the Sea.*

**testacy.**   The condition of a decedent whose will is valid. Compare *intestacy.*

**testamentary trust.**   See *trust.*

**test value.**   A standard for determining transaction value. When appraising an import, a customs agency looks to the value of an import exported from the same source at roughly the same time. When the importer and exporter are affiliated firms involved in related-party transactions, the appraisal uses test value to determine whether the import price is an arm's-length price. When it is not, duties are adjusted to account for the full import transaction value.

**TEU(s).**   The abbreviation for 20-foot container equivalent unit(s). See *container.*

**Textile Program.**  See *Committee for the Implementation of Textile Agreements* and *fiber constraints.*

**Textile Surveillance Board.**  See *MultiFiber Arrangement regarding International Trade in Textiles.*

**The Nine.**  A term that denotes the member states of the European Communities from 1973 to 1979, i.e., Belgium, Denmark, France, Ireland, Italy, Luxembourg, the Netherlands, the United Kingdom, and the former West Germany.

**The Six.**  A reference to the six original signatories to the Treaty of Paris in 1951, the agreement that created the European Communities. The Six include Belgium, France, Italy, Luxembourg, the Netherlands, and the former West Germany.

**The Ten.**  The members of the European Community (EC) from 1979 to 1986, or the Nine plus Greece.

**The Twelve.**  The members of the European Community beginning in 1986, or the Ten plus Portugal and Spain.

**thin capitalization.**  A company with too little subscribed equity and too much debt. In some countries, interest on a portion of the debt is treated as a taxable dividend, thereby reducing the interest deductible from earnings.

**thin market.**  A weak market with low demand and widely fluctuating prices.

**third-country acceptance.**  A banker's acceptance drawn outside the importing or exporting country and paid in a third country's currency. Also called refinance bills, third-country acceptances are used by traders seeking lower financing rates.

**third-country dumper.**  A country that permits its producers to sell below cost in a foreign market. For example, country A allows its exports to be dumped in country B. Country C retaliates against country A because its trade with country B is adversely affected by the trade practices of country A. In the United States, the Omnibus Trade Act of 1988 subjects third-country dumpers to trade penalties, which include increased tariffs or exclusion of imports from the U.S. market.

**third-flag carriage.**  The transport of goods aboard a vessel registered in a country other than the country of origin or destination.

**third market.**  See *over-the-counter market.*

**third-party check.**  See *check.*

**Third World.**  See *developing country* and *less developed country.*

**35 percent value-added.**  In the United States, the domestic content required to qualify imports for trade preferences when some portion of value is added outside a beneficiary country. The rule mandates that 35 percent of an eligible import's total cost, value, or direct processing costs be added in the beneficiary country. The import is thereby transformed into a new and different product in the exporting country. In the United States, U.S. Generalized System of Preferences imports must acquire the value-added in a single beneficiary country. For Caribbean Basin Initiative II imports, the 35 percent value added may be acquired in one or more beneficiary countries, including Puerto Rico and the U.S. Virgin Islands, and 15 percent can be added in the United States. See also *Caribbean Basin Initiative II.*

**threshold price.**  See *Common Agricultural Policy.*

**thrift institution.**  See *savings and loan association.*

**through bill of lading (TBL).**  A bill of lading used to transport cargo to a destination by way of intermediate domestic or foreign ports.

**through railroad bill of lading.**  A railway through bill of lading.

**through rate.**  The rate charged for transporting goods, not including extra surcharges or fees, from the point of pick-up to a discharge site.

**Through Transport Mutual Insurance Association, Limited.**  Also known as the Through Transport Club (TTC), a nonprofit trade association of the marine shipping industry. The association indemnifies its members against losses arising from the use of ocean shipping containers. TTC is headquartered in Bermuda.

**TIB.**  The abbreviation for temporary importation under bond and temporary import bond.

**tick.**  The minimum price movement in a market, i.e., 1/32 of a percentage point. A tick measures price changes in bonds, commodities, interest rate futures, precious metals, and stocks. For example, one upward tick in the price of a $25,000 bond is $781.25.

**TIEA.** The abbreviation for Tax Information Exchange Agreement.

**tied aid.** A conditional grant of aid awarded to enable one government to purchase goods or services from another.

**tied loan.** A variant of tied aid under which loans are granted by one government to another on concessional terms.

**tied outlet.** See *tying contract*.

**tight money.** The result of monetary policy implemented to restrict the availability of money and credit, making loans difficult to obtain or making loans available only at high interest rates.

**TIGR.** The abbreviation for Treasury investment growth receipt.

**timber ton.** A unit of measure for wood products. A timber ton is equal to 40 cubic feet.

**time bargain.** In a stock market, a contract to deliver securities at a future date.

**time bill of exchange.** A bill of exchange payable at a time other than at sight (e.g., pay after 30 days). See also *long bill of exchange*.

**time charter.** A ship or aircraft charter fixed for a specific time period, and not for specific voyages. Compare *voyage charter*.

**time deposit.** Funds deposited in an interest-bearing account for a fixed term. Withdrawals of time deposits before maturity require advance notice to the depository institution, especially when large corporate deposits are involved. Early withdrawals are subject to penalties and loss of interest. Time deposits are also known as time certificates of deposit or investment accounts.

**time draft.** A draft or bill of exchange with a specific maturity after acceptance, or after the date written on its face, e.g., a banker's acceptance.

**time letter of credit.** A letter of credit payable at a specific time, e.g., in 30 days. See also *usance letter of credit*.

**time loan.** A business loan payable at a fixed maturity date, e.g., 60 or 90 days. Time loans are often secured by accounts receivables or inventory. The interest rate can be based on the U.S. fed-

eral funds rate, the London interbank offered rate, the U.S. prime rate, or another index rate. Time loans are usually discounted in advance. Compare *term loan*.

**time lost waiting for berth.** See *lay time*.

**time value.** 1. Also called the time value of money and present value, the current economic value of an asset payable in the future. Time value is current price discounted for interest that could be earned between a specific date and an asset's maturity date. 2. In options trading, a contract's extrinsic value, or the amount paid as a premium above the market value of the underlying commodity.

**time volume rate.** An ocean freight rate covering a stipulated time period at a specified per-unit rate.

**TIR.** The abbreviation for trailer interchange receipt and *transport internationale routier*/international road transport.

**TIR carnet.** See *carnet*.

**title.** A document evidencing ownership of land, or goods.

**Title XI financing.** A federal financing guarantee approved by the U.S. Merchant Marine Act of 1936. The act authorizes the federal government to guarantee certain debts of U.S. citizens who build or purchase ships registered in the United States. See also *construction differential subsidy* and *operational differential subsidy*.

**tlo.** The abbreviation for total loss only.

**TM.** The abbreviation for trademark, indicated by the symbol ™.

**TNC.** The abbreviation for Trade Negotiations Committee.

**to average.** In shipping, a term of art in a charter party that provides for divisible loading and unloading rates. As stipulated in the charter party, credit for unused time in one operation is applied against time used in the other. Compare *average*.

**TOFC.** The abbreviation for trailer-on-flat-car.

**tokkin.** In Japan, a pension fund linked to an investment portfolio.

**Tokyo Declaration.** A communiqué issued by developed nations in 1973 defining negotiating objectives for the Tokyo Round of the General

Agreement on Tariffs and Trade negotiations.The document calls for reductions in trade barriers between developed countries and for nonreciprocal concessions to developing nations. The negotiating objectives are reflected in the Tokyo Round agreements.

**Tokyo Round.**    See *General Agreement on Tariffs and Trade.*

**Tokyo Stock Exchange (TSE).**    The primary stock market in Japan, founded in 1878. Known in Japan as the Nikkei, the TSE trades bonds, convertible bonds, stocks, and warrants. The market's First Section is dedicated to large companies, the Second Section to medium- to small-sized companies. Transactions are completed by the *itayose* method (buy orders and sell orders are compared until a price and quantity match is found) or the *zaraba* method (sales are made using auction rules). Most securities are quoted in yen, although foreign bonds may be quoted in foreign currencies. Prices are published in the *Daily Official List, Statistics Reports,* and the *Fact Book.* The stock-price indexes are the Nikkei, which measures average prices of TSE stocks, and Topix, or the Tokyo Stock Price Index. TSE dealers are known as *saitori,* which denote securities firms specializing in securities trading. Transactions are settled through the Japan Securities Clearing Corporation, a TSE subsidiary. The TSE is a self-regulating organization.

**toll gate tax.**    See *qualified possession source investment income.*

**Tollhusid.**    The customs agency of Iceland.

**Toll-og avgiftsdirektoratet.**    The customs agency of Norway.

**tombstone.**    In finance, a colloquial term for the announcement of a syndicated loan or a bond issue, so called because it is framed in black. Tombstones identify brackets of participants in underwritings and the amount of their subscriptions.

**tomorrow next (tom next).**    In currency and money markets, a 2-day transaction, i.e., a sale executed tomorrow for delivery on the following business day. A premium payable for the extra day is added to the spot price.

**ton (T).**    The international weight measure for heavy cargoes, i.e., a metric ton or *tonne* equal to 1000 kilograms. In the United States, the long ton (2240 pounds) and the short ton (2000 pounds) are still used. For light cargoes, the weight measure is a shipping ton, or 100 cubic feet of cargo space.

**ton mile.**    A measure of the amount of cargo transported per mile. The ton mile is used to compute the weight moved by a carrier, usually a rail or motor carrier, within a given time period.

**tonnage.**    The volume of cargo a ship can transport, i.e., its cargo-carrying capacity. 1. Deadweight tonnage is measured by the number of metric tons (or long tons) of cargo, fuel, and provisions a ship can carry. 2. Displacement tonnage is the weight of water displaced by a ship in motion; one displacement ton is equal to 35 cubic feet of water. 3. Gross register tonnage (GRT) is the stowage volume under the upper deck measured in shipping tons. Docking dues are often determined by GRT. 4. Net register tonnage (NRT) is gross register tonnage less space used for crew and passenger accommodations, engines, fuels, and provisions. Harbor and port dues are usually determined by NRT.

**tonnage tax.**    In the United States, a tax on ships entering from foreign ports. Ships arriving from trading partners covered by treaties or executive orders may be exempt. Tonnage taxes are computed on a per-unit basis at a rate that can be regular or specific. All foreign ships pay at the regular rate, but a lower rate is usually applied to ships originating in the Western Hemisphere. A special rate may be levied in addition to the regular rate. The special rate is based on several factors, including reciprocal port rights in the origin country, the shipowner's or crew's domicile, and the ship's registry.

**tonne.**    French: ton.

**tontine.**    French: share in an annuity. In Francophone Africa, *tontines* are informal financing networks that supplement the formal banking sector by accepting deposits and by lending to borrowers.

**TOP.**    The abbreviation for Trade Opportunities Program.

**TOPIC.**    The abbreviation for teletext output price information computer. See *teletext.*

**topping-up clause.**    A loan clause in a back-to-back loan agreement requiring a borrower to compensate a creditor for currency devaluation. The borrower agrees to pay an additional amount equivalent to the depreciation of the currency in which the loan is repaid. When the creditor does not need the extra currency or must report it as additional income, the exchange risk is often passed to a bank.

**Toronto Stock Exchange (TSE).**    The leading stock exchange in Canada, founded in 1852. The TSE trades primarily in equities and options. In 1985, the exchange permitted options trading by independent traders, known as competitive options traders. The TSE 300 Composite Index measures the average values of leading shares, including securities interlisted in Montreal, New York, and Vancouver. Prices are quoted daily in the Canadian, European, and U.S. press. The TSE is overseen by the Ontario Securities Commission.

**Toronto Terms.**    See *Paris Club.*

**tort.**    An injurious act that causes harm or property loss. The legal remedies for torts are damages and injunction. A grave tort may constitute a criminal act.

**total loss.**    Also known as total loss only, a provision in a marine insurance policy that excludes payments for general average. See also *aversio.*

**touch and stay.**    A marine insurance provision protecting a policyholder from the denial of a claim based on deviation. The provision covers cargo carried aboard ships making intermediate port stops on the way to a discharge port.

**TPRM.**    The abbreviation for Trade Policy Review Mechanism.

**tr.**    The abbreviation for transfer.

**trade acceptance.**    An acceptance honored by a nonbank, such as a manufacturer's agent or a corporation's finance affiliate. Trade acceptances are usually supported by letters of credit. Compare *accommodation endorsement.*

**Trade Act of 1974.**    In the United States, a statute authorizing U.S. participation in the Tokyo Round of the General Agreement on Tariff and Trade negotiations. The act also created the U.S. Generalized System of Preferences (US-GSP), extended most-favored-nation status to some communist countries, changed the name of the U.S. Tariff Commission to the International Trade

Commission (ITC), and authorized the ITC to investigate dumping and subsidy complaints. In addition, the act (1) approves flexible tariffs and orderly marketing agreements, (2) provides adjustment assistance for U.S. workers displaced by import competition and loan guarantees for trade-impacted areas and (3) permits the President to withdraw from injurious trade agreements and suspend US-GSP preferences harmful to domestic industries. Section 201 authorizing safeguard measures for threatened domestic industries and Section 301 permitting retaliation against unfair foreign trade practices are also contained in the 1974 Trade Act. Complaints brought under Section 201 and Section 301 are initiated by the Office of the U.S. Trade Representative.

**Trade Advisory Center.**    See *International Trade Administration.*

**Trade Agreements Act of 1934.**    See *Reciprocal Trade Agreements Act of 1934.*

**Trade Agreements Act of 1979.**    In the United States, the law that adopts the Multinational Trade Negotiation Codes agreed to during the Tokyo Round of the General Agreement on Tariffs and Trade negotiations. The act also (1) opens federal procurements on a reciprocal basis, (2) permits withdrawal of trade concessions when a trading partner's regulatory standards impede trade, (3) repeals the Anti-Dumping Act of 1921 and the Countervailing Duty Law, (4) amends the Tariff Act of 1930 to expand the powers of the International Trade Commission to investigate injury complaints, and (5) abolishes the American selling price and the Final List.

**Trade and Development Board.**    See *United Nations Conference on Trade and Development.*

**Trade and Tariff Act of 1984.**    In the United States, the law that authorizes negotiations leading to the Canada-U.S. Free Trade Agreement and the U.S.-Israel Free Trade Agreement. The act also permits the President to limit U.S. imports of certain steel products.

**trade association.**    An organization representing companies in the same industry in negotiations with governments on business issues. Trade associations also provide members with various services, including arbitration, freight forwarding, information, and self-insurance. Trade associations are financed by membership fees.

**trade balance.** See *balance of payments: balance of trade.*

**trade barrier.** Any official constraint on the free exchange of goods and services in international commerce. Barriers to trade are evidenced by closed procurement procedures, excessive duties, exchange controls, quotas, unnecessarily stringent product standards, and other regulatory rules. Tariff barriers and nontariff barriers are erected to protect domestic industries, preserve foreign exchange, or retaliate against the policies of a trading partner. See also *technical barrier to trade.*

**trade bill.** A bill of exchange that arises from the sale of goods.

**trade bloc.** A cross-border economic association formed to reduce internal trade barriers and negotiate as a unit with third countries. Trade blocs form as a consequence of economic integretion.

**trade creation.** Increased trading between countries when a free trade area, customs union, or common market is formed. In a regional economic association, internal trade grows because of lower tariffs and a reduction in other trade barriers. However, trade with third countries may also grow, since attractive markets in one member country often encourage cross-border trading between other members and nonmember countries. Compare *trade diversion.*

**trade credit.** 1. Credit extended by one government to another to purchase its exports. See *tied aid.* 2. Credit extended to a customer by a commercial supplier, usually on open account. 3. The purchase of a firm's accounts receivable or trade acceptances by a bank or finance company.

**trade creditor.** A company owed for goods and services supplied to a business.

**trade cycle.** The British term for business cycle.

**Trade Data Interchange (TDI).** The standard business format for electronic data interchange used in Europe. See *Electronic Data Interchange for Administration, Commerce and Transport.*

**trade date.** The date an order to buy or sell commodities, financial instruments, or securities is executed. The settlement date, or the day the

account is paid and the commodity is delivered, is 1 day later in options markets, 2 days later in foreign exchange markets, and usually 5 days later in stock markets. Compare *record date.*

**trade declaration charge.** A tax collected on imports and exports. In Hong Kong, the tax is levied on all trade items, except transshipped cargo consigned on through bills of lading. The tax is based on a percentage of the value of a trade item and used to finance trade promotion.

**trade deficit.** A nation's economic loss when its imports reflect adverse terms of trade in its annual balance-of-trade account. Conversely, when a nation's exports are valued higher than its imports, its balance of payments reflects a trade surplus.

**trade deflection.** In a regional trading association, e.g., a common market, the transfer of trade from one country to another. Trade and investment can be deflected by higher duties, complex regulations, currency instability, scarce resources, small market size, or other economic factors. Compare *trade diversion.*

**trade description.** A means of requiring fair product labeling. In Israel, for example, a trade description must be true. Falsely described goods are subject to seizure.

**trade diversion.** A shift in customary patterns of trade when a free trade area, customs union, or common market is formed. Member countries purchase higher-cost imports from one another at the expense of lower-cost producers in nonmember countries. The reduced or zero duties on internal imports offset the cost benefits from cheaper external imports. Compare *trade creation* and *trade deflection.*

**traded option.** See *option.*

**Trade Enhancement Initiative (TEI) for Central and Eastern Europe.** In the United States, a program announced in 1991 to open additional U.S. markets to imports from central and eastern European countries. The program is designed to modify quotas on steel and textiles, two sectors that were previously all but closed to CEEC exports. In addition to enlarging quotas, the TEI provides for technical assistance to CEEC governments seeking benefits under the US Generalized

System of Preferences and establishes expedited review procedures for CEEC-USGSP petitions.

**Trade Expansion Act of 1962.**    In the United States, the law that authorized negotiations for the Kennedy Round of the General Agreement on Tariffs and Trade negotiations. The Kennedy Round set a precedent for across-the-board tariff reductions in international trade agreements.

**trade fair.**    An international exposition organized by a government or industry to increase external trade. Compare *trade mission.*

**trade gap.**    A deficit in a country's balance-of-trade account, a component of national balance of payments.

**trade-impacted area.**    A geographic area where foreign competition causes significant sales and job losses. In the United States, federal loan guarantees to trade-impacted areas are authorized by the Trade Act of 1974. These areas are also eligible for redevelopment assistance under the Public Works and Economic Development Act of 1965.

**Trade Information Center.**    See *Trade Promotion Coordinating Committee.*

**trademark (TM).**    Any name, symbol, or design closely identified with a particular manufacturer's product. Registered trademarks are normally protected under national laws or by international agreement. They are identified by the symbol ™. See also *Lonham Trademark Act of 1946, Paris Convention for the Protection of Industrial Property,* and *Trademark Registration Treaty.*

**Trademark Act of 1946.**    See *Lonham Trademark Act of 1946.*

**Trademark Registration Treaty (TRT).**    A 1973 agreement that permits a single international filing to register a trademark in signatory countries. The TRT differs from the Madrid Agreement Concerning the International Registration of Marks by (1) permitting a single filing with the World Intellectual Property Organization (WIPO) without a prior national filing; (2) authorizing filings in French or English; and (3) preserving the international registration, even when a national registration is canceled within 5 years of the original filing. A TRT registration is effective for 10 years and renewable in perpetuity. The treaty also imposes a 3-year moratorium on enforcing regis-

tration denials in adhering countries. Any country belonging to the Paris Convention for Protection of Industrial Property may join the TRT, but most developed countries are members of the Madrid Agreement. The TRT is administered by WIPO.

**trade mission.**    A government-sponsored visit by a business group to another country, usually to sell products or services. Investment missions are vehicles for increasing foreign direct investment, usually in developing countries. Compare *trade fair.*

**Trade Mission Program.**    In the United States, a program offered by the U.S. Department of Commerce (DOC) to enhance foreign sales of domestic goods and services. Investment missions are sponsored by the Overseas Private Investment Corporation. Trade and investment missions are used to attract sales orders or identify local agents, joint-venture partners, and licensees. The types of missions available through DOC are:

*State and industry-organized government-approved (S&IOGA) trade missions.*    DOC arranges foreign trade missions jointly with state development agencies, trade associations, chambers of commerce, etc. S&IOGA mission organizers must qualify for U.S. government sponsorship.

*U.S. seminar missions.*    DOC offers missions designed for niche market sales of sophisticated products and systems. Seminar teams deliver papers and lead discussion groups, primarily on economic and industrial development.

*U.S. specialized trade missions.*    DOC matches an industry with the itinerary in another country providing the best sales opportunities.

**Trade Negotiations Committee.**    See *General Agreement on Tariffs and Trade.*

**Trade Opportunities Program (TOP).**    In the United States, an export promotion service provided by the U.S. Department of Commerce (DOC). TOP uses computerized lists to match U.S. and foreign firms. TOP notices are also mailed to U.S. subscribers to the service. The lists are obtained from district DOC offices.

**trade paper.**    See *acceptance.*

**trade policy.**    A government's statement of the commercial terms on which it trades with other nations. Trade policy differs from foreign policy, which reflects the terms of political cooperation between nations.

**trade policy review mechanism (TPRM).**    A procedure adopted in 1989 by General Agreement on Tariffs and Trade under which the GATT Council reviews the trade policies and practices of member countries. Periodic TPRM evaluations are designed to permit the GATT Council to render annual assessments of the impact of member countries' conduct on the course of global trade.

**trade preference.**    One country's grant of reduced or eliminated tariffs on foreign exports. Trade preferences are often temporary and restricted to specific products. They are usually granted on a quota basis.

**Trade Promotion Coordinating Committee (TPCC).**    In the United States, a committee created in 1990 to coordinate domestic export policy. Chaired by the secretary of the U.S. Department of Commerce, TPCC represents 18 federal agencies. The committee oversees the Trade Information Center, a national export information clearinghouse.

**trade reference.**    A business credit reference obtained from a credit-reporting agency. The reference reports a firm's payment history with trade creditors, including balances paid or payable during the previous year and delinquencies. The report reflects a firm's capacity to meet current obligations. See also *Dun & Bradstreet.*

**trade-related intellectual property rights.**    See *intellectual property right.*

**trade-related investment measures.**    See *nontariff barrier.*

**trade sanctions.**    See *economic sanctions.*

**trade secret.**    A firm's business proprietary information (BPI), which cannot be disclosed without its permission. Trade secrets include information about a firm's processes and products. In the United States, BPI is protected from unauthorized disclosure by state and federal statutes. Normally, courts also issue injunctions to prevent disclosure and impose damages for injury caused by the theft or unauthorized use of trade secrets.

**trade surplus.**    See *trade deficit.*

**trade terms.**    See *terms of sale* and *terms of trade.*

**Trade Union Congress (TUC).**    In the United Kingdom, the primary organization representing the interests of British trade unions. The TUC negotiates with employers and the British government on behalf of member unions.

**trade war.**    The intentional use of trade measures, such as unilateral increases in duties, to harm the economic interests of an adversary. Tactics used in trade wars include raising internal barriers to an adversary's imports and rigorous price competition in third-country markets. The reciprocal trade commitments and dispute-settlement mechanisms negotiated under the General Agreement on Tariffs and Trade are designed to prevent trade wars.

**trade-weighted.**    See *weighted.*

**trading company.**    A firm specializing in the purchase, distribution, and marketing of another firm's products.

**trading estate.**    See *industrial park.*

**trading house.**    A firm that acts as a principal in international trade transactions involving other companies. Trading houses locate international buyers and sellers, usually in designated regions and for specific product lines. They buy and sell for their own accounts, often arranging substantial countertrade deals. Some trading houses are subsidiaries of large manufacturing concerns.

**trading limit.**    In some markets, the maximum number of trades that can be executed on a stock exchange during a trading session. Trading limits are set by the exchange's rules. Trading limits can be based on price, volume, or other market conditions.

**trading range.**    The spread between high and low prices recorded during a given period. For example, the highs and lows of stock prices displayed on a given day reflect a trading range. High and low bids (or offers) over 12 months are indicators of a market's performance during a stated period.

**trading volume.**    The number of transactions recorded on a securities or commodities exchange during a specific time period.

**Trading with the Enemy Act of 1917.**    In the United States, a law, subsequently amended in 1941, which authorizes the President to ban commerce with unfriendly countries. The authority may be used during wars or national emergencies, although these requirements are often loosely interpreted. The President may prohibit all commercial transactions, investment, and trade with a country covered by the act. See also *Foreign Assets Control Regulations*. Compare *Foreign Securities Act of 1934*.

**traditional option.**    See *option*.

**trailer interchange receipt (TIR).**    A receipt contained in some bills of lading. The receipt is issued by a carrier inspecting shipping containers before transferring them to other carriers.

**trailer-on-flat-car (TOFC).**    Intermodal transport whereby truck trailers containing goods are placed on railroad flatcars for shipment. The use of truck trailers as shipping containers has become less frequent with the growing trend toward standardized ocean containers, which are also transported by trucks.

**tramp ship.**    Also called a tramp, a ship without regular port schedules. A tramp stops at any port where it can deliver goods or acquire a full cargo. Tramps, many of which are tankers, operate under voyage charters or time charters. The charters are arranged between agents and brokers or through the Baltic Exchange in London. Compare *liner*.

**tranche.**    French: slice. 1. One of several classes of bonds issued under a single bond indenture. In the United States, each bond tranche has a different coupon, CUSIP number, and maturity date. Tranches are redeemed in consecutive steps. 2. The preferred International Monetary Fund credit facilities. See also *gold tranche*. 3. Separate funding commitments under a credit facility, e.g., World Bank advances to sovereign borrowers. The separate borrowings are advanced in different tranches, e.g., a sterling tranche, a U.S. dollar tranche, a yen tranche, etc.

**trans.**    The abbreviation for transaction.

**transaction control header record.**    In the United States, the file that identifies a user of the Automated Commercial System and initiates the beginning of a transaction. The record is also known as the A record. Compare *block control header record*.

**transaction control trailer record.**    In the United States, the file that terminates a transaction in the

Automated Commercial System. The record is also known as a Z record. Compare *block control trailer record*.

**transaction costs.**    The price of settling a foreign sale, including financing fees and the cost of foreign exchange.

**transaction statement.**    A document explaining the terms of agreement between a buyer and seller.

**transaction value.**    The basis for calculating import duties adopted by the Customs Valuation Code negotiated during the Tokyo Round of the General Agreement on Tariffs and Trade. Transaction value is determined by an import's selling price. The selling price is the invoice price, if consistent with an arm's-length price, or the appraised value determined in the ordinary course of trade. In the United States, the Customs Service may appraise an import by reference to the import price of identical merchandise or similar merchandise. To determine transaction value, adjustments to price are made according to generally accepted accounting principles. Additions to price include (1) packing costs; (2) the pro rata value of assists; (3) sales commissions, licensing fees, or royalties paid to a buyer; and (4) proceeds earned by the seller from resales. Subtractions from price include (1) domestic assembly costs, (2) domestic excise or other taxes, and (3) insurance and transportation costs. See also *test value* and *valuation*.

**transborder data flow.**    The transfer of data across international boundaries, largely by electronic means. National laws regulating transborder data flows have been enacted in some countries.

**transferable revolving underwriting facility.**    See *revolving underwriting facility*.

**transferable ruble.**    See *International Bank for Economic Cooperation* and *International Investment Bank*.

**Transfer Accounting Lodgement for Investors and Stock Management (TALISMAN).**    In the United Kingdom, an electronic transfer and payments system used to settle transactions on the London Stock Exchange. TALISMAN eliminates the need for a signed transfer form to legalize sales of stock. The system uses SEPON (Stock Exchange Pooled Nominees) as a generic nominee to transfer payments between buyers and sellers. TALIS-MAN also settles dividend claims payable by companies registered with the exchange.

**transfer agent.**   A firm, usually a commercial bank, which registers and redeems securities on behalf of an issuer. The transfer agent maintains records of an issue, i.e., registers sales and purchases; updates records; and cancels redeemed securities. In bond sales, transfer agents are often called registrars.

**Transfer and Automated Registration of Uncertified Stock (TAURUS).**   In the United Kingdom, the electronic stock transfer system of the London Stock Exchange. Ownership of shares is recorded and registered by a paperless system without the need for contract notes or share certificates. TAURUS was fully implemented in 1992.

**transfer costs.**   An accounting term for reporting expenses associated with the international sale of goods. Transfer costs appear as different accounting entries, depending on whether expenses are attributable to transportation and handling or to duties and exchange controls.

**transfer payments.**   A government subsidy granted for purposes other than the purchase of goods or services. Transfer payments include domestic welfare payments, disaster relief, foreign aid grants, etc.

**transfer pricing.**   Price concessions made on sales between affiliated companies. Transfer pricing is frequently used to escape customs duties or, in some instances, to transfer foreign exchange between affiliates. For example, a subsidiary may sell a component to a parent for $100, although the appraised customs price is $200. When transaction value determines duties, the duty owed by the importer is $200.

**transfer risk.**   A foreign exchange risk that arises when a foreign debtor fails to pay in the currency requested by the creditor. See also *country risk*.

**transfer tax.**   A tax payable on the transfer of securities. In the United States, the amount of the tax depends of the jurisdiction of the transfer agent.

**transire.**   A document that verifies the origin of cargo loaded on a lighter. The transire is provided by customs at the port of origin and delivered to officials at the port of destination.

**transit tariff.**   A duty imposed by an intermediate country when goods cross its territory en route to another country. Transit tariffs are still a revenue source for some developing countries, but they have been abolished in developed countries.

**transit zone.**   In coastal nations, a site set aside for landlocked neighbors or for countries with poor port facilities. Transit zones are usually duty-free zones where goods pass under customs bonds. For example, Argentina has 13 transit zones for goods transshipped and destined for neighboring countries.

**transload.**   The transfer of goods from one carrier to another.

**transnational corporation.**   See *multinational corporation.*

**transp.**   The abbreviation for transportation.

**transparency.**   In international trade, public disclosure of import regulations and customs procedures that may have the effect of restraining commerce. In import regulation, tariffs and quotas are the most transparent forms of import regulation. Since the 1980s, establishing a new regime that extends the principle of transparency beyond the merchandise trade to foreign direct investment and trade in services has been a primary objective of the General Agreement on Tariffs and Trade. A regime is transparent when national regulations are published for the interested public and administered in a manner consistent with their stated terms.

**transportation and exportation entry (T/E).**   An expedited customs procedure for clearing imports destined for a third country. In the United States, Customs Form 7512 is filed for T/E goods, which may not be altered or modified during transit.

**Transport internationales routiers (TIR).**   An international carnet agreement originally adopted in 1949 and known as the International Customs Convention on the International Transport of Goods by Road. The 1975 version is called the Customs Convention on the International Transport of Goods under Cover of TIR Carnets. An organization is designated in each adhering country to issue carnets and transit documents. In the United States, the Equipment Interchange Association (EIA) is the TIR agent. The EIA has headquarters in Washington, D.C.

**transshipment.**   A shipment of goods to a destination port by way of a third country. Transshipments are used to avoid embargoes, when there is no direct port service in the importing country, or when a third country provides foreign exchange to pay for a shipment. Transshipments of goods bearing false country-of-origin markings are also used to evade duties and import quotas.

**traveler's check.**   A draft issued by a bank or credit card company payable to the purchaser around the world. Traveler's checks were first issued by American Express. In the United States, the drafts are issued in denominations of $10 to $100. The purchaser signs a draft twice, once when buying it and again when cashing it. Traveler's checks are insured against loss or theft.

**traveler's letter of credit.**   See *circular letter of credit.*

**Treasury.**   1. In the United Kingdom, a division of the Exchequer that manages UK economic policy. 2. In the United States, the popular name for the Department of the Treasury.

**Treasury bill.**   1. Also called a T-bill, a U.S. Treasury security, often repayable within 13, 26, or 52 weeks. Treasury bills are issued at a discount off face value in minimum lots of $10,000. The yield is the difference between the purchase price and the face value at maturity. The Treasury bill is the most frequently used instrument in Federal Reserve open-market operations. 2. A non-interest-bearing bill of exchange issued by the Bank of England. The yield is the difference between the bill's purchase price and redemption price. Treasury bills are tendered in denominations of 5000 to 100,000 pounds, repayable in 90 days. The Bank of England sells Treasury bills weekly to discount houses.

**Treasury bond.**   In the United States, a long-term security issued by the federal government. Treasury bonds are denominated in $1000 or more and mature in 10 years or more. Treasury long bonds mature in 30 years or more. The 30-year Treasury bond is the prime indicator for domestic long-term interest rates and fixed-income investments. Compare *Treasury bill* and *Treasury certificate.*

**Treasury certificate.**   In the United States, a short-term debt obligation used by the U.S.

Department of the Treasury to borrow from the Federal Reserve System through the Federal Reserve Bank of New York. The coupon certificates with maturities under a year cover Treasury's overdrafts at the Federal Reserve. As of 1979, Treasury certificate deposits are approved by the Federal Reserve Board of Governors.

**Treasury investment growth receipt (TIGR, Tiger).**   1. In the United States, a version of the certificate of accrual on Treasury security (CATS). 2. In the United Kingdom, a zero-coupon bond, known as a Tiger, denominated in U.S. dollars and issued in the UK. Linked to U.S. Treasury bonds, Tigers' yields compound semiannually. Income earned on Tigers is taxed in the UK when the bonds are cashed or redeemed.

**Treasury note.**   In the United States, a coupon security issued by the Department of the Treasury in units of $1000 or more. Treasury notes carry original maturities of under 10 years and pay interest semiannually.

**Treasury securities.**   In the United States, a generic term covering Treasury bills, bonds, and notes. Treasury securities are registered in book-entry form. Ownership is evidenced by a receipt, called a statement, issued by the Federal Reserve Bank of New York.

**treasury stock.**   1. A share of stock from a previous securities issue reclaimed and held by the issuer. 2. In the United Kingdom, Treasury stocks are fixed-interest gilt-edged securities issued by the British government.

**treaty.**   In international law, any formal compact between sovereign nations. A treaty becomes effective when adopted or ratified by a country according to its constitutional procedures. See also *enter into force.*

**treaty of amity and economic relations.**   See *treaty of friendship, commerce, and navigation.*

**Treaty of Asunción.**   See *Mercosur.*

**treaty of friendship, commerce, and navigation (FCN).**   In the United States, a generic term for a bilateral commercial treaty. FCNs guarantee freedom of navigation; property rights, including lease protection; most-favored-nation status; and national treatment in taxation and administrative and judicial proceedings. In international parlance, similar friendship accords are also called freedom of commerce and navigation treaties or treaties of amity and economic relations. Compare *bilateral investment treaty*.

**Treaty of Maastricht.** Also known as the Treaties of Maastricht, the treaty of economic and political union in the European Community (EC). The accord was signed by the 12 EC countries at Maastricht, Netherlands, in 1992. Initiated under the Single European Act of 1986, the Maastricht Treaty creates a single regional economic market, beginning January 1, 1993, and anticipates a common currency by 1997. The treaty expands the powers of the European Parliament, provides for uniform defense policies, and contains separate agreements covering labor and social security rights. The labor and social securities provisions are contained in the Social Chapter to the treaty. Different national procedures govern ratification of the treaty. While popular votes approving the treaty were required in some EC countries, others permitted parliamentary ratification. In 1992, referenda failed in Denmark, but were handily approved in Ireland and narrowly accepted in France. As a consequence of its referendum, Denmark was exempted from some of the treaty's provisions, including participation in a common currency. The British House of Commons approved the treaty in 1993, but rejected its labor and monetary-union compacts. As of mid-1993, legal challenges to the treaty's constitutionality and ratification procedures were still pending in Germany and in the United Kingdom. The suits were expected to be settled by the end of 1993, resulting in the unanimous ratification of the Maastricht Treaty. See also *Community Charter of the Fundamental Social Rights of Workers* and *subsidiarity*.

**Treaty of Paris.** The 1951 agreement between European nations to create the European Coal and Steel Community. The treaty established a common market for member states in coal and steel products, harmonized external tariffs in such products, and provided for collective financing of research, production activities, and certain social security benefits for workers in the coal and steel industries.

**Treaty of Rome.** The treaty that created the European Common Market, also known as the European Economic Community, the predecessor of the European Community. The treaty was signed at Rome in 1957 and became effective January 1, 1958. Among other things, the treaty reduced tariffs on internally traded goods, created the Common Agricultural Policy, provided for the continued administration of European non-self-governing territories, and established a precedent for trade and aid preferences accorded newly independent developing countries later authorized by the Lomé Conventions.

**Treaty of Stockholm.** The treaty that created the European Free Trade Association, eliminating tariffs and quotas on most internally traded goods. The treaty was signed at Stockholm and became effective in 1960.

**Treaty on Intellectual Property in Respect of Integrated Circuits.** An international agreement signed at Washington, D.C., in 1989 protecting integrated circuits and designs from unauthorized reproduction. The treaty is open to members of the Berne Union, the Paris Union, and the World Intellectual Property Organization (WIPO). It is administered by the WIPO.

**Treaty on International Registration of Audiovisual Works.** An agreement signed at Geneva in 1989 protecting international registrations of cinematic films. The treaty established the International Register, located at Vienna, and bans unauthorized copying and piracy. A film registered by a national of a signatory country establishes a legal ownership claim in other signatory countries. The treaty is administered by the World Intellectual Property Organization.

**Triangle of Growth.** See *Growth Triangle*.

**Triffin Plan.** A proposal advanced in 1960 by Robert Triffin in *Gold and the Dollar Crisis* to create a uniform system and reserve asset for settling international payments. In the 1940s, the British economist, John Maynard Keynes, had proposed a similar scheme to be managed by the International Clearing Union. In 1969, largely at the behest of the Group of Ten, the International Monetary Fund created the special drawing right, an artificial currency unit used to transfer assets between nations and international financial institutions, thereby reducing liquidity problems in the international monetary system.

**trigger price.** A floor price used by a government or by an international commodity group as a reference price for intervening in commercial markets to support the preferred price of a commodity. Normally, cartel agreements and international commodity accords contain trigger prices. Under the European Community's Common Agricultural Policy, the trigger price is known as the threshold price or intervention price. In the United States, a trigger price mechanism (TPM) was used in the late 1970s, primarily to protect the U.S. steel industry. The floor for the TPM was the price charged by the most efficient foreign producer, adjusted for foreign exchange and transportation costs. When import prices fell below the trigger price, the International Trade Commission was authorized to initiate antidumping investigations.

**trigger price mechanism (TPM).** See *trigger price.*

**trilateral trade.** Any commerce between three countries. Compare *bilateral* and *multilateral trade agreement.*

**TRIM.** The abbreviation for trade-related investment measure. See *nontariff barrier* and *GATT Standing Committees.*

**Trinity House.** In the United Kingdom, a corporation chartered in 1514 that maintains lighthouses and navigation facilities at local ports. Pilotage in the UK remains under the control of port authorities.

**trip charter.** See *voyage charter.*

**TRIP.** The abbreviation for trade-related intellectual property. See *intellectual property right* and *GATT Standing Committees.*

**TRQ.** The abbreviation for tariff rate quota. See *quota.*

**TRT.** The abbreviation for Trademark Registration Treaty.

**true and fair view.** A review standard for auditors of commercial accounts. The auditor is required to determine whether the accounts of an organization reflect fraudulent or misleading accounting. Both omissions and misstatements distort the true state of an organization's finances.

**true interest cost (TIC).** The actual cost of borrowing, including time value, interest , and fees or finance charges payable.

**true lease.** See *lease.*

**trunking.** A popular term for cargo road carriage or distance hauling.

**trunk room.** In Japan, a warehouse for storing small quantities of supplies.

**trust.** A fiduciary arrangement in which property is owned, and sometimes administered, by a trustee for another's benefit. When the trustee performs duties to preserve assets, a trust is active. Conversely, a passive trust does not require affirmative management by the trustee. An express trust is created by a trust deed, will, or other instrument. An implied or constructive trust arises by law, often when a trustee misappropriates or wastes trust assets. A court may imply a precatory trust from a will or trust deed when the instrument's maker expresses a vague wish to benefit another but fails to specify the terms of the trust obligation. A revocable trust can be revoked by the trustor, i.e., the party who created it, while an irrevocable trust can only be revoked with permission of the beneficiary.

**trust company.** A corporation that prepares instruments creating trusts and acts as a trustee. In the United States, trust companies are state-chartered institutions, often permitted to accept deposits, make loans, and act as transfer agents for corporations. The trust departments of most national banks in the United States perform similar services.

**trust deed.** 1. A legal document creating a trust, which identifies the trust property, beneficiary, and the duties and powers of the trustee. In most jurisdictions, a trust deed must be a written document specific enough in its terms to clarify the trustor's intention to dispose of property for the benefit of another. 2. In the United States, a deed to mortgaged real property held by a third party for the benefit of the lender until the mortgage is paid. If the debtor defaults, the trustee is authorized to sell the property, repay the lender, and remit the balance to the debtor.

**trust department.** See *trust company.*

**trustee.** 1. A party named by the person creating a trust to hold and/or administer assets for the benefit of a third party. The trustee may be an individual, trust company, or trust department of a commercial bank designated to invest trust assets and make collections and disbursements on behalf of the beneficiary. 2. In finance, a transfer agent, i.e., the party named to collect and pay principal and interest according to the terms of a bond indenture. 3. A party designated by a court to distribute assets subject to a bankruptcy order.

**trustee investment.**    In the United Kingdom, fiduciary investments regulated by the Trustees Investment Act of 1961. The act specifies the quantities of fixed-interest bonds and equity that must be invested by trustees of fiduciary accounts. All UK trusts are covered, unless expressly excluded by a trust deed after the law was enacted.

**Trusteeship Council.**    An organ created by Chapter XIII of the United Nations Charter to oversee territories placed in the custody of the International Trusteeship System after World War II. The Trusteeship System was established to supervise the administration of territories protected under post-World War I League of Nations mandates, won from powers defeated in World War II, or voluntarily placed in UN custody by colonial powers. Originally, the council supervised 11 territories in Africa and the Pacific administered by Australia, Britain, Belgium, France, Italy, New Zealand, and the United States. After 1960, ten of the dependent territories gained independence, leaving only the Trust Territory of the Pacific Islands within the Trusteeship Council's jurisdiction. The Trust Islands of the Pacific are parties to the Compact of Freely Associated States with the United States.

**trust fund.**    An account containing assets held in trust for another.

**Trust Indenture Act of 1939.**    In the United States, an amendment to the Securities Act of 1933 governing bond issues subject to registration and disclosure rules. The act requires bond issuers to disclose details of issues in indentures, which specify the legal obligations of an issuer and limitations on the redemption rights of bond purchasers. Issuers are required to name registrars, i.e., transfer agents, who make semiannual disclosures related to an issue to bondholders. The act preserves the rights of bondholders to take legal action individually or collectively against securities issuers or their agents.

**trustor.**    Also known as the donor or settlor, a party who establishes a trust to be managed by a trustee for the benefit of a third party.

**trust receipt.**    An instrument used in letter-of-credit financing, whereby a buyer pledges goods as collateral for the credit. When the goods are sold or used for manufacturing, the buyer is obligated to maintain the sales proceeds in trust for the financing bank. Trust receipts secure specific merchandise, clearly identified by a serial number or similar marking. See also *warrant*. Compare *bailee receipt*.

**TSUS.**    The abbreviation for *Tariff Schedules of the United States*.

**TT.**    The abbreviation for telegraphic transfer.

**TTS(rate).**    The abbreviation for telegraphic (funds) transfer rate.

**TUC.**    The abbreviation for Trade Union Congress.

**tugrik.**    The currency of Mongolia.

**turnaround.**    The one-day purchase and sale of securities, usually for speculation.

**turn clause.**    See *berth clause*.

**turnkey project.**    A project managed in all phases by a prime contractor. For example, in a computer systems installation contract, the contractor is responsible for design, development, financing, installation, and training of local users. The buyer receives a fully operational system.

**TVA.**    The abbreviation for tax on value-added and *taxe sur la valeur ajoutée*.

**20-foot equivalent unit (TEU).**    The measure of a vessel's cargo space equivalent to one standard 20-foot ocean container.

**two-name paper.**    Also called double-name paper, a banker's acceptance or a trade acceptance with two signatures. The signatures are most likely those of a drawer and endorser.

**two-party loan.**    See *back-to-back loan*.

**two-sided market.**    A market in which a market maker is prepared to act as buyer or seller. Two-sided markets are made in highly marketable securities with active secondary markets, e.g., national government securities or over-the-counter stocks. One-sided markets are common for less actively traded securities.

**two-tier gold mart.**    A bifurcated system for pricing gold. The official price is used in gold sales between governments, while the market price is determined by dealings in private gold markets.

**two-tier tender offer.**    A takeover bid in which investors with enough stock to maintain a controlling share are offered a higher price than remaining investors. The higher price usually consists of a mixture of cash and equity in a company owned by the bidder. These tenders are made to induce shareholders to respond quickly to takeover offers.

**TWRA.**    The abbreviation for TransPacific Westbound Rate Agreement. See *conference.*

**TWS.**    The abbreviation for timed wire service (telegraph).

**tying contract.**    Also known as tie-in, a seller's sale of a product conditioned on the buyer's agreement to purchase another product. Tying sales are generally prohibited in the United States by the Clayton Act of 1914. Retail stores that sell manufacturers' products on a tie-in basis are known as tied outlets. See also *antitrust laws.*

# U

**u.**   The abbreviation for unit.

**UA.**   The abbreviation for unit of account. See *African Development Bank Group.*

**UAP.**   The abbreviation for *Union des Assurances de Paris.*

**uberrima fides.**   Latin: utmost good faith, or the obligation of full disclosure assumed by a purchaser of insurance. An insurance applicant is obliged to provide relevant information, even though it is not requested. Without full disclosure, an underwriter cannot assess the true insurance risk or accurately calculate a premium. Claims are denied when material facts are withheld or concealed.

**UCC.**   The abbreviation for Uniform Commercial Code.

**UCP.**   The abbreviation for Uniform Customs and Practices for Documentary Credits.

**UDEAC.**   The abbreviation for *Union douanière et économique de l'Afrique Centrale.*

**ugt.**   The abbreviation for urgent.

**UK Balance of Payments.**   See *Pink Book.*

**UKC.**   A cargo marking for United Kingdom–Continent.

**UK National Accounts.**   See *Blue Book.*

**UL.**   The abbreviation for Underwriters Laboratories.

**ULCC.**   The abbreviation for ultra large crude carrier.

**ullage.**   1. A shortage in the liquid contents of a cask or barrel resulting from evaporation, handling, or leakage. 2. The actual contents of a barrel or container imported into a customs territory. The difference between the contents and the container's capacity is called vacuity.

**ult.**   The abbreviation for ultimo.

**ultimate consignee.**   In the United States, the party identified as the authorized importer in a validated export license issued under export administration regulations. As a practical matter, authorized importers or their agents are also approved end users of controlled exports.

**ultimate purchaser.**   In the United States, the last recipient of an import in the same condition as it arrived at the time of customs entry. Ultimate purchasers are identified for, among other things, claiming duty drawbacks. For example, an item imported for sale to consumers in the same condition is not eligible for a duty drawback. Conversely, an item imported and processed by a manufacturer is eligible for drawback.

**ultimo (ult.).**   Latin: in the last month. For example, the 10th ultimo denotes the 10th day of the previous month. Compare *instant* and *proximo.*

**ultra large crude carrier (ULCC).**   A tanker for transporting crude petroleum. The total cargo capacity of an ULCC exceeds 300,000 deadweight tons.

**ultra vires.**   Latin: beyond the powers, i.e., an unauthorized act by a corporation or government agency. The authority of an agency is limited by the statute that creates it, and the powers of a corporation by its articles of incorporation. Government officials acting *ultra vires* can often be sued as individuals without benefit of statutory immunity. Corporate officers who exceed their authority can be replaced or sued by shareholders for damages and/or injunctive relief. Compare *intra vires.*

**umbrella fund.**   An investment account containing funds invested in other accounts, usually offshore.

**umpire.**   An arbitrator. See *arbitration.*

**UN.**   The abbreviation for United Nations.

**unabsorbed cost.**   The deficit in overhead expenses when revenues from production do not cover all costs.

**unauthorized investment.**   An investment that violates a trustor's intent because it is unapproved by a trust deed, will, or other legally valid instrument.

**unbundling.**   The British term for breaking up a company and selling off its parts. In the 1980s, corporate takeovers were often financed by debt and sales of the target company's assets. See also *break-up value*.

**uncalled capital.**   See *reserve capital*.

**UNCDF.**   The abbreviation for United Nations Capital Development Fund. See *United Nations Development Programme*.

**UNCED.**   The abbreviation for United Nations Conference on Environment and Development.

**uncertified units.**   Shares in a mutual fund for which certificates are not issued. When investors buy a small number of shares by reinvesting dividends, the shares are credited to their accounts until holdings are enlarged or divested.

**UNCITRAL.**   The acronym for United Nations Commission on International Trade Law.

**UNCITRAL Arbitration Rules.**   See *United Nations Commission on International Trade Law*.

**UNCITRAL Conciliation Rules.**   See *United Nations Commission on International Trade Law*.

**unclean bill of lading.**   See *foul bill of lading*.

**UNCLOS.**   The abbreviation for United Nations Convention on the Law of the Sea.

**unconditional bid.**   See *takeover*.

**unconfirmed letter of credit.**   See *letter of credit*.

**uncovered option.**   See *option*.

**UNCTAD.**   The abbreviation for United Nations Conference on Trade and Development.

**UNCTAD Certificate of Origin Form A.**   The uniform certificate of origin for imports entering under the Generalized System of Preferences. The form is signed by the exporter and filed with customs authorities at customs entry or during the clearance process, as required by an importing country's customs regulations. Form A is waived at the discretion of a customs agency.

**UNCTAD Code of Conduct for Liner Conferences.**   See *Convention on a Code of Conduct for Liner Conferences*.

**UNCTAD Database on Trade Measures.**   See *United Nations Conference on Trade and Development*.

**undated security.**   A security without a redemption date.

**underdevelopment.**   Principally, the chronic condition of less developed countries (LDCs) with substantially lower gross domestic product and per capita income than the rest of the world. Generally, a developing country is thought to have underdeveloped sectors, but without evoking images of chronic national underdevelopment. LDCs depend on primary commodity exports for income, have severely limited investment capital, and rely on infrastructures inadequate to support even meager industrial development.

**underground economy.**   Known variously as the parallel market or shadow economy, the entrepreneurial market in a heavily regulated or centrally planned economy. The underground market consists of networks of agents and suppliers selling goods and services to companies and consumers willing to pay premiums for products unavailable through regular distribution channels. When illegal goods and services are traded in international commerce, the parallel market is known as the black market.

**underlap.**   In ocean charters, the period of time between the scheduled end of the charter and the earliest date the ship is returned to the owner.

**underlying.**   1. A description of a contract's subject. In a contract for the sale of widgets, widgets are the underlying subject. 2. A description of financial instruments bought and sold in foreign exchange, futures, and options markets.

**underlying lien.**   A legal claim on assets with priority over the claims of other creditors.

**underselling.**   In international trade, selling in an import market at less-than-fair-market value.

**undersubscribed issue.**   See *oversubscribed issue*.

**underwater loan.**   In secondary-market sales, a loan with a lower market value than book value. Loans lose market value when payments are delinquent or the principal exceeds the value of the collateral.

**underwriter.**   1. An insurer who promises to compensate a policyholder for losses in exchange for a premium. The underwriter earns a premium, which is calculated based on the risk reflected in prior claims. Compare *reinsurance*. 2. A merchant bank or an investment bank offering securities under an underwriting agreement. 3. A commercial bank providing a credit facility through syndication. 4. In the United States, a dealer in government securities approved by the Federal Reserve Bank of New York.

**Underwriters Laboratories (UL).**   In the United States, private firms that conduct product testing and evaluate factories. UL's Technical Assistance to Exporters program certifies domestic firms meeting both European and U.S. quality standards. The organization has offices in Northbrook, Illinois; Melville, New York; and Santa Clara, California. See also *Communauté Européenne.*

**underwriting.**   1. The assumption of an insurance risk by an underwriter or syndicate in exchange for a premium. 2. The negotiated purchase of securities for resale by initial public offering or private placement. In the United States, an underwriter buys corporate stocks and bonds, federal agency debt obligations, and municipal bonds from the issuer. U.S. Treasury securities are purchased by underwriters, known as primary securities dealers, at quarterly Treasury bond auctions. Treasury dealers also act as distributors. See also *underwriting agreement.* 3. The process used by commercial banks creating credit facilities through syndication.

**underwriting agreement.**   An agreement, or purchase offer, between an underwriting group and a securities issuer. An underwriting group, also called an underwriting syndicate, is a consortium of commercial banks and investment banks formed to purchase all or part of a new issue. The agreement, negotiated by the managing underwriter on behalf of the group, specifies the terms of the underwriting, including the initial price of the securities and the amount of the issue to be purchased by the group. In the United States, the costs of publishing a prospectus and registering an issue with the Securities and Exchange Commission are borne by the issuer. Compare *syndicate agreement.*

**underwriting group.**   See *underwriting agreement.*

**underwriting spread.**   The underwriting group's profit margin from the sale of a securities issue. Also known as the gross spread, the profit represents the difference between the purchase price paid by the group and the offer price asked for the issue in a public sale.

**undisclosed factoring.**   See *factoring.*

**undisclosed principal.**   A principal whose identity is unknown to other principals in a transaction. In most instances, agents are not required to reveal the identity of a principal, although they must disclose the presence of a third party in the transaction.

**undistributed profit.**   Earnings reserved by a company and not immediately distributed to shareholders. Retained earnings are used to finance operations or expansion, or they are declared as dividends and distributed at a later date.

**undivided interest.**   An unlimited ownership right in assets, as in the claims of owners of a corporation or partnership. Each owner has an unrestricted claim on the assets of the business. See also *tenancy in common.*

**UNDP.**   The abbreviation for United Nations Development Programme.

**unearned income.**   Investment income not earned from a trade or profession. Following World War II, most Western countries taxed unearned income from interest, dividends, and rents at higher rates than earned income. The difference was based on the assumption that a person's limited working life justified lower rates on earned income. In the 1980s, particularly in the United Kingdom and the United States, tax reform measures eliminated distinctions between earned and unearned income, both of which have been recently taxed at the same rate.

**unencumbered property.**   Property free of liens. Unencumbered property may be freely mortgaged, sold, willed, or otherwise conveyed to another.

**unentered goods.**   Goods denied customs entry. In the United States, goods are not entered when the consignee fails to file customs documents within 5 working days of a shipment's arrival at the port of entry. Unentered goods are warehoused under general order, normally for a period of up to 5 years unless redeemed by the owner or disposed of by the U.S. Customs Service. See also *entry documents.*

**UNEP.**   The abbreviation for United Nations Environment Programme.

**UNESCO.**    The abbreviation for United Nations Educational, Scientific and Cultural Organization.

**unfair competition.**    In Anglo-American common law, a broad term covering unethical business conduct. Legal remedies, including damages and injunction, are available to parties injured by wrongful business practices. Stealing trademarks and trade secrets, simulating a competitor's packaging or trade name, and palming off goods as those of a better-known seller are examples of unfair competition. See also *unfair trade practice.*

**unfair prejudice.**    A legal claim lodged by a shareholder alleging inequitable treatment by other owners of a company. The act must prejudice the shareholder's ownership rights or deny an entitlement created by the agreement under which the company was organized.

**unfair trade practice.**    1. In international trade, an action taken by one country that unreasonably burdens the commerce of another. Unfair trade practices are defined differently by countries, but generally include (1) unwarranted discrimination against exports; (2) dumping; (3) industrial espionage; (4) copyright, patent, and trademark infringement; (5) subsidized production for export; and (6) the use of uncompensated labor (e.g., prison labor) to manufacture exports. See also *nontariff barrier* and *unfair competition.* 2. In the United Kingdom, the target of consumer protection laws. Remedies for victims of consumer fraud and similar offenses are specified in the Fair Trading Act of 1973, the Sale of Goods Act of 1979, and the Unfair Contract Terms Act of 1977.

**unfavorable balance.**    A payments deficit. See also *balance of payments.*

**unfranked investment.**    See *franked payment.*

**UNGA.**    The unofficial abbreviation for United Nations General Assembly.

**UNHCR.**    The abbreviation for Office of the United Nations High Commissioner for Refugees.

**UNIDO.**    The abbreviation for United Nations Industrial Development Organization.

**unified gift estate tax.**    See *inter vivos gift.*

**Unified Law on the Boycott of Israel.**    In the Middle East, a law enacted by the Council of the Arab League in 1954 to enforce an international boycott of Israel. Under the law, foreign firms engaged in business with Israel, or its nationals, are blacklisted and denied access to markets in Arab countries. In response, the United States enacted antiboycott legislation in 1976 and 1979. Although the Unified Law is still in effect, it is not generally enforced. See also *antiboycott regulations.*

**uniform bill of lading.**    See *bill of lading.*

**Uniform Central American Customs Code.**    See *Nomenclatura Arancelaria Uniforme Centroamericana II.*

**uniform certificate of manufacture.**    See *certificate of manufacture.*

**Uniform Commercial Code (UCC).**    In the United States, a model code governing commercial transactions, principally the sale of goods in the normal course of trade and negotiable instruments. Drafted by the National Conference of State Law Commissioners, the UCC was ratified by most states and the District of Columbia in the 1950s. (Louisiana has ratified Article 3.) The major sections of the UCC are Article 2: sales; Article 2A: leases; Article 3: negotiable instruments; Article 4: bank deposits and collections; Article 4A: electronic funds transfers; Article 5: letters of credit; Article 6: bulk sales; Article 7: warehouse receipts, bills of lading, and other negotiable documents of title; Article 8: investment securities; and Article 9: secured transactions. The UCC requires a written contract for sales of goods valued at $500 or more.

**Uniform Customs and Practice for Documentary Credits (UCP).**    A set of rules governing the terms and payment of commercial letters of credit. First published by the International Chamber of Commerce in 1933, a revised version of the UCP was adopted in the United States in 1951. The UCP has undergone a number of subsequent revisions, including a 1962 version clarifying rules for accepting on-deck bills of lading. UCP rules currently in effect are contained in the 1983 revision (Publication No. 400), which became effective in 1984. The UCP is not a statute, but its rules are recognized by courts around the world. Typically, letters of credit incorporate UCP principles by reference.

**uniform delivered price.**    A single price offered to all customers within a geographic region, irrespective of actual delivery costs. For large-volume exporters, particularly those selling to governments, a uniform delivered price can prevent price disputes and eliminate repetitious fair pricing certifications.

**Uniform Law on Bills of Exchange.**   A model statute creating a standard form for bills of exchange used in international transactions. Developed by the Convention on Bills of Exchange held at Geneva in 1932 under the auspices of the International Chamber of Commerce (ICC), the Uniform Law has been wholly or partially adopted by most trading nations. It specifies the form, terms, and conditions of negotiability of bills of exchange in international commerce. The ICC has also adopted Uniform Rules for the Collection of Commercial Paper subscribed to by most commercial banks. See also *United Nations Commission on International Trade Law.*

**Uniform Partnership Acts.**   In the United States, laws adopted in the states governing the formation of business partnerships and the distribution of partnership assets. Unless otherwise specified in a partnership agreement, partners share equally in the net profits and losses of the business. Partners may not assign shares in a partnership and are not liable for the financial obligations of other partners unrelated to the conduct of the business. See also *articles of incorporation/partnership* and *tenancy in common.*

**Uniform Product Code (UPC).**   A bar code imprinted on packaged goods and scanned by computers at checkout counters.

**Uniform Rules for the Collection of Commercial Paper.**   See *Uniform Law on Bills of Exchange.*

**Uniform Standard of Weights and Volumes.**   In Israel, the rules governing packaged food imports. Specific metric units for each product are determined by the Department of Weights and Measures in the Ministry of Industry and Trade. See also *Kashrut.*

**UNIIMOG.**   The abbreviation for United Nations Iran-Iraq Military Observer Group.

**unilinear tariff.**   See *customs tariff.*

**uninsurable risk.**   See *risk.*

**uninsured depositor.**   In the United States, a depositor whose assets held in a checking or savings account exceed the $100,000 per depositor maximum insured by the Federal Deposit Insurance Corporation. A depositor avoids the limit by holding funds in trust for another or by owning an account jointly with another party.

**Union d'Assureurs des Crédits Internationaux.** See *Berne Union.*

**Unión de Países Exportadores de Banano (UPEB).**   Also known as the Union of Banana Exporting Countries, a regional commodity group formed at Panama in 1974 to improve prices and the quality of banana exports. UPEB members are Colombia, Costa Rica, Dominican Republic, Guatemala, Honduras, Nicaragua, Panama, and Venezuela. Ecuador, the largest banana exporter in the region, is not a UPEB member.

**union des assurances.**   French: insurance union, i.e., a state-owned insurer.

**Union douanière et économique de l'Afrique Centrale (UDEAC).**   Originally formed as the *Union Douanière Équatoriale (UDE)* in 1959, a customs union of central African states. Restructured in 1964, UDEAC members are Cameroon, Central African Republic, Chad, Congo, and Equatorial Guinea. UDEAC's headquarters are in Bangui, Central African Republic. See also *Communauté Économique des États de l'Afrique Centrale.*

**Union Douanière Équatoriale.**   See *Union douanière et économique de l'Afrique Centrale.*

**Union Douanière et Économique de l'Afrique Centrale.**   See *Communauté Économique des États de l'Afrique Centrale.*

**unitary taxation.**   In the United States, a system of corporate taxation in effect in some states. Under a unitary tax system, the income tax payable by a local subsidiary is based on a pro rata share of a parent's gross profits, including earnings from foreign sources. The subsidiary's tax is the ratio of local assets, payroll, and sales to equivalent factors in the parent's gross income. In 1983, Shell Petroleum, a Netherlands corporation, failed in a U.S. Supreme Court challenge to unitary taxation.

**unit cost.**   The cost of one unit of a product. For example, one automobile represents a unit cost to an automobile manufacturer. For a components manufacturer, the unit cost is that of one component.

**United Nations (UN).**   A multilateral peacekeeping institution created by the United Nations Charter approved by 50 countries at the Conference on International Organization in San Francisco on June 26, 1945. The UN succeeded the League of Nations, established in 1920 and formally dissolved in 1946. The UN is composed of the General Assembly, Security Council, Economic and Social Council, Trusteeship Council, International Court of Justice, and Secretariat, as well as various specialized agencies, commissions, and other subsidiary organizations. UN Charter languages are Chinese, English, French, Russian, and Spanish. Arabic has also been declared an official UN language by the General Assembly. The United Nations is headquartered in New York.

**United Nations Capital Development Fund.** See *United Nations Development Programme.*

**United Nations Centre for Science and Technology for Development.**   An outgrowth of the UN Conference on Science and Technology for Development held at Vienna in 1979, the center is an arm of the Intergovernmental Committee on Science and Technology for Development, also created by the Vienna Conference. An earlier UN convention, the Conference on the Application of Science and Technology for the Benefit of the Less Developed Countries (Geneva, 1963), adopted the principle of accelerating Third World development through access to improved technologies. The center coordinates technology transfers under the Vienna Conference, as well as two other conferences, the Conference on Technical Cooperation among Developing Countries (Buenos Aires, 1978) and the Conference on the Least Developed Countries (Paris, 1981).

**United Nations Centre on Transnational Corporations.**   A body created by the United Nations Economic and Social Council in 1974 to support the United Nations Commission on Transnational Corporations and coordinate the work of the Intergovernmental Working Group of Experts on International Standards of Accounting and Reporting. The center and its regional offices help governments formulate uniform rules for multinational companies, including public accounting and disclosure standards.

**United Nations Charter.**   The founding instrument of the United Nations, signed at San Francisco on June 26, 1945, and effective October 24, 1945. Proposals for the charter were approved at Dumbarton Oaks in 1944 by China, the Soviet Union, the United Kingdom, and the United States. The UN Charter commits signatories to cooperate in peacekeeping missions and programs for global economic and social development; it also provides that members shall respect fundamental human rights and international law. Procedures for membership require that a nation be recommended by the Security Council and admitted by a vote of the General Assembly. The charter contains provisions for the suspension or expulsion of members, which have never been enforced. The agreement is amended by a two-thirds vote of the General Assembly, national ratification by two-thirds of the UN's members, and an affirmative vote by the five permanent members of the Security Council. The UN Charter has been amended four times, essentially to change the majority needed for procedural votes in the Security Council and to increase the membership of the Security Council and the Economic and Social Council.

**United Nations Charter of Economic Rights and Duties of States.**   An instrument adopted by a special session of the General Assembly in 1974 affirming a country's sovereignty over assets and resources located within its territory. Adopted to legalize local regulation of foreign direct investment and compensated nationalization of foreign-owned property, the charter has never been fully implemented. See also *new international economic order.*

**United Nations Commission on International Commodity Trade.**   A body created by the United Nations in 1954 to gather data and report on the impact of commodity markets on developing countries. The commission advises the United Nations Conference on Trade and Development and oversees the Common Fund for Commodities. See *Integrated Programme for Commodities.*

**United Nations Commission on International Trade Law (UNCITRAL).**   A body created by the General Assembly in 1966 to codify international trade law. UNCITRAL prepares model conventions and statutes for international organizations, issues opinions on international law, and promotes uniformity in national trade regimes. UNCITRAL drafted UN conventions on the international sale of goods (1974 and 1980), the carriage of goods by sea (the Hamburg Rules, 1978), multimodal transport of goods (1980), and bills of exchange and promissory notes (1987). The commission also drafted the UNCITRAL Arbitration Rules (1976), the UNCITRAL Conciliation Rules (1980), and the Model Law on International Commercial Arbitration (1985). The 36-nation commission, representing various geographical regions, reports annually to the General Assembly and the United Nations Conference on Trade and Development.

**United Nations Commission on Sustainable Development.**  See *United Nations Conference on Environment and Development.*

**United Nations Commission on Transnational Corporations.**  A standing committee of the United Nations Economic and Social Council. Created in 1974, the 48-member commission advises the United Nations Secretariat on the role and operations of multinational corporations in the global economy. See also *United Nations Centre on Transnational Corporations.*

**United Nations Committee on the Development and Utilization of New and Renewable Sources of Energy.**  An expert body established by the General Assembly in 1982. The committee grew out of a 1981 Nairobi conference that adopted the Programme of Action for the Development and Utilization of New and Renewable Sources of Energy. The committee promotes international cooperation in exploiting and managing global energy resources. See also *United Nations Committee on Natural Resources.*

**United Nations Committee of Experts on the Transport of Dangerous Goods.**  See *dangerous goods.*

**United Nations Committee on Natural Resources.**  A standing committee established in 1970 by the United Nations Economic and Social Council. The committee develops guidelines for natural resource exploitation and advises U.N. members on energy, water, and mineral conservation. The committee's work is supplemented by the UN Revolving Fund for Natural Resources Exploration established in 1975. See also *United Nations Environment Programme.*

**United Nations Common Fund for Commodities.**  See *Common Fund for Commodities.*

**United Nations Conference on Environment and Development (UNCED).**  A global summit on development and environmental issues sponsored by the United Nations in Rio de Janeiro in 1992. The UNCED adoped treaties, known as the Rio Accords, which commit signatories to combat global warming and protect diverse plant and animal species. The latter provisions are contained in the controversial Biodiversity Treaty. The programs recommended by the conference include mechanisms for transferring financial and technical assistance from industrialized countries to developing countries. Following the Rio meeting, the UN established the United Nations Commission on Sustainable Development. See also *Agenda 21* and *sustainable development.*

**United Nations Conference on Trade and Development (UNCTAD).**  A permanent organ of the General Assembly, UNCTAD was established at Geneva in 1964 to encourage cooperation in international trade. At the 1968 New Delhi Conference, UNCTAD adopted policies to stimulate trade in developing countries and sponsored the Generalized System of Preferences accepted by the General Agreement on Tariffs and Trade. UNCTAD oversees negotiations on international commodity agreements, which are designed to stabilize commodity prices. More recently, UNCTAD sponsored the Common Fund for Commodities, an international fund to finance commodity buffer stocks, and the Convention on a Code of Conduct for Liner Conferences, intended to secure a larger share of the cargo carriage trade for ocean carriers registered in developing countries. The UNCTAD Convention on Conditions for Registration of Ships establishes international rules for regulating vessels flying foreign flags. UNCTAD's executive body, the Trade and Development Board, meets semiannually. UNCTAD is headquartered in Geneva.

**United Nations Conventional Arms Register.**  A new mechanism adopted by the United Nations to monitor global traffic in guns, tanks, and other conventional weapons. Under the mechanism, governments file annual accountings listing the armaments that they bought or sold during a given year. Upon receipt of the accountings, the Secretary-General issues a public report disclosing the information provided in them. The first reporting deadline was April 30, 1993.

**United Nations Convention on Arbitration.** An international agreement adopted at Geneva in 1972 to reaffirm the 1923 Geneva Protocol on Arbitration. The 1923 protocol obligates signatories to recognize arbitration clauses in commercial contracts, irrespective of where a contract is executed. The 1972 convention reimposes the obligation on signatories to enforce awards arising from arbitrations that meet the standards of the 1923 protocol. See also *United Nations Convention on the Recognition and Enforcement of Foreign Arbitral Awards.*

**United Nations Convention on Conditions for Registration of Ships.** See *United Nations Conference on Trade and Development.*

**United Nations Convention on Contracts for the International Sale of Goods (CISG).** Also known as the Vienna Sales Convention, an international agreement signed at Vienna in 1980 that applies solely to contracts covering the sale of goods. The convention explicitly excludes services and investment, as well as goods when their sale is incidental to sales of labor or services. Under the rules of the convention, an offer for the sale of goods must stipulate quantity and price. An offer is revoked by rejection, even though expressly irrevocable. Contracts are deemed concluded when acceptances are received, and their terms become effective by mutual agreement between the parties. Signatories may derogate from certain provisions of the convention, including a provision in Article 11 recognizing the enforceability of unwritten contracts. CISG has substantially supplanted the 1964 Convention Relating to a Uniform Law on the Formation of Contracts for the International Sale of Goods, also known as the Hague Formation Convention, and the 1964 Convention Relating to a Uniform Law on the International Sale of Goods, known as the Hague Sales Convention. CISG is complemented by the United Nations Convention on the Limitation

Period in the International Sale of Goods, adopted in 1974, and amended by protocol, adopted in 1980, which establishes an international statute of limitation on breach-of-contract suits. See also *damaged goods.*

**United Nations Convention on International Bills of Exchange and International Promissory Notes.** See *United Nations Commission on International Trade Law.*

**United Nations Convention on International Multimodal Transport of Goods.** See *United Nations Commission on International Trade Law.*

**United Nations Convention on the Carriage of Goods by Sea.** See *Hague-Visby Rules.*

**United Nations Convention on the Law of the Sea.** An international agreement signed at Montego Bay, Jamaica, in 1982 defining the conduct of nations regarding the open seas. The convention covers ocean boundaries, fishing zones, resource conservation and exploration, pollution, and innocent passage. It extends to coastal states sovereignty over open waters within 12 nautical miles of a shoreline, as well as marine exploitation rights within a 200-nautical-mile zone. The convention guarantees landlocked countries access to fishing and navigation rights, so long as the borders of coastal states are not threatened.

**United Nations Convention on the Limitation Period in the International Sale of Goods.** See *United Nations Convention on Contracts for the International Sale of Goods.*

**United Nations Convention on the Recognition and Enforcement of Foreign Arbitral Awards.** Also known as the New York Convention, an international agreement governing private commercial arbitrations. Adopted by the UN Conference on International Commercial Arbitration and signed at New York in 1958, the convention obligates signatory countries to enforce arbitral awards granted under agreements conforming to its terms. Local courts in signatory countries are bound to stay legal proceedings until arbitrations are concluded. Although the convention does not explicitly establish choice of law rules, in practice the law of the arbitration site is usually used. The New York Convention has largely supplanted the 1923 Geneva Protocol on

Arbitration Clauses and the 1927 Geneva Convention on the Execution of Foreign Arbitral Awards, even though substantive provisions of the 1923 Geneva Convention were reaffirmed by the 1972 United Nations Convention on Arbitration. In the United States, the New York Convention was adopted by amendment to the Arbitration Act of 1947.

**United Nations Department of Technical Cooperation for Development (DTCD).**  An agency of the United Nations Secretariat created by the UN General Assembly in 1978 to consolidate the UN's technical assistance operations, including training and advisory services to governments implementing development projects. DTCD is the executing agency for the United Nations Development Programme and the United Nations Population Fund.

**United Nations Development Programme (UNDP).**  An agency created to enable developing countries to cultivate human and natural resources. The UNDP finances feasibility studies and generates capital for high-risk development projects. UNDP programs integrate national and regional economic assistance programs, including those sponsored by other international agencies. The agency administers the United Nations Capital Development Fund, the United Nations Fund for Women, the United Nations Revolving Fund for Natural Resources Exploration, the United Nations Fund for Science and Technology for Development, and the Special Measures Fund for Least Developed Countries. Operating one of the largest procurement programs in the world, the UNDP purchases through its Division for Administrative and Management Services, Inter-Agency Procurement Services Office, and Office for Project Execution.

**United Nations regional economic commissions.** Five regional commissions created to promote global economic development. The commissions identify projects to improve economic performance in the least developed parts of each region and monitor project implementation. The commissions are (1) the Economic Commission for Africa (ECA) in Addis Ababa (Ethopia); (2) the Economic Commission for Europe (ECE) in Geneva; (3) the Economic Commission for Latin America and the Caribbean (ECLAC), also known as *Comisión Económica para América Latina y el Caribe (CEPAL)*, in Santiago (Chile); (4) the Economic and Social Commission for Asia and the Pacific (ESCAP) in Bangkok (Thailand); and (5) the Economic and Social Commission for Western Asia (ESCWA) in Baghdad (Iraq). A sixth commission, the Economic Commission for the Middle East, has been proposed but not established.

**United Nations Educational, Scientific and Cultural Organization (UNESCO).**  A specialized agency of the United Nations proposed by the London Conference in 1945 and created in 1946. UNESCO promotes international collaboration on communications, culture, education, and science. UNESCO's headquarters are in Paris.

**United Nations Electronic Data Interchange Format (UN EDI).**  Any electronic data interchange message format approved by the United Nations Working Party on Trade Facilitation. See also *Electronic Data Interchange for Adminstration, Commerce, and Transport.*

**United Nations Environment Programme (UNEP).**  A program established by the General Assembly in 1977 following the 1972 United Nations Conference on the Human Environment held at Stockholm. UNEP implements, among others, the 1981 Nairobi Programme of Action for the Development and Utilization of New and Renewable Sources of Energy. The organization is headquartered in Nairobi. See also *Earthwatch, United Nations Committee on the Development and Utilization of New and Renewable Sources of Energy,* and *United Nations Conference on Environment and Development.*

**United Nations Food and Agricultural Organization.**  See *Food and Agriculture Organization.*

**United Nations Fund for Science and Technology for Development.**  See *United Nations Development Programme.*

**United Nations Industrial Development Organization (UNIDO).**  An agency created by the General Assembly in 1966 to coordinate international industrial development programs. UNIDO became a UN specialized agency by agreement at Vienna in 1979. The organization promotes the transfer of technical information to developing countries, primarily by financing licensing and industrial pilot projects through the Industrial Development Fund. In the late 1980s, UNIDO shifted some of its funding from large-scale industrial projects to training programs for scientists from developing countries. The International Centre for Science and High Technology and the International Centre for Genetic Engineering and Biotechnology, both at Trieste, are jointly sponsored by UNIDO and the government of Italy. UNIDO also funds projects through the International Centre for Theoretical Physics, operated in association with the International Atomic Energy Agency and the United Nations Educational, Scientific and Cultural Organization. UNIDO is based in Vienna.

**United Nations Information Centres.**   Service centers in major cities around the world operated by the United Nations. The centers provide information on UN programs and services.

**United Nations Institute for Training and Research (UNITAR).**   An institute created in 1965 to train employees of UN permanent missions. UNITAR provides an array of courses and seminars on diplomacy, dispute settlement, the drafting and negotiating of legal instruments, international economics, and so on. UNITAR programs are based in Geneva.

**United Nations Monetary and Financial Conference.**   See *Bretton Woods Conference.*

**United Nations Negotiating Conference on a Common Fund.**   See *Common Fund for Commodities.*

**United Nations Research Institute for Social Development (UNRISD).**   An international research center created to coordinate research on poverty and economic development. UNRISD is located in Geneva.

**United Nations Revolving Fund for Natural Resources Exploration.**   See *United Nations Development Programme.*

**United Nations specialized agencies.**   See *specialized agency.*

**United Nations Standard International Trade Classification.**   See *Standard International Trade Classification.*

**United Nations Water Conference (Mar del Plata, Argentina, 1977).**   A conference that grew out of the work of the Committee on Natural Resources. The conference adopted the Mar del Plata Action Plan, an international program to coordinate the development and management of global water resources.

**United Nations Working Party on Trade Facilitation.**   See *Electronic Data Interchange for Administration, Commerce, and Transport.*

**United States Arbitration Act.**   See *Arbitration Act of 1947.*

**United States–Canada Free Trade Agreement Implementation Act.**   See *Canada–U.S. Free Trade Agreement.*

**United States Customary System.**   The system of weights and measures adopted in 1830 by the predecessor of the U.S. Customs Service and still in use in the United States. The primary units of the Customary System are the inch, foot, and yard (length, area, and volume); the ounce, pint, quart, gallon, and barrel (liquid measure); the pint, quart, peck, and bushel (dry measure); and the avoirdupois grain, dram, ounce, pound, and ton (weight). In 1964, the U.S. National Bureau of Standards approved the use of the *Systeme Internationale* for scientific purposes. The *Systeme Internationale* was officially adopted as the national standard by the Metric Conversion Act of 1975. As of 1992, however, the Customary System was still widely used in the United States, most notably by U.S. Customs Service to calculate and levy specific duties.

**United States value.**   A former basis for levying import duties in the United States. Duties were assessed on the wholesale price of an import, or a like domestic product if an import's value could not be determined. Duties and taxes, ordinary markups, transportation, and insurance were deducted from the import price. Transaction value supplanted U.S. value when the United States adopted the Customs Valuation Code in the Trade Agreements Act of 1979.

**unit investment trust.**   A type of mutual fund in which each investor buys an interest in specific securities. Shares in the trust are purchased from an investment company, and ownership is evidenced by redeemable securities issued by the company. Compare *unit trust.*

**unitization.**   In shipping, consolidating smaller packages into a single unit, e.g., packing cartons onto a pallet. Palletization eases handling.

**unit load device (ULD).**   The container used to consolidate cargo for air transport, usually by freight forwarders. ULDs vary in shape and size, depending on the stowage capacity of the aircraft. They include 20 TEUs, 40 TEUS, pallets, etc.

**unit of account.**   1. In accounting, a function of money that permits a holder to calculate income and expenditures, thereby settling accounts. A unit of account need not be embodied in currency, but may consist solely of accounting credits or debits. 2. The artificial currency unit of the African Development Bank. The value of one unit of account is equal to one special drawing right.

**unit of exchange.**   In accounting, a function of money that permits a holder to purchase goods and services.

**unit of measure.**   In accounting, a function of money that permits a holder to value assets and liabilities.

**unit price.**   In the United States, any one of three tests used by the U.S. Customs Service to determine price for computing deductive value. The applicable tests are (1) the price on or near the importation date for which the largest total quantity of the merchandise is sold; (2) the price after the importation date, but within 90 days of the importation date, for which the largest total quantity of the merchandise is sold; or (3) the further processing price, also known as the superdeductive. The date of importation is a factor in calculating deductive value.

**unit pricing.**   Manufacturer's pricing that displays the cost of a single product packaged in a larger unit.

**unit train.**   In shipping, a train loaded with cargo destined for a single consignee. A unit train usually consists of a minimum of 50 carloads.

**unit trust.**   Outside the United States, an open-end mutual fund. Unlike U.S. mutual funds, however, most unit trusts are managed by commercial banks rather that investment firms dedicated to fund management. Unit trust dividends are usually taxed at the basic rate, and profits earned from divesting holdings are subject to the capital gains tax. Unit trust share prices are quoted in newspapers and financial dailies. Compare *unit investment trust.*

**universal air waybill.**   See *airbill.*

**universal banking system.**   A banking system permitting banks to perform services of commercial banks and investment banks. In a universal system, banks accept deposits, make loans, underwrite securities, and own equities. Universal banking systems are common in Europe, especially in Germany.

**Universal Copyright Convention.**   A 1952 international agreement reached at Geneva protecting works by authors. The convention extends national treatment in signatory countries to published and unpublished literary works for the life of the author plus 50 years, irrespective of the place of first publication. A work is automatically protected when the author's name, the date of publication (or completion), and the copyright symbol are placed on it. The universal copyright symbol is ©. The convention is administered by the United Nations Educational, Scientific and Cultural Organization. The United States adopted the convention in 1955. Compare *Berne Convention for the Protection of Literary and Artistic Works.*

**Universal Postal Union (UPU).**   A specialized agency of the United Nations, the UPU was established to promote universal collaboration in the transmission of mail. The UPU sets postal rates for international mail service, determines conditions of postal acceptance, regulates postal transit and terminal charges, and determines relevant safety and health standards for mail handling. The agency is based in Berne, Switzerland. See *Berne Treaty.*

**unlimited company.**   See *company.*

**unlimited liability.**   The legal liability of a general partner or sole proprietor for the debts of a firm. The liability extends to all personal assets. By contrast, the liabilities of limited partners and company shareholders are limited to the extent of their ownership in the assets of a business.

**unliquidated damages.**   See *damages.*

**unlisted securities.**   Traded securities not listed on a stock exchange. Usually issued by small companies, unlisted securities can be risky investments. In the United Kingdom, these shares are traded on the third market, known as the unlisted securities market. In the United States, unlisted securities are bought and sold in over-the-counter trading.

**unlisted securities market (USM).**    A market for over-the-counter trading, i.e., trading in securities not listed on the main market of a stock exchange. The listing requirements for unlisted markets are less stringent, including lower capital limits. See also *over-the-counter market.*

**unmatched book.**    A portfolio with liabilities in excess of assets. Compare *matched book.*

**unperfected security interest.**    In the United States, a lien on an asset not properly filed as required by the Uniform Commercial Code. A security interest is unperfected when the creditor fails to file a financing statement with a state agency or a continuation statement as required by state law.

**unquoted securities.**    Securities not traded on an exchange. Some exchanges permit occasional unofficial trading of unquoted securities. The shares are usually valued at the balance-sheet price.

**unrealized profit (or loss).**    A paper gain (or loss) from an unsold asset. Normally, unrealized losses caused by a decline in the market value of an asset are noted in a firm's profit and loss statement. Unrealized profits are recognized when an asset is sold.

**unsecured creditor.**    A general creditor without a security interest in the property of a debtor who files for bankruptcy. An unsecured creditor is paid a *pro rata* share of the remaining estate after secured creditors' claims have been satisfied.

**unsecured debenture.**    A debenture for which no fund has been created to pay priority claims. See also *sinking fund.*

**unsecured debt.**    A debt supported by a borrower's creditworthiness and reputation, and not by collateral.

**Unterlassung.**    German: default.

**Unverzinsliche Schatzanweisungen (U-Schätze).**    In Germany, debt obligations of the federal government and its agencies. The instruments are issued at a discount, usually with maturities of less than 2 years.

**unwinding.**    1. In foreign exchange markets, disengaging from a market, usually by placing an order canceling a speculative order. 2. In futures markets, liquidating short and long positions when the difference between the spot price and futures price narrows.

**UPC.**    The abbreviation for Uniform Product Code.

**up-front fee.**    See *origination fee.*

**upstream.**    In sales, the condition of the producer or product closest to the end user. Products move from downstream components to upstream finished manufactures. Pricing by downstream producers are factored into a product's retail price.

**UPU.**    The abbreviation for Universal Postal Union.

**Uruguay Round.**    See *General Agreement on Tariffs and Trade.*

**USAC.**    The abbreviation for U.S. Atlantic Coast.

**U.S. Advisory Committee on Trade Policy Negotiations (ACTPN).**    In the United States, a body authorized by the Omnibus Trade Act of 1988. ACTPN advises the U.S. trade representative on international trade negotiations and on the impact of global trade policies on U.S. industry. Primary business sectors, as well as state and local governments, are represented on ACTPN.

**U.S. Agency for International Development (USAID).**    In the United States, the agency responsible for official development assistance (ODA), including programs first authorized by the Foreign Economic Assistance Act of 1950. USAID also administers the Foreign Assistance Act of 1961, providing direct loans and grants to developing countries for procurement of U.S. commodities. In addition, the agency shares jurisdiction over PL 480 programs with the U.S. Department of Agriculture. USAID Congressional Presentations are valuable sources for developing country economic data, which review USAID projects in a previous year and propose project funding for the next fiscal year. The agency also publishes *Export Opportunities,* a business guide to developing countries. USAID is a division of the U.S. International Development Cooperation Agency.

**USAID.**   The abbreviation for U.S. Agency for International Development.

**usance.**   The time allowed for a bill of exchange to be paid after presentment. Outside the United States, usance generally denotes the time period allotted by custom for payment in a given trade. In the United States, usance means tenor, or the time until a draft matures.

**usance draft.**   See time draft.

**usance letter of credit.**   A time letter of credit specifying maturity date(s) for drafts. The maturity dates are expressed as days after sight or after presentation.

**U.S. & Foreign Commercial Service.**   See *U.S. Department of Commerce.*

**Usanera.**   The acronym for U.S.A./North Europe Rate Agreement. See *conference.*

**U.S.C. The abbreviation for United States Code.** See *U.S. Code.*

**U.S.C.A.**   The abbreviation for United States Code, Annotated. See *U.S. Code.*

**U.S.-Canada Free Trade Agreement.**   See *Canada-U.S. Free Trade Agreement.*

**U-Schätze.**   The short form for Unverzinsliche Schatzanweisungen.

**U.S. Claims Court.**   A federal court reorganized in 1982 by the Federal Courts Improvement Act as the successor to the U.S. Court of Claims, originally established in 1855. The court hears cases arising from claims for monetary damages against the United States, including those involving the U.S. Constitution, acts of Congress, federal agencies, and federal contracts or patent disputes to which the United States is a party. The court is composed of a chief judge and 15 associate judges appointed by the President to 15-year terms.

**U.S. Coast Guard.**   The federal law enforcement agency responsible for enforcing U.S. customs and navigation laws. The Coast Guard is subject to the jurisdiction of the U.S. Department of Transportation in peacetime. During wars or national emergencies, the Coast Guard is controlled by the Department of the Navy.

**U.S. Code.**   The official compilation of laws enacted by the Congress of the United States. Statutes are classified under separate titles by sub-

ject, and supplements are issued after each congressional session. First published in 1926, the code is revised every 6 years. Code revisions are overseen by the Committee on the Judiciary, a permanent body of the House of Representatives.

**U.S. Copyright Office.**   The federal office that registers copyrights, administers U.S. copyright laws, and enforces obligations incurred under international copyright conventions. An agency of the Library of Congress, the Copyright Office protects registered copyright holders from infringing imports by providing registration records to the U.S. Customs Service. The Copyright Office was created by an act of Congress in 1870. See also *Copyright Revision Act of 1976.*

**U.S. Court for the Federal Circuit.**   A specialized appellate court created in 1982 by the Federal Courts Improvement Act. The court succeeded to most of the subject-matter jurisdiction previously granted to the U.S. Court of Customs and Patent Appeals. It hears, among others, appeals from decisions of the U.S. Claims Court and the U.S. Patent and Trademark Office. The court has 12 judges, including a chief judge.

**U.S. Court of Claims.**   See *U.S. Claims Court.*

**U.S. Court of Customs and Patent Appeals (CCPA).**   A specialized court originally created in 1909 as the U.S. Court of Customs Appeals and first authorized to hear patent appeals in 1929. Given constitutional status under Article III of the U.S. Constitution in 1956, the CCPA was abolished in 1982 when its functions were transferred to the U.S. Court for the Federal Circuit and the U.S. Court of International Trade.

**U.S. Court of International Trade.**   A court originally established as the Board of United States General Appraisers in 1890 and reconstituted as the United States Customs Court in 1926. Renamed the Court of Customs and Patent Appeals in 1956 and given constitutional status under Article III of the U.S. Constitution, the court was reorganized as the U.S. Court of International Trade by the Customs Courts Act of 1980. The court hears appeals from antidumping and countervailing orders and U.S. Customs Service import classification and rulings involving valuations, duty refunds, and customs bonds. Cases concerning adjustment assistance originate in the Court of

International Trade. Composed of a chief judge and eight judges, the court sits in New York.

**U.S. Courts of Appeals.** Intermediate appellate courts that hear appeals from decisions of the U.S. District Courts and administrative rulings of most U.S. federal agencies. The appeals courts were known as Circuit Courts of Appeals from 1891 to 1948. The courts sit in 10 circuits and the District of Columbia. Circuit court opinions carry considerable weight because few of their decisions are appealed to the U.S. Supreme Court.

**U.S. Customary units.** See *United States Customary System.*

**U.S. Customs Cooperation Council Explanatory Notes.** The explanatory notes of the Brussels Tariff Nomenclature (BTN) published by the U.S. Customs Service. A guide to import classifications under the BTN, the notes are available in electronic form.

**U.S. Customs Service (USCS).** An agency of the U.S. Department of the Treasury authorized to administer domestic customs laws. Established by Congress in 1789, the Customs Service clears import and export shipments; assesses imports and duties, taxes, and fees; and exercises arrest powers to deter smuggling, fraud, and importation of items infringing intellectual property rights. The Customs Service also administers navigation laws jointly with the U.S. Coast Guard and enforces import quotas, health regulations, and international trade laws at U.S. borders. Divided into nine regions, the largest of which is Region II covering the Port of New York, U.S. Customs territory encompasses the 50 states, the District of Columbia, Puerto Rico, and the U.S. Virgin Islands. The Office of Regulations and Rulings in the Customs Service hears appeals from tariff classifications and valuations. Its rulings are appealed to the U.S. Court of International Trade.

**U.S.** Customs territory. See *U.S. Customs Service.*

**USDA.** The abbreviation for U.S. Department of Agriculture.

**U.S. Department of Agriculture (USDA).** A federal agency created in 1862 and made an executive department in 1889. The USDA sets commodity standards, inspects meat and poultry, and finances agricultural export, support, and rural development programs.

**U.S. Department of Commerce (DOC).** A federal executive department created as the Department of Commerce and Labor in 1903 and reorganized in 1913 to promote domestic commerce and industry. The Bureau of Economic Analysis, the Bureau of Export Administration, the Bureau of Competitive Assessment and Business Policy, the Census Bureau, the Foreign Business Practices Division, the Foreign Trade Zones Board, the International Trade Administration, the Office of Business Liaison, the Office of Export Enforcement, the Office of Maritime Standards, the Office of Textile and Apparel, the Office of Trade Finance, the Travel and Tourism Administration, and the United States & Foreign Commercial Service (US&FCS) are DOC agencies. The US&FCS provides export counseling and market research, country risk assessments, product and service-sector counseling, and trade representation in external markets.

**U.S. Department of Defense (DOD).** A federal executive agency created as the successor to the National Military Establishment in 1949. The DOD contains the Departments of the Air Force, Army, and Navy. It is responsible for military communications, engineering (through the Corps of Engineers), intelligence, international security, logistics, and weapons systems.

**U.S. Department of Energy (DOE).** A federal executive department created in 1977. The DOE administers, among others, the Coal and Technology Export Program, the Export Assistance Initiative, and the Federal International Energy and Trade Development Opportunities Program. The Committee on Renewable Energy Commerce and Trade is an arm of the DOE.

**U.S. Department of Justice (DOJ).** The federal legal department and chief prosecutor of the United States established in 1870. The DOJ represents the United States in cases involving civil rights, foreign claims settlement, immigration and naturalization, internal security, monopolies, and tax collection. The Federal Bureau of Investigation is a DOJ division.

**U.S. Department of State.** The foreign affairs department of the United States created in 1789. The State Department formulates external policy, conducts negotiations with foreign governments, promotes friendly relations with other countries, and issues passports and visas. The department has bureaus for African, East Asian and Pacific, European and Canadian, Inter-American, Near Eastern, and South Asian affairs.

**U.S. Department of the Treasury.**    The finance ministry of the United States created in 1789. The Department of the Treasury collects duties and taxes, enforces export controls and narcotics laws, funds the national debt, investigates counterfeiting, prints currency and stamps, protects the President, and registers foreign agents and ocean vessels. Among others, agencies of the Treasury Department include the Bureau of Alcohol, Tobacco, and Firearms; the Bureau of the Mint; the Bureau of Public Debt; the Comptroller of the Currency; the Customs Service; the Engraving and Printing Bureau; the Financial Management Service; the Internal Revenue Service; and the Secret Service.

**U.S. Department of Transportation (DOT).**    A federal executive department created in 1966 to oversee the national transportation system. DOT contains, among others, the U.S. Coast Guard, the Federal Aviation Administration, the Federal Highway Administration, and the Maritime Administration.

**U.S. District Courts.**    The trial courts of original jurisdiction for most legal cases involving federal matters in the United States. The district courts hear disputes arising under Article III of the U.S. Constitution and have jurisdiction over cases involving admiralty, bankruptcy, copyright, criminal, patent, and postal laws. Three-judge district panels hear petitions for injunctions in certain cases, the decisions of which may be appealed directly to the U.S. Supreme Court. Appeals from most district court decisions lie with the U.S. Courts of Appeals. See also *diversity of citizenship.*

**user fee.**    See *text.*

**U.S. Export/Import Regulations.**    See *Bureau of Export Administration.*

**U.S. Generalized System of Preferences (USGSP).**    A preferential trade program originally enacted for developing countries, Pacific Islands belonging to the Compact of Freely Associated States, and U.S. territories. Authorized by the Trade Act of 1974 and reauthorized by the Trade and Tariff Act of 1984, most USGSP prefer-

ences are not perpetual and are often subject to quantitative limits. The lists of covered countries and products are subject to change. For quota purposes, beneficiary countries belonging to common markets may be treated as one country. The current program took effect January 1, 1976, and expires July 4, 1993. USGSP is governed by Sections 10.171–10.178 of the U.S. Customs Regulations. See also *Generalized System of Preferences; graduation; Harmonized Tariff Schedule of the United States.*

**USGSP.**    The abbreviation for U.S. Generalized System of Preferences.

**USIDCA.**    The abbreviation for U.S. International Development Cooperation Agency.

**U.S. International Development Cooperation Agency (USIDCA).**    A federal agency created in 1979 by amendment to the Foreign Assistance Act of 1961 to coordinate U.S. economic assistance and investment programs for developing countries. The agency oversees official development programs administered by the U.S. Agency for International Development, the Overseas Private Investment Corporation's insurance and credit facilities, and projects financed by the U.S. Trade and Development Program. USIDCA proposes budgets for U.S. contributions to United Nations assistance and development programs, the Organization of American States, the World Bank, and regional development banks.

**USITC.**    The abbreviation for U.S. International Trade Commission.

**USM.**    The abbreviation for unlisted securities market.

**U.S.-Mexican Binational Commission.**    A bilateral body created by a memorandum of understanding signed May 3, 1991. The commission was established to resolve differences over labor and environmental issues. The work of the commission paralleled negotiations leading to the North American Free Trade Agreement.

**U.S.-Mexico Free Trade Agreement.**    See *North American Free Trade Agreement.*

**U.S. Munitions Lists.**    Weapons and military materials lists prepared by the Bureau of Alcohol, Tobacco, and Firearms. The Munitions List identifies arms and similar items subject to International Traffic in Arms Regulations. The Munitions Import List notes weapons eligible for U.S. importation.

**U.S.P.**    The abbreviation for United States Pharmacopoeia.

**U.S. Patent and Trademark Office.**    A federal agency established in 1790 as the U.S. Patent Office. The office accepts and reviews patent and trademark applications and maintains registration records. Registered patents are recorded with the U.S. Customs Service to exclude infringing imports. The office publishes the weekly *Official Gazette,* which lists recent patent and trademark registrations. Domestic and foreign offers to license patents are also published in the *Gazette.*

**USPHS.**    The abbreviation for U.S. Public Health Service.

**U.S. Public Health Service.**    A federal agency that dates to 1798, although authorized under its present name in 1912. The Public Health Service publishes public health information and enforces quarantines at U.S. ports of entry. The agency is authorized to issue import permits for products classified as etiologic agents (i.e., animal, insect, or plant) or as vectors for human disease.

**U.S. shareholder.**    Within the meaning of Section 957 of the Internal Revenue Code, a U.S. person who owns or controls 10 percent or more of the voting shares of a controlled foreign corporation. For purposes of Section 957, a person is a U.S. corporation, citizen, estate, partnership, resident, or trust. See also *Subpart F.*

**U.S. Shipping Board.**    A regulatory body that grew out of hearings conducted by the Alexander Committee. The board was replaced by the Federal Maritime Commission. See also *Shipping Act of 1916.*

**U.S. Supreme Court.**    The court of last resort in the United States created in 1789. Under Article III of the Constitution, the Supreme Court has original jurisdiction in cases affecting ambassadors, consuls, public ministers, and those to which a state is a party. The court's appellate jurisdiction is determined by the Congress with respect to federal matters and by the Eleventh Amendment with respect to the states. The Supreme Court has eight associate justices and a chief justice.

**U.S. territories.**    In the United States, the insular possessions of American Samoa, Guam, and the U.S. Virgin Islands plus Puerto Rico, but excluding the Pacific Islands belonging to the Compact of Freely Associated States.

**U.S. Textile and Apparel Import Program.**    See *Committee for the Implementation of Textile Agreements.*

**USTR.**    The abbreviation for U.S. trade representative.

**U.S. Trade and Development Program (TDP).**    An agency of the U.S. International Development Cooperation Agency established to promote U.S. exports to developing country markets. TDP finances feasibility studies for projects selected in consultation with foreign governments. It also provides grants for consultancies, training programs, and other project support services. Recipient governments must be classified as friendly by the Department of State, demonstrate the utility of a development project, and provide procurement opportunities to U.S. firms. TDP's congressional presentations, published by the Department of State, list the amounts spent by the agency over several years in specific countries.

**U.S. Trade Centers (USTCs).**    Public information centers around the world financed by the U.S. Department of Commerce. The centers post local customs procedures, joint-venture opportunities, and procurement information. Some centers also offer bonded display space and translation and secretarial services.

**U.S. trade representative (USTR).**    The chief officer of the Office of the U.S. Trade Representative created by executive order in 1963. Originally established as the Office of the U.S. Special Representative for Trade Negotiations, the USTR's office was made an executive agency by the Trade Act of 1974. The USTR is the President's chief advisor on international trade policy and the principal U.S. negotiator in all international trade negotiations. In addition to managing trade negotiations and coordinating U.S. trade policy, the USTR is a member of the President's cabinet, vice-chair of the Overseas Private Investment Corporation, and a nonvoting member on the board of the Export-Import Bank of the United States. The USTR holds ambassadorial rank.

**U.S. Travel & Tourism Administration.** See *U.S. Department of Commerce.*

**U.S. Treasury securities.** See *Treasury securities.*

**U.S. trustee.** See *administrator.*

**usury.** See *legal rate of interest.*

**USVI.** The abbreviation for U.S. Virgin Islands.

**utility.** 1. A company supplying a necessary public service, e.g., water, electricity, etc. 2. In classical economics, the usefulness of a product or service. 3. In neoclassical economics, a subjective benefit enjoyed by the consumer of a product or service, usually in direct proportion to its scarcity. Utility in this sense is not measurable, since the concept presumes that, when making purchases, consumers seek maximum benefits, which are largely matters of perception.

**UTU.** The abbreviation for United Transportation Union.

**U/W.** The abbreviation for underwriter.

# V

**v.** An abbreviation for value.

**vacuity.** See *ullage*.

**val.** An abbreviation for value.

**valeur mercuriale.** In some countries, an official value assigned to certain classes of imports and used to compute ad valorem duties. The *valeur mercuriale* is levied only in West Africa, notably Senegal and Benin.

**validated export license.** Also known as an individual validated license, a permit to export a specific commodity to a specified place within a stated period of time. See also *Commerce Control List, periodic requirements license, project license,* and *service supply license.* Compare *general license.*

**valores.** Spanish: securities.

**valorization.** The process of increasing or stabilizing the value of a commodity or currency by government directive. A government valorizes a commodity by controlling supply, usually by creating a buffer stock. Currencies are valorized when given a higher exchange value by decree that market factors justify.

**valuation.** The process of assigning economic value to an import in order to levy duties. Typically, customs agencies use a variety of valuation methods, although transaction value has become the standard method. Other frequently used valuation methods are deductive value, computed value, and net-cost value.

**valuation tariff.** A duty based on government decree rather than commercial value. A valuation tariff is a form of specific duty rarely encountered in international trade.

**value-added.** The amount by which the economic value of a product is enhanced by labor and materials added at different stages of production.

**value-added tax (VAT).** An indirect sales tax on the increase in the economic value of a product or service enhanced by additional materials and processes. Producers pay a sales tax, called an input tax, on materials and services purchased for production. The input tax is deducted from the output tax, or the tax added to goods and services sold by the producer. VATs apply to imports in addition to duties, but are rebated on exports. In countries with VATs, a limited number of goods and services are exempt. Vats are used primarily in Europe. The French term for the VAT is *taxe sur la valeur ajoutée.* In Canada, the value-added tax is known as the goods and services tax, or GST.

**value apportionment process.** The method used by a revenue agency to compute excise taxes on bonus goods. A bonus usually draws a higher tax rate than that imposed on original contract goods. Alternatively, the taxable value of contract goods may be discounted by the amount attributable to the value of the bonus.

**value certificate.** A document certifying the value of an import and the costs declared on an exporter's invoice. In some countries, value certificates are used to verify value for ad valorem duties. See also *certificate.*

**value date.** 1. A date when the economic value of an asset is fixed, usually by agreement. 2. The date on which currency is delivered under a foreign exchange contract, usually within 2 days of a sale. In the Eurobond market, the value date falls one calendar week after the sale. See also *hedge.*

**value determination date.** See *customs entry.*

**value-impaired loan.** A loan to a sovereign borrower on which interest is delinquent, usually for 6 months or more. Loan value is severely impaired when the country has not complied with debt rescheduling terms fixed by agreement with the International Monetary Fund, Paris Club, or commercial banks.

**valuta.** Italian: foreign currency. In banking, a short-term foreign bill of exchange.

**Vancouver Stock Exchange (VSE).** In Canada, an exchange originally established in 1907 as a venture capital market. The VSE's equity market consists primarily of companies engaged in mining and natural resource exploration. There are also commodity options markets, dedicated principally to trading in currency, gold, platinum, and silver, and a stock options market. Prices are quoted in Canadian dollars and U.S. dollars through the Quotation Services Department and in the *Daily Bulletin,* the weekly *Corporate,*

*Financial and Regulatory Services Weekly Summary,* the monthly *Review,* and public media reports. Some shares are interlisted through the Toronto Stock Exchange and several exchanges in Europe and the United States. Corporate takeovers are approved by the VSE, a self-regulating organization, and overseen by the British Columbia Securities Commission and the Ministry of Finance and Corporate Relations. See also *International Options Clearing Corporation.*

**vanning.**   A popular term for loading a container or trailer.

**var.**   The abbreviation for variable and variation.

**variable costs.**   See *overhead costs.*

**variable import levy.**   A duty imposed on some agricultural commodities under the European Community's Common Agricultural Policy. The variable levy is the difference between the threshold price and the minimum adjusted cost, insurance, and freight price. Variable levies are adjusted daily, weekly, monthly, or quarterly, depending on the product. They apply to dairy and poultry products, meat products, and some commodities, such as grain, olive oil, and sugar.

**variable-rate certificate of deposit (CD).**   A time deposit with a yield above a base reference rate. Yields on variable-rate CDs are adjusted quarterly. The reference rate may be a commodity price or an index rate, such as the London interbank offered rate, the U.S. prime rate, etc.

**variable-rate loan.**   Also called a floating-rate loan, a debt with the interest rate pegged to an index rate. The cost of the loan fluctuates with changes in the index rate.

**variation margin.**   A dealer's (or a customer's) profits or losses from an open futures contract. In futures markets, gains and losses are normally credited to accounts at the close of a trading day.

**VAT.**   The abbreviation for value-added tax.

**VD.**   The abbreviation for various dates.

**vehicle emission control information.**   See *Clean Air Act of 1990.*

**velocity of money.**   Also known as velocity of circulation, a currency unit's rate of turnover in an economy. Transaction velocity records the number of times a unit of money is spent, i.e., the ratio of gross national product to the quantity of money in circulation. Income velocity records the number of times money is earned as income, i.e., the ratio of money spent in an economy to the quantity of money in circulation. The speed with which money changes hands reflects the degree of growth or retraction in an economy.

**vendor.**   A person who sells goods or services.

**vendor express.**   In the United States, electronic payments to suppliers of the federal government. The payments are made by the U.S. Department of the Treasury's Financial Management Service and are transmitted through the Automated Clearing House System.

**vendor placing.**   In corporate mergers and acquisitions, the means by which one company acquires another by issuing shares in exchange for equity. The target company trades the shares to its stockholders for cash. Compare *bought deal* and *rights offering.*

**vendor rating.**   A quality rating given to a vendor's goods or services by an independent expert. For example, "star" ratings are provided for films, hotels, and restaurants; i.e., a four-star hotel is a hotel of the highest quality. In the United States, *Good Housekeeping* seals of approval and *Consumers Digest* best-buy labels are well-known ratings of consumer goods.

**Venezuelan Investment Fund.**   See *Inter-American Development Bank.*

**Venice Terms.**   See *Paris Club.*

**venta bajo fórmula.**   Spanish: sale under prescription, i.e., a marking label used in some Latin countries for pharmaceutical imports. Special labels may also be required indicating medical (*médica*), dental (*odontólogica*), and veterinary (*veterinaria*) prescriptions.

**venture capital.**   Risk capital invested in a new company, usually in exchange for equity. In foreign investment, venture capital is often treated more favorably than ordinary investments, particularly in countries with foreign exchange shortages. Some countries offer 100 percent repatriation of capital and profits following disinvestment. Lesser amounts can often be repatriated annually, i.e., roughly one-half of net after-tax profits.

**VER.** The abbreviation for voluntary export restraint.

**vertical foreign investment.** A downstream investment by a firm, usually to locate a plant near foreign sources of raw materials or cheap labor. Vertical investment typically moves from developed countries to developing countries, but diverting investments from high-wage developed countries to lower-wage industrialized countries is no longer uncommon.

**vertical integration.** A business combination of firms engaged in different levels of a production, e.g., a manufacturer of finished goods that owns a distributorship. Compare *horizontal integration.*

**very large crude carrier (VLCC).** An ocean tanker with a deadweight capacity of 200,000 to 300,000 tons.

**ves.** The abbreviation for vessel.

**vessel traffic services system.** An electronic guidance system for monitoring and directing ship movements in waterways. Port authorities use these systems to manage water traffic, particularly along sensitive coastal areas.

**vested interest.** A beneficial interest in property, the ownership of which is not contingent on the occurrence of any event. The owner is entitled to immediate benefits of ownership, irrespective of other claims. For example, an employee becomes entitled to share in a company pension fund after the vesting period.

**Vienna Precious Metals Exchange.** See *Wiener Edele Metalle Warenbörse.*

**Vienna Sales Convention.** See *United Nations Convention on Contracts for the International Sale of Goods.*

**visa.** 1. For a foreign national, an entry permit stamped on the passport by an immigration officer or consular official. 2. In international trade, an export license stamped or sealed on invoices or other shipping documents.

**Visby Amendment.** See *Hague-Visby Rules.*

**visible item of trade.** A transaction involving the sale of merchandise or commodities.

**visibles.** Income from trade in tangible goods reflected in a country's balance of payments.

Visibles include manufactures and commodities. Compare *invisibles.*

**vis major.** In common law, a natural force of catastrophic magnitude causing an unpreventable loss.

**vistos buenos.** In some Latin American countries, a special permit for consumer and pharmaceutical imports. The permits are obtained from government ministries that regulate specific products.

**viz.** Latin: namely. The abbreviation for *videlicet,* used almost exclusively in its abbreviated form preceding a list of items or examples.

**VLCC.** The abbreviation for very large crude carrier.

**Vnesheconombank.** The foreign trade bank of the former Union of Soviet Socialist Republics. Between 1991 and 1992, *Vneshekonombank* became effectively bankrupt and froze all foreign accounts. Its overseas subsidiaries are the Donau Bank in Vienna and the Narodny Bank in London. *Vneshekonombank* is based in Moscow. See also *Rosvneshtorgbank.*

**vol.** The abbreviation for volume.

**volume (vol.).** 1. Capacity, e.g., the maximum amount a container can hold. 2. On a trading exchange, the number of stocks traded or the number of lots sold during a trading period, usually 1 business day.

**volumetric weight.** In transportation, a nominal weight used to price a cargo unit. For example, an air carrier treats 166 cubic inches as 1 pound.

**voluntary bankruptcy.** See *bankruptcy.*

**voluntary export quota.** See *bilateral restraint agreement.*

**voluntary export restraint (VER).** In the United States, a bilateral restraint agreement. No significant difference exists between VERs and earlier agreements, known as orderly marketing agreements (OMAs). However, in contemporary usage, "voluntary" is preferred to "orderly" as a description of the agreements.

**voluntary liquidation.** The winding up of a solvent company. In most jurisdictions, voluntary dissolutions of publicly traded companies are governed by statutes, which provide criminal penalties for false declarations of solvency. A company dissolving, but found to be insolvent, is forced into involuntary bankruptcy to preserve its assets for the benefit of creditors.

**voluntary prior disclosure.**    In the United States, information provided to the U.S. Customs Service by an importer under actual or possible investigation for violations of customs laws. Voluntary disclosure may avert or mitigate penalties, especially for negligence. A penalty may still be imposed for fraud, but probably one less serious in degree.

**voluntary restraint agreement (VRA).**    A bilateral restraint agreement negotiated between a private group and a foreign government (or foreign producers).

**voluntary sharing agreement.**    Also known as vessel sharing, an arrangement between ocean carriers to limit costs and stabilize prices. Sharing arrangements usually involve exchanging equipment, removing tonnage, or withdrawing ships from a given trade route.

**voluntary stranding.**    The grounding of a ship to save it from destruction. Losses from voluntary strandings are recovered in general average, unless the grounding was inevitable.

**vostro account.**    See *nostro account.*

**voting share.**    A stock entitling a shareholder to vote on company management and policy. Common stocks are voting shares, but preferred shares do not carry voting rights.

**voting trust certificate.**    A document issued to holders of common stock in a bankrupt company. The certificates protect shareholders' ownership, but their voting rights are assigned to a voting trust managed by trustees. In the United States, a voting trust usually lasts for 5 years, although stockholders and trustees may agree to extend it.

**voyage charter.**    The hire of a ship or cargo space for a specific number of trips rather than for a fixed time period. Compare *time charter.*

**voyageur, representant et placier (VRP).**    In France, an agent who is also an employee under French agency law. VRPs include sales representatives and traveling salespeople, who must usually be compensated when an agency contract is terminated, irrespective of its terms. See also *civil law.*

**VRA.**    The abbreviation for voluntary restraint agreement.

**Vredling directive.**    A policy enacted by the European Community (EC) in 1979 governing employee participation in a company's management. The directive was proposed by Henk Vredling, an EC commissioner for employment and social affairs. Firms employing 1000 workers or more notify employees of changes in the company's operations and policies, including plant closings. Employees are given a 30-day reply period. The Vredling directive was essentially adopted as EC labor policy in the Community Charter of the Fundamental Social Rights of Workers. The policy applies especially to firms, including foreign firms, operating in two or more EC countries. The United Kingdom derogated from similar provisions in the 1992 Treaty of Maastricht. See also *Mitbestimmung.*

**VRP.**    The abbreviation for *voyageur, représentant et placier.*

**VSA.**    The abbreviation for vessel sharing agreement.

**VSE.**    The abbreviation for Vancouver Stock Exchange.

# W

**WA.** The abbreviation for with average.

**WAEC.** The abbreviation for West African Economic Community.

**wage and price controls.** Government restraints on wages and prices designed to control inflation and maintain employment. See also *price controls*.

**wage earner plan.** See *bankruptcy*.

**wage earner's scheme (WES).** In South Asia, the lower rate paid for labor remittances in a secondary exchange market.

**wages council.** In the United Kingdom, a committee authorized by the Wages Council Act of 1954 to set minimum wage rates. Employees, employers, and unaffiliated bodies are represented on wage councils. The Wages Act of 1986 prohibited the creation of new councils.

**Währung.** German: currency.

**waiting period.** In the United States, the 20-day delay between the registration and sale of a new securities issue. Following the filing of a registration statement, the Securities and Exchange Commission (SEC) imposes a cooling-off period during which the agency can object to actual sales. An SEC objection begins a new 20-day period wherein the agency and issuer have an opportunity to resolve questions surrounding an issue.

**waiver.** In law, the renunciation of a right voluntarily or by operation of law. In a legal or administrative proceeding, a legal right is automatically waived when a party fails to file required documents within the time prescribed by law or regulation.

**walk-on/walk-off (WO/WO).** A ship equipped with ramps for transporting livestock.

**Wall Street.** The site of the American Stock Exchange and the New York Stock Exchange. Wall Street is also the popular name for the New York financial district, where other exchanges, leading banks, insurance companies, and securities firms are located.

**Walras' law.** See *Pareto optimum*.

**W&F.** The abbreviation for water and feed.

**W&I.** The abbreviation for weight and inspection.

**W&R.** The abbreviation for water and rail.

**Ware.** German: offer.

**warehouse.** See *warehousing*.

**warehouse and temporary storage.** In insurance, protection for a policyholder whose goods are stored in a warehouse or other temporary facility.

**warehouse certificate.** See *warehouse receipt*.

**warehouse financing.** See *asset-based lending*.

**Warehouse Information Network Standard.** See *electronic data interchange*.

**warehouse receipt.** A written inventory of goods stored in a warehouse. Warehouse receipts are documents of title used to secure bank financing. In the United States, a negotiable warehouse receipt, made to the order of the owner or an agent, conforms to the Uniform Commercial Code and the Uniform Warehouse Receipt Act. Ownership of the underlying goods is transferred by endorsement *and* delivery. Negotiable warehouse receipts are commonly used when goods are stored pending sale. When the receipt is not negotiable, warehoused goods can only be claimed by the owner or an authorized agent. See also *cedule* and *warrant*.

**warehouse-to-warehouse.** In insurance, a clause protecting a policyholder from financial loss during the period when goods are picked up at a designated facility and transferred to a destination site.

**warehousing.** 1. Storing goods under a warehouse receipt in a temporary facility, such as a bonded or field warehouse. 2. In banking, collecting foreign exchange swaps or interest rate swaps for later trades. 3. In finance, preparing for a hostile takeover by storing stock in the name of another. Warehousing enables the person contemplating the takeover to remain anonymous while buying shares in the target company. In some jurisdictions, warehousing is illegal.

**Warenzeichen.** German: trademark.

**warrant.** 1. A combination warehouse receipt

and trust receipt used to secure bank financing. The warehouse receipt is released to the owner of goods after a trust agreement is executed with the lender. When goods are stored at a dockside warehouse, the receipt is known as a dock warrant or a wharfinger's warrant. 2. A bearer certificate with a conversion option. A warrant is convertible into a commodity, including gold or securities, at a fixed conversion date and exercise price. Although similar to stock options, warrants trade at a premium on exchanges, primarily because the underlying commodity may be less valuable when an option is exercised. By contrast, stock options, usually issued to employees, carry lower prices.

**warranted free.**    In insurance, any exception to coverage. Typically, insurance policies enumerate uncovered risks.

**warranty.**    1. A promise made in a contract. When explicitly stated, the promise is an express warranty. When not explicitly stated, but imposed by law or custom, the promise is an implied warranty. 2. In the United States, certain promises are implied in contracts for the sale of goods, by the Uniform Commercial code (UCC). For example, under §2-312 and §2-314 of the UCC, a merchant implicitly warrants the capacity to transfer title to goods, as well as their merchantability, unless warranties are explicitly disclaimed or modified. Section 2-313 of the UCC creates express warranties when a merchant describes goods or makes representations regarding the terms of a sale. 3. In marine insurance, an agreement by a policyholder to undertake certain measures or refrain from a given course of conduct. When a policyholder fails to honor such warranties, the policy is subject to cancellation.

**war risk.**    A risk of loss from war or insurrection. War risks are normally uninsurable by commercial underwriters, except under country risk coverage provided or subsidized by government agencies. In marine insurance, war risks are insured under separate policies, often purchased as a part of marine perils coverage. See also *export credit insurance, Multilateral Investment Guarantee Agency,* and *Overseas Private Investment Corporation.*

**Warsaw Convention.**    Known formally as the Unification of Certain Rules Relating to International Transportation by Air, an agreement adopted at Warsaw in 1929 setting international limits on an air carrier's liability for death, injury, and property damage. The 1966 Montreal Intercarrier Agreement, which amended the Warsaw Convention, adopted liability limitations of 58,000 to 75,000 U.S. dollars per passenger for injury and death and 1250 U.S. dollars for baggage losses. The Montreal amendments have been accepted in the United States. Proposed protocols to the convention would further increase liability limits, substitute special drawing rights for U.S. dollars to value liability claims, and eliminate carrier liability for air disasters arising from acts of terrorism.

**Warsaw Pact.**    Also known as the Warsaw Treaty Organization (WTO), the defunct military alliance founded in 1945 between the former Union of Soviet Socialist Republics (U.S.S.R.) and its allies. The pact was concluded between the U.S.S.R., Poland, the former Czechoslovakia (i.e., the Czech Republic and Slovakia), Hungary, Romania, the former German Democratic Republic, Bulgaria, and Albania, which resigned in 1968. The WTO and its political arm, the Council for Mutual Economic Assistance, were effectively dissolved between 1990 and 1991.

**Warsaw Treaty Organization.**    See *Warsaw Pact.*

**wash sale.**    In the United States, a transaction involving the sale and repurchase of the same or an identical security by the same parties over a short period of time, i.e., buying and selling within a 61-day period. Losses from wash sales, which are designed to stimulate trading in a given security, are not tax deductible in the United States and are prohibited by stock exchange regulations. A call option is deemed identical to the underlying security. Dissimilar securities require different maturities, voting rights, interest rates, etc.

**waste cube.**    Excess space in a shipping container. The excess occurs when cargo fills the weight capacity, but not the space, of a container.

**wasting asset.**    An asset with a limited useful life. Mineral resources are wasting assets, as are copyrights and patents.

**watered stock.**    Equity in a company diluted by the overall number of outstanding shares when compared with its assets. Shares are said to be diluted when a liquidation would cause a loss of shareholder value, even though a company's operations are profitable.

**waybill.**    See *consignment.*

**W/B, W.B.**    The abbreviations for waybill and westbound.

**W.B./E.I.**    The marking for West Britain/East Ireland.

**wbs.**    The abbreviation for without benefit of salvage.

**wd.**    The abbreviation for warranted.

**WD/Ex.**    The acronym for withdrawal (of goods) for export.

**WD/IT.**    The acronym for warehouse withdrawal (of goods) for immediate transportation.

**WDT.**    The acronym for withdrawal (of goods) for transportation.

**WDT&E.**    The acronym for withdrawal (of goods) for transportation and exportation.

**WDT Rew.**    The acronym for withdrawal (of goods) for transportation and rewarehousing.

**wear and tear.**    Depreciation in the value of an asset through ordinary use. Usually included in leases, the provision protects a lessee from liability for erosions in the value of property occurring as a consequence of normal wear and tear.

**weather insurance.**    See *pluvial insurance.*

**weather permitting.**    A charter party provision covering weather working days. It exempts from lay time hours dedicated for loading and unloading but lost due to bad weather.

**Webb-Pomerene Act of 1918.**    In the United States, a law that exempts export firms from antitrust laws. Companies may combine to form export associations, known as Webb-Pomerene associations, and divide foreign sales territories for setting prices and sales terms. The combinations are allowed so long as their activities do not adversely affect U.S. commerce. The Webb-Pomerene exemption applies to business combinations seeking favorable foreign sales terms, but not to their foreign direct investment activities.

**Wechsel.**    German: bill of exchange.

**WEF.**    The abbreviation for World Economic Forum. See *World Competitiveness Report.*

**weight certificate.**    A document issued by an official weigher. The certificate is used by customs officials to verify weights and measurements for assessing specific duties.

**weighted.**    An arithmetic method of accounting for the relative importance of a given factor in a mathematical calculation. 1. A weighted average reflects the average weight of several similar factors. For example, if a person purchases 50 shares of stock at $2 each and 50 shares at $10 each, the average price is $5 per share. The weighted average $[(50 \times 2) + (50 \times 10)/100]$ is $6 per share. 2. A trade-weighted average is the arithmetic statement of a country's terms of trade, i.e., the relative prices of imports and exports constituting its balance of trade. See also *balance of payments.*

**weight gaining.**    An increase in the bulk weight of a finished product when materials and components are added during the manufacturing process. The reverse is called weight losing.

**weight note.**    A seller's document specifying the gross weight and average tare of packaged goods.

**weight or measurement.**    A provision in a tariff permitting a carrier to levy freight rates for weight *or* measure, i.e., the rate that yields the most revenue.

**W.E.N.**    The abbreviation for waive (foreign) exchange if necessary.

**Werner Report.**    A report issued in 1970 by Pierre Werner, the prime minister of Luxembourg, recommending monetary union in the European Community (EC). The report advocated full economic and monetary integration to lower internal transaction costs. The recommendations of the report were realized in the Treaty of Maastricht adopted by the EC in 1992.

**Wertpapier.**    German: security, i.e., stocks and bonds.

**Wertpapiersammelbank.**    In Germany, a depositary similar to the *Kassenverein.*

**Wertpapiersteuer.**    German: securities transfer tax.

**WES.**    The abbreviation for wage earners' scheme.

**West African Economic Community.** See *Communauté économique de l'Afrique de l'Ouest.*

**Western European Union (WEU).** In Europe, a mutual defense and security alliance that succeeded the Brussels Treaty Organization in 1955. All European Community members belong to WEU, except Denmark, Greece, and Ireland. An enhanced WEU creating a European defense system, possibly associated with the North Atlantic Treaty Organization, is envisioned by some in Europe and elsewhere.

**wet barrel.** In commodities trading, an actual barrel stored at the time of a sale. By contrast, a paper barrel is a paper credit recorded on an accounting ledger.

**WEU.** The abbreviation for Western European Union.

**WFC.** The abbreviation for World Food Council.

**WFP.** The abbreviation for World Food Programme.

**WFTU.** The abbreviation for World Federation of Trade Unions.

**w.g.** The abbreviation for weight guaranteed.

**wharf.** The dock or pier at a port, as well as the surrounding warehouses. The manager of a wharf is known as a wharfinger. The fee charged for the use of a wharf is called wharfage.

**whether in berth or not.** See *berth–no-berth.*

**white goods.** Heavy household appliances (e.g., washing machines, refrigerators, etc.), so named when most were painted with white enamel.

**white knight.** The friendly suitor in a corporate takeover. Companies facing hostile takeovers by black knights often seek out alternative investors. A white knight is a prospective buyer who is preferred to the black knight in terms of reputation, financial solidity, or the attractiveness of a potential offer. Compare *gray knight.*

**WHO.** The abbreviation for World Health Organization.

**wholesale price index.** In the United States, a price index of 22 basic commodities published by the U.S. Department of Labor.

**wholesale (whsle.) trade.** A market composed of distributors who buy large quantities of products for sale to other distributors. In the wholesale trade, bulk quantities of products are divided into lots and sold to retailers.

**Whse.** The abbreviation for warehouse.

**Whse E.** The abbreviation for warehouse entry.

**Whse W.** The abbreviation for warehouse withdrawal.

**whsle.** The abbreviation for wholesale (trade).

**w.i.** The abbreviation for when issued.

**WIBON.** The abbreviation for whether in berth or not.

**wider-range security.** In the United Kingdom, a security eligible for trustee investments under the Trustees Investment Act. Typically, eligible securities are ordinary shares traded on the London Stock Exchange. See also *narrow-range security.*

**Wiener Edele Metalle Warenbörse.** In Austria, the Vienna Precious Metals Exchange, a proposed futures market for precious metals. The exchange will trade, among others, palladium, platinum, and rhodium, mined largely in the Commonwealth of Independent States. Rhodium is used in automobile catalytic converters, an accessory required under most national clean air regulations.

**will.** A document disposing of property after the maker's death. The maker of a will is known as a testator. Normally, a will is written and signed by the testator in the presence of two witnesses, who are not also heirs to the estate. In the United States, oral wills may be valid if witnessed by two or more persons. Handwritten, or holographic, wills are also valid when the handwriting of the testator can be verified.

**windfall profits tax.** A tax on earnings from oil exploration. In the United Kingdom, the tax is known as petroleum revenue tax. The tax is imposed on exportation licensed by the Petroleum Act of 1934 and the Petroleum Act of 1964. In the United States, the tax is authorized by the Crude Oil Windfall Profits Tax of 1980.

**WINS.** The abbreviation for Warehouse Information Network Standard. See *electronic data interchange.*

**WIPO.** The abbreviation for World Intellectual Property Organization.

**WIPON.** The abbreviation for whether in free pratique or not.

**wire fate item.** A bill of exchange or draft forwarded with collection instructions to a collecting bank. The bank wires a notice of payment or dishonor.

**wire transfer (WT).** Also called a bank wire or a telegraphic transfer, an order from a customer to a bank to remit funds to third party by electronic means. In the United States, wire transfers are paid through the Clearing House Interbank Payments System and through the Federal Reserve Wire Network. In the international banking system, instructions to transfer funds are sent to participating banks by the Society for Worldwide Interbank Financial Telecommunications; payments are made through national clearing houses. See also *electronic funds transfer*.

**with average.** See *average*.

**withdrawal.** The removal of goods from a customs warehouse or other customs territory.

**withdrawal price.** The floor price for the European Community Common Agricultural Policy at which domestic farmers may begin to withdraw produce from the market. When the market price falls below the target or intervention price, costs associated with withholding commodities are paid by the EC.

**with exchange.** See *payable with exchange*.

**withholding plan.** A device used by a government or a cartel to reduce supply and stabilize the price of a commodity. Under withholding plans, excess commodities are held as buffer stock or destroyed.

**withholding tax.** 1. In the United States, taxes collected from an employee's earnings by an employer. Employers are assigned an employer identification number, used by the Internal Revenue Service to identify sources of wages or salaries. Employees are identified by Social Security numbers. Taxes withheld include income taxes and the Social Security tax, also known as FICA. See also *backup withholding* and *taxpayer identification number*. 2. Elsewhere, tax deducted from the income of nonresidents, including taxes on dividends and earned interest. Withholding taxes are deducted by the party who distributes the income to the taxpayer. Double-taxation treaties often provide for credits against tax liability attributable to income earned in a foreign country.

**without average.** See *average*.

**without prejudice.** A limitation on the legal effect of an action or document. For example, administrative decisions recorded without prejudice do not affect the rights of the parties in future legal actions. Essentially, a document noted without prejudice verifies the intention of the party signing it not to be bound by its terms.

**without recourse.** French: *sans recours*. 1. In a contract of sale, a seller's disclaimer of liability when a buyer defaults on an obligation to subsequent buyers, especially on warranty obligations. Normally, a nonrecourse disclaimer does not protect a seller from product liability claims. 2. An endorser's disclaimer of liability to subsequent holders of a negotiable instrument. See also *nonrecourse loan*.

**without reserve.** A description of the unconditional authority granted to an agent to vary the original terms of a transaction without further instructions from a principal.

**with particular average.** See *average*.

**with recourse.** A description of the right of one party to a transaction to seek satisfaction from another in the event of a debtor's default or another's failure to fulfill contract terms.

**with the right of survivorship.** See *joint tenants*.

**W/M.** The abbreviation for weight and measurement.

**WMO.** The abbreviation for World Meteorological Organization.

**won.** The currency of Korea.

**worked lumber.** Lumber that has been planed, varnished, or otherwise finished.

**working capital.** Liquid capital or assets easily convertible to cash. The term may apply to gross assets or net assets. However, a company's net assets, or the amount by which assets exceed liabilities, provide the better measure of liquidity and a more accurate description of working capital.

**working days.** See *lay time*.

**work in process (WIP).**   In accounting, work in an intermediate stage for which expense records are maintained. Records are kept on the cost of labor and materials, a pro rata allocation of overhead, and estimated earnings. Work in process is also known as work in progress.

**work interruption surcharge.**   A fee paid to a shipping conference for shipments loaded during port work stoppages. The fee is based on the number of containers shipped to or from the affected port.

**work permit.**   A license to work in another country.

**World Bank (WB) Group.**   A multilateral lending institution created by the 1944 Bretton Woods Conference and formally chartered by Articles of Agreement signed at the United Nations in 1945. The World Bank Group is composed of the International Bank for Reconstruction and Development (IBRD) and the International Development Association, the WB's soft-loan window. The International Centre for Settlement of Investment Disputes, the International Finance Corporation, and the Multilateral Investment Guarantee Agency are affiliated organizations. The World Bank is partially funded through capital subscriptions of member countries, which must also belong to the International Monetary Fund. Its lending facilities are financed from repaid loans, retained earnings, and debt raised on world capital markets. The IBRD is limited, among other things, to lending for productive purposes and is required to establish reasonable terms for repayment. In addition, the World Bank must obtain certain guarantees from the borrowing government, and it lends primarily for specific projects. The World Bank's affairs are overseen by a board of governors, composed of one governor and one alternate from each member state. The board delegates much of its policymaking authority to executive directors, whose selection may be by appointment or election. The World Bank Group is based in Washington, D.C. See also *credits*.

**World Bank International Centre for Settlement of Investment Disputes.**   See *International Centre for Settlement of Investment Disputes*.

**World Climate Programme.**   An international program that originated with the World Climate Conference held in Geneva in 1979. The program provides information on global changes in climate and water resources. The World Climate Programme is sponsored by the World Meteorological Organization.

**World Commercial Holidays.**   In the United States, a reprint of international holiday schedules published in *Business America* and available through the U.S. Department of Commerce.

**World Competitiveness Report (WCR).**   An annual report issued since 1981 by the World Economic Forum (WEF) in association with the International Management Development Institute. WCRs contain data based on 10 measures of national economic competitiveness. The measures are (1) economic growth capacity, (2) financial capacity, (3) future orientation, (4) government policy, (5) human capital, (6) industrial efficiency, (7) international orientation, (8) local market structure, (9) natural resource capacity and use, and (10) sociopolitical structure. The WEF is based in Geneva.

**World Court.**   See *International Court of Justice*.

**World Food Council (WFC).**   A ministerial-level council established by the United Nations to develop international policies to combat global hunger. The WFC promotes international trade as an avenue to global food security.

**World Food Programme (WPF).**   A program sponsored jointly by the United Nations and the Food and Agriculture Organization of the United Nations. The program provides cash and commodities for development programs and emergency food relief.

**World Health Organization (WHO).**   A specialized agency of the United Nations established in 1948 to coordinate and sponsor international health programs. WHO has regional offices in Alexandria (Egypt), Brazzaville (People's Republic of the Congo), Copenhagen, Manila, New Delhi (India), and Washington, D.C.

**World Intellectual Property Organization (WIPO).**   An international organization that became a United Nations specialized agency in 1974. The WIPO was created at Stockholm in 1967 to administer international intellectual property agreements. The organization is based in Geneva.

**World Meteorological Organization (WMO).** The successor organization to the defunct International Meteorological Organization. The WMO was established by convention at Washington, D.C., in 1947 and became a United Nations specialized agency in 1951. The organization promotes uniformity in meteorological facilities and standards, especially in weather-sensitive industries, such as aviation and shipping. Governed by the World Meteorological Congress and composed of representatives of national meteorological centers, the WMO is based in Geneva.

**Worldnet.** In the United States, a business satellite network formed to promote U.S. products and facilitate contacts between domestic firms and foreign buyers. The network is sponsored jointly by the U.S. Department of Commerce, the U.S. Information Agency, and private trade associations.

**world price.** The spot price of a commodity in international markets. A quoted world price is determined by timing, location, and quality. Since most global markets are especially sensitive to political changes, an important news event may also affect world price.

**Worldscale (WS).** Also known as the Worldwide Tanker Nominal Freight Scale, a schedule of nominal freight rates for petroleum products published semiannually on January 1 and July 1. Worldscale lists freight rates quoted in U.S. dollars for transporting products between petroleum ports. The rates are known as Worldscale 100 and Worldscale flat, based on freight charges for a fully stocked tanker weighing 19,500 tons. Worldscale replaced the International Tanker Nominal Freight Scale (London) and the American Tanker Rate Schedule (New York). The schedule is published by the Worldscale Association, which has offices in London and New York.

**world trade center (WTC).** A local affiliate of the World Trade Centers Association founded in 1968. WTCs are located around the world and provide business facilities for firms engaged in international trade. The centers sponsor training programs, trade shows, and international business seminars. Most have library facilities and provide members with secretarial and foreign language translation services. WTCs also sponsor the World Trade Center Network, an electronic bulletin board for advertising products and services in international markets. The World Trade Centers Association is based in New York.

**World Trader's Data Reports (WTDRs).** In the United States, business reports prepared by the U.S. Department of Commerce. WTDRs contain information on foreign firms, including product lines and business reputation. The reports are not available for all countries.

**World Weather Watch.** A system of advanced technology centers operated by the national weather services of the World Meteorological Organization members. The system includes space-based observation systems, which increasingly provide early warning and other weather data to national weather services around the world.

**WO/WO.** The abbreviation for walk-on/walk-off.

**w.p.** The abbreviation for weather permitting.

**W.P.** The abbreviation for wire payment. See *wire transfer.*

**W.P.A.** The abbreviation for with particular average.

**W/R.** The abbreviation for warehouse receipt.

**W.R.** The abbreviation for war risk.

**WRAP policy.** Catastrophic bad debt insurance indemnifying exporters against unanticipated losses, usually arising from sovereign risks. See also *country risk* and *sleep insurance.*

**writ.** A written order issued by a court. An original writ, or summons, initiates a civil action, ordering a defendant to appear and answer a plaintiff's complaint. Judicial writs are issued to enforce court judgments. A writ of attachment, also known as a writ of execution, orders a police officer to seize property. A writ in aid, or a writ of delivery, orders property seized when the writ of execution has failed.

**write off.** 1. To claim a loss for an uncollectible debt in a profit and loss statement. 2. To depreciate (reduce to zero) an asset on a balance sheet.

**written-down value.** The lower market value of an asset when compared with its book value. The process of adjusting accounting values for changes in market value is known as marking to the market. The opposite of writing down is writing up, which occurs when the market value of an asset increases above its book value.

**W.R.O.**   The abbreviation for war risk only.

**wrongful dishonor.**   A bank's failure to honor an otherwise payable check. In the United States, §3-508 of the Uniform Commercial Code requires a bank to pay or dishonor a check by midnight of the day after its presentment. A bank is liable when wrongful dishonor causes injury to the party who presents the check.

**WS.**   The abbreviation for Worldscale.

**wt.**   The abbreviation for warrant and weight.

**WT.**   The abbreviation for wire transfer.

**WTCA.**   The abbreviation for World Trade Centers Association.

**WTDR.**   The abbreviation for World Trade Data Report.

**WTO.**   The abbreviation for Warsaw Treaty Organization. See *Warsaw Pact*.

**W/W.**   The abbreviation for warehouse warrant. See *warehouse receipt*.

**W.W.D.**   The abbreviation for weather working day(s).

# X

**x.**   The marking for unknown quantity.

**X9.**   See *ANSI X9*.

**X12.**   See *ANSI X12*.

**xd.**   The abbreviation for ex dividend.

**x-heavy.**   The marking for extra heavy.

**x/w.**   The marking for without warrants.

**xx-heavy.**   The marking for extra-extra heavy.

**xx-strong.**   The marking for extra-extra strong.

# Y

**¥.** The symbol for yen.

**Y/A.** The abbreviation for York-Antwerp Rules.

**Yankee bond.** A bond denominated in U.S. dollars and registered with the Securities and Exchange Commission, but issued outside the United States. In contrast to Eurobonds, which pay annual interest, Yankee bonds pay interest semiannually.

**Yankee certificate of deposit (CD).** A negotiable time deposit issued by a foreign borrower in the United States, often for minimum investments of $1 million to $5 million. Yankee CDs can carry fixed or variable rates of interest.

**Yaoundé Convention.** See *Lomé Conventions*.

**yd.** The abbreviation for yard.

**yearling.** In the United Kingdom, a share with a maturity of 4 years or less issued by a local government agency. Yearlings are quoted on the discount market or on the London Stock Exchange.

**Yellow Book.** In the United Kingdom, regulations issued by the London Stock Exchange (LSE), also known as the Admission of Securities to Listing. *Yellow Book* regulations specify listing requirements and govern the conduct of issuers trading securities on the LSE.

**yen.** The currency of Japan.

**yen bond.** A bond denominated in yen. Samurai bonds are yen bonds issued in Japan. Euroyen bonds are yen bonds issued in Eurobond markets. Japanese bond purchases were opened to non-Japanese investors in 1984. See also *samurai bond* and *shogun bond*.

**yield (yld.).** Income from an investment expressed as a percentage of the purchase price, i.e., the ratio of income to investment. For example, if income of $10 is earned on a $50 investment, the current yield is 5 percent. 1. For a bond, nominal yield is computed by multiplying the principal by the interest earned and the time until maturity. Current yield is the coupon rate multiplied by the number of times interest is paid, i.e., twice when interest is earned semiannually. Yield to call is the annual return from the purchase date to the first call date specified in the indenture. Yield to maturity, also called the effective rate of return and yield to redemption, is the yearly return earned to the maturity date, including annual interest accruing from the purchase date to maturity. 2. For common or preferred stock, the ratio of annual dividends per share to current market price. See also *effective annual yield*.

**YK.** The abbreviation for *yugen kaisha*.

**yld.** The abbreviation for yield.

**York-Antwerp Rules.** A body of international rules established by the shipping industry for insurance average adjusting. First adopted in 1877, the rules were revised in 1974 and are routinely incorporated into ocean bills of lading. See also *substituted expense*.

**yo-yo stock.** A colloquial term for volatile stock.

**Y record.** See *block control trailer record*.

**YTC.** The abbreviation for yield to call.

**YTM.** The abbreviation for yield to maturity.

**yuan.** The currency of China.

**yugen kaisha (YK).** In Japan, a small limited company. Stock transfers by *yugen kaisha* to nonowners are severely restricted. Compare *kabushiki kaisha*.

# Z

**z.**   The symbol for zero.

**zaibatsu.**   In Japan, a common form of business conglomerate before World War II. The major pre-war *zaibatsu*, e.g., Mitsui, Mitsubishi, Sumitomo, and Yasuda, were ostensibly dismantled after the war. Although most survived in a slightly different form, Japan's Anti-Monopoly Law was enacted in 1947 to prevent the revival of *zaibatsu*. Compare *keiretsu*.

**zaikai.**   In Japan, the business power elite. *Zaikai* consists largely of top-level ministry employees and corporate officials.

**zaire.**   The currency of Zaire.

**zakat.**   In a Moslem country, the 2.5 percent income tax collected for distribution to the poor. Payment of *zakat* is dictated by the *Koran*.

**zengin.**   In Japan, the giro system operated by the Federation of Bankers Associations of Japan. The *zengin* system is used by banks, corporations, and consumers.

**zero-coupon bond.**   A bond redeemed with a single payment. Zero-coupon bonds are often convertible into common stock or exchangeable for coupon bonds after a stipulated time.

**zero haven.**   A tax haven.

**zero inventory.**   A term synonymous with just-in-time.

**zero-rated.**   In a value-added tax system, goods and services with a zero-tax rate. Zero-rated items are not exempt from the VAT, but are untaxed. Although producers of zero-rated items deduct the input tax, consumers are not taxed when the products are purchased.

**ZF.**   The abbreviation for zona franca.

**ZIP code.**   Known as the postcode elsewhere, a postal routing code in the United States.

**zloty.**   The currency of Poland.

**Zoll.**   German: customs. *Zollbehörden, Zollkreisdirektion,* or *Zollverwaltung* refer to customs authorities or a customs agency. *Zollabfertigung* is customs clearance.

**Zolldepot.**   German: bonded warehouse.

**zona franca (ZF).**   Spanish: free trade zone.

**zone-delivered price.**   A uniform price for delivering cargoes to different sites within a geographic zone. The zone-delivered price may be a uniform cost, insurance, and freight price or a free-on-board price. Some carriers offset freight differences by offering discounts for shipping within a zone.

**zone-restricted status.**   The status of otherwise dutiable goods entered into a foreign trade zone to be destroyed or reexported. Zone-restricted goods cannot be altered or processed in the zone, and reentry for consumption is normally prohibited. In the United States, Foreign Trade Zones boards are authorized to permit reentry, but only for public interest reasons.

**Z record.**   See *transaction control trailer record*.